WANDERINGS

'I have talked the book over with many travellers, and we are agreed that here you have all the desert, its hills and plains, the lava fields, the villages, the tents, the men and animals. They are told of the life, with words and phrases fitted to them so perfectly that one cannot dissociate them in memory. It is the true Arabia, the land with its smells and dirt, as well as its nobility and freedom. There is no sentiment, nothing merely picturesque, that most common failing of oriental travel-books. Doughty's completeness is devastating. There is nothing we would take away, little we could add. He took all Arabia for his province, and has left to his successors only the poor part of specialists. We may write books on parts of the desert or some of the history of it; but there can never be another picture of the whole, in our time, because here it is all said.'   T.E. Lawrence

'One of the greatest travel books in literature. No book of Arabian travel is comparable with Doughty's in romantic interest. Not since the Elizabethan voyagers has there been any parallel to it. It is a great story, told in a great manner, a masterpiece of style and a record of heroic doings.'   *The Spectator*

'Mr Doughty's book is surely the supreme book of travel ... It will be studied as long as travel books have any attraction for mankind.'   *Times Literary Supplement*

'Doughty's purpose was to study the people and examine the ancient ruins and monuments of the land. Everything he set out to do he did. He has wonderfully reproduced his impressions. The work is an achievement in the realm of pure literature, apart from its interest as an account of remarkable journeys.'
                               New York Times

'One of the mighty oaks of English travel writing in particular and English literature in general. Beyond its Shakespearean completeness, its immediacy and humanity, and its majestically archaic prose, the special greatness of this book lies in the fact of its author having become an adventurer and explorer of cold necessity rather than by choice. The fact, astonishing as it may seem, must be stated plainly: *Travels in Arabia Deserta* is not only an incomparably better book than *The Seven Pillars of Wisdom*; it is also a vastly more exciting one.'
                               National Review

WANDERINGS IN ARABIA

The Authorised Abridged Edition of 'Travels in Arabia Deserta'

CHARLES DOUGHTY

I.B. TAURIS

LONDON · NEW YORK

Published in 2009 by I.B.Tauris & Co Ltd
6 Salem Road, London W2 4BU
175 Fifth Avenue, New York NY 10010
www.ibtauris.com

In the United States and in Canada distributed by Palgrave
Macmillan a division of St Martin's Press, 175 Fifth Avenue,
New York NY 10010

This Authorised Abridged Edition first published by Duckworth
in 1908

ISBN 978 1 84511 810 5 (hb)
     978 1 84511 766 5 (pb)

A full CIP record for this book is available from the British Library
A full CIP record is available from the Library of Congress

Library of Congress Catalog card: available

Printed and bound in India by Replika Press Pvt. Ltd

CONTENTS

Foreword by Barnaby Rogerson   vii

Map, illustrating Doughty's route   xiv–xv

Part One

I: THE HAJ, OR MECCA PILGRIMAGE   1

II: MEDÂIN [THE "CITIES" OF] SÂLIH   12

III: MEDÂIN SÂLIH AND THE
        INSCRIPTIONS   35

IV: RETURN OF THE HAJ   58

V: THE NOMAD LIFE IN THE DESERT –
        THE FEJÎR BEDUINS   70

VI: LIFE IN THE WANDERING
        VILLAGE   92

VII: THE NOMADS IN THE DESERT; VISIT
        TO TEYMA   113

VIII: THE FUKARA WANDERING AS FUGITIVES
        IN ANOTHER DÎRA   136

IX: PEACE IN THE DESERT   160

X: TEYMA   184

XI: THE DATE HARVEST   204

XII: THE JEBEL   217

XIII: HÂYIL   244

XIV: IBN RASHÎD'S TOWN   269

XV: DEPART FROM HÂYIL: JOURNEY TO
        KHEYBAR   281

CONTENTS

Part Two

I: KHEYBAR "THE APSOTLE'S COUNTRY"   311

II: THE MEDINA LIFE AT KHEYBAR   335

III: GALLA-LAND. MEDINA LORE   348

IV: DELIVERANCE FROM KHEYBAR   362

V: DESERT JOURNEY TO HÂYIL. THE
        NASRÂNY IS DRIVEN FROM THENCE   387

VI: THE SHAMMER AND HARB DESERTS
        IN NEDJ   417

VII: JOURNEY TO EL-KASÎM: BOREYDA   446

VIII: ANEYZA   466

IX: LIFE IN ANEYZA   493

X: THE CHRISTIAN STRANGER DRIVEN
        FROM ANEYZA; AND RECALLED   507

XI: KAHTÂN EXPELLED FROM EL-KASÎM   527

XII: SET OUT FROM EL-KASÎM WITH THE
        BUTTER CARAVAN FOR MECCA   547

XIII: TAYIF. THE SHERÎF, EMIR OF MECCA   581

Short Glossary of Arabic Terms   603

FOREWORD

WILFRID THESIGER annotated the sale-room catalogue which
disposed of his lifelong collection of Arabian travel-books.
Beside Doughty's *Travels in Arabia Deserta* he commented,
"No other book about Arabia can compare with this." T.E.
Lawrence had previously written that it was a, "book not like
other books, but something particular of its kind." A
judgement he made not just from the comfort of a desk but
when he urged the War Office to print a lightweight edition to
be supplied to all British troops assisting in the Arab Revolt.
Amongst other great British explorers of Arabia such as David
Hogarth, Wilfrid Blunt and Harry St John Philby (all men of
determinedly independent if not a frankly contentious frame
of mind) there was no dissension on this one point. Philby,
who wrote half a dozen books of his own about Arabia,
declared that Doughty's travels were, "the finest and most
complete description of the old Arabia produced by anyone, his
predecessors or his successors. I have studied the book on the
spot, and I don't think I have ever been able to detect a flaw or
a mistake in it." Hogarth would add, "Everything about
Arabia seemed to be in the book, if only one read enough of it!"
The Spectator declared that it is, "one of the greatest travel-
books in literature. No other book of Arabian travel is
comparable with Doughty's in romantic interest. Not since the
Elizabethan voyagers has there been any parallel to it. It is a
great story, told in a great manner, a masterpiece of style and
a record of heroic doings." Their review was only superseded
by that of the watchdog itself, the *Times Literary Supplement*,
which declared that, "Mr Doughty's book is surely the
supreme book of travel ... it will be studied as long as travel-
books have any attraction for mankind."

Charles Doughty's *Travels in Arabia Deserta* is most
certainly a travel-book, that species of world literature that
would achieve its most spectacular flowering in English. For a

British travel book is not just the published diary of a journey of exploration, nor is it an historical narrative enlivened by a rigorous inspection of landscape, nor yet a guidebook to selected antiquities though it will freely borrow from all these different forms. It might also shave off into anthropology, art history and comparative mythology but it must also contain something of the narrator, their prejudices and exasperations, not just their powers of professional observation. For the journey must also chronicle an inner sensibility, a form of pilgrimage, that has succeeded in transforming the writer. The travel book is not a pure form, but from the *Odyssey* and *Gilgamesh* onwards, it has always been a multi-cultural fusion, a plum-pudding that draws from all the arts and sciences but to a personal and highly idiosyncratic formula.

Travels in Arabia Deserta is just such a book. Without spoiling the plot and the pure sense of adventure that animates it (a common failing amongst introductions to famous books) Charles Doughty had a particular mission in mind. He wished to be an explorer, the first scholar-traveller to visit the ruined city of Medâin Sâlih in the Arabian desert. To this end he travelled with a stack of blotting paper to make squinches of the inscriptions and a set of scientific instruments that enabled him to record elevation, temperature, longitude, latitude and make maps of the region. This he would achieve quite early on in his travels, sending these records back to the safe-keeping of the British Consulate in Damascus, before he continued the rest of his even more adventurous journey. Thus he was the first European scholar to visit Medâin Sâlih, and his record of the inscriptions that he found positively identified this 'lost city' of the Nabataeans, a southern capital to the more famous Petra, "that rose red city half as old as time." He was also able to report that Medâin Sâlih was not composed of the seven ruined cities of the Arabic imagination, but was a city that had been formed from out of three oasis villages whose mud-brick houses had long since decayed to leave only the outlying rock-cut tombs as a remnant of its past greatness and glory.

This was a considerable achievement in itself, most especially as Charles Doughty was no historian but an eccentric free-scholar who lived abroad in order to continue to study geology and early English poetry. He came from a long line of East Anglian squires, who had succeeded in preserving the size of their ancestral landholdings by encouraging their younger sons to earn their living through taking up one of the professions; either the navy, army, church or the law. Doughty could number amongst his ancestors and relations a colonial governor, a bishop, a judge and a general, though the families chief leaning was towards a career in the Royal Navy, where six Doughtys had achieved the rank of admiral. As a younger son, Charles was sent off at an early age to Beach House, a school near Portsmouth, which specialised in preparing boys for entry into the Royal Navy. The death of his parents followed by the disposal of their family house (to cover his father's debts) further intensified this already bleak childhood. Charles became a loner, a shy boy who delighted in the company of old books and fossil hunting expeditions rather than the rough and tumble of boarding school life. Holidays were taken in the company of his elder brother, the pair of them farmed out to the households of a dutiful rota of aunts and cousins. His rejection by the Naval Board, on grounds of ill-health (which may have been more to do with his character than his physique) was a blow to his dignity and inherited sense of patriotic purpose from which Charles never fully recovered. Instead of serving as a midshipman he went up to Cambridge University to study natural history where the discoveries of Darwin and Lyell had effectively rent the cosy intellectual Anglican world asunder. He even moved to Downing College to escape the clerical loyalties still wrapped around the medieval quad of Caius, his first college. He left Cambridge in 1865 with a few friends and an indifferent degree and then proceeded to make an 'unwise' investment, which blew away a substantial proportion of his inheritance. There was, however, just enough for him to survive without a job and continue his studies in geology and early English poetry in and around the libraries of London and Oxford for another five years. Later he found that his inherited income could be stretched even further by living abroad. So between 1870 and 1875 he travelled the length and breadth of the Mediterranean, from Portugal to the lands of the Ottoman Empire, from Holland to the Sahara with his trunk full of books, staying for months at a time at one agreeable lodging house after another, before moving on. He proved himself a tough and resourceful traveller, passing through a revolution in France, the tale-end of an anti-colonial insurrection in southern Algeria and the Carlist civil war in Spain, without any desire to make a travel-book out of these experiences for his head was still filled with his grand plan for an epic poem rooted in his knowledge of the new eras being mapped out by geologists and natural historians. One of his many problems was that his personal loyalty had long since been pledged to the grand language of the 'believing' ancient past, to the English Bible, to Chaucer, Spenser (and though he denied such a 'modern' influence, to Milton). His powerful description of the eruption of Vesuvius (with which he would later enliven a journey across the lava-fields of the north Arabian desert) gives us a powerful indication into this creative but unpublished period of his life.

The turning-point in these travels and his life as a writer was a chance visit to Nabataean Petra, where the grandeur of the ruins was coupled by that of the barren hills (their geology laid bare by the sun and desert winds) all indelibly mixed up with a Semitic culture of the surrounding Arab herdsmen that could have been taken straight out of the pages of the Bible. Doughty had unexpectedly stumbled across his mission. And the endlessly questing amateur traveller, always off after a new horizon, started to prepare himself with a truly professional zeal. He was a good linguist but transformed his slight command of the local language by an intense six-month study of written and spoken Arabic in Damascus. At the same time he started acclimatising his body to the ordeal of the desert by allowing himself to eat only local foods (milk, dates and barley-bread) and took long trips through the mountains and plateaux of Syria and Lebanon to improve his camel handling (which he would never excel in) and stamina. He would spend twenty days in Maan chatting up Mahmud, a literate and well-travelled secretary who knew the northern desert, whilst a chance meeting in the Syrian desert with Muhammad Said Pasha, an Ottoman officer (and a gentleman scholar like himself), unwittingly provided Doughty with his most sincere friend and his (unknown) but resolute protector. His sudden and over-enthusiastic attempts to interest British officialdom in his desert expedition ended with terse rejections from the RGS in London, the Embassy in Istanbul and the Consulate in Damascus. So without official funding or support, Doughty at last settled down to learn a trade. He learned from the despised class of fast-talking Christian clothe-merchants in the covered markets of Damascus. For they had learned to supplement their income and to make friends amongst the Arab tribes of the desert by carrying a small stock of medicines, some laxatives, aphrodisiacs, painkillers (such as laudanum which is opium dissolved in spirits) as well as anti-malarials such as quinine. Thus equipped, Charles

Doughty tagged onto the tail end of the pilgrimage convoy
being led into the desert by his friend Muhammad Said
Pasha. He lodged with the Persian pilgrims, who, as Shiite
Muslims, kept themselves to themselves at the rear of the
caravan. Said Pasha could not give Doughty, a self-declared
Christian 'doctor' travelling under the name of Khalil, formal
permission to join a Muslim pilgrimage but nevertheless he
turned an official blind eye to his presence. The rest of the
story you can better read for yourself in the *Travels*, though
there are a few things that should yet be clarified.

Doughty made trouble for himself by refusing to pretend to
be a Muslim (unlike Richard Burton who had travelled this
route before him) and was proud throughout his travels to
define himself as a Christian – even if (as we know) his
education at Cambridge had put him outside the Anglican
faith. So when he sounds 'off' against Islam, the reader must
realise that he is criticising all organised religions, for
throughout the book the false pieties of pompous men of
pretension are relentlessly exposed and contrasted with
practical instances of kindness, tolerance and charity. As he
would later explain to his daughter, when she quizzed him
about his lack of enthusiasm for church attendance, "I am
always in Church."

We also know that the journal he made during his year-long
journey across the desert consists of very brief notes. All
reported conversations and poetical observations in the
Travels were created years later – with the benefit of
hindsight. This is not to throw doubt on his written record but
to allow the reader to be aware that these experiences were
sieved through for years afterwards, in order to extract the
true essence of his adventure. The *Travels* would take
Doughty nine years to write and he would prove himself to be
a typical nightmare-like first author who refused all the well-
meaning attempts of his various friends, well-wishers, special-
ist historians of Arabia and editors, to reduce his vast 600,000
word-long work into something more accessible, as well as to
calm down the extraordinary language that he created for
himself from a poetic fusion of Chaucer–Spenser and the
unacknowledged Milton. The monumental first edition came
out in two volumes in 1888 – for which he had to assist his
exasperated publisher with a financial contribution. It was
not until Edward Garnet (a publisher's reader for Duckworths
who had written a very favourable review of this first edition)
undertook to edit it down into the abridged second edition

that it finally got the reviews and readers that it deserved. This edition, known as *Wanderings in Arabia* (which came out in 1908), is the one that you hold in your hand today. Though arguably it was only the passionate championing by T.E. Lawrence at the height of his post-war fame that got Doughty's *Travels in Arabia Deserta* firmly established as a great classic. (Which may usefully be compared to the way that Bruce Chatwin would later raise Robert Byron's *The Road to Oxiana* into the travel-book pantheon.)

Doughty's curious, archaic English will always succeed in repelling the casual reader from his book of Arabian travels. But after a few pages, the interested reader begins to absorb the, "nay Sirs, nay Sirs, why fray ye our mares", with ease and starts to relish his language for the next instance of curiously-wrought beauty such as when he describes, "her clay-built streets are again the blown dust of the wilderness." For it soon becomes apparent that Charles Doughty's ultimate purpose in writing was to somehow catch the beauty of the Arabic language and to record the humour, delight and poetry with which they express themselves. He found the Victorian English of his day an inadequate tool for the task with which to express the elemental dignity of these people ruled by oral traditions and the direct democracy of the tribal counsels. The hunt for ruins, new frontiers and tyrannical Emirs with which the book starts is very soon replaced by a new sort of hero, such as the lone Bedouin woman "full of the godly humanity of the wilderness" who takes pity on an exhausted outcast traveller and declares, "Be not sorrowful for I am thy mother's sister."

Many years later, Doughty would return to the fringes of the desert to show his young bride the landscape and the people who had changed his life and transformed him from a shy and reserved exile into a robust, determined and highly principled man who survived the desert as much through his fluency in Arabic – combined with a quick wit and humour – as through any very slight skill he had with knife, revolver, money, camels or in his dealings with the powerful. At this stage of his life it was his habit to get up at dawn and greet his wife with flowers that he had freshly gathered from the grazing grounds of Arabia. No one can claim that *Travels in Arabia Deserta* is a straightforward or an easy read but it remains, in T.E. Lawrence's carefully chosen words, "the great picture book of nomad life".

Barnaby Rogerson

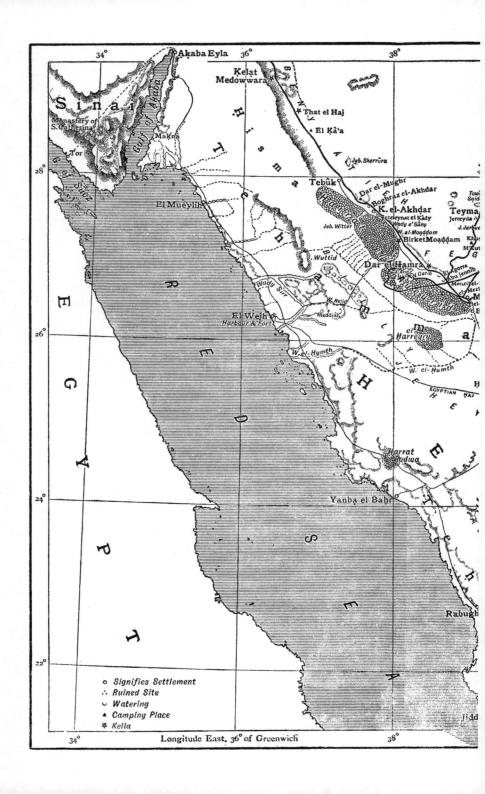

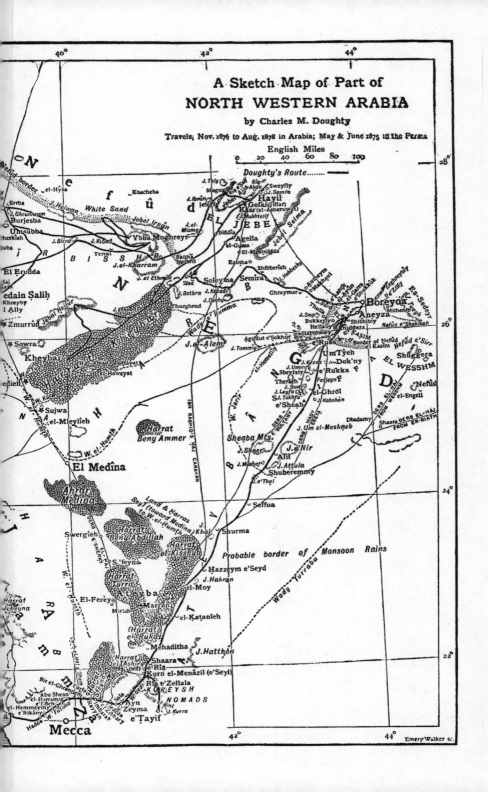

A Sketch Map of Part of
NORTH WESTERN ARABIA
by Charles M. Doughty
Travels; Nov. 1876 to Aug. 1878 in Arabia; May & June 1875 in the Peræa

English Miles

Doughty's Route ....

PART ONE

CHAPTER I

THE HAJ, OR MECCA PILGRIMAGE

A NEW voice hailed me of an old friend when, first returned
from the Peninsula, I paced again in that long street of
Damascus which is called Straight; and suddenly taking me
wondering by the hand "Tell me (said he,) since thou art
here again in the peace and assurance of Ullah, and whilst
we walk, as in the former years, toward the new blossoming
orchards, full of the sweet spring as the garden of God, what
moved thee, or how couldst thou take such journeys into the
fanatic Arabia?"

It was at the latest hour, when in the same day, and after
troubled days of endeavours, I had supposed it impossible.
At first I had asked of the *Wàly*, Governor of Syria, his
licence to accompany the *Haj* caravan to the distance of
Medáin Sâlih. The Waly then privately questioned the
British Consulate, an office which is of high regard in these
countries. The Consul answered, that his was no charge in
any such matter; he had as much regard of me, would I
take such dangerous ways, as of his old hat. This was a man
that, in time past, had proffered to show me a good turn in
my travels, who now told me it was his duty to take no
cognisance of my Arabian journey, lest he might hear any
word of blame, if I miscarried. Thus by the Turkish officers
it was understood that my life, forsaken by mine own Consulate, would not be required of them in this adventure. There
is a merry saying of Sir Henry Wotton, for which he nearly
lost his credit with his sovereign, "an ambassador is a man
who is sent to lie abroad for his country;" to this might be
added, "a Consul is a man who is sent to play the Turk abroad,
to his own countrymen."

That untimely Turkishness was the source to me of nearly
all the mischiefs of these travels in Arabia. And what wonder,

1

none fearing a reckoning, that I should many times come nigh
to be foully murdered! whereas the informal benevolent word,
in the beginning of a Frankish Consulate might have procured
me regard of the great Haj officers, and their letters of com-
mendation, in departing from them, to the Emirs of Arabia.
Thus rejected by the British Consulate, I dreaded to be turned
back altogether if I should now visit certain great personages of
Damascus, as the noble Algerian Prince *Abd el-Kâder ;* for
whose only word, which I am well assured he would have given,
I had been welcome in all the Haj-road towers occupied by
Moorish garrisons, and my life had not been well-nigh lost
amongst them later at Medáin Sâlih.

I went only to the Kurdish Pasha of the Haj, Mohammed
Saîd, who two years before had known me a traveller in the
Lands beyond Jordan, and took me for a well-affected man that
did nothing covertly. It was a time of cholera and the
Christians had fled from the city, when I visited him formerly
in Damascus to prefer the same request, that I might go down
with the pilgrimage to Medáin Sâlih. He had recommended
me then to bring a firmân of the Sultan, saying, "The *hajjàj*
(pilgrims) were a mixed multitude, and if aught befel me, the
harm might be laid at his door, since I was the subject of a
foreign government : " but now he said, ' Well! would I needs
go thither ? it might be with the *Jurdy ;* ' that is the flying provision train which since ancient times is sent down from Syria to
relieve the returning pilgrimage at Medáin Sâlih ; but commonly
lying there only three days, the time would not have sufficed me.

I thought the stars were so disposed that I should not go to
Arabia; but, said my Moslem friends, ' The Pasha himself
could not forbid any taking this journey with the caravan ; and
though I were a *Nasrány,* what hindered! when I went not
down to the *Harameyn* (two sacred cities) but to Medáin Sâlih ;
how! I an honest person might not go, when there went down
every year with the Haj all the desperate cutters of the town ;
nay the most dangerous ribalds of Damascus were already at
Muzeyrîb, to kill and to spoil upon the skirts of the caravan
journeying in the wilderness.' Also they said ' it was but a few
years since Christian masons (there are no Moslems of the craft
in Damascus) had been sent with the Haj to repair the water-
tower or Kella and cistern at the same Medáin Sâlih.'

There is every year a new stirring of this goodly Oriental city
in the days before the Haj ; so many strangers are passing in
the bazaars, of outlandish speech and clothing from far provinces.
The more part are of Asia Minor, many of them bearing over-
great white turbans that might weigh more than their heads :

the most are poor folk of a solemn countenance, which wander
in the streets seeking the bakers' stalls, and I saw that many of
the Damascenes could answer them in their own language. The
town is moved in the departure of the great Pilgrimage of the
Religion and again at the home-coming, which is made a public
spectacle; almost every Moslem household has some one of their
kindred in the caravan. In the markets, there is much taking
up in haste of wares for the road. The tent-makers are busy in
their street overlooking and renewing the old canvas of hundreds
of tents, of tilts and the curtains for litters; the curriers in their
bazaar are selling apace the water-skins and leathern buckets and
saddle-bottles, *matara* or *zemzemieh*; the carpenters' craft are
labouring in all haste for the Haj, the most of them mending
litter-frames. In the *Peraean* out-lying quarter, *el-Medân* is
cheapening and delivery of grain, a provision by the way for
the Haj cattle. Already there come by the streets, passing
daily forth, the *akkâms* with the swaggering litters mounted
high upon the tall pilgrim camels. They are the Haj caravan
drivers, and upon the silent great shuffle-footed beasts, they hold
insolently their path through the narrow bazaars; commonly
ferocious young men, whose mouths are full of horrible cursings:
and whoso is not of this stomach, him they think unmeet for the
road. The *Mukowwems* or Haj camel-masters have called in
their cattle (all are strong males) from the wilderness to the
camel yards in Damascus, where their serving-men are busy
stuffing pillows under the pack-saddle frames, and lapping first
over all the camels' chines, thick blanket-felts of Aleppo, that
they should not be galled; the gear is not lifted till their return
after four months, if they may return alive, from so great a voyage.
The mukowwems are sturdy, weathered men of the road, that
can hold the mastery over their often mutinous crews; it is
written in their hard faces that they are overcomers of the evil
by the evil, and able to deal in the long desert way with the
perfidy of the elvish Beduins. It is the custom in these caravan
countries that all who are to set forth, meet together in some
common place without the city. The assembling of the pilgrim multitude is always by the lake of Muzeyrîb in the
high steppes beyond Jordan two journeys from Damascus.
Here the hajjies who have taken the field are encamped and
lie a week or ten days in the desert before their long voyage.
The Haj Pasha, his affairs despatched with the government
in Damascus, arrives the third day before their departure,
to discharge all first payments to the Beduw and to agree
with the water-carriers, (which are Beduins) for the military
service.

The open ways of Damascus upon that side, lately encumbered with the daily passage of hundreds of litters, and all that, to our eyes strange and motley train, of the Oriental pilgrimage, were again void and silent ; the Haj had departed from among us. A little money is caught at as great gain in these lands long vexed by a criminal government : the hope of silver immediately brought me five or six poorer persons, saying all with great By-Gods they would set their seals to a paper to carry me safely to Medáin Sâlih, whether I would ride upon pack-horses, upon mules, asses, dromedaries, barely upon camel-back, or in a litter. I agreed with a Persian, mukowwem to those of his nation which come every year about from the East by Bagdad, Aleppo, Damascus, to " see the cities " ; and there they join themselves with the great Ottoman Haj caravan. This poor rich man was well content, for a few pounds in his hand which helped him to reckon with his corn-chandler, to convey me to Medáin Sâlih. It was a last moment, the Pasha was departed two days since, and this man must make after with great journeys. I was presently clothed as a Syrian of simple fortune and ready with store of caravan biscuit to ride along with him ; mingled with the Persians in the Haj journey I should be the less noted whether by Persians or Arabs. This mukowwem's servants and his gear were already eight days at Muzeyrîb camp.

It was afternoon when a few Arab friends bade me God-speed, and mounted with my camel bags upon a mule I came riding through Damascus with the Persian, Mohammed Aga, and a small company. As we turned from the long city street, that which in Paul's days was called " The Straight," to go up through the Medân to the Boábat-Ullah, some of the bystanders at the corner, setting upon me their eyes, said to each other, " Who is this ? Eigh ! " Another answered him half jestingly, " It is some one belonging to the Ajamy " (Persian). From the Boábat (great gate of) Ullah, so named of the passing forth of the holy pilgrimage thereat, the high desert lies before us those hundreds of leagues to the Harameyn ; at first a waste plain of gravel and loam upon limestone, for ten or twelve days, and always rising, to Maan in " the mountain of Edom " near to Petra. Twenty-six marches from Muzeyrîb is el-Medina, the prophet's city (Medinat en-Néby, in old time Yathrib) ; at forty marches is Mecca. There were none now in all the road, by which the last hajjies had passed five days before us. The sun setting, we came to the little out-lying village Kesmîh : by the road was showed me a white cupola, the sleeping station of the commander of the pilgrimage, Emir el-Haj, in the evening of his solemn setting forth from Damascus. We came by a beaten way over the wilderness, paved of old at the crossing of winter-stream-beds for the safe passage of the Haj camels, which have no foothold in sliding ground ; by some other are seen ruinous bridges—as all is now ruinous in the Ottoman Empire. There is a block drift strewed over this wilderness ; the like is found, much to our amazement, under all climates of the world. We had sorry night quarters at Kesmîh, to lie out, with falling weather, in a filthy field, nor very long to repose. At three hours past midnight we were again riding. There were come along with us some few other, late and last poor foot wanderers, of the Persian's acquaintance and nation ; blithely they addressed themselves to this sacred voyage, and as the sun began to spring and smile with warmth upon the earth, like awakening birds, they began to warble the sweet bird-like Persian airs. Marching with most alacrity was a yellow-haired young derwîsh, the best minstrel of them all ; with the rest of his breath he laughed and cracked and would hail me cheerfully in the best Arabic that he could. They comforted themselves by the way with tobacco, and there was none, said they, better in the whole world than this sweet leaf of their own country. There arose the high train of Hermon aloft before us, hoar-headed with the first snows and as it were a white cloud hanging in the element, but the autumn in the plain was yet light and warm. At twenty miles we passed before *Salâmen*, an old ruined place with towers and inhabited ruins, such as those seen in the *Hauran :* five miles further another ruined site. Some of my companions were suspicious of a stranger, because I enquired the names. We alighted first at afternoon by a cistern of foul water *Keteyby*, where a guard was set of two ruffian troopers, and when coming there very thirsty I refused to drink, " Oho ! who is here ? " cries one of them with an ill countenance, " it is I guess some Nasrâny ; auh, is this one I say, who should go with the Haj ? " Nine miles from thence we passed before a village, *Meskîn :* faring by the way, we overtook a costard-monger driving his ass with swaggering chests of the half-rotted autumn grapes, to sell his cheap wares to the poor pilgrims for dear money at Muzeyrîb : whilst I bought of his cool bunches, this fellow full of gibes of the road had descried me and " Art thou going. cried he, to Mecca ? Ha ! he is not one to go with the Haj ! and you that come along with him, what is this for an hajjy ? " At foot pace we came to the camp at *Muzeyrîb* after eight o'clock, by dark night ; the forced march was sixteen hours. We had yet to do, shouting for the Aga's people, by their names, to find our tents.

but not much, for after the hundreds of years of the pilgrimage all the Haj service is well ordered. The mukowwems know their own places, and these voices were presently answered by some of his servants who led us to their lodging. The morrow was one of preparation, the day after we should depart. The Aga counselled me not to go abroad from our lodging. The gun would be fired two days earlier this year for the pilgrims' departure, because the season was lateward. We had ten marches through the northern highlands, and the first rains might fall upon us ere we descended to Arabia : in this soil mixed with loam the loaded camels slide, in rainy weather, and cannot safely pass. There was a great stillness in all their camp ; these were the last hours of repose. As it was night there came the waits, of young camp-followers with links ; who saluting every pavilion were last at the Persians' lodgings, (their place as they are strangers and schismatics, doubtless for the avoiding of strifes, is appointed in the rear of all the great caravan) with the refrain *bes-salaamy Ullah yetow-wel ummr-hu, hy el-ády, hy el-ády, Mohammed Aga!* " go in peace, good speed, heigho the largess ! We keep this custom, the Lord give long life to him ; " and the Persian, who durst not break the usage, found his penny with a sorry countenance.

The new dawn appearing we removed not yet. The day risen the tents were dismantled, the camels led in ready to their companies, and halted beside their loads. We waited to hear the cannon shot which should open that year's pilgrimage. It was near ten o'clock when we heard the signal gun fired, and then, without any disorder litters were suddenly heaved and braced upon the bearing beasts, their charges laid upon the kneeling camels, and the thousands of riders, all born in the caravan countries, mounted in silence. As all is up, the drivers are left standing upon their feet, or sit to rest out the latest moments on their heels : they with other camp and tent servants must ride those three hundred leagues upon their bare soles, although they faint ; and are to measure the ground again upward with their weary feet from the holy places. At the second gun, fired a few moments after, the Pasha's litter advances and after him goes the head of the caravan column : other fifteen or twenty minutes we, who have places in the rear, must halt, that is until the long train is unfolded before us ; then we must strike our camels and the great pilgrimage is moving. There go commonly three or four camels abreast and seldom five : the length of the slow-footed multitude of men and cattle is near two miles, and the width some hundred yards in the open plains. The hajjàj were this year by their account

(which may be above the truth) 6000 persons; of these more
than half are serving men on foot; and 10,000 of all kinds of
cattle, the most camels, then mules, hackneys, asses and a few
dromedaries of Arabians returning in security of the great
convoy to their own districts. We march in an empty waste, a
plain of gravel, where nothing appeared and never a road before
us. Hermon, now to the backward, with his mighty shoulders
of snows closes the northern horizon; to the nomads of the
East a noble landmark of Syria, they name it *Towîl éth-Thalj*
' the height of snow ' (of which they have a small experience
in the rainless sun-stricken land of Arabia). It was a Sunday,
when this pilgrimage began, and holiday weather, the summer
azure light was not all faded from the Syrian heaven; the 13th
of November, 1876; and after twelve miles way, (a little, which
seemed long in the beginning,) we came to the second desert
station, where the tents which we had left behind us at Muzeyrîb,
stood already pitched in white ranks before us in the open
wilderness. Thus every day the light tent-servants' train outwent our heavy march, in which, as every company has obtained
their place from the first remove, this they observe continually until their journey's end. Arriving we ride apart,
every company to their proper lodgings: this encampment is
named *Ramta*.

It is their caravan prudence, that in the beginning of a long
way the first shall be a short journey: the beasts feel their
burdens, the passengers have fallen in that to their riding
in the field. Of a few sticks (gathered hastily by the way), of
the desert bushes, cooking fires are soon kindled before all the
tents; and since here are no stones at hand to set under the
pots as Beduins use, the pilgrim hearth is a scraped-out hole,
so that their vessels may stand, with the brands put under,
upon the two brinks, and with very little fuel they make ready
their poor messes. The small military tents of the Haj escort
of troopers and armed dromedary riders, *Ageyl*, (the most *Nejd*
men) are pitched round about the great caravan encampment,
at sixty and sixty paces: in each tent fellowship the watches
are kept till the day dawning. A paper lantern after sunset is
hung before every one to burn all night where a sentinel stands
with his musket, and they suffer none to pass their lines unchal-
lenged. Great is all townsmen's dread of the Beduw, as if they
were the demons of this wild waste earth, ever ready to assail the
Haj passengers; and there is no Beduwy durst chop logic in the
dark with these often ferocious shooters, that might answer
him with lead and who are heard, from time to time, firing
backward into the desert all night; and at every instant crying

down the line kerakô kerakô (sentinel) the next and the next
men thereto answering with *haderûn* (ready). I saw not that
any officer went the rounds. So busy is the first watch, whilst
the camp is waking. These crickets begin to lose their voices
about midnight, when for aught I could see the most of their
lights were out; and it is likely the unpaid men spare their
allowance : those poor soldiers sell their candles privily in the
Haj market.

In the first evening hour there is some merrymake of drum-
beating and soft fluting, and Arcadian sweetness of the Persians
singing in the tents about us ; in others they chant together some
piece of their devotion. In all the pilgrims' lodgings are paper
lanterns with candle burning ; but the camp is weary and all is
soon at rest. The hajjies lie down in their clothes the few
night hours till the morrow gun-fire ; then to rise suddenly for
the march, and not knowing how early they may hear it, but
this is as the rest, after the Pasha's good pleasure and the
weather.

At half past five o'clock was the warning shot for the second
journey. The night sky was dark and showery when we
removed, and cressets of iron cages set upon poles were borne
to light the way, upon serving men's shoulders, in all the companies. The dawn discovered the same barren upland before
us, of shallow gravel and clay ground upon limestone.

The *Derb el-Haj* is no made road, but here a multitude of
cattle-paths beaten hollow by the camels' tread, in the marching
thus once in the year, of so many generations of the motley
pilgrimage over this waste. Such many equal paths lying
together one of the ancient Arabian poets has compared to the
bars of the rayed Arabic mantle. Commonly a shot is heard
near mid-day, the signal to halt ; we have then a short resting-
while, but the beasts are not unloaded and remain standing.
Men alight and the more devout bow down their faces to say
the canonical prayer towards Mecca. Our halt is twenty
minutes ; some days it is less or even omitted, as the Pasha has
deemed expedient, and in easy marches may be lengthened to
forty minutes. "The Pasha (say the caravaners) is our
Sooltan." Having marched twenty miles at our left hand
appeared *Mafrak*, the second Haj road tower, after the great
kella at Muzeyrîb, but it is ruinous and as are some other
towers abandoned. The kellas are fortified water stations
weakly garrisoned ; they may have been built two or three
centuries and are of good masonry. The well is in the midst
of a kella ; the water, raised by a simple machine of drum and
buckets, whose shaft is turned by a mule's labour, flows forth

to fill a cistern or *birket* without the walls. Gear and mules must be fetched down with the Haj from Damascus upon all the desert road, to Medáin Sâlih. The cisterns are jealously guarded; as in them is the life of the great caravan. No Aarab (nomads) are suffered to draw of that water; the garrisons would shoot out upon them from the tower, in which closed with an iron-plated door, they are sheltered themselves all the year from the insolence of the nomads. The kellas stand alone, as it were ships, in the immensity of the desert; they are not built at distances of camps, but according to the opportunity of water; it is more often two or even three marches between them. The most difficult passage of the pilgrim road before Medina is that four or five marches in high ground next above Medáin Sâlih where are neither wells nor springs, but two ruined kellas with their great birkets to be filled only by torrent water, so that many years, in a nearly rainless country they lie dry. A *nejjàb* or post, who is a Beduin dromedary-rider, is therefore sent up every year from Medáin Sâlih, bringing word to Damascus, in *ramathan* before the pilgrimage, whether there be water run in the birket at *Dàr el-Hamra*, and reporting likewise of the state of the next waters. This year he was a messenger of good tidings, (showers and freshets in the mountains had filled the birket) and returned with the Pasha's commandment in his mouth, (since in the garrisons there are few or none lettered) to set a guard over the water. But in years when the birket is empty, some 1500 girbies are taken up in Damascus by the Haj administration to furnish a public supplement of five days water for all the caravan : these water-skins are loaded betwixt the distant waterings, at the government cost, by Beduin carriers.

The caravaners pass the ruined and abandoned kellàs with curses between their teeth, which they cast, I know not how justly, at the Haj officers and say "all the birkets leak and there is no water for the hajjàj ; every year there is money paid out of the treasury that should be for the maintenance of the buildings ; these embezzling pashas swallow the public silver; we may hardly draw now of any cistern before Maan, but after the long marches must send far to seek it, and that we may find is not good to drink." Turkish peculation is notorious in all the Haj service, which somewhat to abate certain Greek Christians, Syrians, are always bursars in Damascus of the great Mohammedan pilgrimage :—this is the law of the road, that all look through their fingers. The decay of the road is also, because much less of the public treasure is now spent for the Haj service. The impoverished Ottoman government has withdrawn the not long established camp at Maan, and greatly diminished the kella allowances ; but the yearly cost of the Haj road is said to be yet £50,000, levied from the province of Syria, where the Christians cry out. it is tyranny that they too must pay from their slender purses, for this seeking hallows of the Moslemîn. A yearly loss to the empire is the *surra* or " bundles of money " to buy a peaceful passage of the abhorred Beduins : the half part of Western Arabia is fed thereby, and yet it were of more cost, for the military escort to pass " by the sword." The destitute Beduins will abate nothing of their yearly pension : that which was paid to their fathers, they believe should be always due to them out of the treasures of the " Sooltan " and if any less be proffered them they would say " The unfaithful pashas have devoured it ! " the pilgrimage should not pass, and none might persuade them, although the *Dowla* (Sultan's Empire) were perishing. It were news to them that the Sultan of Islam is but a Turk and of strange blood : they take him to be as the personage of a prophet, king of the world by the divine will, unto whom all owe obedience. Malcontent, as has been often seen, they would assault the Haj march or set upon some corner of the camp by night, hoping to drive off a booty of camels : in warfare they beset the strait places, where the firing down of a hundred beggarly matchlocks upon the thick multitude must cost many lives ; so an Egyptian army of Ibrahîm Pasha was defeated in the south country by Harb Beduins. * * *

(*After journeying for three weeks through the plains of Moab and through the land of Edom (Arabia Petraea), the Haj reaches the plain of el-Héjr.*)

* * * The name of the strait is *el-Mèzham* " place of thronging." It is short, at first steep, and issues upon the plain of el-Héjr which is Medáin Sâlih ; where the sun coming up showed the singular landscape of this valley-plain, encompassed with mighty sand-rock precipices (which here resemble ranges of city walls, fantastic towers and castle buildings,) and upon

them lie high shouldering sand-drifts. The bottom is sand, with much growth of desert-bushes; and I perceived some thin sprinkled vulcanic drift. Westward is seen the immense mountain blackness, terrible and lowering, of the Harra.

I asked "And where are the *Cities of Sálih?*" It was answered "In none of these precipices about, but in yonder jebel," (Ethlib,) whose sharp crags and spires shot up now above the greenness of a few desert acacia trees, great here as forest timber. "And, Khalîl, thou shalt see wonders to-day of houses hewn in the rock," some added "and the hewn houses standing, wellah, heels uppermost, by miracle!" Other plainer men said "This we saw not, but Khalîl now thy way is ended, look, we have brought thee to Medáin, where we say put not thyself in the danger of the Beduw, but go thou in to lodge at the kella which thou seest yonder with the palms; it is a pleasant one."

The pilgrimage began on a Sunday, this fair morning was the fourth Sunday in the way, therefore the world for me was peace, yet I mused what should become of my life, few miles further at Medáin Sâlih. Whilst we were speaking I heard this disastrous voice before me: "Now only another Nasrâny is in the caravan, curse Ullah his father, he will be dealt with presently." I demanded immediately of Eswad "what was it?" he did not answer again. I could but guess, that some Christian akkâm had been discovered amongst them, and to such the hajjâj were but a confederacy of murderers:—their religion is murderous, and were therefore to be trodden out as fire by the humanity of all the world! I looked continually, and would have attempted somewhat, I was also an European and the caravan is full of reasonable men; but I perceived naught, nor might hear anything further of him. I remembered the chance of a Syrian Christian *mukâry*, or muleteer carrier, whose friends were known to me at Damascus; and who had many times been a driver in the Haj to the Harameyn. The lad's partner on the Syrian roads, was a jolly Moslem that went every year akkâm in the pilgrimage; and would have his fellow along with him, although it were to Mecca. The Christian was willing, and the other taught him praying and prostrations enough for young men of their simple condition. Thus the circumcised and the uncircumcised went down year by year, and returned to make a secret mock together: yet were any such inloper uncased in the Haj, he being but a poor subject of theirs, and none to plead for him, he had sinned against his own soul; except he would abjure his faith, he must die like a dog, he is "an unclean Nasrâny," for the despite done unto Ullah and His Apostle.

CHAPTER II

MEDÁIN [THE " CITIES " OF] SÂLIH

IN a warm and hazy air, we came marching over the loamy sand plain, in two hours, to Medáin Sâlih, a second merkez on the road, and at the midst of their long journey ; where the caravan arriving was saluted with many rounds from the field-pieces and we alighted at our encampment of white tents, pitched a little before the kella.

The Ajamy would have me write him immediately a full release and acquittance. I thought it were better to lodge, if I might, at the kella ; the *kellâjy*, surveyor of this and next towers, had once made me a promise in Damascus, that if I should ever arrive here he would receive me. The Beduins I heard to be come in from three days distance and that to-morrow they would return to their wandering menzils. I asked the Persian to transport my baggage, but because his covenant was out he denied me, although my debtor for medicines which he had upon the road freely, as much as he would. These gracious Orientals are always graceless short-comers at the last, and therefore may they never thrive ! Meanwhile the way-worn people had bought themselves meat in the camp market of the Beduin fleshers, and fresh joints of mutton were hanging soon before all the Haj tents. The weary Damascenes, inhabi-tants of a river city, fell to diligently washing their sullied garments. Those who played the cooks in the fellowships, had gathered sticks and made the little fire pits ; and all was full of business.

Here pilgrims stand much upon their guard, for this is, they think, the most thievish station upon the road to Medina, which " thieves " are the poor Beduins. A tale is told every year after their cooks' wit, how ' the last time, by Ullah, one did but look round to take more sticks and when he turned again the cauldron was lost. This cook stepped upon his feet and through the press he ran, and laid hand upon a bare-foot Beduwy the

first he met; and he was he, the cursed one, who stole back
with the burning pot covered under his beggarly garment.
Friendly persons bade me also have a care, I might lose a thing
in a moment and that should be without remedy. There came
in some of the poor nomads among us; the citizen hajjies cried
upon them "Avaunt!" some with staves thrust them, some
flung them headlong forth by the shoulders as wild creatures;
certain Persians, for fear of their stealing, had armed themselves
with stones.—Yet afterward I knew all these poor people as
friendly neighbours, and without any offence. There were come
in some of their women, offering to sell us bunches of mewed
ostrich feathers, which they had taken up in the desert. The
ribald akkâms proffered them again half-handfuls of broken
biscuit; yet are these fretted short plumes worth above their
weight in silver, at Damascus. Eswad, who was a merry fellow,
offended at this bargaining with a dishonest gesture; " Fie on
thee, ah lad for shame!" exclaimed the poor young woman :—
the nomads much despise the brutish behaviour of the townspeople. I went through the encampment and came under the
kella, where sweetmeat-sellers, with stone counterpoises, were
selling pennyworths of dates upon their spread mantles; which
wares are commonly carried in the desert journeys upon asses.
I spoke to one to lend me his beast for money that I might
fetch in my baggage. "My son, (answered the old man, who took
me for one of the Moorish garrison,) I have therewith to do, I
cannot lend him." I returned to the Ajamy; he would now
lend me a mule, and when I had written him his quittance, the
cloudy villain changed to fair weather; I saw him now a fountain
of smiles and pleasant words, as if he fed only with the bees
among honey flowers, and bidding el-Eswad drive the load he
brought me forward with the dunghill oriental grace and false
courtesy. As I was going "Khalîl Aga (said the best of the
akkâms) forgive us!" they would have me not remember their
sometimes rude and wild behaviour in the way. We found that
kellâjy standing before the gate of his kella (thereover I saw a
well-engraved Arabic inscription); busy he was receiving the
garrison victual and caravan stores. He welcomed me shortly
and bade me enter, until he should be out of hand. Loiterers
of the garrison would hardly let me pass, saying that no
strangers might come in there.

But what marvellous indifference of the weary hajjies! I saw
none of them set forth to view the monuments, though as much
renowned in their religion as Sodom and Gomorrah, and whereof such strange fables are told in the Koran. Pity Mohammed
had not seen Petra! he might have drawn another long-bow

shot in Wady Mûsa : yet hardly from their camp is any of these
wonders of the faith plainly visible. The palmers, who are
besides greatly adread of the Aarab, durst not adventure forth,
unless there go a score of them together. Departing always by
night-time, the pilgrims see not the Cities of Sâlih, but the
ascending Haj see them. Eswad came to the kella at nightfall,
and bade me God-speed and to be very prudent ; for the tower
garrisons are reputed men of violence, as the rest of the Haj
service. So came the kellâjy, who surprised to find me still
sitting obscurely within, by my baggage, assigned me a cell-
chamber. One came then and called him forth to the Pasha ; I
knew afterward that he was summoned upon my account. About
mid-night the warning gunshot sounded in the camp, a second
was the signal to remove ; I heard the last hubbub of the Haj
rising, and in few more moments the solemn jingles of the
takhts er-Rûm journeying again in the darkness, with the
departing caravan. Few miles lower they pass a *boghrâz*, or
strait in the mountains. Their first station is *Zmurrûd*, a forsaken kella ; in another remove they come to *Sawra* kella, then
Hedîeh kella, *Sújwa* kella, *Barraga*, *Oweynat el-Béden ;* there the
Haj camp is pitched a little before Medina. In every step of
the Mecca-bound pilgrims is now heart's rest and religious confidence that they shall see the holy places ; they have passed
here the midst of the long way. In the morning twilight, I
heard a new rumour without, of some wretched nomads, that
with the greediness of unclean birds searched the forsaken
ground of the encampment.

As it was light the Beduins came clamorously flocking into the
tower, and for a day we were over-run by them. Said *Mohammed
Aly* the kellâjy " Wellah, we cannot be sure from hour to hour ;
but their humour changing, they might attempt the kella ! " It
was thus the same Fejîr Beduins had seized this kella few years
before, when the Haj government established a new economy
upon the pilgrimage road, and would have lessened the nomads'
former surra. The caravan gone by, the Aarab that were in
the kella, with their sheykh *Motlog*, suddenly ran upon the weak
guard, to whom they did no hurt but sent them in peace to *el-
Ally*. Then they broke into the sealed chambers and pillaged
all that might come to their hand, the Haj and Jurdy soldiers'
stores with all that lately brought down for the victualling of
this and the other kellas that stand under Medáin Sâlih.
The tribes that year would hardly suffer the caravan to pass
peaceably, and other kellas were in like manner surprised and
mastered by them ; that next below Medáin, and Sújwa kella
were robbed at the same time by the W. Aly. The Beduw said,

they only sought their own ; the custom of surra or payment for right of way could not now be broken. A squadron of Syrian cavalry sent down with the next year's Haj, to protect those towers, was quartered at el-Ally, but when the caravan was gone by, the Beduins (mostly W. Aly) went to surround the oasis, and held them besieged till the second year. I have said to the Beduins, "If the tower-keepers shut their plated door, what were all your threatenings against them ?" Arabians have not wit to burst iron-plate with the brunt of a beam, or by heaping fire-wood to burn the back timber of the door, nor any public courage to adventure their miserable lives under defended walls. They have answered me, "The kella could not be continually shut against us, the Beduins have many sly shifts ; and if not by other means yet by a *thubîha*, (gift of a sheep or other beast for slaughter,) we should not fail sometime to creep in."

In this kella an old Moor of Fez, *Haj Nejm*, was warden (*mohâfuz*) ; the other tower-keepers were *Haj Hasan*, a Moor of Morocco, who was before of this tower service, and coming in our pilgrimage from Damascus, had been stayed here again, at the entreaty of his countryman Nejm. Then *Abd el-Kâder*, (Servitor-of-the-mighty-God) a young man named after the noble Algerian prince, and son of his deceased steward : he growing into fellowship with the muatterîn at Damascus, his "uncle" (whose venerable authority is absolute over all the Moorish emigration) had relegated the lubber into the main deserts for a year, in charge of Mohammed Aly. A fourth was *Mohammed*, a half Beduin lad, son of a former Damascene kella keeper, by a nomad housewife ; and besides, there was only a slave and another poor man that had been sent to keep the water together at the B. Moaddam.

Our few Moors went armed in the tower amongst the treacherous Beduins ; Haj Nejm sat, with his blunderbuss crossed upon his knees, amongst his nomad guests, in the coffee chamber. He was feeble and old, and Hasan the only manful sufficient hand amongst them. This stalwart man was singing all the day at his task and smiling to himself with unabated good humour. Self-minded he was and witty of head to find a shift with any wile, which made all easy to him, yet without his small horizon he was of a barbarous understanding ; so that Mohammed Aly would cry out upon his strongheadedness, "Wellah thou art a *Berber*, Hasan !" (The Berbers, often blue-eyed and yellow-haired, a remnant of the former peoples or Barbary.) Twelve years he had been in the East, and might seem to be a man of middle age, but in his own eyes his years were fifty and more, "And wot you why (he would say and laugh again), my heart is ever green." The Moors are born under wandering stars. Many wearing the white *burnûs*, come in every pilgrimage to Mecca; thence they disperse themselves to Syria, to Mesopotamia, and to all the East Arabic world seeking fortune and service. They labour at their old trades in a new land, and those that have none, (they have all a humour of arms,) will commonly hire themselves as soldiers. They are hired before other men, for their circumspect acrid nature, to be caretakers of orchards at Damascus, and many private trusts are committed to the bold Moghrebies. These Western men are distinguished by their harsh ventriloquial speech, and foreign voices.

Nejm, now a great while upon this side of the sea, was grown infirm more than aged; he could not hope to see his Fez again, that happier soil of which, with a sort of smiling simplicity, he gossiped continually. He had wandered through the Barbary states, he knew even the Algerian *sáhara;* at Tunis he had taken service, then sometime in Egypt far upon the Nile; afterward he was a soldier in Syria, and later of the haj-road service, in the camp at Maan: a fervent Moslem, yet one that had seen and suffered in the world, he could be tolerant, and I was kindly received by him. ' The *Engleys* (said he) at *Jebel Tar* (Gibraltar) were his people's neighbours over the strait.' He had liever Engleys than Stambûlies, Turks that were corrupted and no good Moslems. Only the last year the Sîr Amîn had left a keg of wine with them in the kella, till their coming up again : " a cursed man (he said) to drink of that which is forbidden to the Moslemîn ! " He was father of two children, but, daughters, he seemed not to regard them ; female children are a burden of small joy in a poor Moslem family ; for whom the father shall at last receive but a slender bride-money, when they are divided from his household.

Nature prepared for the lad Mohammed an unhappy age ; vain and timid, the stripling was ambitious to be somewhat, without virtuous endeavour. A loiterer at his labour and a slug in the morning, I heard when Mohammed Aly reprehended him in this manner : " It is good to rise up, my son (as the day is dawning), to the hour of morning prayer. It is then the night angels depart, and the angels of the day arrive, but those that linger and sleep on still, Satan enters into them. Knowest thou I had once in my house a serving lad, a Nasrâny, and although he washed his head with soap and had combed out his hair, yet then his visage always appeared swollen and discoloured, wellah as a swine ; and if you mark them of a morning, you may see the Nasâra to be all of them as swine."

"Ignorant" (*jáhil*) more than ill-given was the young Abd el-Kâder, and hugely overgrown, so that Hasan said one day, observing him, " Abd el-Kâder's costard is as big as the head of our white mule and nothing in it." Thus they pulled his coxcomb in the kella, till it had done the poor lad's heart good to have blubbered; bye and bye he was dismissed to keep the water with another at B. Moaddam.

Mohammed Aly, (by his surname) *el-Mahjûb*, surveyor of the kellas between Tebûk and el-Medina, was an amiable bloody ruffian, a little broken-headed, his part good partly violent nature had been distempered (as many of their unquiet climbing spirits) in the Turkish school of government; he was without letters. His family had inhabited a mountain country (he said, " of uncorrupted ancient manners ") in Algeria: in the conquest, rather than become subjects of the Nasâra, they embarked at their own election in French government vessels, to be landed in Syria. There was a tradition amongst their ancestors, that "very anciently they occupied all that country about Maan, where also Moses fed the flocks of Jethro the prophet; the B. Israel had dispossessed them." Entering the military service, he had fought and suffered with the Syrian troops, in a terrible *jehâd* against the Muscovites, in the Caucasus, where he was twice wounded. The shot, it seemed to me, by his own showing, had entered from the backward, and still the old wounds vexed him in ill weather. Afterward, at the head of a small horse troop, he served in Palestine and the lands beyond Jordan, attaching himself to the fortunes of Mohammed Saîd, from whom he had obtained his present office. The man, half ferocious trooper, could speak fair and reasonably in his better mind; then as there are backwaters in every tide, he seemed humane: the best and the worst Moslemîn can discourse very religiously. He held the valour of the Moghrebies to be incomparable, it were perilous then to contrary him; a tiger he was in his dunghill ill-humour, and had made himself formerly known on this road by his cruelties. Somewhile being lieutenant at Maan, he had hanged (as he vaunted) three men. Then, when it had been committed to him to build a vault over the spring head at the kella Medowwara, and make that water sure from all hostility of the Aarab, he took certain of them prisoners, sheykhs accused of plundering the Haj, and binding them, he fed them every day in the tower with two biscuits, and every day he caused to be ground a measure of meal in an hand-mill (which is of intolerable weight) upon their breasts; until yielding to these extremities, which they bore sometime with manly fortitude, they had sent for that ransom which he

B

would devour of them. A diseased senile body he was, full of ulcers, and past the middle age, so that he looked not to live long, his visage much like a fiend, dim with the leprosy of the soul and half fond ; he shouted when he spoke with a startling voice, as it might have been of the ghrôl : of his dark heart ruled by so weak a head, we had hourly alarms in the lonely kella. Well could he speak (with a certain erudite utterance) to his purpose, in many or in few words. These Orientals study little else, as they sit all day idle at the coffee in their male societies : they learn in this school of infinite human observation to speak to the heart of one another. His tales seasoned with saws, which are the wisdom of the unlearned, we heard for more than two months, they were never ending. He told them so lively to the eye that they could not be bettered, and part were of his own motley experience. Of a licentious military tongue, and now in the shipwreck of a good understanding, with the bestial insane instincts and the like compunctions of a spent humanity, it seemed the jade might have been (if great had been his chance) another Tiberius senex. With all this, he was very devout as only they can be, and in his religion scrupulous ; it lay much upon his conscience to name the Nasrâny *Khalîl*, and he made shift to call me, for one Khalîl, five times Ibrahîm. He returned always with a wonderful solemnity to his prayers, wherein he found a sweet foretaste of Paradise ; this was all the solace here in the deserts of his corrupt mind. A caterpillar himself, he could censure the criminal Ottoman administration, and pinch at all their misdemeanours. At Damascus, he had his name inscribed in the register of French Algerian subjects ; he left this hole to creep into, if aught went hard with him, upon the side of the Dowla ; and in trouble any that can claim their protection in Turkish countries, are very nimble to run to the foreign consuls.

The nomads have an ill opinion of Turkish Haj government, seeing the tyrannical and brutish behaviour of these pretended rulers, their paymasters. All townsmen contemn them again as the most abject of banded robbers. If any nomad be taken in a fault, the military command " Away with this Beduwy " is shouted with the voice of the destroying angel " and bind him to the gun-wheel." Mohammed Aly was mad, in his Moorish pride, and of desperate resentment ; only the last year he durst contend here in the deserts, with his Haj Pasha. In a ground chamber of the kella are sealed government stores and deposits of the mukowwems' furnitures : with the rest was sent in by the paymaster-Pasha a bag of reals, of the public money. When they came again, the Pasha sent his servant to receive the silver. The man, as he held it in his hand, imagining this purse to have leaked, for the Arabs are always full of these canine suspicions, began to accuse Mohammed Aly ; but the Moor, pulling out his scimitar, cut down the rash unarmed slave, flung him forth by the heels, and with frantic maledictions, shut up the iron door after him. The Pasha sent again, bidding Mohammed Aly come to him and answer for this outrage ; but the Syrian Moor, his heart yet boiling, swore desperately he would not go until his humour were satisfied. —"Away and say these words to the Pasha from Mohammed Aly, If Mohammed Saîd have cannon, so have I artillery upon the terrace of this kella,—by God Almighty we will hold out to the last ; and let him remember that we are *Moghrâreba!*" This was a furious playing out friends and playing in mischief, but he trusted that his old service would assure him with the robust Pasha ; at the worst he would excuse himself, attesting his wounds suffered in the sacred cause of their religion ; and after all he could complain " Wellah, his head went not all times well, and that he was a Moghreby," that is one of choleric nature and a generous rashness : at the very worst he could defy them, proving that he was a stranger born and a French subject. His artillery (and such is wont to be the worth of an Arabic boast) were two very small rust-eaten pieces, which for their rudeness, might have been hammered by some nomad smith : years ago they had been brought from the *Borj*, an antique tower half a mile distant, towards the monuments, and were said to have served in old nomad warfare between Annezy and *Harb* tribesmen.

Before the departure of the Aarab, came their sheykh Motlog enquiring for me ; *Wen-hu, wen-hu,* ' where is he, this *dowlâny* or government man ?' He bounced my door up, and I saw a swarthy Beduin that stood to gaze lowering and strangely on one whom he took to be *gomâny*, an enemy. Mohammed Aly had said to them that I was a Sîr Amîn, some secretary sent down upon a government errand. This was a short illusion, for as the Moslems pray openly and Khalîl was not seen to pray, it was soon said that I could not be of the religion. Mohammed Aly was a hater of every other than his own belief and very jealous of the growing despotism in the world of the perilous Nasâra ;—thus they muse with a ferocious gloom over the decay of the militant Islam. Yet he could regard me pleasantly, as a philosopher, in whom was an indulgent natural opinion in all matter of religion.—These were the inhabitants of the kella, a tower seventy feet upon a side, square built. Lurid within are these water-stations, and all that I entered are of one fashion of building. In the midst is the well-court, and about it the stable, the forage and store chambers. Stairs lead upon the gallery which runs round above, whereupon in the north and south sides are the rows of small stone dwelling chambers. Staircases lead from this gallery to the terrace roof, where the garrison may suddenly run up in any need to the defence of the kella.

This tower is built about an ancient well, the *Bîr en-Nâga* where the miraculous she-camel had been watered ; it is the only water that a religious man may drink, in the opinion of their doctors, in " the subverted country : " but by leaking of the cesspool, I fear this well is an occasion of grave vesical diseases. The *bîr*, as the other ancient wells that remain in the plain, is lined with dry-built masonry, twenty-six feet deep to the ground water, which comes up warm and reeking in a winter morning, at a temperature of 66 Fahr. ;—I never found well water not lukewarm in Arabia ! The *Ullema* teach that men's prayers may hardly rise to Heaven from the soil of Medáin Sâlih, and the most perfect of them carry their water over from the last stages, that even of the naga's well they refuse to drink. The kella birket without to the southward, measures eighteen by twenty-two paces ; the depth is three fathoms. Two mules from Damascus wrought singly, turning the rude mill-machine of the well, four and four hours daily ; but that was so badly devised, that nearly a third part of the drawn water as it came up in the buckets, which are hoops of chipwood like corn measures, was spilled back again ; and good part of that which flows out is lost, for all the birket floor leaked or the whole might be filled in ten or twelve days. For the renewing of the well-gear of this and the next kellas stores are brought down here in every Haj from Damascus.

It is remarkable that all the haj-road kellas are said to have been built by Nasâra, nearly to Medina ; Christian masons a few years before repaired this tower of Medáin Sâlih ; I was not then the first Christian man seen within these distant kella walls : they were remembered to have been quiet and hospitable persons. The kella foundations are of stones without mortar laid upon the weak loamy bottom ; the walls above are rude courses of stones raised in clay ; the work is only pointed with mortar. Stone for burning lime must be fetched upon the backs of hired Beduin camels from *Jebel Iss*, which is a sandstone mountain overlaid with limestone in a wady of the same name, two journeys distant under the *Harreyry* or little Harra, below el-Ally. This is not that greater *W. el Iss* of antiquity, wherein are seen many springs with *dôm* palms and the ruins

of villages, which descends from the *Jeheyna* country, beginning
a long journey above *Yánba*, and goes out in the *W. el-Humth*
or *W. Jizzl.*

In Damascus I had heard of the pleasant site of this kella with
its garden of palms. Here were three grown female trees, with
one male stem which made them fruitful. In the orchard plot
closed with a clay wall, Haj Nejm passed his holiday hours in this
immense Beduin wilderness, and raised his salads, his leeks and
other pot-herbs to give a savour to his Arab messes. The tower
stands solitary half a mile before the mountain Ethlib, almost in
the midst of the valley-plain of Medáin. This is Hijr of the
koran, el-Héjr of the Beduins. The place is 'Εγρα of Ptolemy's
geography; in his time an emporium of the caravan road between
el-Yémen and Syria which is since become the derb el-haj. From
the kella roof two may be descried of the greatest monuments,
and the plain is seen as enclosed by cliffs. Only past Ethlib the
plain appears open upon the left hand, with shelves of sand
riding upon the short horizon to the south-eastward : it is
there the haj road passes. Between us and the solitude of the
desert, are the gate Arabs, certain nomad families whose tents
were always pitched before the iron door of the kella. They
are poor Fej(k)îr households, (which wanting camels cannot
follow the wandering camps of their tribesmen,) and a half
dozen ragged tents of *Fehját*, a small very poor kindred of
Heteym, and despised almost as outcasts ; they are clients of
the Fukara and from ancient times, at the service of the kella,
and foragers like the Sweyfly at el-Akhdar, selling their camel
loads of harsh knot-grass, to the pilgrimage caravan, for a
certain government price, which is set at a real. Of the
Fehját, Sweyfly, and the poor Humeydát of Tebûk, is chanted
a ribald rime in the Haj " We have companied with the daughters
of them for a crown." Another poor sort of haj foragers in
these parts are the *Bedówna*, they are also Heteym ; their
home district is *Jebel Dokhàn* below el-Ally : they are fifty
families, sellers here, and at Sawra, of the same tall grass kind,
which grows in low sandy places under the desert mountains ;
the thurrm is not browsed by the small Beduin camels. The
Arabs blame this country as *Béled ej-jûa*, 'a land of hunger':
households seldom here cook anything, a handful of clotted
dates is the most of their commons : also they name it *Béled
el-haramíeh*, 'a land of robbers.' This plain is a path of many
ghrazzûs (ridings on warfare) of hostile tribesmen, so that few
days ever pass without alarms.

The *Medáin Sálih* are, in the koran fable, houses hewn in
the rocks of the idolatrous tribe Thamûd of the ancient

Arabians, which were destroyed already, according to their fantastic chronicles, in the days of Jethro, God's messenger to the Midianites.   Jethro, in the koran, preaches to his incredulous tribesmen of the judgments that had overtaken other peoples sometime despisers of holy prophets *Hejra* in Ptolemy and Pliny, is an oasis staple town of *the gold and frankincense caravan road* from Arabia the Happy.   In the next generations it must needs decay, as this trade road to the North was disused more and more and at last nearly abandoned for the sea carriage.   In Mohammed's time, only five hundred years later, the desolate city had so long passed away that the name was become a marvellous fable.   Mohammed going by, in the Mecca caravans. was doubtless moved seeing from the road the archaic hewn architecture of those " desolate places ": (no one can consider without emotion the severe and proud lineaments of these solemn ranges of caverns!) also he beheld in them a divine testimony of the popular tradition.   The high sententious fantasy of the ignorant Arabs, the same that will not trust the heart of man, is full of infantile credulity in all religious matter ; and already the young religionist was rolling the sentiment of a divine mission in his unquiet spirit.   In his prophetic life the destruction of Thamûd, joined with the like pretended cases of *Aad,* of Midiân and of the cities of Lot, that had "rejected the apostles of Ullah," is become a capital argument in the koran ; words of present persuasion of fear not easily to be answered, since their falsity could only be ascertained by the event. * * *

* * * A week now we had been shut in the kella, and were still weary of our journeys from Syria.   Mohammed Aly would not let me go forth alone : but he had spoken with *Zeyd,* a principal Beduin sheykh, who after other days would return and accompany me to the monuments.   Haj Nejm said of Medáin, "It is a marvel, that you may view their sûks, and even the nail-holes whereupon were hanged their stuffs over the shop doors, and in many of their shops and shelves, spences and little cellars where they laid up their wares ; and, wellah, you may see all full of the bones of *Kôm Thamûd ;* they were *kuffâr,* they would not believe in God until they fell down dead men, when the blast was come upon them."   The worthy old Moor spoke between a confused simplicity and half an honest thought that there failed something in his argument : " and (said he to the aga) knowest thou a new thing was found of late ; certain of the women searching for gunsalt (saltpetre) in the ' houses ', have lighted upon some drug-like matter, which cast on the coals yields an

odour of *bakhúr* (frankincense). Wellah, they have sold it for such at el-Ally." He went and fetched us small crumbling pieces, they were brown and whitish ; "and see you here, said he, three kinds, *bakhúr, aud* and *mubárak.*" He cast them in the hearth and there rose a feeble earthy smoke, with mouldy ill-smelling sweetness of incense. Frankincense is no more of Arabia Felix, and yet the perfume is sovereign in the estimation of all Arabians. The most is brought now in the pilgrimage from the Malay Islands to Mecca ; and from thence is dispersed throughout the Arabian Peninsula, almost to every household. The odour comforts the religious soul and embalms the brain : that we think the incense-odour religious, is by great likelihood the gentile tradition remaining to us of this old gold and frankincense road. The Arabians cast a morsel in a chafing dish, which is sent round from hand to hand in their coffee drinkings, especially in the oases villages in any festival days : each person, as it comes to him in the turn, hides this under his mantle a moment, to make his clothing well smelling ; then he snuffs the sweet reek once or twice, and hands down the perfume dish to his neighbour.

The Beduins had departed. We sat one of these evenings gathered in the small coffee chamber (which is upon the gallery above), about the winter fire of dry acacia timber, when between the clatter of the coffee pestle we thought we heard one hailing under the loop-hole ! all listened ;—an hollow voice called wearily to us. Mohammed Aly shouted down to him in Turkish, which he had learned in his soldier's life : he was answered in the same language. " Ah," said the aga withdrawing his head, " it is some poor hajjy ; up Hasan, and thou run down Mohammed, open the door :" and they hastened with a religious willingness to let the hapless pilgrim in. They led up to us a poor man of a good presence, somewhat entered in years ; he was almost naked and trembled in the night's cold. It was a Turkish derwish who had walked hither upon his feet from his place in Asia Minor, it might be a distance of six hundred miles ; but though robust, his human sufferance was too little for the long way. He had sickened a little after Maan, and the Haj breaking up from Medowwara, left this weary wight still slumbering in the wilderness ; and he had since trudged through the deserts those two hundred miles, on the traces of the caravan, relieved only at the kellas ! The lone and broken wayfarer could no more overtake the hajjàj, which removed continually before him by forced marches. Mohammed Aly brought him an Aleppo felt cloth, in which the poor derwish who had been stripped by Aarab only three hours before Medáin, might wrap himself from the cold.

Kindly they all now received him and, while his supper was being made ready, they bade him be comforted, saying, The next year, and it pleased Ullah, he might fulfil the sacred pilgrimage ; now he might remain with them, and they would find him, in these two and a half months, until the Haj coming again. But he would not! He had left his home to be very unfortunate in strange countries ; he should not see the two blissful cities, he was never to return. The palmer sat at our coffee fire with a devout thankfulness and an honest humility. Restored to the fraternity of mankind, he showed himself to be a poor man of very innocent and gentle manners. When we were glad again, one of the gate-nomads, taking up the music of the desert, opened his lips to make us mirth, sternly braying his Beduin song to the grave chord of the rabeyby. This was *Wady* of the Fejîr Beduins, a comely figure in the firelight company, of a black visage. He had lived a year at Damascus of late, and was become a town-made cozening villain, under the natural semblance of worth. Of sheykhly blood and noble easy countenance, he seemed to be a child of fortune, but the wretch had not camels ; his tent stood therefore continually pitched before .the kella: more than the flies, he haunted the tower coffee chamber, where, rolling his great white eyeballs, he fawned hour by hour with all his white teeth upon Mohammed Aly, assenting with *Ullah Akhbar!* " God most high," to all the sapient saws of this great one of the kella.

Lapped in his cloth, the poor derwish sat a day over, in this sweetness of reposing from his past fatigues. The third morrow come, the last of the customary hospitality, they were already weary of him ; Mohammed Aly. putting a bundle of meal in his hand and a little water-skin upon his shoulders, brought him forth, and showing the direction bade him follow as he could the footprints of the caravan, and God-speed. Infinite are the miseries of the Haj ; religion is a promise of good things to come, to poor folk, and many among them are half destitute persons. This pain, the words of that fatal Arabian, professing himself to be the Messenger of Ullah, have imposed upon ten thousands every year of afflicted mankind! * * *

* * * Beduins soon came in who had seen our derwish slowly travelling upon the lower haj road : clear was the weather, the winter's sun made hot mid-days, but the season was too chill for such a weary man to lie abroad by night. Weeks after other Beduins arrived from Medina, and we enquired if they had seen aught of our derwish ? They hearing how the man was clad, answered " Ay, billah, we saw him lying dead, and the felt was under him ; it was by the way-side, by Sawra, (not far

down,) almost in sight of the kella." Sorry were his benefactors, that he whom they lately dismissed alive lay now a dead carcase in the wilderness; themselves might so mishap another day in the great deserts. All voices cried at once, " He perished for thirst!" They supposed he had poured out his water-skin, which must hang wearily on his feeble neck in the hot noons. The sight was not new to the nomads, of wretched passengers fallen down dying upon the pilgrim way and abandoned; they oftentimes (Beduins have said it in my hearing) see the hyenas stand by glaring and gaping to devour them, as ever the breath should be gone out of the warm body. They pass by:—in Beduins is no pious thought of unpaid charity to bury strangers. —Mohammed Aly told me there is no Haj in which some fail not and are left behind to die. They suffer most between the Harameyn, "where, O Khalîl! the mountains stand walled up to heaven upon either hand!" In the stagnant air there is no covert from the torment of the naked sun: as the breathless *simûm* blows upon them they fall grovelling and are suffocated. There is water by the way, even where the heat is greatest, but the cursed Beduins will not suffer the wayfaring man to drink, except they may have new and new gifts from the Turkish pashas: there is no remedy, nor past this valley of death, is yet an end of mortal evils. The camping ground at Mecca lies too far from the place, the swarm of poor strangers must seek them hired dwelling chambers in the holy city: thus many are commonly stived together in a very narrow room. The most arriving feeble from great journeys, with ill humours increased in their bodies, new and horrible disorders must needs breed among them:—from the Mecca pilgrimage has gone forth many a general pestilence, to the furthest of mankind!

Enormous indeed has been the event of Mohammed's religious faction. The old Semitic currencies in religion were uttered new under that bastard stamp of the (expedite, factious, and liberal) Arabian spirit, and digested to an easy sober rule of human life, (a pleasant carnal congruity looking not above men's possibility). Are not Mohammed's saws to-day the mother belief of a tenth part of mankind? What had the world been? if the tongue had not wagged, of this fatal Ishmaelite! Even a thin-witted religion that can array an human multitude, is a main power in the history of the unjust world. Perilous every bond which can unite many of the human millions, for living and dying! Islam and the commonwealth of Jews are as great secret conspiracies, friends only of themselves and to all without of crude iniquitous heart, unfaithful, implacable.—But the pre-Islamic idolatrous religion of the kaaba was cause that the soon ripe Mawmetry rotted not soon again.   B*

The heart of their dispersed religion is always Mecca, from whence the Moslems of so many lands every year return fanaticised. From how far countries do they assemble to the sacred festival; the pleasant contagion of the Arab's religion has spread nearly as far as the pestilence :—a battle gained and it had overflowed into Europe. The nations of Islam, of a barbarous fox-like understanding, and persuaded in their religion, that " knowledge is only of the koran," cannot now come upon any way that is good.

Other days passed, Mohammed Aly saying every evening " on the morrow he would accompany me to the monuments." These were Turkish promises, I had to deal with one who in his heart already devoured the Nasrâny : in Syria he had admired that curious cupidity of certain Frankish passengers in the purchasing of "antiquities." " What wilt thou give me, said he, to see the monuments ? and remember, I only am thy protection in this wilderness. There be some in the kella, that would kill thee except I forbade them : by Almighty God, I tell thee the truth." I said ' That he set the price of his services, and I would deliver him a bill upon Damascus : '—but distant promises will hardly be accepted by any Arab, their world is so faithless and they themselves make little reckoning of the most solemn engagements.

Now came *Zeyd*, a sheykh of the Fejîr Beduins, riding upon a dromedary from the desert, with his gunbearer seated behind him, and the sheykh's young son riding upon his led mare. Zeyd had been to town in Damascus and learned all the craft of the Ottoman manners, to creep by bribes into official men's favours. Two years before when his mare foaled, and it was not a filly, (they hardly esteem the male worth camel-milk,) this nomad fox bestowed his sterile colt upon the Moorish wolf Mohammed Aly ; the kellâjy had ridden down on this now strong young stallion from Syria. Zeyd had seen nothing again but glozing proffers : now was this occasion of the Nasrâny, and they both looked that I should pay the shot between them. " Give Zeyd ten pound, and Zeyd will mount thee, Khalîl, upon his mare, and convey thee round to all the monuments." The furthest were not two miles from the tower, and the most are within a mile's distance. Zeyd pretended there was I know not what to see besides ' at *Bîr el-Ghrannem*, where we must have taken a *rafîk* of *Billî* Aarab.' Only certain it is that they reckon all that to the overthrown country of el-Héjr which lies between Mûbrak en-Nâga and Bîr el-Ghrannem, which is thirty miles nearly ; and by the old trade-road, along, there are ruins of villages down even to el-Medina. But the nomads say with one voice, there are not anywhere in these parts *byût* or *bébàn*, that is, chambers in the rock, like to those of el-Héjr or Medáin Sâlih.

Zeyd had been busy riding round to his tribesmen's tents and had bound them all with the formula, *Jirak* "I am thy neighbour." If I refused Zeyd, I might hire none of them. The lot had fallen, that we should be companions for a long time to come. Zeyd was a swarthy nearly black sheykh of the desert, of mid stature and middle age, with a hunger-bitten stern visage. So dark a colour is not well seen by the Arabs, who in these uplands are less darkish-brown than ruddy. They think it resembles the ignoble blood of slave races; and therefore even crisp and ringed hair is a deformity in their eyes. We may remember in the Canticles, the paramour excuses the swarthiness of her beautiful looks, "I am black but comely, ye daughters of Jerusalem, as the booths of the Beduw, as the tent-cloths of Solomon;" she magnifies the ruddy white-ness of her beloved. Dark, the privation of light, is the hue of death (*mawt el-aswad*), and, by similitude, of calamity and evil; the wicked man's heart is accounted black (*kalb el-aswad*). According to this fantasy of theirs, the Judge of all the earth in the last judgment hour will hold an Arabian expedite manner of audit, not staying to parley with every soul in the sea of generations, for the leprosy of evil desert rising in their visages, shall appear manifestly in wicked persons as an horrible blackness. In the gospel speech, the sheep shall be sundered from the goats,—wherein is some comparison of colour—and the just shall shine forth as the sunlight. The Arabs say of an unspotted human life, *kalb-hu abiáth*, white is his heart: we in likewise say *candid*. Zeyd uttered his vóice in the deepest tones that I have heard of human throat; such a male light Beduin figure some master painter might have portrayed for an Ishmaelite of the desert. Hollow his cheeks, his eyes looked austerely, from the lawless land of famine, where his most nourishment was to drink coffee from the morning, and tobacco; and where the chiefest Beduin virtue is *es-subbor*, a courageous forbearing and abiding of hunger. "Aha wellah, (said Zeyd,) *el-Aarab fàsidîn* the nomads are dissolute and so are the Dowla": the blight was in his own heart; this Beduish philosopher looked far out upon all human things with a tolerant incredulity. A sheykh among his tribesmen of principal birth, he had yet no honourable estimation; his hospitality was miserable, and that is a reproach to the nomad dwellers in the empty desert. His was a high and liberal understanding becoming a *mejlis* man who had sat in that perfect school of the parliament of the tribe, from his youth, nothing in Zeyd was barbarous and uncivil ; his carriage was that haughty grace of the wild creatures. In him I have not seen any spark of fanatical ill-humour. He could speak with me smilingly of his intolerant countrymen ; for himself he could well imagine that sufficient is Ullah to the governance of the world, without fond man's meddling. This manly man was not of the adventurous brave, or rather he would put nothing rashly in peril. *Mesquin* was his policy at home, which resembled a sordid avarice ; he was wary as a Beduin more than very far-sighted. Zeyd's friendship was true in the main, and he was not to be feared as an enemy. Zeyd could be generous where it cost him naught, and of his sheykhly indolent prudence, he was not hasty to meddle in any unprofitable matter.

Zeyd (that was his desert guile) had brought five mouths to the kella : this hospitality was burdensome to his hosts, and Mohammed Aly, who thought the jest turned against him, came on the morrow to my chamber with a grave countenance. He asked me ' Did I know that all this corn must be carried down upon camels' backs from Damascus ? ' I said, not knowing their crafty drifts, that I had not called them ;—and he aloud, " Agree together or else do not detain him, Khalîl ; this is a sheykh of Aarab, knowest thou not that every Beduin's heart is with his household, and he has no rest in absence, because of the cattle which he has left in the open wilderness ? " I asked, were it not best, before other words, that I see the monuments ? ' It was reasonable,' he said, ' and Zeyd should bring me to the next bébàn.'—" And Khalîl ! it is an unheard-of thing, any Christian to be seen in these countries," (almost at the door of the holy places). I answered, laying my hand upon the rude stones of the kella building, " But these courses witness for me, raised by Christian men's hands."—" That is well spoken, and we are all here become thy friends : Moslem or Nasrâny, Khalîl is now as one of us ; wellah, we would not so suffer another. But go now with Zeyd, and afterward we will make an accord with him, and if not I may send you out myself to see the monuments with some of the kella."

We came in half a mile by those ancient wells, now a watering place of the country Beduins. They are deep as the well in the kella, ten or twelve feet large at the mouth ; the brinks are laid square upon a side, as if they had been platforms of the old wheel-work of irrigation. The well-lining of rude stone courses, without mortar, is deeply scored, (who may look upon the like without emotion ?) by the soft cords of many nomad generations. Now I had sight at little distance, of a first monument, and another hewn above, like the head of some vast frontispice, where yet is but a blind door, little entering into the rock, without chamber. This ambitious sculpture, seventy feet wide, is called *Kasr el-Bint*, " the maiden's bower." It is not, as they pretend, inaccessible; for ascending some ancient steps, entailed in the further end of the cliff, my unshod companions have climbed over all the rocky brow. I saw that tall nightmare frontispice below, of a crystalline symmetry and solemnity, and battled with the strange half-pinnacles of the Petra monuments; also this rock is the same yellow-grey soft sandstone with gritty veins and small quartz pebbles. *Kasr*, in the plural *kassûr*, has commonly the sense in Arabia of ' stable habitation ', whether clay or stone, and opposite to *beyt shaar*, the hair-cloth booth, or removable house, of the nomads. Thus, even the cottages of clay, seen about outlying seed-grounds in the wilderness, and not continually inhabited, are named kassûr At *Hâyil* and *er-Riâth* the prince's residence is named el-Kasr, as it were " the castle." Kasr is also in some desert villages, a cluster of houses, enclosed in one court wall; thus they say of the village *Semîra* " she is three kassûr." Any strong building for defence and security, (such holds are very common in Arabia,) is called gella, for kella. Borj (πύργ-), tower of defence, manifestly a foreign word, I have not heard in Nejd Arabia.

Backward from the Borj rock, we arrived under a principal monument; in the face I saw a table and inscription, and a bird! which are proper to the Héjr frontispice; the width of sculptured architecture with cornices and columns is twenty-two feet.—I mused what might be the sleeping riddle of those strange crawling letters which I had come so far to seek! The whole is wrought in the rock; a bay has been quarried in the soft cliff, and in the midst is sculptured the temple-like monument. The aspect is Corinthian, the stepped pinnacles—an Asiatic ornament, but here so strange to European eyes—I have seen used in their clay house-building at Hâyil. Flat side-pilasters are as the limbs of this body of architecture; the chapiters of a singular severe design, hollowed and square at once, are as all those before seen at Petra. In the midst of this counterfeited temple-face, is sculptured a stately porch, with the ornaments of architecture. Entering, I found but a rough-hewn cavernous chamber, not high, not responding to the dignity of the frontispice: (we are in a sepulchre). I saw in this dim room certain long mural niches or *loculi;* all the floor lies full of driven sand. I thought then, with the help of a

telescope, I might transcribe the epigraph, faintly appearing
in the sun; but the plague of flies at every moment filled my
eyes : such clouds of them, said the Arabs, were because no
rain had fallen here in the last years.

Sultry was that mid-day winter sun, glancing from the sand,
and stagnant the air, under the sun-beaten monuments ; these
loathsome insects were swarming in the odour of the ancient
sepulchres. Zeyd would no further, he said the sun was too hot,
he was already weary. We returned through the Borj rocks ;
and in that passage I saw a few more monuments, which are
also remarkable among the frontispices at el-Héjr: and lying
nigh the caravan camp and the kella they are those first visited
by any curious hajjies. Under the porch of one of them and
over the doorway are sculptured as supporters, some four-footed
beast ; the like are seen in none other. The side pedestal
ornaments upon another are like griffons; these also are
singular. The tablet is here, and in some other, adorned with a
fretwork flower (perhaps pomegranate) of six petals. Over a
third doorway the effigy of a bird is slenderly sculptured upon
the tablet, in low relief, the head yet remaining. Every other
sculptured bird of these monuments we see wrought in high
natural relief, standing upon a pedestal, sculptured upon the
frontispice wall, which springs from the ridge of the pediment :
but among them all, not a head remains ; whether it be they
were wasted by idle stone-casts of the generations of herdsmen,
or the long course of the weather   Having now entered many,
I perceived that all the monument chambers were sepulchral.
The mural loculi in the low hewn walls of these rudely four-
square rooms, are made as shallow shelves, in length, as they
might have been measured to the human body, from the child to
the grown person ; yet their shallowness is such, that they could
not serve, I suppose, to the receipt of the dead. In the rock
floors are seen grave-pits, sunken side by side, full of men's
bones, and bones are strewed upon the sanded floors. A loathsome mummy odour, in certain monuments, is heavy in the
nostrils; we thought our cloaks smelled villanously when we
had stayed within but few minutes. In another of these
monuments, *Beyt es-Sheykh,* I saw the sand floor full of rotten
clouts, shivering in every wind, and taking them up, I found
them to be those dry bones' grave-clothes !

" Khalîl," said Mohammed Aly, " I counsel thee to give Zeyd
three hundred piastres." I consented, but the sheykh had no
mind to be satisfied with less than a thousand. If I had yielded
then to their fantastic cupidity, the rumour would have raised

the country and made my future travels most dangerous. But Zeyd departing, I put a little earnest gold into his hand, that he might not return home scorned; and he promised to come for me at the time of the returning Haj, to carry me to dwell with him among the Beduw: Zeyd hoped that my vaccinating skill might be profitable to himself. The aga had another thought, he coveted my gun, which was an English cavalry carbine: a high value is set in these unquiet countries on all good weapons. "And so you give me this, Khalîl, I will send you every day with some of the kella till you have seen all you would of the monuments, and I will send you, to see more of these things, to el-Ally: and, further, would you to Ibn Rashîd, I will procure even to send you thither."

I went out next with some of the kella to the Kasr el-Bint *bébàn.* The bébàn 'row of doors', are ranges of frontispices upon both sides round of this long crag; the bird is seen upon not a few of them and the epitaph. These are some of the most stately architectural caverns at el-Héjr, the floors are full of men's bones; but not all of them. Showing me a tall monument, "This (said my companions), is the beyt of the father of the bint, and look, Khalîl! here is another, the beyt of the sheykh's bondman, where they all perished together." In this last I saw the most strewed bones: they bade me admire in them the giant stature of Kôm Thamûd. I saw them to be ordinary; but they see in matter of religion less as men with waking eyes than dreaming. Bare rock floors are found in some chambers; the loculi are not found in all. Near the old hewn stair, in the end of the crag, is a double irregular chamber, and this only might seem not sepulchral; yet upon the party wall is a rude sepulchral inscription.

We crossed then to visit the middle rocks (I distinguish them in such manner for clearness), where are many more frontispices and their caverns, but less stately (here are no sculptured eagles, the stone also is softer, the cliff is lower), hewn in all the face of the crag about. I found here an epitaph tablet above a door, banked up with blown sand, so that a man might reach to it with his hands. Amongst them is seen an inconsiderable monument abandoned in the beginning, where only the head of the niche and the upper parts are wrought out. From thence we came to that lofty frontispice within view from the kella, *Beyt es-Sâny,* 'the smith's house.' They showed me 'the smith's blood,' which is but a stain of iron-rust, high upon the battlements. ' This sâny, say the nomads, dishonoured the *bint* or maiden daughter of the sheykh of *The Cities.* Seeing her grow great with child, the sheykh, her father, was moved to take cruel vengeance ; then the valiant smith sallied with his spear to meet them, and in the floor of the sheykh's bondman (that we have seen full of human bones), they all fell down slain.' The porch is simple, and that is marred, as it were with nail-holes, those which Haj Nejm had mentioned ; the like we may see about the doorways of some few other monuments. [Mr. James Fergusson tells me that such holes might be made for pins by which wooden cornices have been fastened in a few frontispices, where the stone was faulty.]

We visited then the western rocks, *K'ssûr* or *Kassûr B'theyny* ; —this is a name as well of all the Héjr monuments, "save only the Beyt es-Sâny." There are many more frontispices in the irregular cliff face and bays of this crag, of the same factitious hewn architecture, not a few with eagles, some are without epitaphs ; in some are seen epitaph tablets yet unwritten. Certain frontispices are seen here nearly wasted away and effaced by the weather.

The crags full of these monuments are " the Cities of Sâlih." We were now five hours abroad : my companions, armed with their long matchlocks, hardly suffered me to linger in any place a breathing-while, saying " It is more than thou canst think a perilous neighbourhood ; from any of these rocks and chambers there might start upon us hostile Beduins." The life of the Arabians is full of suspicion ; they turned their heads with continual apprehension, gazing everywhere about them : also Haj Nejm having once shed the blood of the Wélad Aly, was ever in dread to be overtaken without his kella. In this plain-bottom where we passed, between cliffs and monuments, are seen beds of strewed potsherds and broken glass. We took up also certain small copper pieces called by the Beduins *himmarît* (perhaps *Himyariát*) of rusted ancient money. Silver pieces and gold are only seldom found by the Aarab in ground where the camels have wallowed. A villager of el-Ally thirty years before found in a stone pot, nearly a bushel of old silver coinage. Also two W. Aly tribesmen, one of whom I knew, had found another such treasure in late years. Of the himmarît, some not fully corroded show a stamped Athenian owl, grossly imitated from the Greek moneys ; they are Himyaric. Potsherds and broken glass, nearly indestructible matter, are found upon all the ancient sites in Arabia : none here now-a-days use these brittle wares, but only wood and copper-tinned vessels. Arabia was then more civil with great trading roads of the ancient world ! Arabia of our days has the aspect of a decayed country. All nations trafficked for gold and the sacred incense, to Arabia the Happy : to-day the round world has no need of the daughter of Arabia ; she is forsaken and desolate.

Little remains of the old civil generations of el-Héjr, the caravan city ; her clay-built streets are again the blown dust in the wilderness. Their story is written for us only in the crabbed scrawlings upon many a wild crag of this sinister neighbourhood, and in the engraved titles of their funeral monuments, now solitary rocks, which the fearful passenger admires, in these desolate mountains. The plots of potsherds may mark old inhabited sites, perhaps a cluster of villages : it is an ordinary manner of Semitic settlements in the Oasis countries that they are founded upon veins of ground-water. A sûk perhaps and these suburbs was Hejra emporium, with palm groves walled about.

By the way, returning to the kella, is a low crag full of obscure caverns, and without ornament. In this passage I had viewed nearly all the birds which are proper to the frontispices of Medáin Sâlih. The Arabs say, it is some kind of sea-fowl. The Syrian pilgrims liken them to the falcon ; they are of massy work as in gross grained sand-rock, in which nothing can be finely sculptured. The pediments bear commonly some globular and channeled side ornaments, which are solid, and they are sculptured in the rock.

In other days, I visited the monuments at leisure, and arrived at the last outstanding. The most sumptuous is that, they call *Beyt Akhreymât*. Between the mural cornices there is sculptured an upper rank of four bastard pilasters. There is no bird but only the pedestal ; instead of the channeled urns, there are here pediment side-ornaments of beasts, perhaps hounds or griffons. The bay of the monument (wherein are seen certain shallow loculi, like those found in the walls of the sepulchral chambers) is not hewn down fully to the ground ; so that the heels of the great side pilasters are left growing to the foot of the rock, for the better lasting and defence of this weak sculptured sandstone. The spurious imitating art is seen thus in strange alliance with the chaotic eternity of nature. About the doorway are certain mouldings, barbarously added to the architecture. This goodly work appeared to me not perfectly dressed to the architectural symmetry ; there are few frontispices, which are laboured with the tool to a perfect smoothfacedness. The antique craft-masters (not unlikely hired from Petra,) were of a people of clay builders ; their work in these temple-tombs was imitation : (we saw the like in the South Arabian trade-money). They were Semites, expeditious more than curious, and naturally imperfect workmen.—The interpretation of the inscriptions has confirmed these conjectures.

We were come last to the *Mahál el-Mejlis* or senate house, here the face of a single crag is hewn to a vast monument more than forty feet wide, of a solemn agreeable simplicity. The great side pilasters are in pairs, which is not seen in any other ; notwithstanding this magnificence, the massy frontispice had remained unperfected. Who was the author of this beginning who lies nearly alone in his huge sepulchral vanity ? for all the chamber within is but a little rude cell with one or two grave-places. And doubtless this was his name engrossed in the vast title plate, a single line of such magnitude as there is none other, with deeply engraved cursive characters [now read by the learned interpreters, *For Hail Son of Douna* (and) *his descendants*]. The titles could not be read in Mohammed's time, or the prophet without prophecy had not uttered his folly of these caverns, or could not have escaped derision. The unfinished portal with eagle and side ornaments, is left as it was struck out in the block. The great pilasters are not chiselled fully down to the ground ; the wild reef yet remains before the monument, channeled into blocks nearly ready to be removed,— in which is seen the manner to quarry of those ancient stone cutters. Showing me the blocks my rude companions said, "These were benches of the town councillors."

The covercles of the sepulchres and the doors of the "desolate mansions," have surely been wooden in this country, (where also is no stone for flags) and it is likely they were of acacia or tamarisk timber; which doubtless have been long since consumed at the cheerful watch-fires of the nomads : moreover there should hinder them no religion of the dead in idolatry. Notwithstanding the imitating (Roman) magnificence of these merchants to the Sabeans, there is not a marble plate in all their monuments, nor any strewn marble fragment is seen upon the Héjr plain. It sufficed them to "write with an iron pen for ever" upon the soft sand-rock of these Arabian mountains A mortise is seen in the jambs of all doorways, as it might be to receive the bolt of a wooden lock. The frontispices are often over-scored with the idle wasms of the ancient tribesmen I mused to see how often they resemble the infantile Himyaric letters.

CHAPTER III

MEDÁIN SÀLIH AND THE INSCRIPTIONS

HAVING viewed all the architectural chambers in those few
crags of the plain ; my companions led me to see the *Diwán,*
which only of all the Héjr monuments is in the mount Ethlib,
in a passage beyond a white sand-drift in face of the kella.
Only this *Liwàn* or Diwán, 'hall or council chamber,' of all the
hewn monuments at el-Héjr (besides some few and obscure
caverns,) is plainly not sepulchral. The Diwán alone is lofty
and large, well hewn within, with cornice and pilasters, and
dressed to the square and plummet, yet a little obliquely. The
Diwán alone is an open chamber : the front is of excellent
simplicity, a pair of pilasters to the width of the hewn chamber,
open as the nomad tent. The architrave is fallen with the fore-
part of the flat ceiling. The hall, which is ten paces large and
deep eleven, and high as half the depth ; looks northward. In
the passage, which is fifty paces long, the sun never shines, a
wind breathes there continually, even in summer : this was a
cool site to be chosen in a sultry country. Deep sand lies
drifted in the Diwán floor : the Aarab digging under the walls
for " gun-salt" (the cavern is a noon shelter of the nomad
flocks,) find no bones, neither is there any appearance of burials.
The site resembles the beginning of the Sîk at Wady Mûsa, in
which is the Khazna Pharôun ; in both I have seen, but here
much more, the same strange forms of little plinths and tablets.
The plinths are single, or two or three unevenly standing
together, or there is a single plinth branching above into two
heads ; a few have the sculptured emblems about them of the
great funeral monuments : we cannot doubt that their significance is religious. There is a Nabatean legend lightly entailed
in the rock above one of them. [It is now interpreted *This is
the mesgeda* (beth-el or kneeling stone) *made to Aera, great god.*
This shows them to have been idol-stones.]
We see scored upon the walls, within, a few names of old

Mohammedan passengers, some line or two of Nabatean inscriptions, and the beginning of a word or name of happy augury EYTY- ; these Greek letters only I have found at Medáin Sâlih. Also there are chalked up certain uncouth outlines in shepherd's ruddle, *ghrerra*, (such as they use to mark flocks in Syria,) which are ascribed to the B. Helál. Upon the two cliffs of the passage are many Nabatean inscriptions. Higher this strait rises among the shelves of the mountain, which is full of like clefts,—it is the nature of this sandstone. From thence is a little hewn conduit led down in the rocky side (so in the Sîk), as it were for rain-water, ending in a small cistern-chamber above the Diwán ; it might be a provision for the public hall or temple. Hereabout are four or five obscure hewn caverns in the soft rock. Two of the Fehját accompanied me armed, with Mohammed and Abd el-Kâder from the kella ; whilst we were busy, the kella lads were missing, they, having seen strange riders in the plain, had run to put themselves in safety. Only the Fehjies remained with me ; when I said to them, Will you also run away? the elder poor man answered with great heart, "I am an *Antary* and this is an Antary (of the children of Antar), we will not forsake thee !" (The hero Antar was of these countries, he lived little before Mohammed.) No Beduins were likely to molest the poor and despised Fehjies.

Fourteen days after the Haj passing, came *el-nejjàb*, the haj dromedary post, from Medina ; he carried but a small budget with him of all the hajjies' letters, for Damascus. Postmaster of the wilderness was a W. Aly sheykh, afterward of my acquaintance : he hired this Sherarát tribesman to be his postrider to Syria. The man counted eleven or twelve night stations in his journey thither, which are but waterings and desolate sites in the desert: *el-Jinny, Jeraida, Ghrurrub, Ageyly, W. el-Howga, Moghreyra, Howsa, Bayir.* A signal gun is fired at Damascus when the haj post is come in. The day following the light mail bag is sealed again for the Harameyn. For a piece of money the poor man also carried my letters with him to Syria.

Many were the days to pass within the kella: almost every third day came Beduins, and those of the garrison entertained them with arms in their hands ; in other days there were alarms of ghrazzûs seen or of strange footsteps found in the plain, and the iron door was shut. Not many Beduw are admitted at once into the tower, and then the iron door is barred upon their companions without. Besides Fejîr there came to us Moahîb, nomads of the neighbouring Harra, and

even Beduins of Billî; all sougnt coffee, a night's lodging and
their supper in the kella. The Billî country is the rugged
breadth of the *Tehâma*, beyond the Harra. They pronounced
gîm as the Egyptians. Three men of Billî arriving late in an
evening drank ardently a first draught from the coffee-room
buckets of night-chilled water, and "Ullah be praised! sighed
they, as they were satisfied, wellah we be come over the Harra
and have not drunken these two days!" They arrived now
driving a few sheep in discharge of a *khúwa*, or debt for
"brotherhood," to the Fukara, for safe conduct of late, which
was but to come in to traffic in the Haj market. Said
Mohammed Aly, "Mark well the hostile and necessitous life of
the Beduw! is it to such wild wretches thou wilt another day
trust thy life? See in what manner they hope to live,—by
devouring one another! It is not hard for them to march
without drinking, and they eat, by the way, only, if they may
find aught. The Beduins are *sheyatîn* (of demon-kind;) what
will thy life be amongst them, which, wellah, we ourselves of
the city could not endure!"

How might this largess of the kella hospitality be continually
maintained? "It is all at our own and not at the government
cost," quoth the aga. The Aarab suppose there is certain
money given out of the Haj chest to the purpose; but it seems
to be only of wages spared between the aga and the tower-
warden, who are of a counsel together to hire but half the paid
strength of the garrison. To the victualling of the haj-road
kella there was formerly counted 18 camel loads (three tons
nearly) of Syrian wheat, with 30 cwt. of caravan biscuit (*ozmât*),
and 30 of *bórghrol*, which is bruised, parboiled wheaten grain,
and sun-dried (the household diet of Syria), with 40 lbs. of
samn. But the old allowances had been now reduced, by the
reformed administration, to the year's rations (in wheat only)
of ten men (*nefer*), and to each a salary of 1000 piastres, or £8
sterling; but the warden received for two nefers: thus the cost
of a kella to the Syrian government may be £220 English money
by the year. There is no tower-warden on the road who has
not learned Turkish arts; and with less pay they have found
means to thrive with thankful mind. The warden, who is paymaster for ten, hires but five hands, nor these all at the full
money. The Pasha will never call for the muster of his ten
merry men; they each help other to win and swallow the public
good between them: all is well enough if only the kella be not
lost, and that the caravan find water there.—How may a kella,
nearly unfurnished of defence, be maintained in the land of
Ishmael? How but by making the Beduw their allies, in the

sacrament of the bread and salt : and if thus one man's wages
be spent in twelve months, for coffee and corn and samn, the
warden shall yet fare well enough ;—the two mules' rations of
barley were also embezzled. But I have heard the old man
Nejm complain, that all the fat was licked from his beard by
Mohammed Aly.

Betwixt Wady Zerka in the north and Hedîeh midway from
Medáin upon the derb to Medina, are eleven or twelve inhabited
kellas, manned (in the register) by one hundred and twenty
nefers, said Mohammed Aly ; this were ten for a kella, but
afterward he allowed that only seventy kept them. Thus they
are six-men garrisons, but some are less ; that which is paid
out for the other fifty in the roll, (it may be some £1300,) is
swallowed by the confederate officiality. In former times five
hundred nefers were keepers of these twelve towers, or forty to
a kella ; afterward the garrisons were twenty-five men to a
kella, all Damascenes of the Medân. But the Syrians bred in
happier country were of too soft a spirit, they shut their iron
doors, as soon as the Haj was gone by, ten months, till they
saw the new returning pilgrimage : with easy wages and well
provided, they were content to suffer from year to year this
ship-bound life in the desert. The towers below Maan were
manned by Kurds, sturdy northern men of an outlandish speech
and heavy-handed humour : but a strange nation could have no
long footing in Arabia. After the Emir Abd el-Kâder's seating himself at Damascus and the gathering to him there of
the Moorish emigration, Moghrâreba began to be enrolled for
the haj road. And thenceforth being twenty or twenty-five
men in a tower, the iron doors stood all daylights open. The
valorous Moorish Arabs are well accepted by the Arabians, who
repute them an " old Hejâz folk, and nephews of the Beny
Helál." The adventurous Moors in garrison even made raids on
unfriendly Beduw, and returned to their kellas with booty of
small cattle and camels.

These are the principal tribes of Beduin neighbours : Billî
(singular Belûwy) over the Harra ; next to them at the north
Howeytát (sing. Howeyty): south of them Jeheyna, an ancient
tribe (in the gentile vulg. plur. Jehîn), nomads and villagers,
their country is from Yánba to the derb el-haj. Some fendies
(divisions) of them are el-Kleybát (upon the road between
Sawra and Sujwa), Aroa, G'dah, Merowîn, Zubbián, Grûn and
about Yánba, Beny Ibrahîm, Sieyda, Seràserra. Above Medina
on the derb el-haj were the Saadîn (sing. Saadànny) of Harb ;
westward is Bishr and some fendies of Heteym towards Kheybar.
The successions of nomad tribes which have possessed el-Héjr

since the Beny Helál, or fabled ancient heroic Aarab of Nejd, were they say the Sherarát, (also reckoned to the B. Helál)—these then occupied the Harra, where the *dubbûs*, or club-stick, their cattle mark, remains scored upon the vulcanic rocks —after them are named the *Beny Saíd*, then the *Duffir*, *sheykh Ibn Sweyd* (now in the borders of Mesopotamia), whom the Beny Sókhr expelled ; the Fukara and Moahíb (now a very small tribe) drove out the B. Sókhr from the *Jau*. The Moahíb reckon their generations in this country, thirteen : a sheykh of theirs told me upon his fingers his twelve home-born ancestors this is nearly four centuries. Where any nomad tribe has dwelt, they leave the wild rocks full of their idle wasms ; these are the Beduins' only records and they remain for centuries of years. * * *

(Doughty explores the neighbourhood. Medáin Sálih, el-Ally, and el-Khreyby, and their ruins. He lodges in el-Ally, but returns to Medáin Sálih to finish his task of impressing the epitaphs.)

* * * Upon the morrow I asked of Mohammed Aly to further me in all that he might ; the time was short to accomplish the enterprise of Medáin Sâlih. I did not stick to speak frankly ; but I thought he made me cats'-eyes. " You cannot have forgotten that you made me certain promises ! "—" I will give you the gun again." This was in my chamber ; he stood up, and his fury rising, much to my astonishment, he went to his own, came again with the carbine, turned the back and left me. I set the gun again, with a friendly word, in the door of his chamber,—" Out ! " cried the savage wretch, in that leaping up and laying hold upon my mantle : then as we were on the gallery the Moorish villain suddenly struck me with the flat hand and all his mad force in the face, there wanted little of my falling to the yard below. He shouted also with savage voice, " Dost thou not know me yet ? " He went forward to the kahwa, and I followed him, seeing some Beduins were sitting there ;—the nomads, who observe the religion of the desert, abhor the

homely outrage. I said to them, " *Ya rubbá*, O fellowship, ye are witnesses of this man's misdoing." The nomads looked coldly on aghast; it is damnable among them, a man to do his guest violence, who is a guest of Ullah. Mohammed Aly, trembling and frantic, leaping up then in his place, struck me again in the doorway, with all his tiger's force ; as he heaped blows I seized his two wrists and held them fast. " Now, I said, have done, or else I am a strong man." He struggled, the red cap fell off his Turk's head, and his stomach rising afresh at this new indignity, he broke from me. The sickly captain of ruffian troopers for a short strife had the brawns of a butcher, and I think three peaceable men might not hold him. As for the kella guard, who did not greatly love Mohammed Aly, they stood aloof with Haj Nejm as men in doubt, seeing that if my blood were spilt, this might be required of them by the Pasha. The nomads thought by mild words to appease him, there durst no man put in his arm, betwixt the aga and the Nasrâny. " —Aha ! by Ullah ! shouted the demon or ogre, now I will murder thee." Had any blade or pistol been then by his belt, it is likely he had done nothing less ; but snatching my beard with canine rage, the ruffian plucked me hither and thither, which is a most vile outrage. By this the mad fit abating in his sick body, and somewhat confused as he marked men's sober looks about him, and to see the Nasrâny bleeding, who by the Pasha had been committed to him upon his head, he hastily re-entered the kahwa, where I left them. The better of the kella crew were become well affected towards me, even the generous coxcomb of Haj Hasan was moved to see me mishandled : but at a mischief they were all old homicides, and this aga was their paymaster, though he embezzled some part of their salary, besides he was of their Moorish nation and religion. If M. Aly came with fury upon me again, my life being endangered, I must needs take to the defence of my pistol, in which, unknown to them, were closed the lives of six murderous Arabs, who, as hounds, had all then fallen upon a stranger . and their life had been for my life. As we waken sometime of an horrid dream, I might yet break through this extreme mischief, to the desert ; but my life had been too dearly purchased, when I must wander forth, a manslayer, without way, in the hostile wilderness. All the fatigues of this journey from Syria I saw now likely to be lost, for I could not suffer further this dastardly violence. The mule M. Aly came by and marking me sit peaceably reading at the door of my chamber, with a new gall he bade me quit those quarters, and remove with my baggage to the *liwân*. This is an open arch-chamber to the north in Damascus wise ; there is made the coffee-hearth in summer, but now it was deadly cold in the winter night at this altitude. He gave my chamber to another, and I must exchange to his cell on the chill side, which was near over the cesspool and open to its mephitic emanations when the wind lay to the kella. After this M. Aly sent the young Mohammed to require again, as *rahn*, a pledge, the gun which had been left in my doorway. I carried the gun to M. Aly : he sat now in his chamber, chopfallen and staring on the ground.

At half-afternoon I went over to the kahwa ; Haj Nejm and M. Aly sat there. I must ascertain how the matter stood ; whether I could live longer with them in the kella, or it were better for me to withdraw to el-Ally. I spread my *biuruldi*, a circular passport, before them, from a former governor of Syria. —" Ah ! I have thirty such firmàns at home."—" Are you not servitors of the Dowlat es-Sultàn ? "—" I regard nothing, nor fear creature ; we are Moghràreba, to-day here, to-morrow yonder ; what to us is the Dowla of *Stambûl* or of *Mambûl ?* "— " And would you strike me at Damascus ? "—" By the mighty God men are all days stricken and slain too at es-Shem. Ha ! Englishman, or ha ! Frenchman, ha ! Dowla, will you make me remember these names in land of the Aarab ? "—" At least you reverence es-Sèyid, (Abd-el Kâder)—and if another day I should tell him this ! "—" In the Sèyid is *namûs* (the sting of anger) more than in myself : who has namûs more than the Sèyid ? eigh, Haj Nejm ? wellah, at es-Shem there is no more than the Sèyid and Mohammed Aly (himself)   I have (his mad boast) seven hundred guns there ! "—" You struck me ; now tell me wherefore, I have not to my knowledge offended you in anything."—" Wellah, I had flung thee down from the gallery, but I feared Ullah : and there is none who would ever enquire of thy death. Your own consul expressly renounced before our Wàly (governor of Syria) all charge concerning thee, and said, taking his *bernéta* in his hand, you were to him nothing more than this old hat."— " Such a consul might be called another day to justify himself." —" Well, it is true, and this I have understood, Haj Nejm, that he passed for a *khanzîr* (an animal not eaten by the Turks) among our Pashas at es-Shem, and I make therefore no account of him :—also by this time the nejjàb has delivered Khalîl's letters in Damascus.—It is known there now that you are here, and your life will be required of us." Haj Nejm said, " Ay, and this is one of those, for whose blood is destroyed a city of Islam." (Jidda bombarded and Syria under the rod were yet a bitter memory in their lives.) " Mark you, I said, Haj Nejm, that this man is not very well in his understanding." M. Aly began now in half savage manner to make his excuses ; ' Servitor had

he been of the Dowla these thirty years, he had wounds in his
body ; and M. Aly was a good man, that knew all men.'—
"Enough, enough between you! " cries Haj Nejm, who would
reconcile us ; and M. Aly, half doting-religious and humane
ruffian, named me already *habîb,* ' a beloved '! We drank round
and parted in the form of friends.—Later I came to know the
first cause of this trouble, which was that unlucky Kheybary
elf of Dâhir's, whom I had, with an imprudent humanity, led in to
repose an hour and drink coffee in the kella : once out of my
hearing, although I had paid his wages at el-Ally, he clamoured
for a new shirt-cloth from the aga.   This incensed the Turkish
brains of M. Aly, who thought he had received too little from
me :—more than all had driven him to this excess (he pretended)
that I had called the wild nomads to be my witnesses.   When
afterwards some Beduins asked him wherefore he had done this :
'That Khalîl, he answered, with a lie, had struck off his red
bonnet ;—and wellah the Nasrâny's grasp had so wrung his delicate wrists that he could not hold them to heaven in his prayers
for many a day afterward ; ' also the dastardly villain boasted to
those unwilling hearers that ' he had plucked Khalîl's beard.'

   This storm abated, with no worse hap, they of the kella were
all minded to favour me ; and on the morrow early, leaving one
to drive the well-machine, every man, with Haj Nejm, and Mohammed Aly upon his horse, accompanied the Nasrâny among
the monuments, they having not broken their fasts, until the sun
was setting ; and in the days after, there went out some of them
each morning with me.   Of Haj Nejm I now bought a tamarisk
beam, that had been a make-shift well-shaft, fetched from el-Ally :
the old man hacked notches in my timber for climbing, and
the ladder-post was borne out between two men's shoulders to
the bébàn, and flitted from one to other as the work required.
I went abroad with large sheets of bibulous paper, water, and
a painter's brush and sponge ; and they rearing the timber at a
frontispice, where I would, I climbed, and laboured standing
insecurely at the beam head, or upon the pediment, to impress
the inscription.   The moist paper yielded a faithful stamp (in
which may be seen every grain of sand) of the stony tablet and
the letters.   Haj Nejm would then accompany us to shore
the beam himself, (that I should not take a fall,) having, he said,
always a misgiving.   In few days I impressed all the inscriptions
that were not too high in the frontispices.   We went forward,
whilst the former sheets hanged a-drying in their title plates,
to attempt other.   In returning over the wilderness it was
a new sight to us all, to see the stern sandstone monuments
hewn in an antique rank under the mountain cliff, stand thus

billeted in the sun with the butterfly panes of white paper;
—but I knew that to those light sheets they had rendered, at
length, their strange old enigma! The epitaphs are some quite
undecayed, some are wasted in the long course of the weather.
Our work fortunately ended, there remained more than a half
score of the inscription tablets which were too high for me.

Our going abroad was broken in the next days by the happy
fortune of rain in Arabia. A bluish haze covered the skirts
of the Harra, the troubled sky thundered; as the falling drops
overtook us, the Arabs, hastily folding their matchlocks under
their large mantles, ran towards the kella. Chill gusts blew
out under lowering clouds, the showers fell, and it rained still
at nightfall. The Arabs said then, "The Lord be praised, there
will be plenty of samn this year." On the morrow it rained yet,
and from the kella tower we saw the droughty desert standing full of plashes; the seyl of the Héjr plain did not flow for
all this; I found there but few pools of the sweet rain-water.
"—If only, they said now, the Lord shield us from locusts!"
which their old musing men foretold would return that year:
they think the eggs of former years revive in the earth after
heavy showers. Samn, the riches of the desert, was now after
so long drought hardly a pint for a *real* or crown, at el-Ally.

But what of the sculptured bird in those frontispices of the
sumptuous charnel houses? It was an ancient opinion of the
idolatrous Arabs, that the departing spirit flitted from man's
brain-pan as a wandering fowl, complaining thenceforward in
deadly thirst her unavenged wrong; friends therefore to assuage
the friend's soul-bird, poured upon the grave their pious liba-
tions of wine. The bird is called "a green fowl", it is named
by others an owl or eagle. The eagle's life is a thousand years,
in Semitic tradition. In Syria I have found Greek Christians
who established it with that scripture, "he shall renew his
youth as an eagle." Always the monumental bird is sculptured
as rising to flight, her wings are in part or fully displayed.

In the table of the pediment of a very few monuments, especially in the Kasr el-Bint rocks, is sculptured an effigy (commonly
wasted) of the human face. Standing high upon the ladder
beam, it fortuned me to light upon one of them which only has
remained uninjured; the lower sculptured cornices impending,
it could not be wholly discerned from the ground. I found
this head such as a comic mask, flat-nosed, and with a thin
border of beard about a sun-like visage. This sepulchral image
is grinning with all his teeth, and shooting out the tongue.
The hair of his head is drawn out above either ear like a long
"horn" or hair-lock of the Beduins. Seeing this *larva*, one

might murmur again the words of Isaiah, "Against whom makest thou a wide mouth, and drawest out the tongue?" I called my companions, who mounted after me; and looking on the old stony mocker, they scoffed again, and came down with loud laughter and wondering.

The Semitic East is a land of sepulchres; Syria, a limestone country, is full of tombs, hewn, it may be said, under every hill side. Now they are stables for herdsmen, and open dens of wild creatures. "Kings and counsellors of the earth built them desolate places"; but Isaiah mocked in his time those "habitations of the dead."—These are lands of the faith of the resurrection. Palmyra, Petra, Hejra, in the ways of the desert countries, were all less oases of husbandmen than great caravan stations. In all is seen much sumptuousness of sepulchres; clay buildings served for their short lives and squared stones and columns were for the life of the State. The care of sepulture, the ambitious mind of man's mortality, to lead eternity captive, was beyond measure in the religions of antiquity, which were without humility. The Medáin funeral chambers all together are not, I think, an hundred. An hundred monuments of well-faring families in several generations betoken no great city. Of such we might conjecture an old Arabian population of eight thousand souls; a town such as *Aneyza* at this day, the metropolis of Nejd.

Under the new religion the deceased is wound in a shirt-cloth of calico, (it is the same whether he were a prince or the poorest person, whether villager or one of the restless Beduw,) his corse is laid in the shallow pit of droughty earth, and the friends will set him up a head-stone of the blocks of the desert. Ezekiel sees the burying in hell of the ancient mighty nations: hell, the grave-hole, is the deep of the earth, the dead-kingdom: the graves are disposed (as we see at Medáin Sâlih) in the sides of the pit about a funeral bed (which is here the floor in the midst). We read like words in Isaiah, "Babel shall be brought down to hell, to the sides of the pit." To bury in the sides of the pit was a superstitious usage of the ancient Arabians, it might be for the dread of the hyena. In what manner were the dead laid in the grave at el-Héjr? We have found frankincense or spice-matter, the shreds of winding cloths, and lappets, as of leathern shrouds, in certain monuments: in the most floors lies only deep sand-drift, the bones are not seen in all; and the chamber floor in a few of them is but plain and bare rock. It is not unlikely that they buried the dead nearly as did the Jews about these times with odours, and the corse was swathed in one or several kinds of linen (I find three, finer and grosser webbed, brown-stained and smelling of the drugs of the embalmers) and sewed in some inner leather painted red, and an outer hide, which for the thickness may be goat or else camel-leather, whose welts are seamed with leathern thongs and smeared with asphalte. I saw no mummy flesh, nor hair. In peaceable country the monuments might be one by one explored at leisure. I never went thither alone, but I adventured my life.

In my dealings with Arabs I have commonly despised their pusillanimous prudence. When I told Mohammed Aly that those kassûr chambers were sepulchres, he smiled, though an arrow shot through his barbarous Scriptures, and he could forgive me, seeing me altogether a natural philosopher in religion. " *Yaw!* " said he, with a pleasant stare ; and he had seen himself the rocks plainly full of tombs in many parts of Syria : my word reported seemed afterward to persuade also the Syrian Jurdy and Haj officers, though their Mohammedan hearts despised a Christian man's unbelief. * * *

* * * It was time that my task should be done, and it was well-nigh ended. The Haj were already marching upward from the Harameyn, and the Jurdy descending from Syria, to meet them, here, at the merkez of Medáin. And now the friendly nomads drew hither from their dîras to be dealers in the Haj market. Hostile Beduins hovered upon the borders to waylay them, and our alarms were in these days continual. As fresh traces of a foray of sixteen, habalîs, had been seen in the plain, not a mile from the kella, a messenger was sent up in haste to the kella shepherd Doolan, and his daughter, keeping those few sheep and goats of the garrison in the mountains. He returned the next evening, and the poor man came to my chamber, bringing me a present of fresh sorrel, now newly springing after the late showers ; a herb pleasant to these date-eaters for its grateful sourness. Their mountain lodging was that cold cavern where in our hunting we had rested out the night. There they milked their goats upon sorrel, which milk-meat and wild salads had been all their sustenance ; but I have learned by experience that it may well suffice in the desert. Seeing the skin of my face broken, he enquired quickly how I came by the hurt. When I answered " That ogre ! " showing him with my finger the door of Mohammed Aly's chamber ; said the son of Antar between his teeth : " Akhs ! the Lord do so unto him,

the tyrant that is yonder man; the Lord cut him off!" Doolan himself and the other gate Arabs dwelt here under the savage tyranny of the Moghrebies, in daily awe of their own lives: besides, they lived ever in little quietness themselves, as wretches that had oft-days nothing left to put under their teeth, and men can only live, they think, by devouring one another. One day I heard a strife among the women; soon angry, they filled the air with loud clamouring, every one reviled her neighbour. Their husbands rated them, and cried "Peace!" the askars shouted (from the walls of the kella), "Hush Hareem the Lord curse you!" The young askar-lad Mohammed sallied forth with a stick and flew bravely upon them, and one after another he drubbed them soundly; the men of the tents looking on, and so it stilled their tongues none caring to see his wife corrected.

When I came gipsying again to el-Héjr, after midsummer, with the Fukara Arabs, *eth-Therryeh*, elder son of the sheykh, always of friendly humour towards me, learning here of Mohammed Aly's outrage, enquired of me in his father's tent 'what thought I of the person.' I answered immediately, in the booths of the freeborn, "He is a cursed one or else a madman;" eth-Therryeh assented, and the prudent sheykh his father consented with a nod. Zeyd said another while, "*Kubbak* (he cast thee off) like a sucked lemon peel and deceived me ; very God confound Mohammed Aly!" M. Aly, whether repenting of his former aggression, which I might visit upon him at Damascus, or out of good will towards me, commended me now with a zeal, to all nomads who touched at the kella, and later to the servants of Ibn Rashîd that arrived from Hâyil and Teyma, and warmly at length to the returning Pasha himself. So Mohammed Aly, disposing all these to favour me, furthered the beginning of my travels in Arabia. * * *

(*Doughty describes incidents of life in the kella.*)

APPENDICES TO CHAPTER III

I.—THE NABATEAN INSCRIPTIONS UPON THE MONUMENTS DISCOVERED BY MR. DOUGHTY AT MEDÁIN SÂLIH : translated by M. ERNEST RENAN (*Membre de l'Institut*).

[From the vol published by the *Académie des Inscriptions et Belles-Lettres*, "Documents Épigraphiques recueillis dans le nord de l'Arabie par M. Charles Doughty."

* * *

* * * Quatre ou cinq groupes de faits, qui se rattachaient mal les uns aux autres, se trouvent ainsi réunis et expliqués. La paléographie sémitique en tirera les plus grandes lumières. Nos vingt-deux textes nabatéens, en effet, s'étagent, avec des dates précises, dans un espace d'environ quatre-vingts ans. On peut donc suivre la marche de l'écriture araméenne pendant près d'un siècle, et la voir, presque d'année en année, prendre un caractère de plus en plus cursif. L'écriture de nos monuments est comme le point central d'où l'on découvre le mieux l'affinité du vieil araméen, du caractère carré des Juifs, du palmyrénien, du sinaïtique, de l'estranghélo, du coufique, du neskhi.

L'histoire de l'écriture dans l'ancienne Arabie se trouve de la sorte éclairée en presque toutes ses parties. C'est là un progrès considérable, si l'on songe que, il y a soixante-quinze ans, l'illustre Silvestre de Sacy consacrait un de ses plus savants mémoires à prouver qu'on n'écrivait pas en Arabie avant Mahomet.—ERNEST RENAN.

No. 1.
De l'an 41 de J.-C.

Ceci est le *mesgeda* qu'a fait élever Serouh, fils de Touca, à Aera de Bosra, grand dieu. Dans le mois de nisan de l'an 1 du roi Malchus.

No. 2.
De l'an 2 de J.-C.

C'est ici le caveau que firent faire Camcam, fils de Touallat, fils de Taharam, et Coleibat, sa fille, pour eux, pour leurs enfants et leur descendants, au mois de tebeth de l'année neuvième de Haitat, roi des Nabatéens, aimant son peuple. Que Dusarès et Martaba et Allat........., et Menât et Keïs maudissent celui qui vendrait ce caveau, ou l'achèterait, ou le mettrait en gage, ou le donnerait, ou en tirerait les corps, ou celui qui y enterrerait d'autres que Camcam et sa fille et leurs descendants. Et celui qui ne se conformerait pas à ce qui est ici écrit, qu'il en soit justiciable devant Dusarès et Hobal et Menât, gardiens de ce lieu, et qu'il paye une amende de mille *selaïn*......, à l'exception de celui qui produirait un écrit de Camcam ou de Coleibat, sa fille, ainsi conçu : " Qu'un tel soit admis dans ce caveau."

Wahbélahi, fils de Abdobodat, a fait.

No. 3.

De l'an 40 de J.-C.

Ceci est le caveau qu'a fait faire Mati, le stratège, fils d'Euphronius, l'éparque, pour lui-même et pour ses enfants, et pour Vaal, sa femme, et pour ses fils, dans le mois de nisan de l'année quarante-huitième de Hartat, roi des Nabatéens, aimant son peuple. Que personne n'ose ni vendre, ni mettre en gage, ni louer ce caveau-ci.

Wahbélahi, fils de Abdobodat, a fait. A perpétuité.

No. 4.

Date illisible, vers 25 après J.-C.

Ce caveau a été fait construire par Seli, fils de Riswa, pour lui et pour ses fils et pour ses descendants en ligne légitime. Que ce caveau ne soit point vendu, qu'il ne soit point mis en gage, et quiconque fera autrement que ce qui est marqué ici, il sera redevable au dieu Dusarès, notre Seigneur, de mille *selaïn*... Dans le mois de nisan de l'année.........de Hartat, roi des Nabatéens, aimant son peuple. Aftah le tailleur de pierre a fait.

No. 5.

Date illisible, au moins pour le premier chiffre, peut-être de l'an 16 après J.-C.

Ce caveau a été fait construire par Teimélahi, fils de Hamlat, pour lui-même, et il a donné ce caveau à Ammah, sa femme, fille de Golhom. En vertu de l'acte de donation qui est dans sa main, elle peut en faire ce qu'elle voudra. En l'année 3 de Hartat, roi des Nabatéens, aimant son peuple.

No. 6.

Date en partie illisible ; de l'an 3, 13, 23 ou 33 de J.-C.

Ceci est le caveau que...................................et à leurs descendants et à quiconque viendra........................... tout

homme qui..et quiconque le
mettra en gage.. Et quiconque fera
autrement que ce qui est écrit, aura sur lui le double de la valeur de
tout ce lieu-ci, et la malédiction de Dusarès et de Menât. Dans le
mois de nisan de l'an......de Hartat, roi des Nabatéens, aimant son
peuple. Et quiconque.........dans ce caveau ou changera quelque
chose à ce qui est écrit, il aura à payer à Dusarès mille *selaïn*......
Aftah [le tailleur de pierre a fait].

No. 7.

De l'an 3 avant J.-C.

C'est ici le caveau que fit Khaled, fils de Xanten, pour lui et pour
Saïd, son fils, et pour les frères quels qu'ils soient de ce dernier,
enfants mâles qui naîtraient à Khaled, et pour leurs fils et leurs
descendants, par descendance légitime, à perpétuité. Et que soient
enterrés dans ce caveau les enfants de Saïd......... Soleimat, fille
de Khaled............. ....tout homme, hors Saïd et ses frères
mâles, et leurs enfants et leurs descendants, qui vendra ce caveau et
en écrira une donation ou...............à n'importe qui, excepté celui
qui aurait un écrit en forme dans sa main,..................................
....
Celui qui ferait autrement que ceci devra au dieu Dusarès, notre
Seigneur, une amende de cinquante *selaïn* d'argent.........notre
Seigneur.........Keïs. Dans le mois de nisan de la quatrième année
de Hartat, roi des Nabatéens, aimant son peuple. Douma et Abdobodat, sculpteurs.

No. 8.

Date illisible ; vers l'époque même de notre ére.

Ceci est le caveau que firent Anam, fils de Gozeiat, et Arsacès,
fils de Tateim le stratège...............et Calba, son frère. A Anamou
appartiendra le tiers de ce caveau et sépulcre, et à Arsacès les deux
autres tiers de ce caveau et sépulcre, et la moitié des niches du côté
est et les *loculi* [qui y sont]. A Anemou appartiendra la moitié des
niches du côté sud, et les *loculi* qui y sont. (Ces *loculi* appartien-
dront) à eux et à leurs enfants en ligne légitime. Dans le mois de
tebeth de l'année...........de Hartat, roi des Nabatéens, aimant son
peuple. Aftah, le tailleur de pierre, a fait.

No. 9.

A l'intérieur d'un caveau ; de l'an 16 de J.-C.

Ce *loculus* a été fait par Tousouh, fils de..................., pour lui,
de son vivant, et pour ses filles Et quiconque le...............ou le
tirera hors de la fosse,.......................qu'il paye à notre Seigneur
Hartat, roi des Nabatéens, ami de son peuple, mille *selaïn*.....; et au

dieu Dusarès, seigneur de tous les dieux. Celui qui.....................
la fosse......................la malédiction de Dusarès et de tous les
dieux.........Dans le mois de..............de l'année 23 de Hartat, roi
des Nabatéens, ami de son peuple.

No. 10.

De l'an 77 après J.-C.

Ceci est le caveau de Hoinat, fille d'Abdobodat, pour elle, pour
son fils et ses descendants, et pour ceux qui produiront en leur main,
de la main de Hoinat, un écrit en cette forme : " Qu'un tel soit enterré en tel caveau."
Ce caveau a appartenu à Abdobodat,...
....
à Hoinat ou Abdobodat, fils de Malikàt,................................
soit Abdobodat, soit Hoinat, soit tous ceux qui..................ce
caveau............l'écrit que voici : " Qu'il soit enterré dans ce caveau,
à côté d'Abdobodat." Que personne n'ose vendre ce caveau, ni le
mettre en gage, ni..................dans ce caveau. Et quiconque fera
autrement, qu'il doive à Dusarès et à Menât mille *selaïn* d'argent, et
autant à notre Seigneur Dabel, roi des Nabatéens. Dans le mois
d'iyyar de l'année deuxième de Dabel, roi des Nabatéens. Dans le
mois d'iyyar de l'année deuxième de Dabel, roi des Nabatéens.

No. 11.

De l'an 61 de J.-C.

Ceci est le caveau qu'a fait construire Hoinat, fille de Wahb, pour
elle-même, et pour ses enfants et ses descendants, à perpétuité. Et
que personne n'ose le vendre, ou le mettre en gage ou écrire............
dans ce caveau-ci, et quiconque fera autrement que ceci, que sa part
..............En l'année vingt et unième du roi Malchus, roi des
Nabatéens.

No. 12.

Date illisible, antérieure à l'an 40 de notre ère.

Ce caveau a été fait par Maénat et Higr, fils de Amiérah, fils de
Wahb, pour eux et leurs enfants et leurs descendants,...................
Maénat................une part de ce caveau-ci..............dans le lieu de
Higr............une part......Maénat........il devra au dieu Dusarès
mille *selaïn* d'argent..................mille *selaïn*......................
la malédiction de Dusarès. Dans le mois de tisri de l'année...........
de Hartat, roi des Nabatéens, aimant son peuple.

No. 13.

De l'an 6 de J.-C.

Cette fosse................................ ....sa fille...............
tous ceux qui y seront enterrés...

dans toutes les fosses qui sont dans ce caveau autres que..............
autre que cette fosse-ci..
....
il devra à Dusarès cent *selaïn*......et à notre Seigneur le roi Hartat
tout autant. Dans le mois de thébet de l'année 13 de Hartat, roi
des Nabatéens, aimant son peuple.

No. 14.
De l'an 40 de J.-C.

C'est ici le caveau de Sabou, fils de Moqimou, et de Meikat, son
fils,......leurs enfants et leurs descendants légitimes, et de quiconque
apportera dans sa main, de la part de Sabou et de Meikat, un écrit
....................qu'il y soit enterré,..............enterré............
Sabou..............En l'année quarante-hu tième de Hartat, roi des
Nabatéens, aimant son peuple.

No. 15.
An 49 de J.-C.

C'est ici le caveau de Banou, fils de Saïd, pour lui-même et ses
enfants et ses descendants et ses *asdaq*. Et que personne n'ait le
droit de vendre ou de louer ce caveau. A perpétuité. En l'année
neuvième du roi Malchus, roi des Nabatéens. Hono [fils de] Obeidat,
sculpteur.

No. 16.
Date illisible, entre 40 et 75 après J.-C.

Caveau destiné à Abda, à Aliël, à Géro, fils de Aut, et à Ahadilou,
leur mère, fille de Hamin, et à quiconque produira en sa main un
écrit ainsi conçu : "Qu'il soit enterré dans mon tombeau." A eux
et à leurs descendants. En l'année neuvième de Malchus.

No. 17.
Non datée.

Ceci est le *loculus* qu'a fait Tahged pour Mesalmana, son frère, et
pour Mahmit, sa fille. Qu'on n'ouvre pas sur eux durant l'éternité.

No. 18.
De l'an 17 après J.-C.

Ceci est le caveau et tombeau que fit construire Maénat, fils
d'Anban, pour lui-même et ses fils et ses filles et leurs enfants. En
l'année vingt-quatrième de Hartat, roi des Nabatéens, aimant son
peuple.

No. 19.

De l'an 79 après J.-C.

Ceci est le caveau d'Amlat, fils de Meleikat, pour lui et pour ses enfants après lui. En l'année quatrième de Dabel, roi des Nabatéens.

No. 20.

Date illisible.

C'est ici le caveau de Higr, fils de............et de.........ilat, pour eux-mêmes et pour leurs enfants et leurs descendants.................
En l'année..

No. 21.

Non datée.

Ce caveau est pour Sakinat, fils de Tamrat......et ses fils et ses filles et leurs enfants.

No. 22.

Pour Haïl, fils de Douna, (et) ses descendants.

Il est remarquable que dans cette liste on ne trouve aucun nom grec bien caractérisé. La civilisation nabatéenne avait cependant été pénétrée par la civilisation grecque, comme le prouvent certains noms propres, des mots tels que $\sigma\tau\rho\alpha\tau\eta\gamma\delta\varsigma$, $\check{\epsilon}\pi\alpha\rho\chi o\varsigma$ et plus encore le style des monuments.

Le caractère des inscriptions de Medaïn-Salih témoigne d'un état social où l'on écrivait beaucoup et où les scribes se livraient à de grands caprices de calligraphie, ainsi que cela eut lieu plus tard pour l'écriture coufique.—E. R.

MEDÁIN SÂLIH.—*Note par M. Philippe Berger, Sous-Bibliothécaire de l'Institut.* [L'ARABIE AVANT MAHOMET D'APRÈS LES INSCRIP-TIONS: Conférence faite à la Sorbonne, *Mars* 1885.]—Voici toute une vallée pleine de sépultures de famille: car chacune de ces constructions n'est pas une sépulture particulière; ce sont de véritables caveaux de famille, où les ayants droit sont spécifiés et qui sont entourés de toutes les formalités et de toutes les garanties que nous donnons à nos actes officiels.

Mais alors où étaient les maisons?—Ce problème, qui nous embar-rasse, a dû dérouter les Arabes du temps de Mahomet. On conçoit qu'en présence de ces monuments dont ils ne comprenaient plus la signification, ils se soient dit: ce sont les demeures des anciens habi-

tants du pays, d'impies, de géants : les deux choses se touchent ; et
que, pénétrant dans l'intérieur et voyant des cadavres, ils les aient
pris pour les ossements des infidèles, frappés par le ciel dans leurs
demeures. Ils ont dû être confirmés dans cette opinion par l'aspect
de ces monuments. Les créneaux qui les surmontent et qui sont un
des motifs habituels de l'architecture assyrienne, leur donnent un
faux air de fortifications.

Un autre fait qui ressort clairement de ces légendes, c'est qu'à
l'époque de Mahomet on ne comprenait plus ces inscriptions, dont en
était séparé par cinq cents ans à peine, et *cela nous montre combien
l'horizon des Arabes était borné du côté de ses origines.* Qui sait
pourtant s'ils n'en ont pas eu encore un vague sentiment, au moins
par tradition. Ces inscriptions, qui présentent un singulier mélange
d'araméen et d'arabe, commencent par un mot qui n'est pas araméen,
qui est arabe : *Dena Kafrâ* "Ceci est le tombeau." Or le même mot
signifie en arabe *tombeau* et *impie.* Qui sait si, à une époque déjà
éloignée de la dynastie nabatéenne, quand le souvenir de la langue
araméenne commençait à se perdre, la confusion ne s'est pas faite
entre les deux mots, et si, en répétant machinalement cette formule,
les Arabes ne se sont pas dit : Voilà les mécréants écrasés par le ciel
dans leurs demeures.

Il est un point sur lequel ils ne s'étaient pas trompés : c'est que
ces anciens habitants du pays étaient bien des mécréants et des ido-
lâtres. A l'une des entrées de la vallée de Medaïn-Saleh se trouve
une gorge, taillée à pic, comme elles le sont toutes dans cette région.
D'un des côtés on voit les restes d'une salle qui est creusée dans le
roc ; seulement, au lieu d'être fermée par devant, elle est ouverte sur
toute la largeur de la façade. Elle ne présente pas de niches : quelques figures, grossièrement dessinées au trait sur les murs ; rien de
plus. C'est la seule construction qui n'ait pas de caractère funéraire.
On l'appelle le Divan. Sur la paroi opposée de la gorge, au même
niveau et dominant le précipice, on découvre toute une série de niches
dans lesquelles se trouvent des pierres dressées, tantôt isolées, tantôt
réunies par groupes de deux ou de trois.

La vue de ces petits monuments, dessinés avec soin par M.
Doughty, a été pour nous une véritable révélation. Nous avions
déjà rencontré des monuments analogues à l'autre extrémite du
monde sémitique. Il y a trois ans, on n'en connaissait qu'un ex-
emple : un bas-relief, trouvé en Sicile, et qui représentait un homme
en adoration devant une petite triade de pierre. Ce monument isolé
était inexplicable ; mais il avait frappé l'attention de M. Renan,
quand, quelque temps après (une découverte ne marche jamais seule),
M. l'abbé Trihidez en rapporta plusieurs de même genre qui venaient
d'Hadrumète, en Tunisie. Ces pierres, accouplées trois par trois,
étaient des représentations divines, de véritables triades, il n'y avait
pas de doute à avoir. S'il en restait encore, ils sont levés par les
découvertes de M. Doughty. Voilà les dieux qu'allaient adorer les
habitants de Medaïn-Saleh. Une inscription placée au-dessus d'une
de ces niches le dit expressément :

"Ceci est le *mesgeda* qu'a fait élever Serouh, fils de Touca, à Aouda (ou Aera) de Bostra, grand dieu. Dans le mois de Nisan de l'an I du roi Malchus." [*See above*, p 47.] Une autre niche porte une inscription analogue. Le *mesgeda*, c'est-à-dire la mosquée, n'est donc pas la salle située de l'autre côté du ravin, mais la niche avec la pierre qui est dedans. Voilà le Beth-El devant lequel les Nabatéens allaient se prosterner ; cette pierre n'est autre que le dieu Aouda.

* * *

On se demande où est, au milieu de tout cela, l'Arabe des Coréischites et de Mahomet ? Il nous apparaît comme un dialecte excessivement restreint, comme la langue d'une toute petite tribu, qui, par suite de circonstances, très locales, est arrivée à un degré de perfection extraordinaire. C'est à l'islamisme qu'elle a dû toute sa fortune.

L'islamisme de même a imposé sa langue avec sa religion à toute l'Arabie, et de là il s'est répandu de proche en proche, sur l'Afrique et sur l'Asie, créant, partout où il s'établit, une puissance qui pénètre tout, mais qui ferme la porte à tout ce qui n'est pas elle. Nulle part l'unité n'a été réalisée d'un façon aussi absolue. De là viennent les obstacles toujours renaissants que l'on trouve à pénétrer dans ces contrées fanatiques et désertes, obstacles si grands qu'on hésite à désirer que d'autres cherchent à les surmonter : le prix en est trop cher. Ils le seront pourtant, car il est une autre puissance que rien n'arrête, *c'est la force intérieure qui pousse l'homme à la recherche de la vérité.*

II.—THE NABATEAN SCULPTURED ARCHITECTURE AT MEDÁIN SÂLIH.
Note by M. LE MARQUIS DE VOGÜÉ (*Membre de l'Institut*).

Funchal, 24 janvier, 1886.

Vous me demandez, Monsieur, de vous donner mon avis sur le style des monuments que vous avez découverts, au prix de si grands efforts et de si grands dangers. Votre question m'embarrasse un peu : je suis à Madère, séparé, depuis plus d'un an, de mes livres et de mes notes : je ne puis donc écrire que de souvenir : les réflexions que me suggèrent vos dessins n'auront pas le développement que j'aurais aimé à leur donner : je vous les adresse néanmoins, avec l'espoir qu'elles pourront vous être de quelque utilité.

Le principal intérêt du groupe de tombeaux de Médaïn-Salih réside dans ce fait qu'il est daté : il offre donc une base indiscutable pour les rapprochements archéologiques. Tous ces monuments ont été exécutés dans le premier siècle de notre ère, et, pour la plupart, dans la première moitié de ce même siècle. Ils sont d'une remarquable uniformité. On voit qu'ils ont tous été exécutés à la même époque par des artistes de la même école, en possession d'un petit nombre de modèles. On s'étonnerait, à première vue, qu'une région aussi

anciennement habitée ne renfermât pas de monuments de sa longue
existence, si le fait n'était pas général. Sa Syrie et la Palestine,
malgré la grande antiquité de la civilisation dans ces contrées, ne
renferment presque plus de monuments antérieurs à l'époque grecque:
à part quelques rares exceptions, les innombrables tombeaux, taillés
dans le roc, qui sillonnent toutes les montagnes de ces régions, sont
postérieurs à Alexandre, et généralement même postérieurs à Jésus
Christ.   Telle est du moins mon opinion, et les monuments que vous
avez découverts lui apportent une confirmation nouvelle.

La forme générale de ces tombeaux est celle d'une tour à demi
évidée dans la surface du rocher : à la base de la tour une porte
donne accès dans la chambre sépulcrale. la surface de la tour est
coupée par des bandeaux, ou corniches, qui en rompent l'uniformité ;
le sommet est couronné par une sorte de crénelage à merlons taillés
en escalier.   Quelques unes des façades de ces tours sont décorées de
pilastres : c'est le petit nombre ; vos dessins en mentionnent surtout
quatre qui méritent de nous arrêter quelque temps : ce sont les monuments provenant l'un du Borj, l'autre de Kasr-el-Bint, reproduits à
la page 104 et à la page 105 de votre volume, puis les monuments
désignés sous les noms de Beït-Akhraémat (p. 114) et Mahal-el-Mejlis
(p. 116).   (See *Travels in Arabia Deserta*, vol. i., 1888.)

Le premier est orné de deux pilastres portant une architrave et
une corniche ; les pilastres devaient avoir des chapiteaux corinthiens :
mais ils sont restés inachevés : le tailleur de pierre s'est borné à les
dégrossir : il a ménagé, à leur base, des anneaux pour les deux
rangées de feuilles d'acanthe ;—à leurs angles supérieurs, deux
saillies pour les volutes et les feuilles qui les supportent ;—au centre
de l'abaque, une saillie pour le fleuron.   Les moulures de l'architrave
sont empruntées à l'art grec ; la corniche est au contraire imitée
de la corniche égyptienne ; quant aux créneaux ou pinnacles, imités des tombeaux de Pétra, ils semblent un souvenir de l'art
Assyrien.   La porte est décorée dans le même style hybride : les
pilastres qui la flanquent sont corinthiens inachevés ; l'architrave
est imitée du dorique de basse époque ; le fronton est imité de
l'ionique ; des acrotères informes ornent les angles du fronton, que
surmonte la figure grossière d'un aigle.   Le dessin que vous avez
donné (Pl. xli de la publication de l'Académie), à une plus grande
échelle, d'une porte semblable, permet d'en apprécier plus com-
plètement le caractère.   Les triglyphes et les rosaces sont du style
que l'on appellerait *toscan*, si la date et le lieu n'excluaient toute
intervention des architectes romains.   Il faut se reporter à Jérusalem, aux tombeaux de la vallée de Josaphat, pour en trouver d'analogues.

Le second tombeau, celui de Kasr-el-Bint, est presque semblable
au précédent : l'architrave est plus complète et surmontée d'une frise :
mais les détails sont absolument les mêmes : les chapiteaux ne sont
qu'ébauchés.

Les monuments dits Mahal-el-Mejlis et Beït-Akhraémat ne dif-
fèrent des deux premiers que par de plus grandes dimensions et une

plus grande richesse. L'un a quatre pilastres et une succession de bandeaux ; l'autre a deux ordres de pilastres et une porte très ornée : mais le style est identiquement le même ; ils sont également inachevés.

La disposition intérieure de ces tombeaux est celle des monuments analogues de Syrie et de Palestine : une chambre sépulcrale, taillée dans le roc, et munie de *loculi* pour recevoir les corps : les *loculi* sont creusés ou dans le sol de la chambre, ou dans les parois latérales, parallèlement à ces parois : on en trouve qui sont superposés trois à trois, de chaque côté d'une grande niche rectangulaire : toutes ces formes se retrouvent en Syrie et Palestine : mais les tombeaux de ces régions renferment en outre deux formes que nous ne voyons pas ici, du moins dans les monuments que vous avez dessinés : c'est la forme dite *arcosolium* si répandue dans la Syrie du Nord, et les *fours* perpendiculaires à la paroi du rocher, si nombreux autour de Jérusalem. Néanmoins tous ces monuments sont de la même famille. Les *loculi* portent, dans les inscriptions de Médaïn-Salih, le nom de *Goukh*, très voisin du mot *Kouk* par lesquels les Juifs les désignent.

Le seul monument non funéraire de ce groupe est celui qui est désigné sous le nom de Liwân. C'est une grotte artificielle, ouverte au dehors par un portique aujourd'hui écroulé, et qui servait de lieu de prière ; les nombreuses stèles votives sculptées sur le rocher ne laissent aucun doute à ce sujet. L'une d'elles est accompagnée d'une inscription où se lit le mot *mesgeda* qui est caractéristique, et qui est devenu le mot arabe *mesjed*, "mosquée." La grotte a été exécutée avec soin : une corniche en fait le tour à l'intérieur ; des pilastres ornent les angles ; le tout est formé d'éléments grecs.

Les détails reproduits sur les planches XXXVIII, XL, XLI de la publication de l'Académie sont aussi empruntés à l'art grec ; mais on les dirait imités de monuments de basse époque : les colonnettes accouplées, les arcs placés soit en décharge, soit en porte-à-faux sur des architraves ou des pilastres sont des formes que nous étions habitués à considérer comme l'œuvre des architectes romains : les monuments de Pétra avaient bien déjà ébranlé cette opinion ; mais comme ils ne sont pas datés, la discussion était permise ; tandis qu'à Médaïn Salih la présence des dates défie toute contradiction.

En résumé, les monuments que vous avez découverts confirment ce que l'étude des monuments de Pétra et de Siah, dans le Haouran, ainsi que la numismatique, avaient déjà fait connaître, c'est qu'au point de vue de l'art le royaume Nabatéen était profondément pénétré par la Grèce : à peine les arts antérieurs de l'Asie sont-ils représentés par quelques rares réminiscences. Les artistes étaient nabatéens ; ceux de Siah et de Pétra avaient un véritable talent ; ceux de Médaïn Salih étaient des tailleurs de pierre qui attaquaient le rocher avec vigueur et ampleur, mais ne savaient pas sculpter les détails : pour achever leurs œuvres ils attendirent sans doute de Pétra des sculpteurs qui ne vinrent jamais.

Les modèles grecs imités per ces artistes orientaux renfermaient des formes dites de décadence : il faut donc faire remonter avant

l'ère chrétienne l'origine de ces formes. Enfin, en imitant les monuments grecs, les artistes orientaux en mélangeaient les ordres, as-
sociant les triglyphes doriques aux chapiteaux corinthiens, aux frises
ioniques, et même à la corniche égyptienne. Ces associations hy-
brides déjà remarquées dans les tombeaux qui entourent Jérusalem,
cessent donc d'être une exception : elles constituent un fait général
qui caractérise une région et une époque (la fin de l'ancienne ère et
le commencement de la nouvelle) ; la discussion que les monuments
de Jérusalem avaient soulevée se trouve ainsi définitivement close, et
ce n'est pas un des moindres services rendus par votre courageuse
exploration que d'avoir débarrassé la science des théories fantaisistes
qui ont un moment égaré certains esprits.

Veuillez agréer, Monsieur, l'expression de ma sincère estime et
de mes sentiments très distingués.

M. De Vogüé.

CHAPTER IV

* * * The Haj was late, and the Beduish multitude, which were come to market without their booths, lay out sheltering under the bushes in these bitter cold nights ; their cheerful watch-fires appeared glimpsing up and down in the dark, nigh the camp, in the wilderness. In the watch before midnight shells were shot from the Jurdy cannon east and west over their treasonable heads into the empty waste. Long now and chill at this altitude were the winter nights ; the gate Arabs these two months could not sleep past midnight, but lay writhing, with only their poor mantles lapped about them, in the cold sand and groaning for the morning. But especially their women suffer in the ragged tents : some of them, bare of all world's good, have not more than a cotton smock upon their bodies ; for where might they find silver to buy any mantle to cover them ? Snow falls not in the plain, but some years it whitens the Harra, above 3000 feet height. A dromedary rider, sent down to meet the Haj, brought word that the pilgrims had been delayed, in their camps, by (tropical) rains, betwixt the Harameyn. Now the caravan approaching, it was rumoured they brought the small-pox among them. Beduins of my acquaintance, who cared not to receive it before as a gift, now entreated me to sell them vaccination ; and they reproached me when in this busy stir and preparation to depart, I could not hear them.

The same evening we saw flights of locusts, an ill augury of the opening spring season ; they would devour the *rabía*. The people cried, " They come driving from el-Ally." The bird-like insects flitting upon their glassy feeble wings in the southern wind, fell about the camp ; these locusts were toasted presently at all watch-fires and eaten. The women on the morrow had gathered great heaps, and were busy singeing them in shallow pits, with a weak fire of herbs ; they give up a sickly odour of fried fish oil. Thus cured and a little salt cast in, the locust

meat is stived in leathern sacks, and will keep good a long while :
they mingle this, brayed small, with their often only liquid diet
of sour buttermilk. Locust powder is not victual to set before
guests; and I have seen poor nomads (more often women) a
little out of countenance to confess that (to beguile hunger)
they were eating this wretchedness. The best is the fat spring
locust, and "fretting every green thing," the Aarab account
them medicinal. The later broods, *dubba*, born of these, sex-
less, or imperfect females, finding only a burned-up herbage,
are dry and unwholesome. This early locust, toasted, is reckoned
a sweetmeat in town and in desert.

In these days whilst we awaited the pilgrimage, so incurious
were the weary Damascenes who came with the Jurdy, that only
two parties, and they upon account of my being there, went a
mile abroad to visit the monuments at Medáin Sâlih. The
Jurdy pasha, with the Turkish lieutenant and his troop,
Mohammed Aly guiding them, galloped another day to see what
they were, for whose sake the Engleysy was come down, so far,
from Syria. A lonely Christian in the midst of a stirring
multitude of Moslemîn, assembled at el-Héjr, I lived among
Syrians, and under that somewhat burdensome jealousy of the
tolerant better sort of Arabians. Mohammed Aly also recommended me to every one who might further my adventure in
Arabia ; from which, notwithstanding, all the friendly and well-
disposed persons very heartily dissuaded me : it is not of their
easy religious minds to attempt anything untried. "Whither
would I go, said they, to lose myself in lawless land, to be an
outlaw, if only for my name of Nasrâny, and far from all
succour ; where they themselves, that were of the religion and
of the tongue, durst not adventure ? Khalîl, think better for
thyself, and return with us, whilst the way is open, from this
hunger-stricken wilderness and consumed by the sun ; thou
wast not bred, and God calls thee not, to this suffering in a land
which only demons, *afarît*, can inhabit ; the Beduw are demons,
but thou art a Nasrâny,—there every one that seeth thee will
kill thee ! And if the Lord's singular grace save thy life to the
end, yet what fruit shouldst thou have for all those great pains ?
Other men jeopardy somewhat in hope of winning, but thou
wilt adventure all, having no need." And some good hearts of
them looked between kindness and wonder upon me, that born
to the Frankish living, full of superfluity, I should carelessly
think to endure the Aarab's suffering and barren life. And they
said, " In a day or two we return to Syria, leave thou this purpose, and go up in our company : and is not Damascus a
pleasant city to dwell in ? " The like said also the blind Mehsan,

he too would honestly dissuade me, a man of the town-life, and
a Nasrâny : " Hear," said he, " a friendly counsel ; return now,
Khalîl, with the Haj to es-Sham : here is only a land of Beduw
under no rule, and where thou art named Nasrâny ; do not
jeopardy thy life : and yet I tell thee, wilt thou needs adventure,
the Aarab are good folk, and thou wilt enlarge thy breast (feel
thy heart to be free) amongst them." M. Aly answered,
" Khalîl is a man too adventurous ; there may nothing persuade
him." Said a sheykh, " If one go to the Aarab, he should carry
his shroud under his arm with him ; " others said, " Khalîl, see
thou trust not thyself to any of them all ; the Beduw are elfin."
The Jurdy officers blamed me, saying, " And why cast your life
away ? you know them not, but we know them ; the Beduins are
fiends." And the lieutenant said, " Even we which are soldiers
cannot pass, but by paying them surra. They are rebels, and
(he added as a Turk) deserve to lose their heads. How durst
they gainsay the authority of the Sûltàn ! " They asked me,
" What think you of this desert ? " " I warrant you (answered
M. Aly, the Algerian), if *Fransa* had it, there would be towns
and villages." I told them I thought the country would not be
worth the pains.

Secretary with the Jurdy was a swarthy Ageyly Arabian, a
lettered man of the Waháby country, and very unlike all those
Syrian faces about him. And yet the eyes of his dark visage
regarded me with goodwill, without fanatical envy, as a simple
Nasrâny traveller in land of the Arabs : he said he would tell
me of a wonder in his country where I might come another
day. " Write!...*Siddûs*, in *W. Halîfa*, in the dîrat *Umseylmy*
(Moseilima) *el-kitthâb* (the false prophet), there is set up a *mîl*
(needle, or pillar) with an unknown writing, no man can tell
what ; but it was of those Nasâra or kafirs which in old time
inhabited the land."

It was now ascertained that the Haj brought the small-pox
among them. This terrible disease and cholera fever are the
destruction of nomad Arabia. In their weakly nourished bodies
is only little resistance to any malignant sickness. The pilgrimage caravans, (many from the provinces of Arabia herself,)
are as torrents of the cities' infection flowing every year through
the waste Peninsula.

The eighth morrow of this long expectation, the Haj, which
had journeyed all night, were seen arriving in the plain. The
Jurdy troop mounted and galloped with their officers to salute
the Pasha. The tent-pitchers came before : in few more
minutes they had raised the pilgrims' town of tents, by the Jurdy

camp. The jingles sounded again in our ears, measured to the solemn gait of the colossal bearing camels, of the pageant-like (but now few returning) takhts er-Rûm. The motley multitude of the Haj came riding after. Their straggling trains passed by for half an hour, when the last of the company re-entered their lodgings. Twice every year stands this canvas city of a day, in the Thamudite plain, full of traffic! Cobblers sat at the sûk corners to drive their trade; they had by them raw soles of camels fallen by the way; and with such they clouted shoes for those who fared so far on foot. The Jurdy street of tent-shops was soon enlarged by the new merchants' tents. The price of small commodities is, at this mid-way station, five to eight times the market worth at Damascus. The Jurdy have brought down Syrian olives, leeks and cheese and caravan biscuit. The Jurdy baker was busy with his fire-pit of sticks in the earth and his girdle pans, tannûr, to make fine white flat bread, for the pennies of the poor pilgrims. The refreshing sweet and sour lemons and helw dates, from el-Ally, I saw very soon sold out. The merchants upon camels from Damascus opened their bales in the tents and set out coffee-cups, iron ware, precious carpets (like gardens of fresh colours and soft as the spring meadows,)— fairings for great sheykhs! and clothing stuffs for the poor Beduw. The returning Haj tradesmen bring up merchandise from Mecca; now in their tent stalls I saw heaps of coffee from el-Yémen (Arabia the Happy).

In little outlying tents I found spices set to sale from the Malay islands. India or Mecca perfumes, and trifles in porcelain from the China Seas; all brought by the Mohammedan pilgrims, assembling to the Holy Fair, of many strange distant nations. The keeper of one of them cried to the Beduins, "Come up and buy, ya Aarab!" women who went by, seeking for some drugs and spicery, answered again very soberly, "What hast thou, young man?" When they murmured at his price, "How is this? (exclaimed the seller) do ye take me for one that could defraud you, a man come up from beholding the temple of Ullah!"— Then, seeing me, he stayed in his talk to salute me! the fellow made me all the false smiling excuses in the world in the name of the Persian Mohammed Aga, because he was not come this way again (as his feigned promise had been to me, to convey me to es-Shem), but gone about by sea to Bagdad. The Persian feared in his conscience, I might another day accuse him at Damascus. There I afterwards saw him again, when I had returned in peace from Arabia; but so many world's waves were gone over my head, that when he spoke to me in the market-place I remembered him not, only of the cankered visage there

lingered some uneasy remembrance; he might be sure that I
intended no unkindness "Ah! (he said then to my companion,
a Damascene) what have I suffered for your friend because I
conveyed him to Medáin Sâlih, at Maan and all along the road!
What happened to me then at el-Medina! Wellah! I would
not undertake the like again;—no, not for five times the money.
At Medina I was examined before their council, day by day, and
they regarded not my solemn oaths, but would compel me to
acknowledge where I had hidden the Nasrâny. I was never in
such trouble in my life."

Poor Beduins flitted up and down in the street of tent-shops,
to sell their few pints of samn for silver, and hoping to have
therefore a new mantle this year and a *shâmy* (Damascus ware)
shirt-cloth. The pilgrims who have journeyed through the
night are now reposing in the tents, and the pleasant water-
pipe and the cup are made ready at a hundred coffee fires: but
the large white faces of girded Damascenes, their heavy foreheads wound round with solemn turbans, their citizen clothing
and superfluous slops, are now quaint to the eye disused a
while in the wilderness. Great press of their waterers was
about the birket, to fill the girbies and draw for the multitude
of cattle. The kella cistern was already green and fermenting.
Even the nomads (who are not wont to find good water),
refused to drink; it was become to us abominable by the
nasty ablutions to prayerward of the odious Alowna, who made
no conscience to go down and wash their bodies in the public
water.

In this great company I met with a swarthy Beduwy of the
Murra Aarab, a tribe far in the south, by Wady Dauâsir. The
man was going up in the Haj caravan to Syria! when I asked
him of his country, he answered me with that common sorry
saying of the Beduins, *Ma biha kheyr*, "little or no good to find
in her." He would say, "an open soil without villages, land of
dearth and hunger." *Béled biha kheyr*, "a good land," they
use to say of a country whose inhabitants do eat and are
satisfied.

I had been in friendly wise commended by the Jurdy officers,
and praised by Mohammed Aly to the Pasha; but I did not
think it well so early in the busy day to visit him, who of my
coming to Medáin Sâlih had formerly conceived a grave displeasure. From M. Aly, both in his better mind and in his
angry moments, I had heard all that matter. In the December
night of the Haj departure from Medáin, the Turkish Sîr Amîn
and Mohammed Saîd Pasha had sent, before they removed, to
call again M. Aly. "Wellah, they said to him, hast thou

not hidden the Nasrâny, to send him secretly to Medina and Mecca?" "God is my witness, no your lordships, but this man certainly has adventured hither only to see Medáin Sâlih: trust me he shall not pass a step further: in any case I shall know how to let him; but I go to bring him before you: he shall answer for himself." "No," said the Pasha, "I will not see his face, and I have a dignity to keep." (It might be when I visited him in Damascus, I had not observed to call the old portly embezzler of public moneys "Your Magnificence!") Said the Sîr Amîn (of Stambûl), "Hearken, kellâjy; if this Engleysy should follow us but one footstep further to Medina, thou art to bring me the dog's head." [Englishmen, who help these barbarians at Constantinople that cannot be taught, they would murder you secretly, and let hounds live, at Medina and Mecca!] The Pasha said to Mohammed Aly, "Let him remain with you in the kella, and you are to send him round to all the monuments, that no more Franks come hither hereafter. Look to it, that no evil befall this man: for wellah we will require his life at thy hand." *Sir Amîn:* "By Almighty God, except we find him alive at our coming again, we will hang thee, Mohammed Aly, above the door of thine own kella." Sore adread are they of late to be called in question for the life of European citizens.—M. Aly looked stoutly upon it, and answered to their beards, that 'he would obey his orders, but by High God, he was a Moghreby, and not to be put in awe by living creature.' Now I must ask a boon of the Pasha, namely, that he would commend me to the wild Beduins of the road. When the caravan removed in the morning, I should go forth to wander with the Aarab in the immense wilderness. The Jurdy officers had dissuaded Zeyd, so had even the Pasha himself; but Zeyd hoped to win silver, and they had no power at all with a free Beduin.

Some Algerian derwishes were evening guests at the kella. Willingly they allowed to me—I might seem to them a Moslem stranger,—that they had both liberty of religion, and justice, under their Christian rulers. There were also Moorish askars come in from the kellas to the southward; for here they draw their stipends, which upon the haj way are paid for the year beforehand, although all other men's wages of the Ottoman Dowla be as much or more in arrear:—which of them would otherwise remain cut off, in the midst of great deserts, waiting for his pay? that were much the same to them as if they should never receive it. Merry were these men of the settled countries, used to stout hackneys, to look upon the lean and scald gift-

mare of the Nejd prince. 'A beggarly scorn, to send this
carrion, not worth thirty crown pieces; and the Pasha would
not accept her!' Some Beduins who were present boasted her
worth to be thirty camels. A Syrian said, "A month at Shem,
and she will seem better than now. A mare another year, lean
as a faggot, sent by this Beduin emir Ibn Rashîd or what you
call him, grew in the Pasha's stable, with plenty of corn and
green provender, to be big—ay as this coffee-chamber!" The
best brood-mares of pure blood are valued in the Aarab tribes,
where they are few, at twenty-five camels, that is £130 at
least, or at most £150 sterling; and the worst at five camels,
which is the price of the best thelûls. The Beduin prince's
yearly gift of a mare to Mohammed Saîd was a sop in the
mouth of the great Syrian pasha. The Pasha at his coming
down again with the next year's pilgrimage sends his messenger
from hence to Hâyil, bearer of counter-gifts for the Arabian
emir. These are revolver pistols, rifle-guns, telescopes, and the
like Western wares from Stambûl.

Upon the morrow at eight, when the signal gun was fired,
the Haj caravan set forward, and I rode after them with Zeyd,
upon a young camel he had bought me for thirty reals. In
departing he asked Mohammed Aly to remember him at
Damascus (for his gift-foal), and bring him down, in the next
Haj, at least, a furred winter cloak [the town guise: Syrian
Aarab wear a warm jerkin of sheep skins; Sinai Beduins a
gazelle or other skin hanging from the neck, which they shift
round their bodies as the wind blows]. Little the other
answered again; they were both deceivers, and we saw him no
more. We journeyed through the Héjr plain, full of little
sand-hillocks blown about *rimth* bushes. A Wélad Aly tribesman reviling me as we rode (neighbours to Medina, they have I
know not what ill savour of the town, with their nomad
fanatical malignity,) said he, "Wouldst thou bring upon us the
Muscôv? O thou enemy! (he levelled his matchlock;) but
know that thus we will do with them, we have many guns like
this and every Beduwy in battle is worth, wellah, ten
Muscovies." I said to him, "By my faith, one of them I can
think were a match for many idle vaunters of you weleds; I
am no enemy, simpleton: there is no nation in all the world
which envies you your sand deserts. I am of the part of the
Sûltàn, and against those Muscôv, if they came hither." We
alighted a moment, to let the caravan pass upward before
Mubrak en-Nâga. It was a mirth to hear the solemn loud
hooting and pistol firing of the devout hajjies. For the Beduw,

ignorant of the koran mythology, here (as said) is but "The thronging place": it might be such in former times when the pilgrimage was a multitude. As we rode I saw that the east cliff was full of antique scored inscriptions: but I could not now alight to transcribe them. Looking here from the height of my camel, I thought I saw the caravan much diminished; hardly two-third parts returned of the Haj which had gone down to Mecca: there was not a Persian fur cap amongst them. The holy visitation accomplished, many go home by sea ; a few have died in the way. With the Haj returning from Mecca, are brought the African slaves, for all the north-west of the Mohammedan world, but gazing all day up and down, I could not count five among them.

Seeing that some Beduins who marched with us had stopped their nostrils, I enquired the cause. The men told me "they had never been inoculated, and they doubted sore to smell the Haj." Nomads living always in an incorrupt atmosphere, are very imaginative of all odours. In entering towns, where they are sensible of diverse strange, pungent and ungrateful airs, it is common to see them breathe with a sort of loathing, through a lap of their kerchiefs. Sultry was that afternoon, and we were thirsty. A poor derwish, who went by on foot, hearing one say "water," laid hand, with a pleasant look, upon the bridle of my camel, and lifting his little girby he said heartily, "Drink of this, O pilgrim, and refresh thyself." Seeing but foul rotten water in the leathern bag and discoloured, I gave him his own again ; but he would not hear my excuses. It seemed by his looks he thought the rider on the camel had ill requited his religious gentleness, for all charity is rare in the struggle of the haj road. A moment he gazed in anger, his merit lost ; and passing on wearily might guess the man who would not drink water with other pilgrims to be no right Moslem.

The ascending Haj came to their camping-ground before sunset. We alighted and I went to commit my large roll of inscriptions, impressed at Medáin Sâlih, to Mohammed Tâhir ; he laid my commission in his camel-chests, and promised with good humour to deliver them at Damascus to the British Consulate:—and very honourably he did so, indeed. I enquired if there were any political tidings in Medina. He said thus: 'The Powers had exhibited certain requisitions to the Porte, threatening if they were not satisfied to make common cause against the Sûltàn.'—"And England?"—"Ay, and Inghilterra! Ha now! who can tell how the world will go?" There was standing by a young Turkish officer of the Haj soldiery,

and he said to me, "We know that the Frenjies talk these
many years of dividing the Empire of the Sooltàn: but what
says the Sooltàn? 'Well, and it must be so, *hŷ yellah*, let
them come, one or all together and unto whom it shall please
the Lord, to them be the victory!'" He said this in a young
man's melancholy, as if the divine decree were about to go forth
and they must march soon to put all upon that final adventure.
—The most fanatic and wild Mohammedan region lay before
me, where the name of Nasrâny is only wont to be said as an
injury; how might I have passage amongst a frenetic and
sanguinary population, and not be taken for a spy, one of their
imagined hereditary enemies? Because their political talk was
full of solecisms, I judged the truth might be less, and thought
not now to return from this enterprise. Was this a year of
the jehâd? yet another time I might have no list to travel in
Arabia. The two officers turning at unawares looked to read
in my looks how I received and did digest this news of their
dying religion, whether with no secret exultation? foreseeing
the Christian triumph to be nearly ready in the world: but
when they marked evidently that I was not glad of their
sorrow, but pensive, this lifted me to the height of their good
opinion.

I awaited Zeyd; when we alighted the guileful Beduin would
lead, he said, our camels to pasture; and then we could go
together to find the Pasha. He eluded me till nightfall, when
weary and fasting since yesterday, I returned through the
sentinels to the fires of my Beduin company: there I found
Zeyd, who sat sipping coffee. He made me place, and with
smiles dissembled out the matter. Later, re-entering the Haj
menzil, I went alone to visit the Pasha; but stumbling at the
cords of his pavilion, for the lights were out, I understood from
the watchman that the great man was already at rest. I saw
there the empty bearing-frame, standing without, of the Mahmal
camel; and next to the great tent was made a small pole-and-
curtain court, "for an apartment of the hareem." I came then
to the military surgeon, whom they call *el-jábbar*, or the bone-
setter; he had promised to read me a lesson in the art of medicine. I found him a worthy person, and his few instructions
of one hour availed me long afterwards; for I had lost my book
of pharmacy. I said the names over of my drugs, and wrote
down the simple usage of each of them, from his lips. At his
desire I had brought him, for a patient of his, a little laudanum
powder; he was too weary himself to open his field-chests. I
enquired 'what to do if having given any one many doses of
that medicine to keep by him, he in ignorance swallowed them

all together, *wa yuskut el-kalb ;* ' I would have said, "and his heart ceased to beat," but all for weariness I pronounced simple *k*, (not *ḳ* with a guggle in the throat,) for *heart* mis-saying, "and the *dog*, is silenced." My false word tumbled to the mind of the pleasant hakîm : after the first smiles, stroking down a russet beard, the algebrist composed his rising mirth, which he held over (I am in dread) till the morrow, when he should be sitting at the pasha's dish. In this there enters a young derwish of the Medân, a giant of stature, and who had very often seen me, a Frenjy, pacing in that open quarter of Damascus. He came in to ask men's alms, some biscuit for his supper ; and, having eyes seven feet above his heels, he stood gazing to see one so like me sitting there in the Haj, and in this array. "Biscuits (ozmât) are dear," quoth the charitable surgeon, "but to-morrow and the day after they will be at better price, then I will buy, and so come thou to me." Carried upon camels, the price of all provisions in the caravan sûk, is after every march enhanced or diminished as the Haj is nearer the midst or the ends of their journey. Ozmât were sold at Medáin for seven times their worth at Damascus.

Challenged civilly by the sentinels, I passed out of the camp to the Arabs' firelight, and came again to our Beduin bush ; where in the pure sand, with their camel-saddles piled against the wind, we had our night's shelter. In this company sat a devout Fejîry, who had been to the Harameyn and now returned with the pilgrimage ; he was busily kneading a barley cake, when upon a sudden, a clear great meteor sliding under the stars, with luminous train, casting a broad blue gleam, drooped and brake before our eyes. "Eigh ! (sighed the man full of the religious sight of Mecca) these things, my God, be past understanding, of Thy wonderful works ! " Then having raked the cake under the ashes, and his fingers still cloyed, he rose quickly, seeing a nâga staling, and ran to take water in the hollow of his hands and rinsed them :—their cattle's excrement is pure in the opinion of the nomads. Then I understood the perpetual penury of waters in yonder desert land, where we should come on the morrow. I found with our Beduins some Kasîm men ; who, leaving the Syrian Haj service, would go this way home, more than three hundred miles, upon their feet, by Teyma and Jebel Shammar. They told me if ever I went to their country, I might thrive there by my medicines. "But wherefore, said they, proclaim thyself Nasrâny ? this thou mayest do at Damascus, but not in Nejd, where the people having no notice of the world, it will endanger thee." And as we drank round, they bade me call myself a "Misslim", and in my heart be still of what opinion I would, (this indulgence is permitted in the koran to any persecuted Moslemîn)—words not far from wisdom; and I have often felt the iniquitous fortune of travelling thus, an outlawed man (and in their sight worthy of death), only for a name, in Arabia. It had cost me little or naught, to confess Konfuchu or Socrates to be apostles of Ullah; but I could not find it in my life to confess the barbaric prophet of Mecca and enter, under the yoke, into their solemn fools' paradise.

At the first gunfire, before dawn, the Beduins charged their camels and departed. I saw by the stars our course lay much over to the eastward. Because the Aarab are full of all guile which may profit them, I had then almost a doubt of my company, until the light breaking I espied the B. Sókhr haj-carriers, coming on disorderly with their wild Beduin canticles; the main body of the caravan, far in the rear, was not yet in sight; I saw also the old wheel-ruts of the Jurdy cannon, and knew thereby certainly, that we were in the road. But for more surety, I dismounted to walk; and took an oath of Zeyd, who yesterday had not kept touch, to ride with me before the Pasha. Bye and bye we had sight of the Pasha, riding far in front, with his officers and a few soldiery; it was near Shuk el-Ajûz. I mounted then with Zeyd on his thelûl, (my camel was sick,) and we rode to them at a round trot. Zeyd greeted with the noble Beduin simplicity in his deep stern tones, and as a landlord in his own country, " Peace be with thee." Mohammed Saîd, hearing the Beduish voice behind him, said only " Ho! " again, without turning, but looking aside under the sun, he saw and knew me; and immediately with good humour he said to my Beduin companion,—" I commit him to thee, and (laying the right hand over his heart,) have thou a care of him as of mine own eye." So he said to me, " Have you ended all at Medáin Sâlih? The epigraphs, are what? believe you there be any in your countries able to read them? And what of the houses? have you not said they were no houses, but sepulchres? —But have you not found any treasure?—Good bye." I delayed yet, I spoke to the Pasha of the sick camel which Zeyd had bought for me : so he said to Zeyd, " Hearken! thou shalt restore the camel to his owner, and require the money again;—and (he said to me) if this Beduwy do not so I myself will require it of him at Damascus.—(To Zeyd) Where be now your Aarab? "—" About a day eastward of this, and the face of them is toward Teyma." The Pasha asked me anew, " And where are you going? "—" To Teyma, to Hâyil, I hope also to Kheybar." The Pasha drew a breath; he misliked my visiting

Kheybar, which is in the circuit of Medina: he answered, "But it is very difficult." Here Mohammed Tâhir, who came on riding with the Pasha, said friendly, "He has the vaccination with him, and that will be for his security among the Aarab; I saw it myself." He added, "Are all your inscriptions together in the roll which you have committed to me?" I answered immediately, "All are there, and I trust in God to show them one day to your worships at Damascus." The Pasha answered gravely, *Insha 'lla,* 'if the Lord will,' doubtless his thought was that I might very hardly return from this Arabian adventure.—Afterwards Zeyd, reporting the Pasha's discourse in the nomad tents, put in my mouth so many Beduin *billahs* ('by-Gods'), and never uttered, that I listened to him as one who dreams.

Departing from them, we rode aside from the haj-road, and went to fill our girby at a pool of sweet rain-water. Then entering eastward in the wild sandstone upland *Borj Selmàn,* we found before us an infinite swarm of locusts, flying together and alighting under all the desert bushes, it is their breeding-time ; the natural office accomplished, it seems they bye and bye perish. As we went fasting, Zeyd found a few wild leeks and small tubers, *thunma* or *sbeydy,* which baked are not unlike the potato. He plucked also the twigs of a pleasant-tasting salad bush, *thalûk,* and wild sorrel, and offered me to eat; and taking from his saddle-bags a piece of a barley-cake, he broke and divided it between us. "This, he said, is of our surra; canst thou eat Beduins' bread, eigh Khalîl?" The upland through which we passed, that they call the Borj Selmàn (an ancient name from the heroic time of the Beny Helál), is a waste land-breadth of gravel and sand, full of sandstone crags. This, said Zeyd, showing me the wild earth with his swarthy hand, is the land of the Beduw. He watched to see if the townling were discouraged, in viewing only their empty desert before him. And he said, "Hear, O Khalîl; so thou wilt live here with us, thy silver may be sent down to thee year by year with the Haj, and we will give thee a maiden to wife: if any children be born to thee, when thou wouldst go from hence, they shall be as mine own, billah, and remain with me."—Also of his stock he would give me a camel.

CHAPTER V

WE journeyed taking turns to walk and ride, and as Zeyd would changing our mantles, till the late afternoon; he doubted then if we might come to the Aarab in this daylight. They often removing, Zeyd could not tell their camping-ground within a dozen or score miles. One of the last night's Ageylies went along with us ; armed with a hammer, he drove my sick camel forward. As we looked for our Aarab we were suddenly in sight of the slow wavering bulks of camels feeding dispersedly under the horizon ; the sun nigh setting, they were driven in towards the Beduin camp, *menzil*, another hour distant. Come to the herdsmen, we alighted and sat down, and one of the lads receiving our bowl, ran under his nâgas to milk for us. This is *kheyr Ullah* ("the Lord's bounty"), not to be withheld from any wayfaring man, even though the poor owners should go supperless themselves. A little after, my companions enquired, if I felt the worse ; " because, said they, strangers commonly feel a pain after their first drinking camel-milk." This some-what harsh thin milk runs presently to hard curds in the stomach.

In approaching the Beduin tents I held back, with the Ageyly, observing the desert courtesy, whilst our host Zeyd pre-ceded us. We found his to be a small summer or " flitting-tent " which they call *héjra*, "built" (thus they speak) upon the desert sand. Poor and low it seemed, unbecoming a great sheykh, and there was no gay carpet spread within: here was not the welfar-ing which I had known hitherto, of the northern Beduins. Zeyd led me in with his stern smiling ; and, a little to my surprise, I must step after him into the woman's apartment. These some-time emigrated Beduins, have no suspicion of Nasrânies, whom they have seen in the north, and heard them reputed honest folk, more than the Moslemîn. There he presented me to his young wife : " Khalîl (said he), here is thy new ' aunt ' (*ammatak*,—

hostess); and, *Hirfa*, this is Khalîl; and see thou take good care of him." Before the morning the absent tribesmen had returned from the haj market; the nomads lodged yet one day in the Borj Selmàn : the third morrow we removed. The height of this country is nearly 4500 feet.

The removing of the camp of the Aarab, and driving the cattle with them from one to another pasture ground, is called *ráhla*. In their yesterday's mejlis they have determined whither and how early; or was it left in the sheykh's hand, those in the neighbour booths watch when the day is light, to see if the sheykh's hareem yet strike his tent ; and, seeing this, it is the ráhla. The Beduish housewives hasten then to pluck up the tent-pegs, and their booths fall ; the tent-cloth is rolled up, the tent-poles are gathered together and bound in a faggot : so they drag out the household stuff, (bestowed in worsted sacks of their own weaving,) to load upon the burden-camels. As neighbours see them and the next neighbours see those, all booths are presently cast in the wide dispersed menzil. The herdsmen now drive forward; the hareem [plur. of *horma*, woman] mount with their baggage ; the men, with only their arms, sword or matchlock, hanging at the saddle-tree behind them, and the long lances in their hands, ride forth upon their thelûls, they follow with the sheykh :—and this is the march of the nomad village. But if the sheykh's tent remain standing and it is already an hour past sun-rising, when their cattle should be dismissed to pasture, the people begin to say, " Let the beasts go feed then, there will be no ráhla to-day."

This dawn, about the 16th February, was blustering and chill in that high country. *Shîl*, ' load now ! ' cried Zeyd ; and Hirfa, shivering and sighing, made up their household gear. Sheykhly husbands help not their feeble housewives to truss the baggage ; it were an indignity even in the women's eyes. The men sit on, warming themselves over any blazing sticks they have gathered, till the latest moment, and commonly Zeyd made coffee. The bearing-camels are led in and couched between the burdens ; only the herdsman helps Hirfa to charge them upon the rude pack-saddles, *hadàj*, a wooden frame of desert acacia timber, the labour of some nomad sâny or Solubby. The underset pad of old tent-cloth, *wittr*, is stuffed with some dry herbage, and all is girded under the camel's belly with a simple cord. Zeyd called to help lift the loads, for they were over-heavy, did it grudgingly, murmuring, ' Was a sheykh a porter to bear burdens ? ' I also helped them to stay up the weighty half-loads in the sides of the saddles until both were laid even and coupled. Zeyd was a lordling in no contemptible

tribe. Such a sheykh should not in men's sight put the hand
to any drudgery ; he leaves it to his hind. A great sheykh
may take upon him part care of his own mare, in the menzil,
whilst the hinds are all day herding in the field ; yet having
led her to the well, if there be any, by, of the common tribesmen the sheykh will call him to draw her water. Nevertheless
sheykhs' sons whilst they are children, and later as young men
armed, are much abroad with the tribes' cattle and companions
with the herdsmen. I have seen Zeyd go out with a grass-hook
to cut his mare's forage and bring again a mantle-full on his
back, and murmuring, with woe in his black visage, it was
Selîm his son's duty : and the boy, oftentimes disobedient, he
upbraided, calling him his life's torment, *Sheytàn,* only never
menacing him, for that were far from a Beduin father's mind.

We removed hardly ten miles, and pitched four hours to the
eastward of Dàr el-Hamra. The hareem busily " build " their
tents ; but the men, as they have alighted, are idle, that when
not herding or riding in a foray sit all day at home only lazing
and lording. "The *jowwár* (Bed. housewives), say they, are
for the labour of the household and to be under discipline "
Zeyd, with a footcast in the sand-bank where we had taken
shelter from the gusty wind till the *beyts* were standing, had
made an hearth ; then he kneeled with the Beduin cheerfulness to kindle our gipsy fire. Selîm gathered sticks, and we
sat down to warm ourselves and roast locusts.

Here we lodged two days, and removed anew five hours
eastward through the same sandy moorland, with mild weather,
and pitched in the camping-ground *el-Antaríeh.* Sweet and
light in these high deserts is the uncorrupt air, but the water is
scant and infected with camel urine. Hirfa doled out to me, at
Zeyd's commandment, hardly an ounce or two of the precious
water every morning, that I might wash " as the townspeople."
She thought it unthrift to pour out water thus when all day
the thirsty tribesmen have not enough to drink. Many times
between their waterings, there is not a pint of water left in the
greatest sheykhs' tents ; and when the good-man bids his housewife fill the bowl to make his guests' coffee, it is answered from
their side, " We have no water." Too much of a great sheykh's
provision is consumed by his mare ; the horse, of all cattle in
the desert, is most impatient of thirst. Zeyd used oftentimes
this fair excuse, (being miserable even in the poor dispense of
coffee,) " There is no water." Motlog the great sheykh coming
one of these mornings to visit me, enquired first, " Hast thou
drunk coffee ?"—" Not to-day, they say *there is no water.*"—
"What ! he asked, has not Zeyd made you coffee this morning ? "

for even poorer sheykhs will not fail to serve the morrow's cup, each one to his own fellowship. Motlog knew his cousin Zeyd, and smiled, saying, " What is this, Zeyd has no water! but, Khalîl, come over to us, and I will make thee coffee." He led me to his tent, which was not far off, where, sitting at the hearth, and being himself the sheykh of his tribe, he roasted, brayed and boiled, and prepared this cup of hospitality for the Christian stranger. In that place it chanced Zeyd to lose a camel, which had been frayed by wolves. He mounted his mare at the morrow's light, and rode forth with the long shivering horseman's lance upon his shoulder to follow her traces. The day after Zeyd returned to us, driving in his lost beast: he had found her near Birket Moaddam

After three days the Aarab removed south-eastward twelve miles, and pitched at the camping ground *Khussherkish*. It was now the 22nd February, and we found here the rabîa, or new spring of sweet blossoming herbage ; the most was of wild rape kind, pimpernel and sorrel, *humsîs*. The rabîa is the yearly refreshment, nay, the life, of the nomads' cattle. Delightful to the eye, in the desert land, was that poor faery garden of blossoms. When the Beduins saw me pensive, to admire the divine architecture of those living jewels, they thought it but childish fondness in the stranger. If I did but ask the names of the simples it was roughly answered, " The name of them all is *el-usshb*, ' the spring forage,' very good for our small cattle and camels." This high droughty country is plain for some days' journeys ; mostly sand soil and sandstone gravel, without furrows of seyls or wadies ; it is an upland, which in the light Arabian rains never runs down with water. * * *

* * * The camels now feeding of the sappy rabîa were *jezzîn* or ' not drinking.' In good spring years they are in these dîras almost two and a half months jezzîn, and not driven to the watering. Then the force of life is spent of the herb lately so fresh upon the earth, and withering under the sun it is dried up. If, after some shower, the great drinkless cattle find rain-water lodged in any hollow rocks, I have seen them slow to put down their heavy long necks; so they snuff to it, and bathing but the borders of their flaggy lips, blow them out and shake the head again as it were with loathing. The nomads' camels are strong and frolic in these fat weeks of the spring pasture. Now it is they lay up flesh, and grease in their humps,

for the languor of the desert summer and the long year. Driven home full-bellied at sunset, they come hugely bouncing in before their herdsmen : the householders, going forth from the booths, lure to them as they run lurching by, with loud *Wolloo-wolloo-wolloo*, and to stay them *Wòh-ho, wòh-ho, wòh-ho!* they chide any that strikes a tent-cord with *hutch !* The camels are couched every troop beside, about, and the more of them before the booth of their household ; there all night they lie ruckling and chawing their huge cuds till the light of the morrow. The Aarab · say that their camels never sleep ; the weary brute may stretch down his long neck upon the ground, closing awhile his great liquid eyes ; but after a space he will right again the great languid carcase and fall to chawing. In this fresh season they rise to graze anew in the moonlight, and roam from the booths of the slumbering Aarab ; but fearful by nature, they stray not then very far off. Sometimes wakening after midnight and seeing our camels strayed, I went out to bring them in ; but the Beduins said, " Sleep on, Khalîl, there is no cause ; let them go feeding as they will." They would see them pasture now all they can ; but not seldom they are bereaved thus of their cattle by prowling night-robbers. Camels, the only substance of the nomads, are the occasion of all their contending. " *Neshîl*, we load, say they, upon them, and we drink halîb, the milk, of them." The cows go twelve months with young ; now was their time of calving, which falls at the beginning of the rabîa. The nomad year is divided in this sort ; *er-rabîa*, springtime of three months ; *el-gáyth*, midsummer, three months ; *es-sferry*, fall of the year, three months ; *es-shítá* (pronounce *és-sh'tá*), winter. To be a ready man in this kind of lore, is clerkship with the Beduw, and to have a wayfarer's knowledge of the stars. When they found good pasture the Beduins encamped, and we lodged upon that ground mostly till the third or fourth morrow. The nomads dwelling, the day over, in any place, they say " el-Aarab *um-jemmîn*" (*j* for *k* guttural), or the camp is standing. The herdsmen bring word of the pasture about them, and as the sheykhs determine in the mejlis the people will remove again, it was commonly to twelve or thirteen miles distance ; and now their " face was toward " Teyma.

If the rábla be short the Beduw march at leisure, the while their beasts feed under them. The sheykhs are riding together in advance, and the hareem come riding in their trains of baggage-camels ; if aught be amiss the herdsmen are nigh at hand to help them : neighbours will dismount to help neighbours and even a stranger. The great and small cattle are driven along with their households. You shall see housewives dismount, and gossips walk on together barefoot (all go here unshod,) and spinning beside their slow-pacing camels. But say the Beduin husbands, " We would have the hareem ride always and not weary themselves, for their tasks are many at home." The Fukara women alighted an hour before noon, in the march, to milk their few ewes and goats. Every family and kindred are seen wayfaring by themselves with their cattle. The Aarab thus wandering are dispersed widely; and in the vast uneven ground (the most plain indeed but full of crags), although many hundreds be on foot together, commonly we see only those which go next about us. The Beduins coming near a stead where they will encamp, Zeyd returned to us; and where he thought good there struck down the heel of his tall horseman's lance *shelfa* or *romhh*, stepping it in some sandy desert bush: this is the standard of Zeyd's fellowship,—they that encamp with him, and are called his people. Hirfa makes her camel kneel; she will " build " the booth there: the rest of Zeyd's kindred and clients coming up, they alight, each family going a little apart, to pitch their booths about him. This is " Zeyd's menzil " and the people are Zeyd's Aarab. The bearing-camels they make to kneel under their burdens with the guttural voice, *ikh-kh-kh!* The stiff neck of any reluctant brute is gently stricken down with the driving-stick or an hand is imposed upon his heavy halse; any yet resisting is plucked by the beard; then without more he will fall groaning to his knees. Their loads discharged, and the pack-saddles lifted, with a spurn of the master's foot the bearing-camels rise heavily again and are dismissed to pasture. The housewives spread the tent-cloths, taking out the corner and side-cords; and finding some wild stone for a hammer, they beat down their tent-pegs into the ground, and under-setting the tent-stakes or " pillars " (*am'dàn*) they heave and stretch the tent-cloth: and now their booths are standing. The wife enters, and when she has bestowed her stuff, she brings forth the man's breakfast; that is a bowl of léban, poured from the sour milk-skin, or it is a clot of dates with a bowl of the desert water: for guest-days it is dates and buttermilk with a piece of sweet butter. After that she sits within, rocking upon her knees the *semíla* or sour milk-skin, to make this day's butter.

As Zeyd so is every principal person of these Beduins, the chief of a little menzil by itself: the general encampment is not disposed (as is the custom of the northern Aarab) in any formal circuit. The nomads of these marches pitch up and down in all the "alighting place " at their own pleasure. The Fejîr or

Fukara never wandered in *ferjàn* (*j* for *k* guttural) or nomad hamlets, dispersedly after their kindreds, which is everywhere the nomad manner, for the advantage of pasture; but they journey and encamp always together. And cause was that, with but half-friends, and those mostly outraged upon their borders, or wholly enemies, there were too many reckonings required of them; and their country lies open. Zeyd's Aarab were six booths : a divorced wife's tent, mother of his young and only son, was next him; then the tent of another cast-off housewife, mother of a ward of his, *Settàm*, and by whom he had himself a daughter; and besides these, (Zeyd had no near kinsfolk,) a camel-herd with the old hind his father, of Zeyd's father's time, and the shepherd, with their alliance. Forlorn persons will join themselves to some sheykh's menzil, and there was with us an aged widow, in wretchedness, who played the mother to her dead daughter's fatherless children, a son so deformed that like a beast he crept upon the sand [*ya latif*, " oh happy sight! " said this most poor and desolate grandam, with religious irony, in her patient sighing]—and an elf-haired girl wonderfully foul-looking. Boothless, they led their lives under the skies of God, the boy was naked as he came into the desert world. The camel upon which they rode was an oblation of the common charity ; but what were their daily food only that God knoweth which feedeth all life's creatures. There is no Beduwy so impious that will chide and bite at such, his own tribesfolk, or mock those whom God has so sorely afflicted; nor any may repulse them wheresoever they will alight in the common wilderness soil. Sometimes there stood a stranger's booth among us, of nomad passengers or an household in exile from the neighbour tribesmen : such will come in to pitch by a sheykh of their acquaintance.

Hirfa ever demanded of her husband toward which part should "the house" be built. "Dress the face, Zeyd would answer, to this part," showing her with his hand the south, for if his booth's face be all day turned to the hot sun there will come in fewer young loitering and parasitical fellows that would be his coffee-drinkers. Since the sheukh, or heads, alone receive their tribe's surra, it is not much that they should be to the arms coffee-hosts. I have seen Zeyd avoid as he saw them approach, or even rise ungraciously upon such men's presenting themselves, (the half of every booth, namely the men's side, is at all times open, and any enters there that will, in the free desert,) and they murmuring he tells them, wellah, his affairs do call him forth, adieu, he must away to the mejlis, go they and seek the coffee elsewhere. But were there any sheykh

with them, a coffee lord, Zeyd could not honestly choose but
abide and serve them with coffee ; and if he be absent himself,
yet any sheykhly man coming to a sheykh's tent, coffee must
be made for him, except he gently protest, " billah, he would
not drink." Hirfa, a sheykh's daughter and his nigh kinswoman,
was a faithful make to Zeyd in all his sparing policy.

Our menzil now standing, the men step over to Zeyd's coffee-
fire, if the sheykh be not gone forth to the mejlis to drink his
mid-day cup there. A few gathered sticks are flung down
beside the hearth : with flint and steel one stoops and strikes
fire in tinder, he blows and cherishes those seeds of the cheerful
flame in some dry camel-dung, sets the burning sherd under dry
straws, and powders over more dry camel-dung. As the fire
kindles, the sheykh reaches for his *dellâl*, coffee-pots, which are
carried in the *fatya*, coffee-gear basket ; this people of a nomad
life bestow each thing of theirs in a proper *beyt*, it would otherwise be lost in their daily removing. One rises to go fill up the
pots at the water-skins, or a bowl of water is handed over the
curtain from the woman's side ; the pot at the fire, Hirfa reaches
over her little palm-full of green coffee-berries. We sit in a
half ring about the hearth ; there come in perhaps some acquaintance or tribesmen straying between the next menzils.
Zeyd prepared coffee at the hours ; afterward, when he saw in
me little liking of his coffee-water, he went to drink the cup
abroad ; if he went not to the mejlis, he has hidden himself two
or three hours like an owl, or they would say as a dog, in my
little close tent, although intolerably heated through the thin
canvas in the mid-day sun. It was a mirth to see Zeyd lie and
swelter, and in a trouble of mind bid us report to all comers
that ' Zeyd was from home ' : and where his elvish tribesmen
were merry as beggars to detect him. *Mukkarîn el-Beduw !*
" the nomads (say the settled Arabs) are full of wily evasions."

The sheykhs and principal persons assemble at the great
sheykh's or another chief tent, when they have alighted upon
any new camping-ground ; there they drink coffee, the most
holding yet the camel-stick, *mishaab, mehján* or *bakhorra*, as a
sceptre, (a usage of the ancient world,) in their hands. The few
first questions among them are commonly of the new dispositions
of their several menzils : as, " *Rahŷel !* (the sheykh's brother),
fen ahl-ak ? where be thy people (pitched) ?—*Eth-Therrŷeh* (the
sheykh's son), *fen ahl-ak ?*—*Mehsan* (a good simple man, and
who had married Zeyd's only sister,)—*Khálaf* and the rest,
where be your menzils ?—*Zeyd* is not here ! who has seen Zeyd?
—and *Mijwel*, where are his Aarab ?" for every new march
displaces these nomads, and few booths in the shortness of the

desert horizon are anywhere in sight. You see the Beduins silent whilst coffee is being made ready, for all their common talk has been uttered an hundred times already, and some sit beating the time away and for pastime limning with their driving-sticks in the idle sand. They walk about with these gay sticks, in the daytime: but where menzils are far asunder, or after nightfall, they carry the sword in their hands: the sword is suspended with a cord from the shoulder. The best metal is the Ajamy, a little bent with a simple crossed hilt (beautiful is the form), wound about with metal wire; next to the Persian they reckon the Indian blade, *el-Hindy*.

In nomad ears this word, Aarab, signifies "the people". Beduin passengers when they meet with herdsmen in the desert enquire, *Fen el-Aarab?* "where is the folk?" Of the multitude of nomad tribes east and west, they say in plural wise, *el-Arbân*. This other word, Beduin, received into all our languages, is in the Arabian speech Bedùwy, that is to say inhabitant of the waste, (*bâdia*,) in the plural *Bedaùwy* (*aù* dipth.), but commonly *èl-Bèduw*. As we sit, the little cup, of a few black drops, is served twice round. When they have swallowed those boiling sips of coffee-water, and any little news has been related among them, the men rise one after other to go home over the hot sand: all are barefoot, and very rarely any of those Aarab has a pair of sandals. So every one is come again to his own, they say the mid-day prayers; and when they have breakfasted, they will mostly slumber out the sultry mid-day hours in their house-wife's closed apartment. I have asked an honest wife, "How may your lubbers slug out these long days till evening?" and she answered, demurely smiling, "How, sir, but in solace with the hareem!"

The héjra, or small flitting-tent, laid out by the housewife, with its cords stretched to the pins upon the ground, before the am'dàn or props be set up under, is in this form: to every pair of cords, is a pair of stakes; there are three stakes to every pair of cords in the waist of the tent. Greater booths are stayed by more pairs of waist-cords, and stand upon taller staves. The Aarab tent, which they call the *beyt* [pl. *byût*] *es-shaar*, "abode, booth, or house of hair," that is of black worsted or hair-cloth, has, with its pent roof, somewhat the form of a cottage. The tent-stuff, strong and rude, is defended by a list sewed under at the heads of the am'dàn, and may last out, they say, a generation, only wearing thinner; but when their roof-cloth is thread-bare it is a feeble shelter, thrilled by the darting beams of the Arabian sun, and casting only a grey shadow. The Arabian tent strains strongly upon all the staves and in good holding ground, may resist the boisterous blasts which happen at the crises of the year, especially in some deep mountainous valleys. Even in weak sand the tents are seldom overblown. Yet the cords, *tunb el-beyt*, which are worsted-twist of the women's spinning, oft-times burst: who therefore (as greater sheykhs) can spend silver, will have them of hempen purchased in the town. In all the road tribes they every year receive rope, with certain clothing and utensils, on account of their haj surra. The tent-stuff is seamed of narrow lengths of the housewives' rude worsted weaving; the yarn is their own spinning, of the mingled wool of the sheep and camels' and goats' hair together. Thus it is that the cloth is blackish: we read in the Hebrew Scripture, "Black as the tents of Kedar." Good webster-wives weave in white borders made of their sheep's wool, or else of their gross-spun cotton yarn (the cotton wool is purchased from Medina or the sea coast).

When the tent-cloth is stretched upon the stakes, to this roof they hang the tent-curtains, often one long skirt-cloth which becomes the walling of the nomad booth: the selvedges are broached together with wooden skewers. The booth front is commonly left open, to the half at least we have seen, for the *mukaad* or men's sitting-room: the other which is the women's and household side, is sometimes seen closed (when they would not be espied, whether sleeping or cooking) with a fore-cloth; the woman's part is always separated from the men's apartment by a hanging, commonly not much more than breast or neck high, at the waist poles of the tent. The mukaad is never fenced in front with a tent-cloth, only in rain they incline the am'dàn and draw down the tent eaves lower. The nomad tents are thus very ill lodging, and the Beduins, clothed no better than the dead, suffer in cold and stormy weather. In winter they sometimes load the back-cloth ground-hem with great stones, and fence their open front at the men's side with dry bushes. The tent side-cloths can be shifted according to the wind and sun: thus the back of the Beduin booth may become in a moment the new front. A good housewife will bethink herself to unpin and shift the curtain, that her husband's guests may have shadow and the air, or shelter.

Upon the side of the hareem, that is the household apartment, is stored all their husbandry. At the woman's curtain stand the few tent-cloth sacks of their poor baggage, *él-gush* : in these is bestowed their corn and rice if they have any ; certain lumps of rock-salt, for they will eat nothing insipid ; also the housewife's thrift of wool and her spun yarn,—to be a good wool-wife is honourable among Aarab women ; and some fathoms perhaps of new calico. There may be with the rest a root of *er'n* or tan wood, the scarlet chips are steeped in water, and in two or three days, between ráhlas, they cure therein their goat-skins for girbies and semîlies, besides the leather for watering-buckets, watering-troughs, and other nomad gear. The poorest wife will have some box, (commonly a fairing from the town,) in which are laid up her few household medicines, her comb and her mirror, *mèrguba*, her poor inherited ornaments, the ear-rings and nose-ring of silver or even golden (from the former generations); and with these any small things of her husband's, (no pockets are made in their clothing,) which she has in her keeping. But if her good-man be of substance, a sheykh of surra, for his bundle of reals and her few precious things she has a locked coffer painted with vermilion from Medina, which in the ráhla is trussed (also a mark of sheykhly estate) upon her bearing-camel.— Like to this I have mused, might be that ark of things sacred to the public religion, which was in the nomad life of B. Israel.

Commonly the housewife's key of her box is seen as a glittering pendant, upon her veil backward; and hangs, with her thimble and pincers, (to pluck the thorns out of their bare soles,) by a gay scarlet lace, from the circlet of the head-band. Their clotted dates, if they have any, are stived in heavy pokes of camel-hide, that in the ráhla are seen fluttering upon the bearing-cattle with long thongs of leather. This apparel of fringes and tassels is always to the Semitic humour; of the like we read in Moses, and see them in the antique Jewish sculptures. Of their old camel sack-leather, moisty with the juice of the dates, they cut the best sandals. The full-bellied sweating water-skins are laid, not to fret at the ground, upon fresh sprays of broom or other green in the desert; amongst all stands the great brazen pot, *jidda*, tinned within by the nomad smith, or by the artificer in their market village. They boil in it their butter, (when they have any, to make samn,) and their few household messes; they seethe the guest-meal therein in the day of hospitality.

The Aarab *byút shaar* are thus tents of haircloth made housewise. The "houses of hair" accord with that sorry landscape! Tent is the Semitic house: their clay house is built in like manner; a public hall for the men and guests, and an inner woman's and household apartment. Like to this was Moses' adorned house of the nomad God in the wilderness. Also the firmament, in the Hebrew prophet, is a tabernacle of the one household of God's creation. These flitting-houses in

the wilderness, dwelt in by robbers, are also sanctuaries of
"God's guests," *theĩf Ullah*, the passengers and who they be
that haply alight before them. Perilous rovers in the field, the
herdsmen of the desert are kings at home, fathers of hospitality
to all that seek to them for the night's harbour. " Be we not
all, say the poor nomads, *guests of Ullah ?* " Has God given
unto them, God's guest shall partake with them thereof : if
they will not for God render His own, it should not go well
with them. The guest entered, and sitting down amongst them,
they observe an honourable silence, asking no untimely questions,
(such is school and nurture of the desert,) until he have eaten
or drunk somewhat at the least, and by "the bread and salt"
there is peace established between them, for a time (that is
counted two nights and the day in the midst, whilst their food
is in him). Such is the golden world and the "assurance of
Ullah" in the midst of the wilderness : travelled Beduins are
amazed to see the sordid inhospitality of the towns ;—but where
it were impossible that the nomad custom should hold.

Zeyd told us one day his old chance at Damascus (the tribe
was then in the North) ; and how he had disputed in this sense
with a government man (Dowlâny) of late, some Haj officer,
*Whether were nigher unto God the life of townsfolk or of the
Aarab.*—*Officer:* "Some of you neither pray nor fast, the
Beduw are incessantly riding in forays ; ye are manslayers for
a little booty, and violent reavers of other men's goods. God
wot, and though your mouths confess the Prophet, ye be little
better than the *kuffâr* (heathen,—Jews and Christians). Ye
discern not betwixt the *halàl* and the *harrâm ;* but we, knowing
the good and the evil, are the better Moslemîn." *Zeyd :* "All
this I can grant ; but hearken ! a stranger alighting at a Beduin
booth, we welcome him, and are busy to serve him and we
prepare the guest-supper ; and when he has eaten, in the same
place he sleeps, in the assurance of Ullah, and with the morning
light he rises up refreshed to hold on his journey. But ha!
when I came to es-Shaïn, riding upon my thelûl, it was an
evening (at the supping hour), and passing weary and hungry
by the sûk, I alighted before some door where I thought to
take my night-lodging. As I knocked, one cries within, *Min?*
Who ? who ? I answered ' *Thaif !* (a guest) and O thou behind
the door, open quickly ! ' But the voice said, ' O thou which
standest knocking, seek further down the sûk, where is many
a house, and there is nothing here ; go in peace, good man.'
This is the manner with them all, and they are not ashamed,
billah ! Then, not having tasted food that day (the wayfaring
nomad eats not till his alighting), I lay me down in the dust of

your street, slain with hunger and seeking to slumber. This is their dealing with strangers which enter your towns!—And wellah the Dowlâny allowed our life to be nigher unto God, because of the hospitality." So much they hold of this godly human virtue, as wherein a man may be just before the "Bountiful Ullah", and like to a poor player of the Divine Providence. With all this, there lacks not Arabic hospitality in the good city of Damascus; it is little less than I have afterwards seen in the upland Arabian towns. There are worthy sheykhs in the Medân, that village quarter of es-Shem, men of the antique simplicity, which keep nearly the open hospitality of the outlying villages. * * *

* * * The waste circuit of the Fukara begins about Dàr el-Hamra and reaches to Bîr el-Ghrannem : it is not less wide from the derb el-haj eastward to the mountain Birrd, at the border of Nejd. This is as much as certain of our English counties; and they are nearly eight hundred souls. Their tents are two hundred ; I have been able to survey them at once, when we were summering later about the wells of el-Héjr. Small is these nomads' horizon ; few of them know much land beyond their own dîras or out of common ways, as the paths to Hâyil their political or Medina their religious metropolis. In distant forays they must hire a dalîl or land-pilot to ride with them ; he is commonly some former exile or guest in that country of which he will now betray the hospitality. Seldom (as in any general migrations) do they come to a knowledge of strange dîras. The whole world they can hardly imagine to be other than their Arabian sun-stricken wilderness, with little water and few palm-villages, with perhaps some populous border city as Mecca Nomad children have bid me tell them 'how many were the camels of ed-Dowla?' The Ottoman Empire they could only think to be a tribe, whereof they see the Haj descending by them every year. The eldest son of the great W. Aly sheykh, who may live to be the head of that tribe after him, a wooden-headed young man, having enquired of me in which part of the world lay the dîrat of the Engleys, would know further the name of our market village ; and said earnestly, "Tell me, Khalîl, the names of the tribes your foemen : " if he heard them he thought he might happen to know them. He could understand that we were kafirs, but not that we should be other than the tribes of Arabs.

And now to speak of Zeyd's household. He had another
wife, but she was fled from him—this is common, in their male
tyranny of many marriages—and now dwelt in her mother's
tribe, the Bishr; they were pasturing nigh before us in this
wilderness. Zeyd rode over to his neighbours, and with pleasant
promises, which well he knew to forge and feign, he wooed her
home again. A sheykh told me she was beautiful, "she has egg-
great eyes;" but that, when I saw her, was all her pallid
beauty. The returned wife would not pitch with us, where
jealous Hirfa was, but 'built" her booth with some kindred in
another menzil. Zeyd and Hirfa were next cousins; Hirfa was
a sheykh's orphan, whom it seems he had taken partly for her
few inherited camels. Hirfa was an undergrown thick Beduin
lass, her age might be twenty; the golden youth was faded
almost to autumn in her childish face, but not unpleasing; there
was a merry wooden laughter always in her mouth, which ended
commonly, from the unsatisfied heart, in sighing. 'The woman
sighs (says the proverb) who has an ill husband.' Hirfa sighed
for motherhood: she had been these two years with an husband
and was yet *bint*, as the nomads say, 'in her girlhood'; and
she wept inwardly with a Semitic woman's grief. Zeyd and
Hirfa were as Isaac and Rebecca; with the Beduin simplicity
they sat daily sporting lovingly together before us, for we were
all one family and friendly eyes, but oftentimes in the midst
Hirfa pouted; then Zeyd would coldly forsake her, and their
souls were anew divided. Hirfa in her weary spirit desired
some fresh young husband, instead of this palled Zeyd, that she
mistrusted could not give her children. Again and again they
bade the Christian stranger deliver judgment of their fruitless
marriage, whether it had been lawful, as betwixt brothers'
children. Hirfa, a testy little body, of her high birth in
sheykhs' booths was a *sheykha* among the hareem, and so even
by the men regarded; all the principal sheukh were her nigh
kinsmen. In the Arabian small tribes and villages there is a
perpetual mingling of kindred blood: to-day after so many
generations who may think this Semitic race has been impaired
thereby?—but truly we see not few brain-sick and cripples
amongst them.

Self-minded, a bold-faced wench, mistress Hirfa cast as she
should not a pair of eyes upon their herdsman, a likely young
man, whom in her husband's absence she wooed openly and in
Zeyd's despite; but he was prudent, and faithful to his sheykh's
service. Here, and though bordering the jealous Hejâz and
the austere Waháby Nejd, the Fukara women go open-faced,
and (where all are kindred) I could never perceive amongst them

any jealousy of the husbands. In this tribe of date-eaters, there was not almost a well-grown man, besides the sheykh Motlog and his sons, nor any comely woman. Zeyd would tame his little wilful wife; and upon a time he corrected her with the rod in the night.

The comedy of Hirfa and Zeyd was become matter of daily raillery in the mejlis of the coffee-drinking sheukh their cousins; where, arriving alone, I might hear them say, "Eigh! here comes Khalîl: *márhabba*, welcome, O Khalîl; make place for Khalîl; pass up, Khalîl, and sit thou here beside me."—"Well met, Khalîl! but where is thine uncle Zeyd to-day?"—"Zeyd is *zahlán*, or melancholy; he lies in this mood wilfully slumbering out the day at home:"—in the lands of the sun, men willingly sleep out their sorrow. "But tell us, knowst thou was Hirfa beat? what news to-day? Khalîl, do you love your uncle?" One said who did not love him (*Khálaf Allàyda*, an exile, of the sheukh of W. Aly), "Zeyd is not a man, who beats his wife; it is a *marra*, woman, that will strike a *marra*; do your people so, Khalîl?" I answered, "Nay, surely; unless it be some ungracious wretch." And he, "It is thus amongst us Beduw, *ayb*, a shame, wellah." The wales of Zeyd's driving-stick were ever in her stubborn little spirit; and at the next alighting from a ráhla, when she had hastily built the booth and Zeyd was walked to the mejlis, leaving all, Hirfa ran back embittered into the wilderness. A devout Beduin of our menzil, he of the meteors, held awhile her two little hands, beseeching her to return to her patience; but, a sheykh's daughter, she would not be held and peevishly she broke from him.

Of a disaffected Beduin wife, such is the public remedy; to show herself to be alienated from her husband, and ready to forsake his wedlock and household, thus putting upon him a common scorn, because he will not dismiss her. There followed after Hirfa, as soon as he heard the tidings, her next kinsman of the mother's side, one that resembled Hirfa as if he had been her brother: she was running like an ostrich alone in the wild desert. An hour passed till he led her home to us, and left her again sorrowful at her own and Zeyd's tent. " Ha, Khalîl," said he, what wilt thou give me now that I have fetched in thine aunt again, who pours thee out léban and water? and (showing me his cutlass), Wellah, I have brought her *bes-seyf* by constraint of the sword." Zeyd, displeased, now ranged some nights to his Bishr wife's booth; and jealous Hirfa, not suffering this new despite, another day, even in the presence of strangers, Zeyd's guests, fled forth in the gall of her heart from the newly pitched tent when the people alighted at a menzil; Zeyd sat on, as a man aggrieved, only looking after her, but not hindering (in their eyes it had been unseemly, that man's life is free). The fugitive Beduin wife has good leave to run whithersoever she would; she is free as the desert, there is none can detain her. Hirfa hied then to her mother's kindred, and sat down, all sighs, in her aunt's booth; and in what beyt soever a running wife have taken refuge, not her own wedded husband may honestly appear to reclaim his part in her.

The strangers departed, and Zeyd sat by his now desolate booth in long heaviness of mind; but to show any lively resentment, only by occasion of a woman, had been ill nurture and unmanly. He stretched himself upon the sand to sleep out his grief, and slumbered with his head in the scalding sun. The nomads make religion, to observe this mildness and forbearance in the household life! " God's peace " is in that parcel of the great and terrible wilderness, which is shadowed by every poor herdsman's booth. Bye and bye I shook him and said, " It is not good so to sleep and swoon in the sun." We went then together to seek coffee at the mejlis, where, some malicious ones smiling at his sadness and new troubled looks, Zeyd complained in his great, now untoned voice, ' that he had no longer an household,—unless it were that Khalîl (their guest) would fetch Hirfa home.' Every tiding is presently wide blown in all the open tents of a nomad menzil, and there is no idle tale that will not ride upon the tongues, light as leaves, of witless Beduins, to drive the empty hours

The common voice blamed Hirfa's second flight : "How, they said, abandon Zeyd's tent in the presence of guests, and they were strangers!"—"Ha!" there answered an aged mother of our menzil to the old hind her husband, "dost hear, Sâlih? The hareem be good for little now-a-days,—ay, billah! I say they are all corrupted-like; but it be only myself!" Those strangers were certain Howeytát (*Terabîn*) Beduw and merchantmen, from the Syrian seabord desert, under Gaza, and who every spring-time return hither, as camel brokers, among the Aarab. They passing by us in the end of the râhla, Zeyd had called them from his menzil to alight with him and rest themselves. They sat down on the sand, whilst the tents were building, and he brought them forth the mid-day commons of their wretched country, a bowl of musty dates and another of the foul desert water. They, seeing this hap of the host's renegade wife, as men that could their courtesy, dispatched themselves and rising from the slender breakfast, gave thanks; yet a little with that unhandsome citizens' humility which is not in the easy carriage of the nomads: Beduins bless the host

and yield their thanks unto God ; but these were border countrymen, and had almost the daunted looks of townspeople, in the
deep wilderness. They purchase only of the best beasts:
although they bid high prices the Aarab are never very willing
to sell them. The camel they think is a profitable possession,
a camel will bring forth the camel, but money is barren good
that passes quite away in the using. Commonly they will sell
of their beasts only when they have some present need of reals,
and then sooner of the males; but they are the better for
carriage.

For robust he-camels of good stature was paid, by the brokers,
as much as fifty reals ; the half told in the hand, the rest is
counted out in calico, which the nomad may readily sell away
again, for shirt-cloths, in the desert. This the traders brought
from Syria ; and, selling here at the price of Teyma, they gain
for their risks and charges not above the fourth part. The
purchased camels they will sell again in Egypt and Syria.
Such brokers travel, most years, through all parts of the upland
Arabia, to buy for the border-countries, and thereby the price of
camels had been doubled within few years ; it is now almost one
throughout the northern country: and any need rising in the
border lands, as for a war declared with Abyssinia, Arabia
might be searched in few weeks by these emissaries, and, an
advance offered. there could be brought forth many thousands
of camels. But this is very costly carriage in an expedition,
since six camels' backs must be set under every ton burden.

The Howeytát asked me what I did there in that Beduin
world ? I told them I had visited their country, and lodged in
their circle-villages of tents, and seen how they plough the wild
sand with camels. "To-morrow's dawn (said they, friendly)
we ride homeward. Were it not better for thee to return with
us ? " * * *

* * * I enquired of those dealers, how they hoped to pass
safely with their merchandise to Howeytát country, which begins
about two hundred and fifty miles from hence at J. Sherra ?
They told me, "We have taken a *rafîk* from every tribe upon
the way thither." The Arabian rafîk, often an enemy, is a
paid brother-of-the-road, that for a modest fee takes upon him
to quit the convoy from all hostile question and encounter of
his own tribesmen. Thus Arabian wayfarers may ride with
little dread through hostile marches, and be received even to
their enemies' hospitality.

When I understood in our menzil that this is the guest's
honourable office, I went the next afternoon to call Hirfa home
to Zeyd's household; where else she had been abashed to return
of herself and they to seek her.   I found Hirfa a little shame-
faced, sitting in the midst of her gossips; old wife-folk that
had been friends of her dead mother; they were come together
to the aunt's booth to comfort her, and there were the young
men her cousins.   Sad-faced sat the childless young wife, she
was playing fondly with a neighbour's babe. ' Khalîl, she said,
must fill her great tobacco pipe, galliûn, or she would not hear
my words.'   The old wives cried out, "Thou art, Khalîl, to fill
all our galliûns (they are great tobacco ' bibbers '), and else we
will not let Hirfa go."   The young men said they would keep
Hirfa, and marry her themselves, and not give her again "to
that wicked Zeyd."

The tobacco distributed, I took Hirfa by the little Beduish
hand (never labouring, they have all these little hands), and
bidding her rise, the little peevish housewife answered me,
' But she would not be held, Khalîl must let go her hand.'   I
said then, "I will bring thee home, hostess, return with me;
and else I must alight to pitch my tent by thee, from the next
ráhla."   Hirfa: "That do, Khalîl, and welcome: I and thou
will go,—ah! where we shall eat a camel together (she would
say a bountiful household), only fill thou again my galliûn."
The Aunt: " And mine, Khalîl; or Hirfa is ours, ay, and we
will not let her go."   Having filled the galliûns of them all, I
asked if our mistress Hirfa were not now coming.   A young
cousin said 'I am her father, and Hirfa is mine, Khalîl; no! we
will not give her more to Zeyd."   Said her aunt: "Well, go
over, Khalîl; Hirfa follows, and all we (the bevy of old women)
accompany her " (to bring her home honourably).   Soon after,
arriving before my tent-door, they called me out to pay them
another dole of tobacco:—And Hirfa sat again in her own
beyt.

The woman's lot is here unequal concubinage, and in this
necessitous life a weary servitude.   The possession in her of
parents and tutors has been yielded at some price, (in contempt
and constraint of her weaker sex,) to an husband, by whom she
may be dismissed in what day he shall have no more pleasure
in her.   It may be, (though seldom among nomads their will is
forced,) that those few flowering years of her youth, with her
virginity have been yielded to some man of unlikely age.   And
his heart is not hers alone; but, if not divided already, she
must look to divide her marriage in a time to come with other.
And certainly as she withers, which is not long to come, or

having no fair adventure to bear male children, she will as thing unprofitable be cast off; meanwhile all the house-labour is hers, and with his love will be lost. What oneness of hearts can be betwixt these lemans, whose lots are not faithfully joined? Sweet natural love may bud for a moment, but not abide in so uneven ways. Love is a dovelike confidence, and thereto consents not the woman's heart that is wronged.

Few then are the nomad wives whose years can be long happy in marriage! they are few indeed or nearly none that continue in their first husband's household. Such are commonly mothers of many children, or wedded in needy families, so that the house-fathers are not able to maintain another housewife. But substantial and sheykhly persons will have done betimes with these old wives, and pass to new bride-beds, or they were not Moslemîn; and being rich men they spend cheerfully for new wives as they will spend for the seasonable change of clothing. The cast housewife may be taken up by another worthy man, in favour of some old liking, or pass to the new marriage and household service of some poorer person. The woman's joy and her comfort is to be mother of sons, that at least she may remain a matron in her boy's tent, when even his hard father shall have repudiated her. It was thus with *Ghrobny*, Zeyd's young son Selím's mother. Zeyd, pitying her tears, had found her another husband of poor Khamâla folk, by whom she had now a new babe: but the man dealt unkindly with her; wherefore returning to her young son, she was pitched again as an uncheerful widow to live by Zeyd. A day dawned, and Ghrobny's booth was away! the Arabs stood half laughing and wondering, for it was a poor-spirited creature, that had been a fair woman in her youth, till we understood of Selím she had loaded upon her camel in the night-time and was stolen away to the Khamâly in a distant menzil. The wretch, the day before, coming hither, had kissed her and vowed like a smooth lover to receive her again. But after two days the poor fond woman, and now little pleasing, returned to us with red eyes, to embrace her child, who had remained in the meanwhile confused with his father; and from the next râhla, the drivelling and desolate wife alighted as before to encamp by Zeyd.

These Aarab say, "the hareem are twice the men, in number." If that be so, natural reason should teach that a man may have more wives than one; and I can think that the womankind exceed them. From spring months to spring months, nine months in the year, the most nomad women are languishing with hunger: they bear few children; of two at a birth I have heard no mention among them. They are good mothers, and will suckle the babe very long at their meagre breasts, if they be not again with child. In Zeyd's encampment was a little damsel of four years, not yet weaned ; and the mother said, " We have no goats, there is naught in this waste, and what else might I do for my little bint ? They wash their babes in camel-urine, and think thus to help them from insects : it is acrid, especially when the cattle have browsed of certain alkaline bushes, as the rimth. And in this water they all comb out their long hair, both men and women, yet sometimes thereby bleaching their locks, so that I have seen young men's braided "horns" grizzled. There is a strange custom, (not only of nomad women, but in the Arabic countries even among Christians, which may seem to remain of the old idolatry among them,) of mothers, their gossips, and even young maidens, visiting married women to kiss with a kind of devotion the *hammam* of the male children.

In all Arabia both men and women, townsfolk, and Beduins, where they may come by it, paint the whites of their eyes blue, with *kahl* or antimony ; thus Mohammed Ibn Rashîd has his bird-like eyes painted. Not only would they be more love-looking, in the sight of their women, who have painted them, and that braid their long manly side-locks ; but they hold that this sharpens too and will preserve their vision. With long hair shed in the midst, and hanging down at either side in braided horns, and false eyes painted blue, the Arabian man's long head under the coloured kerchief, is in our eyes more than half feminine ; and in much they resemble women.

Townswomen of well-faring families, in all the old government of the Waháby are taught the prayers ; and there are some that have learned to read. In the nomad tribes women are seldom seen to pray, except in *ramathán*, the month of bodily abstinence and devotion : they are few which know the prayers ; I suppose even the half of the men have not learned them. The Beduwy, in Arabia, passes for as good as a clerk that can say his formal devotion : the nomads which have much praying amongst them, are the more ill-natured. Women pray not as the men, falling upon their faces ; but they recite the form of words with folded arms and kneeling. " *El-entha*, the female (mild to labour and bringing forth the pastoral riches) is, of all animals, the better, say the Arabians, save only in mankind." Yet this is not an opinion of all Arabs, for the *hurr*, or dromedary stallion, is preferred for his masculine strength by the Moors or Western Arabs. Upon the human entha the Semites cast all their blame. Hers is, they think, a maleficent nature, and the Aarab complain that "she has seven lives."

D*

The Arabs are contrary to womankind, upon whom they would have God's curse; "some (say the Beduw) are poisoners of husbands, and there are many adulteresses." They, being full of impotent iniquity themselves, too lightly reproach the honest housewives, although not without some cause : but what might not those find to tell all day again of the malignant inconstancy of husbands ? The *horma* they would have under subjection : admitted (they say) to an equality, the ineptitude of her evil nature will break forth. They check her all day at home, and let her never be enfranchised from servitude. If the sapient king in Jerusalem found never a good woman; many a better man has found one better than himself. The veil and the jealous lattice are rather of the obscene Mohammedan austerity in the towns : among the mild tent-dwellers in the open wilderness the housewives have a liberty, as where all are kindred; yet their hareem are now seen in the most Arabian tribes half veiled. When some asked me, at Zeyd's coffee-fire, if our hareem went veiled, I answered, "No! they are open-faced, there is no need of face-clouts among honest folk; also I think among you Aarab, they which have their women's faces veiled, are the more dissolute tribes." The Beduins are always glad to hear other tribesmen blamed. It was answered, "Ay, billah, they are corrupted." I asked Zeyd, "Art thou of this opinion ? " "Khalîl—he said in his heart, 'Thou thinkest as the kuffâr '— the face of a wife should be seen of no man besides her own husband."

The woman's sex is despised by the old nomad and divine law in Moses; for a female birth the days of her purification are doubled, also the estimation of her babe shall be at the half. Did she utter any vow, it is void if her husband say no. But the Semitic mother of a son is in honour. We read : " Let a man obey his mother and his father," the Semitic scribe writing his mother first. And commonly it is seen amongst rude Arabs, the grown son has a tender regard toward his mother, that she is his dam, before the teeming love even of his fresh young wife. So the mother's love in the tribes is womanly, tender ; and naming her sons she will add some loving superstitious saw, as *el-agal Ullah*, "The Lord preserve them ! " The nomad hareem are delivered as other mothers, with pangs, after a labour of certain hours. It is a fond opinion that the daughters of the desert are as the wild creatures, that suffer not in childbearing. But her household and nation is migratory ; there is no indolent hope before her of comfort and repose. The herb is consumed daily about them, the thirsty cattle are ever advancing to pasture and water, the people is incessantly removing: in the camping-ground of to-day, they cannot perhaps lie upon the morrow. Their bed is a mantle or tent-cloth spread upon the earth; they live indeed in the necessitous simplicity almost of the wild creatures. The nomad woman has therefore, of custom, of necessity! another courage. Are the Aarab in a journey when her time is come? her family halt, and alighting, they build the booth over her. Are the tribesmen encamped? with certain elder women friends she steals forth to be delivered, apart in the wilderness. The nomads about journeying, when it were peril to be left behind, she is gently lifted and seated as any other sick and infirm person in a nest made of her carpet or her tent-cloth wound down upon the camel pack-saddle, to follow riding with them in the ráhla: and that they pass their lives thus nomads feel little fatigue, but rather take rest in riding. * * *

CHAPTER VI

LIFE IN THE WANDERING VILLAGE

THE camels now jezzîn, we wandered without care of great watering places; the people drinking of any small waters of the *suffa*, or ground rock. There are in all this desert mountain soil pit-like places of rock choked with old blown sand. In these sand-pools a water, of the winter rains, is long time preserved, but commonly thick and ill-smelling in the wet sand, and putrefying with rotten fibres of plants and urea of the nomads' cattle, which have been watered here from the beginning. Of such the Aarab (they prefer the thick desert water to pure water) now boiled their daily coffee, which is not then ill-tasting. The worst is that blackish water drawn from pits long forsaken, until they have been voided once; and sooner than drink their water I suffered thirst, and very oft passed the nights half sleepless. Strange are the often forms in this desert of wasted sand-rock, spires, needles, pinnacles, and battled mountains, which are good landmarks. I asked Zeyd, ' Did he know them all?' *Answer:* " From my childhood, I know as good as every great stone upon all our marches," that may be over three or four thousand square miles. Mountain (*jebel* in the settled countries) is commonly *thulla*—" rib," (and dim. *thulleya*,) with the nomads;—we say *coast* almost in like wise. Any tall peak, berg or monticule, serving for a landmark, they call *towîl;* a headland is *khusshm*, "naze, snout;" (khusshm is said in Arabia for man's nose.) Some hilly mountain-coasts are named *huthb; bottin* in the mouths of the Moahîb Beduins is said of any blunt hilly height. The desert waste is called *khála*, " the land that is empty;" the soil, *béled.* —And such is desert Arabia.

— But to speak now of the nomad inhabitants and how they lead their lives. El-Beduw *ma yetaabun*, " toil not " (say they,) that is not bodily; but their spirits are made weary with incessant apprehension of their enemies, and their flesh with continual thirst and hunger The necessitous lives of the Aarab may hardly reach to a virtuous mediocrity; they are constrained to be robbers. " The life in the desert is better than any, *if there were not the Beduw*," is said proverbially by oases' Arabians; the poor Beduins they think to be full of iniquity, *melaun el-weyladeyn*, " of cursed kind, upon both sides, of their father and mother " Pleasant is the sojourn in the wandering village, in this purest earth and air, with the human fellowship, which is all day met at leisure about the cheerful coffee fire, and amidst a thousand new prospects.   Here, where we now alighted, is, this day's rest, to-morrow our home will be yonder.   The desert day returning from the east, warns the Beduin awake, who rises to his prayers ; or it may be, unwitting of the form, he will but murmur toward heaven the supplication of his fearful human nature, and say, " Ah Lord my God ! " and, " Oh that this day may be fortunate ; give Thou that we see not the evil ! " Of daily food they have not half enough, and if any head of the cattle be taken !—how may his household yet live ? Bye and bye the herdsman is ready, and his beasts are driven far from his sight.

No sweet chittering of birds greets the coming of the desert light, besides man there is no voice in this waste drought.   The Beduins, that lay down in their cloaks upon the sandy mother-earth in the open tents, hardly before the middle night, are already up and bestirring themselves.   In every coffee-sheykh's tent, there is new fire blown in the hearth, and he sets on his coffee-pots ; then snatching a coal in his fingers, he will lay it in his tobacco-pipe. The few coffee-beans received from his housewife are roasted and brayed ; as all is boiling, he sets out the little cups, *fenjeyl* (for *fenjeyn*) which we saw have been made, for the uningenious Arabs, in the West. When, with a pleasant gravity, he has unbuckled his *gutîa* or cup-box, we see the nomad has not above three or four fenjeyns, wrapt in a rusty clout, with which he scours them busily, as if this should make his cups clean The roasted beans are pounded amongst Arabs with a magnanimous rattle—and (as all their labour) rhythmical—in brass of the town, or an old wooden mortar, gaily studded with nails, the work of some nomad smith. The water bubbling in the small dellàl, he casts in his fine coffee powder, *el-bunn*, and withdraws the pot to simmer a moment. From a knot in his kerchief he takes then an head of cloves, a piece of cinnamon or other spice, *bahar*, and braying these, he casts their dust in after. Soon he pours out some hot drops to essay his coffee; if the taste be to his liking, making dexterously a nest of all the cups in his hand

with pleasant clattering, he is ready to pour out for the company,
and begins upon his right hand; and first, if such be present,
to any considerable sheykh and principal persons. The *fenjeyn
kahwa* is but four sips: to fill it up to a guest, as in the
northern towns, were among Beduins an injury, and of such
bitter meaning, "This drink thou and depart." Then is often
seen a contention in courtesy amongst them, especially in any
greater assemblies, who shall drink first. Some man that
receives the fenjeyn in his turn, will not drink yet,—he proffers it to one sitting in order under him, as to the more
honourable: but the other putting off with his hand will answer
ebbeden, "nay, it shall never be, by Ullah! but do thou drink!"
Thus licensed, the humble man is despatched in three sips, and
hands up his empty fenjeyn. But if he have much insisted, by
this he opens his willingness to be reconciled with one not his
friend. That neighbour, seeing the company of coffee-drinkers
watching him, may with an honest grace receive the cup, and
let it seem not willingly: but an hard man will sometimes rebut
the other's gentle proffer.

Some may have taken lower seats than becoming their
sheykhly blood, of which the nomads are jealous; entering
untimely, they sat down out of order, sooner than trouble all
the company. A sheykh, coming late and any business going
forward, will often sit far out in the assembly; and show himself
a popular person in this kind of honourable humility. The
more inward in the booths is the higher place; where also is,
with the sheykhs, the seat of a stranger. To sit in the loose
circuit without and before the tent, is for the common sort.
A tribesman arriving presents himself at that part, or a little
lower, where in the eyes of all men his pretension will be well
allowed; and in such observances of good nature, is a nomad
man's honour among his tribesmen. And this is nigh all that
serves the nomad for a conscience, namely, that which men
will hold of him. A poor person approaching from behind,
stands obscurely, wrapped in his tattered mantle, with grave
ceremonial, until those sitting indolently before him in the sand
shall vouchsafe to take notice of him: then they rise unwillingly,
and giving back enlarge the coffee-circle to receive him. But
if there arrive a sheykh, a coffee-host, a richard amongst them
of a few cattle, all the coxcomb companions within will hail
him with their pleasant adulation, *taad hennéyi*, "Step thou up
hither."

The astute Fukara sheukh surpass all men in their coffee-
drinking courtesy, and Zeyd himself was more than any large
of this gentleman-like imposture: he was full of swaggering

complacence and compliments to an humbler person. With
what suavity could he encourage, and gently too compel a man,
and rising himself yield him parcel of another man's room! In
such fashions Zeyd showed himself a bountiful great man, who
indeed was the greatest niggard. The cups are drunk twice
about, each one sipping after other's lips without misliking; to
the great coffee sheykhs the cup may be filled more times, but
this is an adulation of the coffee-server. There are some of the
Fukara sheukh so delicate Sybarites, that of those three bitter
sips, to draw out all their joyance, twisting, turning and tossing
again the cup, they could make ten. The coffee-service ended,
the grounds are poured out from the small into the great
store-pot that is reserved full of warm water : with the bitter
lye, the nomads will make their next bever, and think they
spare coffee.

— This of the greater coffee gatherings : but to speak rather
of the small daily company in a private sheykh's menzil, drawn
together to the clatter of the good man's *surbût* or coffee-pestle.
Grave, with levity, is the indolent nomad man's countenance.
As many Beduin heads, so many galliûns or tobacco-pipes, with
commonly nothing to put in them. Is any man seen to have
a little of the coveted leaf, knotted in his kerchief, he durst
not deny to divide it with them,—which if he withheld, yet
pretending mirth, the rest would have it from him, perforce.
If there be none found among them, they sit raking the old
filth out of their galliûns and, with sorry cheer, put the coal
upon that, which they have mixed with a little powdered dry
camel-dung or some sere herbage : thus they taste at least a
savour (such sweetness to them) of tobacco, whereof, when they
are any while deprived, I have seen them chop their pipe-stems
small for the little tobacco moisture which remained in them ;
and laying a coal upon this drenched wood they " drink " in the
fume with a last solace.

The best pipe-heads are those wrought in stone by the hands
of the Beduins ; the better stone is found two days below Héjr,
and by Teyma. Besides they use the *scbíl*, or earthenware bent
tube of the Syrian haj market. Their galliûn stem is made of
the branch of some wild fig-tree, grown by desert waters, or
of plum-tree from the oasis ; they bore it with a red-hot iron
over the evening watch-fires. Comfortatives of the brain and
vital spirits, and stay of importunate hunger, we find the
Arabian nomads abandoned to the usage of coffee and tobacco ;
in both they all observe the same customs and ceremony, which
we might imagine therefore, without book, to be come down in
their generations from some high antiquity. So much are they

idly given to these tent pleasures, that many Beduins think
they may hardly remember themselves of a morning, till they
have sipped coffee, and " drunk " upon it a galliûn of tobacco.
The coveted solace of the grape, in the veins of their old idol-
worshipping fathers, is no more remembered by the Beduin
tradition ; even their former artillery, the bows and arrows,
hardly two centuries laid down, I have found almost out of mind
amongst them. We see the Arabian race lasting without change,
only less than their eternal deserts ; but certain inventions
(guns, tobacco, coffee) sprung up in the world, and falling,
like their religion, to the national humour, have as hastily
prevailed among them. Even the outlying great waste
Peninsula is carried by the world's great changes! History
shows a marvellous levity of their hundred tribes ; part fearing
for themselves, and partly in the hope of booty, converting
(so they will ever to the stronger), in one generation, from
their ancient idols to the new and soon grown faction of
Mohammed in religion. * * *

* * * For the Beduins sitting in the coffee-tent of their menzil,
when the sun mounts it, is time to go over to the mejlis, "sitting,"
the congregation or parliament of the tribesmen.   There also is
the public coffee drinking, held at Motlog's or some other one of
the chief sheykhs' worsted "houses "; where the great sheykh
and the coffee companions may that morrow be assembled : for
where their king bee is found, there will the tribesmen assemble
together.   The mejlis-seekers wending through the wide encampment, enquire of any they meet, "The mejlis, where ?
eigh weled! hast thou seen the sheukh sitting? "   In this
parliament they commune together of the common affairs; they
reason of their policy in regard of Ibn Rashîd, the Dowla, the
tribes about them.   Here is reported what any may have
heard of the movement of foemen, or have signs been seen of a
ghrazzu : tidings from time to time are brought in of their own
or foreign waters ; householders tell of the pasture found yesterday by their dispersed herdsmen.   Let him speak here who will,
the voice of the least is heard among them ; he is a tribesman.
The mejlis forecast the next journeys of the tribe, whereof a
kind of running advice remains in all their minds, which they
call es-shor ; this is often made known to their allies, and is very
necessary to any of themselves that are about to take a journey.
   This is the council of the elders and the public tribunal :
hither the tribesmen bring their causes at all times, and it is

pleaded by the maintainers of both sides with busy clamour; and every one may say his word that will. The sheykh meanwhile takes counsel with the sheukh, elder men and more considerable persons; and judgment is given commonly without partiality and always without bribes. This sentence is final. The loser is mulcted in heads of small cattle or camels, which he must pay anon, or go into exile, before the great sheykh send executors to distrain any beasts of his, to the estimation of the debt. The poor Beduins are very unwilling payers, and often think themselves unable at present: thus, in every tribe, some households may be seen of other tribes' exiles.

Their justice is such, that in the opinion of the next governed countries, the Arabs of the wilderness are the justest of mortals. Seldom the judge and elders err, in these small societies of kindred, where the life of every tribesman lies open from his infancy and his state is to all men well known. Even their suits are expedite, as all the other works of the Arabs. Seldom is a matter not heard and resolved in one sitting. Where the accusation is grave and some are found absent that should be witnesses, their cause is held over to another hearing. The nomad justice is mild where the Hebrew law, in this smelling of the settled countries, is crude. In the desert there is no human forfeit, there is nothing even in homicide, if the next to the blood withhold not their assent, which may not be composed, the guilty paying the amends (rated in heads of cattle). The Hebrew law excised the sores in the commonwealth, and the certainty of retaliation must weigh and prick in the mind of evil-doers. The Beduwy has no more to fear before him than a fine afar off; he may escape all if his evil heart sufficeth him, only going from his own kin into perpetual exile. * * *

* * * As for the head of the tribe, Motlog, he was a personable strong man and well proportioned, of the middle stature, of middle age, and with a comely Jewish visage; and thereto the Arabian honour of a thick black beard, and he looked forth with a manly assurance under that specious brow of his sheykhly moderation. A fair-spoken man, as they be all in fair weather, full of the inborn Beduin arts when his interest was touched. Simple in his manners, he alone went with no gay camel-stick in his hand and never carried a sword; by which politic urbanity, he covered a superfluous insolence of the nobleman, which became him well. When the mejlis assembled numerous at his booth, he, the great sheykh and

host, would sit out with a proud humility among the common
people, holding still his looks at the ground; but they were
full of unquiet side-glances, as his mind was erect and watching.
His authority slumbered, till, there being some just occasion,
he ruled with a word the unruly Beduw. A rude son of the
desert sat down by me in the mejlis at my first coming, the
shepherd of Zeyd's menzil. I asked him in his ear, "Which of
them is Motlog?" *Answer:* " Yonder is Motlog!" and he added
boisterously, to the stranger, "The man there is our Pasha;
for right as the haj pasha, this Motlog governs the Aarab.
When he says 'The ráhla!' we all mount and set forth; and
where he alights there we pitch our booths.—Oho, thou Motlog!
speak I not well to this Nasrâny?—and, Khalîl, if he would,
he might cut off the heads, wellah-billah, of us all." Motlog
lifted his eyes upon us for a moment with half a smile, and
then reverted to himself. The sheykh of a nomad tribe is no
tyrant; a great sheykh striking a tribesman he should bruise
his own honour: man-striking is a very bestiality, in their sight,
at home.

The sheukh (*pl.* of sheykh, an elder) are nobles of the blood,
of a common ancestor, the reputed Jid or father of the tribe;
the great sheykh's dignity he has of inheritance. Motlog *el-
Hameydy* succeeded his father Hameydy, who fell in a foray,
and was sheykh of the Fejîr, as all his fathers before him,
ascending to the patriarch; and this dignity, which in their
sight is a disposition of Providence, there is no man certainly
who will gainsay. No commoner, nor any of strange blood,
even though he surpassed all men in wealth and sufficiency, can
come to be the head of a nomad ashîra, or even to be named of
the sheykhly kindred, which, as has been said, are a noble
lineage in the tribe. Sheukh match sooner with sheykhs'
daughters; and between all the Fejîr was now a certain, so to
say, feminine resemblance of voice and manners: the sheykh
of the tribe is as well, agîd, of his own right, conductor of the
general ghrazzus; his is the fourth part of the booty. If he
ride not himself, he will send a son or another of the sheukh,
his deputy, it might be Zeyd, who leads for him. I asked Zeyd,
" But if the inheriting sheykh doted, or he were a man
notoriously insufficient?" Zeyd had not heard of such a chance.
" He would be set aside," he answered, " and the next after him
would become our sheykh."

The sun setting, the loitering coffee-companions turn again
homeward to pray and to their suppers. At first, when the
Aarab saw me wander in the cool of the evening, I heard them
say "Khalîl goes forth to pray after his religion;" but bye and

bye, since I would not by any feints deceive my hosts, they began to account me a prayerless one of the heathen, living in the world without conscience of Ullah. An hour or two passed, the sheukh companions will *sayer*, " sally " or stray away, again to coffeeward and the evening mejlis, where they will linger on till midnight. For dread they have of treading in the darkness upon serpents, a sheykh may be seen then to draw on some quaint pair of old boots, such as he may have long since purchased at Medina. Arabian Beduins are not wearers of the high red clanking boots, which are a proud token of sheykhly estate in Syria.

The Fukara are of the fanatical tribes ; but they are nearly all thus in Arabia. Motlog, the sheykhs and tribesmen, had been displeased with Zeyd that (for his cupidity, so well known to them,) he had brought in a kafir, and none such as those home-bred Nasrânies, which they had seen themselves in Syria, but of a formidable foreign nation and government, (the sheykh heard this from the Jurdy and Haj officers,) to wander amongst them. And yet, even the great sheykh's authority could hardly go between any hospitality of the poorest tribesman among them. But now as they knew me better, they welcomed the Nasrâny with friendly words at all their coffee fires, and I sat every day with Zeyd in the mejlis. Only Zeyd would have me often remember it was only himself, who sheltered me from the murderous wildness of the Beduins. He would not have me venture, even with himself when he went abroad, after the day's light, but sit at home by our tent-fire with Hirfa and the men of our menzil : ' what if some wretch, he said, stabbed me in the darkness, and the doer of it might never be known.' Those of our encampment, with whom I had eaten bread and salt, confirmed Zeyd's words, with many billahs, bidding me not trust to any creature, beside themselves. The Arabs are full of great words ; and I did not disquiet myself for their fanatical wild talk. " Wellah ! " said Zeyd, " it was never seen before that any Nasrâny should sit in the Beduins' mejlis, or be seen riding aloft upon a camel and to follow the râhla."

My practice in medicine was yet to begin ; now, in most un-happy hour, my vaccination failed me ! The lymph was purchased of a fawning Christian vaccinator of Damascus : I had more sent to me by the Jurdy ; but, exposed in open quills, the virtue was lost even before they could be delivered to me at Medáin Sâlih. I had used the lately learned art with good success in Syrian villages. For the benefit of vaccination, the Beduw would have almost pardoned my misbelief ; and I might have lived thereby competently in a country where it is peril of death to be

accounted the bearer of a little silver. No more than a sick
camel now remained to me, and little gold in my purse, and I
began to think of quitting this tedious soil, where henceforth
without a pretext, I must needs appear as a spy intruded among
them ; and—since it were impossible for me to conform to their
barbaric religion—where my neck would be for every lawless
and fanatic wretch's knife; and in what part soever I should
pass, with great extremities, every soul would curse me.

I was not the first Christian vaccinator in land of the southern
Aarab. They had all to tell me of one *Abu Fâris*, who came
to them with this craft many years before me : a man of an up-
landish Syrian village, part inhabited by Nasâra. He was well
remembered among the Aarab : for his sake I can think them,
where I came, to have been often less fanatically minded towards
me.—And who comes after me may, I confide in God ! find the
(before reproachful) Christian name respectable over large provinces of the fanatical Peninsula. Abu Fâris led a year of his
life with the nomads ;—only touching at the towns, for doubt
of their less tolerant humanity. Teyma he visited and Hâyil ;
he was even in Kasîm, and had vaccinated at Aneyza. There
was after him a second Abu Fâris : he came to the tribes ten
years later, also a Nasrâny ; his own name was *Sleymàn*, but,
professing the art of Abu Fâris, he was called by the nomads
Abu Fâris. * * *

  * * * The later Abu Fâris was less a man of his meat among
the Beduw : when word was brought to the mejlis of the massacre
of the Nasâra in Syria, they saw him, between grief and fear,
sobbing and sighing before them. When the kind Beduw said,
" *Meskîn !* poor man, why will he lament thus ? Abu Fâris, take
thy heart again, dost thou not believe, also in thy religion, that
althing is from Ullah ? " he answered them, " Alas I am thinking
of my parentage, ah Lord God ! and lie they now dead ? woe is
me, all cruelly murdered ! " and half womanized he added, " *Ya
rubba,* Aha! this friendly company, will ye now slay me also ? *La,
la, dakhîlakom,* nay, nay, do it not ! I cast myself upon you, I do
entreat you ; " then abjectly, so that the citizens of the wilderness laughed out, " *Udkhul hareemakom,* I do enter even to
your women, that they protect me ! " " Wellah, answered the
Aarab, the man is *mejnûn,* beside himself. Now look up man !
Abu Fâris ! How, thou Sleymàn ! " And said many magnanimous desert voices, " Hast thou not eaten with us the bread and
salt ? *bess !* it is enough, *khàlas !* all doubts are ended between

us; as for this doing in es-Sham, we judge not whether it were good or evil; but *henna* (we are) *el-Beduw*, we make no account of the Shwâm (Damascenes). Let no fear be in thee here amongst us, thy friends; *henna el-Beduw, wa eth-thaif azîz*, and the guest is as one dearly beloved."

It was Khálaf Allàyda who had fetched and fathered this Sleymàn the vaccinator, *mujeddir*. They came riding down together upon his thelûl with the Haj from Syria, and the Beduin's share was to be a third in this profitable adventure. I heard the tale from Khálaf's mouth; he had since a mind to have fetched another mujeddir; but the poor man's heart failed him when he saw the Beduwy's gaunt thelûl at his door and only the wilderness before him.—The Aarab had been faithful to Abu Fâris, nor envied they the man's good fortune; every one of them paying gladly the ransom for his life from the horrible sickness, the fourth part of the mejîdy, or a shilling. His year ended, they sent him home in peace, with not a little substance, which he had gathered amongst them : his cattle were driven up before him, by the Beduin herdsmen, to Syria.

The Arabs, until now using inoculation, being once vaccinated, are in no fear of the disease for the rest of their lives. If I said " It is not so sure," they answered, " But it has been approved among hundreds, and whosoever was vaccinated with the *taam* (lymph) of Abu Fâris, when the *jídery* (small-pox) was in again, wellah *ma sáb-hu*, it never attained him." The Aarab are cured in their maladies by the hareem, who have all some little store of drugs, spices and perfumes fetched from Medina, and their grandam's skill of simples, which are not many to find in their desert dîras. The nomads had little expectation of better remedies in the hands of Khalîl, which were dearer "government medicines " and strange among them. They bade me show my drugs to the hareem who, they supposed, should certainly know them. The practice of the poor affectionate women, is not all (in some malignant husbands' surmising) to their health; men too often ascribe their slow and obscure maladies to ' witchcraft of the hareem.' " See, Khalîl, some patient has said, how dead is my body and wasted: I am in doubt of a jealous wife, and that she has given me some cold drink." Poisoning is familiar to the criminal imagination of all the Arabs. They call medicaments *dawwa*, as in the settled countries; and the Beduins give the name to those few herbs and condiments which they put to their food to give a pleasant savour and colour.

Hirfa, as a principal sheykh's daughter, was reputed to be seen in leechcraft. Hirfa one day calling her gossips together, they sat down before me to see my medicine-box opened. The silly bewildered hareem took my foreign drugs in their hands, one by one; and, smelling to them, they wavered their heads with a wifely gravity. And all these they allowed to be to them unknown, but sure they were they had smelled out *haltîta*, or gum asafœtida, a drug which the Arabs have in sovereign estimation. But what was their wonder to see me make an effervescing drink! Hirfa oftentimes entreated me to show her gossips this marvellous feat of " boiling water without fire ". It is strange how, for remedies, the Arabs make no more a nice account of halàl and harrâm ; they will take of the unclean and even abominable, saying : " dawwa! it is medicine." These Beduins give the sick to eat of the *rákham* or small white carrion eagle. Upon a day I found a poor woman of our menzil seething asses' dung in the pot ; she would give the water to drink with milk, to her sick brother : the Arabs think the ass unclean, but especially the excrement.

Now were I to speak of my medical practice plainly, I think it a desperation to cure the Arabs, and that a perfect physician would hardly be praised amongst them. He is lost whose science is slow, and the honest man of few promises ; they will despise his doubts and his tentatives. He who would thrive must re- semble them, some glozing Asiatic that can file his tongue to the baseness of those Semitic minds. Their wild impatience looks to see marvels : the right physician, only handling a pulse, they think, should be able to divine a man's state and all his past infirmities ; and some specific must he have for every disease, because ' there is a salve in nature for every sore '; yet so knavish are they that for all his skill they would pay him only upon a day which is ever to come. The Arabians are ill nourished, and they think themselves always ailing. The no- mads live nearly as the wild creatures, without certain diet, and they drink infected waters. Few have not some visceral in- firmities—*el-kibd;* and, the wind breathing upon their nearly naked bodies, they are crazed with all kinds of rheums, *er-rîhh;* a name they give to all obscure, aching diseases. Every sick- ness they name *wajjá,* " pain, disease; " the patient *wajjân.* * * *

* * * It is said in the towns, " *the Beduwy's mind is in his eyes.*" Negligent and impatient, they judge, as they are pas- sionately persuaded, in the seeing of the moment, and revert to their slumbering indolence. They cannot be persuaded that

a little powder of quinine should be truly sold for a silverling, when their housewives buy their hands full of beggarly drugs at Medina, for a piece of small money. Others imagined the Mudowwy himself had made all the medicines, of some common earths and simples. Where they proved some marvellous effect of a remedy, as morphia (a grave anguish relieved with one drop of the medicine-water), neither could this move them: for all is as nothing, in comparison of God's miracles. Nor enquired they for it again of the man of medicine; since they must pay the second time, if only with the gift of a little rice, or with the promise of a bowl of sour butter-milk. Others, having received my medicines, the elves withheld the price; for all that the Beduin can catch of another man's good is his booty. There were some so ungracious ones that they have stolen away the cups in which, with much pains, I had charitably mixed them medicines; poor losses, but that cannot be repaired in the desert. So said the men at our homely evening fire, "The people come to Khalîl's tent for medicines; and Khalîl, not distinguishing them, will give to all of them in trust: the people *yegôtarun*, go their ways, and he sees them no more, wellah! Khalîl, there is no wit in thee at all for buying and selling."

And were I to wander there again, I would carry with me only a few, that are called quack-salving medicines, of an easy application and like to specific remedies. Who has not made the experience, can hardly think how tedious it is to prepare medicines in the wilderness; in that sun-stricken languishing and indigence of all things and often confusion of the nomad tent, to weigh out grains in the balance, the sand blowing, and there is no pure water: but when the potions are ready and the lotions, your nomad patients will hardly be able to find any phial, *garrôra*, to receive them. After my return a friend said to me, "Your Beduins have a good custom,—I would God we had it here! Let physicians be paid only upon the patients' amendment! A bold man to take upon you an art unlearned!"—"I relieved many, the most part freely; I hurt none; I have deluded no man."

All the Aarab would have hijabs sooner than medicaments, which they find so unprofitable in the hands of their hareem. The Moghrâreba, Moors or "Occidental Arabs," are esteemed in Arabia, the best scriveners of these magical scriptures; and the people suppose them to be of a wonderful subtlety, in the finding of hid treasures. There are hijabs for the relief of several diseases, and against possession of the jan or earth-demons: also hijabs which should preserve life in dangers, as hijabs

written against lead. *Metaab Ibn Rashíd,* prince of Shammar
after his brother *Tellál,* had worn one of this kind of amulets;
and his murderous nephews, who thought they might not pre-
vail with common shot, killed him therefore with a silver bullet.
The lieutenant of Turkish soldiery at Kheybar told in my
hearing, long after, of one who, taken in a revolt at Medina,
had been sentenced by the military court to be shot. Brought
forth to execution, the bullets which struck the condemned,
fell down as from a wall, and he remained unwounded: so one
fired a pistol in his bosom, but the lead fell from him. The
unhappy man cried out in his suffering, " Sirs! I have no defence against iron!" so they bound him to a cannon's mouth,
and at the blast, he perished. The Turk swore to us mighty
oaths he was there, he had seen the thing with his eyes; and
others said they had known the like, "ay, billah!"—Such are
everyday miracles, heard and confirmed and believed in among
them. * * *

* * * Pleasant, as the fiery heat of the desert daylight is
done, is our homely evening fire. The sun gone down upon
a highland steppe of Arabia, whose common altitude is above
three thousand feet, the thin dry air is presently refreshed, the
sand is soon cold; wherein yet at three fingers' depth is left
a sunny warmth of the past day's heat until the new sunrise.
After a half hour it is the blue night, and the clear hoary starlight in which there shines the girdle of the milky way, with
a marvellous clarity. As the sun is setting, the nomad housewife brings in a truss of sticks and dry bushes, which she has
pulled or hoed with a mattock (a tool they have seldom) in
the wilderness; she casts down this provision by our hearth-
side, for the sweet-smelling evening fire. But to Hirfa, his
sheykhly young wife, Zeyd had given a little Beduin maid to
help her. The housewife has upon her woman's side an hearth
apart, which is the cooking-fire. Commonly Hirfa baked then,
under the ashes, a bread-cake for the stranger: Zeyd her
husband, who is miserable, or for other cause, eats not yet,
but only near midnight, as he is come again from the mejlis
and would go in to sleep.

At this first evening hour, the Beduw are all *fi ahl-ha,*
in their households, to sup of such wretchedness as they may
have; there is no more wandering through the wide encampment, and the coming in then of any persons, not strangers,

were an unseemly " ignorance ". The foster-camels lie couched, before the booth of hair: and these Beduins let them lie still an hour, before the milking. The great feeble brutes have wandered all day upon the droughty face of the wilderness; they may hardly crop their fills, in those many hours, of so slender pastures. The mare stands tethered before the booth at the woman's side, where there is not much passage. Such dry wire-grass forage as they find in that waste, is cast down beside her. When the Arabs have eaten their morsel and drunken léban of the flock, the few men of our menzil begin to assemble about the sheykh's hearth, where is some expectation of coffee. The younger or meanest of the company, who is sitting or leaning on his elbow or lies next the faggot, will indolently reach back his hand from time to time for more dry rimth, to cast on the fire, and other sweet resinous twigs, till the flaming light leaps up again in the vast uncheerful darkness. The nomads will not burn the good pasture bushes, *gussha*, even in their enemies' country. It is the bread of the cattle. I have sometimes unwittingly offended them, until I knew the plants, plucking up and giving to the flames some which grew in the soil nigh my hand; then children and women and the men of little understanding blamed me, and said wondering, " It was an heathenish deed."

Glad at the fall of the empty daylight, the householders sit again to make talk, or silent and listless, with the drooping gravity of brute animals. Old men, always weary, and the herdmen, which were all day abroad in the sun, are lying now upon an elbow (this is the right Aarab posture, and which Zeyd would have me learn and use), about the common fire. But the reposing of the common sort at home is to lie heels out backward, about the hearth, as the spokes of a wheel, and flat upon their bellies (which they even think appeases the gnawing of hunger); and a little raising themselves, they discourse staying upon their breasts and two elbows: thus the men of this lean nation will later sleep, spreading only their tattered cloaks under them, upon the wild soil (béled), a posture even reproved by themselves. Béled, we saw in the mouth of the nomads, is the inhabited soil of the open desert and also of the oasis ; they say of the dead, " He is under the béled." Dîra, the Beduin circuit, is heard also in some oases for their town settlement.—I asked Zeyd, " Then say ye the béled is our mother ? "— " Ay well, and surely, Khalîl ; for out of the ground took God man and all return thither." They asking me of our custom, I said " You are ground-sitters, but we sit high upon stools like the Tûrk."—The legs of chair-sitters to hang all day they

thought an insufferable fatigue. " Khalîl says well," answered
Zeyd, who, a sheykh of Aarab, had been in high presence of
pashas and government men at Damascus ; and he told how
he found them sitting in arm-chairs and (they are all cross-
leg Orientals) with a leg crossed over the other, a shank or
a foot : ' a simple crossed foot is of the under functionaries :
but to lap a man's shin, (Zeyd showed us the manner,) he
said to be of their principal personages.' The Arabs asked
me often, if we sat gathered in this kindly sort about our
evening fires ? and if neighbours went about to neighbour
byût, seeking company of friends and coffee-drinking ?

Sitting thus, if there any one rises, the mare snorts softly,
looking that it is he who should now bring her delicious bever
of warm camel-milk, and gazing after him, she whinnies with
pleasance. There is a foster camel to every nomad mare, since
they taste no corn, and the harsh desert stalks could not else
sustain her : the horse, not ruminating and losing much moisture by the skin, is a creature very impatient of hunger and
thirst. His mare is therefore not a little chargeable to a sheykh
in the desert, who must burden oftentimes another camel with
her provision of water. Twice she will drink, and at the
hottest of the summer season, even thrice in a daylight ; and
a camel-load of girbies may hardly water her over two days.
Who has wife or horse, after the ancient proverb, may rue, he
shall never be in rest, for such brittle possessions are likely to
be always ailing. Yet under that serene climate, where the
element is the tent of the world, the Beduw have little other
care of their mares ; it is unknown in the desert so much as to
rub them. They milk first for the mare and then (often in the
same vessel) for the nomad household. She stands straining
upon her tether, looking toward the pleasant sound of milking :
the bowl frothing from the udder is carried to her in the
herdsman's hand and she sups through her teeth the sweet warm
milk, at a long draught. The milking time of camels is but
once in the day, at evening, unless a little be drawn for some
sick person or stranger in the morning, or for any wayfaring
man in the daytime. The small cattle, *ghrannen* or *dubbush*,
are milked at sunset ; only in rich spring districts, the housewives may draw their teats again in the morning. The dubbush
are milked by their housewives, the milch camels by the men
and lads only. Spring is the milky season, when men and beasts,
(if the winter rain failed not) fare at the best in the wilderness.
With small cattle, it lasts only few weeks from the yeaning till the
withering of the year be again upon them, when the herb is
dried up ; but the camel kine are nearly eleven months in milk.

So needful is the supplement of milk to the desert horses, that when, in the dry summer or at some other low times, the camels are driven wide from the standing menzil to be *azab*, absent certain days, that is in quest of pasture, the mare also is led along with them in her master's troop, to drink the foster milk. But if the sheykh have need of his mare then at home, he will nourish her, as he may, without the wet-nurse, mixing at evening a bowl of *mereesy* or dry milk rubbed in water. Mereesy is the butter-milk of the flock, dried by boiling to the hard shard, and resembles chalk. It is a drink much to thank God for, in lean times, and in the heat of the year, in the wilderness; in the long dead months when there is no milk, it is every day dearer and hard to be come by. Excellent to take upon journeys, mereesy is gipsy drink and no dainty in the border countries; but in the Arabian oases it is much esteemed to use with their unwholesome date diet, which alone were too heating. Mereesy ('that which rubbed between the palms of the hands, can be mingled with water,') or dry milk, is called by many other names in the provinces of Arabia, as *thiràn* and *bùggila, baggl*, in West Nejd; in the South and towards Mecca, *mùthir*. Butter is the poor nomad's market ware: with this they can buy somewhat in the towns for their household necessities. Having only mereesy in the saddle-bags and water before us every third day on the road, I have not doubted to set out upon long voyages in the khála. Mereesy will remain unaltered till the next season; it is good in the second year, only growing harder. The best were to grind it to flour, as they do in Kasîm: and this stirred, with a little sugar, in a bowl of the desert water is a grateful refreshment after the toil and heat of the desert journey.

A pleasure it is to listen to the cheerful musing Beduin talk, a lesson in the travellers' school of mere humanity,—and there is no land so perilous which by humanity he may not pass, for man is of one mind everywhere, ay, and in their kind, even the brute animals of the same foster earth—a timely vacancy of the busy-idle cares which cloud upon us that would live peaceably in the moral desolation of the world. And pleasant those sounds of the spretting milk under the udders in the Arabs' vessels! food for man and health at a draught in a languishing country. The bowl brought in foaming, the children gather to it, and the guest is often bidden to sup with them, with his fingers, the sweet froth, *orghra* or *roghrwa, irtugh*: or this milk poured into the sour milk-skin and shaken there a moment, the house-wife serves it forth again to their suppers, with that now gathered sourness which they think the more refreshing.

The nomad's eyes are fixed upon the crude congruity of
Nature ; even the indolence in them is austere. They speak of
the things within their horizon. Those loose "Arabian tales"
of the great border-cities, were but profane ninnery to their
stern natural judgments. Yet so much they have of the Semitic
Oriental vein, without the doting citizen fantasy, that many
dream all their lives of hidden treasures ; wealth that may fall
to them upon a day out of the lap of heaven. Instead of the
cities' taling, the Aarab have their braying rhapsodies, which
may be heard in every wild nomad hamlet, as those of the Beny
Helál. The Arabs are very credulous of all that is told beyond
their knowledge, as of foreign countries. All their speech is
homely ; they tell of bygone forays and of adventures in their
desert lives. You may often hear them in their tale quote the
rhythms between wisdom and mirth of the *kusasîd* (riming
desert poets without letters) ; the best are often widely current
among the tribes. In every tribe are makers : better than any
in this country were the kassâds of Bishr. The *kassâd* recites,
and it is a pleasant adulation of the friendly audience to take
up his last words in every couplet. In this poetical eloquence
I might not very well, or hardly at all, distinguish what they
had to say ; it is as strange language. The word *shâer*, he that
'*feeleth*', a poet, is unused by them ; the Beduins knew not the
word, Zeyd answered " it is *nadêm*." The Beduin singer draws
forth stern and horrid sounds from the rabeyby or viol of one
bass string, and delivers his mind, braying forcedly in the nose.
It is doubtless a very archaic minstrelsy, in these lands, but a
hideous desolation to our ears. It is the hinds, all day in the
wilderness with the cattle, who sing most lustily in their
evening home-coming to the humanity of the byût. I often
asked for a *kasída* of Abeyd Ibn Rashîd, and have found no
singer in this country who was not ready with some of them.
The young herdsmen of Zeyd's menzil would chant for the
stranger the most evening-times the robust *hadú*, or herding-
song. [This word *rabeyby* is perhaps the Spaniard's *rabel*, and
that was in Ancient England *revel*, *rebibel*.] The Beduw make
the instrument of any box-frame they may have from the towns :
a stick is thrust through, and in this they pierce an eye above
for the peg ; a kid-skin is stretched upon the hollow box ; the
hoarse string is plucked from the mare's tail ; and setting
under a bent twig, for the bridge, their music is ready.

The nomad's fantasy is high, and that is ever clothed in
religion. They see but the indigence of the open soil about,
full of dangers, and hardly sustaining them, and the firmament
above them, habitation of the Divine salvation. These Ish-

maelites have a natural musing conscience of the good and evil, more than other men; but none observe them less in all their dealings with mankind. The civil understanding of the desert citizens is found in their discourse (tempered between mild and a severe manly grace) and liberal behaviour. * * *

* * * The nomads, at leisure and lively minds, have little other than this study to be eloquent. Their utterance is short and with emphasis. There is a perspicuous propriety in their speech, with quick significance. The Arabian town-dwellers contemn this boisterous utterance of the sons of the wilderness; they themselves are fanatic sectators of the old koran reading. Asiatics, the Aarab are smiling speakers. All Beduin talk is one manner of Arabic, but every tribe has a use, *loghra*, and neighbours are ever chiders of their neighbours' tongue. " The speech of them, they will say, is somewhat 'awry,' *awaj.*" In the mouth of the Fukara sheykhs, was a lisping of the terminal consonants. The Moahîb talk was open and manly. In that dry serenity of the air, and largely exercised utterance of the many difficult articulations of their language, the human voice, *hess*, is here mostly clear and well-sounding; unless it be in some husk choking throat of heart-sore misery.

There is as well that which is displeasing in their homely talk. The mind is distempered by idleness and malice; they will hardly be at pains to remember suddenly, in speech, their next tribesman's name; and with this is their barbarous meddling curiosity, stickling mistrust one of another and beggarly haggling for any trifle, with glosing caresses, (would they obtain a thing, and which are always in guile,) impudent promises and petulant importunity. And their hypocrite iniquitous words, begetting the like, often end in hideous clamour, which troubling " the peace of Ullah " in the nomad booth, are rebuked by the silent impatience of the rest, of whom the better will then proffer themselves as peace-makers. The herdsmen's tongue is full of infantile raillery and, in sight and hearing of the other sex, of jesting ribaldry : they think it innocent mirth, since it is God that has founded thus our nature. Semites, it is impossible that they should ever blaspheme, in manner of those of our blood, against the Heavenly Providence. Semitic religion is the natural growth of the soil in their Semitic souls; in which is any remiss, farewell life's luck, farewell his worldly estimation : their criminal hearts are capable of all mischief, only not of this enormous desperation to lede the sovereign majesty of Ullah. Out of that religious persuasion of theirs that a man's life should be smitten to death, who is rebel unto God and despiser of the faith, comes the sharp danger of our travelling among them ; where of every ten, there is commonly some one, making religion of his peevish bestiality, who would slay us, (which all men may do religiously and help divine justice). But otherwise they all day take God's name in vain (as it was perhaps in ancient Israel), confirming every light and laughing word with cheerful billahs. The herdsmen's grossness is never out of the Semitic nature, the soul of them is greedy first of their proper subsistence and then of their proper increase. Though Israel is scattered among the most polite nations, who has not noted this humour in them ? Little Joseph is a tale-bearer to their father of his brethren's lewd conversation in the field ; such are always the Semitic nomads. Palestine, the countries beyond Jordan and Edom, given to the children and nephews of Abraham, spued out the nations which dwelled before in them, and had defiled the land : the Beny Israel are admonished, lest the soil cast out them also. In Moses is remembered the nomad offence of lying with cattle ; the people are commanded to put away guiltiness from the land by stoning them : in Arabia that is but a villanous mock, and which the elder sort acknowledge with groans and cursing. The pastoral race being such, Israel must naturally slide back from Moses' religion to the easy and carnal idolatry of the old Canaanites.

To speak of the Arabs at the worst, in one word, the mouth of the Arabs is full of cursing and lies and prayers ; their heart is a deceitful labyrinth. We have seen their urbanity ; gall and venom is in their least ill-humour ; disdainful, cruel, outrageous is their malediction. " Curse Ullah, thy father (that is better than thou), the father of the likes of thee ! burn thy father ! this is a man fuel for hell-burning ! bless thee not God ! make thee no partaker of His good ! thy house fall upon thee ! " I have heard one, in other things a very worthy man, in such form chide his unruly young son : " Ullah rip up that belly in thee ! Curse the father (thy body) of that head and belly ! Punish that hateful face ! " And I have heard one burden another thus ; " Curse thee all the angels, curse thee all the Moslemîn, let all the heathen curse thee ! " The raging of the tongue is natural to the half-feminine Semitic race. The prophet prayeth against some which disquieted him : " Pour out their blood by the sword, let their children consume with famine, their women be childless and their wives widows : they shall cry out from the houses as the ghrazzu is suddenly upon them. Forgive not, Lord, their trespass, give to them trouble of spirit, destroy them from under the heaven, and let Thy very curse abide upon them." Another holy man curses to death petulant children. The Aarab confirm all their words by oaths, which are very brittle, and though they say *Wa hyât Ullah*, " As the Lord liveth," or a man swear by himself, *aly lahyaty*, or *Wa hyât dúkny*, " Upon (the honour of) my beard." He will perform such oaths if they cost him nothing, this is if he be not crossed in the mean while, or have become unwilling. If a man swear by his religion, it is often lightly and with mental reservation. For the better assurance of a promise they ask and give the hand ; it is a visible pledge. So in Ezekiel, the sheukh of the captivity promise and plight their hands. A Beduin will swear to some true matter Wellâhi, or doubly, which is less to trust, Wellâhi-Billâhi. It is a word he will observe if he may, for nothing can bind them against their own profit; and they may lawfully break through all at an extremity. Another form is Wullah-Bullah, often said in mocking uncertainty and hypocrisy. That is a faithful form of swearing which they call *halif yemîn :* one takes a grass stalk in his fist, and his words are : *"Wa hyât hâtha el-aûd*, By the life of this stem, *wa'r-rubb el-mabûd*, and the adorable Lord." When I have required new wayfaring companions to swear me this at the setting out, and add *inny má adeshurak,* " I will not (for any hap) forsake thee," they have answered, " Our lot is one whilst we are in the way, whether to live or die together; and what more can I say, I will conduct thee thither, but I die, and by very God I will not forsake thee." I laid hold on their hands and compelled them, but they swore (to a kafir) unwillingly ; and some have afterward betrayed me: when then I reproached them to the heart, they answered me, " Oaths taken to a kafir be not binding ! " Magnanimous fortitude in a man, to the despising of death, where his honour is engaged, were in their seeing the hardihood of a madman : where mortal brittleness is fatally overmatched we have a merciful God, and human flesh, they think, may draw back from the unequal contention. * * *

* * * There are certain gestures used among them, which are tokens of great significance. I smooth my beard toward one to admonish him, in his wrongful dealing with me, and have put him in mind of his honour. If I touch his beard, I put him in remembrance of our common humanity and of the witness of God which is above us. Beard is taken in Arabia for human honour, and to pluck it is the highest indignity ; of an honest

man they say, *lahyat-hu taîba*, "His is a good beard ; " of a vile
covetous heart *mâ lihu lahya*, " He has no beard." The sup-
pliant who may bind, as I have heard, a certain knot in the
other's kerchief, has saved himself : and were the other the
avenger for blood, yet he must forbear for God! Kiss an angry
man's forehead, and his rancour will fall ; but the adversary
must be taken by surprise, or he will put forth stern hostile
hands to oppose thee. Surely a very ancient example of the
Semitic sacramental gestures is that recorded of Abraham, who
bids his steward put the hand under his thigh, to make his oath
sure. A simple form of requiring an honourable tolerance and
protection is to say ; *Ana nuzîlak*, " I have alighted at thy tent,"
or say where thou fearest treachery, *ana nusik*, and again, *Ana
bi wejhak ya sheykh*, "Sir, I am under thy countenance ; " more
solemnly, and touching him, *Terâny billah ya sheykh ; wa bak
ana dakhîlak*, which may signify, " By the Lord thou seest me,
and I do enter, Sir under thy protection." In my long
dangerous wanderings in the Arabian peninsula I have thrice
said this one word *dakhîlak :* twice when, forsaken in the deserts,
I came to strange tents of Heteym (they are less honourable
than Beduins, and had repulsed me) ; once to the captain of the
guard at Hâyil, when I was maltreated by the emir's slaves in
the market-place. He immediately drove them from me ; and
in the former adventure it made that I was received with
tolerance. * * *

    * * * The Aarab's leave-taking is wonderfully ungracious to
the European sense, and austere. The Arab, until now so gentle a
companion, will turn his back with stony strange countenance,
to leave thee for ever. Also the Arabs speak the last words as
they have turned the back ; and they pass upon their way not
regarding again. This is their national usage, and not of a
barbarous inhumanity ; nay, it were for thee to speak when any
departs company, saying : " Go in peace." You have not eaten
together, there was nothing then between you why this must
take his leave ; all men being in their estimation but simple
grains, under the Throne of God, of the common seed of
humanity. But the guest will say as he goes forth, and having
turned his face, with a frank simplicity, *nesellem aleyk*, " We bid
thee peace." The Arabs are little grateful for the gift which is
not food, receive they with never so large a hand ; " So little !
they will say, put to, put to ; " but the gentler spirits will cry out
soon, *bess ! wâjed ! keffy !* "enough, there is found, it sufficeth me
heartily."

CHAPTER VII

THE NOMADS IN THE DESERT; VISIT TO TEYMA

THIS was a formidable year for the Fukara : they were in dread of Ibn Rashîd ; they feared also that Kheybar would be barred to them,—" Kheybar the patrimony of Annezy," from whence those tribes in the South eat (the date fruit), eight in the twelve months. Besides it was a year of locusts. The tribesmen disputed in the mejlis, "should they go up anew to the Hauran," the land of bread; and that which they call, (nearly as nomad Israel coming from the lower deserts,) "The good Land of the North, where is milk enough; " this is Shàm or High Syria. They would remain as before in the *Niggera* (Batanea,) which is in the marches of their kinsmen the northern half-tribe of W. Aly : they count it fifteen removes, journeying with all their cattle and families, beyond Teyma. They had few years before forsaken their land upon this occasion : the Fejîr in a debate with their sister tribe, the southern W. Aly, had set upon them at Dàr el-Hamra, and taken their camels. Many were slain, and the mishandled kinsmen, appealing to Ibn Rashîd, the Prince gave judgment that satisfaction be made. The Aarab will hardly restore a gotten booty, especially where there is evil meaning between them ; and to live without fear of the Emir, they withdrew to a far-off Syrian country, where slenderly clad and not inured to that harsh and longer winter, and what for a contagious fever which happened in the second year, there perished many among them; the most, as it is the weak which go to the wall, were poor Fehját, wretches whom the iniquity of fortune ceases not to pursue until the end of all natural evils.—The Fehját buried, in the north, the half of their grown males, which were twenty persons. There is always living with the northern W. Aly, a body of the Fukara, *el-Kleyb, sheykh Fendy*, which for a blood feud with Bishr, might not inherit in their own country.

The presence of the Nasrâny in land of the Aarab was an enigma to them ; they put me to the question with a thousand

sudden demands, which were often checked by the urbanity of
the rest. 'At what distance (they enquired), in which part lay
my country?' I said, "A thelûl rider might alight among my
neighbours, a little before the year's end."—They had not
thought the world was so large! So they said, "Khalîl's
country lies at very great distance, and can it be he has passed
all that great way, only to visit the Aarab! now what can this
mean? Tell us by Ullah, Khalîl, art thou not come to spy
out the country? For there will no man take upon himself
immense fatigues for naught. Khalîl, say it once, what thy purpose is? Art thou not some banished man? comest thou of thine
own will, or have other sent thee hither?—Khalîl loves well the
Moslemîn, and yet these books of his be what? Also, is he
not 'writing' the country as he has 'written up' el-Héjr and
el-Ally?" I said, "I was living at Damascus and am a *Sâiehh;*
is not the sâiehh a walker about the world?—and who will say
him nay! also I wander wilfully."—"Now well! Khalîl is a
Sûwahh; wander where you list, Khalîl, and keep to the settled
countries, there is nothing to hinder; but come not into the
wilderness of the Beduw; for there you will be stripped and
they will cut thy throat: wellah, in all the desert no man fears
to kill a stranger; what then when they know that thou art a
Nasrâny!—A sûwahh! eigh! but the Aarab are so ignorant
that this will not help thee; a day may come Khalîl, the end of
all this rashness, when some one will murder thee miserably!"—
Sâiehh in the Mohammedan countries is God's wanderer, who,
not looking back to his worldly interest, betakes himself to the
contemplative life's pilgrimage. They would not hold me for a
derwish. "Nay, said they, derawîsh are of small or no regard;
but Khalîl was a care to the Dowla." Also they had word I was
some rich man in Damascus. How then, they wondered, could
I forsake Damascus, *jinnat ed-dinnea,* "the world's garden or
paradise," to dwell in the waste land of the Aarab!—It is
always a melancholy fantasy of the upland Arabians, who have
seen or heard anything of the plentiful border provinces, to
complain of their own extreme country. The Southern Arabs
lead their lives in long disease of hunger and nakedness:
to see good days in the northern land, which is watered with
seasonable rains and is wet with the dew of heaven, they think
should be a wonderful sweetness. The "garden" of all is
Damascus, the Arabs' belly-cheer "paradise"; for there is
great cheap of all that can ease a poor man, which is food and
raiment. And such, as Semites, is all they intend, in their
word of Damascus, "the garden or paradise."
    I passed for a seeker of treasure with some who had seen me
sitting under the great acacia, which they believe to be possessed

by the jan, at el-Héjr ; now they said to me, " Didst thou take
up anything, Khalîl, tell us boldly ? " and a neighbour whispered in my ear, " Tell thy counsel to me only, good Khalîl,
and I will keep it close."—" There is no lore, I answered, to find
treasures ; your finders are I know not what ignorant sots, and
so are all that believe in their imposture."—" God wot it may
be so ; Khalîl is an honest-speaking man ;—but in roaming up
and down, you lighted upon naught ? Hearken ! we grant you
are disinterested—have patience ! and say only, if you find a
thing will you not give some of it to your uncle Zeyd ? "—" The
whole, I promise you."—" Wellah, in Khalîl's talk is sincerity,
but what does he, always asking of the Aarab an hundred vain
questions ?—Though thou shouldst know, O Khalîl, the name
of all our camping grounds and of every jebel, what were all
this worth when thou art at home, in a far country ? If thou
be'st no spy, how can the Aarab think thee a man of good understanding ? " In other times and places whilst I was yet a
stranger little known among them, the Beduin people did not
always speak so mildly, many murmured and several tribesmen
have cruelly threatened that ' could it be known, I came about
spying the land, they would cast me, billah, on a fire, with my
books, and burn all together.' In such case, they might break
the cobweb customs of hospitality : the treacherous enemy is
led forth, and drawn to the hindward of the tent there they cut
his throat. Many times good Beduin friends predicted to me
this sharp ending of my incurable imprudence, when leaving
their friendly tribes I should pass through strange dîras : but as
I lingered long in the country, I afterward came almost no-
whither, where some fair report was not already wafted before
me. " Friends, I have said, I am come to you in no disguises ;
I have hidden nothing from you ; I have always acknowledged
myself a Nasrâny, which was a name infamous among you."
And they : " Well, but the war with those of your kindred and
the Sooltân !—Is he not killing up the Nasâra like sheep flocks ?
so God gave him the victory !—say this, Khalîl, *Ullah Tunsur
es-Sooltân*."

As we hearken to strange tales, so they would ask me of
the far Nasarene country ; were we *ahl tîn*, ' a people dwelling
in clay (houses),' or else *ahl byût shaar*, ' wandering Aarab
dwelling in houses of hair ' ? When I answered, " We have
no other nomad folk, than a few gipsies ; "—" it is plain (they
said) that Khalîl's Arabs are *hâthir*," or settled on the land :
and they enquired which were our cattle. It was marvels to
them, that in all our béled was not one camel.—" Lord ! upon
what beasts do they carry ? "—" Ours is a land of horses, which
are many there as your camels ; with a kind of labouring horses

we plough the fallows: besides, we have the swiftest running horses, of stature as your thelûls." There lives not an Arab who does not believe, next to his creed, that the stock of horses is only of the Arabs, and namely, the five strains, educated in Arabia. 'And to which of these (they would know) reckoned we our horses?' It perplexed and displeased them that our béled should be full of horses:—'had Ullah given horses also to the Nasâra!'—"Listen! (said Zeyd, who loved well to show his sharp wit,—the child's vanity not dead in the saturnine grown man,) and I can declare Khalîl's words; it is that we have seen also in es-Sham: Khalîl's coursers be all *kudsh*, or pack-horses." When I answered, 'he was mistaken;' they cried me down; " Khalîl, in other things we grant you may know more than we, but of horses thou canst have no knowledge, for they are of the Aarab." The Fejîr are reckoned a tribe of horsemen, yet all their mares were not a score : Beduins of tribes in which were very few horses I have found mistrustful of their own blunt judgment; they supposed also I might tell them many subtle skills from a far country.

They enquired of our ghrazzus, and what number of fighting men could we send to the field. Hearing from my mouth that many times all the Haj were but a small army of our great nations, they gasped for fear, thinking that el-Islam was lost, and " wherefore, they asked quickly, being such multitudes, did we not foray upon them (as they would have overridden us):— Ah God! (they cried), help Thou the Moslemîn!" "Comfort yourselves, I answered, that we, being the stronger, make no unjust wars: ours is a religion of peace ; the weak may live in quietness for us."—" It is good that God has given you this mind, to the welfare of el-Islam, yet one Moslem (they confided) should be able to drive before him an hundred of the Nasâra." I told them we had made the great war of *Krîm* (the Crimea) for the Sûltân and their sake ; in which were fallen the flower of our young men, and that women yet weep for them in our land." They enquired coldly, " Were your dead two or three hundred, or not so many ? " When I said their number might be 60,000, (and they believing I could not lie,) as men confounded they cried, " Ah Lord God! is not that more than all the men together in these parts ? " (there may not be so many grown males in the nomad tribes of upland Arabia !) " And have your people any great towns, Khalîl ? "—" Great indeed, so that all the Beduw gathered out of your deserts might hardly more than fill some one great city."—" God (they exclaimed) is almighty ! but have we not heard of Khalîl's people, is it not of them that is said *el-Engreys akhuâl es-Sûltàn* (the English are

uncles of the Sûltàn on the mother's side); the Sûltàns do well
to ally in their friendly Christian blood,"—which always they
esteem above their own. They say in Arabia, "the Nasâra
never ail anything in their lives, nor suffer in their flesh, but
only in the agony of dying; their head aching, it is a sign to
them that they are nigh their end; the flesh of the Nasâra
is better than ours." Beduins have curiously observed me in
their camps, waiting to see the truth of their opinion fulfilled,
if at any time I sat wearily with the head in my hand; some
would then say, "Eigh! what ails thee? does thy head ache?
—it is likely that he will die, poor Khalîl!"
And our béled, "a land without palms," this was as a fable
to them.—"There are no dates! How then do your people live,
or what sweetness taste they! Yet Khalil may say sooth:
companions, have we not found the like in the North? Which
of us saw any palms at Damascus? Khalîl's folk may have honey
there, and sugar;—(the sweet and the fat comfort the health of
the ill dieted under these climates.) We too have seen the north
country; all that grows out of the soil is there, and that oil of a
tree which is better than samn." These hungry Beduins being
in the Hauran, where they had corn enough, yet so longed in
the autumn for the new date berries, that it drew them home
to their hungry desert, only "to eat of their own palms at
Kheybar." The nomads think they cannot be in health, except
they taste this seasonable sweetmeat; although they reckon it
not wholesome diet.
The Beduw very often asked me "Beyond how many floods
lies the land of the Nasâra?" They heard say we dwelt behind
seven floods; other said, "It is three, and if you will not believe
this, ask Khalîl." Ullah bring thee home, Khalîl! and being
come again to thy house, if the Lord will, in peace, thou wilt
have much to relate of the Aarab's land? and wilt thou not
receive some large reward? for else, we think, thou wouldst
never adventure to pass by this wilderness, wherein even we,
the Beduw, are all our lives in danger of robbers: thou art
alone, and if thou wast made away, there is none would avenge
thee. There is not, Khalîl, a man of us all which sit here, that
meeting thee abroad in the khála, had not slain thee. Thy
camel bags, they say, are full of money, but, billah, were it only
for the beast which is under thee; and lucky were he that
should possess them. *The stranger is for the wolf!* you heard
not this proverb in your own country?"—"By God (one cries),
I had killed Khalîl!"—"And I" (said another).—"Wellah, I
had waylaid him (says another); I think I see Khalîl come riding,
and I with my matchlock am hidden behind some crag or bush;

he had never seen it :—*deh* ! Khalîl tumbles shot through the body and his camel and the gear had been all mine : and were it not lawful, what think ye, mates ? to have killed him, a God's adversary ? This had been the end of Khalîl." I said, " God give thee a punishment, and I might happen to prevent thee." —" Wellah (answered the rest), we had not spared him neither ; but beware thou, the Beduw are all robbers. Khalîl ! the stronger eat the weaker in this miserable soil, where men only live by devouring one another. But we are Zeyd's Aarab, and have this carefulness of thee for Zeyd's sake, and for the bread and salt : so thou mayest trust us, and beside us, we warn thee, by Ullah, that thou trust not in any man. Thou wilt hardly receive instruction, more than one possessed by the jan ; and we dread for thee every morrow lest we should hear of thy death ; the people will say, ' Khalîl was slain to-day,'—but we all wash our hands of it, by Ullah ! The Aarab are against thee, a Nasrâny, and they say, ' He is spying the country : ' and only we are thy friends which know thee better. Khalîl may trust to the Dowla, but this is a land under no rule, save only of the Lord above us. We but waste breath, companions ; and if God have blinded this man, let him alone ; he may die if he will, for who can persuade the foolhardy ? " When I told them that far from looking for any reward, I thought, were I come home, I might hardly purchase, at need, the livelihood of a day with all this extreme adventure, they answered, ' Were the Nasâra inhospitable ? '

The Arab travels with his rafîk, they wondered therefore how I came unaccompanied : " Khalîl, where is thy companion, that each might help other ? " They wondered hearing that all ours was peaceable land, and that we carried no arms, in our own country. " Khalîl, be there no Beduins at all, in the land of the Nasâra ? " I told them of the Lapland nomads in the cold height of the north, their round hoop-tents of skins, and clothing of the same : some bid me name them, and held that " they had heard such a name." " What are their cattle in so cold a béled ? the winter snow lying the more months of the year, it were unfit for camels !"—" You will not believe me : their beasts are a kind of gazelles, big as asses, and upon their heads stand wide branching horns, with whose tines they dig in the snow to a wort, which is their daily pasture Their winter's night, betwixt the sunsetting and the sunrising, is three months ; and midsummer is a long daylight, over their heads, of equal length. There I have seen the eye of the sun a spear's height above the face of the earth at midnight." Some thought it a fabulous tale that I told in scorn of them

"We believe him rather," said other. Nothing in this tale seemed so quaint to them, as that of those beasts' branching horns, which I showed them in the sand with my camel-stick; for it is the nature of horns, as they see any, to be simple. They asked, "Should not such be of buffalo kind?" But of that strange coming and going of the sun, the herdsmen's mirth rising, "How, laughed they, should those Aarab say their prayers? would it be enough to say them there but once, in a three-months' winter night!"

"And are your settled countries so populous? tell us, wellah, Khalîl, have you many villages? an hundred?"—"Hundreds, friends, and thousands: look up! I can think as many as these stars shining above us:" a word which drew from them long sighing eighs! of apprehension and *glucks!* upon their Beduish tongues, of admiration. Meteors are seen to glance at every few moments in the luminous Arabian night. I asked, "What say the Aarab of these flitting stars?" *Answer:* "They go to tumble upon the heads of the heathen, O Khalîl! fall there none upon the Nasâra? Ullah shortly confound all the kuffâr!" Zeyd said with a sober countenance, "Your towns-folk know better than we, but ye be also uncunning in many things, which the Aarab ken.—Khalîl now, I durst say, could not tell the names of the stars yonder," and pointing here and there, Zeyd said over a few names of greater stars and constellations, in what sort the author of Job in his old nomad-wise, "The Bear, Orion and the Pleiades." I asked, "How name you this glorious girdle of the heavens?"—"*El-Mujjir;*" and they smiled at our homely name, "The Milky Way." I told them, This we see in our glasses to be a cloud of stars; all our lore is not to call a few stars by their names. Our star-gazing men have numbered the stars, and set upon every one a certain name, and by "art-Indian," they may reckon from a hundred ages before our births, or after our deaths, all the courses of the host of heaven.—But those wandering stars stedfastly shining, are like to this earth, we may see seas and lands in them." Some of the younger sort asked then, "Were there Aarab in them?—and the moon is what, Khalîl?"

There is a proverb which says, "Misfortunes never come single;" my vaccination had failed, and now *Abán*, my camel, failed me. Abán (to every beast of their cattle is a several name, as these are of camels: *Areymîsh, Ghrallâb, er-Rahîfa, ed-Dònnebil, Dánna, el-Mûs, Aitha, Atsha*) was a strong young he-camel and rising in value; but Zeyd had it in his double mind to persuade me otherwise, hoping in the end to usurp it himself.

Upon a morrow the unhappy brute was led home, and then we saw the under-jaw bleeding miserably, it was hanging broken. It happened that a great coffee company was assembled at Zeyd's, from the sunrise, and now they all rose to see this chance. The groaning camel was made to kneel; some bound the limbs, and with strength of their arms careened and laid his great bulk upon the side; and whoso were expert of these camel-masters searched the hurt. Zeyd laid his searing irons in the embers ready for firing, which is seldom spared in any practice of their desert surgery. All hearkened to the opinion of a nomad smith, which kindred of men are as well the desert farriers and, skilled in handling tools, oftentimes their surgeons. This sâny cured the broken jaw with splints, which he lapped about with rags daubed with rice cinder and red earth. The camel, said he, being fed by hand, might be whole in forty days. The like accident, I heard it said among them, had happened once in their memories to a tribesman's camel, and the beast had been cured in this manner; but I felt in my heart that it might never be. The wound was presently full of flies, and the dressing, never unbound, bred worms in so great heat; the dead bone blackened, and in few days fell away of itself. My watch also failed me, by which I made account of distances: from thenceforth I have used cross-reckonings of camel journeys.

It was March; already the summer entered with breathless heat, and in face of these contradictions of fortune, I thought to depart out of the desert country. I would return to el-Ally, and there await some rice-caravan returning to Wejh, from whence by any of the small Arab hoys, upon which they use to ship camels, I might sail for Egypt. But Zeyd and Motlog bade me have patience, until after the spring season; when the tribe in their journeys should again approach the Héjr country, from which we were already very far divided. 'The forsaken deserts behind us being now infested by habalîs, I should not find any willing, and they moreover would suffer none to accompany me.' The habalîs, 'desert fiends,' are dreaded by the nomad tribesmen, as the Beduw themselves among settled country and oasis folk. Commonly the habalîs are some young miscreants that, having hardly any head of cattle at home, will desperately cast themselves upon every cruel hazard: yet others are strenuous solitary men, whose unquiet mettle moves them from slothing in the tent's shadow to prowl as the wolf in the wilderness. These outlaws, enduring intolerable hardships, are often of an heathenish cruelty, it is pretended they willingly leave none alive. Nearly always footmen, they are more hardly perceived, lurking under crag or bush.

The waste (sand-plain) landscape of these mountain solitudes is overgrown with rare pasture bushes. The desert bushes, heaped about the roots with sand, grow as out of little hillocks. The bushes dying, the heaps which were under them remain almost everlastingly, and they are infinite up and down in all the wilderness : in some is the quantity of two or three or more wagon loads. These nomads bury in them their superfluous carriage of dates every year, as their camels come up overloaded with the summer gathering from Kheybar: that they may find their own again they observe well the landmarks. Some sheykhs will leave their winter beyt thus committed to the sand of the desert : in the hot months, with scarcity of pasture, and when the cattle are least patient of thirst, if they would not have them lean they must lessen their burdens. These nomad deposits lying months in the dry ground are not spoiled ; and there is none of their tribesmen that will ever disturb them : the householder shall be sure to find his own again where he buried it. The nomad tribes have all this manner of the summer deposit ; some leave their cumber in the villages with their hosts, and such trust is (in nearly all men's hands) inviolable. The Moahîb have a secret cave known to none living but themselves, in their desolate Harra ; there they lay up, as in a sanctuary, what they will, and a poor tribesman may leave his pound of samn.—Passing through a valley apart from the common resort in the solitudes of Sinai, I saw a new Beduin mantle, hanging on a thorn. My nomad camel-driver went to take it down, and turning it in his hand "Ay billah (said he), a good new cloak enough!" and hanged it on the bough again : such goods of tribesmen are, as it were, committed to God. So we came to some of those Sinai stone cottages, which they call 'Nasarene houses' (they would say, of the antique people of the land, before the Moslemîn), in which they used to leave their heavy quern-stones ; and there are certain locked barns of the few traffickers bringing in corn from Gaza, among the Beduw. We entered one of them, and as I was looking at something of their gear, my companion, with altered looks, bade me put it up again ; as if even the handling were sacrilege. Sheykhs receiving surra of the haj road, have also their stores of heavy stuff and utensils in the kellas, as those of the Fejîr at Medáin ; and I heard they paid a fee to Haj Nejm, one real for every camel load. The sand upon all this high inland is not laid in any ripples (as that at the Red Sea border, rippled, in this latitude, from the north) ; here are no strong or prevailing winds.

E *

As we went by to the mejlis, "Yonder (said Zeyd) I shall
show thee some of a people of antiquity " This was a family
which then arrived of poor wanderers, *Solubba*. I admired the
full-faced shining flesh-beauty of their ragged children, and
have always remarked the like as well of the Heteym nomads.
These alien and outcast kindreds are of fairer looks than the
hunger-bitten Beduw. The Heteym, rich in small cattle, have
food enough in the desert, and the Solubba of their hunting and
gipsy labour : for they are tinkers of kettles and menders of
arms, in the Beduin menzils. They batter out upon the anvil
hatchets, *jedûm*, (with which shepherds lop down the sweet
acacia boughs, to feed their flocks,) and grass-hooks for cutting
forage, and steels for striking fire with the flint, and the like.
They are besides woodworkers, in the desert acacia timber,
of rude saddle-trees for the burden-camels, and of the thelûl
saddle-frames, of pulley reels (*máhal*) for drawing at any deeper
wells of the desert, also of rude milk vessels, and other such
husbandry : besides, they are cattle surgeons, and in all their
trade (only ruder of skill) like the smiths' caste or *Sunna*.
The Solubba obey the precept of their patriarch, who forbade
them to be cattle-keepers, and bade them live of their hunting
in the wilderness, and alight before the Beduin booths, that
they might become their guests, and to labour as smiths in the
tribes for their living. Having no milch beasts, whereso they
ask it at a Beduin tent, the housewife will pour out léban from
her semîla, but it is in their own bowl, to the poor Solubba :
for Beduins, otherwise little nice, will not willingly drink after
Solubbies, that might have eaten of some *futís*, or the thing
that is dead of itself. Also the Beduw say of them, "they eat
of vile insects and worms : " the last is fable, they eat no such
vermin. Rashly the evil tongue of the Beduw rates them as
'kuffâr', because only few Solubbies can say the formal prayers,
the Beduins are themselves not better esteemed in the towns.
The Solubba show a good humble zeal for the country religion
in which they were born, and have no notice of any other ; they
are tolerant and, in their wretched manner, humane, as they
themselves are despised and oppressed persons.

In summer, when the Beduw have no more milk, loading
their light tents and household stuff, with what they have
gained, upon asses, which are their only cattle, they forsake
the Aarab encampment, and hold on their journey through
the wide khála. The Solubby household go then to settle
themselves remotely, upon a good well of water, in some un-
frequented wilderness, where there is game. They only (of all
men) are free of the Arabian deserts to travel whithersoever

they would; paying to all men a petty tribute, they are molested by none of them. Home-born, yet have they no citizen-
ship in the Peninsula. No Beduwy, they say, will rob a
Solubby, although he met him alone, in the deep of the wilderness, and with the skin of an ostrich in his hand, that is worth
a thelûl. But the wayfaring Beduwy would be well content to
espy, pitched upon some lone watering, the booth of a Solubby,
and hope to eat there of his hunter's pot; and the poor Solubby
will make the man good cheer of his venison. They ride even
hunting upon ass-back. It is also on these weak brutes, which
must drink every second day, (but otherwise the ass is hardly
less than the camel a beast of the desert,) that they journey
with their families through great waterless regions, where the
Beduwy upon his swift and puissant thelûl, three days patient
of thirst, may not lightly pass. This dispersed kindred of desert
men in Arabia, outgo the herdsmen Beduw in all land-craft, as
much as these go before the tardy oases villagers. The Solubba
(in all else ignorant wretches,) have inherited a land-lore from
sire to son, of the least finding-places of water. They wander
upon the immense face of Arabia, from the height of Syria to
el-Yémen, beyond *et-Táif*, and I know not how much further!
—and for things within their rat-like understanding, Arabians
tell me, it were of them that a man may best enquire.

They must be masters in hunting, that can nourish themselves in a dead land; and where other men may hardly see a
footprint of venison, there oftentimes, the poor Solubbies are
seething sweet flesh of gazelles and bedûn, and, in certain sand
districts, of the antelope; everywhere they know their quarries'
paths and flight It is the Beduw who tell these wonders of
them; they say, "the S'lubba are like herdsmen of the wild
game, for when they see a troop they can break them and
choose of them as it were a flock, and say, 'These will we have
to-day, as for those other heads there, we can take them after
to-morrow'."—It is human to magnify, and find a pleasant
wonder, this kind of large speaking is a magnanimity of the
Arabs; but out of doubt, the Solubba are admirable wayfarers
and hardy men, keen, as living of their two hands, and the best
sighted of them are very excellent hunters. The Solubba or
Slèyb, besides this proper name of their nation, have some other
which are epithets. West of Hâyil they are more often called
el-Khlûa or *Kheluîy*, " the desolate," because they dwell apart
from the *Kabâil*, having no cattle nor fellowship;—a word
which the Beduw say of themselves, when in a journey, finding
no menzil of the Aarab, they must lie down to sleep " solitaries "
in the empty khâla. They are called as well in the despiteful

tongue of this country, Kiláb el-Khála, 'hounds of the wilderness.' *El-Ghrúnemy* is the name of another kindred of the
Slèyb in East Nejd; and it is said, they marry not with the
former. The Arabians commonly suppose them all to be come
of some old kafir kind, or Nasâra. * * *

* * * Wandering and encamping, we had approached Teyma;
and now being hardly a journey distant, some of our people would
go a-marketing thither, and Zeyd with them, to buy provisions:
I should ride also in the company with Zeyd. We set out upon
the morrow, a ragged fellowship, mostly Fehját, of thirty men
and their camels. We passed soon from the sandy highlands
to a most sterile waste of rising grounds and hollows, a rocky
floor, and shingle of ironstone. This is that extreme barrenness
of the desert which lies about Teyma, without blade or bush.
We passed a deep ground, *M'hai*, and rode there by obscure
signs of some ancient settlement, *Jerèyda*, where are seen a few
old circles of flag-stones, pitched edgewise, of eight or nine
yards over, seeming such as might have fenced winter tents of
the antique Aarab, sheltered in this hollow. In the Moallakát,
or elect poems of ancient Arabia, is some mention of round
tents, but the booths of all the Arab nomads are now foursquare
only. The company hailed me, " See here! Khalîl, a village of
the *Auellín*, those of old time."—" And what ancients were
these?"—" Some say the Sherarát, others the *Beny Kelâb* or
Chelb, and theirs, billah, was the Borj Selmàn and the ground
Umsheyrifa." Zeyd added: " This was of the *Ahl Theyma* (not
Teyma), and sheykh of them *Aly es-Sweysy* the Yahûdy."
Come upon the highest ground beyond, Zeyd showed me the
mountain landmarks, westward *Muntar B. Atíeh*, next *Twoyel
Saída, Helaima* before us, in front *el-Ghrenèym*, which is behind
the oasis. Some murmured, " Why did Zeyd show him our
landmarks?"—" I would have Khalîl, said he, become a
Beduwy."
Delightful now was the green sight of Teyma, the haven of
our desert; we approached the tall island of palms, enclosed by
long clay orchard-walls, fortified with high towers. Teyma is a
shallow, loamy, and very fertile old flood-bottom in these high
open plains, which lie out from the west of Nejd. Those lighthouse-like turrets, very well built of sun-dried brick, are from
the insecure times before the government of Ibn Rashîd, when,
as the most Arabian places, Teyma was troubled by the sheykhs'
factions, and the town quarters divided by their hereditary

enmities. Every well-faring person, when he had fortified his palms with a high clay-brick wall, built his tower upon it; also in every sûk of the town was a clay turret of defence and refuge for the people of that street. In a private danger one withdrew with his family to their walled plantation : in that enclosure, they might labour and eat the fruits, although his old foes held him beleaguered for a year or two. Any enemy approaching by day-light was seen from the watch-tower. Such walling may be thought a weak defence; but for all the fox-like subtlety of Semitic minds, they are of nearly no invention. A powder blast, the running brunt of a palm beam, had broken up this clay resistance; but a child might sooner find, and madmen as soon unite to attempt anything untried. In the Gospel parables, when one had planted a vineyard, he built a tower therein to keep it. The watch-tower in the orchard is yet seen upon all desert borders. We entered between grey orchard walls, overlaid with blossoming boughs of plum trees; of how much amorous contentment to our parched eyes! I read the oasis height 3400 ft. We dismounted at the head of the first sûk before the *dàr*, house or court of a young man our acquaintance, *Sleymàn*, who in the Haj time had been one of the kella guests at Medáin Here he lived with his brother, who was Zeyd's date merchant; we were received therefore in friendly wise, and entertained. The hareem led in Hirfa, who had ridden along with us, to their apartment.

As the coffee pestle (which with the mortars, are here of limestone marble, sunna's work, from Jauf,) begins to ring out at the coming of guests; neighbours enter gravely from the sûk, and to every one our sheykh Zeyd arose, large of his friendly greeting, and with the old courtesy took their hands and embraced them.

Teyma is a Nejd colony of Shammar, their fathers came to settle here, by their saying, not above two hundred years past : from which time remain the few lofty palms that are seen grown to fifteen fathoms, by the great well-pit, *Haddàj;* and only few there are, negroes, who durst climb to gather the fruits of them. All their palm kinds have been brought from Jebel Shammar, except the *helw*, which was fetched from el-Ally. Theirs is even now, in another dîra, the speech of Shammar. Here first we see the slender Nejd figures, elated, bold tongued, of ready specious hospitality, and to the stranger, arriving from the Hejâz, they nearly resemble the Beduins. They go bare-footed, and bravely clad of the Hâyil merchandise from *el-Iràk*, and inhabit clay-built spacious houses, mostly with an upper floor; the windows are open casements for the light and air, their flooring the beaten earth, the rude door is of palm boards, as in all the oases. This open Shammar town was never wasted by plagues, the *burr* or high desert of uncorrupt air lies all round about them from the walls: only Beduins from the dry desert complain here of the night (the evaporation from irrigated soil), which gives them cold in the head, *zikma*. Here are no house-ruins, broken walls and abandoned acres, that are seen in the most Arabian places. Prosperous is this outlying settlement from Nejd, above any which I have seen in my Arabian travels. If any one here discover an antique well, without the walls, it is his own; and he encloses so much of the waste soil about as may suffice to the watering; after a ploughing his new acre is fit for sowing, and planting of palms, and fifteen years later every stem will be worth a camel. Teyma, till then a free township, surrendered without resistance to the government of Ibn Rashîd. They are skilful husbandmen to use that they have, without any ingenuity: their wells are only the wells of the ancients, which finding again, they have digged them out for themselves: barren of all invention, they sink none, and think themselves unable to bore a last fathom in the soft sand-rock which lies at the bottom of the seven-fathom wells. Moslemîn, they say, cannot make such wells, but only Nasâra should be good to such work and Yahûdies. Arabian well-sinkers in stone there are none nearer than Kasîm, and these supine Arabs will call in no foreign workmen. They trust in God for their living, which, say the hearts of these penny-wise men, is better than to put their silver in adventure.

There was none here who asked alms in the street; indeed it is not common to see any destitute persons in West Nejd. I knew in Teyma but one such poor man, helpless with no great age. In what house he entered at supper time, he might sit down with the rest to eat and welcome, but they grudged that he should carry any morsel away. There were in the town one or two destitute Beduins, who entered to sup and "to coffee" in which households they would, no man forbidding them. At night they lay down in their cloaks, in what coffee hall they were; or went out to sleep, in the freshing air, upon some of the street clay benches.

Old Teyma of the Jews, according to their tradition, had been (twice) destroyed by a flood. From those times there remain some great rude stone buildings; the work is dry-laid with balks and transoms of the same iron-stone. Besides, there is a great circuit (I suppose almost three miles) of stone wall-ing, which enclosed the ancient city. This *sûr* lies somewhat above the oasis. The prince of old Mosaic Teyma is named in their tradition *Béder Ibn Jòher.* Nomad masters of new Teyma were at first B. Sókhr, unto whom even now they yield a yearly khûwa; and else they should not be delivered from their distant foraying. Fever is unknown at Teyma. Their water, and such I have found all Arabian ground-water, is flat, lukewarm and unwholesome. Of this they think it is that amongst them almost no man is seen of robust growth; but they are the lean shot-up figures of Nejd, with the great startling eyes, long oval shallow faces, and hanging jaws: you might think them Beduins. The women are goodly, more than the men, loose-fleshed large village faces, but without ruddiness, they have dissonant voices. as the neighbour tribeswomen of the B. Wáhab, they go unveiled. I saw in the town no aged persons. Of the two hundred houses here, are three sheykhs' sûks or parishes and fifteen *hárats* or smaller wards; in every one there is some little mesjid or public oratory (often but a penthouse) of poor clay walling without ornaments, the flooring is of gravel. Such are as well places of repose, where the stranger may go in to sleep under a still shadow, at the gate of heaven. But the great mosque, whither all the males resort for the Friday mid-day prayers, preaching, and koran-reading, stands a little without the sûks to the eastward. It is perhaps the site of some ancient temple, for I found certain great rude pillars lying about it. At el-Ally, (a Hejâz oasis, and never entered by the Waháby,) I saw the mosques nearly such as are those in the Syrian villages.

We were led round to drink in the coffee-halls of other house-holders, with whom Zeyd dealt, for some part of his victual of grain and dates. As they have little fuel of that barren land about them, and out of their plantations no more than for the daily cooking,—the palm timber is besides "as vinegar to the teeth and smoke to the eyes" in burning—they use here the easy and cleanly Nejd manner of a charcoal coffee-fire, which is blown in a clay hearth with a pair of smith's bellows: this coal is brought by men who go out to make it, in the further desert. The smiling oasis host spares not, sitting at his coals, to blow and sweat like a Solubby for his visiting guests; and if thou his acquaintance be the guest of another, "Why, he will ask thee with a smooth rebuke, didst thou not alight at my dàr?" Coffee is thus made, with all diligence, twice or thrice over in an hour: prepared of a dozen beans for as many persons, their coffee drink is very small at Teyma. The coffee-hall, built Nejd-wise, is the better part of every house building. The lofty proportion of their clay-house walls is of a noble simplicity, and ceiled with ethl beams or long tamarisk, which is grown in all the oases for timber. The close mat of palm stalks laid upon the rafters, is seen pleasantly stained and shining with the Arabs' daily hospitable smoke, thereabove is a span deep of rammed earth. The light of the room is from the entry, and in many halls, as well, by open casements, and certain holes made high upon the walls. The sitting-place (*múkaad*) of the earthen floor and about the sunken hearth, is spread with palm mat or nomad tent cloth. Upon the walls in some sheykhs' houses is seen a range of tenter-pegs, where guesting sheykhs of the Aarab may lay up their *romhh* or long horseman's lance. In these dârs you shall hear no minstrelsy, the grave viol sounds in Wahâby ears are of an irreligious levity, and the Teyâmena had received a solemn rescript from Ibn Rashîd, forbidding them to sound the rabeyby ! *Khâlaf*, the emir, a liberal-minded person, told it to some Beduins in my hearing, not without a gesture of his private repugnance.

We met Motlog's brother in the streets ; he was come into Teyma before us. I marked how preciously the nomad man went, looking upon the ground, I thought him dazing in the stagnant air of the oases, and half melancholy : *Rahyel* might be called in English the complete gentleman of his tribe ; a pensive and a merry errand he had now upon hand. The sheykh was come in to wed a town wife : for as some villager, trafficking to the nomads, will have his Beduwîa always abiding him in the desert, so it is the sick fantasy of many a Beduwy to be a wedded man in the market settlement, that when he is there he may go home to his wife, though he should not meet with her again in a round year. At evening we heard loud hand-clapping, the women's merrymaking for this bridal, in one of the next houses. This is a general and ancient Semitic wise of striking sounds in measure, to accompany the lively motions of their minds ; in the Hebrew Scriptures it is said, ' The floods and the trees of the field clap their hands.' The friends of the spouse fired off their match-locks. This pairing was under a cloud, for there happened at the moment a strange accident ; it was very unlucky I came not provided with an almanac. Seeing the moon wane, the housewives made great clangour of pans to help the labouring planet, whose bright hue at length was quite lost. I began to expound the canonical nature of eclipses, which could be calculated for all times past and to come. The coffee drinkers answered soberly, " It may well be true, but the Arabs are ignorant and rude ! We cannot approach to so high and per-fect kinds of learning."

Upon the morrow, whilst we sat at coffee, there enters one,

walking stately, upon his long tipstaff, and ruffling in glorious
garments : this was the Resident for Ibn Rashîd at Teyma.
The emir's gentleman, who seemed to have swallowed a stake,
passed forth, looking upon no man, till he sat down in his
solemnity ; and then hardly vouchsafed he to answer the
coffee-drinkers' cheerful morning greetings. This is the great
carriage of Hâyil, imitated from the Arabian Prince Ibn
Rashîd, who carries his coxcomb like an eagle to overawe the
unruly Beduw. The man was Saîd, a personage of African
blood, one of the libertines of the emir's household. He sat
before us with that countenance and stiff neck, which by his
estimation should magnify his office : he was lieutenant of the
lord of the land's dignity in these parts. Spoke there any man
to him, with the homely Arabian grace *ya Saîd !* he affecting
not to look again, seemed to stare in the air, casting eyes over
your head and making merchant's ears ; bye and bye to awaken,
with displeasure, after a mighty pause : when he questioned any
himself, he turned the back, and coldly averting his head he
feigned not to attend your answer. Saîd was but the ruler's
shadow in office for this good outlying village : his was the pro-
curation and espial of his master's high affairs ; but the town
government is, by the politic princely house of Shammar, left in
the hands of the natural sheykhs. Said dwelt in a great Teyma
house, next by the Haddàj : miserably he lived alone to himself
and unwived ; at evening he sparred the door, and as he went
not forth to his master's subjects, so he let in no coffee-fellowship.
The Prince's slave gentleman has a large allowance, so much
by the month, taken upon the tribute of the town : unlettered
himself, a son was here his clerk. Now he thought good to
see that Nasrâny come to town, who was dwelling he heard,
since the Haj, amongst the Beduw of Ibn Rashîd. Saîd, with
a distant look, now enquired of the company "Where is he?"
as if his two eyes had not met with mine already. After
he had asked such questions as "When came he hither?—
He is with thee, Zeyd?" he kept awful silence a set space ;
then he uttered a few words towards me and looked upon
the ground. "The Engleys, have they slaves in their country?"
I answered, "We purge the world of this cursed traffic, our ships
overrun the slave vessels in all seas; what blacks we find in
them we set free, sending them home, or we give them land and
palms in a country of ours. As for the slave shippers, we set
them upon the next land and let them learn to walk home ; we
sink their prize-craft, or burn them. We have also a treaty with
the Sûltàn : God made not a man to be sold like an head
of cattle. This is well, what thinkest thou?" The gross

negro lineaments of Saîd, in which yet appeared some token
of gentle Arabic blood, relented into a peaceful smiling, and
then he answered pleasantly, "It is very well." Now Saîd had
opened his mouth, his tongue began to wag: he told us he
had gone once (very likely with Nejd horses) as far as Egypt,
and there he had seen these Frenjies. So rising with lofty state,
and taking again his court countenance, he bade Zeyd bring
me presently, and come himself to his dàr, to drink coffee.
When we arrived thither, Saîd had doffed this mockery of
lordship, and sat but homely in old clothes in his own house.
He led me to the highest place; and there wanting leaning
pillows, he drew under my elbow his *shidàd* or thelûl saddle,
as is the usage in the nomad booths. These Beduin manners
are seen in the oases' coffee-halls, where (the Semites inventing
nothing of themselves) they have almost no other moveables.—
And seeing them in their clay halls in town and village one
might say, "Every Arab is a wayfaring man, and ready for the
journey." Saîd brought paper and ink, and a loose volume or
two, which were all his books; he would see me write. So I
wrote his name and quality, *Saîd Zèlamat Ibn Rashîd;* and the
great man, smiling, knew the letters which should be the signs
of his own name. So when we had drunk coffee, he led me out
beyond his yard to a great building, in stone, of ancient Teyma,
hoping I might interpret for him an antique inscription ; which
he showed me in the jamb of the doorway, made (and the beams
likewise, such as we have seen in the basaltic Hauran) of great
balks of sandstone. These strange characters, like nothing I
had seen before, were in the midst obliterated by a later cross-
mark. Saîd's thought was that this might be the token of an
hid treasure ; and he told us "one such had been raised at
Feyd,"—a village betwixt Shammar and Kasîm.—Is not this a
mad opinion ? that the ancients, burying treasure, should have
set up a guidestone and written upon it ! Returning, I found
in the street wall near his door, an inscription stone with
four lines sharply engraved of the same strange antique Teyma
writing.

Zeyd went out to buy his provision, and no one molesting
me, I walked on through the place and stayed to consider their
great well-pit, El-Haddàj ; a work of the ancients which is in
the midst of the new Teyma. That pit is unequally four-sided,
some fifty feet over, and to the water are seven fathoms. The
Haddàj is as a great heart of Teyma, her many waters, led outward to all sides in little channels, making green the whole
oasis ; other well-pits there are only in the outlying hamlets.
The shrill draw-wheel frames, *suàny* are sixty, set up all round,

commonly by twos and threes mounted together; they are
seldom seen all in working together   The well-camels walking
downwards from the four sides of the pit, draw by their weight
each one a vast horn-shaped camel-leather bucket, *dullû* : the
lower neck is an open mouth, which, rising in the well, is sustained by a string, but come to the brink, and passing over a
roller the dullû belly is drawn highest, whilst the string is
slackened, and the neck falling forward, pours forth a roaring
cataract of water   Afterward, I saw the like in India.   The
shrieking suâny and noise of tumbling water is, as it were, the
lamentable voice of the rainless land in all Nejd villages.   Day
and night this labour of the water may not be intermitted.
The strength ot oxen cannot profitably draw wells of above
three or four fathoms and, if God had not made the camel,
Nejd, they say, had been without inhabitant.   Their Haddàj
is so called, they told me, " for the plenty of waters," which
bluish-reeking are seen in the pit's depth, welling strongly from
the sand-rock : this vein they imagine to come from the Harra.

Returned to the coffee-hall I found only Sleymàn ; we sat
down and there timidly entered the wives and sisters of his
household.   The open-faced Teyma hareem are frank and
smiling with strangers, as I have not seen elsewhere in Arabia :
yet sometimes they seem bold-tongued, of too free manners,
without grace.   The simple blue smock of calico dipped in
indigo, the woman's garment in all the Arab countries, they
wear here with a large-made and flowing grace of their own ;
the sleeves are embroidered with needlework of red worsted,
and lozenges sewed upon them of red cotton.   The most have
bracelets, *hadŷd*, of beautiful great beads of unwrought amber,
brought, as they tell me, anciently from Hâyil.   The fairer of
them have pleasant looks, yet dull as it were and bovine for the
blindness of the soul ; their skin, as among the nomads, is early
withered ; spring-time and summer are short between the slender
novice and the homely woman of middle age.   Tamar's garment
of patches and party-colours was perchance of such sort as now
these Arabian women's worked gown.   His old loving father
made for little Joseph a motley coat ; and it may seem more
than likely, that the patriarch seamed it with his own hands.
Amongst the nomads men are hardly less ready-handed to cut,
and to stitch too, their tunics, than the hareem.   *Sleymàn :* "See
Khalîl I have this little sister here, a pretty one, and she shall
be thine, if thou wouldest be a wedded man, so thou wilt number
me the bride-money in my hand ; but well I warn thee it is not
small."   The bevy of hareem, standing to gaze upon a stranger,
now asked me, " Wherefore art thou come to Teyma? "—"It

were enough if only to see you my sisters." But when their tongues were loosed, and they spoke on with a kine-like stolidity, Sleymàn cried full of impatience, " Are your hareem, Khalîl, such dull cattle? Why dost thou trouble thyself to answer them? Hence, women, ye stay too long, away with you!" and they obeyed the beardless lad with a feminine submission ; for every Arab son and brother is a ruler over all woman-kind in the paternal household. This fresh and ruddy young man, more than any in the town, but not well minded, I found no more at my coming again : he lay some months already in an untimely grave! * * *

* * * Sultry seemed this stagnant air to us, come in from the high desert, we could not sleep in their clay houses. My thirst was inextinguishable ; and finding here the first clean water, after weeks of drought, I went on drinking till some said, " Khalîl is come to Teyma only to drink water ; will he drink up the Haddàj?" When Zeyd returned not yet, I went out to visit some great ancient ruin, *Kasr Zellûm,* named after a former possessor of the ground. A sturdy young half-blooded negro guided me, but whose ferocious looks by the way, brain-sick and often villanous behaviour, made me pensive : he was strong as a camel, and had brought a sword with him, I was infirm and came (for the heat) unarmed. We passed the outer walls, and when I found the place lay further in the desert, and by the eyes and unsettling looks of this ribald I might divine that his thought was in that solitary way to kill me, I made some delay ; I saw a poor man in a field, and said, I would go over to him, and drink a little water. It was a nomad, building up an orchard clay wall for the villager's hire, paid in pottles of dates. In this, there came to us from the town, a young man of a principal sheykhly family, *er-Romàn,* and another with him. They had been sent after me in haste by Zeyd, as he had news in what company I was gone :—and in a later dissension Zeyd said, "I saved thy life, Khalîl! rememberest thou not that day at Teyma, when the black fellow went out to murder thee?" I knew these young smilers, so not much trusting them, we walked on together. I must run this risk to-day, I might no more perhaps come to Teyma ; but all that I found for a weapon, a pen-knife, I held ready open under my mantle, that I might not perish like a slaughter-beast, if these should treacherously set upon me.

Kasr Zellûm I found to be a great four-square fort-like

building; it may be fifty or sixty paces upon a side. The walls
are five feet thick, in height fifteen feet, laid of dry masonry.
A part within is divided into chambers, the rest is yard, in the
midst they think a great well lies buried. The site of the kasr
is a little below those great town walls of ancient Teyma,
which are seen as sand-banks, riding upon the plain ; the head
of the masonry only appearing. In the midst of the kasr wall,
I found another inscription stone, laid sideways, in that strange
Teyma character ; and above the writing, are portrayed human
eyes.—We read that the augurs of the antique Arabs scored
two lines as eyes, the wise men naming them their ",children of
vision." At the rendering of Teyma to Abeyd Ibn Rashîd, he
left this injunction with the Teyâmena, " Ye are not to build
up to the walls of that kasr ! " * * *

* * * At evening we were gathered a great coffee company
at our host's fire, and some beginning their talk of the Christian
religion, were offended that " the Nasâra worship idols, and this
not only, but that they blaspheme the apostle." Also they
said, " It is a people that know no kind of lawful wedlock, but
as beasts, they follow their natural affection ; the lights
quenched in their religious assemblies, there is a cursed meddling among them in strange and horrible manner, the son it
may be lying in savage blindness with his own mother, in
manner, wellah, as the hounds :—in such wise be gotten the
cursed generation of Nasrânies, that very God confound them !
(the speaker dared to add) and this Nasrâny I durst say cannot
know his own father. Besides, they have other heathenish
customs among them, as when a Christian woman dies to bury
her living husband along with her." Almost the like con-
tumelies are forged by the malicious Christian sects, of the
Druses their neighbours in the mountain villages of Syria.
" Friends, I answered, these are fables of a land far off, and old
wives' malice of things unknown ; but listen and I will tell you
the sooth in all." A Fejîry Beduin here exclaimed, " Life of
this fire ! Khalîl lies not; wellah even though he be a Nasrâny,
he speaks the truth in all among the Aarab; there could no
Musslim be more true spoken. Hear him !—and say on,
Khalîl."—" This is the law of marriage given by God in the
holy religion of the *Messîah*, ' the son of Miriam from the Spirit
of Ullah,'—it is thus spoken of him in your own Scriptures."—
" *Sully Ullah aley-hu* (they all answered), whom the Lord
bless, the Lord's grace be with him," breathing the accustomed

benediction as the name is uttered in their hearing of a greater prophet.—" As God gave to Adam *Hawwa*, one woman, so is the Christian man espoused to one wife. It is a bond of religion until the dying of either of them ; it is a faithful fellowship in sickness, in health, in the felicity and in the calamity of the world, and whether she bear children or is barren : and that may never be broken, saving by cause of adultery."—" But, said they, the woman is sooner old than her husband ; if one may not go from his wife past age to wed another, your law is not just." One said, laughing, " Khalîl, we have a better religion, thy rule were too strait for us ; I myself have wedded one with another wives fifteen. What say you, companions ? in the hareem are many crooked conditions ? I took some, I put away some, ay billah ! until I found some with whom I might live." * * *

* * * Nejd Beduins are more fanatic, in the magnanimous ignorance of their wild heads, but with all this less dangerous than the village inhabitants, soberly instructed and settled in their koran reading. There was a scowling fellow at my elbow who had murmured all the evening ; now as I rested he said, ' I was like a fiend in the land, akhs ! a Yahûdy ! ' As I turned from him, neighbours bade me not to mind this despiteful tongue, saying " Khalîl, it is only a Beduwy." The poor man, who was of Bishr, abashed to be named Beduwy among them in the town, cast down his eyes and kept silence. One whispered to Zeyd, " If anything happen to him have you not to answer to the Dowla ? he might die among you of some disease." But Zeyd answered with a magnanimity in his great tones, " *Henna mà na sadikîn billah*, Are we not confiding in God ! "—The company rose little before midnight, and left us to lie down in our mantles, on the coffee-house floor. Sleymàn said a last petulant word, ' How could I, a civil man, wander with the wild Beduw that were melaun el-weyladeyn, of cursed kind ? '

It was not long before we heard one feeling by the walls. Zeyd cried, " Who is there ? " and sat up leaning on his elbow in the feeble moonlight. " Rise, Zeyd, (said an old wife's voice,) I come from Hirfa, the Aarab are about removing." Zeyd answered, wearily stretching himself, " A punishment fall upon them : '—we must needs then march all this night. As we stood up we were ready ; there is no superstitious leave-taking among them ; and we stepped through our host Sleymàn's dark gate into the street, never to meet with him again, and came at the end of the walled ways to the Beduins, who were already loading in the dark. Zeyd, reproving their changeable humour, asked a reason of this untimely wandering; "We would not, they answered, be longer guests, to eat the bread of the Teyâmena." They being all poor folk, had seen perhaps but cold hospitality.

We held south, and rode soon by some ruins, "of ancient Teyma, (they told me) and old wells there." They alighted near dawn; discharging the beasts, we made fires, and lay down to slumber awhile. Remounting from thence, after few miles, we passed some appearance of ruins, *Burjesba*, having upon the south a mountain, *J. Jerbûa*. At the mid-afternoon we met with our tribesmen marching; they had removed twice in our absence: the Aarab halted to encamp few miles further. As said, this year was big with troubles, the Fukara were now fugitives. The Beny Wáhab, as borderers, having least profit of Ibn Rashîd's government, are not cheerful payers of his *zikâ*. The Fejîr had withheld the light tax, five years, until the Emir, returning last summer with his booty of the W. Aly, visited them in the wilderness, and exacted his arrears, only leaving them their own, because they had submitted themselves. The Fukara were not yet in open enmity with the Wélad Aly, as the Prince had prescribed to them, only they were "not well" together; but our Fejîr were daily more in mistrust of the terrible Emir. Every hour they thought they saw his riders upon them, and the menzil taken. They would go therefore from their own wandering ground, and pass from his sight into the next Bishr dîra.

CHAPTER VIII

IN this menzil, because the people must march from the morrow, the booths were struck and their baggage had been made up before they slept. The Beduin families lay abroad under the stars, beside their household stuff and the unshapely full sweating water-skins. The night was cold, at an altitude of 3600 feet. I saw the nomads stretched upon the sand, wrapped in their mantles : a few have sleeping carpets, *ekîm*, under them, made of black worsted stuff like their tent-cloth, but of the finer yarn and better weaving, adorned with a border of chequerwork of white and coloured wool and fringes gaily dyed. The ekîms of Teyma have a name in this country.

It was chill under the stars at this season, marching before the sun in the open wilderness. The children of the poor have not a mantle, only a cotton smock covers their tender bodies ; some babes are even seen naked. I found 48° F., and when the sun was fairly up 86°. It was a forced march ; the flocks and the herds, *et-tursh*, were driven forth beside us. At a need the Beduw spare not the cattle which are all their wealth, but think they do well to save themselves and their substance, even were it with the marring of some of them ; their camel kine great with young were now daily calving. The new-yeaned lambs and kids, the tottering camel-calf of less than five days old, little whelps, which they would rear, of the hounds of the encampment, are laid by the housewives, with their own children, upon the burden camels. Each mother is seen riding upon a camel in the midst of the roll of her tent-cloth or carpet, in the folds lie nested also the young animals ; she holds her little children before her. Small children, the aged, the sick, and even bed rid folk, carried long hours, show no great signs of weariness in camel-riding. Their suffering persons ride seated in a nest of tent-cloth ; others, who have been herdsmen, kneel or lie along, not fearing to fall, and seem to repose thus

upon the rolling camel's bare back. It is a custom of the desert
to travel fasting: however long be the ráhla, the Aarab eat only
when they have alighted at the menzil; yet mothers will give
their children to drink, or a morsel in their mouths, by the long
way.

Journeying in this tedious heat, we saw first, in the afternoon
horizon, the high solitary sandstone mountain J. Birrd. "Yonder thulla," cried my neighbours in their laughing *argot*, "is the
sheykh of our dîra." Birrd has a height of nearly 5000 feet.
At the right hand there stretches a line of acacia trees in the
wilderness plain, the token of a dry seyl bed, *Gô*, which descends,
they said, from a day westward of Kheybar, and ends here in
the desert. In all this high country, between Teyma and
Tebûk and Medáin Sâlih, there are no wadies. The little latter
rain that may fall in the year is but sprinkled in the sand.
Still journeying, this March sun which had seen our ráhla,
rising, set behind us in a stupendous pavilion of Oriental glories,
which is not seldom in these Arabian waste marches, where the
atmosphere is never quite unclouded. We saw again the cold
starlight before the fainting households alighted under Birrd
till the morrow, when they would remove anew; the weary
hareem making only a shelter from the night wind of the tent-
cloths spread upon two stakes. It was in vain to seek milk of
the over-driven cattle with dry udders. This day the nomad
village was removed at once more than forty miles. In common times these wandering graziers take their menzils and
dismiss the cattle to pasture, before high noon.—Hastily, as we
saw the new day, we removed, and pitched few miles beyond
in the Bishr dîra; from hence they reckoned three journeys
to Hâyil, the like from Dàr el-Hamra, a day and a-half to Teyma.

A poor woman came weeping to my tent, entreating me to
see and divine in my books what were become of her child.
The little bare-foot boy was with the sheep, and had been missing after yesterday's long ráhla. The mother was hardly to be
persuaded, in her grief, that my books were not cabalistical.
I could not persuade the dreary indifference of the Arabs in her
menzil to send back some of them, besides the child's father,
to seek him: of their own motion they know not any such
charity. If the camel of some poor widow woman be strayed,
there is no man will ride upon the traces for human kindness,
unless she can pay a real. The little herd-boy was found in
the end of the encampment, where first he had lighted upon a
kinsman's tent.

We removed from thence a little within the high white
borders of the Nefûd, marching through a sand country full of

last year's plants of the "rose of Jericho". These Beduw call them *ch(k)ef Marhab*. *Kef* is the hollow palm, with the fingers clenching upon it. Marhab is in their tradition sheykh of old Jewish Kheybar. We found also the young herb, two velvet green leaves, which has the wholesome smack of cresses, and is good for the nomad cattle. The Aarab alighted afterward in the camping ground *Ghrormùl el-Mosubba;* known from far by the landmark of a singular tower-like needle of sandstone, sixty feet high, the *Towîlan.* The third day we removed from thence, with mist and chill wind blowing, to *J. Chebàd :* from Chebàd we went to the rugged district *el-Jebâl.* After another journey, we came to pitch before the great sandstone mountain chine of Irnàn, in Nejd. Beyond this we advanced south-eastward to the rugged coast of *Ybba Moghrair;* the Beduins, removing every second or third day, journeyed seven or eight miles and alighted. I saw about el-Jebâl other circles of rude flag-stones, set edgewise, as those of Jerèyda. In another place certain two cornered wall-enclosures, of few loose courses; they were made upon low rising grounds, and I thought might have been a sort of breastworks; the nomads could give me no account of them, as of things before their time and tradition. East of Ybba Moghrair, we passed the foot of a little antique rude turret in the desert soil. I showed it to some riding next me in the ráhla. "Works (they answered) remaining from the creation of the world; what profit is there to enquire of them?" "But all such to be nothing (said Zeyd) in comparison with that he would show me on the morrow, which was a marvel: the effigy of *Abu Zeyd*, a fabulous heroic personage, and dame *Alîa* his wife, portrayed upon some cliff of yonder mountain Ybba Moghrair."

Wandering in all the waste Arabia, we often see rude trivet stones set by threes together: such are of old nomad pot-fires; and it is a comfortable human token, that some have found to cheer themselves, before us, in land where man's life seems nearly cast away, but at what time is uncertain; for stones, as they were pitched in that forsaken drought, may so continue for ages. The harder and gravel wilderness is seen cross-lined everywhere with old trodden camel paths; these are also from the old generations, and there is not any place of the immense waste, which is not at some time visited in the Aarab's wanderings; and yet whilst we pass, no other life, it may be, is in the compass of a hundred miles about us. There is almost no parcel of soil where fuel may not be found, of old camel dung, *jella,* bleaching in the sun; it may lie three years, and a little sand blown upon it, sometime longer. There is another human sign

in the wilderness, which mothers look upon; we see almost in
every new ráhla, little ovals of stones, which mark the untimely
died of the nomads: but grown persons dying in their own dîras,
are borne (if it be not too difficult) to the next common burying
place.

On the morrow betimes, Zeyd took his mare and his lance,
and we set out to visit Abu Zeyd's image, the wonder of this
desert. We crossed the sand plain, till the noon was hot over
us; and come to the mountain, we rounded it some while in
vain : Zeyd could not find the place. White stains, like sea-
marks, are seen upon certain of those desolate cliffs, they are
roosting-places of birds of prey, falcons, buzzards and owls:
their great nests of sticks are often seen in wild crags of these
sandstone marches. In the waterless soil live many small animals which drink not, as rats and lizards and hares. We heard
scritching owls sometimes in the still night; then the nomad
wives and children answered them with mocking again *Ymgebâs!*
Ymgebâs ! The hareem said, " It is a wailful woman, seeking
her lost child through the wilderness, which was turned into this
forlorn bird." Fehjies eat the owl ; for which they are laughed
to scorn by the Beduw, that are devourers of some other vermin.
We went upon those mountain sides until we were weary.
A sheykh's son, a coffee companion from his youth, and here in
another dîra, Zeyd could not remember his landmarks. It was
high noon ; we wandered at random, and, for hunger and thirst,
plucking wild dandelions sprung since some showers in those
rocks, we began to break our fast. At length, looking down at
a deep place, we espied camels, which went pasturing under the
mountain: there we found Fehját herdsmen. The images, they
said, were not far before us, they would put us in the way, but
first they bade us sit down to refresh ourselves. The poor men
then ran for us under the nâgas' udders, and drew their milk-
skin full of that warm sustenance.—Heaven remember for good
the poor charitable nomads ! When we had drunk they came
along with us, driving the cattle : a little strait opened further,
it was a long inlet in the mountain bosom, teeming green
with incomparable freshness, to our sense, of rank herbage. At
the head of this garden of weeds is an oozy slumbering pool ;
and thereabove I perceived the rocks to be full of scored inscriptions, and Abu Zeyd's yard-high image, having in his hand the
crooked camel stick, bakhorra, or, as the Aarab say, who cannot
judge of portraiture, a sword ; beside him, is a lesser, perhaps
a female figure, which they call " Alîa his wife ". It is likely
that these old lively shapes were battered, with a stone, upon

the sandstone; they are not as the squalid scrawling portraiture of the Beduw, but limned roundly to the natural with the antique diligence. Here are mostly short Himyaric legends, written (as is common in these deserts) from above downwards; the names, the saws, the salaams, of many passengers and cameleers of the antique generations. *Ybba*, is said for *Abu*, father, in these parts of Arabia, and at Medina; *Moghrair*, is perhaps cave. I bade Zeyd let me have a milch nâga and abandon me here with Abu Zeyd. Zeyd answered (with a fable), he had already paid a camel to Bishr, for license to show me their Abu Zeyd. The Fehját answered simply, " A man might not dwell here alone, in the night time, the demons would affray him."

As we came again, Zeyd lighted upon a natural sanded basin among the rocks, under the mountain, and there sounding with his hands to the elbow, he reached to a little stinking moisture. Zeyd smiled vaingloriously, and cried, ' Ha! we had discovered a new water. Wellah, here is water a little under the mire, the hind shall come hither to morrow and fill our girbies.' Thereby grew a nightshade weed, now in the berry; the Beduin man had not seen the like before, and bade me bear it home to the menzil, to be conned by the hareem:—none of whom, for all their wise looking, knew it. " A stranger plant (said they) in this dîra:" it is housewifely amongst them to be esteemed cunning in drugs and simples. Lower, we came to a small pool in the rock; the water showed ruddy-brown and ammoniacal, the going down was stained with old filth of camels. " Ay (he said) of this water would we draw for our coffee, were there none other." Upon the stone I saw other Himyaric legends. And here sat two young shepherd lasses; they seeing men approach, had left playing, their little flock wandered near them. Zeyd, a great sheykh, hailed them with the hilarity of the desert, and the ragged maidens answered him in mirth again: they fear none of their tribesmen, and herding maidens may go alone with the flocks far out of seeing of the menzil in the empty wilderness. We looked up and down, but could not espy Zeyd's mare, which, entering the mountain, he had left bound below, the headstall tied back, by the halter, to an hind limb in the nomad manner. Thus, making a leg at every pace, the Beduin mare may graze at large; but cannot wander wide. At length, from a high place, we had sight of her, returning upon her traces to the distant camp. " She is thirsty (said Zeyd), let her alone and she will find the way home:"—although the black booths were yet under our horizon. So the nomad horses come again of them-selves, and seek their own households, when they would drink water. Daily, when the sun is well risen, the Beduin mare is hop-shackled with iron links which are opened with a key, and loosed out to feed from her master's tent. The horses wander, seeking each other, if the menzils be not wide scattered, and go on pasturing and sporting together: their sheykhly masters take no more heed of them than of the hounds of the encampment, until high noon, when the mares, returning homeward of themselves, are led in to water. They will go then anew to pasture, or stand shadowing out that hot hour in the master's booth (if it be a great one). They are grazing not far off till the sun is setting, when they draw to their menzils, or are fetched home and tethered for the night.

There hopped before our feet, as we came, a minute brood of second locusts, of a leaden colour, with budding wings like the spring leaves, and born of those gay swarms which, a few weeks before, had passed over and despoiled the desert. After forty days these also would fly as a pestilence, yet more hungry than the former, and fill the atmosphere. We saw a dark sky over the black nomad tents, and I showed Zeyd a shower falling before the westing sun.—" Would God, he answered, it might reach us ! " Their cattle's life in this languishing soil is of a very little rain. The Arabian sky, seldom clear, weeps as the weeping of hypocrites.

We removed from hence, and pitched the black booths upon that bleakness of white sand which is, here, the Nefûd, whose edge shows all along upon the brown sandstone desert : a seyl bed, *Terrai*, sharply divides them. The Aarab would next remove to a good well, *el-Hyza*, in the Nefûd country, where in good years they find the spring of new pasture : but there being little to see upon this border, we returned another day towards the *Helwàn* mountain ; in which march I saw other (eight or nine yards large) circles of sandstone flags. Dreary was this Arabian ráhla ; from the March skies there soon fell a tempest of cold rain, and, alighting quickly, the Beduin women had hardly breath in the whirling shower to build their booths :—a héjra may be put up in three minutes. In the tents, we sat out the stormy hours upon the moist sand in our stiffened wet mantles ; and the windy drops fell through the ragged tilt upon us. In the Nefûd, towards el-Hŷza, are certain booming sand hills, *Rowsa, Deffafîat, Subbîa* and *Irzûm*, such as the sand drift of *J. Nagûs*, by the sea village of *Tor*, in Sinai : the upper sand sliding down under the foot of the passenger, there arises, of the infinite fretting grains, such a giddy loud swelling sound, as when your wetted finger is drawn about the lip of a glass of water, and like that swooning din after the chime of a great

bell, or cup of metal.—*Nagûs* is the name of the sounding-board
in the belfry of the Greek monastery, whereupon as the sacristan
plays with his hammer, the timber yields a pleasant musical
note, which calls forth the formal *colieros* to their prayers:
another such singing sand drift, *el-Howayria*, is in the cliffs
(east of the Mezham,) of Medáin Sâlih

The afternoon was clear ; the sun dried our wet clothing, and
a great coffee party assembled at Zeyd's tent.   He had promised
Khalîl would make *chai* (tea), "which is the coffee-drink, he
told them, of the Nasâra.—And, good Khalîl, since the sheykhs
would taste thy chai, look thou put in much sugar "   I had to-
day pure water of the rain in the desert, and that tea was
excellent.   Zeyd cried to them, "And how liketh you the
kahwat of the Nasâra ? "   They answered, "The sugar is good,
but as for this which Khalîl calls *chai*, the smack of it is little
better than warm water "   They would say "Thin drink, and
not gross tasting " as is their foul-water coffee.   Rahŷel drank
his first cup out, and returned it mouth downward (a token
with them that he would no more of it), saying, "Khalîl is not
this *el-khamr ? the fermented* or wine of the Nasâra : " and for
conscience sake he would not drink , but the company sipped
their sugar-drink to the dregs, and bade the stranger pour out
more.   I called to Rahŷel's remembrance the Persians drinking
chai in the Haj caravan.   Beduins who tasted tea the second
time, seeing how highly I esteemed it, and feeling themselves
refreshed, afterward desired it extremely, imagining this drink
with sugar to be the comfort of all human infirmities.   But I
could never have, for my asking, a cup of their fresh milk ; they
put none in their coffee, and to put whole milk to this *kahwat
en-Nasâra* seemed to them a very outlandish and waste using of
God's benefit.   When I made tea at home, I called in Hirfa to
drink the first cup, saying to the Beduins that this was our
country manner, where the weaker sex was honourably regarded.
Hirfa answered, "Ah ! that we might be there among you !
Khalîl, these Beduw here are good for nothing, billah, they are
wild beasts ; to-day they beat and to-morrow they abandon the
hareem : the woman is born to labour and suffering, and in the
sorrow of her heart, it nothing avails that she can speak."
The men sitting at the hearths laughed when Hirfa preached.
She cried peevishly again, "Yes, laugh loud ye wild beasts !—
Khalîl, the Beduw are heathens ! " and the not happy young
wife smiled closely to the company, and sadly to herself again.

Evening clouds gathered ; the sheykhs going homewards had
wet mantles.   The mare returned of herself through the falling
weather, and came and stood at our coffee fire, in half human

wise, to dry her soaked skin and warm herself, as one among us.
It may be said of the weak nomad horses, that they have no gall.
I have seen a mare, stabling herself in the mid-day shadow of
the master's booth, that approached the sitters about the coffee
hearth and putting down her soft nose the next turned their
heads to kiss her, till the sheykh rose to scold his mare away.
They are feeble, of the slender and harsh desert forage ; and
gentle to that hand of man, which is as the mother's teat to them
in the wilderness. Wild and dizzy camels are daily seen, but
seldom impetuous horses, and perverse never : the most are of
the bay colour. The sheykh's hope is in his mare to bear him
with advantage upon his enemy, or to save him hastily from the
field ; it is upon her back he may best take a spoil and outride
all who are mounted upon thelûls. Nor she (nor any life, of
man or beast, besides the hounds) is ever mishandled amongst
them. The mare is not cherished by the master's household,
yet her natural dwelling is at the mild nomad tent. She is allied
to the beneficent companionship of man ; his shape is pleasant
to her in the inhospitable khála. The mildness of the Arab's
home is that published by their prophet of the divine household ;
mild-hearted is the koran Ullah, a sovereign Semitic house-
father, how indulgent to his people ! The same is an adversary,
cruel and hard, to an alien people.

The nomad horse we see here shod as in Syria with a plate
open in the midst, which is the Turkish manner ; these sheukh
purchase their yearly provision of horse-shoes in the Haj market.
I have seen the nomads' horses shod even in the sand country
of Arabia : yet upon the Syrian borders a few are left without
shoes, and some are seen only hind-shod. The sâny who followed our tribe—he was accounted the best smith, in all work
of iron, of that country side, not excepted Teyma—was their
farrier. One day I went with Zeyd to see his work. We found
the man of metal firing Rahyel's mare, which had a drawn hind
leg, and as they are ready-handed with a few tools he did it
with his ramrod of iron ; the end being made red-hot in the fire,
he sealed and seared the infirm muscles. I saw the suffering
creature without voice, standing upon three legs, for the fourth
was heaved by a cord in stiff hands. The Beduw, using to fire
their camels' bodies up and down, make not much more account
of the mare's skin, how whole it be or branded. They look only
that she be of the blood, a good breeder, and able to serve her
master in warfare. Rahýel quitted the sâny's hire ; Zeyd, who
waited for the ends of the smith's labour, had brought his hands
full of old horse-shoes, and bade him beat them into nails,
against his mare should be shod. Zeyd went to pull dry sticks,

kindled a bonfire, and when it had burned awhile he quenched
all with sand ; and taking up the weak charcoal in his mantle,
he went to lay it upon the forge fire (a hearth-pit in the sand).
Then this great sheykh sat down himself to the pair of goat-skin
bellows, and blew the sâny a blast. It was a mirth to see how
Zeyd, to save his penny, could play the Solubby, and such he
seemed sweating between two fires of the hot coals and the
scalding sun at high noon, till the hunger-bitten chaps were
begrimed of his black and, in fatigue, hard-favoured visage.
Finally, rising with a sigh, " Khalîl, he said, art thou not weary
sitting abroad in the sun ? yonder is Rahŷel's booth, let us enter
in the shadow ; he is a good man, and will make us coffee."
Thus even the Beduins are impatient of the Arabian sun's
beating upon their pates, unless in the râhla, that is, when the
air about them is moving.—" Peace be with thee, Rahŷel, I
bring Khalîl ; sit thee down by me, Khalîl, and let us see thee
write Rahyel's name ; write ' Rahŷel el-Fejîry, the sheykh, he
that wedded the bint at Teyma ':" they kneeled about me with
the pleased conceit of unlettered mortals, to see their fugitive
words detained and laid up in writing.

There arrived at our camp some Beduin traders, come over
the Nefûd from Jauf : they were of Bishr. And there are such
in the tribes, prudent poor men, that would add to their livelihood by the peaceable and lawful gain of merchandise, rather
than by riding upon ungodly and uncertain ghrazzus. The men
brought down samn and tobacco, which they offered at two-
thirds of the price which was now paid in these sterile regions.
Yet the Aarab, iniquitous in all bargains, would hardly purchase
of them at so honest and easy a rate ; they would higgle-haggle
for a little lower, and finally bought not at all ;—sooner than
those strangers should win, they would pay double the money
later at el-Ally ! and they can wait wretchedly thus, as the dead,
whilst a time passes over them. A little more of government,
and men such as these traders would leave the insecure
wandering life, (which all the Aarab, for the incessant weariness
and their very emptiness of heart, have partly in aversio ,) to
become settlers. Beduins complain in their long hours of the
wretchedness of their lives ; and they seem then wonderfully
pensive, as men disinherited of the world. Human necessitous
malice has added this to the affliction of nature, that there
should be no sure passage in Arabia : and when there is dearth
in any dîra, because no autumn rain has fallen there, or their hope
was devoured by the locusts, the land traffic may hardly reach
them.

The destitute Beduw, in their idle tents, are full of musing melancholy; if any blame them they answer in this pensive humour: " Aha, truly the Aarab are *baháim*, brute beasts; *mesakín*, mesquins; *kutaat ghranem*, *dubbush*, a drove of silly sheep, a mixed herd of small cattle; *juhál*, ignorant wretches; *mejanín*, lunatic folk; *affinín*, corrupt to rottenness; *haramíyeh*, law-breakers, thieves; *kuffár*, heathen men; *míthil es-seyd*, like as the fallow beasts, scatterlings in the wilderness, and not having human understanding." And when they have said all, they will add, for despite, of themselves, *wellah, el-Aarab kîlâb*, "and the nomads are hounds, God knoweth." But some will make a beggarly vaunt of themselves, "the Aarab are jinnies and sheyatîn," that is witty fiends to do a thing hardily and endure the worst, without fear of God. Between this sorry idleness in the menzils and their wandering fatigue they all dote, men and women, upon *tittun*, tobacco. The dry leaf (which they draw from el-Ally and Teyma) is green, whether, as they say, because this country is dewless, or the Arabian villagers have not learned to prepare it. They smoke the green dried leaf, rubbed between the palms from the hard stalks, with a coal burning upon it. I have seen this kind as far as the borders of Syria, where the best is from Shobek and J. Kerak, it is bitter tasting; the sweetest in this country is that raised by Beduin husbandmen of the Moahîb, in *Wady Aurush* upon the sea side of the *Aueyrid* Harra, over against el-Héjr.

Our wandering village maintained a tobacco seller, an Ally villager, who lived amongst them in nomad wise in the desert, and was wedded with a tribeswoman of theirs. The man had gathered a little stock, and was thriving in this base and extortionate traffic. It irked the lean Beduin souls to see the parasite grow fat of that which he licked vilely from their beards. Seeing him merry they felt themselves sad, and for a thing too which lay upon their consciences. The fault bewitched them; also they could not forbid a neighbour the face of the free desert. Thus the bread of the poor, who before had not half enough, was turned to ashes. He let them have here for twelve pence only so much as was two penny-worth at el-Ally; the poor soul who brought him a kid in payment, to-day, that would be valued before the year was out at two crowns, comforted himself with his pipe seven days for this loss of a head of cattle, having a half groat to "drink" of the villager's tobacco, or rather the half of two pence, for, wetting the leaves, that malicious Alowwy had devised to make the half part fill his pint measure. After the men, I saw poor tobacco-sick hareem come clamouring to his tent, and holding in their weak

F

hands bottoms of their spun wool and pints of samn which they
have spared perhaps to buy some poor clothing, but now they
cannot forbear to spend and 'drink' smoke: or else having
naught, they borrow of him, with thanksgiving, at an excessive
usury. And if the extortioner will not trust one, she pitifully
entreats him, that only this once, he would fill her cold galliûn,
and say not nay, for old kindness sake. Zeyd though so principal a sheykh, would buy no tobacco himself, but begged all
day, were it even of the poorest person in a coffee company:
then looking lovely he would cry, *min y'ámir-ly,* "Who (is
he the friend) will replenish (this sebîl) for my sake?" For
faintness of mind in this deadly soil they are all parasites
and live basely one upon another: Beduins will abjectly beg
tobacco even of their poor tribeswomen. Zeyd came one day
into the mejlis complaining of the price of tittun, and though it
cost him little or naught; and sitting down he detested, with
an embittered roughness in his superhuman comely voice, all the
father s kin of Alowna. "Ullah! (he cried) curse this Sleymàn
the tittun-seller! I think verily he will leave this people ere-
long not even their camels!" Tobacco is this world's bliss of
many in the idle desert, against whom the verses of a Beduin
maker are currently recited in all their tribes: "For three
things a man should not 'drink' smoke: is not he a sot that
will burn his own fingers (in taking up a coal from the hearth
to lay it in his pipe-head), and he that willingly wasteth his
substance (spending for that which is not bread), and withal he
doth it ungodly."

The Fejîr wandered in the strange Bishr marches not without apprehension and some alarms,—then the sheykhs pricked
forth upon their mares, and the most morrows, they rode out
two hours to convoy the pasturing great cattle of the tribe,
el-'bil. The first locusts had devoured the rabîa before us;
there was now scarcity, and our Beduins must divide themselves into two camps. Motlog removed with his part, in which
were the most sheykhs, making half a journey from us to the
westward. Zeyd remained with his fellow Rahÿel, who had the
sheykh's charge in this other part. We marched and encamped
divided, for many days, in before determined and equal manner.

I saw often the *samhh* plant growing, but not abundantly;
now a leafless green wort, a hand high, with fleshy stems and
branches full of brine, like samphire. At each finger end is an
eye, where, the plant drying up in the early summer, a grain is
ripened. In the Sherarát country, where the samhh grows
more plentifully, their housewives and children gather in this

wild harvest. The dry stalks are steeped in water, they beat out the seed with rods ; and of this small grain their hareem grind flour for the daily mess. I had eaten of this wild-bread at Maan ; it was black and bitter, but afterward I thought it sweet-meat, in the further desert of Arabia. The samhh porridge is good, and the taste " as camel milk " : but the best is of the flour, kneaded with dates and a little samn, to be eaten raw : —a very pleasant and wholesome diet for travellers, who in many open passages durst not kindle fire.

Now I was free of the Beduins' camp, and welcomed at all coffee hearths ; only a few minds were hostile still, of more fanatical tribesmen. Often, where I passed, a householder called me in from his booth, and when I sat down, with smiles of a gentle host, he brought forth dates and léban : this is ' the bread and salt,' which a good man will offer once, and confirm fellowship with the stranger. The Aarab, although they pardoned my person, yet thought me to blame for my religion. There happened another day a thing which, since they put all to the hand of Ullah, might seem to them some token of a Providence which cared for me. Weary, alighting from the ráhla in blustering weather, I cast my mantle upon the next bush, and sat down upon it. In the same place I raised my tent and remained sheltered till evening, when the cripple child of our menzil came to me upon all fours for his dole of a handful of dates, but at my little tent door he shrieked and recoiled hastily. He had seen shining folds of a venomous serpent, under the bush,—so they will lie close in windy weather. At his cry Zeyd's shepherd caught a stake from the next beyt, and running to, with a sturdy stroke he beat in pieces the poisonous vermin The viper was horned, more than two feet long, the body swollen in front, with brassy speckled scales, and a broad white belly, ending in a whip-like tail. A herdsman had been bitten, last year, by one of this kind in a ráhla ; they laid him upon a camel, but he died, with anguish and swelling, before the people were come to the menzil. A camel stung " will die in an hour ", and the humour in so desiccated a soil must be very virulent, yet such accidents are seldom in the nomad life. I had certainly passed many times over the adder, the Beduwy bore it away upon a stick, to make some " salve very good for the camels ". We had killed such an adder at Medáin. Haj Nejm was with us ; they called it *umm-jeneyb*, ' that moves upon her side.' The lad Mohammed divided the head with a cutlass stroke, as she lay sleeping deafly in the sand against the sun, in many S-shaped boughts : the old Moor would have her horns. " Wot ye, in the left horn

lies the venom, and the antidote is in her other, if it be
drunken with milk :—or said I amiss! let me think in which
of them—: well lads let her be, for I have not this thing certainly in mind." There is a horned adder in the deserts of
Barbary. This tale was told immediately in the nomad camp,
'the Nasrâny escaped from the poisonous serpent,' and some
asked me in the mejlis, How " saw " I the adventure? Zeyd
answered them, " It was God's mercy indeed." There was
sitting by our fire a rude herding-lad, a stranger of Ruwàlla,
one of those poor young men of the tribes, who will seek
service abroad, that is with other Beduins: for they think, in
every other dîra may be better life, and they would see the
world. " Auh! said he, had she bitten thee, Khalîl, thou
shouldst never have seen thy mother again." ' The guilty
overtaken from Heaven upon a day,' such is the superstition
of mankind; and in such case the Beduins would have said,
" Of a truth he was God's adversary, the event has declared it."

Surely these pastoral people are the least ingenious of all
mankind; is any man or beast bitten, they know nothing better
than to " read " over him (el-kirreya). Some spells they have
learned to babble by heart, of words fetched out of the koran;
the power of " God's Word ", (which commandeth and it is
made,) they think, should be able to overcome the malignity of
venom. Some wiseacre " reader " may be found in nearly every
wandering village ; they are men commonly of an infirm understanding and no good conditions, superstitiously deceiving themselves and not unwilling to deceive others. The patient's friends
send for one, weeping, to be their helper ; and between his
breaths their " reader ' will spit upon the wound, and sprinkle a
little salt. The poor Beduins are good to each other, and there is
sometimes found one who will suck his friend's or a kinsman's
poisoned wound. Yet all availeth less, they think, than the
" Word of God ", were it rightly " read "; upon their part, the
desert " readers ", without letters, acknowledge themselves to be
unlearned. There is also many a bold spirit among the Aarab,
of men and women, that being hurt, snatching a brand from
the hearth, will sear his wounded flesh, till the fire be quenched
in the suffering fibre: and they can endure pain (necessitous
persons, whose livelihood is as a long punishment,) with constant fortitude.

The ligature is unknown to them, but I once found a
Solubby who had used it: when his wife had been bitten in the
shin by an adder, he hastily bound the leg above the knee,
and sucked the venom. A night and a day his wife lay
dead-like and blackened ; then she revived little and little, and

came to herself : the woman recovered, but was for a long while
after discoloured. Charity, that would suck the bite of a serpent,
must consider, is there no hurt in her own lips and mouth, for so
one might envenom himself. There came to me a man seeking
medicine, all whose lower lip to the chin was an open ulcer :
huskily he told me, (for the horrible virus corrupted his voice,)
that the mischief came to him after sucking a serpent-bite, a year
past. I said, I hoped to help him with medicines, and freely,
as his courage had deserved ; but the impatient wretch disdained a physician that could not cure him anon. I saw him
six months later at Teyma, when he said, " See thou ! I am
well again ; " all the flesh was now as jasper, where the wound
had been, which was healed in appearance. * * *

* * * One evening a man was led to me bleeding in the arm,
he had but now received a sword-cut of a Fehjy : they strove for
a goat, which each maintained to be his own. The poor Fehjy,
thinking himself falsely overborne, had pulled out his cutlass
and struck at the oppressor,—neighbours running in laid hands
upon them both. Zeyd murmured at our fire, "—That any
Fehjy should be an aggressor ! (The Fehját, born under a
lowly star, are of a certain base alloy, an abject kind amongst
the Aarab.) It was never seen before, that any Fehjy had lifted
his weapon against a Fejîry." That small kindred of Heteym
are their hereditary clients and dwellers in their menzils. The
Fukara sheykhs on the morrow, and Zeyd a chief one with
them, must judge between the men indifferently : and for aught
I have learned they amerced the Fejîry, condemning him to
pay certain small cattle ; for which, some time after, I found
him and his next kinsmen dwelling as exiles in another tribe.
Satisfaction may be yielded (and the same number will be
accepted) in any year to come, of the natural increase of his
stock, and the exiles reestablish themselves : for the malicious
subtlety of usury is foreign to the brotherly dealing of the
nomad tribesmen.
  Passengers in the land say proverbially of these poor Fehját,
" The Fehjies are always blithe." And what care should he
have who lives as the fowls of the air, almost not hoping to gain
or fearing to lose anything in the world : and commonly they
are full of light jesting humour, and merry as beggars. Their
father is that Marhab, say they, sheykh next after the
Mohammedan conquest of ancient Kheybar.—Are they then
the Yahûd Kheybar ? I have seen Doolan, the prowest and

the poorest of these Antarids, cast down a night and a day after his lips had uttered to us this magnanimous confession; as his grandsire Antara could proudly acknowledge his illiberal blood of the mother's side, and be a sad man afterward. Believing themselves such, they would sometime have the Nasrâny to be an ancient kinsman of theirs; and being accused for the name of my religion, this procured me the good will of such persons, which were themselves the thralls of an insane fortune. Sometimes they said I should take a wife of the fairest daughters amongst them; and Fehjiát (Heteym) were, I think, the only two well favoured forms of women in this great encampment. As I rode in the midst of a ráhla, the husband of one of them hailed me cheerfully—I had hardly seen them before —" Ho there, Khalîl!"—" *Weysh widdak ya zillamy*, O man, what is thy will?"—" I say, hast thou any liking to wed?— is not this (his wife) a fair woman?" And between their beggarly mirth and looking for gain, he cries in merry earnest, " Wellah, if this like you, I will let her go (saying the word of divorce); only Khalîl, thou wilt *súk* (drive up cattle, that is, pay over to me) five camels,"—which he swore fast he had given himself for her bride-money. Tall was this fair young wife and freshly clad as a beloved; her middle small girt with a gay scarlet lace : barefoot she went upon the waste sand with a beautiful erect confidence of the hinds, in their native wilderness. " And what (I asked) is thy mind, my sister?" She answered, " So thou wouldst receive me, Khalîl, I am willing."—Thus light are they in their marriages, and nearly all unhappy! I passed from them in silence at the pace of my thelûl. Another day, seeing her come to a circumcision festival, I saluted her by name, but for some laughing word maliciously reported, she showed me, with a wounded look, that I was fallen under her beautiful displeasure * * *

* * * Long were our sultry days since the tribe was divided, and without mejlis; yet the fewer neighbours were now more friendly drawn together. Zeyd was always at home, to his beyt resorted the sheukh companions, and he made them coffee. All cousins together, the host far from all jealousy, and Beduins fain to be merry, their often game was of the late passages betwixt Hirfa and Zeyd ; they twitted the young wife's demure ill humour. " Hirfa ho! Hirfa, sittest thou silent behind the curtain, and have not the hareem a tongue? Stand up there and let that little face of thine be seen above the cloth, and clear thyself, before the company. Hirfa! what is this we hear of thee, art thou still contrary to Zeyd? Didst thou not forsake

Zeyd? and leave Zeyd without an household? and must Khalîl bring thee home again? what hast thou to answer for thyself?" *Khâlaf Allayda:* "Say thy opinion, Khalîl, of my mare colt. She is well worth thirty-five camels, and her mother is worth twenty-five; but Zeyd's mare is not worth five camels:—and hast thou seen my *jâra* (housewife)? tell us now whether Hirfa be the fairer faced, or she that is mine." Hirfa, showing herself with a little pouting look, said she would not suffer these comparisons; "Khalîl, do not answer." The Aarab playing thus in the tent-life, and their mouths full of the broadest raillery, often called for the stranger, to be judge of their laughing contentions: as, "Is not this a gomâny (enemy)? Khalîl, he is a *hablûs;* what shall be done to him? shall I take off his head?—and this old fellow here, they say, is naught with his wife; for pity, canst thou not help him? is there not a medicine?"—And the old sire, "Do not listen to these young fools." So they said, "This Zeyd is good for nothing, why do you live with him? and Hirfa, is she good to you? she pours you out lében; and is she beautiful, *mez'ûna?*" Hirfa herself, were there no strangers, would come in at such times to sit down and jest her part with us: she was a sheykha, and Zeyd, a manly jaded man, was of this liberality more than is often seen among Beduins. Sometimes for pastime they would ask for words of my Nasrâny language, and as they had them presently by heart, they called loud for Hirfa, in plain English, "*Girl, bring milk!*—by thy life, Hirfa, this evening we have learned Enghreys." *Hirfa:* "And tittun, what is it in the tongue of Khalîl?"—"Tobacco."—"Then give me some of this good word in my galliûn, fill for me, Khalîl!"—Another day, a tribesman arriving sat down by Hirfa, in her side of the booth; and seeing the stranger, "Tell me, he said, is not Hirfa mez'ûna? oh, that she were mine!" and the fellow discovered his mind with knavish gestures. Hirfa, seeing herself courted, (though he was not a sheykh,) sat still and smiled demurely; and Zeyd, who could well play the shrew in other men's wedlock, sitting by himself, looked manly on and smiling.

Zeyd might balance in his mind to be some day quit of Hirfa, for what a cumber to man's heart is an irksome woman!—As we sat, few together, about another evening fire, said Zeyd, "Wellah, Khalîl, I and thou are brethren. In proof of this, I ask thee, hast thou any mind to be wedded amongst us? See, I have two wives, and, billah, I will give thee to choose between them; say which hast thou rather, and I will leave her and she shall become thy wife. Here is thy hostess Hirfa; the other is the *Bishrîa,* and I think thou hast seen her yonder."—Perhaps

he would have given me Hirfa, to take her again (amended) at
my departure and in the meanwhile not to miss her camels;
for it seemed he had married the orphan's camels. To this
gentle proffer I answered, ' Would they needs marry me, then
be it not with other men's wives, which were contrary to our
belief, but give me my pretty *Rakhŷeh :* ' this was Zeyd's
sister's child, that came daily playing to our booth with her
infant brothers. "Hearest thou, Hirfa? answered Zeyd; I
gave thee now to Khalîl, but he has preferred a child before
thee." And Hirfa a little discontented: " Well, be it so, and I
make no account of Khalîl's opinions."—The great-eyed Bishr
wife, meeting me some day after in the camp, proffered, betwixt
earnest and game, without my asking, to take me for her
husband, ' as ever her husband would divorce her : but I must
buy some small cattle, a worsted booth, and camels ; we should
live then (she thought) in happy accord, as the Nasrânies put
not away their wives.' Sometimes in the coffee tents a father
proffered his child, commending her beauty, and took witness
of all that sat there ; young men said they gave me their sisters :
and this was because Zeyd had formerly given out that Khalîl,
coming to live with him, would ride in the ghrazzus and be a
wedded man.—For all their jealousy is between themselves ;
there had no man not been contented with the Nasrány
parentage, since better in their belief is the Christian blood ;
and the white skin betokens in their eyes an ingenuous lineage,
more than their own. Human spirits of an high fantasy, they
imagine themselves discoloured and full of ailing ; this is their
melancholy. I have known Beduin women that disdained, as
they said, to wed with a Beduwy ; and oasis women who disdained to wed among their villagers. They might think it an
advancement, if it fell to them to be matched with some man
from the settled countries. Beduin daughters are easily given
in marriage to the kella keepers.

Only young hinds, abiding in the master's booth, and lads
under age, can worthily remain unmarried. A lonely man, in
the desert tribes, were a wretch indeed, without tent, since the
household service is wholly of the hareem : and among so many
forsaken women, and widows, there is no man so poor who may
not find a make to ' build ' with him, to load, to grind, to fetch
water and wood : he shall but kill a sheep (or a goat, if he be
of so little substance,) for the marriage supper. Incredible it
seems to the hareem, that any man should choose to dwell
alone, when the benefit of marriage lies so unequally upon his
part. Gentle Beduin women timidly ask the stranger, of very
womanhood, " And hast thou not hareem that weep for thee in

thy land?"—When the man's help is gone from their indigent house of marriage, they are left widows indeed. It is a common smiling talk to say to the passenger guest, and the stranger in their tents, *nejowwazak bint*, "We will give thee a maiden to wife, and dwell thou among us." I have said, "What should she do in my country? can she forget her language and her people leading their lives in this wilderness?" And they have answered, "Here is but famine and thirst and nakedness, and yours is a good béled; a wife would follow, and also serve thee by the way, this were better for thee: the lonely man is sorrowful, and she would learn your tongue, as thou hast learned *Araby*." But some murmured, "It is rather a malice of the Nasâra, Khalîl will none, lest the religion of Islam should grow thereby." Others guessed ' It were meritorious to give me a wife, to this end, that true worshippers might arise among them, of him who knew not Ullah.' Also this I have heard, " Wed thou, and leave us a white bint, that she may in time be for some great sheykh's wife." Large is the nomad housewives' liberty. The few good women, sorted with worthy men, to whom they have borne sons, are seen of comely, and hardly less than matronly carriage. In hareem of small worth, fallen from marriage to marriage, from one concubinage to another, and always lower, is often found the license of the nomad tongue, with the shameless words and gestures of abandoned women. The depraved in both sexes are called by the tribesmen *affûn*, putrid or rotten persons. The maidens in the nomad booths are of a virginal circumspect verecundity, wards of their fathers and brethren, and in tutelage of an austere public opinion. When daughters of some lone tents must go herding, as the *Midianite* daughters of Jethro, we have seen, they may drive their flocks into the wilderness and fear no evil ; there is not a young tribesman (vile though many of them be,—but never impious,) who will do her oppression. It were in all their eyes harrâm, breach of the desert faith and the religion of Islam; the guilty would be henceforth unworthy to sit amongst men, in the booths of the Aarab.

Now longwhile our black booths had been built upon the sandy stretches, lying before the swelling white Nefûd side: the lofty coast of Irnân in front, whose cragged breaches, where is any footing for small herbs nourished of this barren atmosphere, are the harbour of wild goats, which never drink. The summer's night at end, the sun stands up as a crown of hostile flames from that huge covert of inhospitable sandstone bergs; the desert day dawns not little and little, but it is noontide in

F*

an hour. The sun, entering as a tyrant upon the waste landscape, darts upon us a torment of fiery beams, not to be remitted
till the far-off evening.—No matins here of birds; not a rock
partridge-cock, calling with blithesome chuckle over the extreme
waterless desolation. Grave is that giddy heat upon the crown
of the head; the ears tingle with a flickering shrillness, a subtle
crepitation it seems, in the glassiness of this sun-stricken
nature: the hot sand-blink is in the eyes, and there is little
refreshment to find in the tents' shelter; the worsted booths
leak to this fiery rain of sunny light. Mountains looming like
dry bones through the thin air, stand far around about us: the
savage flank of Ybba Moghrair, the high spire and ruinous
stacks of el-Jebâl, Chebâd, the coast of Helwàn! Herds of the
weak nomad camels waver dispersedly, seeking pasture in the
midst of this hollow fainting country, where but lately the
swarming locusts have fretted every green thing. This silent
air burning about us, we endure breathless till the assr: when
the dazing Arabs in the tents revive after their heavy hours.
The lingering day draws down to the sun-setting; the herdsmen, weary of the sun, come again with the cattle, to taste in
their menzils the first sweetness of mirth and repose.—The
day is done, and there rises the nightly freshness of this purest
mountain air: and then to the cheerful song and the cup at
the common fire. The moon rises ruddy from that solemn
obscurity of jebel like a mighty beacon:—and the morrow will
be as this day, days deadly drowned in the sun of the summer
wilderness.

The rugged country eastward, where we came in another
remove, was little known to our Beduins; only an elder generation had wandered there : and yet they found even the lesser
waters. We journeyed forth in high plains, (the altitude always
nearly 4000 feet,) and in passages, stretching betwixt mountain
cliffs of sandstone, cumbered with infinite ruins of fallen crags,
in whose eternal shadows we built the booths of a day. One of
these quarters of rock had not tumbled perhaps in a human
generation ; but they mark years of the sun, as the sand, a little
thing in the lifetime of a planet!

The short spring season is the only refreshment of the desert
year. Beasts and men swim upon this prosperous tide ; the
cattle have their fill of sweet pasture, butter-milk is in the
booths of the Aarab ; but there was little or none in Zeyd's
tent. The kids and lambs stand all tied, each little neck in a
noose, upon a ground line which is stretched in the nomad
booth. At day-break the bleating younglings are put under the
dams, and each mother receives her own, (it is by the scent)—

she will put by every other. When the flock is led forth to
pasture, the little ones are still bound at home ; for following
the dams, they would drink dry the dugs, and leave no food
for the Arabs. The worsted tent is full all day of small hungry
bleatings, until the ghrannem come home at evening, when they
are loosed again, and run to drink, butting under the mothers'
teats, with their wiggle tails ; and in these spring weeks, there
is little rest for their feeble cries, all night in the booths of the
Aarab : the housewives draw what remains of the sweet milk
after them. The B. Wáhab tribes of these open highlands, are
camel Beduins ; the small cattle are few among them : they
have new spring milk when their hinds have calved. The
yeaning camel cow, lying upon her side, is delivered without
voice, the fallen calf is big as a grown man : the herdsman
stretches out its legs, with all his might ; and draws the calf,
as dead, before the dam. She smells to her young, rises
and stands upon her feet to lick it over. With a great clap of
the man's palm upon that horny sole, zóra, (which, like a pillar,
Nature has set under the camel's breast, to bear up the huge
neck,) the calf revives : at three hours end, yet feeble and
tottering, and after many falls, it is able to stand reaching up the
long neck and feeling for the mother's teat. The next morrow
this new born camel will follow to the field with the dam. The
cow may be milked immediately, but that which is drawn
from her, for a day or two, is purgative. The first voice of the
calf is a sheep-like complaint, báh-báh, loud and well sounding.
The fleece is silken soft, the head round and high ; and this
with a short body, borne arch-wise, and a leaping gait upon so
long legs, makes that, a little closing the eyes, you might take
them for fledglings of some colossal bird. Till twelve months be
out they follow the teat ; but when a few weeks old they begin,
already, to crop for themselves the tops of the desert bushes ;
and their necks being not yet of proportionate reach, it is only
betwixt the straddled fore legs, that they can feed at the
ground. One evening, as I stroked the soft woolly chines of the
new-born camels, " Khalíl ! said the hind (coming with a hostile
face), see thou do no more so,—they will be hide-bound and not
grow well ; thou knowest not this ! " He thought the stranger
was about some maleficence ; but Zeyd, whose spirit was far from
all superstition with an easy smile appeased him, and they were
his own camels.

The camel calf at the birth is worth a real, and every
month rises as much in value. In some "weak" households the
veal is slaughtered, where they must drink themselves all their
camel milk. The bereaved dam wanders, lowing softly, and

smelling for her calf; and as she mourns, you shall see her
deer-like pupils, say the Arabs, 'standing full of tears.' Other
ten days, and her brutish distress is gone over to forgetfulness;
she will feed again full at the pasture, and yield her foster milk
to the Aarab.   Then three good pints may be drawn from her
at morning, and as much to their supper : the udder of these
huge frugal animals is not greater than I have seen the dugs
of Malta goats.   A milch cow with the calf is milked only at
evening.   Her udder has four teats, which the southern nomads
divide thus : two they tie up with a worsted twine and wooden
pegs, for themselves, the other they leave to the suckling.   The
Aarab of the north make their camel udders sure, with a
worsted bag-netting.   Upon a journey, or when she is thirsting, the nâga's milk is lessened to the half.   All their nâgas
give not milk alike.   Whilst the spring milk is in, the nomads
nourish themselves of little else.   In poorer households it is all
their victual those two months.   The Beduins drink no whole-
milk, save that of their camels ; of their small cattle they drink
but the butter-milk.   The hareem make butter, busily rocking
the (blown) sour milk-skin upon their knees.   In the plenteous
northern wilderness the semîly is greater ; and is hanged to be
rocked in the fork of a robust bearing-stake of the nomad tent.
As for this milk diet, I find it, by proof in the Beduin life, to be
the best of human food.   But in every nomad menzil, there are
some stomachs, which may never well bear it ; and strong men
using this sliding drink-meat feel always an hungry disease in
their bodies ; though they seem in never so good plight.   The
Beduins speak thus of the several kinds of milk : " Goat milk is
sweet, it fattens more than strengthens the body ; ewe's milk
very sweet, and fattest of all, it is unwholesome to drink whole :"
so they say, " it kills people," that is, with the colic.   In spite
of their saws, I have many times drunk it warm from the dug,
with great comfort of languishing fatigue.   It is very rich in
the best samn : ewe butter-milk " should be let sour somewhile
in the semîly, with other milk, till all be tempered together,
and then it is fit to drink."   Camel milk is they think the
best of all sustenance, and that most, (as lightly purgative,)
of the *bukkra*, or young nâga with her first calf, and the most
sober of them add with a Beduish simplicity, " who drinks and
has a jâra he would not abide an hour."   The goat and nâga
milk savour of the plants where the cattle are pastured ; in
some cankered grounds I have found it as wormwood.   One of
those Allayda sheykhs called to me in the ráhla, " Hast thou
not some Damascus *kaak* (biscuit cakes) to give me to eat?
wellah, it is six weeks since I have chewed anything with the

teeth; all our food is now this flood of milk. Seest thou not
what is the Beduins' life; they are like game scattered in all
the wilderness." Another craved of me a handful of dates;
"with this milk, only, he felt such a creeping hunger within
him." Of any dividing food with them the Beduins keep a
kindly remembrance; and when they have aught will call thee
heartily again.

The milk-dieted Aarab are glad to take any mouthful of
small game. Besides the desert hare which is often startled
in the ráhlas, before other is the thób; which they call here
pleasantly 'Master Hamed, sheykh of wild beasts,' and say he
is human, *zillamy*,—this is their elvish smiling and playing—
and in proof they hold up his little five-fingered hands. They
eat not his palms, nor the seven latter thorny-rings of sheykh
Hamed's long tail, which, say they, is 'man's flesh.' His pasture
is most of the sweet-smelling Nejd bush, *el-arrafej*. Sprawling
wide and flat is the body, ending in a training tail of even
length, where I have counted twenty-three rings. The colour
is blackish and green-speckled, above the pale yellowish and
dull belly: of his skin the nomads make small herdmen's
milk-bottles. The manikin saurian, with the robust hands,
digs his burrow under the hard gravel soil, wherein he lies
all the winter, dreaming. The thób-catcher, finding the hole,
and putting in his long reed armed with an iron hook, draws
Hamed forth. His throat cut, they fling the carcase, whole,
upon the coals; and thus baked they think it a delicate roast.
His capital enemy among beasts, "which undermines and devours him, is, they say, the *thurbàn*," I know not whether a
living or fabulous animal. The *jerboa*, or spring rat, is a small
white aery creature in the wide waterless deserts, of a pitiful
beauty. These lesser desert creatures lie underground in the
daylight, they never drink. The hedgehog, which they call
kúnfuth and *abu shauk*, 'father prickles,' is eaten in these parts
by Fejîr tribesmen, but by their neighbours disdained, although
they be one stock with them of Annezy. Selím brought in an
urchin which he had knocked on the head, he roasted Prickles
in the coals and rent and distributed the morsels, to every
one his part. That which fell to me I put away bye and bye
to the starveling greyhound; but the dog smelling to the meat
rejected it. When another day I told this tale in the next
tribes, they laughed maliciously, that the Fukara should eat
that which the hounds would not of. The porcupine is eaten
by all the nomads, and the *wabbar*. I have seen this thick-
bodied beast as much as an heavy hare, and resembling the
great Alpine rat; they go by pairs, or four, six, eight, ten,

together. The wabbar is found under the border of the sandstone mountains, where tender herbs nourish him, and the gum-acacia leaves, upon which tree he climbs nimbly, holding with his pad feet without claws ; the fore-paws have four toes, the hind-paws three : the flesh is fat and sweet : they are not seen to sit upon the hind quarters ; the pelt is grey, and like the bear's coat.

Rarely do any nomad gunners kill the wolf, but if any fall to their shot he is eaten by the Beduins, (the wolf was eaten in mediæval Europe). The Aarab think the flesh medicinal, " very good they say for aches in the shins," which are so common with them that go bare-legs and bare-footed in all the seasons. Zeyd had eaten the wolf, but he allowed it to be of dog's kind, " Eigh, billah (he answered me), the wolf's mother, that is the hound's aunt." The fox, *hosseny*, is often taken by their greyhounds, and eaten by the Fejîr ; the flesh is " sweet, and next to the hare." They will even eat the foul hyena when they may take her, and say, " she is good meat." Of great desert game, but seldom slain by the shot of these pastoral and tent-dwelling people, is the bédan of the mountains (the wild goat of Scripture, *pl.* bedûn ; with the Kahtân *waúl*, as in Syria). The massy horns grow to a palm-breadth, I have seen them two and a half feet long ; they grow stretching back upon the chine to the haunch. The beast at need, as all hunters relate, will cast himself down headlong upon them backwards : he is nigh of kin to the stone-buck of the European Alps.

The gazelle, *ghrazel*, pl. *ghrazlán*, is of the plains ; the Arabians say more often *thobby* (the N. T. Tabitha). They are white in the great sand-plains, and swart-grey upon the black Harra ; these are the roes of the scriptures. There is yet a noble wild creature of the Arabian deserts, which was hitherto unknown among us, the *wothŷhi*, or " wild cow " above mentioned. I saw later the male and female living at Hâyil ; it is an antelope, *Beatrix*, akin to the beautiful animals of Africa. It seems that this is not the " wild ox " of Moses : but is not this the (Hebr.) *reem*, the " *unicorn* " of the Septuagint translators ?—Her horns are such slender rods as from our childhood we have seen pictured " the horns of the unicorns ". We read in Balaam's parable, " EL brought them out of Egypt ; He hath as it were the strength of a *reem :* " and in Moses' blessing of the tribes, ' Joseph's horns are the *two* horns of reems." In Job especially, are shown the headstrong conditions of this *velox* wild creature. " Will the reem be willing to serve thee—canst thou bind the reem in thy furrow ? " The wounded wothŷhi is perilous to be approached ; this antelope, with a cast of her sharp horns, may strike through a man's body ; hunters await therefore the last moments to run in and cut their quarry's throat. It was a monkish darkness in natural knowledge to ascribe a single horn to a double forehead !—and we sin not less by addition, putting wings to the pagan images of gods and angels ; so they should have two pairs of fore-limbs! The wothŷhi falls only to the keenest hunters : the wotŷhies accompany in the waterless desert by troops of three and five together.

Of vermin, there are many snakes and adders ; none of them eaten by these tribes of nomads. *Jelámy* is that small brown lizard of the wilderness which starts from every footstep. Scorpions lurk under the cool stones ; I have found them in my tent, upon my clothing, but never had any hurt. I have seen many grown persons and children bitten, but the sting is not perilous ; some wise man is called to " read " over them. The wounded part throbs with numbness and aching till the third day, there is not much swelling. Many are the cities, under this desert sand, of seed-gathering ants ; I have measured some watling-street of theirs, eighty-five paces : to speed once this length and come again, loaded as camels, is these small busybodies' summer day's journey.

Besides, of the great predatory wild animals, most common is the *thùbba*, hyena ; then the *nimmr*, a leopard, brindled black and brown and spotted : little common is the *fáhd*, a wild cat no bigger than the fox ; he is red and brown brindled, and spotted. In these Beduins' memory a young fáhd was bred up amongst Bishr, which (they are wonderfully swift footed) had been used by his nomad master to take gazelles. In all the Arabic countries there is a strange superstition of parents, (and this as well among the Christian sects of Syria,) that if any child seem to be sickly, of infirm understanding, or his brethren have died before, they will put upon him a wild beast's name, (especially, wolf, leopard, wolverine,)—that their human fragility may take on as it were a temper of the kind of those animals. Hawks and buzzards are often seen wheeling in the desert sky, and *el-ágab*, which is a small black eagle, and *er-rákham*, the small white carrion eagle,—flying in the air they resemble sea-mews : I have not seen vultures, nor any greater eagle in the deserts (save in Sinai). These are the most of living creatures, and there are few besides in the wilderness of Arabia.

CHAPTER IX

PEACE IN THE DESERT

UPON a morrow, when there was a great coffee-drinking at Zeyd's, one cries over his cup, *bahhir!* " Look there !—who come riding yonder ? " All shadowing with their hands, and fixing the eyes, it was answered, " Are they not tradesmen of Teyma, that ride to sell calico ; or some that would take up well-camels ; or the sheukh perhaps, that ride to Hâyil ? " The Beduw make no common proof that I can find of extraordinary vision. True it is, that as they sit the day long in the open tents, their sight is ever indolently wavering in the wide horizon before them, where any stirring or strangeness in the wonted aspect of the desert must suspend their wandering cogitation. But the Arabs also suffer more of eye diseases than any nation. It was not long before the weak-eyed Arabs discovered the comers, by their frank riding, to be Beduins ; but only a little before they alighted, the company knew them to be their own sheykh Motlog and his son, and a tribesman with them. Motlog had mounted very early from the other camp. Our company, of nigh fifty persons, rose to welcome their chief sheykhs ; Motlog re-entered cordially amongst them, with a stately modesty ; and every man came forward in his place, to salute them, as kins-men returning from an absence, with *gowwak ya Motlog*, ' The Lord strengthen thee.' *Answer : Ullah gowwîk*, ' May He give thee strength : ' so, falling upon each other's necks, they kiss gravely together, upon this and upon the other cheek   Room now is made for them in the highest place, where they sit down, smiling easily ; and the Fukara sheukh, noblemen born, of some-what an effeminate countenance, excel, as said, in specious and amiable mejlis manners : yet their Asiatic hearts are full of corruption inwardly, and iniquity. Roasting anew and braying and boiling are taken in hand, to make them coffee ; and Zeyd, as an host, brings them forth a bowl of his musty dates to breakfast, (he would spend for none better at Teyma,) and

160

another of butter-milk, and those in small measure ;—it was Hirfa and Zeyd's known illiberality, for which cause, there alighted almost no guests at Zeyd's beyt in the round year. This is the goodly custom in the wilderness, that somewhat be served immediately, (however early it be,) to the guest alighting from his journey. The sheykhs consented to join our camps from the next ráhla, and we should remove further into the Bishr country. * * *

* * * As our Aarab were pitched together again, there arrived a principal sheykh of Teyma, *Abd el-Azíz er-Román*, riding round to the Aarab, to buy well camels. The price is two or three camel-loads of dates or a load of corn, *aysh*, for a good nâga. He alighted at Motlog's, and I went down to the coffee meeting, to hear the country news. Motlog welcomed me graciously, and called, " Bring a shidâd for Khalîl." The Teyma sheykh was a well clad, comely, stirring man, in the favour of Ibn Rashîd, collector of the prince's revenue in his oasis ; presumptuous, penetrating-malicious, and, "as all the Teyâmena," in the opinion of the nomads, *jâhil*, of a certain broken-headed ineptitude, and rusticity. In the nomad-like village, he had not learned letters : Motlog, among Beduins, was the friend of his youth. As we sat on, Abd el-Azíz, turning abruptly, demanded of me, ' What did I there in the wilderness, and wherefore had I banished myself from all world's good,' (that is, from the shadow by day, bread and dates sure, and water enough, and the stable dwelling). " I take the air."—" If this be all, thou mightest as good take the air upon yonder top of Irnàn." His rafîk enquired in his ear, yet so that I heard it, "Is not this a Yahûdy ? "—" Jew, there is no doubt (answered Abd el-Azíz), or what they tell me Nasrâny, a difference in the names only." The other then, with a ghastly look, as if he beheld a limb of Sheytan, " Lord, for thy mercy ! and is this—akhs !—a Yahûdy ? Ullah confound all the kuffâr." Abd el-Azíz, when I came again to Teyma, had put on a new courtesy, since he heard the stranger had publicly pronounced him, " Ignorant ass, and sheykh of all the Yahûd of Teyma : " for the Arabs, who covet to be praised, are tender as vain women of men's opinions. They brought tidings of a disaster at home, the Haddàj was fallen ! yet he looked merrily upon it, because his two or three draw-wheels and the side which belonged to his own sûk, were yet standing; the loss was not of his faction.

The knavish Beduins heard unmoved of the mischance of the Teyâmena ; those merchants of dates and corn, that beguile, they think, their uncunning with false measures. Of some who

came later from the oasis, we heard that the townspeople and
fanatics laid all to the charge of the Nasrâny. 'The Haddàj
fell only few days after my being there, I had overthrown it
with mine eye;' but the graver sort said, 'it was not fallen but
by the permission of Ullah.' I asked a plain worthy man of the
town, "How could I have cast down your well?" And he:
"Khalîl, I believe not it was thy doing; (he added darkly,) I
think rather it was of Ibn Rashîd!" The prince and his riders
(perhaps three hundred men), returning from the raid upon
W. Aly, had encamped without Teyma walls a day or twain.
He added, "The multitude of them was as the sand, *ouff!*"—
"Was it the tread of their waterers about the Haddàj?"—
"Not this, but *el-âyn*, the eye!" The evil eye is part of the
Semitic superstition. The darling of the body is the eye, the
window of the soul, and they imagine her malign influence to
stream forth thereat. Fanatical nomads, from that day, looked
upon me as a yet more perilous ' God's adversary '.

One of these evenings there rode into our encampment a
main ghrazzu, eighty men of Bishr, that had mounted to go set
upon their foemen W. Aly; they passed this night as guests of
the Fukara, in their own dîra. They were friendly entertained,
and heard after their suppers the latest advice of the W. Aly's
being pitched about the wells *Mogeyra;* about eighty miles from
hence, at the haj road, a journey below el-Héjr. I enquired of
Zeyd, Would they not send this night to warn their cousins of
the sister tribe? *Answer:* " Ha, no! but let them all be taken,
for us." Months later, being with some W Aly tribesmen I
heard them censure this treacherous malice of the Fukara; and
yet being full of the like themselves, which in truth is the
natural condition of Beduins. Of the Annezy nation, unto
which all these tribes belong, and that is greatest of all ashîrats
in the Peninsula, it is spoken in proverb, "God increased
Annezy, and He has appointed divisions among them:" there is
no time when some of the kindreds are not *gôm*, or robber
enemies, of some other. The Annezy have been compared with
B. Israel; they are not without resemblance. The seat of this
people, in the first Mohammedan ages, was, according to their
tradition, the dîra lying a little north of Medina, which is now
of the W. Aly. Then they conquered Kheybar, whose feverish
palm valleys became their patrimony to this day.

It happened strangely that whilst Bishr was out against them
a main ghrazzu of the Wélad Aly had mounted to go and set
upon Bishr. These hostile squadrons by a new adventure met
with each other in the wilderness. An hundred thelûl riders

cover the ground of a regiment. It is a brave sight, as they come on with a song, bowing in the tall saddles, upon the necks of their gaunt stalking beasts, with a martial shining of arms. The foemen in sight, the sheukh descend with the long lances upon their led horses; and every sheykh's back-rider, *radíf*, who is also his gun-bearer, now rides in the thelûl saddle. Those thelûl riders, upon the slower sheep-like beasts, are in comparison of their few light horsemen, like a kind of heavy infantry of matchlock men. The nomad cavalier, sitting loosely upon a pad without stirrups, can carry no long and heavy firearm, which he could not reload. Only few amongst these southern sheykhs are possessors of some old flint horse-pistols, which abandoned in our grandsires' time, have been sold away from Europe. Their hope is in the romhh or shelfa, the Beduin lance: the beam, made of a light reed of the rivers of Mesopotamia, is nearly two of their short horse-lengths; they charge them above their heads. Agîd or conductor of the W. Aly part, was a beardless and raw young man, *Fáhd*, their great sheykh's son; and *Askar* of the other, son of *Misshel*, the great sheykh above mentioned: these young hostile Annezy leaders were sisters' sons. Fáhd, tilting impetuously, pierced his cousin Askar; but, overborne by strong men's hands, he was himself taken alive. The W. Aly, glorious and confident in the tents, were seized with panic terror in the field, in presence of the warlike Auájy, the most big of bone and resolute of that country Beduins; in each of whom they looked for an avenger of the blood slain before Kheybar. They cried out therefore that they were brethren! and those W. Aly, which were one hundred and twentv riders with arms in their hands, submitted to the eighty lion-like men of Bishr; every one pitifully intreating his spoiler, "*akhyey, ya akhyey*, ah, little brother mine! take thou then my thelûl, have here my arms, and even my mantle; take all, only let me go alive." No more than a few sheykhs of them, who were horsemen, escaped that day upon their mares. Yet of the thelûl riders there broke away three hardy men, mountaineers; they were Moahîb, that had ridden with them in hope to divide the spoils of the common enemy.—Before the year was out, the Moahîb by the same Bishr were miserably bereaved, in one day, of all their cattle. The sheykhs upon all sides were, at some time, of my acquaintance; and I had this tale among them.

The Bishr received their *dakhíls* to quarter; they would not, only remembering the vengeance, make a butchery of their kinsmen; and, as the southern Aarab use not to take human lives to ransom, they let their enemies go. in their shirts, to ride

home to their wives, upon their bare feet. It is contrary to the
Arabian conscience to extinguish a kabîla. There are tribes of
neighbours, cruel gomânies since their granddames' days, as the
Fejîr and B. Atîeh, that have never met in general battles, when,
in a day, they might void so long controversies, by the destruction of one of them. Even the Beduins' old cruel rancours are
often less than the golden piety of the wilderness. The danger
past, they can think of the defeated foemen with kindness;
having compassion of an Arab lineage of common ancestry with
themselves. When men fall down wounded in a foray the
enemies which had the upper hand will often send again far
back, and bear them to their menzil: and there they nourish
their languishing foemen, until they be whole again; when they
give to each a water-skin and say to him *ruhh*, "depart," without taking promises, putting only their trust in Ullah to obtain
the like at need for themselves. But Fáhd was led away with
the Bishr, since he must answer for the life of Askar: if his
cousin died he must die for his death, unless the next of kin
should consent to receive the blood ransom; he would be entertained in the meanwhile in his hostile kinsmen's tents. Askar
recovered slowly, in the next months. I asked, "When those
shearers of W. Aly came home shorn, with what dances and
lullilooing will the hareem sally forth to meet them!" It was
answered, "Ay billah, they had merited the women's derision!"
—"But how, being one hundred and twenty strong, had they
submitted to the fewer in number?" *Answer:* "Are they not
W. Aly? and this is the manner of them." They are unwarlike, but the Fejîr, the sister tribe, were never contemned by
their enemies, which are all those strong free tribes behind
them, B. Atîeh, Howeytát, Bíllî, Jeheyna.

The clouds of the second locust brood which the Aarab call
am'dàn, ' pillars ' [it is the word we read in Exodus—the *ammud*
of cloud and fire], wreathing and flickering as motes in the sun-
beam, flew over us for some days, thick as rain, from near the
soil to great height in the atmosphere. They alight as birds,
letting down their long shanks to the ground; these invaded the
booths, and for blind hunger, even bit our shins, as we sat at
coffee. They are borne feebly flying at the wind's list, as in the
Psalms, "I am tossed up and down as the locust." There fell
of them every moment upon the earth, and were dashed upon
the stones. After this we saw them drifted to the southward:
and the Aarab, knowing they must now devour Kheybar, where
their dates would be lost, came forth, and stood to gaze after
them with a fatal indifference; and with *aha!* they went in to
sit down again, leaving their lot in the hands of Ullah, who

they say is Bountiful. And oftener than no, the Arabs will smile in such mishaps, over their own broken hopes, with a kind of godly melancholy. The children bring in gathered locusts, broached upon a twig. and the nomads toast them on the coals; then plucking the scorched members, they break away the head, and the insect body which remains is good meat; but not of these latter swarms, born in time of the dried-up herbage. A young man at our fire breaking the toasted body of the first, there fell out a worm, and he cast it from him with loathing; and cried, ' akhs ! Wellah this cured him of all locust eating.' Yet women went out to gather them; they were of some poor households. The coffee-drinkers asked of me, " Eat you the locusts in your béled, Khalîl; tell us, be they wholesome ? " (We read in Leviticus that the children of Jacob might eat the kinds of locust.) Nearly every seventh year, in the Arabians' opinion, is a season of locusts.—This year was remembered for the locust swarms and for the great summer heat. The male insect is yellow, spotted brown. the female somewhat greater and of a leaden colour. The pair of glassy wings are spotted, the inner pair are wide and folded under. Her length to the end of the closed wing is nearly three inches. The Beduins say, " This is not the eye which appears such, in the head, but that clear spot under the short first legs." I took a pen and made the outline of a locust, and upon the next leaf was another of Abu Zeyd; all the Arabs came to see these two pictures. " Very well, Khalîl," said the simple gazers, " and ha ! his image wellah, without any difference ! " And one smutched the lines of the locust with his fingers, seldom washed, to know if this lay even upon the smooth paper, and *yeteyr* quoth he "it will rise and fly ! " And ever as there came coffee-bibbers to Zeyd's menzil, they asked for Khalil, and " Let him show us Abu Zeyd and his book of pictures ; " these were a few prints in my book of medicine. Then they wondered to look through my telescope, in which, levelling at any camel a mile distant, they saw her as it were pasturing before their faces. Nevertheless, as a thing which passed their minds, they did not learn to covet it ; and yet to sharpen their vision the best sighted of them, seeing as falcons, would needs essay all my eye-washes ; for there is no endowment of nature so profitable to them in this life of the open wilderness.

Only the starveling hounds of the menzils, in these days, greedily swallowing up locusts, seemed to be in better plight, running gaily in the encampment, sleeping with their fills, and now sullenly careless of the Aarab. Their hounds, say the nomads, "bite the wolf:" they waken all night whilst the Aarab slumber. With the Fejîr, Beduins of a " camel dîra ", the "wolf-eaters " are not many, and those of currish kind, nearly like the street dogs of Syria. The best I have seen with any Aarab, were the great shagged dogs of Bíllî, in the Tehâma. The common nomad hound is yellowish, shaped as the fox ; the like is seen over most wild parts of the world. A few Beduins have their greyhounds, light with hunger, and very swift to course the hare ; and by these the gazelle fawn is taken. The common barkers of every Beduin village (for they go not out with the flocks), in tribes where the house-mothers have little or no milk to give them, are carrion lean, and in hunger-times they receive no sustenance of man's hand but a little water : it were hard to say of what uncleanness they then live. Only for a few days once in the long year they are well refreshed : these are in the date-gathering at Kheybar, when the fruit abounding in the Beduins' not improvident hands (above that they may carry,) they give to the camels and asses their fill of dates, and fling also to their wretched hounds largely.

The hounds for their jealous service have never a good word. It is the only life mishandled at home by the gentle Aarab, who with spurns and blows cast out these profane creatures from the beyt, and never touch them (unless it be the unweaned whelps) with their hands. If any dog be an house-thief, a robber of human food, he is chased with hue and cry, and will be most cruelly beaten ; the men swear great oaths ' he shall be dead, he has it well deserved.' This makes that the parasite creature, in these countries, is of more diffident behaviour, towards his masters : only to the nomad greyhound is granted, as of noble kind, to lie down in the booth. The hounds watch all day in the menzil, every one by his household, *ahlahu.* They follow in the râhla with the baggage-train and their mistress ; pacing, with a half reasonable gait, in the shadows of the lofty moving camels : impatient of heat and the sand burning under their paws, where they spy any shelter of crag or bush, there they will go in to pant awhile. At the alighting, the booth-cloth is hardly raised, when (if suffered—this is in the sheep-keeper tribes) they creep into the shadow and scrabble the hot sand, and dig with their paws under them, to make their lair upon the cool soil beneath. A dog strayed at the menzil, and running by strange tents, is hooted—*ahl-ak, ahl-ak !* 'to thy household, sirra!' The loud nomad dogs, worrying about the heels of all strange comers, are a sort of police of the nomad encampment. A few of them are perilous snatchers with their teeth ; a man may come by, skirmishing with his camel-stick behind him, and the people call off their dogs. But if there be only hareem at home, which do but look on with a feminine malice, a stranger must beat them off with stone-casts. Some woman may then cry, " Oh ! oh ! wherefore dost thou stone our dog ? " And he, "The accursed would have eaten me."—" But, O thou ! cast not at him."—" Then call him in thou foolish woman and that quickly, or with this block now, I may happen to kill him." —" Eigh me ! do not so, this eats the wolf, he watches for the enemy, he is the guard of our beyt and the ghrannem ; I pray thee, no, not another stone."—" Mad woman, before he eat me I will break all the bones in his skin, and cursed be thy tongue ! with less breath thou canst call him off ! " In such case, I have not spared for stones, and the silly wife thought herself wronged ; but the men answered, " It was well enough." The hareem, as to whom little is attributed, are naturally of infirmer reason, and liker children in the sentiment of honour ; so there are tents, where the passing guest may not greatly trust them, nor their children.

The sharp-set nomad hounds fall upon aught they may find abroad, as the baggage (when sometimes it is left without the booth) of any stranger guest : then they rend up all with their eager teeth and sharp claws; therefore to carry in the guests' bags is accounted a charitable deed. Men who are pilferers of others' provision, are often called "hounds " by the Beduins. Hirfa called one of these mornings at my tent door, " Where art thou, Khalîl ? I go abroad, and wilt thou the while mind my household ? "—" And whither will my hostess to-day ? "— " I go to buy us yarn : Khalîl, open the eyes and beware, that there come no dogs to my beyt." When she returned some hours after, Hirfa came to chide me, " Ha ! careless Khalîl, the dogs have been here ! why hast thou not kept my beyt ? and did I not bid thee ? "—" I have watched for thee, Hirfa, every moment, by thy life ! sitting before the booth in the sun, and not a hair of any dog has entered."—" Alas, Khalîl does not understand that ' the dogs ' are men ; tell me, Khalîl, who has been here whilst I was out ? "—" There came two men, and when I saw them sheltering in thy apartment, I guessed them to be of kindred and acquaintance; could I suppose there would any tribesman steal from a tribesman's beyt ? "—" But these have stolen, said she, a peck of dates, and all by thy fault." In the popular sort of nomads is little or no conscience to rob food (only) ; they holding it as common, kheyr Ullah.

The cheerful summer nights are cool from the sunset in these dry uplands. As they have supped, men wander forth to talk with neighbours, coffee drinkers seek the evening cup ; in the mejlis coffee company, the Aarab gossip till midnight.

Often in our menzil only the herdsman remains at home, who wakens to his rough song the grave chord of the rabeyby.

Some moonlight evenings the children hied by us : boys and girls troop together from the mothers' beyts, and over the sand they leap to play at horses, till they find where they may climb upon some sand-hillock or rock. A chorus of the elder girls assemble hither, that with hand-clapping chant the same and ever the same refrain, of a single verse. Little wild boys stripping off their tunics, and flinging down kerchiefs, or that have left all in the mothers' beyts, run out naked ; there being only the *haggu* wound about their slender loins : this is the plaited leathern ribbon, which is worn, and never left, by all the right Arabians, both men and hareem. Every boy-horse has chosen a make, his *fáras* or mare ; they course hand in hand together, and away, away, every pair skipping after other and are held themselves in chase in the moonlight wilderness. He kicks back to the horses which chevy after them so fast, and escapes again neighing. And this pastime of Aarab children, of pure race, is without strife of envious hearts, an angry voice is not heard, a blow is not struck among them. The nomads are never brutal. This may last for an hour or two : the younger men will sometimes draw to the merry-make where the young maidens be : they frolic like great camels amongst the small ghrannem ; but not unclad, nor save with the eyes approach they to that charming bevy of young damsels; an ill-blooded nature appearing in any young man, he shall have the less estimation among them. After the child's age, these indolent Arabians have not any kind of manly pastime among them. Of Ahl Gibly, or southern nomads, I have not seen horsemen so much as exercise themselves upon their mares. Child's play it were in their eyes, to weary themselves, and be never the better. They have none other sport than to fire off their matchlocks in any household festivals. Herdsmen, they are naturally of the contemplative life : weakly fed, there can be little flushing of gross sanguine spirits in their veins, which might move them to manly games ; very rarely is any Beduin robust. Southward of Hâyil I did not see any young woman with the rose blood in her cheeks ; even they are of the summer's drought, and palled at their freshest age.

Now in the mild summer is the season of *muzayyins*, the Nomad children's circumcision feasts : the mother's booth is set out with beggarly fringes of scarlet shreds, tufts of mewed ostrich feathers, and such gay gauds as they may borrow or find. Hither a chorus assembles of slender daughters of their neighbours, that should chant at this festival in their best array.

A fresh kerchief binds about every damsel's forehead with a feather; she has ear-rings great as bracelets, and wears to-day her nose-ring, *zmèyem :* they are jewels in silver ; and a few, as said, from old time, are fine gold metal, *thahab el-asfr.* These are ornaments of the Beduin women, hardly seen at other times (in the pierced nostril, they wear for every day a head of cloves), and she has bracelets of beads and metal finger-rings. The thin black tresses loosed to-day and not long, hang down upon their slight shoulders, and shine in the sun, freshly combed out with camel urine. The lasses have borrowed new cloaks, which are the same for man or woman. Making a fairy ring apart, they begin, clapping the palms of their little hands, to trip it round together, chanting ever the same cadence of few words, which is a single verse. Hungered young faces, you might take them for some gipsy daughters; wayward not seldom in their mother's households, now they go playing before men's eyes, with downcast looks and a virginal timidity. But the Aarab raillery is never long silent, and often young men, in this day-light feast, stand jesting about them. Some even pluck roughly at the feathers of the lasses, their own near cousins, in the dance, which durst answer them nothing, but only with reproachful eyes : or laughing loud the weleds have bye and bye divided this gentle bevy among them for their wives; and if a stranger be there, they will bid him choose which one he would marry among them. "Heigh-ho ! what thinkest thou of these maidens of ours, and her, and her, be they not fair-faced ? " But the virgins smile not, and if any look up, their wild eyes are seen estranged and pensive. They are like children under the rod, they should keep here a studied demeanour ; and for all this they are not Sirens. In that male tyranny of the Mohammedan religion regard is had to a distant maidenly behaviour of the young daughters ; and here they dance as the tender candidates for happy marriage, and the blessed motherhood of sons. May their morrow approach ! which shall be as this joyful day, whose hap they now sing, wherein a man-child is joined to the religion of Islam ; it is better than the day of his birth. The nomad son is circumcised being come to the strength of three full years; and then as the season may serve without any superstition of days, and as the mother shall be able to provide corn or rice enough for her guests' supper. They sometimes put off the surgery till the morrow, in any rough windy weather, or because of the Aarab's ráhla.

The friends of the father will come in to be his guests : some of them have adorned themselves with the gunner's belt and gay baldric, rattling with the many little steel chains and brass powder-cases; and they bear upon their shoulders the long matchlocks. Therewith they would prove their hand to shoot, at the sheep's skull, which the child's *babbu* has sacrificed to ' the hospitality'. Every man kills his sacrifice, as in the ancient world, with his own hands, and the carcase is flayed and brittled with the Arabs' expedition. Nomads are all expert fleshers; the quarters hang now upon some bush or boughs, which wandering in an open wilderness, they have sought perhaps upon a far mountain side. As the sun goes low the meat is cast into the caldron, jidda. The great inwards remain suspended upon their trophy bush. After the flesh, a mess is cooked in the broth of such grain as they have. The sun setting, the maidens of the ring-dance disperse: the men now draw apart to their prayers, and in this time the cattle of every household are driven in. The men risen from their prayers, the supper is served in the tent: often thirty men's meat is in that shield-wide wooden platter which is set before them. A little later some will come hither of the young herdsmen returning boisterous from the field; they draw to the merry noise of the muzayyin that feel a lightness in their knees to the dance. A-row, every one his arm upon the next one's shoulder, these laughing weleds stand, full of good humour; and with a shout they foot it forth, reeling and wavering, advancing, recoiling in their chorus together; the while they hoarsely chant the ballad of a single verse. The housewives at the booth clap their palms, and one rising with a rod in her hand, as the dancing men advance, she dances out to meet them; it is the mother by likelihood, and joyously she answers them in her song: whilst they come on bending and tottering a-row together, with their perpetual refrain. They advancing upon her, she dances backward, feinting defence with the rod; her face is turned towards them, who maintain themselves, with that chanted verse of their manly throats, as it were pursuing and pressing upon her.—The nomads imagine even the necessity of circumcision: graziers, they will allege the examples of all cattle, that only in the son of Adam may be found this matter of impediment. When they questioned me I have said, " You can amend then the work of Ullah! "—" Of that we speak not, they answered, but only of the expediency." Questioned, What be the duties of a Moslem? they responded "That a man fast in the month, and recite his daily prayers;"— making no mention of the circumcision, which they call " purification".

The 15th of April, after a morning wind, blustering cold from the north-eastward, I found early in the afternoon, with

still air and sunshine, the altitude being 4000 feet, 95 deg. F.
in the booth's shelter. The drooping herb withered, the summer
drought entering, the wilderness changed colour; the spring
was ended. The Beduins removed and lodged in their desolate
camps: upon a morrow, when the camels had been driven forth
an hour, an alarm was given from the front, of gôm. A herdsman came riding in, who had escaped, upon a thelûl, and told
it in the mejlis, " *él-'bil*, the camel-herds are taken." The
sheukh rose from the hearth and left their cups with grave
startled looks: all went hardily out, and hastily, to find their
mares. Hovering haramîyeh had been seen yesterday, and
now every man hied to take arms. The people ran, like angry
wasps, from the booths : some were matchlock men, some had
spears, all were afoot, save the horsemen sheykhs, and hastened
forth to require their enemies, which could not be seen in
that short desert horizon: bye and bye only the housewives,
children and a few sick and old men were left in the encampment. Some asked me would I not ride to set upon the
thieves ; for Zeyd's talk had been that Khalîl would foray with
them. " Khalîl (cried the housewives), look for us in your wise
books ; canst thou not prophesy by them (*shûf f'il ghraib*) :
read thou and tell us what seest thou in them of these gomânies.—A punishment fall upon them ! they certainly espied
the people's watch-fires here this last night, and have been
lurking behind yonder mountain until the camels were driven
out."—The long morning passed over us, in the cold incertitude of this misadventure.

Motlog had ridden days before to Hâyil to treat with the
emir, and left Rahŷel to govern the tribe ; a man of perplexed
mind in this sudden kind of conjuncture. The armed tribesmen returning after midday, we went to sit in the mejlis and
talk over this mishap. I heard no word spoken yet of pursuing ;
and enquiring of my neighbour, " Ay, they would mount their
thelûls, said he, so soon as the 'bil were come home at evening ; "
for all the great cattle were not taken, but those which had been
driven forth from the north side of the menzil. Celerity is
double strokes in warfare, but these Beduins sat still the long
day and let the robbers run, to wonder what they were; they
all said, "some Aarab of the North," for they had seen them
armed with pistols. They reasoned whether those should be
Sherarát or Howeytát Ibn Jàsy (Beduins from about Maan); or
else of the Ruwàlla. " Hear me, and I shall make it known to
you, said Zeyd (who had this vanity among them), what they
were. I say then, *es-Sokhûr*, and ye shall find it true." The
few words which had fallen from the foemen's lips were now

curiously examined. They had challenged the camel herds, "What Aarab be ye—ha! the Fejîr?" but this could not suffice to distinguish the *loghrat* of a tribe. The gôm were thirteen horsemen, and twenty riders upon thelûls. In driving off the booty a mare broke loose from them, and she was led into the encampment, but of that nothing could be learned, the nomad sheykhs not using to brand their horses with the tribe's cattle-mark. This mare, by the third day, perished of thirst! that none would pour out to her of their little water. If a tribes-man's goat stray among them, and her owner be not known, none will water her. In the time when I was with them, I saved the lives of a strayed beast or two, persuading some of my patients to give them drink.

They now reckoned in the mejlis the number of camels taken, saying over the owners' names : Zeyd kept count, scoring a new line for every ten in the sand; so he told them and found six score and seven camels—the value of £600 or more. All this tribes' camels were not so many as 2000, nor I think fully 1500 ; and the whole fortune of the Fukara Beduins in the field, two hundred households, their great and small cattle with the booths and utensils, I suppose, not to exceed £17,000. Besides which is their landed patrimony at Kheybar, that may be worth £7000 more. A household of these poor southern Beduins may thus, I think, possess the capital value of £120 sterling; and much like to them are their nomad neighbours about. In the same small tribe there are nobles and commons, the sufficient livelihood, and the pittance, and abject misery. The great sheykh Motlog, possessing more than other men, had not so many of his own as twenty-five camels. There is difference also between tribe and tribe ; the great tribes of the north, as the Annezy in Syria, and the northern Shammar upon Mesopotamia, wandering in plenteous country, are rich in cattle and horses : so also may be reckoned Kahtân and *Ateyby* of the southern tribes, (their dîras we shall see are watered by the yearly monsoon ;) but these middle tribes of nomads, in a rainless land, are "weaker". Those at the haj road which receive a surra, are the most coffee-lazing, beggarly and pithless minded of them all. The Fejîr sheukh divided between them, every year, I think about £600 of these pay-ments ! whereof almost an hundred pounds fell to Zeyd, who received his father's surra, and £160 to Motlog : besides some changes of clothing, grain, and certain allowances for their tents, and utensils ; yet poor they all were, and never the better. Motlog's halàl, or 'lawful own' of cattle, his mare and his tent and household gear together, were worth, I think, not £300 :

add to this for his funded property at Kheybar, and we may find he possessed hardly above £500.

The Aarab trifled time which could never be theirs again ; the housewives made some provision ready for those that should mount at evening. This mounting is at every man's free will, and yet the possessor of a thelûl cannot shun the common service and keep his honest name. Rahŷel led the pursuit. Some as they sat boasted, "This night or towards morning, when the haramîyeh think themselves come in security, and are first reposing, we shall be suddenly upon them, and recover our own, if the Lord will, and take their beasts from under them." As camels are driven off in a foray, the robbers chase them all that day at a run before them, hoping to outgo the pursuit; and now as the sun was setting, these might be gotten almost fifty miles in advance. The last words were, as they rose, "Please God, every camel of those taken shall be couched again, to-morrow about this time, before the booth of his household:" and with this good augury the company dispersed, going to their suppers, and afterward the riders would take their thelûls, the sheykhs (for a long pursuit) not leading their mares with them. Zeyd sat still at home ; he had two thelûls, he said "they were ailing". Khálaf sat also close in his booth, a man who, though vaunting his mare's worth at so many camels and himself of the principal W. Aly sheykhs, had not a beast to mount. A weak reason is found too light in the balance of public estimation ; and Zeyd all the next day sitting melancholy, sipping much coffee, vehemently protested to be ever since sorry, by Ullah, that he was not ridden along with them.

His camels were saved that day, feeding on the other side of the desert ; but a calamity as this is general; and to be borne by the tribe. None which had lost their cattle to-day would be left destitute ; but the governing sheykh taxing all the tribesmen, the like would be rendered to them, out of the common contribution, in a day or two. He will send some round as assessors to the menzils, where every man's state being known, the computation is made of the cattle of every household. There was levied of Zeyd the next day, of less than twenty that he had, a camel, and the value of certain head of small cattle. The nomad tribes we have seen to be commonwealths of brethren, ruled by their sheykhs with an equitable moderation. They divide each others' losses, and even in such there is community between whole tribes. Mischief is never far from them, an evil day may chance which has not befallen them in many years, when a tribe is stripped at a stroke, of nearly all its cattle, as later in my knowledge, the Moahîb.—And what then? The next Bîllî of free-will gave them, of their own, much cattle. * * *

* * * Their ghrazzus and counter-ghrazzus are the destruction of the Aarab. Reaving and bereaved they may never thrive ; in the end of every tide it is but an ill exchange of cattle. So in the eyes of nomads, the camel troops of the Fukara were all "mingled" cattle and uneven, that is, not home-born-like, but showing to be robbed beasts out of several dîras. Motlog's son said to me, he who should be great sheykh after him, "Ay, wellah! all our camels are harrâm, (of prey taken in the forays,) and not our lawful own." The Fejîr were impoverished of late years, by their neighbours' incursions : Bishr, and after them the W. Aly, had taken their flocks; but they lost most by a murrain, in these hot sandy marches, a kind of colic, in which there had died nearly all the remnant of their small cattle. A year before, Zeyd had a great mixed herd of goats and sheep, so that Hirfa, the last spring time, made a camel load and a half (as much as £18 worth) of samn. Now I saw but an ewe and two milch goats left to them, which yielded in the day but a short bowl of milk, and, discouraged, he would not buy more. Zeyd had inherited of his father, who was the former great sheykh's brother, a large landed patrimony of palm-stems at Kheybar: the half fruit being to the negro husbandmen, his own rent was, he told me, nearly 200 reals. Thus Zeyd, with his surra, had spending silver for every day, in good years, of nearly two reals, the value of a goat, which is much money in the khála: yet the man was miserable, and loving to defer payments, he was always behind the hand with old usury. Sheykhs of the B. Wáhab lay up their money, tháhab, (spared from the haj surra,) at el-Ally ; out of this, one who is low will increase his "halàl" silently, and may sometime go to the bottom of his bag to purchase him a new mare.

Rahŷel's pursuing party was three nights out. The men left in camp being now very few, they came continually together to drink coffee. The affectionate housewives sat abroad all day watching: at mid-afternoon, the fourth after, we heard the hareem's jubilee, lullilu!—but the merry note died away in their throats when, the longer they looked, they saw those that came riding in the horizon were leading nothing home with them. The men rose together, and going forth, they gazed fixedly. "What, said they, means this cry of the hareem? for look, they arrive empty-handed, and every man is riding apart to alight at his own household!" so returning to their fatal indolence, they reentered as men that are losers, and sat down again. " Some of them, they said, will presently bring us tidings." Rahŷel soon after dismounted at his tent, pitched near behind us.—The housewife comes forth as her husband makes his thelûl kneel; she réceives him in silence, unsaddles the beast, and carries in his gear. The man does not often salute her openly, nor, if he would to the mejlis, will he speak to his wife yet; so Rahŷel, without entering his booth, stepped over to us.—" Peace be with you ! " said he from a dry throat; and seating himself with the sigh of a weary man, in some sadness, he told us, ' that in the second day, following the enemy upon the Nefûd, they came where a wind had blown out the prints,' and said he, " So Ullah willed it ! " They turned then their beasts' heads,—they had no list to cast further about, to come again upon the robbers' traces. " Ha well! God would have it so! " responded the indolent Aarab. A weak enemy they thus faintly let slip through their fingers, for a little wind, though these were driving with them nearly a tithe of all their camels. But Rahŷel, to knit up his sorry tale with a good ending, exclaimed, ' Wellah, they had found water at the wells el-Hŷza in the Nefûd; and as they came again by Teyma, he heard word that some of the gôm had touched there, and they were of the Sherarát: "—Rahŷel, with his troop, had ridden nearly two hundred idle miles. " Bye and bye we shall know (said the Beduins) which tribesmen robbed our camels; then will we *ghrazzy* upon them, and God willing, take as many of them again." But the ghrazzus often return empty : a party of Fukara, " twenty *rikáb* " or warfaring thelûls, which rode lately upon the Beny Atîeh, had taken nothing.

Every man leans upon his own hand in the open desert, and there will none for naught take upon him a public service. The sheykh may persuade, he cannot compel any man ; and if the malcontent will go apart, he cannot detain them. The common body is weak, of members so loosely knit together, and there befalls them many an evil hap, which by a public policy might have been avoided.—" Why send you not out scouts, (thus I reasoned with Zeyd,) which might explore the khála in advance of your pasturing cattle? or cannot you set some to watch in the tops of the rocks, for the appearing of an enemy! Why commit yourselves thus to wild hazard, who are living openly in the midst of danger? " When Zeyd gravely repeated my words in the mejlis, the sheykh's son answered readily, " Ay, and that were very well, if we might put it in practice ; but know, Khalîl, there are none of the Beduw will thus adventure themselves by twos or threes together, for fear of the habalîs, we cannot tell where they lie until thou hearest from behind a crag or bush *deh!* and the shot strikes thee."

Later in the week Motlog came again from Hâvil: he had not before been thither, nor his companions; but they crossed an hundred miles over the open khála guided by sight only of the mountain landmarks, which they had enquired beforehand. We had shifted ground many times in his absence; and it was strange for me to see them ride in, without having erred, to our menzil. As the journeys of the tribesmen are determined beforehand, they might reckon, within a day's distance, where riding they should fall upon our traces, which finding they will follow the fresh footing of our late ráhla; and climbing on all heights as they come, they look for the black booths of their Aarab. Thus these land-navigators arrive bye and bye at the unstable village port of their voyage. All the tribesmen which were not abroad herding, assembled to parliament, where they heard Motlog was gone down, to his brother Rahŷel's tent, to hear their sheykh give account of his embassy to the emir, which imported so much to the policy of their little desert nation.—Every man had armed his hand with the tobacco-pipe, and, said each one arriving, "Strengthen thee, O Motlog!" and to the great sheykh he handed up his galliûn. Motlog sat freshly before them, in his new apparel, the accustomed gift of the emir, and he filled all their pipe-heads benignly, with the aromatic tittun *el-Hameydy* of Mesopotamia; of which he had brought with him a few weeks' cheer, from the village capital. The coffee was slowly served round, to so great an assembly. Burdensome was that day's heat, and now the mid-day's sun overhead, yet there was none who thought of going to his slumber, or even to eat; such was all the people's expectation to hear the mind of the terrible emir. They sat this day out, no man moving from his place, and yet fasting, except only from coffee and tittun, till the evening.—The prince licensed them to return, without fear, into their own dîra.

The vassals of Ibn Rashîd receive, after the audience, a change of clothing; besides, the emir bestowed sixty silver reals upon Motlog, and gave ten pieces to each of his wayfellows. These are arts of the Arabian governors, to retain, with a pretended bounty, the slippery wills of the wild Beduw; and well sown is the emir's penny, if he should reap, in the next years, ten-fold. Motlog was sheykh of one of the tributary tribes, a little wide of his reach. The tax upon the nomads is light, and otherwise it could never be gathered; a crown piece is payment for every five camels, or for thirty head of small cattle. Of the Fukara was levied thus but four hundred reals, which is somewhat as eight or nine shillings for every household: yet the free-born, forlorn and predatory Beduw grimly fret their hearts under these small burdens; the emir's custom is ever untimely, the exaction, they think, of a stronger and plain tyranny: yet yielding this tribute, they become of the prince's federation, and are sheltered from all hostility of the Aarab in front. Motlog was a prudent man, of reach and sight; but he could not see through sixty reals. This was a pleasant policy of the emir, and by the like the wisest man's heart is touched; and the nomad sheykh brought back, in his new smelling clothes, a favourable opinion, for the while, of the flattering prince, and Hâyil government; and thought in his heart, to be the prince's liegeman, for the present, of whom he had received so gentle entertainment. But the haughty Mohammed Ibn Rashîd, who paid the scot, had another opinion of him; the emir afterward told me, with his own mouth, that he misliked this Motlog.

Blithe were the Fukara to return to their home marches, and better to them than all this high desolate country, which (said they) is '*ghror*, a land wherein is nothing good, for man nor cattle.' Also, they think that dîra better, by which the derb el-haj passes; they say, "We have a kella," that is a house of call, and store-chambers, the caravan market is held there, and their sheukh receive surra. On the morrow we marched; and the Beduins henceforth removed every day by short journeys; now their face was homeward. Behind us we left J. Misma, then some mountain which I heard named *Roaf*. the third day we came to drink upon the upland, at a wide standing water, in a gravel bed, which in winter is a lake-plash, of the ponded rain, *Therrai*.

We marched then in a sandstone country, where, for crags, thick as loaves in a baker's oven, we could not see the next riders about us. From the fifth march, we alighted again under Birrd, to water, in the natural deep chaps of the precipitous sandstone mountain: the herdsmen, digging shallow pits with their hands in the fetid sand, took up in buckets, with their waterer's song, a sandy foul water. We removed now daily, loading before dawn, and alighting at high noon. In another march we came, under the flaming sun, over the high open plain, a barren floor of gravel, towards a great watering-place and summer station of the tribe, *el-Erudda*. These uplands are mostly without growth of the desert acacia

G

trees: woe is therefore the housewife, for any tent-peg lost in the ráhla. Yet now appeared a long line of acacias, and a white swelling country, these are the landmarks of el-Erudda; and here, at the midst of their dîra, is a *mákbara*, or common burying-place of the tribe, with few barren plants of wild palms. It is hardly a journey from hence to el-Héjr: the Beduins would be here umjemmîn, for many days.

Camels strayed the next night from Zeyd's menzil; the owners scoured the country, hoping to have sight of them, for where all the soil was trodden down with innumerable footprints of the tribe's cattle, they could not distinguish the traces. It was not that they feared their beasts, losing themselves, must in few days perish with thirst: the great dull and sheeplike cattle have a perfect conscience of all watering-places of their home dîra; though, for all their long necks, in but very few of them might they attain to drink. Three years before, when the Fukara were in Syria, some camels of theirs, frayed and lost near the Hauran, had been recovered by tribesmen returning later in the year from Medina, who, crossing their own dîra, found those beasts feeding about a watering, in the border of the Hejâz. The men knew them, by the brand, to be some of their tribe's cattle, and brought up again those fugitive camels, which had fled to their native marches, over seven geographical degrees.

We had no more notice of the haramîyeh.—Then, by a Solubby family which arrived from over the Harra, there came uncertain tidings, that their cattle had been retaken by the Moahîb: a small Moahîb foray riding in the north had crossed the robbers; (hostile ghrazzus, meeting in the wilderness, hail each other, *ya gôm!* "ho! ye enemies,") but not able to overtake the main body of them, they had cut off but fifteen camels. The custom of one real salvage, for a head, is paid between friendly tribes, and they are restored to the owners.

At length we understood that the robbers, as Zeyd foretold, had been a party of Beny Sókhr, who from their tents in Syria, to the place where they met with us had ridden out not less than four hundred miles; and in their company there rode a few men of the Sherarát nomads who are part friends, part "not well" with the Fejîr. As for the Sokhûr, our Beduins reckoned them hitherto neither friends nor enemies; yet certain Fukara households, of the northern migration, were wandering with that tribe to this day. A ragged rout of B. Sókhr, carriers to the Haj, must every year pass, with the caravan, through the Fukara country.— On behalf of the Fejîr a young sheykh, *Mijwel*, was sent after this to the North, to treat peaceably with the B. Sókhr for the restitution of his tribe's camels. The elders of B. Sókhr responded in the mejlis, "They that had reaved the Fukara cattle were a company of ignorant young men; but their ignorance to be less blameworthy because they found the Fejîr wandering out of their own dîra." The sheykhs promised that good part of the cattle should be brought again with the Haj; the rest they would have conceded to the turbulent young men, "which must be appeased, with somewhat for their pains, and that for an end of strife." More might not Mijwel obtain: and this is as much justice as may commonly be had in the world.

Now, arrived at el-Erudda, my mind was to forsake the Beduin life and pass by el-Ally to the sea coast at el-Wejh. My friends bade me speak with Motlog in the matter of my camel. Why did not Zeyd obey the pasha's injunction?—and then this mischief had not chanced. I had not the price of another camel,—hard must be my adventure henceforth in land of Arabia. The custom of the desert is that of Moses, "If any man's beast hurt the beast of another man, the loss shall be divided." Frolic in the succulent spring herbage, the great unwieldly brutes rise in the night with full cuds to play their whale-sports together; some camel then, as the Beduins held, had fallen upon the neck of my gaping young camel: whether it happened then, or in the camels' bouncing forth to their morning pasture, it was among Zeyd's troop of camels. I must bring witnesses: but who would give testimony against a sheykh of his tribe, for the Nasrâny? Amongst Mohammedans, and though they be the Beduins of the wilderness, there is equity only between themselves. I found Motlog in his tent, who with a woollen thread was stitching in his mare's saddle-pad. "A pity, said the sheykh, that any controversy should grow betwixt Khalîl and Zeyd, who were brethren, but the Pasha's words ought to have been observed." Zeyd was disappointed in me of his greedy hopes; fortune had given us both checkmate since the hope of my vaccination had failed; there remained only my saddle-bags, and his eyes daily devoured them. Great they were, and stuffed to a fault, in a land where passengers ride without baggage. Heavy Zeyd found their draught, and he felt in them elbow-deep day by day, which was contrary to the honourable dealing of an host;—besides my apprehension that he might thus light upon my pistol and instruments, which lay hidden at the bottom in our menzils.

For these displeasures, in a last râhla I had forsaken Zeyd, and came on walking over the waste gravel, under the scalding sun many miles till the Aarab alighted. Zeyd found in his heart that he had done me wrong, I had not deceived him, and he respected my person : I also heedfully avoided to rake up the wild unknown depths of their Mohammedan resentment. I entered Motlog's tent, the sheykhly man sat playing with his children, he was a very affectionate father. Thither came Zeyd soon and sat down to drink coffee ; then raising his portentous voice said he, " If I had not intended to devour him, wellah, I had not received the Nasrâny ; I would not have suffered him to accompany the Aarab, no not in a râhla. The Nasrâny gave sixty reals (a fable) to Mohammed Aly, and I require the like to be paid me in this hour " " No, (Motlog answered from behind the women's curtain, whither he was gone for somewhat,) this is not in thy hand, O Zeyd " Zeyd complaining that my being in his menzil was an expense to him, I proved that Zeyd had received of me certain reals, and besides a little milk I had taken of him nothing : but his meaning was that I brought too many coffee guests, who all came thither to see the stranger. Zeyd had bought two reals worth in the haj market. " Here (I said) is that money, and let Zeyd trust further to my friendly possibility. Zeyd complains of me with little cause ; I might complain with reason ; should one treat his guest's baggage as thing which is taken in the ghrazzu ? he seeks even in my purse for money, and in my belt, and ransacks my bags."—" Ha ! how does Zeyd ? " said some sheykh's voice. I answered, in my haste, " Billah, like an hablûs." Motlog shrank at the word, which had been better unsaid ; the Beduins doubted if they heard Khalîl aright : the worst was that Zeyd in all his life came so near to merit this reproachful word, which uttered thus in the mejlis, must cleave to him in the malicious memory of his enemies. He rose as he had sipped the cup and left us. In our evening mirth the hinds often called to each other, hablûs ! hablûs ! which hearing, and I must needs learn their speech of the Arabs, I had not supposed it amiss : but Zeyd vaunted himself sherîf. When he was gone out some said, so had Zeyd done to such and such other, Zeyd was a bad man ; (the Beduw easily blame each other). Said Motlog, ' in the question of the camel I must bring witnesses, but he would defend me from all wrongful demands of Zeyd.'

As we sat, one came in who but then returned from an absence ; as the custom is he would first declare his tidings in the mejlis, and afterward go home to his own household. He sat down on his knee, but was so poor a man, there was none in the sheykhly company that rose to kiss him : with a solemn look he stayed him a moment on his camel-stick, and then pointing gravely with it to every man, one after other, he saluted him with an hollow voice, by his name, saying, " The Lord strengthen thee ! " A poor old Beduin wife, when she heard that her son was come again, had followed him over the hot sand hither ; now she stood to await him, faintly leaning upon a stake of the beyt a little without, since it is not for any woman to enter where the men's mejlis is sitting. His tidings told, he stepped abroad to greet his mother, who ran, and cast her weak arms about his manly neck, trembling for age and tenderness, to see him alive again and sound ; and kissing him she could not speak, but uttered little cries. Some of the coffee-drinkers laughed roughly, and mocked her drivelling, but Motlog said, " Wherefore laugh ? is not this the love of a mother ? "

Selím came soon to call me from his father; " Well, go with Selím, said Motlog, and be reconciled to Zeyd ; and see that neither require aught of the other." Zeyd invited me into his wife's closed apartment, where we sat down, and Hirfa with us, to eat again the bread and salt together. Zeyd soon returned from these rubs, when he could not find his ' brother ' in fault, to the Beduin good humour, and leaning on his elbow he would reach over, pledge of our friendship, the peaceable sebîl, I should ' drink ' with him tobacco :—and such are the nomads. Our late contention was no more mentioned, but it was long after branded in Zeyd's mind, that Khalîl had called him hablûs. In the autumn of this year, when the Fukara lay encamped at el-Héjr, and I was again with them, as I passed by Zeyd's menzil, he called me from the beyt, " ya Khalîl taal ! come hither," I greeted him, and also the housewife behind the curtain " gowwich Hirfa, the Lord strengthen thee."—Zeyd answered, " It is the voice of Khalîl, and the words of a Beduwy ; " and he rose to bring me in to eat a bowl of rice with him, which was then ready. After meat, " he was glad to see me, he said, once more here in his beyt, it was like the old times ; " then a little casting down his eyes he added, " but after our friendship I was wounded, Khalîl, when you named me hablûs, and that before the sheukh."—" Because you had threatened and displeased me; but, Zeyd, let not this trouble thee ; how could I know all the words of you Beduins ? Seest thou these black worsted tents ? Are they not all booths of hablûses ? " We walked down to the mejlis, where Zeyd related, smiling, that my meaning had been but to name him " thou Beduwy ".

—When I reasoned with Zeyd, " Why didst thou not do as the Pasha commanded ? " cried he, " Who commands me ! henna (we are) *el-Beduw:* what is Pasha, or what is the Dowla here? save only that they pay us our surra, and else we would take it by force."—"What is your force? were an hundred of you, with club-sticks, lances, and old matchlocks, worth ten of the haj soldiery?"—"We would shoot down upon them in the boghrazát." "And how far may your old rusty irons shoot?" Zeyd answered, between jest and solemnity, "*Arbaa saa,*" to four hours distance: Saat is with the Aarab 'a siound', a second or third space between the times of prayer Often they asked me, "How many hours be there in the day? We know not well *saa.*" Their partitions of the daylight are *el-féjr,* the dawning before the sun; *el-gaila,* the sun rising towards noon; *eththóhr,* the sun in the mid-day height; *el-assr,* the sun descended to mid-afternoon; *ghraibat es-shems,* the sun going down to the setting:—*mághrib* is a strange town speaking in their ears.

The nomads' summer station at el-Erudda was now as an uncheerful village. In the time of wandering since the Haj, the sheykhs had spent their slender stores of coffee; and "where no coffee is, there is not merry company," say the Aarab. Their coffee hearths now cold, every man sat drooping and dull, *fi ahlahu,* in his own household. Said Zeyd, "This was the life of the old nomads in the days before coffee." The sheukh would soon send down for more coffee of theirs which was stored at Medáin; and Zeyd must go thither to fetch up a sack of rice, which he had also deposited in the kella: I would then ride with him, intending to pass by el-Ally to the Red Sea coast. The wilderness fainted before the sunny drought; the harvest was past, and I desired to be gone. The Aarab languished lying in the tents; we seemed to breathe flames. All day I gasped and hardly remained alive, since I was breathless, and could not eat. I had sometimes a thought in the long days to teach Selím letters: but when his son had learned the alphabet Zeyd would no more, lest the child should take of me some faulty utterance; my tongue he said was not yet " loosed ". Having a vocabulary in my hand, now and then I read out a page or two to the company. Certainly I could not err much in the utterance of many words that were before well known to me; but no small part of these town and bookish terms were quite unknown to all my nomad hearers! of some it seemed they had not the roots, of many they use other forms. They wondered themselves, and as Arabs will (who have so much feeling in their language and leisure to be eloquent) considered word after word with a patient attention. * * *

* * * The evening before our departure, Mehsan had sacrificed a sheep, the year's-mind of his father here lying buried, and brought us of his cooked meat; he was Zeyd's brother-in-law, and we were a homely company. I made them sweet tea; and distributed presents of the things which I had. As we sat I asked these Beduins if my *gaûd* (young camel) with the broken mouth could carry me a hundred and fifty miles to el-Wejh? One sitting with us proffered, so I would give him ten reals, to exchange his own nâga for mine. Zeyd and Mehsan approving, I gave the money; but the meditations of the Arabs are always of treachery. The poor man's wife and children also playing the weepers, I gave them besides all that I might spare of clothing, of which they have so much need in the desert; but after other days I saw my things put to sale at Teyma. I bought thus upon their trust, a dizzy camel, old, and nearly past labour and, having lost her front teeth, that was of no more value, in the sight of the nomads, than my wounded camel. I was new in their skill; the camels are known and valued after their teeth, and with regard to the hump. They are named by the teeth till the coming of the canines in this manner: the calf of one year, *howwar;* of two, *libny;* the third, *hej;* the fourth, *jitha;* the fifth, *thènny;* the sixth, *ròbba;* the seventh, *siddes;* and the eighth, *shâgg en-naba, wafiat, mùfter.*

(*Doughty revisits Medâin with Zeyd, and, later, attaches himself to the Moahîb tribe in their wanderings upon the Harra. The Moahîb forsake the Harra, and descend to their summer station in Wady Thirba. Doughty summers* (1877) *with the Fukara tribe at el-Héjr, and revisits el-Ally.*)

CHAPTER X

FINALLY, after other days of great heat, which were the last
of that summer, the 28th of August, the Aarab removed from
el-Héjr. Once more their " faces were toward " the Teyma country, and I mounted among them with such comfort of heart as
is in the going home from a scurvy school-house ;—delivered,
at length, from the eye-sore and nose-sore of those mawkish
mummy-house cliffs, the sordid kella and perilous Moghrâreba
of Medáin Sâlih. Now, leaving the Turkish haj-road country,
I had Nejd before me, the free High Arabia !

We passed the enclosed plain to the south-eastward. I saw
many falcons carried out by the thelûl riders in this ráhla ;
they had purchased the birds of the gate Arabs ; and there are
Beduin masters who in the march carry their greyhounds upon
camel-back, lest the burning sand should scald their tender
feet. Four days we journeyed by short marches to the eastward, and the nomads alighting every forenoon dismissed their
cattle to pasture. The summer heat was ended for us in those
airy uplands. At the morrow's sunrise whilst we sat a moment, before the ráhla, over a hasty fire, I read the thermometer, 73° F. ; yet it seemed a cold wind that was blowing
upon us.

I would leave now the wandering village, and set out with
Méhsan, and a company of poorer tribesmen who went to pass
Ramathán at Teyma, where the new dates were ripening. The
tribe would come thither a month later in the last days of Lent,
to keep their (Bairam) festival at the village and in the date
gathering to buy themselves victuals.

When the sun rose of the first of September, and we were
departing from the menzils, we heard cries, in the side of the
camp, *El-Gôm !* Tribesmen ran from the byût girded in their
jingling gunners' belts, with long matchlocks, or armed with
pikes and lances. The sheykhs went to take their horses,

foot-farers hastened forward, and shouted. Only a few aged men remained behind with the hareem ; bye and bye they 'thought they heard shots yonder'. Now Zeyd went by us, a little tardy, at a hand gallop. Stern were the withered looks of his black visage and pricking sheykhly upon the mare to his endeavour, with the long wavering lance upon his virile shoulder, and the Ishmaelite side-locks flying backward in the wind, the son of Sbeychan seemed a martial figure. Even boys of mettle leapt upon thelûls which were theirs, and rode to see the battle : this forwardness in them is well viewed by the elders. Méhsan cast down his load and followed them, unarmed, upon his mad thelûl. It was not much before we saw the head of our tribespeople's squadron return-ing :—the riding of an hundred mounted upon dromedaries is (as said) a gallant spectacle ; they come on nodding in the lofty saddles to the deep gait of their cattle, with a glitter of iron, and the song of war, in a sort of long flocking order.

Then we heard a sorry tiding of the calamity of our friends ! The herdsmen first abroad had found strange camels in the desert ; they knew them by the brand ⌒ to be cattle of the Moahîb and shouted, and the cry taken up behind them was heard back in the menzils.—Therrŷeh leading out the armed band, the keepers of those cattle came to greet them—with ' Gowwak ya Therrŷeh, we are of the Auwájy and have "taken " the Moahîb yesterday ; wellah, all their camels in the Héjr plain, beside Thirba.'—The Fukara being their friends upon both sides, could not now go between them ; but if the Moahîb had been removing and encamping with the Fukara in their dîra, the Bishr might not have molested them. Silent and pensive our Teyma company gathered again, we were forty riders ; and many a man went musing of his own perpetual insecurity in the face of these extreme slips of fortune. Our familiar friends had been bereaved in one hour of all their living ; and their disaster seemed the greater, since we have seen their sheykhs had ridden—it was to have outgone this danger, but they came too late—to make their humble submission to the Emir. The Aarab sigh a word in sadness which is without contradiction, and cease complaining, "It has happened by the appointment of Ullah ! "

After two hours' riding we come to drink and fill our girbies at a solitary well-pit of the ancients, cased with dry stonework ; there grew a barren wild fig-tree. In that day's march we went by three more small well-pits, which are many (wherever the ground-water lies not deep) in all the waste emptiness of the Arabian wilderness: these may suffice to the watering of their lesser cattle.

Sultry was our journey, and we alighted at half-afternoon, where we found shadows of some great rocks with tolh trees, and pasture for the camels. The men rested and drank coffee: the housewives also kindled fires and baked scanty cakes, under the ashes, of their last barley meal. After an hour or two, when men and beasts were a little refreshed from the burdenous heat, we mounted and rode on again in the desert plain, till the sun was nigh setting; then they drew bridle in ground where an encampment of ours had been in the spring time. "Companions, I exclaimed, this is Umsubba!" but it dismayed the Aarab, with a sort of fear of enemies, to hear a stranger name the place, and though it is marked by that tall singular needle of sandstone.

At the watch-fires they questioned among them, had they well done to break their fasts to-day, which some of these Beduin heads accounted to be the first in the holy month: but Méhsan, who was of an easy liberal humour, held that no man were to blame for eating ' until he saw the new moon (it is commonly at the third evening), and then let him fast out his month of days'. Some answered: " In the town they reckon now by el-Hindy (Indian art, arithmetic), and they say it is unfailing, but what wot any man of us the Beduw!" Now in the glooming we perceived the new moon nigh her setting, and of the third day's age: the Beduins greeted this sign in heaven with devout aspirations, which brought in their month of devotion. The dwellers in the desert fast all months in their lives, and they observe this day-fasting of a month for the religion. But Ramathán is to the Beduins an immoderate weariness full of groans and complaining; so hard it is for them to abstain from drinking and even from tobacco till the summer sun sets: in those weeks is even a separation of wedded folk. The month of Lent which should be kept clean and holy, is rather, say the nomads and villagers, a season of wickedness, when the worst sores break forth and run afresh of human nature. Not more than a good half of these fanatical nomads observe the day-fasting and prayers;—the rest are "ignorants ",—this is to say they have not learned to pray, yet they cherish little less fanaticism in their factious hearts, which is a kind of national envy or Semitic patriotism.—For herding-men, fried all day in the desert heat, it is very hard and nearly impossible not to drink till the furnace sun be set. Men in a journey have a dispensation ; the koran bids them fast to the number of days omitted and hallow the month, at their home-coming.

We set forward very early on the morrow, long and sultry lay the way before us, which to-day the Beduins must pass thirsting; and when the morning heat arose upon us, we were well advanced towards Teyma,—the landmark J. Ghrenèym now appearing—and came to that bald soil which lies before the town, a floor of purple sand-rock with iron-stone and shingles, where the grassy blade springs not and you may seldom see any desert bush. We perceived in the early afternoon the heads of the oasis palms, and approached the old circuit of town walling. The first outlying orchards are nigh before us,—an Eden to our parched eyes from the desert; then we see those full palm-bosoms, under the beautiful tressed crowns, the golden and purple-coloured food-fruits. Locust flights had passed this year over all the villages, and hardly more than half their trees had been saved at Teyma. The company dispersed, every fellowship going to pitch upon their friends' grounds. I followed with Méhsan's fellowship, we made our camels stumble over some broken clay walls into an empty field : the men as we alighted cried impatiently to their housewives to build the booths; for the thirsty Beduins would be out of this intolerable sun-burning.

Some labourers, with hoes in their hands, came out of the next gates; I asked them to fetch a twig of the new dates (their Semitic goodness to strangers), and to bring me a cup of water. "Auh! what man is this with you, O ye of the Fukara (said the villagers, wondering), who eats and drinks in Rama-thán, and the sun is yet high !—for shame ! dost thou not know Ullah ? " and the torpid souls gaped and fleered upon me. One said, "Is not this Khalîl the kafir, he that was here before ? ay, he is he."—"Upon you be the shame, who forbid my eating, that am a wayfaring man, musáfir."—"Ha! (said the voice of a poor woman, who came by and overheard them) this stranger says truth, it is ye the men of Teyma, who fear not Ullah," and she passed on hastily. Bye and bye as I was going in with them, she, who seemed a poor Bedlam creature, met me again running, and took hold without saying word on my mantle, and opening her veil, with a harrowed look she stretched me out her meagre hands, full of dates and pomegranates, nodding to me in sign that I should receive them; she lived where we went in to water.—The poor woman came to me again at evening like one half distracted, and shrinking from sight. "Stranger, she said, eigh me ! why didst thou not eat all my fruit ? I ran for them as ever I heard thee speak. Know that I am a poor woman afflicted in my mind.—Ah Lord! He who has given has taken them away; I have lost my children, one after other, four sons, and for the last I besought my Lord that He would leave me this child, but he died also—aha me!—and he was come almost to manly age. And there are times when this sorrow so taketh me, that I fare like a madwoman; but tell me, O stranger, hast thou no counsel in this case? and as for me I do that which thou seest,—ministering to the wants of others —in hope that my Lord, at the last, will have mercy upon me."

— The Teyma men had thwacked their well-team, with alacrity, and made them draw for the guests. Our host's place was a poor grange, lying a little before the main orchard walls of Teyma. In the midst was his house-building, kasr.—dark clay-built rooms about a long-square space, which was shadowed from the sun by a loose thatch upon poles of the palm leaf-branches. His was a good walled palm-orchard and corn ground, watered day and night from a well of two reels and dullûs: yet such a possession may hardly suffice to the simple living of an Arabic household from year to year. Of the uncertain fruits of his trees and seed-plots, that which was above their eating, he sold for silver to the Beduw; he must pay for timely help of hands, the hire of well-camels, for his tools, for his leathern well-gear; and the most such small owners will tell you, what for their many outgoings and what for their old indebtedness, they may hardly hold up their heads in the world.

The Arabs very impatiently suffering the thirst of the first Ramathán days, lie on their breasts sighing out the slow hours, and watching the empty daylight till the " eye of the sun " shall be gone down from them. When five or six days are past, they begin to be inured to this daylight abstinence, having so large leave in the night-time. If their Lent fall in the corn harvest, or at the ingathering of dates, the harvesters must endure for the religion an extremity of thirst: but in Ramathán the villagers give over all that they may of earnest labour, save the well-driving that may never be intermitted. Their most kinds of dates were ripe in the midst of the fast; but they let them still hang in the trees.—The owner of the plantation, to whom I said again my request, delayed, as it were with unwillingness. " It is a pain (one whispered to me) for men, weak with thirst and hunger, to see another eat the sweet and drink water; "—the master lingered also to make a little raillery (as the Arabs will, for they love it) at that contempt in the stranger of their high religious custom. Then he went out and gathered me date-twigs of the best stems, upon which hanged, with the ripe, half-ripe purple berries, which thus at the mellowing, and full of sappy sweetness, they call *belah;* the Arabs account them very wholesome and refreshing. Even the common kinds of dates are better meat now than at any time after,—the hard berry, melted to ripeness in the trees, is softly swelling under the sun with the genial honey moisture.

We returned to our cottage friends at evening, when the Arabs refreshed, and kindling their cheerful galliûns, seemed to themselves to drink in solace again. Fire was made in the cold hearth-pit, and coffee-pots were set, a drink not often seen in that poor place. Later came in some persons from the town, and their talk with us new-comers was of the ruined haddàj, 'The Teyâmena, they told us, were persuaded that the pit fell-in after my having "written it," and when they saw me again in their town, wellah, the angry people would kill me.' Because they had thus drunk with me in fellowship, they counselled me not to adventure myself in Teyma;—let my Beduin friends look to it, as they would have my life saved. Méhsan answered (who was a timid man), "As ever the morrow is light, Khalîl must mount upon his nâga, and ride back to Zeyd."—"Consider! I said to them, if I were guilty of the haddàj falling, I had not returned hither of my free will. May our bodies endure for ever? ancient house-buildings fall, also that old well must decay at some time."— "But after it was fallen, we heard that you refused to rebuild it!"—So we left them for the night.

The first moments of the morning sun, were of those which I oftentimes passed very heavily in Arabia, when I understood of my bread-and-salt friends, that my lonely life was atrociously threatened, and they earnestly persuaded me to sudden flight. Some of our hareem came to me when I awoke,—Méhsan was gone out in the cool, before dawn, to sell a new saffron gown-cloth in the town; and the men were abroad with him—Zeyd's sister, my hostess, and the women besought me to depart in haste, 'lest I should be slain before their eyes.'—The nomad wives had been over-night to visit their gossips in the settlement, and in their talk they said the Nasrâny had arrived in the company. "The Nasrâny! cried the Teyma housewives,— is not that, as they say, a son of the Evil One? is he come among you! Now if ye have any care of Khalîl's life, let him not enter the town,—where yet would God! he may come, and be slain to-morrow : some of our men are sworn upon the death of him."—"And why think ye evil of this man? now a long time he is living among the Beduw, and other than his name

of Nasrâny, they find no cause in him."—"Yet know certainly
that he is a wicked person, and of the adversaries of Ullah;
they say moreover, he is a sorcerer. Heard you not tell that
the haddàj was fallen? and men do say it was his eye.—Ye
have not found him maleficent? but what he may be no man
can tell, nor wherefore he may be come into the land of the
Aarab. Who ever heard before that a Nasrâny came hither?
and our people say he ought not to live; it were also a merit
to kill him."

"Khalîl, said Méhsan's wife, the Teyâmena are determined
to kill thee for the haddàj, and if they come, we are few and
cannot resist them. They are not the Beduw, that have a good
mind towards you, and a regard for the Dowla, but the headstrong and high-minded people of Teyma, so that whilst we
lodge here, we live ourselves wellah in dread of them: the
Teyâmena are treacherous, *melaunnîn*, of cursed counsels!"—
Said Méhsan, who now arrived, "Akhs! while Khalîl sits here,
some of them will be coming; Ullah confound the Teyâmena!
Mount, Khalîl, and prevent them!"—The women added, "And
that quickly, we would not have thee slain." The children
cried, "Ride fast from them, uncle Khalîl." Sâlih the old
grey-headed gun-bearer of Zeyd's father, and Zeyd's own man,
was very instant with me that I should mount immediately
and escape to the Beduw, "Our Aarab (he said) are yet where
we left them, and my son and another are about to ride back
with the camels; mount thou and save thyself with the young
men; and remain with Zeyd, and amongst thy friends, until
time when the Haj arrive."—"And if all this cannot move
thee, said the old man and Méhsan, Khalîl, thou hast lost
thy understanding!—and companions, this man whom we
esteemed prudent (in his wise books), is like to one that hath
a jin: up now! that thy blood be not spilt before our faces.
When they come, we can but entreat and not withhold them,
—wellah it is a cursed people of this town.—We know not
what he may have seen (in his books); yet stay not, Khalîl,
rise quickly, and do thou escape from them with the lads! Ah,
for these delays! he does not hear the words of us all, and
sitting on here he may have but few moments to live:—and yet
Khalîl does nothing!" *Another voice*, "It may be that Ullah
has determined his perdition; well! let him alone." I blamed
them that trusted to the fond words of silly hareem.—"And
what if the Teyâmena come, I might not dissuade them with
reason?"—"They that will be here presently are hot-heads, and
hear no words."—There is an itch between pain and pleasure,
which is such a mastering cruelty in children, to see one

shaped like themselves overtaken in some mortal agony, and his calamitous case not to touch them; and now, as I looked about me, I saw a strange kindling in some of this ring of watching wild eyes, there a writhing lip, and there some inhuman flushing even in those faded women's cheeks. "Eigh! what and if the Lord have determined his death!—we see, he cannot hear, or hearing that he cannot understand! We say but this once more; mount, Khalîl! whilst there is any space. Wellah we would not that thy blood be spilt beside our byût, by the rash-handed people of Teyma, and we cannot deliver thee."—"Friends, when I was here before, I found them well disposed."—"Then thou wast in company with a great sheykh, Zeyd, and now there is none here to shelter thee!—but since we have endeavoured and cannot persuade thee, may not the event be such as we would not!—it is now too late, and Ullah will provide."

In this there approached two younger men of the town, and they spoke pleasantly with us. One of them, Hásan Ibn Salâmy, the Beduins told me, was of the principal town sheukh; that other was a Shammar Beduwy of the north, lately become a flesher at Teyma,—he brought this new trade into the Beduin-like town. The Shammary boasted to be a travelled young man, he had visited Sham as well as Irâk, and now he looked for the praise of a liberal mind. Being one of the most removable heads, he had gone out at the first rumour of the stranger's arriving, and led that sheykh, his neighbour in the sûk, along with him. The weled would see for himself, and bring word whether that Nasrâny were not of some people or tribe he had visited, or it might be he had passed by their béled in his caravan journeys: besides, he had a thought, there might be a *shatâra*, or mastery in the hand of the Nasrâny, for building up their haddàj, and he would win a thank for himself from the village sheukh. The Teyâmena had built their well-wall, since the spring, now three times, and the work was fallen. The best village architect of the spacious and lofty clay-brick Teyma houses was their master-builder in the second and third essays, for not a small reward,—fifty reals. As ever the walling was up, the landowners had mounted their wheel-gear; and the teams were immediately set labouring upon the distempered carth, so that the work could not stand many days; the weak soil parted forward, and all had fallen again. The Teyâmena knew not what more to do, and when Ramathán was in, they let it lie: also the workmen (seeing their time) demanded higher wages,—and they labour in Lent only half-days.

The last ruin of the walls had been a fortnight before. 'If I had a shatâra to build, said the Beduwy, the sheykhs

would enrich me, giving me what I myself would in reason.'
Hásan confirmed the word, being himself *râiyat*, or one of the
principal owners, with his sûk, of the haddàj, and namely of that
part which was fallen. I said, ' I would go in to see it, if they
thought the town was safe.'—" Fear nothing, and I am *thâmin*
(said Hásan) engaged for thee to these friends here ; and if thou
art not fasting come down to my house, where I will have thy
breakfast made ready ; and we will afterward go to visit the
haddàj ; but as for the wall falling, it was from Ullah, and
not of man's deed." I was fainting with hunger, and had
my weapon bound under my tunic, so hearing they would lead
me to breakfast, I rose to follow them. " And these thou
mayest trust," said the Beduins ; nevertheless, Méhsan's wife
took me by the sleeve as I departed, to whisper, " Khalîl, we
know him—a great sheykh, yet he may be leading thee to
destruction : have a care of them, *iftah ayûn-ak*, open thine
eyes, for they are all treacherous Teyâmena."

As we were entering at the town's end I called to him,
" Hásan ! art thou able to defend me if there should meet
with us any evil persons ? " And he, with the slippery smiling
security of an Arab, who by adventure is engaged for another,
and in the Semitic phrase of their speech ; " There is nothing
to fear, and I have all this people in my belly." We came
in by alleys of the town to the threshold of Hásan's large
dàr. We sat down on a gay Turkey carpet, in the court
before his kahwa, and under a wide sheltering vine, whose
old outspread arms upon trellises, were like a wood before the
sun of sappy greenness : there came in a neighbour or two.
Water from the metal, *'brîk*, was poured upon my hands, and
the host set a tray before me of helw dates—this kind is
full of a honey-like melting sweetness—gathered warm out
of the sun, and pomegranates.—They wondered to see me
eat without regarding the public fast, but as smiling hosts
were appeased with this word : *Imma ana musâfir*, " but I
am a wayfaring man." They smiled when I told of the
nomads' distrust of them, for my sake, and said, " It is like
the Beduw ! but here, Khalîl, thou hast nothing to fear,
although there be some dizzy-headed among us like themselves ;
but they fear the sheûkh, and, when they see I am with thee,
khálas ! there an end of danger."

We walked forth to the great well-pit, where I heard such
voices, of idle young men and Beduins—" Look, here he comes,
look, look, it is the kafir ! will the sheykhs kill him ? is not this
he who has overthrown the haddàj ? Or will they have him
build it again, and give him a reward, and they say it shall be

better than before." Hásan bade me not mind their knavish talk ; and when we had passed round he left me there, and said that none would offer me an injury. This butterfly gallant, the only ornament of whose bird's soul was a gay kerchief of a real, would not be seen in the kafir's company,—it was not honest : and where is question of religion, there is no sparkle of singular courage in these pretended magnanimous, to set one's face against the faces of many. So I came to some grave elder men who sat communing together under a wheel-frame : as I saluted them with peace, they greeted me mildly again ; I asked would there be any danger in my walking in the town ? " Doubt nothing, come and go, they said, at thine own pleasure in all the ways of Teyma, and give no heed to the ungracious talk of a few blameworthy young men."—The Shammary was gone with word to "the *Emir*"; thus he called the chief sheykh in the town (under Ibn Rashîd), *Khálaf el-Ammr.*— He (for the Arabs) is Emir, in whom is the word of command, *amr:* thus, *emir el-káfila*, ruler of an Arabian town-caravan ; and in arms they say, likewise, ' emir of ten ' and ' emir of an hundred.' The Beduwy told how he had found me willing, and he made them this argument, ' Their ancient well is of the old kafirs' work, and Khalîl is a kafir, therefore could Khalîl best of all rebuild the haddàj.'

I asked my way to *Aj(k)eyl's* dàr, he had been one of those Teyma merchant-guests in the kella (before the Haj) at Medáin. With a sort of friendliness he had then bidden me, if I came afterward to Teyma, to lodge in his house. Homely was his speech, and with that bluntness which persuaded me of the man's true meaning. Nevertheless the Beduins bade me mistrust Ajeyl, "a dark-hearted covetous fellow that would murder me in his house, for that tháhab" or metal of money, which Arabians can imagine to be in every stranger's hold. Zeyd had said to me, " Ajeyl killed his own brother, in disputing over a piece of silver ! " Therrŷeh added, " Have a care of him, that certainly Ajeyl is a churl."—Zeyd said then a good word, " Thou art too simple, Khalîl, if thou hast not discerned it already, that coveting of money is before all things in the Aarab: having this in mind, thou wilt not be deceived; trust me, it is but upon some hope of winning, if any man bind himself to further a Nasrány. It is hard for thee to pass the distance from hence, to the Ghrenèym mountain; but this must thou do,—I tell thee, Khalîl, thou mayest travel in the Aarab's country only by tóma ; "—that is in casting back morsels to their sordid avarice.

I went now to see if after his promises I might not lodge in some room of Ajeyl's house. 'Every place, he answered, is taken up, but he would speak with his father.'—A young man of the town led me away to visit his sick mother. In another large dàr I found the woman lying on the ground far gone in a vesical disease, which only death could remedy. Thâhir the householder promised me much for the healing of this old wife, and would have the hakîm lodge in his house; but the man was of such a grim inflamed visage, with a pair of violent eyes, and let me divine so much of his fanatical meaning (as if he would have me made a Mosleman perforce), that, with a civil excuse, I was glad to be abroad again and out of their neighbourhood.—Another led me to see a dropsical woman near the haddàj; the patient was lying (so swollen that those who entered with me mocked) under a palm, where her friends had made her an awning. She promised, she would not fail to pay the hakîm, when he had cured her. In visiting the sick I desired in my heart to allay their heathenish humour with the Christian charity; but I considered that whatso I might do, it must ever be unavailing, and that it would endanger me to empty a part of my small stock of medicines;—my only passport when all else should fail in this hostile country.

A young mother, yet a slender girl, brought her wretched babe, and bade me spit upon the child's sore eyes; this ancient Semitic opinion and custom I have afterwards found wherever I came in Arabia.—Meteyr nomads in el-Kasîm, have brought me some of them bread and some salt, that I should spit in it for their sick friends.—Her gossips followed to make this request with her, and when I blamed their superstition they answered simply, that 'such was the custom here from time out of mind.' —Also the Arabians will spit upon a lock which cannot easily be opened.

Ajeyl excused himself saying 'a Beduin woman of their acquaintance had alighted here yesterday, who occupied their only room, and that to dismiss the guest became not his beard: yet he would help me, so that I should not be deceived, when I would buy anything in the town.' Nevertheless, as I bought wheat another day of himself, the sahs which Ajeyl numbered to me were of short measure.

I thought if I might lodge at Khálaf's, it would be well. He had spoken of my rebuilding the haddàj; I might resolve that simple problem, when I should be a little refreshed,—so to wall up the great water-pit that it should stand fast, more than before, and leave them this memorial of a Christian man's passage; also the fair report would open the country before me. Khálaf with the men of his household and certain guests were sitting crosslegs on the clay bench at his own court door in the street, whereover was made a rude awning of palm branches, and silently awaiting the sun's going down, that he might enter to his evening breakfast. I saw him a slender tall man of mild demeanour, somewhat past the middle age ; and have found in him a tolerant goodness and such liberality of mind as becomes a sheykh : he was a prudent householder, more than large in his hospitality. Khálaf's world being this little palm village in the immense deserts, and Hâyil the village capital, and his townspeople fewer than the souls in a great ship's company, yet there appeared in him the perspicuous understanding, and, without sign of natural rudeness, an easy assured nobility of manners (of their male society), which may be seen in the best of nearly all the Arab blood. The Arabs are never barbarous, they are of purer race than to be brutish ; and if they step from their Arabian simplicity, into the hive of our civil life (as it is seen in Bombay), their footing is not less sure than another's, and they begin bye and bye to prosper there.

I sat down in his company, and few words were spoken besides greetings ; they were weak with fasting. When I rose to be gone he beckoned me friendly to sit still : as the sun was sinking, Khálaf and they all rising with him, he led me in, ' to drink coffee, the evening, he said, was come.' Within was his pleasant house-court, the walls I saw decently whitened with *jiss*, gypsum ; we sat down upon long carpets before the hearth-pit, whited as well, in the Nejd-wise, and where already his slave-lad stooped to blow the cheerful flames, and prepared coffee ;—this, when the sun was gone down, should be their first refreshment. You will see a bevy of great and smaller tinned coffee-pots in the Nejd village fire-pits which they use for old coffee-water store, pouring from one to another. They sat now, with empty stomachs, watching earnestly the fading sunlight in the tops of the palm trees, till we heard the welcome cry of the muétthin praising God, and calling the devout Moslemîn to their prayers. It is then a pious man may first put in his mouth a morsel and strengthen himself ; the coffee was immediately served, and as one had drunk the cup, he went aside, and spreading down his mantle evenly before him towards the Sanctuary of Mecca, he began to recite the formal devotion. After prayers there is fetched-in the first night-meal *futûr* or breakfast ; this was, at Khálaf's, bare date-stalks fresh gathered from the tree. They took their food, though they had been languishing all day with thirst, without drinking till the end·; and after the dates slices were set before us of a great ripe but nearly tasteless melon, an autumn kind which is common at Teyma. * * *

* * * Later in the evening came in some Fukara, *Weyrid*, *Jèllowwy*, *Feràya*, that arrived after us, and they being men of my friendly acquaintance, we sat coffee-drinking till late hours. It was not well to go out then in the moonless night, to seek my Beduin fellowship that had removed I knew not whither, and I lay down with my arm for a pillow by the hearth-side to sleep. It seemed to me little past midnight when the company rose to eat the second night-meal, it was of dates only,—this is a wretched nourishment; and then the Arabs lay down anew under the cool stars, till the grey daylight of the returning fast, when they rose to their prayers. I spoke to Khálaf, on the morrow, and he said, 'He would give me a chamber in his house-building, in a day or two:'—but at that time, he answered, 'It was a store-room, full of corn, which his house-wife said could not be voided at present.'—His superstitious hareem might think it not lucky to harbour the Nasrâny in their dàr. * * *

* * * There was a young smith *Seydàn* who sought me out; and many an Arabian sâny imagined he might learn a mastery of the Nasrâny, since from us they suppose the arts to spring and all knowledge. When a lad he had come with his family, footing it over the deserts two hundred miles from Hâyil, his birth-place, to settle at Teyma. He was one of those who last winter passed by the kella of Medáin to el-Ally. I entered their workshop to bespeak a steel to strike fire with the flint,— a piece of gear of great price in the poor desert life, where so cheerful is the gipsy fire of sweet-smelling bushes :—there is a winter proverb of the poor in Europe, " Fire is half bread ! " Their steel is a band of four inches, which is made two inches, the ends being drawn backward upon itself. When he had beat out the piece, the long sunlight was low in the west. " We may not all day labour, said the young smith, in Rama-thán;" and rising, with a damp clout he wiped his honest smutched face, and as he shut up the shop he invited me home to drink coffee in his dàr. He led me round by the way, to see some inscription that was in a neighbour's house. There I found a few great antique embossed letters upon the threshold of dark bluish limestone, in the kind which I had found before at Teyma. [*Doc. Epigr.* pl. XXVII.] The smith's house was the

last in going out of the town beyond Khálaf's, small, but well-built of clay bricks. The former year he and his brother had made it with their own hands upon a waste plot next the wilderness, and in Hâyil wise; they thought but meanly of the Teyma architecture.

Another time he brought me a little out of the town (yet within the walls) eastward, to see some great antique pillars. We came to a field of two acres, wherein stands their great clay-built mesjid. I saw certain huge chapiters, lying there, and drums of smooth columns, their thickness might be twenty-seven inches, of some bluish limestone, and such as there is none (I believe) in a great circuit about. The sculpture is next to naught; we found not any inscription. These mighty stones have not, surely, been transported upon the backs of camels. I thought this might be the temple site of ancient Teyma; and wonderful are such great monuments to look upon in that abandonment of human arts and death of nature which is now Arabia! A stranger in these countries should not be seen to linger about ruins, and we returned soon.

Seydàn was telling me great things by the way of Hâyil: he supposed his Arabian town (nearly three thousand souls), for the well-purveyed sûks, the many dàrs of welfaring persons, the easy civil life and the multitude of persons, who go by shoals in the public place, and the great mesjid able to receive them all, should be as much as es-Sham [Damascus, 130,000]! We sought further by the town and through the grave-yard, looking (in vain) upon all headstones for more antique inscriptions. There was one till lately seen upon a lintel in Ajeyl's camel yard, but it had fallen and was broken, and the pieces they told us could no more be found; also a long inscription was on a stone of the haddàj walls, which were fallen down. [Since writing these words in 1879 the haddàj inscription has been seen by Huber and the learned epigraphist Euting some years after me. Euting supposes the inscription, which is dedicatory, and in the same Aramaic letters as the other inscriptions which I found at Teyma, may be of four or five centuries before Jesus Christ.]

Sometimes in these Ramathán half days we walked a mile over the desert to an uncle of his, who with the gain of his smith's labour had bought a good *hauta* (orchard) in the *Ghrerb*, or outlying little west oasis. When we came thither the sâny, who would have me cure his son's eyes, fetched lemons and pomegranates, and leaving me seated under his fruit-tree shadows, they went in to labour at the anvil, which the good-man had here in his house in the midst of his homestead. One day the young smith, who thought vastly of these petty hospitalities, said to me, " Khalîl ! if I were come to your country wouldst thou kill a sheep for me, and give me somewhat in money, and a maiden to wife ? " I said, ' I would not kill any beast, we buy our meat in the market-place ; I would give him money if he were in want ; and he might have a wife if he would observe our law ; he should find that welcome in my dàr which became his worth and my honour.' We sat at Khálaf's ; and the young smith answered : " See what men of truth and moderation in their words are the Nasâra ! Khalîl might have promised now—as had one of us—many gay things, but he would not." To reward Seydàn I could but show him the iron-stone veins of the desert about ; he wondered to hear that in such shales was the smith's metal ;—but how now to melt it ! Their iron, which must be brought in over the desert five or six hundred miles, upon camels, from the coast, is dear-worth in Arabia.

Teyma oasis is three : the main, lying in the midst, is called of the Haddàj ; outlying from the two ends are *es-Sherg* and *el-Ghrerb*, the " east and west hamlets," and these are watered only from wells of the ancients which have been found from time to time. In all of them, as the " man of medicine ", I had friends and acquaintance, especially in the Sherg ; and whereso I entered, they spread the guest-carpet under some shadowing greenness of palms or fig-trees : then the householder brought the stranger a cooling cucumber or date-stalks, and they bade me repose whilst they went about their garden labour.—Cheerful is the bare Arabic livelihood in the common air, which has sufficiency in few things snatched incuriously as upon a journey ! so it is a life little full of superfluous cares. Their ignorance is not brutish, their poverty is not baseness. But rude are their homes ; and with all the amorous gentleness of their senses, they have not learned to cherish a flower for the sweetness and beauty, or to desire the airy captivity of any singing bird.

Shâfy, one among them, led me out one morrow ere the sun was risen (that we might return before the heat), to visit some antique inscription in the desert. When we had walked a mile he asked me if I were a good runner.—" Though (he said) I am past my youth, I may yet outrun a thelûl and take her ; see thou if I am nimble," and he ran from me. While he was out I saw there came one with the ganna or Arab club-stick in his hand ; and from Teyma a horseman sallied to meet me. I began to wish that I had not gone to this length unarmed.

Those were men from the Sherg, though they seemed Beduins, who came to see whether we found any treasures. The rider with a long lance came galloping a strange crippling pace ; and now I saw that this mare went upon three legs ! her fourth was sinew-tied. The rest laughed, but said the cavalier *Atullah*, ' his mare was of the best blood, billah, and he was thus early abroad to breathe her ; she bred him every year a good filly or a foal.' The inscription was but a rude scoring in Arabic. Atullah, a prosperous rich man and bountiful householder, would have us return with him. His orchard grounds were some of the best in Teyma : and besides this fortune he had lighted lately upon the mouth of an ancient well nigh his place, in the desert. The welfaring man brought me a large basket of his best fruits, and bade me return often.

Where I walked round the oasis I found some little rude buildings of two or three courses of stones, thatched with sticks and earth. They are gunners' shrouds, they may contain a man lying along upon his breast. At a loop in the end his gun is put forth, and a little clay pan is made there without, to be filled, by the hareem, before the sun, with two or three girbies of water. The wild birds, wheeling in the height of the air and seeing glistering of water, stoop thither to drink from great distances ; their gun is loaded with very small stones. Commonly five birds are killed from such a kennel, ere the half-afternoon, when the villagers, that are not labourers, go home to coffee and think the busy-idle day is done : I have seen nearly all their dead birds were buzzards and falcons and the rákham, in a word only birds of prey,—and yet it is seldom one may perceive them riding aloft in the desert. I asked of some " Do you eat these puttocks ? "—" We eat them, ay billah, for what else should we shoot them ? if they be not very good meat, it is the best we may take ; and what we would not eat ourselves we may cast to the hareem, for the hareem anything is good enough."—The Teyâmena are blamed for eating vile birds ; most nomads would loathe to eat them. So the answer was easy when Arabians have cast it in my beard that the Nasâra eat swine's flesh. " If God have commanded you anything, keep it ; I see you eat crows and kites, and the lesser carrion eagle. Some of you eat owls, some eat serpents, the great lizard you all eat, and locusts, and the spring-rat ; many eat the hedgehog, in certain (Hejâz) villages they eat rats, you cannot deny it ! you eat the wolf too, and the fox and the foul hyena, in a word, there is nothing so vile that some of you will not eat." These young villagers' pastime is much in gunning.

They pace with their long guns, in the sunny hours, in all the orchard ways, and there is no sparrow sitting upon a leaf that possesseth her soul in peace. You hear their shots around you, and the oft singing of their balls over your head. Here also in the time they strike down certain migratory birds. I have seen small white and crested water-fowl, and a crane, *saady*, shot at this season in their plantations; the weary birds had lighted at the pools of irrigation water. The Arabs think these passing fowl come to them from the watered Mesopotamia (four hundred miles distant). In the spring they will return upwards. Being at Tôr, the Sinai coast village, in March 1875, I saw a flight, coming in from the seaward, of great white birds innumerable,—whether storks or rákhams I cannot tell; they passed overhead tending northward.

When certain of the town were offended with the Nasrâny because I kept not their fast, others answered for me, "But why should we be hard on him, when billah the half of the Beduw fast not, whom we grant to be of el-Islam; Khalîl is born in another way of religion, and they keep other times of fasting Are not en-Nasâra the people of the Enjîl, which is likewise Word of Ullah, although now annulled by the koran *el-furkán.*" —In the Medina country I heard their book, besides *furkán* ('the reading which separates the people of God from the worldly ignorance'), named more commonly "The Seal," *el-khâtm*, a word which they extended also, for simplicity, to any book; for they hardly know other than books of the religion. As I walked about the town some from their house doors bade me come in; and, whilst I sat to speak with them, dates were put before me;—yet first to satisfy their consciences they asked, "Art thou a musâfir?"

Méhsan, Sâlih, and our nomad households' booths were now pitched in an orchard field of Féjr's, my host in the spring, when with Zeyd I had visited Teyma. The camels being in the wilderness, they had removed upon asses borrowed of their acquaintance; and commonly if one speak for an ass in the Arabian villages (though no hire will be asked) it is not denied him. [Comp. Matt. xxi. 2, 3; Mark xi 2—6; Lu xix. 30—34.] In this hauta at the walls of the oasis I pitched my little tent with them. Here were corn plots, and a few palm trees full of fruit; yet the nomads and their children will not put forth their hand to the dates which are not fallen from the trees. Méhsan, when his last real was spent, knew not how longer to live;—these are the yearly extremities of all poorer Beduins! They must go knock at men's doors in the market

village, to see "who will show them any good " and lend them
at thirty in the hundred above the market price, till their next
tide, which is here of the haj surra. Méhsan purchased upon
credence the fruit of a good date tree in our field to satisfy his
children's hunger this month; and when they were hungry
they climbed to the palm top to eat.

Méhsan was a sickly man, and very irksome was the fast,
which divided our Beduins all day from their galliûns and even
from the water-skin; they slumbered under the palms from the
rising sun, only shifting themselves as the shadows wore round
till the mid-afternoon. The summer heat was not all past,
I found most mid-days 97° Fahrenheit under the palm-leaf
awnings of the coffee-courts of Teyma houses. At noon the
fasting Beduins wakened to rehearse their formal prayers, when
they feel a little relief in the ceremonial washing of the hands,
forearms and feet with water—which they need not spare in
the oasis—and to cool their tongue; for taking water into the
mouth they spout it forth with much ado again. Coming to
themselves at vespers, they assembled after their prayers under
the high western wall, which already cast the evening shadow,
there to play at the game of *beatta*, which may be called a
kind of draughts; the field is two rows of seven holes each,
beyts, which in the settled countries are made in a piece of
timber, *múngola;* but with these nomads and in the Hejâz
villages they are little pits in the earth. I have not seen this
playing in Nejd, where all their light pastimes were laid down
in the Waháby reformation, as dividing men's souls from the
meditation of the Living God. In every hole are seven stones;
the minkala was the long summer game of Haj Nejm in the
kella at Medáin, and these Beduins had been his patient play-
fellows. "Ay wellah (said the old man Sâlih), Haj Nejm is
min ashíraty, as mine own tribesman." Instead of the clear
pebbles of the Héjr plain (which are carried even to Damascus),
they took up bullets of camel-dung, *jella,*—naming their pieces
gaûd (camel foals), and the like. I never saw right Arabians
play to win or lose anything;—nay certes they would account
one an impious sot who committed that (God-given) good
which is in his hand to an uncertain adventure. We saw
carders at el-Ally and shall see them at Kheybar, but these are
villages of the Hejâz infected from the Holy Cities.—Galla
slaves have told me that the minkala game is used in their
country, and it is doubtless seen very wide in the world.

Who had the most pain in this fast? Surely Méhsan's
sheykhly wife with a suckling babe at her breast; for with a
virile constancy Zeyd's sister kept her Lent, neither drinking

nor eating until the long going-down of the sun. For this I
heard her commended by women of the town,—' her merit was
much to admire in a simple 'Beduish creature!' Even religious
women with child fast and fulfil the crude dream of their
religion, to this they compel also their young children. She
was a good woman, and kind mother, a strenuous housewife,
full of affectionate service and sufferance to the poor man her
husband; her's was a vein like Zeyd's, betwixt earnest and
merry, of the desert humanity. The poor man's sheykhly wife
was full of children; which, though the fruitful womb be
God's foison amongst them, had made his slender portion bare,
for their cattle were but five camels and half a score of dubbush,
besides the worsted booth and utensils :—hardly £60 worth in
all. Therefore Méhsan's livelihood must be chiefly of the haj
surra. Because he was an infirm man to bear the churlish looks
of fortune, he snibbed them early and late, both wife and
children, but she took all in wifely patience. There is among
them no complaining of outrageous words (not being biting
injuries as *ent kelb*, 'thou an hound!'); such in a family and
betwixt kindred and tribesmen have lost the sound of malevolence in their ears. Now this child,—now he would cry
down that, with "Subbak! the Lord rip up thy belly, curse
that face!" or his wife, not in an instant answering to his call,
he upbraided as a Solubbîa, gipsy woman, or *bàghrila*, she-
mule (this beast they see at the kellas); and then he would cry
frenetically, *Inhaddem beytich*, the Lord - undo thee, or *Ullah
yafúkk'ny minch*, the Lord loose me from thee! and less
conveniently, "Wellah some bondman shall know thee!"
But commonly a nomad father will entreat his son, if he
would have him do aught, as it were one better than himself,
and out of his correction. When he had chided thus and
checked all the household as undutiful to him, Méhsan would
revert to the smiling-eyed and musing nomad benevolence with
us his friends.

A light wind rising breathed through our trees,—first bathing, after the many summer months' long heat, our languishing
bodies! We were thus refreshed now the most afternoons,
and the sun rose no more so high; the year went over to the
autumn. At the sun's going down, if any one had invited us,
we walked together into the town ; or when we had supped we
went thither "seeking coffee" and where with friendly talk
we might pass an evening. The tent-lazing Beduins are of
softer humour than the villagers inured to till the stubborn
metal of the soil, with a daily diligence :—the nomads surpass
them in sufferance of hunger and in the long journey. As we

sit one will reach his galliûn to another, and he says, *Issherub wa keyyif râs-ak*, Drink! and make thy head dream with pleasance. All that is genial solace to the soul and to the sense is *keyyif*,—the quietness after trouble, repose from labour, a beautiful mare or thelûl, the amiable beauty of a fair woman.

Some nights if any nomad weleds visited us, our hauta resounded, as the wilderness, with their harsh swelling song, to the long-drawn bass notes of the rabeyby. I asked, "What think ye then of the Emir's letter?" [his injunction to the Teyâmena to put away the viol.] *Answer:* "Ibn Rashîd may command the villagers, but we are the Beduw!"—As this was a great war-time, their thoughts fell somewhiles upon that jehâd which was now between Nasâra and Islam. A Beduwy arriving from Jauf brought in false tidings,—'The Sooltàn of the Moslemîn had sallied from Stambûl, to take the field, and the lately deposed Murâd marched forth with him, bearing the banner of the Prophet!'—"But wot well (sighed Méhsan) whenever it may be at the worst for el-Islam, that the conquering enemies *shall be repulsed at the houses of hair!* [the religion of the Apostle shall be saved by the Beduw.] Wellah *wakîd!* it is well ascertained, this is written in the book!"— also the poor man was recomforted since this end of miseries was foretold to the honour of the Aarab. I said, "Yet for all your boasting ye never give a crown, nor send an armed man for the service of the Sooltàn!"—"What need, they answered, could the [magnific] Sooltàn have of us *mesakin* (mesquins)?"

Sometimes the Beduw questioned me of our fasting; I told them the Nasâra use to fast one day in the week, and they keep a Lenten month; some observe two or even more.—"And what is their fasting?—till the going down of the sun?"— "Not thus, but they abstain from flesh meat, and some of them from all that issues from the flesh, as milk and eggs, eating only the fruit of the ground, as bread, salads, oil of olive, and the like;—in the time of abstinence they may eat when they will." "Ah-ha-ha! but call you this to fast? nay wellah, Khalîl! you laugh and jest!"—"But they think it a fasting diet, 'as the death,' in those plentiful countries,—to eat such weak wretchedness and poor man's victuals."—"God is Almighty! Well, that were a good fasting!—and they cried between wonder and laughter—Oh that the Lord would give us thus every day to fast!"

CHAPTER XI

In the field, where we dwelt, I received my patients. Here I found the strangest adventure. A young unwedded woman in Teyma, hearing that the stranger was a Dowlâny, or government man, came to treat of marriage: she gave tittun to Méhsan's wife and promised her more only to bring this match about; my hostess commended her to me as 'a fair young woman and well grown; her eyes, billah, egg-great, and she smelled of nothing but ambergris.' The kind damsel was the daughter of a Damascene (perhaps a kella keeper) formerly in this country, and she disdained therefore that any should be her mate of these heartless villagers or nomad people We have seen all the inhabitants of the Arabian countries contemned in the speech of the border-country dwellers as " Beduw ",—and they say well, for be not all the Nejd Arabians (besides the smiths) of the pure nomad lineage? The Shâmy's daughter resorted to Méhsan's tent, where, sitting in the woman's apartment and a little aloof she might view the white-skinned man from her father's countries ;—I saw then her pale face and not very fair eyes, and could conjecture by her careful voice and countenance—Arabs have never any happy opinion of present things,—that she was loath to live in this place, and would fain escape with an husband, one likely to be of good faith and kind ; which things she heard to be in the Nasâra. When it was told her I made but light of her earnest matter, the poor maiden came no more ; and left me to wonder what could have moved her lonely young heart : ' Her mind had been, she said, to become the wife of a Dowlâny.'

Some of the Teyâmena bade me remain and dwell among them, ' since I was come so far hither from my country '—it seemed to them almost beyond return,—and say *La ilah ill' Ullah wa Mohammed rasúl Ullah.* They would bestow upon me a possession, such as might suffice for me and mine when I was a wedded man. But seeing an indifferent mind in me, "Ha! he has reason, they said, is not their flesh better than ours? the Nasâra have no diseases,—their hareem are fairer in his eyes than the daughters of Islam : besides, a man of the Nasâra may not wed except he have slain a Moslem; he is to bathe himself in the blood, and then he shall be reputed purified." But others answered, "We do not believe this; Khalîl denies it:" one added, "Have we not heard from some who were in the north, that no kind of wedlock is known amongst them?" I answered, "This, O thou possessed by a jin! is told of the Druses; your lips all day drop lewdness, but a vile and unbecoming word is not heard amongst them."—"The Druses, quoth he? Ullah! is not that the name of the most pestilent adversaries of el-Islam?—Well, Khalîl, we allow all you say, and further, we would see thee well and happy; take then a wife of those they offer you, and you will be the more easy, having some one of your own about you: and whenever you would you may put her away."—"But not in the religion of the Messîh."—"Yet there is a good proverb, It is wisdom to fall in with the manner, where a man may be."

When they said to me, "We have a liberty to take wives and to put them away, which is better than yours:" the answer was ready, "God gave to Adam one wife;" and they silently wondered in themselves that the Scriptures seemed to make against them.—There was another young woman of some Dowlâny father in the town; and as I sat one day in the smith's forge she came in to speak with us: and after the first word she enquired very demurely if I would wed with her. *Seydàn:* "It is a fair proffer, and thou seest if the woman be well-looking! she is a widow, Khalîl, and has besides two young sons:"—Seydàn would say, 'also the boys shall be a clear gain to thee, and like as when in buying a mare the foal is given in with her.'—"Shall I marry thee alone, mistress, or thee and thy children? Come I will give thee a friend of mine, this proper young man; or wouldest thou have the other yonder, his brother, a likely fellow too if his face were not smutched." But the young widow woman a little in disdain: "Thinkest thou that I would take any sâny (artificer) for my husband!"

The fairest of women in the town were Féjr our host's wife —fair but little esteemed, "because her hand was not liberal" —and another the daughter of one Ibrahîm an Egyptian, banishing himself at Teyma, for danger of his country's laws or of some private talion. One day I was sitting on the benches when the stately virgin came pacing to us, with a careless grace of nature; I marked then her frank and pleasant upland looks, without other beauty : the bench-sitters were silent as she went by them, with their lovely eye-glances only following this amiable vision. One of them said, as he fetched his breath again, " You saw her, Khalîl ! it is she of whom the young men make songs to chant them under her casement in the night-time ; where didst thou see the like till now ? Tell us what were she worth, that one, happy in possessing much, might offer to her father for the bride money ? " *Ibrahîm el-Misry* had lived some years at Teyma, he dealt in dates to the Beduins ; he was from the Delta, and doubtless had seen the Europeans ; if he were seated before his coffee-door, and I went by, he rose to greet me. Some day when he found me poring in a book of geography at Khálaf's, I turned the leaf, and read forward of that river country ; and he heard with joy, after many years, the names of his own towns and villages, often staying me to amend my utterance from the skeleton Arabic writing. Said some who came in, " Is Khalîl *kottîb !* (*lit* a scribe) a man who knows letters." Khálaf answered, " He can read as well as any of us ; " the sheykh himself read slowly spelling before him :—and what should their letters profit them ? The sheykh of the religion reads publicly to all the people in the mosque on Fridays, out of the koran ; and he is their lawyer and scrivener of simple contracts,—and besides these, almost no record remains in the oases : they cannot speak certainly of anything that was done before their grand-fathers' days.

Abd el-Azîz er-Romàn, sheykh of one of the three sûks, was unlettered ; there was no school in Teyma, and the sons must take up this learning from their fathers. Some young men of the same sheykhly family told me they had learned as far as the letters of the alphabet,—they made me hear them say their *álef, ba, ta, tha, jîm*—but come thus far in schooling, they *yakub-hu,* cast it down again : they might not cumber their quick spirits, or bind themselves to this sore constraint of learning. Every morrow the sun-shiny heat calls them abroad to the easy and pleasant and like to an holiday labour of their simple lives. Learning is but a painful curiosity to the Arabs, which may little avail them,—an ornament bred of the yawning superfluity of welfaring men's lives. These Shammar villagers are commonly of the shallowest Arabian mind, without fore-wit, without after-wit ; and in the present doing of a plain matter, they are suddenly at their wits' end. Therefore it is said of them, " the Teyâmena are juhâl, untaught, not under-standing the time." The Annezy say this saw, " *Es-Shammar, ayûnuhum humr,*—of the red eyes ; they will show a man hospi-

tality, yet the stranger is not safe amongst them; " but this is
no more than the riming proverbs which may be heard in all
the tribes of their neighbours.

These townsmen's heartless levity and shrewish looseness of
the tongue is noted by the comely Beduw. Teyma is not
further spoken of in Arabia for their haddàj, than for that
uncivil word, which they must twitter at every turn, "The
devil is in it, *iblis! iblis*"—as thus: "This child does not hear
me, *iblis!* dost thou disobey me? *iblis!* What is this broken,
lost, spoiled, thing done amiss? It is the devil, *iblis! iblis!*"
So, at anything troublesome, they will cry out "alack! and
iblis!" It is a lightness of young men's lips, and of the
women and children; their riper men of age learn to abstain
from the unprofitable utterance. When I have asked wherefore
they used it, they answered, "And wast thou two years at
Teyma, thou couldst not choose but say it thyself!" I found
the lighter nomad women, whilst they stayed at Teyma, became infected with this infirmity, they babbled among many
words, the unbecoming *iblis*: but the men said scornfully,
"This *iblis*, now in the mouths of our hareem, will hardly
be heard beyond the first ráhla; their *iblis* cannot be carried
upon the backs of camels, *henna el-Beduw!*"—The strong contagion of a false currency in speech we must needs acknowledge
with "harms at the heart" in some land where we are not
strangers!—where after Titanic births of the mind there
remains to us an illiberal remissness of language which is not
known in any barbarous nation.—Foul-mouthed are the Teyâmena, because evil-minded; and the nomads say, "If we had
anything to set before the guest, wellah the Beduins were
better than they:" and, comparing the inhabitants of el-Ally
and Teyma, "Among the Alowna, they say, are none good, and
all the Teyâmena are of a corrupt heart."—Their building is
high and spacious at Teyma, their desert is open, whereas
everything is narrow and straitness at el-Ally.

The building-up again (*towwy*) of the haddàj was for the
time abandoned: forty-four wheels remained standing, which
were of the other two sheykhs' quarters. Khálaf and those of
his sûk whose side was fallen, wrought upon the other sûks'
suânies in bye-hours, when the owners had taken off their well-
teams. The well nâgas, for they are all females—the bull
camel, though of more strength, they think should not work so
smoothly and is not so soon taught—are put to the draught-
ropes in the third hour after midnight, and the shrieking of all
the running well-wheels in the oasis awakens the (Beduin)
marketing strangers with discomfort out of their second sleep.

The Teyma housewives bring in baskets of provender, from the orchards, for their well camels, about sun-rising; it is that corn straw, sprinkled down with water, which is bruised small in treading out the grain, and with which they have mingled leaves of gourds and melons and what green stuff they find. Though such forage would be thought too weak in Kasîm, the camels lose little flesh, and the hunch, which is their health, is well maintained; and sometimes a feed is given them in this season of the unripe date berries. Good camels are hired by the month, from the nomads, for an hundred measures of dates each beast, that is five reals.—Their sweet-smelling fodder is laid to the weak labouring brutes in an earthen manger, made at the bottom of every well-walk. Thus the nâgas when they come down in their drawing, can take up a mouthful as they wend to go upward. They are loosed before nine, the sun is then rising high, and stay to sup water in the *suryân* (running channels),—a little, and not more, since labouring in the oasis they drink daily: they are driven then to their yards and unharnessed; there they lie down to rest, and chew the cud, and the weary teamsters may go home to sleep awhile. The draught-ropes of the camel harness are of the palm fibre, rudely twisted by the well-drivers, in all the oases; —and who is there in Arabia that cannot expeditely make a thread or a cable, rolling and wrapping between his palms the two strands? To help against the fretting of the harsh ropes upon their galled nâgas, the drivers envelop them with some list of their old cotton clothing. At two in the afternoon the camels are driven forth again to labour, and they draw till the sun-setting, when it is the time of prayers, and the people go home to sup. They reckon it a hard lot to be a well-driver, and break the night's rest,—when step-mother Nature rocks us again in her nourishing womb and the builder brain solaces with many a pageant the most miserable of mankind,— and hours which in comparison of the daylight, are often very cold. They are the poorest young men of the village, without inheritance, and often of the servile condition, that handle the well-ropes, and who have hired themselves to this painful trade.

Later I saw them set up two wheel-frames at the ruined border of the haddàj, and men laboured half days with camels to dig and draw up baskets of the fallen stones and earth. Seeing the labourers wrought but weakly in these fasting days, I said to a friend, "This is slack work." He answered, "Their work is *fâsid*, corrupt, and naught worth."—"Why hire you not poor Beduins, since many offer themselves?"—"This is no labour

of Beduins, they are too light-headed, and have little enduring
to such work."

Khálaf, Hásan and Salâmy, the sheykhs of the sûk, sent for
their thelûls (which are always at pasture with the nomads in
the desert): they would ride with Beduin radîfs to Hâyil, and
speak to the Emir for some remission of taxes until they might
repair the damage. Villager passengers in the summer heat
yugáillún, alight in every journey for 'nooning', where they
may find shadow. The sheykhs fasted not by the way—they
were musâfirs, though in full Ramathán: villagers pass in
seven days thelûl riding to J. Shammar,—it is five Beduin
journeys.

The well side fallen, one might go down in it, so did many
(the most were Beduins), to bathe and refresh themselves in
these days. That is the only water to drink, but the Arabs
are less nice in this than might be looked for: I felt the
water tepid even in that summer heat. There remains very
little in the haddàj walls of the ancient masonry, which has
fallen from time to time, and been renewed with new pans of
walling, rudely put up. The old stone-laying is excellent, but
not cemented. In the west walling they showed me a double
course of great antique masonry; and where one stone is
wanting, they imagine to be the appearance of a door, "where
the hareem descended to draw water in the times of Jewish
Teyma." As I was at the bottom, some knavish children cast
down stones upon the Nasrâny. Oftentimes I saw Beduins
swimming there, and wondered at this watercraft in men of the
dry deserts; they answered me, "We learned to swim, O stranger,
at Kheybar, where there are certain tarns in the Harra borders,
as you go down to the W. el-Humth," that is by the *Tubj*: they
were tribesmen of Bishr.

I had imagined, if those sheukh would trust me in it, how
the haddàj might be rebuilt: but since they were ridden to
Hâyil, the work must lie until their coming again. In their
former building the villagers had loosely heaped soil from the
backward; but I would put in good dry earth and well rammed;
or were this too much enlarging the cost I thought that the
rotten ground mixed with gravel grit might be made lighter,
and binding under the ram likely to stand. The most stones
of their old walling were rude; I would draw some camel-loads
of better squared blocks from the old town ruins. And to make
the new walls stand, I thought to raise them upon easy curves,
confirmed against the thrust by tie-walls built back, as it were
roots in the new ground, and partings ending as knees toward
the water. I confided that the whole thus built would be

H

steadfast, even where the courses must be laid without mortar. That the well-building might remain (which I promised them) an hundred years after me, I devised to shore all the walling with a frame of long palm-beams set athwart between their rights and workings.—But I found them lukewarm, as Arabs, and suspicious upon it, some would ascertain from me how I composed the stones, that the work should not slide; they enquired 'if I were a mason, or had I any former experience of stone-building?' and because I stood upon no rewards, and would be content with a thelûl saddled, they judged it to be of my insufficiency, and that should little avail them.

Upon a clay bench by the haddàj sat oftentimes, in the afternoons, Ibn Rashîd's officer or *mutasállim*, and in passing I saluted him, friendly, but he never responded. One day sitting down near him,—he was alone, for no man desired Saîd's company,—" What ails thee? I said, thou art deaf, man, or dost thou take me for an enemy?" Saîd, who sat with his slow-spirited swelling solemnity, unbent a little, since he could not escape me, that dangerous brow, and made his excuses: 'Well, he had been in Egypt, and had seen some like me there, and—no, he could not regard me as an enemy; the Engleys also *yuháshimûn* (favour) the Sûltàn el-Islam.' The great man asked me now quite familiarly, "Tell me, were the ancients of this town Yahûd or Nasâra?"—"For anything I can tell they were like this people!—I showed him the many kerchiefed and mantled Arabs that went loitering about the well—Yahûdies, billah." Saîd shrewdly smiled, he might think the stranger said not amiss of the Teyámena.—The sum of all I could learn (enquiring of the Arabs) of Ibn Rashîd's custom of government is this : ' He makes them sure that may be won by gifts, he draws the sword against his adversaries, he treads them down that fear him;' and the nomads say, "He were no right *Hâkim* (ruler), and he hewed no heads off." Though hard things be said of the Ruler by some of the nomads, full of slipping and defection, one may hear little or no lamenting in the villages. The villagers think themselves well enough, because justly handled.

When Kheybar was occupied, the Turkish government of Medina had a mind to take Teyma.—The year before this a squadron of Ageyl, with infantry and a field-piece, had been sent from thence upon a secret expedition to the north ; it was whispered they went to occupy Teyma : but when the soldiery had made two marches a new order recalled them, and they wheeled again for Kheybar. It was believed that the great ones in Medina had been bought off, in time, with a bribe from Hâyil. The Turks love silver, and to be well mounted; and the Shammar "*Sûltàn el-Aarab*" is wont to help himself with them in both kinds; he fishes with these Turkish baits in the apostle's city. The Teyâmena live more to their minds under the frank Nejd government; they would none of your motley Turkish rule of Medina, to be made dogs under the churlish tyranny of the Dowla.—It was affirmed to me by credible persons, that a stranger who visited Teyma few years before, had been afterward waylaid in the desert and slain, by order of Khâlaf, because they guessed him to be a spy of the Dowla! The poor man was murdered, lest he should bring the ugly Dowla upon them; I heard among the Fukara that 'he was *abd*, a negro'.

I could not thrive in curing the sick at Teyma; they who made great instance to-day for medicines will hardly accept them to-morrow with a wretched indifference; the best of them can keep no precept, and are impatient to swallow up their remedies. *Dareyem*, one of the sheykhs, was dropsical; his friends were very earnest with me for him. Coming home heated from a Friday noon prayer, before Ramathán, he had drunk a cold draught from the girby; and from that time he began to swell. I mixed him cream of tartar, which he drank and was the better, but soon began to neglect it, 'because in seven nights I had not cured him,' and he refused to take more. I said to the friends, "I suppose then he may hardly live a year or two!"—but now they heard this with a wonderful indifference, which made my heart cold. "The death and the life, they answered, are in the hands of Ullah!" There came others to me, for their eyes; but they feared to lay out sixpence or two pottles of dates for the doctor's stuff, and some of them, because they had not received it for a gift, went home cursing me. Nomads in the village resorted to the hakîm more frankly, and with better faith, for the old cough, aching in the bones, their many intestinal diseases,—the mischiefs of the desert; and Annezy tribesmen, for the throbbing ague-cake of Kheybar.

In the month of Lent a kind of rheumatic ophthalmia is rife; the cause of it (which may hardly be imagined in countries of a better diet) is the drinking of cold water to bedward, as it is chilled in the girbies; and perhaps they slept abroad or uncovered, and the night's chill fell upon them towards morning, when they are in danger to waken with the rime about their swollen eyelids. The course of the disease is ten days with a painful feeling in the nearly closed eyes of dust and soreness, and not without danger of infiltration under the cornea of an opaque matter; and so common is this malady in the Nejd settlements, that amongst three persons, there is commonly some one purblind. Ophthalmia is a besetting disease of all the Arab blood, and in this soil even of strangers : we see the Gallas suffer thus and their children, but very few of the negroes; I found the evil was hardly known at Kheybar, though they all lead their lives in the same country manner. Méhsan and another in our field, encamping upon the oasis soil, *gára*, had already been in the dark with prickly eyes; but it passed lightly, for the malady is of the oases, and not of the dry deserts. I drank every evening a large draught out of the suspended girbies, looking devoutly upon the infinity of stars!— of which divine night spectacle no troublous passing of the days of this world could deprive me : I drank again at its most chillness, a little before the dawning. One morrow in the midst of Ramathán, I felt the eyes swell; and then, not following the precept of the Arabs but grounding upon my medical book, I continually sponged them. "In this disease put no water to the eyes," say the Arabs; washing purged the acrid humour a moment and opened the eyes, yet did, I believe, exasperate the malady.— But the Arabians carry too far their superstition against water, forbidding to use it in every kind of inflammation.

Ten twilight days passed over me, and I thought 'If the eyes should fail me!—and in this hostile land, so far from any good' Some of the village, as I went painfully creeping by the ways, and hardly seeing the ground, asked me, "Where be now thy medicines !" and they said again the old saw, "Apothecary heal thyself." After a fortnight, leaving the water, the inflammation began to abate ; I recovered my eyes and, Heaven be praised! without worse accident. The eyesight remained for a time very weak, and I could not see so well as before, in the time of my being in Arabia; and always I felt a twitching at the eyes, and returning grudges of that suffered ophthalmia, if I but sipped cold water by night,—save the few times when I had supped of flesh meat. I have seen by experience, that one should not spare to drink water (competently) in the droughty heat of the day, to drink only when the sun is set ; and in the people's proverbs, in the water-drinking Arabic countries, it is counted 'one of the three most wasting excesses of the body to drink water to bedward'. Some friendly Teyâmena, sorry to see my suffering plight, said to me : "This is because thou hast been eye-struck—what! you do not understand *eye-struck?* Certainly they have looked in your eyes, Khalîl! We have lookers (God cut them off!) among us,

that with their only (malignant) eye-glances may strike
down a fowl flying; and you shall see the bird tumble in the
air with loud shrieking *kâk-kâ-kâ-kâ-kâ* Wellah their looking can blast a palm tree so that you shall see it wither
away.—These are things well ascertained by many faithful
witnesses." * * *

(*Doughty describes the ruined site of Mosaic Teyma. The
Fukara arrive The date harvest.*)

* * * There fell daily showers, and a cold wind breathed
over the desert, the sky was continually overcast. The visiting
nomads were about to depart, and I desired to go eastward
with them,—forsaking the well-building, rather than longer
abide their loitering leisure. The year was changing, and must
I always banish my life in Arabia! My friends were very slow
to help me forward, saying, 'What had I to do in Hâyil that
I must go thither? and after Teyma I should no longer be safe
with Aarab that knew not the Dowla.' As for Ibn Rashîd,
they said, "He is *néjis* (polluted, profane), a cutter-off of his
nigh kinsfolk with the sword:" and said Abd el-Azîz, who collected the Emir's dues, "Word is come of thee to Ibn Rashîd!
—that 'a Nasrâny, whom no man knoweth, is wandering with
the Aarab and *writing*,' and he was much displeased. The
Beduw eastward will fear to receive thee lest the Emir should
require it of them."
I hoped to depart with Bishr, their marketing families lay
in an outlying hauta of Thuèyny's; there I went to visit them.
Each household lodged apart upon the ground amongst their
pack saddles and baggage, and in the rain by day and night
they were without shelter: only the sheykh Misshel lay under
a tent-cloth awning. Misshel was coffee-drinking in the town,
but I found Askar (he who had been wounded), a young man in
whom was a certain goodness and generosity of nature, more
than in his blunt-witted father: Askar received my greeting
with a comely *yâ hulla!* he was pleased when the stranger
enquired of his hurt, and that thus I should know him.
The rain fell as we sat about the camp-fire, where they were
making coffee: theirs was the best I had tasted in Arabia,—
not of casting in a few beans Teyma-wise, but as Nejders the
best part of an handful. Bye and bye I asked, which of them

would accompany me to Hâyil? one said, ' He cared not if it
were he; when they returned from Teyma, he must needs go
thither: what would Khalîl give, and he would set me down in
the midst of the town?'—"I will give thee three reals." The
rest and Askar dissuaded him, but the man accepted it, and
gave his right hand in mine, that he would not draw back from
this accord, and Askar was our witness. The help to needy
Beduins of a very little money, to buy them a shirt-cloth and a
mantle, made my journeys possible (as Zeyd foretold), among
lawless and fanatical tribes of Arabia:—but I have hardly
found Beduins not better than the Fukara. These Bishr
nomads, not pensioners of the haj road, but tribesmen living
by their right hands in their own marches, are more robust-
natured, and resemble the northern Beduins. They are clad
from el-Irâk, and they bind the kerchief upon their foreheads
with a worsted head-band in great rolls as it were a turban.

On the morrow one of those nomads took me by the mantle
in the street to ask me, ' Would I go to his dîra to cure
a tribesman who had suffered many years a disease of the
stomach, so that what food he took he rejected again?' I saw
the speaker was a sheykh, and of Zeyd who was standing by he
enquired ' had they found the Nasrâny a good hakîm, in the
time of my living amongst them?' I was pleased with the
man's plain behaviour and open looks. Though he seemed a
great personage, he was an Heteymy, *Hannas Ibn Nômus*,
sheykh of the *Noâmsy*;—that is a kindred of Heteym now
living in alliance with Misshel, and inhabiting the nomad
district of the Auájy, where they had found a refuge from their
enemies. Zeyd said to me, "There is nothing to fear if thou
go with him: Hannas is a very honest man: billah I would not
so leave thee in the hands of another."

The Fejîr watered once more at Teyma; I saw the great
cattle of our households driven in, and after the watering their
burden camels were couched by the booths: for Méhsan and
the rest would remove in the morning and return to the desert.
Among the beasts I found my old nâga, and saw that she was
badly galled on the chine; the wound might hardly be healed
in fifteen or twenty days, but I must journey to-morrow. I
brought nomad friends to look at her, who found that she had
been ridden and mishandled, the marks of the saddle-tree cords
yet appearing in the hairy hide. It could not be other than
the fault of Zeyd's herdsman Îsa, a young man, whom I had
befriended. So taking him by the beard before them all, I
cursed ' the father of this Yahûdy '. The young man, strong

and resolute, laid hands upon my shoulders and reviled me for a
Nasrâny ; but I said, " Sirrah, thou shouldst have kept her
better," and held him fast by the beard. The tribesmen
gathered about us kept silence, even his own family, all being
my friends, and they had so good an opinion of my moving only
in a just matter. Isa seeing that his fault was blamed, must
suffer this rebuke, so I plucked down the weled's comely head
to his breast, and let him go. An effort of strength had been
unbecoming, and folly it were to suffer any perturbation for
thing that is without remedy ; I had passed over his fault, but
I thought that to take it hardly was a necessary policy. Also
the Arabs would have a man like the pomegranate, a bitter-
sweet, mild and affectionate with his friends in security, but
tempered with a just anger if the time call him to be a defender
in his own or in his neighbour's cause. Isa's father came bye
and bye to my tent, and in a demiss voice the old hind acknowledged his son's error ; " Yet, Khalîl, why didst thou lay upon
me that reproach, when we have been thy friends, to name me
before the people Yahûdy ? " But as old Sâlih saw me smile
he smiled again, and took the right hand which I held forth
to him.

I found Zeyd, at evening, sitting upon one of the clay
benches near the haddàj ; he was waiting in the midst of the
town, in hope that some acquaintance of the villagers coming by,
before the sun's going down, might call him to supper. Returning after an hour I found Zeyd yet in the place, his almost black
visage set betwixt the nomad patience of hunger and his lordly
disdain of the Teyâmena. Zeyd might have seemed a pros
perous man, if he had been liberal, to lay up friendship in
heaven and in this world ; but the shallow hand must bring
forth leanness and faint willing of a man's neighbours again.
I stayed to speak a word with Zeyd, and saw him draw at last
his galliûn, the remedy of hunger : then he called a lad, who
issued from the next dàr, to fetch a live coal, and the young
villager obeyed him.

In the first hour of this night there fell upon us a tempest
of wind and rain. The tall palms rocked, and bowing in all
their length to the roaring gusts it seemed they would be rent
by the roots. I found shelter with Méhsan in the house of Féjr
our host ; but the flat roof of stalks and rammed earth was
soon drenched, and the unwonted wet streamed down inwardly
by the walls. Méhsan spoke of my setting forth to-morrow
with the Bishr, and, calling Féjr to witness, the timid friendly
man sought to dissuade me, ' also Zeyd, he said, had forsaken
me, who should have commended me to them ; it was likely I

should see him no more.'—" Should I wonder at that?—Zeyd
has no heart," they answered both together : " Ay, billah, Zeyd
has no heart," and repeated *ma láhu kalb,* He has no heart!
Féjr was suffering an acute pain of 'the stone', *el-hása,* a
malady common in these parts, though the country is sandstone ; yet sometimes it may be rather an inflammation, for
they think it comes of their going unshod upon the burning
soil.   When the weather lulled, we went towards our wet tents
to sleep out the last night at Teyma.

CHAPTER XII

THE JEBEL

THE women of the hauta loaded the tents and their gear, and I saw our Aarab departing before the morning light. Zeyd rode in upon his mare, from the village where he had slept; 'If I would go now with him, he would bring me, he said, to the Bishr and bind them for my better security;' but Zeyd could not dwell, he must follow his Aarab, and I could not be ready in a moment; I saw the Fukara companions no more. A stranger, who passed by, lent me a hand in haste, as I loaded upon my old nâga: and I drove her, still resisting and striving to follow the rest, half a mile about the walls to those Bishr, who by fortune were not so early movers. There, I betook myself to *Hayzàr*, the man who had agreed to conduct me: and of another I bought the frame of a riding-saddle, that I might lay the load upon my wounded camel. They were charging their cattle, and we set forward immediately.

Leaving Teyma on the right hand, we passed forth, between the Érbah peaks and Ghrenèym, to the desert; soon after the bleak border was in sight of the Nefûd, also trending eastward. We journeyed on in rain and thick weather; at four of the afternoon they alighted, in the wet wilderness, at an height of 600 feet above Teyma, and the hungry camels were dismissed to pasture. The Beduin passengers kindled fires, laying on a certain resinous bush, although it be a plant eaten by the cattle, and though full of the drops of the rain, it immediately blazed up. They fenced themselves as they could from the moist wind and the driving showers, building bushes about them; and these they anchored with heavy stones.

We removed at sunrise: the sudden roaring and ruckling hubbub of the Beduins' many camels grudging to be loaded, made me remember the last year's haj journeys! before ten in the morning, we had Helwàn in front, and clearer weather. The Bishr journeyed a little southward of east, Birrd (Bírd) was visible : at two, afternoon, we alighted, and dismissed the camels to pasture ; the height was here as yesterday, nearly 4000 feet. The rain had ceased and Hayzàn went out hawking. There were two or three men in this company who carried their falcons with them, riding on the saddle peaks, in their hoods and jesses, or sitting upon the master's fist. Sometimes the birds were cast off, as we journeyed, at the few starting small hares of the desert ; the hawks' wings were all draggled in the wet: the birds flew without courage wheeling at little height, after a turn or two they soused, and the falconer running in, poor Wat is taken. Thus Hayzàn took a hare every day, he brought me a portion from his pot at evening, and that was much to the comfort of our extenuated bodies. I missed Hannas and his cousin *Rayyàn*, in the way ; they had left our journeying Aarab to go to their people encamped more to the southward, above the *Harrat Kheybar*. To-day I was left alone with the Auájy,—somewhat violent dealing and always inhospitable Beduins, but in good hope of the sooner arriving at Hâyil. We sat down to drink coffee with the sheykh, Misshel, who would make it himself. This "ruler of the seven tribes" roasted, pounded, boiled, and served the cheerful mixture with his own hand. Misshel poured me out but one cup, and to his tribesmen two or three. Because this shrew's deed was in disgrace of my being a Nasràny I exclaimed, " Here is billah a great sheykh and little kahwa ! Is it the custom of the Auájy, O Misshel, that a guest sit among you who are all drinking, with his cup empty ? " Thus challenged, Misshel poured me out unwillingly, muttering between the teeth some word of his fanatical humour, *yà fàrkah !*

The third day early, we came in sight of J. Irnàn ; and I said to my neighbour, " Ha, Irnàn ! " A chiding woman, who was riding within ear-shot, cried out, " Oh, what hast thou to do with Irnàn ? " At half-afternoon we alighted in high ground, upon the rising of Ybba Moghrair, where I found by the instrument, 4000 feet. Some camels were now seen at a distance, of Aarab *Ibn Mertaad*, allies of theirs. When we were lodged, there came a woman to my tent ; who asked for needles and thread (such trifles are acceptable gifts in the khála) ; but as she would harshly bargain with the weary stranger I bade her begone. She answered, with an ill look, " Ha ! Nasràny, but ere long we shall take all these things from thee." I saw, with an aversion [of race], that all these Bishr housewives wore the *berkoa* or heathenish face-clout, above which only the two hollow ill-affected eyes appeared.

This desolation of the woman's face was a sign to me that I journeyed now in another country, that is jealous (and Waháby) Nejd;—for even the waste soil of Arabia is full of variety.

The fourth morning from Teyma, we were crossing the high rugged ground of sandstone rocks behind Ybba Moghrair. Strange is the discomfort of rain and raw air in Arabia, when our eyes, wont to be full of the sun, look upon wan mists drooping to the skirts of these bone-dry mountains! wind, with rain, blew strongly through the open wilderness in the night-time. We lodged, at evening, beside some booths of Mertaad Arabs, and I went over bye and bye to their cheerful watch-fires. Where I entered the fire-light before a principal beyt, the householder received me kindly and soon brought me in a vast bowl of fresh camel-milk. They asked me no questions,—to keep silence is the host's gentleness, and they had seen my white tent standing before sunset. When I was rising to depart, the man, with a mild gesture, bade me sit still. I saw a sheep led in to be sacrificed;—because Misshel had alighted by them, he would make a guest-supper. *Aÿid* Ibn Mertaad, this good sheykh, told me his Aarab went up in droughty years to the Shimbel, and as far as Palmyra, and Keriateyn! I lay down and slumbered in the hospitable security of his worsted tent till his feast was ready, and then they sent and called Misshel and the Auájy sheykhs. Their boiled mutton (so far from the Red Sea coast) was served upon a mess of that other rice-kind, temmn, which is brought from el-Irâk, and is (though they esteem it less) of better savour and sustenance. Misshel, and every man of these Bishr tribesmen, when they rose after supper and had blessed their host, bore away—I had not seen it before—a piece of the meat and a bone, and that was for his housewife journeying with him.

Upon the morrow, the fifth from Teyma, we ascended over the very rugged highlands eastward by a way named the *Derb Zilláj*, where the height was 4500 feet, and I saw little flowerets, daughters of the rain, already sprung in the desert. At noon we reached Misshel's menzil of only few tents standing together upon this wide sandstone mountain platform where we now arrived, *el-Kharram*, the altitude is 5400 feet: the thermometer in the open showed 80° F. From hence the long mountain train appeared above the clouds of Irnàn, in the north, nearly a day distant.

At afternoon there came in two strange tribesmen, that arrived from a dîra in the southward near Medina: they said, there was no rain fallen in the Jeheyna dîra, nor in all the country of the W. el-Humth! A bowl of dates was set before them;

and the Beduin guests, with the desert comity, bade me [a guest] draw near to eat with them :—Misshel, although I was sitting in his tent, had not bidden the Nasrâny! I took and ate two of the fruits, that there might be " the bread and salt " between us. I had with me a large Moorish girdle of red woollen; Misshel now said, I should give it him, or else, billah, he would ' take me ' and my things for a booty. The girdle of the settled countries, _kúmr_, is coveted by the nomad horsemen, that binding thus the infirmer parts of the body they think a man may put forth his strength the better. ' The girdle, I said, was necessary to me; yet let Misshel give me a strong young camel, and I would give him my old nâga and the girdle.'—This man's camels were many more than two hundred! ' Well then, Misshel answered, he would take me.'—" See the date-stones in my hand, thou canst not, Misshel, there is now ' bread and salt ' between us."—" But that will not avail thee; what and if to-morrow I drive thee from us, thou and thy old nâga, canst thou find a way in the wilderness and return to el-Héjr ? "— " I know it is four journeys south of west, God visit it upon thee, and I doubt not it may please Ullah, I shall yet come forth."— " But all the country is full of habalîs."—" Rich Misshel, wouldst thou strip a poor man! but all these threats are idle, I am thy guest."—They believe the Nasâra to be expert riders, so it was said to me, ' To-morrow would I meet Misshel on horse-back, and I should be armed with a pistol ? ' I answered, ' If it must be so, I would do my endeavour.'—" Nay, in the morning Khalîl shall mount his old nâga (said Misshel again) and ride to Medáin Sâlih ; " so with a sturdy smile he gave up the quest, seeing he could not move me. His younger son, who sat dropsical in the father's tent, here said a good word, ' Well, let Khalîl sleep upon it,—and to-morrow they would give me a nâga for the Khuèyra and the girdle.'—In their greediness to spoil the castaway life, whom they will not help forward, the Arabs are viler than any nation !

Hayzàn in the morning bade me prepare to depart, Askar and some companions were setting out for Hâyil, and we might ride with them; he enquired ' Was my old nâga able to run with thelûls? '—" She is an old camel, and no dromedary."— " Then we must ride apart from them." Hayzàn, when he had received his money, said he could not accompany me himself, ' _but this other man_,' whom he feigned to be his brother, besides he named him falsely.—Hard it were to avoid such frauds of the Beduins ! Misshel said, " Well, I warrant him, go in peace " I made the condition that my bags should be laid upon his thelûl, and I might mount her myself; so we set forward.

This rafîk looked like a wild man : Askar and his fellowship were already in the way before us ; we passed by some shallow water-holes that had been newly cleared ; I wondered to see them in this high ground. We came then to the brow, on the north, of the Kharram mountain, here very deep and precipitous to the plain below ; in such a difficult place the camels, holding the fore-legs stiff and plumping from ledge to ledge, make a shift to climb downward. So, descending, as we could, painfully to the underlying sand desert, and riding towards a low sandstone coast, *Abbassîeh*, west of Misma, we bye and bye overtook Askar's company. Coming nigh the east end of the mountain, they thought they espied habalîs lurking in the rocks, " Heteym of the Nefûd, and foemen," where landlopers had been seen the day before. " Khalîl (said Askar), can your nâga keep pace with us ? we are Beduw, and *nenhash* (*nahájj*) ! we will hie from any danger upon our thelûls ; hasten now the best thou canst, or we must needs leave thee behind us, so thou wilt fall alone into the hands of the robbers." They all put their light and fresh thelûls to the trot : my old loaded nâga, and jaded after the long journey from Teyma, fell immediately behind them, and such was her wooden gait I could not almost suffer it. I saw all would be a vain effort in any peril ; the stars were contrary for this voyage, none of my companions had any human good in them, but Askar only. My wild rafîk, whom I had bound at our setting out by the most solemn oath, ' upon the herb stem,' that he would not forsake me, now cried out, ' Wellah-billah, he would abandon me if I mended not my pace (which was impossible) ; he must follow his companions, and was their rafîk,' so they ran on a mile or two.

The last days' rain had cooled the air ; this forenoon was overcast, but the sun sometimes shone out warmly. When with much ado I came up to my flying fellowship, I said to Askar, " Were the enemies upon you, would you forsake me who am your way-fellow ? " " I would, he said, take thee up back-rider on my thelûl, and we will run one fortune together ; Khalîl, I will not forsake thee." They were in hope to lodge with Aarab that night, before we came to the Misma mountain, now before us. The plain was sand, and reefs of sandstone rocks, in whose hollows were little pools of the sweet rain-water. At half-afternoon they descried camels very far in front ; we alighted, and some climbed upon the next crags to look out, who soon reported that those Aarab were rahîl, and they seemed about to encamp. We rode then towards the Misma mountain, till we came to those Beduins ; they were but a family of Shammar, faring in the immense solitudes. And doubtless, seeing us, they had felt a cold dread in their loins, for we found them shrunk down in a low ground, with their few camels couched by them, and the housewife had not built the beyt. They watched us ride by them, with inquiet looks, for there is no amity between Annezy and Shammar.— That which contains their enmities is only the injunction of the Emir. I would have asked these Beduins to let me drink water, for all day we had ridden vehemently without drawing bridle, and the light was now nearly spent; but my companions pricked forward. I bade my rafîk lend me at last his more easy thelûl, that such had been our covenant; but the wild fellow denied me, and would not slack his pace. I was often, whilst they trotted, fallen so far back as to be in danger of losing them out of sight, and always in dread that my worn-out nâga might sink under me, and also cast her young.

At Askar's word, when they saw I might not longer endure the fellow assented to exchange riding with me, and I mounted his dromedary ; we entered then at a low gap in the Misma near the eastern end of this long-ranging sandstone reef. My companions looked from the brow, for any black booths of Aarab, in the plain desert beyond to the horizon   One thought he saw tents very far distant, but the rest doubted, and now the sun was setting. We came down by the deep driven sand upon the sides of the mountain, at a windy rush, which seemed like a bird's flight, of the thelûls under us, though in the even any horse may overtake them. The seat upon a good thelûl " swimming ", as say their ancient poets, over sand-ground, is so easy that an inured rider may sometimes hardly feel his saddle.

We descended to a large rain-pool in the sand-rock, where they alighted, and washed, and kneeling in the desert began to say their sunset prayers ; but Askar, though the night was coming on, and having nothing to dry him, washed all his body, and his companions questioning with him, " That thus behoved a man, he said, who has slept with his wife; " and then let him return with confidence to ask his petition of Ullah :—the like Moses commanded. Moslems, whether in sickness or health, if the body be sullied by any natural impurity, durst not say their formal prayers. Many patients have come to me lamenting that, for an infirmity, ' they might not pray '; and then they seem to themselves as the shut out from grace, and profane. Thus they make God a looker upon the skin, rather than the Weigher and Searcher-out of the secret truth of man's heart. We rode now in the glooming ; this easy-riding lasted for me not far, for the

darkness coming on, *Nasr* my rafîk could not be appeased, and
I must needs return to my old nâga's back, ' For, he said, I
might break away with her (his thelûl) in the night-time.' In
Nasr's eyes, as formerly for Horeysh, I was a Beduin, and a
camel-thief ; and with this mad fantasy in him he had not
suffered me earlier in the day to mount his rikâb, that was
indeed the swiftest in the company ; for Askar and the rest who
were sheykhs had left at home their better beasts, which they
reserve unwearied for warfare.

We had ridden two hours since the sunset, and in this long
day's race the best part of fifty miles ; and now they consulted
together, were it not best to dismount and pass the night as we
were ?   We had not broken our fast to-day, and carried neither
food nor water, so confident they were that every night we
should sup with Aarab.   They agreed to ride somewhat further ;
and it was not long before we saw a glimpsing of Beduin watch-
fires.   We drew near them in an hour more, and I heard the
evening sounds of a nomad menzil ; the monotonous mirth of
the children, straying round from the watch-fires and singing at
the houses of hair.   We arrived so silently, the dogs had not
barked.   There were two or three booths.   When the Aarab
perceived us, all voices were hushed : their cheerful fires,
where a moment before we saw the people sitting, were
suddenly quenched with sand.   We were six or seven riders,
and they thought we might be an hostile ghrazzu.   Alighting
in silence, we sat down a little aloof: none of us so much as
whispered to his companion by name ; for the open desert is
full of old debts for blood.   At a strange meeting, and yet more
at such hours, the nomads are in suspense of mind and mistrust
of each other.   When, impatient of their mumming, I would
have said Salaam ! they prayed me be silent.   After the
whisperers within had sufficiently taken knowledge of our
peaceable demeanour, one approaching circumspectly, gave us
the word of peace, *Salaam aleyk*, and it was readily answered
by us all again, *Aleykom es-salaam*.   After this sacrament of the
lips between Beduw, there is no more doubt among them of any
evil turn.   The man led Askar and his fellowship to his beyt,
and I went over to another with Nasr my rafîk and a nomad
whom we had met riding with his son in the desert beyond
Misma.   The covered coals were raked up, and we saw the fires
again.

What these Aarab were we could not tell ; neither knew
they what men we were ; we have seen the desert people ask no
questions of the guest, until he have eaten meat ; yet after
some little discoursing between them, as of the rain this year,

and the pasture, they may each commonly come to guess the other's tribe. When I asked my rough companion "What tribesmen be these?" he answered in a whisper, 'he knew not yet;' soon after we understood by the voices that they had recognised Askar in the other tent. He was the son of their own high-sheykh; and these Aarab were Wélad Sleyman, a division of Bishr, though the men's faces were nearly unknown to each other Our host having walked over to the chief tent to hear the news, we were left with his housewife, and I saw her beginning to bray corn with a bat, in a wooden mortar, a manner not used by the southern Beduw of my former acquaintance; but bruised corn is here as often served for the guest-meal as temmn. The year was now turned to winter in the waste wilderness, they had fenced round their booths from the late bitter rain and wind with dry bushes.

There came in one from the third remaining tent, and supped with us. I wondered, seeing this tribesman, and he wondered to look upon me: he a Beduwy, wearing the Turkey red cap, *tarbûsh*, and an old striped gown *kumbâz*, the use of the civil border countries! When I asked what man he was, he answered that being " weak " he was gone a soldiering to Sham and had served the Dowla for reals: and now he was come home to the nomad life, with that which he esteemed a pretty bundle of silver. In this the beginning of his prosperity he had bought himself camels, and goats and sheep, he would buy also my old nâga for the price I set upon her, seven reals, to slaughter in the feast for his deceased father.—Where Beduins are soldiery, this seemed to me a new world! Yet afterwards, I have learned that there are tribesmen of Bishr and Harb, Ageyl riders in the great cities. The Beduin who saw in the stranger his own town life at Damascus, was pleased to chat long with me, were it only to say over the names of the chief sûks of the plenteous great city. He should bring his reals in the morning; and, would I stay here, he would provide for my further journey to Hâyil, whither he must go himself shortly.—But when my rafîk called me to mount before the dawn, I could not stay to expect him. Afterwards finding me at Hâyil, he blamed me that I had not awaited him, and enquired for my nâga, which I had already sold at a loss He told me that at our arriving that night, they had taken their matchlocks to shoot at us; but seeing the great bags on my camel, and hearing my voice, they knew me to be none of the nomads, and that we were not riding in a ghrazzu.

We hasted again over the face of the wilderness to find a

great menzil of Aarab, where my fellowship promised themselves to drink coffee. Sheykhs accustomed to the coffee-tent think it no day of their lives, if they have not sipped kahwa; and riding thus, they smoked tittun in their pipe-heads incessantly. We arrived in the dawning and dismounted, as before, in two fellowships, Askar and his companions going over to the sheykhly coffee-tent : this is their desert courtesy, not to lay a burden upon any household. The people were Shammar, and they received us with their wonted hospitality. Excellent dates (of other savour and colour than those of el-Ally and Teyma) were here set before us, and a vast bowl—that most comfortable refreshment in the wilderness—of their camels' léban. Then we were called to the sheykh's tent, where the sheykh himself, with magnanimous smiles, already prepared coffee. When he heard I was an hakîm, he bade bring in his little ailing granddaughter. I told the mother that we were but in passage, and my remedy could only little avail her child. The sheykh, turning to my companions, said therefore, 'That I must be some very honest person.'—" It is thus, Askar answered him, and ye may be sure of him in all." The sheykh reached me the bowl, and after I had supped a draught, he asked me, ' What countryman I was?' I answered "An Engleysy," so he whispered in my ear, " Engreys!—then a Nasrâny?" I said aloud, "Ay billah; " the good sneykh gave me a smile again, in which his soul said, " I will not betray thee."—The coffee ready, he poured out for me before them all. When my companions had swallowed the scalding second cup, they rose in their unlucky running haste to depart : the sheykh bade me stay a moment, to drink a little more of his pleasant milk and strengthen myself.

We rode on in the waste wilderness eastward, here passing out of the Misma district, and having upon the right-hand certain mountains, landmarks of that great watering-place, *Baitha Nethîl.* From the Kharram we might have ridden to Hâyil eastward of the mountain *Ajja;* but that part they thought would be now empty of the wandering Beduins. This high and open plain,—3800 feet, is all strewed with shales as it were of iron-stone ; but towards noon I saw we were come in a granite country, and we passed under a small basalt mountain, coal-black and shining. The crags rising from this soil were grey granite; *Ibrân,* a blackish mountain, appeared upon our horizon, some hours distant, ranging to the northward. A little later we came in Nefûd sand and, finding there wild hay, the Beduins alighted, to gather provender. This was to bait their cattle in the time when they should be lying at Hâyil, where the country next about is *mâhal*, a barrenness of soil hardly less than that which lies about Teyma. To make hay were unbecoming a great sheykh : and whilst the rest were busy, Askar digged with his hands in the sand to the elbow, to sound the depth of the late fallen rain, this being all they might look for till another autumn, and whereof the new year's herb must spring. Showers had lately fallen, sixteen days together ; yet we saw almost no sign in the wilderness soil of small freshets. When Askar had put down his bare arm nearly to the shoulder, he took up the old sandy drought; the moisture of the rain had not sunk to a full yard ! The seasonable rains are partial in Arabia, which in these latitudes is justly accounted a nearly rainless country. Whilst it rained in the Kharram no showers were fallen in the Jeheyna dîra ; and so little fell at Kheybar, a hundred miles distant, that in the new year's months there sprang nearly no rabîa in those lava mountains.

We had not ridden far in this Nefûd, when at half-after-noon we saw a herd of camels moving before us at pasture in their slow dispersed manner; we found beyond where the nomad booths were pitched in an hollow place. Beduins, when encamping few together, choose deep ground, where they are sheltered from the weather, and by day the black beyts are not so soon discerned, nor their watch-fires in the night-time. These also were Shammar, which tribe held all the country now before us to the Jebel villages ;—they were scattered by families as in a peaceable country of the Emir's dominion, with many wells about them. Flies swarming here upon the sand, were a sign that we approached the palm settlements. Whenever we came to tents in this country the Aarab immediately asked of us, very earnestly, " What of the rain ? tell us is there much fallen in the Auájy dîra ? " My companions ever answered with the same word, *Lá tanshud*, " Ask not of it." If any questioned them, 'Who was this stranger they brought with them ?' the Auájy responded, with what meaning I could not tell, " *El-kheyr Ullah.*" The sheykh in this menzil would have bought my nâga, engaging as well to convey me to Hâyil after a few days in which I should be his guest.

I thought at least we should have rested here this night over ; but my companions when they rose from supper took again their thelûls to ride and run, and Nasr with them ; they would not tarry a moment for me at the bargain of the nâga.— Better I thought to depart then with these whom I know, and be sure to arrive at Hâyil, than remain behind them in booths of unknown Beduins ; besides, we heard that a large Shammar

encampment lay not much before us, and a coffee-sheykh : Askar
promised to commit me to those Aarab, if he might persuade my rafîk to remain with me.   I was broken with this
rough riding ; the heart every moment leaping to my throat,
which torment they call *katu 'l-kalb,* or heart-cutting.   They
scoured before me all the hours of the day, in their light
riding, so that with less than keeping a good will, death at
length would have been a welcome deliverance out of present
miseries.   The Aarab lay pitched under the next mountain ;
but riding further in the darkness two hours, and not seeing
their watch-fires, the Auájy would then have ridden on all that
long night, to come the earlier, they said, to Hâyil.   They must
soon have forsaken me, I could not go much further, and my
decrepit nâga fainted under me : bye and bye Askar, overcome
by drowsiness, murmured to his companions, "Let us alight
then and sleep "   A watch-fire now appeared upon our right
hand, which had been hidden by some unevenness of the ground,
but they neglected it, for the present sweetness of sleeping : we
alighted, and binding the camels' knees, lay down to rest by
our cattle in the sandy desert.

We had not ridden on the morrow an hour when, at sun-
rising, we descried many black booths of a Beduin encampment, where the Auájy had promised me rest : but as ever
the scalding coffee was past their throats, and they had swallowed a few of the Shammary's dates, they rose to take their
dromedaries again.   Such promises of nomads are but sounds in
the air ; neither would my wild and brutish rafîk hear my
words, nor could Askar persuade him : " Wellah, I have no authority," said he ; and Nasr cried, "Choose thee, Khalîl, whether
thou wilt sit here or else ride with us ; but I go in my company."   What remained, but to hold the race with them ?
now to me an agony, and my nâga was ready to fall under me.
As we rode, "It is plain, said Askar, that Khalîl may not hold
out ; wilt thou turn back, Khalîl, to the booths ? and doubt not
that they will receive thee."—"How receive me ? you even
now lied to them at the kahwa, saying ye were not Auájy,
and you have not commended me to them : what when they
understand that I am a Nasrâny ? also this Nasr, my rafîk,
forsakes me ! "—" We shall come to-day, they said, to a settlement, and will leave thee there."   We had neglected to
drink at the tents, and riding very thirsty, when the sun rose
high, we had little hope to find more rain-pools in a sandy
wilderness.   Afterward espying some little gleam under the
sun far off, they hastened thither,—but it was a glistering clay

bottom, and in the midst a puddle, which we all forsook. The altitude of this plain is 3700 feet, and it seemed to fall before us to J. Ajja which now appeared as a mighty bank of not very high granite mountain, and stretching north and south. The soil is granite-sand and grit, and rolling stones and rotten granite rock. We passed, two hours before noon, the ruins of a hamlet of one well which had been forsaken five years before. Askar said, "The cattle perished after some rainless years for want of pasture, and the few people died of the small-pox,"—not seldom calamities of the small out-settlements, in Arabia. When I asked the name of the place, he answered shortly, *Melûn Tâlibuhu,* which might mean " Cursed is everyone that enquireth thereof."

We found a pool of clear rain in the rock, which, warmed in the sun, seemed to us sweeter than milk. There we satisfied our thirst, and led our beasts to drink, which had run an hundred and thirty miles without pasture or water, since the Kharram. His companions before we mounted went to cut a little more dry grass, and Askar said to me, " Khalîl, the people where we are going are jealous. Let them not see thee writing, for be sure they will take it amiss ; but wouldst thou write, write covertly, and put away these leaves of books. Thou wast hitherto with the Beduw, and the Beduw have known thee what thou art ; but, hearest thou ? they are not like good-hearted, in yonder villages ! " We rode again an hour or two and saw the green heads of palms, under the mountain, of a small village, where, they said, five or six families dwelt, *Jefeyfa.* Upon the north I saw *J. Tâly,* a solitary granitic mountain on the wilderness horizon. My company, always far in advance, were now ridden out of my sight. I let them pass, I could no longer follow them, not doubting that with these land-marks before me I should shortly come to the inhabited. There I lighted upon a deep-beaten path,—such are worn in the hard desert soil, near settlements which lie upon common ways, by the generations of nomad passengers. I went on foot, leading my fainting camel at a slow pace, till I espied the first heads of palms, and green lines of the plantations of Môgug. At length I descried Nasr returning out of the dis-tance to meet me. At the entering of the place my jaded camel fell down bellowing, this a little delayed us ; but Nasr raised and driving her with cruel blows, we entered Môgug about an hour and a half after noon.

I wondered to see the village full of ruins and that many of their palms were dead and sere, till I learned that Môg(k)ug(k) had been wasted by the plague a few years before.

Their house-building is no more the neat clay-brick work which we see at Teyma, but earthen walls in layers, with some cores of hard sun-dried brick laid athwart in them; the soil is here granitic. The crumbling aspect of the place made me think of certain oases which I had seen years before in the Algerian Sáhara. Their ground-water is luke-warm, as in all the Arabian country, and of a corrupt savour; the site is feverish, their dates are scaly, dry, and not well-tasting. We went towards the sheykh's kahwa, where the companions had preceded us, and met with the good sheykh who was coming forth to meet me. He led me friendly by the hand, and bade his man straw down green garden stalks for our camels. When we were seated in the coffee-room there entered many of the villagers, who without showing any altered countenance—it might be for some well-said word of Askar beforehand—seemed to regard me favourably. Seeing all so well disposed, I laid before the sheykh my quarrel with Nasr, and was supported by Askar, he allowing that my nâga could not go forward.

Even now they would mount immediately, and ride all night to be at Hâyil ere day. ' He would go in their company, said Nasr, and if I could not ride with them, he must for-sake me here.' The sheykh of Môgug ruled that since the camel could not proceed, Nasr, who had taken wages, must remain with me, or leaving so much of his money as might pay another man (to convey me to Hâyil) he might depart freely. The elf, having, by the sheykh's judgment, to disburse a real, chose rather to remain with me. Askar and his fellowship rose again hastily from the dates and water, to ride to Hâyil. This long way from the Kharram they had ridden, in a continued run-ning, carrying with them neither food nor water-skins, nor coffee: they trusted to their good eyesight to find every day the Aarab. All were young men in the heat of their blood, they rode in a sort of boast of their fresh endurance and ability. I asked Askar, wherefore this haste, and why they did not in any place take a little repose. *Answer:* " That we may be the sooner at home again; and to stay at the menzils by the way were un-becoming (*ayb*)." When they were gone, the villagers sitting in the kahwa—they were Shammar—blamed my companions as *Annezy!* These narrow jealousies of neighbours often fur-thered me, as I journeyed without favour in this vast land of Arabia.

Here first I saw Bagdad wares, from the sûk at Hâyil: the men of Môgug no longer kindled the galliûns with flint and

steel, but with the world-wide Vienna *Zündhölzer*,—we were in
the world again! Dim was their rudely-built coffee-hall, and
less cleanly than hospitable; the earthen floor where we sat
was littered with old date-stones of the common service to daily
guests. The villagers were of a kindly humour; and pleased
themselves in conversing with the stranger, so far as their short
notice might stretch, of foreign countries and religions: they
lamented that the heathen yet resisted the truth, and more
especially the Nasâra, in whom was a well of the arts, and
learning. They reached me from time to time their peaceable
galliûns. I thought the taste of their bitter green tobacco, in
this extremity of fatigue, of incomparable sweetness, and there
was a comfortable repose in those civil voices after the wild
malignity of the Bishr tongues. A young man asked me,
'Could I read?—had I any books?' He was of Môgug, and
their schoolmaster. I put in his hand a geography written in
the Arabic tongue by a learned American missionary of Beyrût.
—The young man perused and hung his head over it in the dull
chamber, with such a thirsty affection to letters, as might in a
happier land have ripened in the large field of learnings: at
last closing the book, when the sun was going down, he laid it
on his head in token how highly he esteemed it,—an Oriental
gesture which I have not seen again in Arabia, where is so
little (or nothing) of "*Orientalism*". He asked me, 'Might he
buy the book?—(and because I said nay) might he take it
home then to read in the night?' which I granted.

A tall dark man entered the kahwa, I saw he was a stranger
from the north, of a proud carriage and very well clad. Coldly
he saluted the company, and sat down; he arrived from *Gofar*
where he had mounted this morning. The dates were set
before him, and looking round when he remembered one or
two sitting here, with whom he had met in former years, he
greeted them and, rising solemnly, kissed and asked of their
welfare. He was a Shammary of Irâk; his Beduin dîra lay
250 miles from hence. Long and enviously he looked upon me,
as I sat with my kerchief cast back in the heat, then he
enquired, " Who is he?—eigh! a Nasrâny, say ye! and I knew
it: this is one, O people! who has some dangerous project, and
ye cannot tell what; this man is one of the Frankish nation!"
I answered, " It is known to all who sit here, that I am an
Engleysy, and should I be ashamed of that? what man art
thou, and wherefore in these parts?"—"I am at Hâyil for the
Emir's business!—wellah, he said, turning to the company, he
can be none other than a spy, one come to search out the
country! tell me what is reported of this man; if he question

the Aarab, and does he write their answers ?"—A villager said, ' Years before one had been here, a stranger, who named himself a Moslem, but he could guess, he was such as Khalîl, and he had written whatsoever he enquired of them.'

The villagers sat on with little care of *Nasr's* talk (that was also his name), misliking, perhaps, the northern man's lofty looks, and besides they were well persuaded of me. The sheykh answered him, "If there be any fault in Khalîl, he is going to Hâyil, and let the Emir look to it." Nasr, seeing the company was not for him, laid down his hostile looks and began to discourse friendly with me. At evening we were called out to a house in the village ; a large supper was set before us, of boiled mutton and temmn, and we ate together.

Nasr told me the northern horses abound in his dîra ; he had five mares, though he was not a sheykh, and his camels were many ; for their wilderness is not like these extreme southern countries, but full of the bounty of Ullah. As he saw my clothing worn and rent—so long had I led my life in the khála —he bade me go better clad before the Emir at Hâyil, and be very circumspect to give no cause, even of a word that might be taken amiss, amongst a people light and heady, soon angry, and [in which lies all the hardship of travelling in Arabia] unused to the sight of a stranger. Here first in Nejd I heard the *nûn* in the ending of nouns pronounced indefinitely, it is like an Attic sweetness in the Arabian tongue, and savours at the first hearing of self-pleasing, but it is with them a natural erudition. The sultry evening closed in with a storm of lightning and rain ; these were the last days of October. In this small village might be hardly 150 souls.

Upon the morrow we stayed to drink the early kahwa ; and then riding over a last mile of the plain, with blue and red granite rocks, to the steep sides of Ajja, I saw a passage before us in a cleft which opens through the midst of the mountain, eighteen long miles to the plain beyond ; this strait is named, *Ría es-Self*. The way at first is steep and rugged : about nine o'clock we went by a cold spring, which tumbled from the cliff above !—I have not seen another falling water in the waterless Arabia. There we filled our girby, and the Arabs, stripping off their clothing, ran to wash themselves ;—the nomads, at every opportunity of water, will plash like sparrows. Not much further are rude ground-walls of an ancient dam, and in a bay of the mountain unhusbanded palms of the Beduins ; there was some tillage in time past. At the highest of the ría, I found 5100 feet.

A poor Beduwy had joined our company in the plain, he

came, driving an ass, along with us, and was glad when I reached him an handful of Teyma dates to his breakfast. Later, at a turn of the rock, there met us three rough-looking tribesmen of Shammar, coming on in hot haste, with arms in their hands. These men stayed us; and whilst we stood, as the Arabs will, to hear and tell tidings, ·they eyed me like fiends. They understanding, perhaps, from some of Askar's malicious fellowship, of the Nasrâny's passing to-day by the rîa, had a mind to assail me. Now seeing themselves evenly matched, they said to him of the ass, and who was their tribesman, "Turn thou and let us kill him!"—"God forbid it (the poor man answered them), he is my fellow!" They grinning savagely then with all their teeth, passed from us. "Now Khalîl! (said Nasr,) hast thou seen?—and this is that I told thee, the peril of lonely riding through their country! these are the cursed Shammar, and, had we been by ourselves, they would have set upon thee,—Ullah curse the Shammar!"— "Have we not in the last days tasted of their hospitality?"— "Well, I tell thee they are fair-faced and good to the guests in the beyts, but if they meet a solitary man, kh'lûy, in the khála, and none is by to see it, they will kill him! and those were murderers we saw now, lurkers behind rocks, to cut off any whom they may find without defence."

There is but the Emir's peace and no love between Bishr and Shammar. Not many years before, a bitter quarrel for the rights of the principal water station of their deserts, Baitha Nethîl, had divided these nigh dwellers. Baitha Nethîl is in the Bishr borders, and they could not suffer it patiently, that Shammar came down to water there, and in that were supported by the Emir Telâl. For this they forsook even their own dira, and migrating northward, wandered in the wilderness of their Annezy kindred in Syria, and there remained two or three years : but, because they were new comers in those strange marches, many foraying enemies lifted their cattle ;—and the Bishr returned to their own country and the Emir.

— In the midst of the rîa the granite mountain recedes upon the north side and there are low domes of plutonic basalt, which resemble cones of volcanoes. We heard there a galloping tumult behind us, and a great shuffling of camels' feet over the gritty rocks; it was a loose troop of ajlâb, or "fetched," dromedaries, the drove of a camel-broker. The drovers went to sell them "in Jebel Shammar". These tribesmen were Bishr, and in their company our apprehensions were ended. A driving lad cried to me, "Hast thou not some kaak (biscuit cake of Damascus) to give me? in all this day's going and running I have tasted nothing." It was late in the afternoon when we came forth, and as I looked down over the plain of Gofar, the oasis greenness of palms lay a little before us. The sun was setting, and Nasr showed me the two-horned basalt mountain, *Sumrá* Hâyil, which stands a little behind the village capital, upon the northward. Gofar, written Káfar, and in the mouth of the nomads Jiffar, lies, like Môgug, enclosed by orchard walling from the desert. In the plain before the town, I read the altitude 4300 feet. We entered by a broad empty way, between long walls, where we saw no one, nor the houses of the place. It was sunset, when the Arabian villagers go in to their suppers. There met us only a woman,—loathly to look upon! for the feminine face was blotted out by the sordid veil-clout; in our eyes, an heathenish Asiatic villany! and the gentle blooded Arabian race, in the matter of the hareem, are become churls.—Beginning at Káfar, all their women's faces, which God created for the cheerfulness of the human world, are turned to this jealous horror ; and there is nothing seen of their wimpled wives, in sorry garments, but the hands ! We dismounted by a mosque at the *munákh*, or couching place of strangers' camels, where all passengers alight and are received to supper : the public charge for hospitality is here (upon a common way) very great, for, by the Arabian custom, wayfarers depart at afternoon, and those who ride from Hâyil to the southward pass only that first short stage, to sleep at Gofar.

Arriving with the drovers, we were bidden in together to sup of their scaly lean dates and water ; dates, even the best, are accounted no evening fare to set before strangers. He who served us made his excuses, saying that the householder was in Hâyil. The citizens of Gofar, *Beny Temîm*, are not praised for hospitality, which were sooner to find in Hâyil, inhabited by Shammar Nasr my rafîk, who had showed him-self more treatable since the others' departure, afterwards began to blame the passers-by in the street, because none had bidden me to coffee and to sleep in their houses, saying, 'Would they leave an honourable person to lodge in the open ways !' Nasr strawed down equally, of his store of dry pro-vender, to his thelûl and to my poor nâga ; then he made dough of some barley-meal I had bought at Môgug and kneaded it with dates, and thrusting this paste into her mouth by handfuls, he fed my weary beast. There we lay down by our cattle, to pass this starry night, in the dust of their village street.

We mounted at break of day : Nasr would be at Hâyil in time to go to breakfast in the guest-hall, with Askar and his fellowship. I wondered, to see that all that side of Gofar town, towards Hâyil, was ruinous, and the once fruitful orchard-grounds were now like the soil of the empty desert,—and tall stems, yet standing in their ranks, of sere and dead palms. We rode by cavernous labyrinths of clay-building under broken house-walling, whose timbers had been taken away, and over sunken paths of the draught-camels, where their wells now lay abandoned. When I asked, "What is this?" Nasr answered, *Béled mât*, "a died-out place." The villagers had perished, as those of Môgug, in a plague which came upon them seven years before. Now their wells were fallen in, which must be sunk in this settlement to more than twenty-five fathoms. The owners of the ground, after the pestilence, lacked strength to labour, and had retired to the inner oasis.

Beyond Gofar's orchard walls is that extreme barrenness of desert plain (máhal) which lies before Hâyil; the soil, a sharp granite-grit, is spread out between the desolate mountains Ajja and *Selma*, barren as a sea-strand and lifeless as the dust of our streets; and yet therein are hamlets and villages, upon veins of ground-water. It is a mountain ground where almost nothing may spring of itself, but irrigated it will yield barley and wheat, and the other Nejd grains. Though their palms grow high they bear only small and hot, and therefore less wholesome kinds of date-berries. We found hardly a blade or a bush besides the senna plant, flowering with yellow pea-like blossoms. The few goats of the town must be driven far back under the coast of Ajja to find pasture. After two hours Nasr said, "Hâyil is little further, we are here at the mid-way; women and children go between Hâyil and Gofar before their (noon) breakfast." Thus the road may be eleven miles nearly. Hâyil was yet hidden by the brow of the desert,—everywhere the horizon seemed to me very near in Nomad Arabia. Between these towns is a trodden path; and now we met those coming out from Hâyil. They were hareem and children on foot, and some men riding upon asses: "Ha! (said a fellow, and then another, and another, to Nasr) why dost thou bring him?"— So I knew that the Nasrány's coming had been published in Hâyil! and Nasr hearing their words began to be aghast. 'What, he said, if his head should be taken off!'—"And Khalîl, where is the tobacco-bag? and reach me that galliûn, for billah, my head turns." We had ridden a mile further, when I espied two horsemen galloping towards us in a great dust. I began to muse, were these hot riders some cruel messengers of the Emir, chevying out from Hâyil upon my

account ?—The name of Nasrâny was yet an execration in this
country, and even among nomads a man will say to another,
" Dost thou take me for a Nasrâny ! that I should do such
[iniquitous] thing."—Already the cavaliers were upon us, and
as only may riders of the mild Arabian mares, they reined up
suddenly abreast of us, their garments flying before them in
the still air ; and one of them shouted in a harsh voice to Nasr
(who answered nothing, for he was afraid), " All that baggage
is whose, ha ? "—so they rode on from us as before ; I sat
drooping upon my camel with fatigue, and had not much
regarded what men they were.

We saw afterward some high building with battled towers.
These well-built and stately Nejd turrets of clay-brick are
shaped like our light-houses ; and, said Nasr, who since Telâl's
time had not been to Hâyil, " That is the Emir's summer residence." As we approached Hâyil I saw that the walls extended
backward, making of the town a vast enclosure of palms. Upon
our right hand I saw a long grove of palms in the desert,
closed by high walls ; upon the left lies another outlying in
the wilderness and larger, which Abeyd planted for the inheritance of his children. Now appeared as it were suspended
above the town, the whitened donjon of the *Kasr*,—such clay
buildings they whiten with jiss. We rode by that summer
residence which stands at the way-side ; in the tower, they
say, is mounted a small piece of artillery. Under the summer-
house wall is a new conduit, by which there flows out irrigation
water to a public tank, and townswomen come hither to fetch
water. This, which they call *mâ es-Sáma*, is reckoned the best
water in the town ; from all their other wells the water comes
up with some savour of salty and bitter minerals, " which
(though never so slight) is an occasion of fever." We alighted,
and at my bidding a woman took down the great (metal) water-
pan upon her head to give us to drink. Nasr spoke to me not
to mount anew ; he said we had certain low gateways to pass.
That was but guile of the wild Beduwy, who with his long
matted locks seemed less man than satyr or werwolf. They
are in dread to be cried down for a word, and even mishandled
in the towns ; his wit was therefore not to bring in the Nasrâny
riding at the (proud) height of his camel.

I went on walking by the short outer street, and came to
the rude two-leaved gateway (which is closed by night) of the
inner sûk of Hâyil. There I saw the face of an old acquaintance who awaited me,—Abd el-Azîz, he who was conductor of
Ibn Rashîd's gift-mare, now twelve months past, to the kella
at el Héjr. I greeted him, and he greeted me, asking kindly of

my health, and bade me enter. He went before me, by another way, to bring the tiding to the Emir, and I passed on, walking through the public sûk, full of tradesmen and Beduw at this hour, and I saw many in the small dark Arab shops, busy about their buying and selling. Where we came by the throng of men and camels, the people hardly noted the stranger; some only turned to look after us. A little further there stepped out a well-clad merchant, with a saffron-dye beard, who in the Arabian guise took me by the hand, and led me some steps forward, only to enquire courteously of the stranger 'From whence I came?' A few saffron beards are seen at Hâyil: in his last years Abeyd ibn Rashîd had turned his grey hairs to a saffron beard. It is the Persian manner, and I may put that to my good fortune, being a traveller of the English colour, in Arabia. The welfaring men stain their eyes with kahl; and of these bird-like Arabians it is the male sex which is bright-feathered and adorned. Near the sûk's end is their corn market, and where are sold camel-loads of fire-wood, and wild hay from the wilderness. Lower I saw veiled women-sellers under a porch with baskets where they sit daily from the sunrise to sell dates and pumpkins; and some of them sell poor ornaments from the north, for the hareem.

We came into the long-square public place, *el-Méshab*, which is before the castle, *el-Kasr*. Under the next porch, which is a refuge of poor Beduin passengers, Nasr couched my camel, hastily, and setting down the bags, he withdrew from me; the poor nomad was afraid. Abd el-Azîz, coming again from the Kasr, asked me why I was sitting in that place? he sat down by me to enquire again of my health. He seemed to wish the stranger well, but in that to have a fear of blame,—had he not also encouraged my coming hither? He left me and entered the Kasr gate, to speak anew with the Emir. Abd el-Azîz, in the rest a worthy man, was timid and ungenerous, the end of life to them all is the least displeasure of Ibn Rashîd, and he was a servant of the Emir. A certain public seat is appointed him, under the Prince's private kahwa upon the Méshab, where he sat in attendance with his company at every mejlis. The people in the square had not yet observed the Nasrâny, and I sat on three-quarters of an hour, in the midst of Hâyil;—in the meanwhile they debated perhaps of my life within yonder earthen walls of the castle. I thought the Arabian curiosity and avarice would procure me a respite: at least I hoped that someone would call me in from this pain of famine to breakfast.

In the further end of the Méshab were troops of couched

thelûls ; they were of Beduin fellowships which arrived daily, to
treat of their affairs with the Emir. Certain of the Beduw now
gathered about me, who wondered to see the stranger sitting
under this porch. I saw also some personage that issued from
the castle gate under a clay tower, in goodly fresh apparel,
walking upon his stick of office, and he approached me. This
was *Mufarrij, rájul el-Mothîf,* or marshal of the Prince's guest-
hall, a foreigner, as are so many at Hâyil of those that serve
the Emir. His town was Aneyza in Kasîm (which he had
forsaken upon a horrible misadventure, afterwards to be related). The comely steward came to bid the stranger in to
breakfast; but first he led me and my nâga through the
Méshab, and allotted me a lodging, the last in the row of
guest-chambers, *mákhzans,* which are in the long side of this
public place in front of the Kasr : then he brought me in by
the castle-gate, to the great coffee-hall, which is of the guests,
and the castle service of the Emir. At this hour—long after
all had breakfasted and gone forth—it was empty, but they
sent for the coffee-server. I admired the noble proportions of
this clay hall, as before of the huge Kasr ; the lofty walls,
painted in device with ochre and jiss, and the rank of tall
pillars, which in the midst upheld the simple flat roof, of ethel
timbers and palm-stalk mat-work, goodly stained and varnished
with the smoke of the daily hospitality. Under the walls are
benches of clay overspread with Bagdad carpets By the entry
stands a mighty copper-tinned basin or " sea " of water, with a
chained cup (daily replenished by the hareem of the public
kitchen from the mâ es-Sáma) ; from thence the coffee-server
draws, and he may drink who thirsts. In the upper end of
this princely kahwa are two fire-pits, like shallow graves,
where desert bushes are burned in colder weather ; they lack
good fuel, and fire is blown commonly under the giant coffee-
pots in a clay hearth like a smith's furnace. I was soon called
out by Mufarrij to the guest-hall, *mothîf ;* this guest-house is
made within the castle buildings, a square court cloistered, and
upon the cloisters is a gallery. Guests pass in by the Prince's
artillery, which are five or six small pieces of cannon ; the iron
is old, the wood is ruinous.

The Beduins eat below, but principal sheykhs and their
fellowships in the galleries ; Mufarrij led me upstairs, to a
place where a carpet was belittered with old date-stones. Here
I sat down and dates were brought me,—the worst dates of
their desert world—in a metal standish, thick with greasy
dust ; they left me to eat, but I chose still to fast. Such is the
Arabian Ruler's morning cheer to his guests—they are Beduw—

and unlike the desert cleanness of the most Arabian villages, where there is water enough. Till they should call me away I walked in the galleries, where small white house-doves of Irâk were flittering, and so tame that I took them in my hands. I found these clay-floor galleries eighty feet long ; they are borne upon five round pillars with rude shark's-tooth chapiters. Mufarrij appearing again we returned to the kahwa where coffee was now ready. A young man soon entered shining in silken clothing, and he began to question me. This Arabian cockney was the Prince's secretary, his few words sounded disdainfully: "I say, eigh ! what art thou ?—whence comest thou, and wherefore hast thou come?" I answered after the nomad sort, "Weled, I can but answer one question at once ; let me hear what is thy first request : " he showed himself a little out of countenance at a poor man's liberal speech, and some friendly voice whispered to me, "Treat him with more regard, for this is *Nasr* " So said this Nasr, "Up! the Emir calls thee : " and we went out towards the Prince's quarters.

There is made a long gallery under the body of the clay castle-building, next the outer wall upon the Méshab ; by this we passed, and at the midst is an iron-plated door, kept by a young Galla slave within ; and there we knocked. The door opens into a small inner court, where a few of the Emir's men-at-arms sit in attendance upon him ; at the south side is his chamber. We went through and entered from the doorway of his open chamber into a dim light, for their windows are but casements to the air, and no glass panes are seen in all Nejd. The ruler Mohammed—a younger son of Abdullah ibn Rashîd, the first prince of Shammar, and the fourth Emir since his father—was lying half along upon his elbow, with leaning-cushions under him, by his fire-pit side, where a fire of the desert bushes was burning before him. I saluted him "*Salaam aleyk,* Peace be with thee; " he lifted the right hand to his head, the manner he had seen in the border countries, but made me no answer;—their hostile opinion that none out of the saving religion may give the word of God's peace ! He wore the long braided hair-locks for whose beauty he is commended in the desert as 'a fresh young man'. His skin is more than commonly tawny, and even yellowish ; lean of flesh and hollow as the Nejders, he is of middle height : his is a shallow Nejd visage, and Mohammed's bird-like looks are like the looks of one survived out of much disease of the world,—and what likelihood was there formerly that he should ever be the Emir?

"Sit down ! " he said. Mohammed, who under the former

Princes was conductor of the "Persian" Haj, had visited the cities of Mesopotamia, and seen the manners of the Dowla.— The chief of the guard led me to the stranger's seat. In the midst of a long carpet spread under the clay wall, between my place and the Emir, sat some personage leaning upon cushions; he was, I heard, a kinsman of Ibn Rashîd, a venerable man of age and mild countenance. The Emir questioned me, " From whence comest thou, and what is the purpose of thy voyage?"—"I am arrived from Teyma, and el-Héjr, and I came down from Syria to visit Medáin Sâlih."—" *Rájul sadûk*, wellah! a man to trust (exclaimed that old sheykh). This is not like him who came hither, thou canst remember Mohammed in what year, but one that tells us all things plainly." *Emir:* "And now from Teyma, well! and what sawest thou at Teyma—anything?"—"Teyma is a pleasant place of palms in a good air."—"Your name?"—"Khalîl."—"Ha! and you have been with the Beduw, eigh Khalîl, what dost thou think of the Beduw? *Of the Beduw there are none good:*—thou wast with which Beduins?"—"The Fukara, the Moahîb, the Sehamma beyond the Harra."—"And what dost thou think of the Fejîr, and of their sheykhs? Motlog, he is not good?"—"The Fukara are not unlike their name, their neighbours call them Yahûd Kheybar." The Emir, half wondering and smiling, took up my words (as will the Arabians) and repeated them to those present: "He says they are the Yahûd Kheybar! and well, Khalîl, how did the Aarab deal with thee? they milked for thee, they showed thee hospitality?"—"Their milk is too little for themselves." The Emir mused and looked down, for he had heard that I wandered with the Beduins to drink camel milk. "Ha! and the Moahîb, he asked, are they good? and Tollog, is he good?"—The Emir waited that I should say nay, for Tollog was an old enemy or 'rebel' of theirs.—"The man was very good to me, I think he is a worthy Beduin person." To this he said, "*Hmm hmm!*—and the Sehamma, who is their sheykh?"—"Mahanna and Fóthil."—"And how many byût are they?"

He said now, "Have you anything with you (to sell)? and what is thy calling?"—"I have medicines with me, I am an hakîm."—"What medicines? *kanakîna* (quinine)?"—"This I have of the best."—"And what besides?"—"I have this and that, but the names are many; also I have some very good *chai*, which I will present to thee, Emir!"—"We have chai here, from Bagdad; no, no, we have enough." [Afterward it was said to me, in another place,—"He would not accept thy chai, though it were never so good: Ibn Rashîd will eat or

drink of nothing which is not prepared for him by a certain
slave of his; he lives continually in dread to be poisoned."]
Emir: "Well! thou curest what diseases? canst thou cure the
mejnûn?" (the troubled, by the jan, in their understanding):—
the Emir has some afflicted cousins in the family of Abeyd,
and in his heart might be his brother Telâl's sorrowful remembrance. I answered, "*El-mejnûn hu mejnûn,* who is a fool
by nature, he is a fool indeed." The Emir repeated this wisdom
after me, and solemnly assenting with his head, he said to those
present, "*Hu sâdik,* he saith truth!" Some courtiers answered
him "*Fî tarîk,* but there is a way in this also." The Aarab suppose there is a *tarîk,* if a man might find it, a God-given way,
to come to what end he will.—"And tell me, which beasts thou
sawest in the wilderness?"—"Hares and gazelles, I am not a
hunter."—"Is the hare unlawful meat!—you eat it? (he would
know thus if I were truly a Christian). And the swine you
eat?" I said, "There is a strange beast in the Sherarât wilderness, which they call wild ox or wothŷhi, and I have some horns
of it from Teyma."—"Wouldst thou see the wothŷhi? we have
one of them here, and will show it thee." Finally he said,
"Dost thou 'drink' smoke?" The use of tobacco, not yet seen
in the Nejd streets but tolerated within doors, is they think
unbecoming in persons of more than the common people's dignity and religion. Mohammed himself and Hamûd his cousin
were formerly honest brothers of the galliûn; but come up
to estimation, they had forsaken their solace of the aromatic
Hameydy. The Emir said further, "So you are Mesîhy?"
—that was a generous word! he would not call me by
the reproachful name of Nasrâny; also the Emir, they say,
"has a Christian woman among his wives."—Christians of the
Arabic tongue in the great border lands name themselves
Mesîhiyûn.

He bade Nasr read in a great historical book which lay upon
a shelf, bound in red (*Akhbâru-'d-Dúal wa athâru-'l-Uwwal*),
what was written therein of the prophet *Isa ibn Miriam;*—and
the secretary read it aloud. The Mohammedan author tells us
of the person, the colour, the human lineaments of Jesus,
"son of the virgin;" and the manner of his prophetic life,
how he walked with his disciples in the land of Israel, and that
his wont was to rest in the place where the sun went down
upon him. The Emir listened sternly to this tale, and impatiently.—"And well, well! but what could move thee (he
said) to take such a journey?" I responded suddenly, "*El-
elûm!* the liberal sciences;" but the sense of this plural is, in
Nejd and in the Beduin talk, *tidings.* The Ruler answered

hastily, ' And is it for this thou art come hither!'" It was difficult to show him what I intended by the sciences, for they have no experience of ways so sequestered from the common mouth-labours of mankind. He said then, " And this language, didst thou learn it among the Beduw, readest thou *Araby?* "— He bade Nasr bring the book, and put it in Khalîl's hands. Mohammed rose himself from his place, [he is said to be very well read in the Arabic letters, and a gentle poet though, in the dispatch of present affairs of state, he is too busy-headed to be longer a prentice in unprofitable learning]—and with the impatient half-childish curiosity of the Arabians the Emir Ibn Rashîd himself came over and sat down beside me.—" Where shall I read ? "—" Begin anywhere at a chapter,—there ! and he pointed with his finger. So I read the place, ' *The king* (such an one) *slew all his brethren and kindred.* It was *Sheytân* that I had lighted upon such a bloody text; the Emir was visibly moved ! and, with the quick feeling of the Arabs, he knew that I regarded him as a murderous man. "Not there ! he said hastily, but read here !—out of this chapter above " (beating the place with his finger); so I read again some passage. *Emir :* " Ha, well ! I see thou canst read a little," so rising he went again to his place. Afterward he said, " And whither wouldst thou go now ? "—" To Bagdad."—" Very well, we will send thee to Bagdad," and with this word the Emir rose and those about him to go forth into his palm grounds, where he would show me the ' wild kine.'

Nasr then came with a letter-envelope in his hand, and asked me to read the superscription. " Well, I said, this is not Arabic ! "—" Ay, and therefore we wish thee to read it."— "From whom had ye this letter ? "—" From a Nasrâny, who came from the Haurân hither, and *this we took from him.*" Upon the seal I found in Greek letters *Patriarchate of Damascus,* and the legend about it was in Latin, *Go ye into all the world and preach this gospel to every creature.* They were stooping to put on their sandals, and awaited a moment to hear my response; and when I recited aloud the sense *Ukhruju fi kull el-âlam* ...... the venerable sheykh said piously to the Emir: "Mohammed, hearest thou this ?—and they be the words of the Messîah ! "

All they that were in his chamber now followed abroad with the Emir ; these being his courtier friends and attendance. Besides the old sheykh, the captain of the guard, and Nasr, there was not any man of a good countenance amongst them. They of the palace and the Prince's men wear the city gown, but go ungirded. Mohammed the Emir appeared to me, when we came into the light, like a somewhat undergrown and hard-favoured Beduwy of the poorer sort; but he walked loftily and with somewhat unquiet glancing looks. At the irrigation well, nigh his castle walls, he paused, and showing me with his hand the shrill running wheel-work, he asked suddenly, "Had I seen such gear?"—"How many fathoms have ye here?"—"Fifteen." He said truly his princely word, though I thought it was not so, —for what could it profit them to draw upon the land from so great depths? I walked on with Mohammed and the old sheykh, till we came to his plantation, enclosed in the castle wall; it seemed to me not well maintained. The Emir stayed at a castor-oil plant (there was not another in Hâyil) to ask "What is that?" He questioned me, between impatient authority and the untaught curiosity of Arabians, of his plants and trees,—palms and lemons, and the thick-rinded citron ; then he showed me a seedling of the excellent pot-herb *bámiya* and thyme, and single roots of other herbs and salads. All such green things they eat not! so unlike is the diet of Nejd Arabia to the common use in the Arabic border countries

Gazelles were running in the further walled grounds ; the Emir stood and pointed with his finger, "There (he said) is the wothŷhi!" This was a male of a year and a half, no bigger than a great white goat; he lay sick under a fig-tree. *Emir :—* "But look yonder, where is a better, and that is the cow."— "Stand back for fear of her horns! the courtiers said about me, do not approach her." One went out with a bunch of date twigs to the perilous beast, and stroked her; her horns were like sharp rods, set upright, the length I suppose of twenty-seven inches. I saw her, about five yards off, less than a small ass ; the hide was ash-coloured going over to a clear yellow, there was a slight rising near the root of her neck, and no hump, her smooth long tail ended in a bunch. She might indeed be said "to resemble a little cow"; but very finely moulded was this creature of the waterless wilderness, to that fiery alacrity of their wild limbs. " *Uktub-ha !* write, that is portray, her!" exclaimed the Emir. As we returned, he chatted with me pleasantly ; at last he said "Where are thy sandals ?"—" Little wonder if you see me unshod and my clothing rent, it is a year since I am with the Beduw in the khála."—" And though he go without soles (answered the kind old sheykh), it is not amiss, for thus went even the prophets of Ullah."—This venerable man was, I heard, the Emir's mother's brother : he showed me that mild and benevolent countenance, which the Arabs bear for those to whom they wish a good adventure.

The Emir in his spirituous humour, and haughty familiar manners, was much like a great sheykh of the Aarab. In him is the mark of a former contrary fortune, with some sign perhaps of a natural baseness of mind; Mohammed was now "fully forty years old", but he looked less. We came again into the Kasr yard, where the wood is stored, and there are two-leaved drooping gates upon the Méshab; here is the further end of that gallery under the castle, by which we had entered. The passage is closed by an iron-plated door; the plates (in their indigence of the arts) are the shield-like iron pans (*tannûr*) upon which the town housewives bake their girdle-bread.—But see the just retribution of tyrants! they fear most that make all men afraid. Where is—the sweetest of human things—their repose? for that which they have gotten from many by their power, they know by the many to be required of them again! There the Emir dismissed the Nasrâny, with a friendly gesture, and bade one accompany me to my beyt or lodging.

CHAPTER XIII

WHEN this day's sun was setting, Mufarrij called me to the Mothîf gallery, where a supper-dish was set before me of mutton and temmn. When I came again into the coffee-hall, as the cup went round, there began to be questioning among the Beduin guests and those of the castle service, of my religion. I returned early to my beyt, and then I was called away by his servants to see one, whom they named "The Great Sheykh".—'Who was, I asked, that great sheykh?' they answered "*El-Emir!*" So they brought me to a dàr, which was nearly next by, and this is named Kahwat Abeyd. They knocked and a Galla slave opened the door. We passed in by a short entry, which smelled cheerfully of rose-water, to that which seemed to my eyes, full of the desert, a goodly hall-chamber. The Oriental rooms are enclosures of the air, without moveables, and their only ornaments are the carpets for sitting-places, here laid upon the three sides of the upper end, with pillowed places for "the Emir" and his next kinsman. All was clay, the floor is beaten clay, the clay walls I saw were coloured in ochre ; the sitters were principal persons of the town, a Beduin sheykh or two, and men of the princely service ; and bright seemed the civil clothing of these fortunate Arabs.—They had said ' *The Emir* ' ! and in the chief place I saw a great noble figure half lying along upon his elbow !—but had I not seen the Prince Ibn Rashîd himself this morning? If the common sort of Arabs may see a stranger bewildered among them, it is much to their knavish pleasure.

This personage was *Hamûd*, heir, although not the eldest son, of his father Abeyd ; for *Fàhd*, the elder, was *khîbel*, of a troubled understanding, but otherwise of a good and upright behaviour ; the poor gentleman was always much my friend.— The princely Hamûd has bound his soul by oath to his cousin the Emir, to live and to die with him ; their fathers were brethren and, as none remain of age of the Prince's house, Hamûd ibn Rashîd is next after Mohammed in authority, is his deputy at

home, fights by his side in the field, and he bears the style of
Emir. Hamûd is the Ruler's companion in all daily service
and counsel.—The son of Abeyd made me a pleasant countenance, and bade me be seated at his right hand ; and when he
saw I was very weary, he bade me stretch the legs out easily,
and sit without any ceremony.

Hamûd spoke friendly to the Nasrâny stranger ; I saw he
was of goodly great stature, with painted eyes, hair shed [as we
use to see in the images of Christ] and hanging down from the
midst in tresses, and with little beard. His is a pleasant man-
like countenance, he dissembles cheerfully a slight crick in the
neck, and turns it to a grace, he seems to lean forward. In
our talk he enquired of those marvellous things of the Nasâra,
the telegraph, 'and glass, was made of what ? also they had
heard to be in our Christian countries a palace of crystal ; and
Barıs (Paris) a city builded all of crystal ; also what thing was
rock oil,' of which there stood a lamp burning on a stool before
them : it is now used in the principal houses of Hâyil, and
they have a saying that the oil is made from human urine.
He wondered when I told them it is drawn from wells in
the New World ; he had heard of that *Dinya el-jedîda,* and
enquired to which quarter it lay, and beyond what seas. He
asked me of my medicines, and then he said, " Lean towards
me, I would enquire a thing of thee." Hamûd whispered,
under the wing of his perfumed kerchief, " Hast thou no medicine, that may enable a man ? " I answered immediately,
" No, by thy life."—" No, by my life ! " he repeated, turning
again, and smiled over to the audience, and laughed cheerfully,
" ha ! ha ! "—for some crabbed soul might misdeem that he had
whispered of poison. Also that common oath of the desert,
" By thy life," is blamed among these half-Wahábies. Hamûd
said, with the same smiling demeanour, " Seest thou here those
two horsemen which met with thee upon the road ? "—" I
cannot tell, for I was most weary."—" Ay, he said with the
Arabian humanity, thou wast very weary ; ask him ! " Hamûd
showed me with his finger a personage, one of the saffron-
beards of Hâyil, who sat leaning upon cushions, in the place
next by him, as next in dignity to himself. This was a dull-
witted man, *Sleymàn,* and his cousin. I asked him, " Was it
thou ? " but he, only smiling, answered nothing. *Hamûd :*
" Look well ! were they like us ? be we not the two horsemen ?
—It was a match, Khalîl, to try which were the better breathed
of our two mares ; how seest thou ? the horses of the Engleys
are better, or our Nejd horses ? "—Hamûd now rising to go to
rest (his house is in another part), we all rose with him. In

that house—it stands by the public birket which is fed from the irrigation of this kahwa palm-yard—are his children, a wife and her mother, and his younger brothers ; but, as a prince of the blood, he has a lodging for himself (where he sleeps) within the castle building. The Hâyil Princes are clad as the nomads, but fresh and cleanly and in the best stuffs; their long wide tunic is, here in the town, washed white as a surplice, and upon their shoulders is the Aarab mantle of finer Bagdad woollen, or of the black cloth of Europe. They wear the haggu upon their bodies, as in all nomad Arabia.

I was but ill-housed in my narrow, dark, and unswept cell:— they told me, a Yahûdy also, at his first coming, had lodged there before me ! This was a Bagdad Jew, now a prosperous Moslem dwelling at Hâyil and married, and continually increasing with the benediction of the son-in-law of Laban ; the man had a good house in the town, and a shop in the sûk, where he sold clothing and dates and coffee to the nomads : his Hâyil wife had borne him two children. The gaping people cried upon me, "Confess thou likewise, Khalîl, 'There is one God, and His apostle is Mohammed,' and thine shall be an equal fortune, which the Emir himself will provide." From the morrow's light there was a gathering of sick and idle townsmen to the Nasrâny's door, where they sat out long hours bibble-babbling, and left me no moment of repose. They asked for medicines, promising, 'If they found them good remedies they would pay me, but not now.' When I answered they might pay me the first cost for the drugs, this discouraged them ; and nothing can be devised to content their knavish meaning. I said at length, "None of you come here to chaffer with me, for I will not hear you," and putting my door to upon them, I went out. As I sat at my threshold in the cool of the afternoon, Hamûd went by with his friends ; he stayed to greet me, and bade me come to supper, and showed me his sword, which he carries loosely in his hand with the baldric, like the nomads, saying, "What thinkest thou of it ? "—they suppose that every son of the Nasâra should be schooled in metal-craft. As I drew his large and heavy blade out of the scabbard—the steel was not Damascened—Hamûd added, "It is Engleys " (of the best Christian countries' work): he had this sabre from Ibn Saûd, and "paid for it one thousand reals ". "It seems to be excellent," I said to him, and he repeated the words smiling in their manner, "It is excellent." The sword is valued by the Arabians as the surest weapon ; they all covet to have swords of the finest temper.

At sunset came a slave from Abeyd's coffee-hall to lead

me to supper. Hamûd sups there when he is not called to eat with the Emir; his elder son *Mâjid*, and the boy's tutor, eat with him; and after them, the same dish is set before the men of his household. His simple diet is of great nourishment, boiled mutton upon a mess of temmn, with butter, seasoned with onions, and a kind of curry. When the slave has poured water upon our hands, from a metal ewer, over a laver, we sit down square-legged about the great brazen tinned dish upon the carpet floor. "*Mudd yédak*, Reach forth thine hand" is the Arab's bidding, and with "*Bismillah*, In the name of God," they begin to eat with their fingers. They sit at meat not above eight or ten minutes, when they are fully satisfied; the slave now proffers the bowl, and they drink a little water; so rising they say "*El-hamd illah*, The Lord be praised," and go apart to rinse the mouth, and wash their hands :—the slave lad brought us grated soap. So they return to their places refreshed, and the cheerful cup is served round ; but the coffee-server—for the fear of princes—tasted before Hamûd. There is no banqueting among them. Arabians would not be able to believe, that the food-creatures of the three inhabited elements (in some happier lands) may hardly sustain an human entrail ; and men's sitting to drink away their understanding must seem to them a very horrible heathenish living. Here are no inordinate expenses of the palace, no homicide largesses to smooth favourites of the spoil of the lean people. Soon after the sunrising, the Shammar princes breakfasted of girdle-bread and butter with a draught of milk; at noon a dish of dates is set before them ; at sunset they sup as we have now seen : Prince and people, they are all alike soberly dieted. The devil is not in their dish ; all the riot and wantonness of their human nature lies in the Mohammedan luxury of hareem.—I remember to have heard, from some who knew him, of the diet of the late Sultan of Islam, Abd el-Azîz, otherwise reproached for his insatiable luxury. Only one dish—which his mother had tasted and sealed—was set before him, and that was the Turks' every-day *pilaw* (which they say came in with Tamerlane) of boiled rice and mutton ; he abstained (for a cause which may be divined) from coffee and tobacco. I heard Hamûd say he had killed the sheep in my honour; but commonly his supper mutton is bought in the sûk.

An hour or two after, when the voice of the muétthin is heard in the night calling to the last prayer, Hamûd never fails to rise with the company. A slave precedes him with a flaming palm leaf-branch; and they go out to pray in the mosque, which is upon the further part of the Méshab, ranging with the guest-chambers, but separated by a small thorough-fare from them.—Princes of men, they are bond-servants to a doting religion !

When Hamûd returns, a little *sajjeydy* or kneeling-carpet reserved only to this use is unrolled by the slave in waiting before him ; and the princely man falling upon his knees towards Mecca says on to great length more his formal devotion   One evening I asked him, ' But had he not already said his prayers in the mesjid ? '—" Those, Hamûd answered, which we say in the mesjid are a man's legal prayers, and these are of the tradition, sunna." The sitters in the coffee-hall did not stint their chatting, whilst Hamûd prayed,—there prayed no man with him. The rest were not princes, why should they take upon them this superfluous religion ! and the higher is a Moslem's estate, by so much the more he must show himself devoted and as it were deserving of God's benefits. Hamûd never fails at the mosque in the hours ; and in all the rest, with the cheerful air of a strong man, he carries his own great fortune, and puts by the tediousness of the world. He might be a little less of age than the Emir ; in his manly large stature he nearly resembles, they say, the warlike poet his father : Hamûd and the Emir Mohammed are not novices in the gentle skill, inherited from their fathers in this princely family ;—their new making is extolled by the common voice above the old.

The Prince Mohammed goes but once, at el-assr, to prayers in the great mesjid ; he prays in an oratory within the castle, or standing formally in his own chamber. And else so many times to issue from the palace to their public devotion, were a tediousness to himself and to his servitors, and to the towns-people, for all fear when they see him, since he bears the tyrant's sword. And Mohammed fears !—the sword which has entered this princely house ' shall never depart from them —so the Aarab muse—until they be destroyed ' He cut down all the high heads of his kindred about him, leaving only Hamûd ; the younger sort are growing to age ; and Mohammed must see many dreams of dread, and for all his strong security, is ever looking for the retribution of mankind. Should he trust himself to pass the Méshab oftentimes daily at certain hours ?—but many have miscarried thus. Both Hamûd and the Emir Mohammed affect popular manners : Hamûd with an easy frankness, and that smiling countenance which seems not too far distant from the speech of the common people ; Mohammed with some softening, where he may securely, of his princely asperity, and sowing his pleasant word between ; he is a man very subtle witted, and of an acrid understanding.

Mohammed as he comes abroad casts his unquiet eyes like a falcon ; he walks, with somewhat the strut of a stage-player, in advance of his chamber-followers, and men-at-arms. When Hamûd is with him, the Princes walk before the rout. The townspeople (however this be deemed impossible) say ' they *love him and fear him* : '—they praise the prince under whose sufficient hand they fare the better, and live securely, and see all prosper about them ; but they dread the sharpness, so much fleshed already, of the Ruler's sword.

The evening after Mohammed sent for me to his apartment : the clay walls are stained with ochre. When I said to the Emir, I was an Englishman, this he had not understood before ! he was now pleasant and easy. There sat with him a great swarthy man, Sâlih, (I heard he was of the nomads,) who watched me with fanatical and cruel eyes, saying at length in a fierce sinister voice, " Lookest thou to see thy land again ? "— " All things, I answered, are in the power of Ullah."—" Nay, nay, Sâlih ! exclaimed the Emir, and Khalîl has said very well, that all things are in the hand of Ullah." Mohammed then asked me nearly Hamûd's questions. " The telegraph is what ? and we have seen it (at Bagdad in time of his old conductorship of the ' Persian ' pilgrims) : but canst thou not make known to us the working, which is wonderful? "—" It is a trepidation— therewith we may make certain signs—engendered in the corrosion of metals, by strong medicines like vinegar." *Emir :* " Then it is an operation of medicine, canst thou not declare it ? "—" If we may suppose a man laid head and heels between Hâyil and Stambûl, of such stature that he touched them both ; if one burned his feet at Hâyil, should he not feel it at the instant in his head, which is at Stambûl? "—" And glass is what ? " He asked also of petroleum ; and of the New Con- tinent, where it lay, and whether within ' the Ocean '. He listened coldly to my tale of the finding of the New Land over the great seas, and enquired, " Were no people dwelling in the country when it was discovered? " At length he asked me, ' How did I see Hâyil ? and the market street, was it well ? but ah, (he answered himself) it is a *sûk Aarab !* ' little in comparison with the chief cities of the world. He asked ' Had I heard of J. Shammar in my own country? ' The ruler was pleased to understand that the Nasâra were not gaping after his desert provinces ; but it displeased the vain-glory of the man that of all this troublous tide of human things under his govern- ance, nearly no rumour was come to our ears in a distant land. Hamûd asked of me, another while, the like question,

1*

and added, "What! have ye never heard of Ibn Saûd the Waháby!" When I had sat two hours, and it might be ten o'clock, the Emir said to the captain of the guard, who is groom of his chamber, "It is time to shut the doors;" and I departed.

In the early days of my being in Hâyil, if I walked through their sûk, children and the ignorant and poor Beduw flocked to me; and I passed as the cuckoo with his cloud of wondering small birds, until some citizen of more authority delivered me, saying to them, 'Wellah, thus to molest the stranger would be displeasing to the Emir!' Daily some worthy persons called me to coffee and to breakfast; the most of them sought counsel of the hakîm for their diseases, few were moved by mere hospitality, for their conscience bids them show no goodness to an adversary of the saving religion; but a Moslem coming to Hâyil, or even a Frankish stranger easily bending and assenting to them, might find the Shammar townspeople hospitable, and they are accounted such.

And first I was called to one *Ghrânim*, the Prince's jeweller, and his brother *Ghruneym.* They were rich men, of the smiths' caste, formerly of Jauf, where are some of the best sânies, for their work in metal, wood, and stone, in nomad Arabia. Abeyd at the taking of the place found these men the best of their craft, and he brought them perforce to Hayil. They are continually busied to labour for the princes, in the making and embellishing of sword-hilts with silver and gold wire, and the inlaying of gun-stocks with glittering scales of the same. All the best sword-blades and matchlocks, taken (from the Beduw) in Ibn Rashîd's forays, are sent to them to be remounted, and are then laid up in the castle armoury. Of these some very good Persian and Indian blades are put in the hands of the Emir's men-at-arms. In his youth, Ghrânim had wandered in his metal trade about the Haurân, and now he asked me of the sheykhs of the Druses, such and such whom he had known, were they yet alive. The man was fanatical, his understanding was in his hands, and his meditations were not always of the wise in the world: so daily meeting me, Ghrânim said before other words, "Khalîl, I am thine enemy!" and in the end he would proffer his friendly counsels.—He had made this new clay house and adorned it with all his smith's art. Upon the earthen walls, stained with ochre, were devices of birds and flowers, and koran versets in white daubing of jiss,—which is found everywhere in the desert sand: the most houses at Hâyil are very well built, though the matter be rude. He had built a double wall with a casement in each, to let the light pass, and not the weather. I saw no sooty smith's forge within, but Ghrânim was sitting freshly clad at his labour, in his best chamber; his floor was spread with fine matting, and the sitting places were Bagdad carpets. His brother Ghruneym called away the hakîm to his own house to breakfast: he was hindered in his craft by sickness, and the Emir ofttimes threatened to forsake him. His son showed me an army rifle [from India] whereupon I found the Tower mark; the sights —they not understanding their use!—had been taken away.

The Jew-Moslem—he had received the name *Abdullah*, "the Lord's servitor," and the neophyte surname *el-Moslemanny*— came to bid me to coffee. His companion asked me, ' Did my nation love the Yahûd?' "We enquire not, I answered, of men's religions, so they be good subjects." We came to the Jew's gate, and entered his house; the walls within were pleasantly stained with ochre, and over-written with white flowerets and religious versets, in daubing of gypsum. I read: "THERE IS NO POWER BUT OF GOD;" and in the apostate's entry, instead of Moses' words, was scored up in great letters the Mohammedan testimony, "There is none other god than (very) God, and Mohammed is the apostle of (very) God." Abdullah was a well-grown man of Bagdad with the pleasant elated countenance of the Moslemîn, save for that mark (with peace be it spoken) which God has set upon the Hebrew lineaments. Whilst his companion was absent a moment, he asked me under his breath " Had I with me any—" (I could not hear what).—" What sayest thou?" "*Brandi*, you do not know this (English Persian Gulf word)—brandi?" His fellow entering, it might be his wife's brother, Abdullah said now in a loud voice, ' Would I become a Moslem, his house should be mine along with him.' He had whispered besides a word in my ear —" I have a thing to say to thee, but not at this time." It was seven years since this Bagdad Jew arrived at Hâyil. After the days of hospitality he went to Abeyd saying, he would make profession of the religion of Islam ' upon his hand ';—and Abeyd accepted the Jew's words upon his formal hand full of old bloodshed and violence. The princely family had endowed the Moslemanny at his conversion with " a thousand reals ", and the Emir licensed him to live at Hâyil, where buying and selling,—and Abdullah knew the old art,—he was now a thriving tradesman. I had heard of him at Teyma, and that ' he read in such books as those they saw me have ': yet I found him a man without instruction,—doubtless he read Hebrew, yet now he denied it.

A merchant in the town, *Jâr Ullah*, brought me a great

foreign folio. It was a tome printed at Amsterdam in the last century, in Hebrew letters! so I said to him, "Carry it to Abdullah, this is the Jews' language."—"Abdullah tells me he knows it not."—This book was brought hither years before from the salvage of a Bagdad caravan, that had perished of thirst in the way to Syria. Their dalîl, "because Ullah had troubled his mind," led them astray in the wilderness; the caravaners could not find the wells, and only few that had more strength saved themselves, riding at adventure and happily lighting upon Beduins. The nomads fetched away what they would of the fallen-down camel-loads, ' for a month and more.' There were certain books found amongst them, a few only of such unprofitable wares had been brought in to Hâyil.

It was boasted to me that the Jew-born Abdullah was most happy here; ' many letters had been sent to him by his parents, with the largest proffers if he would return, but he always refused to receive them.' He had forsaken the Law and the Promises;—but a man who is moved by the affections of human nature, may not so lightly pass from all that in which he has been cherished and bred up in the world!

Jâr Ullah invited me up to his spacious house, which stands in the upper street near the Gofar gate: he was a principal corn-merchant. One *Nasr*, a fanatical Harb Beduwy of the *rajajîl*, meeting with us in the way, and *Aneybar* coming by then, we were all bidden in together: our worthy host, otherwise a little fanatical, made us an excellent breakfast. Aneybar was a *Hábashy*, a home-born Galla in Abdullah ibn Rashîd's household, and therefore to be accounted slave-brother of Telâl, Metaab and Mohammed: also his name is of the lord's house, Ibn Rashîd. This libertine was a principal personage in Hâyil, in affairs of state-trust under the Emirs since Telâl's time. The man was of a lively clear understanding, and courtly manners, yet in his breast was the timid soul-not-his-own of a slave: bred in this land, he had that suddenness of speech and the suspicious-mindedness of the Arabians.— When I came again to Hâyil Aneybar had the disposing of my life;—it was a fair chance, to-day, that I broke bread with him!

Hamûd bade me again to supper, and as I was washing, "How white (said one) is his skin!" Hamûd answered in a whisper, "It is the leprosy."—"Praised be God, I exclaimed, there are no lepers in my land."—"Eigh! said Hamûd (a little out of countenance, because I overheard his words), is it so? eigh! eigh! (for he found nothing better to say, and he added after me) the Lord be praised." Another said, "Wellah in Bagdad I have seen a maiden thus white, with

yellow hair, that you might say she were Khalîl's daughter."—
"But tell me (said the son of Abeyd), do the better sort in your
country never buy the Circass women?—or how is it among
you to be the son of a bought-woman, and even of a bond-
woman, I say is it not-convenient in your eyes?"—When it
seemed the barbaric man would have me to be, for that uncommon whiteness, the son of a Circass bond-woman, I responded with some warmth, "To buy human flesh is not so
much as named in my country; as for all who deal in slaves we
are appointed by God to their undoing. We hunt the cursed
slave-sail upon all seas, as you hunt the hyena." Hamûd was
a little troubled, because I showed him some flaws in their
manners, some heathenish shadows in his religion where there
was no spot in ours, and had vaunted our naval hostility,
(whereby they all have damage in their purses, to the ends
of the Mohammedan world).—"And Khalîl, the Nasâra eat
swine's flesh?"—"Ay billah, and that is not much unlike
the meat of the wabar which ye eat, or of the porcupine.
Do not the Beduw eat wolves and the hyena, the fox, the
thób, and the spring-rat?—owls, kites, the carrion eagle? but
I would taste of none such." Hamûd answered, with his
easy humanity, "My meaning was not to say, Khalîl, that for
any filth or sickliness of the meat we abstain from swine's
flesh, but because the Néby has bidden us;" and turning to
Sleymàn, he said, "I remember *Abdullah,* he that came to Hâyil
in Telâl's time, and cured *Bunder,* told my father that the
swine's flesh is very good meat."—"And what (asked that
heavy head, now finding the tongue to utter his scurvy soul) is
the wedlock of the Nasâra? as the horse covers the mare it is
said [in all Nejd] the Nasâra be engendered,—wellah like the
hounds!"

And though they eat no profane flesh, yet some at Hâyil
drink the blood of the grape, *mâ el-enab,* the juice fermented of the fruit of the few vines of their orchards, here
ripened in the midsummer season. Mâjid told me, that it
is prepared in his father's household; the boy asked me if I
had none such, and that was by likelihood his father's request.
The Moslemîn, in their religious luxury, extremely covet the
forbidden drink, imagining it should enable them with their
wives.

When coffee was served at Hamûd's, I always sat wondering that to me only the cup was not poured; this evening,
as the servitor passed by with the pot and the cups,
I made him a sign, and he immediately poured for me.

Another day Majid, who sat next me, exclaimed, "Drinkest thou no kahwa, Khalîl?" As I answered, "Be sure I drink it," the cup was poured out to me,—Hamûd looked up towards us, as if he would have said something I could suppose it had been a friendly charge of his, to make me the more easy. In the Mohammedan countries a man's secret death is often in the fenjeyn kahwa. The Emir where he enters a house is not served with coffee, nor is coffee served to any in the Prince's apartment, but the Prince called for a cup when he desired it; such horrible apprehensions are in their daily lives!

Among the evening sitters visiting Hamûd in the Kahwat Abeyd was a personage whom they named as a nobleman, and yet he was but a rich foreign merchant, *Seyyid Mahmûd*, the chief of the *Meshâhada* or tradesmen of Méshed, some thirty-five families, who are established in Hâyil; the bazaar merchandise (wares of Mesopotamia) is mostly in their hands; Méshed (place of the martyrdom of) Aly is at the ruins of *Kûfa*, they are Moslems of the Persian sect in religion.

These ungracious schismatics are tolerated and misliked in Ibn Rashîd's town, howbeit they are formal worshippers with the people in the common mesjid. They are much hated by the fanatical Beduins, so I have heard them say, "Nothing, billah, is more néjis than the accursed Meshâhada." Men of the civil North, they have itching ears for political tidings, and when they saw the Engleysy pass, some of them have called me into their shops to enquire news of the war,—as if dwelling this great while in the deserts I had any new thing to relate!—for of the Turkish Sûltàn's "victories" they believed nothing! The (Beduin-like) princes in Hâyil have learned some things of them of the States of the world, and Hamûd said to me very soberly: "What is your opinion, may the Dowlat of the Sûltàn continue much longer?"—"*Ullah Âlem* (God knoweth)."—"Ay! ay! but tell us, what is that your countrymen think?"—"The Sûltàn is become very weak."—Hamûd was not sorry (they love not the Turk), and he asked me if I had been in el-Hind;—the Prince every year sends his sale-horses thither, and the Indian government they hear to be of the Engleys. Hamûd had a lettered man in his household, Mâjid's tutor, one formed by nature to liberal studies. The tutor asked me tidings of the several Nasâra nations whose names he had heard, and more especially of Fransa and Brûssia, and *el-Nemsa*, that is the Austrian empire. "All this, I said, you might read excellently set out in a book I have of geography, written in Arabic by one of us long resident in es-Sham, it is in my chamber."

—"Go Khalîl, and bring it to me," said Hamûd, and he sent one of his service to light before me, with a flaming palm-branch

"How! (said Hamûd, when we came again,) your people learn Arabic!" I opened my volume at the chapter, *Peninsula of the Aarab.* Hamûd himself turned the leaves, and found the sweet verses, "Oh! hail to thee, beloved Nejd, the whole world to me is not as the air of Nejd, the Lord prosper Nejd;" and with a smile of happiness and half a sigh, the patriot, a kassâd himself, gave up the book to his man of letters, and added, wondering, "How is this?—are the Nasâra then *ahl athâb,* polite nations! and is there any such beautiful speaking used amongst them? heigh!—Khalîl, are there many who speak thus?" For all this the work was unwelcome among them, being written by one without the saving religion! I showed the lettered man the place where Hâyil is mentioned, which he read aloud, and as he closed the book I said I would lend it him, which was (coldly) accepted. I put also in their hands the Psalter in Arabic of "Daûd Father of Sleymàn," names which they hear with a certain reverence, but whose *kitâb* they had never seen. Even this might not please them! as coming from the Nasâra, those 'corruptors of the scriptures'; and doubtless the title savoured to them of 'idolatry',—*el-Mizamîr* (as it were songs to the pipe); and they would not read.

"Khalîl, said Hamûd, this is the Seyyid Mahmûd, and he is pleased to hear about medicines; visit him in his house, and he will set before thee a water-pipe,"—it is a keyif of foreigners and not used in Nejd. Hamûd told me another time he had never known any one of the tradesmen in Hâyil whose principal was above a thousand reals; only the Seyyid Mahmûd and other two or three wholesale merchants in the town, he said, might have a little more. Of the foreign traders, besides those of Méshed, was one of Bagdad, and of Medina one other;—from Egypt and Syria no man. Hamûd bade me view the Emir's cannon when I passed by to the Mothîf:—I found them, then, to be five or six small ruinous field-pieces, and upon two were old German in-scriptions. Such artillery could be of little service in the best hands; yet their shot might break the clay walling of Nejd towns. The Shammar princes had them formerly from the Gulf, yet few persons remembered when they had been used in the Prince's warfare, save that one cannon was drawn out in the late expedi-tion with Boreyda against Aneyza; but the Emir's servants could not handle it. Two shots and no more were fired against the town; the first flew sky-high, and the second shot drove with an hideous dint before their feet into the desert soil.

— To speak now of the public day at Hâyil: it is near two
hours after sunrise, when the Emir comes forth publicly to the
Méshab to hold his morning mejlis, which is like the mejlis of
the nomads. The great sheykh sits openly with the sheukh
before the people; the Prince's mejlis is likewise the public
tribunal, he sitting as president and judge amongst them. A
bench of clay is made all along under the Kasr wall of the
Méshab, in face of the mesjid, to the tower-gate; in the midst,
raised as much as a degree and in the same clay-work (whereupon in their austere simplicity no carpet is spread), is the
high settle of the Emir, with a single step beneath, upon
which sits his clerk or secretary Nasr, at the Prince's feet.
Hamûd's seat (such another clay settle and step, but a little
lower) is that made nigh the castle door. A like ranging
bank and high settle are seen under the opposite mesjid walls,
where the sheukh sit in the afternoon shadow, holding the
second mejlis, at el-assr. Upon the side, in face of the Emir,
sits always the kâdy, or man of the religious law; of which
sort there is more than one at Hâyil, who in any difficult process
may record to the Emir the words, and expound the sense, of
the koran scripture. At either side of the Prince sit sheykhly
men, and court companions; the Prince's slaves stand before
them; at the sides of the sheukh, upon the long clay bank, sit
the chiefs of the public service and their companies; and mingled
with them all, beginning from the next highest place after
the Prince, there sit any visiting Beduins after their dignities.
—You see men sitting as the bent of a bow before all this
mejlis, in the dust of the Méshab, the *rajajíl*, leaning upon their
swords and scabbards, commonly to the number of one hundred
and fifty; they are the men-at-arms, executors of the terrible
Emir, and riders in his ghrazzus; they sit here (before the tyrant)
in the place of the people in the nomads' mejlis. The mejlis
at Hâyil is thus a daily muster of this mixed body of swordsmen, many of whom in other hours of the day are civilly
occupied in the town. Into that armed circuit suitors enter
with the accused and suppliants, and in a word all who have
any question (not of state), or appear to answer in public audience
before the Emir; and he hears their causes, to every one shortly
defining justice: and what judgments issue from the Prince's
mouth are instantly executed. In the month of my being at
Hâyil might be daily numbered sitting at the mejlis with the
Emir about four hundred persons.

The Emir is thus brought nigh to the people, and he is
acquainted with the most of their affairs. Mohammed's judgment and popular wisdom is the better, that he has some-

time himself tasted of adversity. He is a judge with an indulgent equity, like a sheykh in the Beduin commonwealths, and just, with a crude severity : I have never heard anyone speak against the Emir's true administration of justice. When I asked, if there were no handling of bribes at Hâyil, by those who are nigh the Prince's ear, it was answered, " Nay." The Byzantine corruption cannot enter into the eternal and noble simplicity of this people's (airy) life, in the poor nomad country ; but (we have seen) the art is not unknown to the subtle-headed Shammar princes, who thereby help themselves with the neighbour Turkish governments. Some also of Ibn Rashîd's Aarab, tribesmen of the Medina dîras, have seen the evil custom : a tale was told me of one of them who brought a bribe to advance his cause at Hâyil ; and when his matter was about to be examined he privily put ten reals into the kâdy's hand. But the kâdy rising, with his stick laid load upon the guilty Beduin's shoulders until he was weary, and then he led him over to the Prince, sitting in his stall, who gave him many more blows himself, and commanded his slaves to beat him. The mejlis is seldom sitting above twenty minutes, and commonly there is little to hear, so that the Prince being unwell for some days (his ordinary suffering of head-ache and bile), I have seen it intermitted ;—and after that the causes of seven days were despatched in a morning's sitting ! The mejlis rising and dispersing, as the Prince is up, they say *Thâr el-Emir ;*—and then, what for the fluttering of hundreds of gay cotton kerchiefs in the Méshab, we seem to see a fall of butterflies. The town Arabians go clean and honourably clad ; but the Beduins are ragged and even naked in their wandering villages.

The Emir walks commonly from the mejlis, with his companions of the chamber, to a house of his at the upper end of the Méshab, where they drink coffee, and sit awhile : and from thence he goes with a small attendance of his rajajîl to visit the stud ; there are thirty of the Prince's mares in the town, tethered in a ground next the clay castle, and nearly in face of the Kahwat Abeyd. After this the Emir dismisses his men, saying to them, " Ye may go, *eyyâl,*" and re-enters the Kasr ; or sometimes with Hamûd and his chamber-friends he walks abroad to breathe the air, it may be to his summer residence by the mâ es-Sáma, or to Abeyd's plantation : or he makes but a passage through the sûk to visit someone in the town, as Ghrânim the smith, to see how his orders are executed ;—and so he returned to the castle, when if he have any business with Beduins, or men from his villages, and messengers awaiting him, they will be admitted to his presence. It is a busy pensive life to be the ruler at Hâyil, and his witty head was always full of the perplexity of this world's affairs. Theirs is a very subtle Asiatic policy. In it is not the clement fallacy of the (Christian) Occident, to build so much as a rush upon the natural goodness (fondly imagined to be) in any man's breast; for it is certain they do account most basely of all men, and esteem without remorse every human spirit to be a dunghill solitude by itself. Their (feline) prudence is for the time rather than seeing very far off, and always savours of the impotent suddenness of the Arab impatience. He rules as the hawk among buzzards, with eyes and claws in a land of ravin, yet in general not cruelly, for that would weaken him. An Arab stays not in long questioning, tedious knots are in peril to be resolved by the sword. Sometimes the Prince Ibn Rashîd rides to take the air on horseback, upon a white mare, and undergrown, as are the Nejd horses in their own country, nor very fairly shaped. I was sitting one after-sunset upon the clay benching at the castle-gate when the Prince himself arrived, riding alone: I stood up to salute the Emir and his horse startled, seeing in the dusk my large white kerchief. Mohammed rode with stirrups, he urged his mare once, but she not obeying, the witty Arab ceded to his unreasonable beast; and lightly dismounting the Emir led in and delivered her to the first-coming hand of his castle service.

Beduin companies arrived every day for their affairs with the Prince, and to every such company or *rubba* is allotted a makhzan, and they are public guests (commonly till the third day) in the town. Besides the tribesmen his tributaries, I have seen at Hâyil many foreign Beduins as *Thuffîr* and *Meteyr*, that were friendly Aarab without his confederacy and dominion, yet from whom Ibn Rashîd is wont to receive some yearly presents. Moreover there arrived tribesmen of the free Northern Annezy, and of Northern Shammar, and certain migrated Kahtân now wandering in el-Kasîm.

An hour before the morning's mejlis the common business of the day is begun in the oasis. The inhabitants are husbandmen, tradesmen (mostly strangers) in the sûk, the *rajajîl es-sheukh*, and the not many household slaves. When the sun is risen, the husbandmen go out to labour. In an hour the sûk is opened: the *delâls*, running brokers of all that is put to sale, new or old, whether clothing or arms, cry up and down the street, and spread their wares to all whom they meet, and entering the shops as they go by, with this illiberal noise, they sell to the highest bidders ; and thus upon an early day I sold my nâga the Khuèyra. I measured their sûk, which is between the Méshab and the inner gate towards Gofar, two hundred paces ; upon both sides are the shops, small ware-rooms built backward, into which the light enters by the doorway,—they are in number about one hundred and thirty, all held and hired of the Emir. The butchers' market was in a court next without the upper gate of the sûk : there excellent mutton was hastily sold for an hour after sunrise, at less than two-pence a pound, and a small leg cost sixpence, in a time when nine shillings was paid for a live sheep at Hâyil, and for a goat hardly six shillings. So I have seen Beduins turn back with their small cattle, rather than sell them here at so low prices :—they would drive them down then, nearly three hundred miles more, to market at Medina ! where the present value of sheep they heard to be as much again as in the Jebel. The butchers' trade, though all the nomads are slaughterers, is not of persons of liberal condition in the townships of Nejd.

Mufarrij towards evening walks again in the Méshab : he comes forth at the castle gate, or sends a servant of the kitchen, as often as the courses of guests rise, to call in other Beduin rubbas to the public supper, which is but a lean dish of boiled temmn seconds and barley, anointed with a very little samn. Mufarrij bids them in his comely-wise, with due discretion and observance of their sheykhly or common condition, of their being here more or less welcome to the Emir, and the alliance or enmities of tribesmen. Also I, the Nasrâny, was daily called to supper in the gallery ; and this for two reasons I accepted, —I was infirm, so that the labour had been grievous to me if I must cook anything for myself, and I had not fuel, and where there was no chimney, I should have been suffocated in my makhzan by the smoke ; also whilst I ate bread and salt in the Mothîf I was, I thought, in less danger of any sudden tyranny of the Emir ; but the Mothîf breakfast I forsook, since I might have the best dates in the market for a little money. If I had been able to dispend freely, I had sojourned more agreeably at Hâyil ; it was now a year since my coming to Arabia, and there remained but little in my purse to be husbanded for the greatest necessities.

In the Jebel villages the guest is bidden with : *summ !* or the like is said when the meat is put before him. This may be rather *'smm* for *ism*, in *b' ismi 'llah* or bismillah, " in God's name." But when first I heard this summ ! as a boy of the

Mothîf set down the dish of temmn before me, I thought he had said (in malice) *simm*, which is ' poison ' ; and the child was not less amazed, when with the suddenness of the Arabs, I prayed Ullah to curse his parentage :—in this uncertainty whether he had said poison, I supped of their mess ; for if they would so deal with me, I thought I might not escape them. From supping, the Beduins resort in their rubbas to the public kahwa : after the guests' supper, the rajajîl are served in like manner by messes, in the court of the Mothîf ; there they eat also at noon their lean collation of the date-tribute, in like manner as the public guests. The sorry dates and corn of the public kitchen have been received on account of the government-tax of the Emir, from his several hamlets and villages ; the best of all is reserved for the households of the sheykhly families. As the public supper is ended, you may see many poor women, and some children, waiting to enter, with their bowls, at the gate of the Kasr. These are they to whom the Emir has granted an evening ration, of that which is left, for themselves, and for other wretched persons. There were daily served in the Mothîf to the guests, and the rajajîl, 180 messes of barley-bread and temmn of second quality, each might be three and a quarter pints ; there was a certain allowance of samn. This samn for the public hospitality is taken from the Emir's Beduins, so much from every beyt, to be paid at an old rate, that is only sometimes seen in the spring, two shillings for three pints, which cost now in Hâyil a real. A camel or smaller beast is killed, and a little flesh meat is served to the first-called guests, once in eight or ten days. When the Prince is absent, there come no Beduins to Hâyil, and then (I have seen) there are no guests. So I have computed may be disbursed for the yearly expenses of the Prince's guest-house, about £1500 sterling.

— Now in the public kahwa the evening coffee is made and served round. As often as I sat with them, the mixed rubbas of Beduins observed towards me the tolerant behaviour which is used in their tents ;—and here were we not all guests together of the Emir ? The princely coffee-hall is open, soon after the dawn prayers, to these bibbers of the morning cup ; the door is shut again, when all are gone forth about the time of the first mejlis. It is opened afresh, and coffee is served again after vespers. To every guest the cup is filled twice and a third is offered, when, if he would not drink, a Beduwy of the Nejd tribes will say shortly, with the desert courtesy, *Káramak Ullah*, ' the Lord requite thee.' The door of the kahwa is shut for the night as the coffee-drivelling Beduw are gone forth to the last prayers in the mesjid. After that time, the rude two-leaved gates of this (the Prince's) quarter and the market street are shut,—not to be opened again ' for prayer nor for hire ' till the morrow's light ; and Beduins arriving late must lodge without :—but the rest of Hâyil lies open, which is all that built towards Gofar, and the mountain Ajja.

The Emir Mohammed rode out one half-afternoon, with the companions of his chamber and attendance, to visit *ed-dubbush*, his live wealth in the desert. The Nejd prince is a very rich cattle-master, so that if you will believe them he possesses " forty thousand " camels. His stud is of good Nejd blood, and as *Aly el-Aŷid* told me, (an honest man, and my neighbour, who was beforetime in the stud service,—he had conducted horses for the former Emirs, to the Pashas of Egypt,) some three hundred mares, and an hundred horses, with many foals and fillies. After others' telling Ibn Rashîd has four hundred free and bond soldiery, two hundred mares of the blood, one hundred horses : they are herded apart in the deserts ; and he has " an hundred bond-servants " (living with their families in booths of hair-cloth, as the nomads), to keep them Another told me the Emir's stud is divided in troops of fifty or sixty, all mares or all horses together ; the foals and fillies after the weaning are herded likewise by themselves. The horse-troops are dispersed in the wilderness, now here, now there, near or far off,—according to the yearly springing of the wild herbage The Emir's horses are grazed in nomad wise ; the fore-feet hop-shackled, they are dismissed to range from the morning. Barley or other grain they taste not : they are led home to the booths, and tethered at evening, and drink the night's milk of the she-camels, their foster mothers.—So that it may seem the West Nejd Prince possesses horses and camels to the value of about a quarter of a million of pounds sterling ; and that has been gotten in two generations of the spoil of the poor Beduw. He has besides great private riches laid up in metal ; but his public taxes are carried into the government treasury, *beyt el-mâl*, and bestowed in sacks and in pits. He possesses much in land, and not only in Hâyil, but he has great plantations also at Jauf, and in some other conquered oases.—I saw Mohammed mount, at the castle gate, upon a tall dromedary, bravely caparisoned In the few days of this his peaceable sojourn in the khála, the Prince is lodged with his company in booths like the Beduins. He left Hamûd in Hâyil, to hold the now small daily mejlis ;—the son of Abeyd sits not then in the Prince's settle, but in his own lower seat by the tower.

Hamûd sent for me in his afternoon leisure ; " Mohammed is

gone, he said, and we remain to become friends." He showed
me now his cheap Gulf watches, of which he wore two upon his
breast, and so does his son Mâjid who has a curious mind in
such newels,—it was said he could clean watches! and that
Hamûd possessed not so few as an hundred, and the Emir many
more than he. Hamûd asked me, if these were not "Engleys",
he would say 'of the best Nasâra work'. He was greedy to
understand of me if I brought not many gay things in my deep
saddle-bags of the fine workmanship of the Nasâra : he would
give for them, he promised me with a barbarous emphasis,
FELÛS ! 'silver scales' or money, which the miserable Arab
people believe that all men do cherish as the blood of their own
lives. I found Hamûd lying along as the nomads, idle and
yawning, in the plantation of Abeyd's kahwa, which, as said,
extends behind the makhzans to his family house in the town
(that is not indeed one of the best). In this palm-ground he
has many gazelles, which feed of vetches daily littered down to
them, but they were shy of man's approach : there I saw also
a bédan-buck. This robust wild goat of the mountain would
follow a man and even pursue him, and come without fear into
the kahwa. The beast is of greater bulk and strength than
any he-goat, with thick short hair ; his colour purple-ruddy ; or
nearly as that blushing before the sunset of dark mountains.

This is a palm-ground of Abeyd, planted in the best manner.
The stems in the harsh and lean soil of Hâyil, are set in rows,
very wide asunder. I spoke with Aly, that half-good fanatical
neighbour of mine, one who at my first coming had felt in my
girdle for gold, he was of Môgug, but now overseer at Hâyil of the
Prince's husbandry. This palm foster answered, that ' in such
earth (granite grit) where the palms have more room they bear
the better ; the (fivefold) manner which I showed him of setting
trees could not avail them.' Hamûd's large well in this ground
was of fifteen fathoms, sunk in that hard gritty earth ; the upright sides, baked in the sun, stand fast without inner building
or framework. The pit had been dug by the labour of fifteen
journeymen, each receiving three or four piastres, in twenty
days, this is a cost of some £10. Three of the best she-camels
drew upon the wheels, every one was worth thirty-five reals.
The price of camels in Arabia had been nearly doubled of late
years after the great draughts for Egypt, the Abyssinian wars,
and for Syria. It surprised me to hear a Beduwy talk in this
manner,—"And billah a cause is the lessened value of money"!
If rainless years follow rainless years, there comes in the end a
murrain. It was not many years since such a season, when a
camel was sold for a crown by the nomads, and languishing

thelûls, before worth sixty in their health, for two or three
reals, (that was to the villagers in Kasîm,) sooner than the
beasts remaining upon their hands should perish in the khála.

Mâjid, the elder of Hamûd's children, was a boy of fifteen
years, small for his age, of a feminine beauty, the son (the Emirs
also match with the nomads) of a Beduin woman. There accompanied him always a dissolute young man, one Aly, who had
four wives and was attached to Hamûd's service. This lovely
pair continually invaded me in my beyt, with the infantile
curiosity of Arabs, intent to lay their knavish fingers upon any
foreign thing of the Nasâra,—and such they hoped to find in
my much baggage; and lighting upon aught Mâjid and his
villanous fellow Aly had it away perforce.—When I considered
that they might thus come upon my pistol and instruments, I
wrested the things from their iniquitous fingers, and reminded
them of the honest example of the nomads, whom they despise.
Mâjid answered me with a childish wantonness: "But thou,
Khalîl, art in our power, and the Emir can cut off thy head at
his pleasure!" One day as I heard them at the door, I cast
the coverlet over my loose things, and sat upon it, but nothing
could be hidden from their impudence, with *bethr-ak ! bethr-ak !*
" by thy leave ; "—it happened that they found me sitting upon
the koran. "Ha! said they now with fanatical bitterness, he
is sitting upon the koran ! "—this tale was presently carried in
Mâjid's mouth to the castle ; and the elf Mâjid returned to tell
me that the Emir had been much displeased.

Mâjid showed himself to be of an affectionate temper, with
the easy fortunate disposition of his father, and often childishly
exulting, but in his nature too self-loving and tyrannical. He
would strike at the poorer children with his stick as he passed
by them in the street, and cry " Ullah curse thy father ! " they
not daring to resent the injury or resist him,—the best of the
eyyál es-sheuhk ; for thus are called the children of the princely
house. For his age he was corrupt of heart and covetous ; but
they are all brought up by slaves ! If he ever come to be the
Prince, I muse it will be an evil day for Hâyil, except, with good
mind enough to amend, he grow up to a more humane understanding. Mâjid, full of facility and the felicity of the Arabs,
with a persuading smile, affected to treat me always according
to his father's benevolence, naming me ' his dear friend ' ; and
yet he felt that I had a cold insight to his ambitious meaning.
So much of the peddling Semite was in him, that he played
huckster and bargained for my nâga at the lowest price, imagining to have the double for her (when she would be a milch cow

with the calf) in the coming spring : this I readily yielded, but
'nay, said then the young princeling, except I would give him
her harness too,' (which was worth a third more).—I have many
times mused what could be their estimation of honour! They
think they do that well enough in the world which succeeds to
them ; human deeds imitating our dream of the divine ways are
beautiful words of their poets, and otherwise unknown to these
Orientals.

As I walked through their clean and well-built clay town I
thought it were pleasant to live here,—save for the awe of the
Ruler and their lives disquieted to ride in the yearly forays of
the Emir : yet what discomfort to our eyes is that squalor of
the desert soil which lies about them! Hâyil for the unlikeli-
hood of the site is town rather than oasis, or it is, as it were, an
oasis made *ghrósb*, perforce. The circuit, for their plantations
are not very wide, may be nearly an hour ; the town lies as far
distant from the Ajja cliffs (there named *el-M'nîf*). Their
town, fenced from the wholesome northern· air by the bergs
Sumrá Hâyil, is very breathless in the long summer months.
The Sumrâ, of plutonic basalt, poured forth (it may be seen in
face of the Méshed gate) upon the half-burned grey-red granite
of Ajja, is two members which stand a little beyond the town,
in a half moon, and the seyl bed of Hâyil, which comes they say
from Gofar, passes out between them. That upon the west is
lower ; the eastern part rises to a height of five hundred feet,
upon the crest are cairns ; and there was formerly the look-out
station, when Hâyil was weaker.

The higher Samrâ, *Umm Arkab*, is steep, and I hired one
morning an ass, *jáhash*, for eightpence to ride thither. The
thick strewed stones upon this berg, are of the same rusty black
basalt which they call *hurrî* or *hurra*, heavy and hard as iron,
and ringing like bell-metal. Samrâ in the nomadic speech of
Nejd is any rusty black berg of hard stone in the desert ; and
in the great plutonic country from hence to Mecca the samrâs
are always basalt. The same, when any bushes grow upon it,
is called *házm*, and házm is such a vulcanic hill upon the
Harras. I saw from the cairns that Hâyil is placed at the
midst in a long plain, which is named *Sâhilat el-Khammashîeh*,
and lies between the M'nîf of Ajja (which may rise in the
highest above the plain to 1500 feet), and that low broken
hilly train, by which the Sâhilat is bounded along, two leagues
eastward, toward Selma, *J. Fittij ;* and under us north-eastward
from Hâyil is seen *el-Khreyma*, a great possession of young
palms,—the Emir's ; and there are springs, they say, which
water them !

Some young men labouring in the fields had seen the Nasrâny ascending, and they mounted after us. In the desert below, they said, is hidden much treasure, if a man had wit to find it, and they filled my ears with their "*Jebel Tommîeh!*" renowned, "for the riches which lie there buried," in all Nejd ; —Tommîeh in the Wady er-Rummah, south of the *Abanât* twin mountains. After this, one among them who was lettered, sat down and wrote for me the landmarks, that we saw in that empty wilderness about us. Upon a height to the northward they showed me *Kabr es-Sâny*, 'the smith's grave,' laid out to a length of three fathoms : "Of such stature was the man ; he lived in time of the Beny Helâl: pursued by the enemies' horsemen, he ran before them with his little son upon his shoulder, and fell there." All this plain upon the north is *G(k)isan M'jelly*, to the mountain peaks, *Tuâl Aly*, at the borders of the Nefûd, and to the solitary small mountain *Jildiyyah*, which being less than a journey from Hâyil, is often named for an assembling place of the Emir's ghrazzus. There is a village northward of Hâyil two miles beyond the Sumrâ, *S'weyfly ;* and before S'weyfly is seen a ruined village and rude palm planting and corn grounds, *Kasr Arbŷiyyah.* Arbŷiyyah and S'weyfly are old Hâyil ; this is to say the ancient town was built, in much better soil and site, upon the north side of the Sumrâ. Then he showed me with his hand under the M'nîf of Ajja the place of the *Ria Ag(k)da*, which is a gap or strait of the mountain giving upon a deep plain-bosom in the midst of Ajja, and large so that it might, after their speaking, contain *rúba ed-dínya*, "a fourth part of their (thinly) inhabited world." There are palms in a compass of mighty rocks ; it is a moun- tain-bay which looks eastward, very hot in summer. The narrow inlet is shut by gates, and Abeyd had fortified the passage with a piece of cannon The Riâ Agda is accounted a sure refuge for the people of Hâyil, with all their goods, as Abeyd had destined, in the case of any military expedition of the Dowla, against "the JEBEL," of which they have some- times been in dread. Northward beyond el-M'nîf the Ajja coast is named *el-Aueyrith.*

I came down in the young men's company, and they invited me to their noonday breakfast of dates which was brought out to them in the fields. Near by I found a street of tottering walls and ruinous clay houses, and the ground-wall of an ancient massy building in clay-brick, which is no more used at Hâyil. The foundation of this settlement by Shammar is from an high antiquity ; some of them say "the place was named at first, *Hâyer*, for the plentiful (veins of ground-) water ", yet

Hâyil is found written in the ancient poem of Antar. [Ptolemy has here 'Αρρη κώμη.—v. Sprenger in *Die alte Geogr. Arabiens.*] The town is removed from beyond the Sumrâ, the cause was, they say, the failing little and little of their ground-water. Hâyil, in the last generation, before the beginning of the government of Ibn Rashîd, was an oasis half as great as Gofar, which is a better site by nature; yet Hâyil, Abdullah Ibn Rashîd's town, when he became *Muhafûth*, or constable under the Wahâby for West Nejd, was always the capital. To-day the neighbour towns are almost equal, and in Hâyil I have estimated to be 3000 souls; the people of Gofar, who are Beny Temîm, and nearly all husbandmen, do yet, they say, a little exceed them. In returning home towards the northern gate, I visited a ruined suburb *Wâsit* "middle" (building), which by the seyl and her fields only is divided from Hâyil town. There were few years ago in the street, now ruins, "forty kahwas," that is forty welfaring households receiving their friends daily to coffee.

Wâsit to-day is ruins without inhabitant; her people (as those in the ruined quarter of Gofar and in ruined Môgug) died seven years before in the plague, *wába*. I saw their earthen house-walls unroofed and now ready to fall, for the timbers had been taken away: the fields and the wells lay abandoned. The owners and heirs of the soil had so long left the waterer's labour that the palm-trees were dead and sere · few palms yet showed in their rusty crowns any languishing greenness. Before I left Hâyil I saw those lifeless stems cut down, and the earth laid out anew in seed-plots There died in Wâsit three hundred persons; in Hâyil, 'one or two perished in every household (that were seven hundred or eight hundred); but now, the Lord be praised, the children were sprung up and nearly filled their rooms.' Of the well-dieted princely and sheykhly families there died no man! Beduins that visited Hayil in time of the pestilence perished sooner than townsfolk; yet the contagion was lighter in the desert and never prevailed in their menzils as a mortal sickness. The disease seized upon the head and bowels; some died the same day, some lingered awhile longer Signs in the plague-struck were a black spot which appeared upon the nose, and a discolouring of the nails; the sufferings were nearly those of cholera. After the pest a malignant fever afflicted the country two years, when the feeble survivors loading the dead upon asses (for they had no more strength to carry out piously themselves) were weary to bury. A townsman who brought down, at that time, some quinine from the north, had dispensed 'ten or twelve grains to the sick at five reals; and taken after a purging dose of magnesia, he told me, it commonly relieved them.' This great death fell in the short time of *Bunder's* playing the Prince in Hâyil, and little before the beginning of Mohammed's government, which is a reign they think of prosperity " such as was not seen before, and in which there has happened no public calamity." Now first the lordship of Shammar is fully ripe: after such soon-ripeness we may look for rottenness, as men succeed of less endowments to administer that which was acquired of late by warlike violence, or when this tide of the world shall be returning from them.

After Wâsit, in a waste, which lies between the town walls and the low crags of the Sumrâ, is the wide grave-yard of Hâyil. Poor and rich whose world is ended, lie there alike indigently together in the desert earth which once fostered them, and unless it be for the sites here and there, we see small or no difference of burial. Telâl and Abeyd were laid among them. The first grave is a little heap whose rude headstone is a wild block from the basalt hill, and the last is like it, and such is every grave; you shall hardly see a scratched epitaph, where so much is written as the name which was a name. In the border Semitic countries is a long superstition of the grave; here is but the simple nomad guise, without other last loving care or adornment. At a side in the mákbara is the grave-heap of Abeyd, a man of so much might and glory in his days: now these are but a long remembrance; he lies a yard under the squalid gravel in his shirt, and upon his stone is rudely scored, with a nail, this only word, *Abeyd bin-Rashîd*. When I questioned Mâjid, 'And did his grandsire, the old man Abeyd, lie now so simply in the earth?' my words sounded coldly and strange in his ears; since in this land of dearth, where no piece of money is laid out upon thing not to their lives' need, they are nearly of the Wife of Bath's opinion, " it were but waste to bury him preciously," —whom otherwise they follow in her luxury. When one is dead, they say, *khálas!* " he is ended," and they wisely dismiss this last sorrowful case of all men's days without extreme mourning.

Between the mákbara and the town gate is seen a small menzil of resident nomads. They are pensioners of the palace; and notwithstanding their appearance of misery some of them are of kin to the princely house. Their Beduin booths are fenced from the backward with earthen walling, and certain of them have a chamber (kasr) roofed with a tent-cloth, or low tower of the same clay building. They are Shammar, whose few cattle are with their tribesfolk in the wilderness; in the spring months they also remove thither, and refresh themselves in the short season of milk. As I went by, a woman called me from a ragged booth, the widest among them; ' had I a medicine for her sore eyes?' She told me in her talk that her sister had been a wife of Metaab, and she was "aunt" of Mohammed now Emir. Her sons fled in the troubled times and lived yet in the northern dîras. When she named the Emir she spoke in a whisper, looking always towards the Kasr, as if she dreaded the wings of the air might carry her word into the Prince's hearing. Her grown daughter stood by us, braying temmn in a great wooden mortar, and I wondered to see her unveiled; perhaps she was not married, and Moslems have no jealous opinion of a Nasrâny. The comely maiden's cheeks glowed at her labour; such little flesh colour I had not seen before in a nomad woman, so lean and bloodless they all are, but she was a stalwart one bred in the plenteous northern dîras. I counted their tents, thirty; nearer the Gofar gate were other fifteen booths of half-resident Shammar, pitched without clay building.

CHAPTER XIV

IBN RASHÎDS TOWN

(*Doughty describes the great Kasr and the public guest-chambers. Hamûd sends his sick infant son to him, to cure ; and talks much with the Nasrâny.*)

* * * A week passed and then the Emir Mohammed came again from the wilderness : the next afternoon he called for me after the mejlis. His usher found me slumbering in my makhzan. Worn and broken in this long year of famine and fatigues, I was fallen into a great languor. The Prince's man roused me with haste and violence in their vernile manner : " Stand up thou and come off ; the Emir calls thee ; " and because I stayed to take the kerchief and mantle, even this, when we entered the audience, was laid against me, the slave saying to the Emir that ' Khalîl had not been willing to follow him ' !

Mohammed had gone over from the mejlis with the rajajîl to Abeyd's kahwa. The Emir sat now in Hamûd's place, and Hamûd where Sleymàn daily sat. The light scimitar, with golden hilt, that Mohammed carried loose in his hand, was leaned up to the wall beside him ; the blade is said to be of some extremely fine temper. He sat as an Arabian, in his loose cotton tunic, mantle and kerchief, with naked shanks and feet, his sandals, which he had put off at the carpet, were set out before him. I saluted the Emir, *Salaam aleyk.*—No answer : then I greeted Hamûd and Sleymàn, now of friendly acquaintance, in the same words, and with *aleykom es-salaam* they hailed me smiling comfortably again. One showed me to a place where I should sit down before the Emir, who said shortly " From whence ? "—" From my makhzan."—' And what found I there to do all the day, ha ! and what had I seen in the time of my being at Hâyil, was it well ? ' When the Prince said, " Khalîl ! " I should have responded in their manner *Aunak* or *Labbeyk* or *Tawîl el-Ummr,* " O Long-of-age ! and what is thy sweet will ? " but feeling as an European among these light-tongued Asiatics, and full of mortal weariness, I kept silence. So the Emir, who had not responded to my salutation, turned abruptly to ask Hamûd and Sleymân : *Má yarúdd?* 'how! he returns not one's word who speaks with him?' Hamûd responded kindly for me, 'He could not tell, it might be Khalîl is tired.' I answered after the pause, " I am lately arrived in this place, but *aghrúty,* I suppose it is very well." The Emir opened his great feminine Arab eyes upon me as if he wondered at the not flattering plainness of my speech ; and he said suddenly, with an emphasis, before the company, " Ay, I think so indeed, it is very well !—and what think you Khalîl, it is a good air ? "—" I think so, but the flies are very thick."— " Hmm, the flies are very thick! and went you in the pilgrimage to the Holy City (Jerusalem) ? "—" Twice or thrice, and to *J. Tôr,* where is the mountain of our Lord Mûsa."—Some among them said to the Emir, " We have heard that monks of the Nasâra dwell there, their habitation is built like a castle in the midst of the khála, and the entry is by a window upon the wall ; and who would come in there must be drawn up by a wheelwork and ropes." The Emir asked, " And have they riches ? "—" They have a revenue of alms." The Emir rose, and taking his sandals, all the people stood up with him,—he beckoned them to be seated still, and went out to the plantation. In the time of his absence there was silence in all the company ; when he returned he sat down again without ceremony. The Prince, who would discern my mind in my answers, asked me, " Were dates good or else bad ? " and I answered " *battâl, battâl,* very bad."—" Bread is better? and what in your tongue is bread ? ' he repeated to himself the name which he had heard in Turkish, and he knew it in the Persian ; Mohammed, formerly conductor of the pilgrimage, can also speak in that language.

The Emir spoke to me with the light impatient gestures of Arabs not too well pleased, and who play the first parts,—a sudden shooting of the brows, and that shallow extending of the head from the neck, which are of the bird-like inhabitants of nomadic Nejd, and whilst at their every inept word's end they expect thy answer. The Emir was favourably minded toward me, but the company of malignant young fanatics always about him, continually traduced the Nasrâny. Mohammed now Prince was as much better than they, as he was of an higher understanding. When to some new question of the Emir I confirmed my answer in the Beduin wise, By his life, *hayátak,* he said to Hamûd, " Seest thou ? Khalîl has learned to speak (Arabic) among the Annezy, he says *aghrûty*."—"And what might I say, O el-Muhafûth? I speak as I heard it of the Beduw." The Prince would not that I should question him of grammar, but hearing me name him so justly by his title, Warden (which is nearly that in our history of Protector), he said mildly, "Well, swear By the life of Ullah!" (The other, since they are become so clear-sighted with the Waháby, is an oath savouring of idolatry.) I answered somewhat out of the Prince's season, "—and thus even the nomads use, in a greater occasion, but they say, *By the life of thee*, in a little matter." As the Prince could not draw from me any smooth words of courtiers, Hamûd and Sleymàn hastened, with their fair speech, to help forth the matter and excuse me. "Certainly, they said, Khalîl is not very well to-day, eigh, the poor man! he looks sick indeed!"—And I passed the most daylight hours, stretched weakly upon the unswept floor of my makhzan, when the malignants told the Emir I was writing up his béled: so there ofttimes came in spies from the Castle, who opened upon me suddenly, to see in what manner the Nasrâny were busied.—*Emir*: "And thy medicines are what? hast thou *tiryâk* [thus our fathers said treacle, θηριακ-, the antidote of therine poisons]. In an extreme faintness, I was now almost falling into a slumber, and my attention beginning to waver I could but say,—"What is tiryâk?—I remember; but I have it not, by God there is no such thing." *Sleymàn*: "Khalîl has plenty of salts Engleys (magnesia)—hast thou not, Khalîl?" At this dull sally, and the Arabian Emir being so much in thought of poison, I could not forbear to smile,—an offence before rulers. Sleymàn then beginning to call me to give account in that presence of the New Continent,—he would I should say, if we had not dates there; but the "Long-of-Days" rose abruptly, and haughtily,—so rose all the rest with him, and they departed.

A word now of the princely family and of the state of J. Shammar: and first of the tragedies in the house of Ibn Rashîd. Telâl returning from er-Riâth (whither he was accustomed, as holding of the Waháby, to go every year with a present of horses) fell sick, *musky*, poisoned, it was said, in his cup, in East Nejd. His health decayed, and the Prince fell into a sort of melancholy frenzy. Telâl sent to Bagdad for a certain Persian hakîm. The hakîm journeyed down to Hâyil, and when he had visited the Prince, he gave his judgment unadvisedly: "This sickness is not unto death, it is rather a long disease which must waste thy understanding."—Telâl answered, "Aha, shall I be a fool?—wellah *mejnûn!* *wa ana el-*HÀKIM, and I being the Ruler?" And because his high heart might not longer endure to live in the common pity; one day when he had shut himself in his chamber, he set his pistols against his manly breast, and fired them and ended. So Metaab, his brother, became Emir at Hâyil, as the elder of the princely house inheriting Abdullah their father's dignity: Telâl's children were (legally) passed by, of whom the eldest, Bunder, afterwards by his murderous deed Emir, was then a young man of seventeen years. Metaab I have often heard praised as a man of mild demeanour, and not common understanding; he was princely and popular at once, as the most of his house, politic, such as the great sheukh el-Aarab, and a fortunate governor. Metaab sat not fully two years,—always in the ambitious misliking of his nephew Bunder, a raw and strong-headed young man. Bunder, conspiring with his next brother, Bedr, against their uncle, the ungracious young men determined to kill him.

They knew that their uncle wore upon his arm "an amulet which assured his life from lead", therefore the young parricides found means to cast a silver bullet   Metaab sat in his fatal hour with his friends and the men-at-arms before him in the afternoon mejlis, which is held, as said, upon the further side of the Méshab, twenty-five paces over in face of the Kasr.—Bunder and Bedr were secretly gone up from the apartments within to the head of the castle wall, where is a terrace and parapet. Bunder pointing down his matchlock through a small trap in the wall, fired first ; and very likely his hand wavered when all hanged upon that shot, for his ball went a little awry and razed the thick head-band of a great Beduin sheykh *Ibn Shalàn,* chief of the strong and not unfriendly Annezy tribe er-Ruwàlla in the north, who that day arrived from his dîra, to visit Prince Ibn Rashîd. Ibn Shalàn, hearing the shot sing about his ears, started up, and (cried he) putting a hand to his head, " Akhs, Mohafûth, wouldst thou murder me!" The Prince, who sat on, and would not save himself by an unseemly flight, answered the sheykh with a constant mild face, " Fear not; thou wilt see that the shot was levelled at myself." A second shot struck the Emir in the breast, which was Bedr's.

Bunder being now Prince, sat not a full year out, and could not prosper: in his time, was that plague which so greatly wasted the country. Mohammed who is now Emir, when his brother Metaab was fallen, fled to er-Riâth, where he lived awhile. The Wahâby prince, Abdullah Ibn Saûd, was a mean to reconcile them, and Bunder, by letters, promising peace, invited his uncle to return home. So Mohammed came, and receiving his old office, was governor again of the Bagdad haj caravan. Mohammed went by, with the convoy returning from Mecca to Mesopotamia, and there he was to take up the year's provision of temmn for the Mothîf, (if you would believe them, a thousand camel-loads,—150 tons!). Mohammed finding only Thuffîr Aarab at el-Méshed, hired camels of them with promise of safe conduct going and returning, in the estates of Ibn Rashîd; for they were Beduw from without, and not friendly with the Jebel. The journey is two weeks' marches of the nomads for loaded camels.—Mohammed approaching Hâyil, sent before him to salute the Emir saying, "Mohammed greets thee, and has brought down thy purveyance of temmn for the Mothîf."—"Ha! is Mohammed come? answered Bunder,— he shall not enter Hâyil." Then Bunder, Bedr, and Hamûd rode forth, these three together, to meet Mohammed; and at Bunder's commandment the town gates behind them were shut.

Mohammed sat upon his thelûl, when they met with him as he had ridden down from the north; and said Bunder, "Mohammed, what Beduw hast thou brought to Hâyil?—the Thuffîr! and yet thou knowest them to be gôm with us!" *Mohammed:* "Wellah, yâ el-Mohafûth, I have brought them *bi wéjhy*, under my countenance! (and in the Arabian guise he stroked down his visage to the beard)—because I found none other for the carriage of your temmn." Whilst Bunder lowered upon him, Hamûd, who was in covenant with his cousin Mohammed, made him a sign that his life was in doubt,—by drawing (it is told) the forefinger upon his gullet. Mohammed spoke to one of the town who came by on horseback, "Ho there! lend me thy mare awhile," making as though he would go and see to the entry and unloading of his caravan. Mohammed, when he was settled on horseback, drew over to the young Prince and caught Bunder's "horns", and with his other hand he took the crooked broad dagger, which upon a journey they wear at the belt.—"*La ameymy, la ameymy*, do it not, do it not, little 'nuncle!" exclaimed Bunder in the horror and anguish of death. Mohammed answered with a deadly stern voice, "Wherefore didst thou kill thine uncle? *wa hu fî batn-ak*, and he is in thy belly (thou hast devoured him, dignity, life, and all)," and with a murderous hand-cast he struck the blade into his nephew's bowels! —There remained no choice to Mohammed, when he had received the sign, he must slay his elder brother's son, or himself be lost; for if he should fly, how might he have outgone the godless young parricides? his thelûl was weary, he

K

was weary himself; and he must forsake the Thuffîr, to whom his princely word had been plighted.—Devouring is the impotent ambition to rule, of all Arabians, who are born near the sheykhly state. Mohammed had been a loyal private man under Metaab; his brother fallen, what remained but to avenge him? and the garland should be his own.

Bunder slain, he must cut off kindred, which else would endanger him. The iniquity of fortune executed these crimes by Mohammed's hand, rather than his own execrable ambition.—These are the tragedies of the house of Ibn Rashîd! their beginning was from Telâl, the murderer of himself : the fault of one extends far round, such is the cursed nature of evil, as the rundles of a stone dashed into water, trouble all the pool. There are some who say, that Hamûd made Bunder's dying sure with a pistol-shot,—he might do this, because his lot was bound up in Mohammed's life : but trustworthy persons in Hâyil have assured me that Hamûd had no violent hand in it.—Hamûd turning his horse's head, galloped to town and commanded to 'keep the gates close, and let no man pass out or enter for any cause'; and riding in to the Méshab he cried : "Hearken, all of you ! a Rashîdy has slain a Rashîdy,—there is no word for any of you to say ! let no man raise his voice or make stir, upon pain of my hewing off his head wellah with this sword "

In Hâyil there was a long silence, the subject people shrunk in from the streets to their houses ! Beduins in the town were aghast, inhabitants of the khála, to which no man "may set doors and bars ", seeing the gates of Hâyil to be shut round about them.

An horrible slaughter was begun in the Kasr, for Mohammed commanded that all the children of Telâl should be put to death, and the four children of his own sister, widow of one el-Jabbâr, of the house Ibn Aly, (that, till Abdullah won all, were formerly at strife with the Rashîdy family, for the sheykhship of Hâyil, —and of them was Mohammed's own mother). Their uncle's bloody command was fulfilled, and the bleeding warm corses, deceived of their young lives, were carried out the same hour to the burial ; there died with them also the slaves, their equals in age, brought up in their fathers' households,—their servile brethren, that else might, at any time, be willing instruments to avenge them.

All Hâyil trembled that day till evening and the long night till morning ; when Mohammed, standing in the Méshab with a drawn sword, called to those who sat timidly on the clay banks,—the most were Beduins—"Yâ Moslemîn ! I had not so dealt with them, but because I was afraid for this! (he clapped the left palm to the side of his neck), and as they went about to kill me, *ana sabáktahum*, I have prevented them." Afterward he said:—" And they which killed my brother Metaab, think ye, they had spared me?" " And hearing his voice, we sat (an eyewitness, of the Meteyr, told me) astonished, every one seeing the black death before him."—Then Mohammed sat down in the Emir's place as Muhâfuth. Bye and bye, some of the principal persons at Hâyil came into the Méshab bending to this new lord of their lives, and giving him joy of his seized authority. Thus ' out dock in nettle', Bunder away, Mohammed began to rule; and never was the government, they say, in more sufficient handling.

— Bedr had started away upon his mare, for bitter-sweet life, to the waste wilderness: he fled at assr. On the morrow, fainting with hunger and thirst, and the suffered desolation of mind and weariness, he shot away his spent horse, and climbed upon a mountain.—From thence he might look far out over the horror of the world, become to him a vast dying place! Mohammed had sent horsemen to scour the khála, and take him; and when they found Bedr in the rocks they would not listen to his lamentable petitions: they killed him there, without remedy; and hastily loading his body they came again the same day to Hâyil. The chief of them as he entered, all heated, to Mohammed, exclaimed joyfully, " Wellah, O Muhâfûth, I bring thee glad tidings! it may please thee come with me, whereas I will show thee Bedr lies dead; this hand did it, and so perish all the enemies of the Emir!" But Mohammed looked grimly upon the man, and cried, " Who commanded thee to kill him? I commanded thee, son of an hound? when, thou cursed one? Ullah curse thy father, akhs! hast thou slain Bedr?" and, drawing his sword, he fetched him a clean back-stroke upon the neck-bone, and swapt off at once (they pretend) the miserable man's head. Mohammed used an old bitter policy of tyrants, by which they hope to make their perplexed causes seem the more honest in the thick eyesight of the common people. "How happened it, I asked, that Bedr, who must know the wilderness far about, since the princely children accompany the ghrazzus, had not ridden hardily in some way of escape? Could not his mare have borne him an hundred miles?—a man of sober courage, in an extremity, might have endured, until he had passed the dominion of Ibn Rashîd, and entered into the first free town of el-Kasîm." It was answered, " The young man was confused in so great a calamity, and jâhil, of an inept humour, and there was none to deliver him."

Hamûd and Mohammed allied together, there was danger between them and Teiâl's sons; and if they had not forestalled Bunder and Bedr, they had paid it with their lives. The massacres were surely contrary to the clement nature of the strong man Hamûd. Hamûd, who for his pleasant equal countenance, in the people's eyes, has deserved to be named by his fellow citizens *Azíz*, "a beloved," is for all that, when contraried out of friendship, a lordly man of outrageous incontinent tongue and jabbâr, as his father was; and doubtless he would be a high-handed Nimrod in any instant peril. Besides, it is thus that Arabs deal with Arabs; there are none more pestilent, and ungenerous enemies. Hamûd out of hospitality, is as all the Arabs of a somewhat miserable humour, and I have heard it uttered at Hâyil, "Hamûd *khára!*" that is draffe or worse. These are vile terms of the Hejâz, spread from the dens of savage life, under criminal governors, in the Holy Cities; and not of those schools of speaking well and of comely manners, which are the kahwa, in the Arabian oases and the mejlis in the open khâla.—A fearful necessity was laid upon Mohammed: for save by these murders of his own nigh blood, he could not have sat in any daily assurance. Mohammed is childless, and ajjr, a man barren in himself; the loyal Hamûd el-Abeyd has many children.

His instant dangers being thus dispersed, Mohammed set himself to the work of government, to win opinion of his proper merit; and affecting popular manners, he is easier of his dispense than was formerly Telâl. Never Prince used his authority, where not resisted, with more stern moderation at home, but he is pitiless in the excision of any unsound parts of the commonwealth. When Jauf fell to him again, by the mutiny of the few Moghrâreba left in garrison, it is said, he commanded to cut off the right hands of many that were gone over to the faith of the Dowla. Yet Jauf had not been a full generation under the Jebel; for Mohammed himself, then a young man, was with his uncle Abeyd at the taking of it, and he was wounded then by a ball in the foot which lodged in the bone;—the shot had lately been taken from him in Hâyil by a Persian hakîm, come down, for the purpose, from Mesopotamia.

As for any bounty in such Arabian Princes, it is rather good laid out by them to usury. They are easy to loose a pound to-day, which within a while may return with ten in his mouth. The Arabs say, "Ibn Rashîd uses to deal with every man *aly aklu*, according to his understanding." Fortune was to Mohammed's youth contrary, a bloody chance has made him Ruler. In his government he bears with that which may not be soon

amended ; he cannot, by force only, bridle the slippery wills of
the nomads ; and though his heart swell secretly, he receives all
with his fair-weather countenance, and to friendly discourse :
and of few words, in wisely questioning them, he discerns their
minds. Motlog, sheykh of the Fejîr, whom he misliked, he
sends home smiling ; and the Prince will levy his next year's
mîry from the Fukara, without those tribesmen's unwillingness.
The principal men of Teyma, his good outlying town, whose
well was fallen, depart from him with rewards. Mohammed
smooths the minds of the common people ; if any rude Beduin
lad call to him in the street, or from the mejlis (they are
all arrant beggars), "Aha! el-Muhafûth, God give thee long
life ! as truly as I came hither, in such a rubba, and wellah am
naked," he will graciously dismiss him with " *bismillah*, in
God's name ! go with such an one, and he will give thee
garments,"—that is a tunic worth two shillings at Hâyil, a
coarse worsted cloak of nine shillings, a kerchief of sixpence ;
and since they are purchased in the gross at Bagdad, and
brought down upon the Emir's own camels, they may cost him
not ten shillings. * * *

* * * The Prince Mohammed is pitiless in battle, he shoots
with an European rifle ; Hamûd, of ponderous strength, is seen
raging in arms by the Emir's side, and, if need were, since they
are sworn together to the death, he would cover him with his
body. The princes, descended from their thelûls, and sitting
upon horseback in their "David shirts of mail ", are among the
forefighters, and the wings of the men-at-arms, shooting against
the enemy, close them upon either hand. The Emir's battle
bears down the poor Beduw, by weight and numbers ; for the
rajajîl, and his riders of the villages, used to the civil life, hear
the words of command, and can maintain themselves in a body
together. But the bird-witted Beduins who, in their herding
life, have no thought of martial exercises, may hardly gather,
in the day of battle, under their sheukh, but like screaming
hawks they fight dispersedly, tilting hither and thither, every
man with less regard of the common than of his private
interest, and that is to catch a beggarly booty : the poor
nomads acknowledge themselves to be betrayed by tóma, the
greediness of gain. Thus their resistance is weak, and woe to
the broken and turned to flight ! None of the Emir's enemies
are taken to quarter, until they be destroyed : and cruel are
the mercies of the rajajîl and the dire-hearted slaves of Ibn
Rashîd. I have known when some miserable tribesmen, mad-
prisoners, were cast by the Emir's band into their own well

pits:—the Arabians take no captives. The battles with nomads are commonly fought in the summer, about their principal water-stations; where they are long lodged in great standing camps.

Thus the Beduins say "It is Ibn Rashîd that weakens the Beduw!" Their resistance broken, he receives them among his confederate tributaries, and delivers them from all their enemies from his side. A part of the public spoil is divided to the rajajîl, and every man's is that commonly upon which he first laid his hand. Ibrahîm the Algerian, one of them who often came to speak with me of his West Country, said that to every man of the Emir's rajajîl are delivered three or four reals at the setting out, that he may buy himself wheat, dates and ammunition : and there is carried with them sometimes as much as four camel loads of powder and lead from Hâyil ; which is partly for the Beduw that will join him by the way.

But to circumscribe the principality or dominion in the deserts of Ibn Rashîd :—his borders in the North are the Ruwàlla, northern Shammar and Thuffîr marches, nomad tribes friendly to the Jebel, but not his tributaries. Upon the East his limits are at the dominion of Boreyda, which we shall see is a principality of many good villages in the Nefûd of Kasîm, as el-Ayûn, Khubbera, er-Russ, but with no subject Beduw. The princely house of Hâyil is by marriage allied to that usurping peasant *Weled Mahanna*, tyrant of Boreyda, and they are accorded together against the East, that is Aneyza, and the now decayed power of the Wahâby beyond the mountain. In the South, having lost Kheybar, his limits are at about an hundred miles from el-Medina ; the deserts of his dominion are bounded westwards by the great haj-way from Syria,—if we leave out the B. Atîeh—and all the next territory of the Sherarât is subject to him, which ascends to J. Sherra and so turns about by the *W. Sirhân* to his good northern towns of Jauf and Sh'kâky and their suburbs. In a word, all that is Ibn Rashîd's desert country lying between Jauf, el-Kasîm and the Derb el-Haj ; north and south some ninety leagues over, and between east and west it may be one hundred and seventy leagues over. And the whole he keeps continually subdued to him with a force (by their own saying) of about five hundred thelûl riders, his rajajîl and villagers ; for who may assemble in equal numbers out of the dead wilderness, or what were twice so many wild Beduins, the half being almost without arms, to resist him ? * * *

(Doughty describes life in Hâyil. Anecdotes of Ibn Rashíd's rule. Kâhtan tribesmen and travelled men at Hâyil.)

* * * The weather, sultry awhile after my coming to Hâyil, was now grown cold. Snow, which may be seen the most winters upon a few heads of Arabian mountains, is almost not known to fall in the Nejd wilderness, although the mean altitude be nearly 4000 feet. They say such happens about " once in forty years ". It had been seen two winters before, when snow lay on the soil three days : the camels were couched in the menzils, and many of them perished in that unwonted cold and hunger.

A fire was kindled morning and evening in the great kahwa, and I went there to warm myself with the Beduins. One evening before almost anyone came in, I approached to warm myself at the fire-pit.—"Away ! (cried the coffee-server, who was of a very splenetic fanatical humour) and leave the fire to the guests that will presently arrive." Some Beduins entered and sat down by me. " I say, go back ! " cries the coffee-keeper. " A moment, man, and I am warm ; be we not all the Prince's guests ? " Some of the Beduw said in my ear : " It were better to remove, not to give them an occasion." That káhwajy daily showed his rancour, breaking into my talk with the Beduw, as when someone asked me " Whither wilt thou next, Khalîl ? "—" May it please Ullah (cries the coffee-server) to jehennem ! " I have heard he was one of servile condition from Aneyza in Kasîm ; but being daily worshipfully saluted by guesting Beduin sheykhs, he was come to some solemn opinion of himself. To cede to the tyranny of a servant, might, I thought, hearten other fanatics' audacity in Hâyil. The coffee-server, with a frenetic voice, cried to a Beduwy sitting by, " Reach me that camel-stick," (which the nomads have always in their hands,) and having snatched it from him, the slave struck me with all his decrepit force. The Beduins had risen round me with troubled looks,—they might feel that they were not themselves safe ; none of these were sheykhs, that durst say any word, only they beckoned me to withdraw with them, and sit down with them at a little distance. It had been perilous to defend myself among dastards ; for if it were told in the town that the Nasrâny laid heavy hands on a Moslem,

then the wild fire had kindled in many hearts to avenge him.
The Emir must therefore hear of the matter and do justice, or
so long as I remained in Hâyil every shrew would think he had
as good leave to insult me. I passed by the gallery to the
Emir's apartment, and knocking on the iron door, I heard the
slave-boy who kept it within say to the guard that it was Khalîl
the Nasrâny. The Emir sent out Nasr to enquire my business,
and I went to sit in the Méshab. Later someone coming from
the Kasr, who had been with the Emir, said that the Emir sent
for the coffee-server immediately, and said to him, "Why!
Ullah curse thy father, hast thou struck the Nasrâny?"—
"Wellah, O el-Muhafûth (the trembling wretch answered) I
touched him not!"—so he feared the Emir, who said then to
some of the guard "Beat him!" but Hamûd rose and going
over to Mohammed, he kissed his cousin's hand, asking him, for
his sake, to spare the coffee-server, 'who was a *mesquin* (meskîn).' "Go káhwajy, said the Emir, and if I hear any more
there shall nothing save thee, but thou shalt lose thy office."
Because I forsook the coffee-hall, the second coffee-server came
many times to my makhzan, and wooed me to return among
them ; but I responded, "Where the guests of the Emir are not
safe from outrage—!"

CHAPTER XV

THE Haj were approaching;—this is Ibn Rashîd's convoy
from Mesopotamia of the so-called 'Persian pilgrimage' to
Mecca:—and seeing the child Feysal had nearly recovered,
I thought after that to depart; for I found little rest at all or
refreshment at Hâyil.   Because the Emir had spoken to me
of mines and minerals, I conjectured that he would have sent
some with me on horseback, seeking up and down for metals:
—but when he added "There is a glancing sand in some parts
of the khála like scaly gold," I had answered with a plainness
which must discourage an Arab.   Also Hamûd had spoken to
me of seeking for metals.

Imbârak invited me one morning to go home with him " to
kahwa", he had a good house beside the mesjid, backward from
the Méshab.   We found his little son playing in the court: the
martial father took him in his arms with the tenderness of
the Arabians for their children.   An European would bestow the
first home love upon the child's mother; but the Arabian oases'
housewives come not forth with meeting smiles and the eyes
of love, to welcome-in their husbands, for they are his espoused
servants, he purchased them of their parents, and at best, his
liking is divided.   The child cried out, "Ho! Nasrâny, thou
canst not look to the heaven!"—"See, my son, I may look
upon it as well, I said, as another and better;—taal húbbiny!
come thou and kiss me;" for the Arab strangers kiss their
hosts' young children.—When some of the young courtiers had
asked me, Fen rubbuk, 'Where is thy Lord God?' I answered
them very gravely, Fî kull makán, 'The Lord is in every
place:' which word of the Nasrâny pleased them strangely
and was soon upon all their tongues in the Kasr.

"Khalil, said Imbârak, as we sat at the hearth, we would
have thee to dwell with us in Hâyil; only become a Moslem, it

K*

is a little word and soon said. Also wouldst thou know more
of this country, thou shalt have then many occasions, in being
sent for the Emir's business here and there. The Emir will
promote thee to an high place and give thee a house; where
thou mayest pass thy life in much repose, free from all cares,
wellah in only stretching the limbs at thy own hearth-side.
Although that which we can offer be not more than a man
as thou art might find at home in his country, yet consider it
is very far to come again thither, and that thou must return
through as many new dangers."—Imbârak was doubtless a
spokesman of the Emir, he promised fair, and this office I
thought might be the collecting of taxes; for in handling of
money they would all sooner trust a Nasrâny.

Those six or seven reals which came in by the sale of my
nâga,—I had cast them with a few small pieces of silver into a
paper box with my medicines, I found one day had been stolen,
saving two reals and the small money; that either the Arab
piety of the thief had left me, or his superstition, lest he
should draw upon himself the Christian's curse and a chastise-
ment of heaven. My friends' suspicion fell upon two persons.
The dumb man, who very often entered my lodging, for little
cause, and a certain Beduwy, of the rajajîl at Hâyil, of a
melancholy scelerat humour; he had bought my camel, and
afterward he came many times to my makhzan, to be treated
for ophthalmia. I now heard him named a cut-purse of the
Persian Haj, and the neighbours even affirmed that he had cut
some of their wezands. When I spoke of this mischief to
Hamûd, he affected with the barbaric sleight of the Arabs not
to believe me. I looked then in my purse, and there were not
thirty reals! I gave my tent to the running broker and gained
four or five more. The dellâl sold it to some young patrician,
who would ride in this winter pilgrimage of 160 leagues and
more in the khâla, to Mecca. Imbârak set his sword to the
dumb man's throat, but the dumb protested with all the
vehement signs in the world that this guilt was not in him.
As for the Beduwy he was not found in Hâyil!

Already the fore-riders of the Haj arrived : we heard that the
pilgrims this year were few in number. I saw now the yearly
gathering in Hâyil of men from the villages and the tribes that
would follow with the caravan on pilgrimage, and of petty tradesmen that come to traffic with the passing haj :—some of them
brought dates from Kasîm above a hundred miles distant. A
company from the Jauf villages lodged in the next makhzans;
they were more than fifty persons, that had journeyed ten days

tardily over the Nefûd in winter rain and rough weather: but that is hardly a third of their long march (of seven hundred miles) to Mecca. I asked some weary man of them, who came to me trembling in the chill morning, how he looked to accomplish his religious voyage and return upwards in the cold months without shelter. "Those, he answered, that die, they die; and who live, God has preserved them." These men told me they reckon from Jauf eight, to el-Méshed, and to Damascus nine camel journeys; to Maan are five thelûl days, or nine nights out with loaded camels. Many poor Jaufies come every year into the Haurân seeking labour, and are hired by the Druses to cleanse and repair their pools of rain-water:—it is the jealous manner of the Druses, who would live by themselves, *to inhabit where there is scarcity of water.* Much salt also of the Jauf deserts is continually carried thither. The Jauf villagers say that they are descended from Mesopotamians, Syrians and from the Nejd Arabians. The sûk in Hâyil was in these days thronged with Beduins that had business in the yearly concourse, especially to sell camels. The Méshab was now full of their couching thelûls. The multitude of visiting people were bidden, at the hours, in courses, by Mufarrij and those of the public kitchen; and led in to break their fasts and to sup in the Mothîf.

Three days later the Haj arrived, they were mostly *Ajam*, strangers ' of outlandish speech '; but this word is commonly understood of Persia. They came early in an afternoon, by my reckoning, the 14th of November. Before them rode a great company of Beduins on pilgrimage; there might be in all a thousand persons. Many of the Aarab that arrived in Hâyil were of the Syrian Annezy, Sbáa, whose dîra is far in the northwest near Aleppo. With this great yearly convoy came down trains of laden camels with wares for the tradesmen of Hâyil; and I saw a dozen camels driven in through the castle gate, which carried bales of clothing, for the Emir's daily gifts of changes of garments to his visiting Beduins. The Haj passed westwards about the town, and went to encamp before the Gofar gate, and the summer residency, and the Mâ es-Sáma. The caravan was twelve nights out from Bagdad. I numbered about fifty great tents: they were not more, I heard, than half the hajjies of the former season; but this was a year of that great jehâd which troubled el-Islam, and the most Persians were gone (for fear) the long sea way about to the port of Mecca. I saw none of them wear the Persian bonnets or clad as Persians : the returning pilgrimage is increased by those who visit el-Medina, and would go home by el-Méshed.

I wondered to mark the perfect resemblance of the weary,
travel-stained, and ruffianly clad Bagdad akkâms to those of
Damascus; the same moon-like white faces are of both the
great mixed cities. In their menzil was already a butchers'
market, and I saw saleswomen of the town sitting there with
baskets of excellent girdle-bread and dates , some of those wives
—so wimpled that none might know them—sold also butter-
milk! a traffic which passes for less than honest, even in the
towns of nomad Arabia. Two days the pilgrims take rest in
Hâyil, and the third morrow they depart. The last evening, one
stayed me in the street, to enquire, whether I would go with the
Haj to Mecca! When I knew his voice in the dusk I answered
only, *"Ambar,* no!" and he was satisfied. Ambar, a home-
born Galla of Ibn Rashîd's house, was now *Emir el-Haj,*
conductor of the pilgrim convoy—this was, we have seen, the
Emir Mohammed's former office; Aneybar was his elder
brother, and they were freemen, but their father was a slave of
Abdullah ibn Rashîd. Aneybar and Ambar, being thus libertine brethren of the succeeding Emirs, were holders of trusts
under them; they were also welfaring men in Hâyil.

On the morrow of the setting out of the Haj, I stood in the
menzil to watch their departure. One who walked by in the
company of some Bagdad merchants, clad like them and girded
in a kumbâz, stayed to speak with me. I asked, ' What did he
seek?'—I thought the hajjy would say *medicines:* but he
answered, " *If I speak in the French language, will you understand me?* "—" I shall understand it! but what countryman
art thou?" I beheld a pale alien's face with a chestnut
beard :—who has not met with the like in the mixed cities of
the Levant? He responded, " I am an Italian, a Piedmontese
of Turin."—" And what brings you hither upon this hazardous
voyage? good Lord! you might have your throat cut among
them ; are you a Moslem? "—" Ay."—" You confess then their
'none îlah but Ullah, and Mahound, apostle of Ullah '—which
they shall never hear me utter, may Ullah confound them ! "—
" Ay, I say it, and I am a Moslem; as such I make this
pilgrimage."

— He told me he was come to the Mohammedan countries,
eight years before ; he was then but sixteen years of age, and
from Damascus he had passed to Mesopotamia : the last three
years he had studied in a Mohammedan college, near Bagdad,
and received the circumcision. He was erudite in the not short
task of the Arabic tongue, to read, and to write scholarly, and
could speak it with the best, as he said, " without difference."
For a moment, he treated in school Arabic, of the variance of

the later Arabian from the antique tongue, as it is found in the
koran, which he named with a Mohammedan aspiration, *es-sherîf!*
'the venerable or exalted scripture.' With his pedant teachers,
he dispraised the easy babble-talk of the Aarab. When I said
I could never find better than a headache in the farrago of the
koran ; and it amazed me that one born in the Roman country,
and under the name of Christ, should waive these prerogatives,
to become the brother of Asiatic barbarians, in a fond religion !
he answered with the Italic *mollitia* and half urbanity,—"Aha !
well, a man may not always choose, but he must sometime go
with the world." He hoped to fulfil this voyage, and ascend
with the returning Syrian Haj : he had a mind to visit the
lands beyond Jordan, and those tribes [B. Hameydy, B. Sokhr],
possessors of the best blood horses, in Moab ; but when he understood that I had wandered there, he seemed to pass over so
much of his purpose. It was in his mind to publish his Travels
when he returned to Europe. Poor (he added) he was in the
world, and made his pilgrimages at the charges, and in the company, of some bountiful Persian personage of much devotion and
learning :—but once returned to Italy, he would wipe off all
this rust of the Mohammedan life. He said he heard of me,
"the Nasrâny ", at his coming to Hâyil, and of the Jew-born
Abdullah : he had visited the Moslemanny, but " found him to
be a man altogether without instruction ".

There was a hubbub now in the camp of the taking up tents
and loading of baggage and litters; some were already mounted :
—and as we took hands, I asked, " What is your name ? and remember mine, for these are hazardous times and places." The
Italian responded with a little hesitation—it might be true, or
it might be he would put me off—*Francesco Ferrari*. Now the
caravan was moving, and he hastened to climb upon his camel.

From Hâyil to Mecca are five hundred miles at least, over vast
deserts, which they pass in fifteen long marches, not all years
journeying by the same landmarks, but according to that which
is reported of the waterings (which are wells of the Aarab), and
of the peace or dangers of the wilderness before them. Ibn
Rashîd's Haj have been known to go near by Kheybar, but they
commonly hold a course from Mustajidda or the great watering
of *Semîra,* to pass east of the *Harrat el-Kesshub,* and from
thence in other two days descend to the underlying Mecca
country, by *W. Laymûn.* It is a wonder that the Ateyba (the
Prince's strong and capital enemies) do not waylay them : but
a squadron of his rajajîl ride to defend the Haj. * * *

 * * * When in the favourable revolution of the stars I was

come again to peaceable countries, I left notice of the Italian wanderer " Ferrari " at his consulate in Syria, and have vainly enquired for him in Italy :—I thought it my duty, for how dire is the incertitude which hangs over the heads of any aliens that will adventure themselves in Mecca,—where, I have heard it from credible Moslems, that *nearly no Haj passes in which some unhappy persons are not put to death as intruded Christians.* A trooper and his comrade, who rode with the yearly Haj caravans, speaking (unaffectedly) with certain Christian Damascenes (my familiar acquaintance), the year before my setting out, said ' They saw two strangers taken at Mona in the last pilgrimage, that had been detected writing in pocket-books. The strangers being examined were found to be " Christians " ; they saw them executed, and the like happened most years ! ' Our Christian governments too long suffer this religious brigandage ! Why have they no Residents, for the police of nations in Mecca ? Why have they not occupied the direful city, in the name of the health of nations, in the name of the common religion of humanity, *and because the head of the slave trade is there ?* It were good for the Christian governments, which hold any of the Mohammedan provinces, to consider that till then they may never quietly possess them. Each year at Mecca every other name is trodden down, and the " Country of the Apostle " is they pretend inviolable, where no worldly power may reach them. It is " The city of God's house ",—and the only God is God only of the Moslemîn.

Few or none of the pilgrim strangers, while lying at Hâyil, had entered the town,—it might be their fear of the Arabians. Only certain Bagdad derwishes came in, to eat of the public hospitality ; and I saw besides but a company of merry adventurers, who would be bidden to a supper in Arabia, for the novelty. In that day's press even the galleries of the Mothîf were thronged ; there I supped in the dusk, and when I rose, my sandals, the gift of Hamûd, were taken. From four till halfpast six o'clock rations had been served for "two to three thousand" persons ; the Emir's cheer was but boiled temmn and a little samn.

It is a passion to be a pointing-stock for every finger and to maintain even a just opinion against the half-reason of the world. I have felt this in the passage of Arabia more than the daily hazards and long bodily sufferance : yet some leaven is in the lump of pleasant remembrance ; it is oftentimes by the hearty ineptitude of the nomads. In the throng of Aarab in these days in the Méshab, many came to me to speak of their infirmities; strangers where I passed called to me, not knowing my name, "Ho! thou that goest by, el-hakîm there!" others, when they had received of me (freely) some faithful counsel, blessed me with the Semitic grace, "God give peace to that head, the Lord suffer not thy face to see the evil." And such are phrases which, like their brand-marks, declare the tribes of nomads: these were, I believe, northern men. One, as I came, showed me to his rafîk, with this word: *Urraie urraie, hu hu!* 'Look there! he (is) he, this is the Nasrâny.'—*Cheyf Nasrâny?* (I heard the other answer, with the hollow drought of the desert in his manly throat), *agûl! weysh yùnsurhu?* He would say, "How is this man victorious, what giveth him the victory?" In this strange word to him the poor Beduwy thought he heard *nasr*, which is *victory*. A poor nomad of Ruwàlla cried out simply, when he received his medicines: 'Money he had none to give the hakîm, wellah! he prayed me be content to receive his shirt.' And, had I suffered it, he would have stripped himself, and gone away naked in his sorry open cloak, as there are seen many men in the indigence of the wilderness and, like the people of India, with no more than a clout to cover the human shame; and when I let him go, he murmured, *Jízak Ullah kheyr*, 'God recompense thee with good,' and went on wondering, whether the things 'which the Nasrâny had given him for nothing, could be good medicines'?

I thought no more of Bagdad, but of Kheybar; already I stayed too long in Hâyil. At evening I went to Abeyd's kahwa to speak with Hamûd; he was bowing then in the beginning of his private devotion, and I sat down silently, awaiting his leisure. The son of Abeyd, at the end of the first bout, looked up, and nodding cheerfully, enquired, "Khalîl, is there need, wouldst thou anything immediately?"—"There is nothing, the Lord be praised."—"Then I shall soon have ended." As Hamûd sat again in his place, I said, 'I saw the child Feysal's health returning, I desired to depart, and would he send me to Kheybar?' Hamûd answered, 'If I wished it.'—"But why, Khalîl, to Kheybar, what is there at Kheybar? go not to Kheybar, thou mayest die of fever at Kheybar; and they are not our friends, Khalîl, I am afraid of that journey for thee." I answered, "I must needs adventure thither, I would see the antiquities of the Yahûd, as I have seen el-Héjr."—"Well, I will find some means to send thee; but the fever is deadly, go not thither, eigh Khalîl! lest thou die there."—Since I had passed the great Aueyrid, I desired to discover also the Harrat

Kheybar, such another vulcanic Arabian country, and wherein
I heard to be the heads of the W. er-Rummah, which westward
of the Tueyk mountains is the dry waterway of all northern
Arabia. This great valley, which descends from the heads above
el-Hâyat and Howeyat to the Euphrates valley at ez-Zbeyer,
a suburb of Bosra, has a winding course of "fifty camel
marches."

Hamûd, then stretching out his manly great arm, bade me
try his pulse; the strokes of his heart-blood were greater than
I had felt any man's among the Arabians, the man was strong as
a champion. When they hold out their forearms to the hakîm,
they think he may well perceive all their health : I was cried
down, when I said it was imposture. " Yesterday a Persian
medicaster in the Haj was called to the Kasr to feel the Emir's
pulse. The Persian said, ' Have you not a pain, Sir, in the left
knee?' the Prince responded, 'Ay I feel a pain there by God!'
—and no man knew it ! "

The Haj had left some sick ones behind them in Hâyil :
there was a welfaring Bagdad tradesman, whose old infirmities
had returned upon him in the way, a foot-sore camel driver,
and some poor derwishes. The morrow after, all these went
to present themselves before the Emir in the mejlis, and the
derawîsh cried with a lamentable voice in their bastard town
Arabic, *Janâbak !* ' may it please your grace.' Their clownish
carriage and torpid manners, the barbarous border speech
of the north, and their illiberal voices, strangely discorded with
the bird-like ease and alacrity and the frank propriety in the
tongue of the poorest Arabians. The Emir made them a
gracious gesture, and appointed them their daily rations in
the Mothîf. Also to the tradesman was assigned a makhzan ;
and at Hâyil he would pass those two or three months well
enough, sitting in the sun and gossiping up and down the
sûk, till he might ride homeward. Afterward I saw led-in
a wretched young man of the Aarab, who was blind; and
spreading his pitiful hands towards the Emir's seat, he cried
out, *Yâ Tawîl el-Ummr ! yâ Weled Abdullah !* 'Help, O
Long-of-days, thou Child of Abdullah !' The Emir spoke
immediately to one over the wardrobe, and the poor weled was
led away to receive the change of clothing.

Afterwards, I met with Imbârak. "Wouldst thou (he said)
to Kheybar? there are some Annezy here, who will convey
thee." When I heard their menzils were in the Kharram, and
that they could only carry me again to Misshel, and were to
depart immediately : I said that I could not so soon be ready to
take a long journey, and must call in the debts for medicines.

" We will gather them for thee; but longer we cannot suffer thee to remain in our country : if thou wouldst go to Kheybar, we will send thee to Kheybar, or to el-Kasîm, we will send thee to el-Kasîm."—" To Kheybar, yet warn me a day or two beforehand, that I may be ready."

The morning next but one after, I was drinking kahwa with those of er-Riâth, when a young man entered out of breath, he came, he said, to call me from Imbârak. Imbârak when I met him said, " We have found some Heteym who will convey thee to Kheybar."—' And when would they depart ? '—" To-morrow or the morning after." But he sent for me in an hour to say he had given them handsel, and I must set out immediately. " Why didst thou deceive me with *to-morrow*? "—" Put up thy things and mount."—" But will you send me with Heteym ! " —" Ay, ay, give me the key of the makhzan and make up, for thou art to mount immediately."—" And I cannot speak with the Emir ? "—" *Ukhlus*! have done, delay not, or wellah ! the Emir will send, to take off thy head."—" Is this driving me into the desert to make me away, covertly ? "—" Nay, nothing will happen to thee."—" Now well let me first see Hamûd." There came then a slave of Hamûd, bringing in his hand four reals, which he said his " uncle " sent to me. So there came Zeyd, the Moghreby porter of the Kasr ; I had shown him a good turn by the gift of medicines, but now quoth the burly villain, " Thou hast no heart (understanding) if thou wouldst resist Imbârak ; for this is the captain and there ride behind him five hundred men."

I delayed to give the wooden key of my door, fearing lest if they had flung the things forth my aneroid had been broken, or if they searched them my pistol had been taken ; also I doubted whether the captain of the guard (who at every moment laid hand to the hilt of his sword) had not some secret commission to slay the Nasrâny there within. His slaves already came about me, some plucked my clothes, some thrust me forward ; they would drive me perforce to the makhzan.—" Is the makhzan thine or ours, Khalîl ? "—" But Imbârak, I no longer trust thee : bear my word to the Emir, ' I came from the Dowla, send me back to the Dowla '." The Arab swordsman with *fugh*! spat in my face. " Heaven send thee confusion that art not ashamed to spit in a man's face."—" Khalîl, I did it because thou saidst ' I will not trust thee '." I saw the Moghreby porter go and break open my makhzan door, bursting the clay mortice of the wooden lock. The slaves plucking me savagely again, I let go the loose Arab upper garments in their hands, and stood before the wondering wretches in my

shirt. "A shame! I said to them, and thou Imbârak *dakhîl-ak*,
defend me from their insolence." As Imbârak heard 'dakhîl-
ak', he snatched a camel-stick from one who stood by, and beat
them and drove them from me.

They left me in the makhzan and I quickly put my things
in order, and took my arms secretly. Fáhd now came by, going
to Abeyd's kahwa : I said to him, "Fáhd, I will enter with
thee, for here I am in doubt, and where is Hamûd?" The
poor man answered friendly, "Hamûd is not yet abroad, but it
will not be long, Khalîl, before he come."—*Imbârak :* "Wellah,
I say the Emir will send immediately to cut off thy head!"
Mâjid (who passed us at the same time, going towards Abeyd's
kahwa): "Eigh! Imbârak, will the Emir do so indeed?" and
the boy smiled with a child's dishonest curiosity of an atrocious
spectacle. As I walked on with Fáhd, Imbârak retired from
us, and passed through the Kasr gate, perhaps then he went
to the Emir.—Fáhd sighed, as we were beyond the door, and
"Khalîl, please Ullah, said the poor man, it may yet fall out
well, and Hamûd will very soon be here." I had not sat long,
when they came to tell me, 'the Emir desired to see me.' I
said, "Do not deceive me, it is but Imbârak who knocks."
Fáhd : "Nay, go Khalîl, it is the Emir."

When I went out, I found it was Imbârak, who with the old
menaces, called upon me to mount immediately. "I will first,
I answered, see Hamûd : " so he left me. The door had been
shut behind me, I returned to the makhzan, and saw my baggage was safe ; and Fáhd coming by again, "Hamûd, he said,
is now in the house," and at my request he sent back a servant
to let me in. After a little, Hamûd entering, greeted me, and
took me by the hand. I asked, 'Was this done at the commandment of the Emir?' *Hamûd :* "By God, Khalîl, I can
do nothing with the Emir; *hu yáhkam aleyna* he rules
over us all."—"Some books of mine, and other things, were
brought here."—"Ha! the eyyâl have taken them from
thy makhzan, they shall be restored." When I spoke of a
knavish theft of his man Aly—he was gone now on pilgrimage
—Hamûd exclaimed : "The Lord take away his breath!"—He
were not an Arab, if he had proffered to make good his man's
larceny. "What intended you by that money you lately sent
me?"—"My liberality, Khalîl, why didst thou refuse it?"—"Is
it for medicine and a month's daily care of thy child, who is
now restored to health?"—"It was for this I offered it, and we
have plenty of quinine ; wilt thou buy an handful of me for two
reals?" He was washing to go to the mid-day public prayer,
and whilst the strong man stayed to speak with me it was late.

"There is a thing, Hamûd."—" What is that, Khalîl?" and he looked up cheerfully   " Help me in this trouble, for that bread and salt which is between us."—"And what can I do? Mohammed rules us all."—"Well, speak to Imbârak to do nothing till the hour of the afternoon mejlis, when I may speak with the Emir."—"I will say this to him," and Hamûd went to the mesjid.

After the prayer I met the Prince himself in the Méshab ; he walks, as said, ın an insolent cluster of young fanatics, and a half score of his swordsmen close behind them.—Whenever I had encountered the Emir and his company of late in the streets, I thought he had answered my greeting with a strutting look. Now, as he came on with his stare, I said, without a salutation, *Arûhh*, 'I depart.' "*Rûhh*, So go," answered Mohammed "Shall I come in to speak with thee?"—" *Meshghrûl !* we are too busy."

When at length the afternoon mejlis was sitting, I crossed through them and approached the Emir, who sat enforcing himself to look gallantly before the people ; and he talked then with some great sheykh of the Beduw, who was seated next him. Mohammed ibn Rashîd looked towards me, I thought with displeasure and somewhat a base countenance, which is of evil augury among the Arabs.   "What (he said) is thy matter?"— "I am about to depart, but I would it were with assurance. To-day I was mishandled in this place, in a manner which has made me afraid. Thy slaves drew me hither and thither, and have rent my clothing; it was by the setting on of Imbârak, who stands here : he also threatened me, and even spat in my face."   The Emir enquired, under his voice, of Imbârak, 'what had he done,' who answered, excusing himself. I added, "And now he would compel me to go with Heteym ; and I foresee only mischance."   " Nay (said the Emir, striking his breast), fear not ; but ours be the care for thy safety, and we will give thee a passport,"—and he said to Nasr, his secretary, who sat at his feet —" Write him a schedule of safe-conduct."

I said, "I brought thee from my country an excellent. telescope."   The cost had been three or four pounds ; and I thought 'if Ibn Rashîd receive my gift, I might ask of him a camel' : but when he said, " We have many, and have no need," I answered the Emir with a frank word of the desert, *weysh aad*, as one might say, 'What odds !'   Mohammed ibn Rashîd shrunk back in his seat, as if I had disparaged his dignity before the people ; but recovering himself, he said, with better looks and a friendly voice, " Sit down."   Mohammed is not ungenerous, he might remember in the stranger his own evil times.   Nasr having ended his writing, upon a small square of paper, handed it up to the Emir, who perused it, and daubing his Arabic copper seal in the ink, he sealed it with the print of his name. I asked Nasr, "Read me what is written herein," and he read, "That all unto whose hands this bill may come, who owe obedience to Ibn Rashîd, know it is the will of the Emir that no one *yaarud aley*, should do any offence to, this Nasrâny." Ibn Rashîd rising at the moment, the mejlis rose with him and dispersed. I asked, as the Emir was going, "When shall I depart?"— "At thy pleasure."—"To-morrow?"—"Nay, to-day." He had turned the back, and was crossing the Méshab.

"Mount!" cries Imbârak: but, when he heard I had not broken my fast he led me through the Kasr, to the Mothîf and to a room behind, which is the public kitchen, to ask the cooks what was ready. Here they all kindly welcomed me, and Mufarrij would give me dates, flour and samn for the way, the accustomed provision from the Emir, but I would not receive them. The kitchen is a poor hall, with a clay floor, in which is a pool and conduit. The temmn and barley is boiled in four or five coppers: other three stand there for flesh days (which are not many), and they are so great that in one of them may be seethed the brittled meat of a camel. So simple is this palace kitchen of nomadic Arabia, a country in which he is feasting who is not hungry! The kitchen servants were one poor man, perhaps of servile condition, a patient of mine, and five or six women under him; besides there were boys, bearers of the metal trays of victual for the guests' suppers.—When I returned to the Méshab, a nomad was come with his camel to load my baggage: yet first he entreated Imbârak to take back his real of earnest-money and let him go. The Emir had ordered four reals to be given for this voyage, whether I would or no, and I accepted it in lieu of that which was robbed from my makhzan; also I accepted the four reals from Hamûd for medicines.

"Imbârak, swear, I said as we walked together to the sûk, where the nomads would mount, that you are not sending me to the death."—"No, by Ullah, and Khalîl nothing I trust will happen to thee."—"And after two journeys in the desert will the Aarab any more observe the word of Ibn Rashîd?"—"We rule over them!—and he said to the nomads, Ye are to carry him to *Kâsim ibn Barák* (a great sheykh of the midland Heteym, his byût were pitched seventy miles to the southward), and he will send him to Kheybar."—The seller of drugs from Medina, a good liberal Hejâz man, as are many of that partly Arabian city, came out, as we passed his shop, to bid me God speed, "Thou mayest be sure, he said, that there is no treachery, but

understand that the people (of Hâyil and Nejd) are Beduw."—
"O thou (said the nomad to me) make haste along with us out
of Hâyil, stand not, nor return upon thy footsteps, for then they
will kill thee."

Because I would not that his camel should kneel, but had
climbed upon the overloaded beast's neck standing, the poor
pleased nomad cried out, "Lend me a grip of thy five!" that is
the five fingers. A young man, Ibrahîm, one of the Emir's men—
his shop was in the end of the town, and I had dealt with him—
seeing us go by, came out to bid me farewell, and brought me
forward. He spoke sternly to the nomads that they should have
a care for me, and threatened them, that 'If anything befell me,
the Emir would have their heads.' Come to the Mâ es-Sáma,
I reached down my water-skin to one of the men, bidding him
go fill it. "Fill the kafir's girby! nay, said he, alight, Nasrâwy,
and fill it thyself." Ibrahîm then went to fill it, and hanged
the water at my saddle-bow. We passed forth and the sun was
now set. My companions were three,—the poor owner of my
camel, a timid smiling man, and his fanatic neighbour, who
called me always the Nasrâwy (and not Nasrâny), and another
and older Heteymy, a somewhat strong-headed holder of his
own counsel, and speaking the truth uprightly. So short is
the twilight that the night closed suddenly upon our march,
with a welcome silence and solitude, after the tumult of the
town. When I responded to all the questions of my nomad
company with the courtesy of the desert, "Oh! wherefore, cried
they, did those of Hâyil persecute him? Wellah the people of
Hâyil are the true Nasâra!" We held on our dark way three
and a half hours till we came before Gofar; there we alighted
and lay down in the wilderness.

When the morrow was light we went to an outlying kasr,
a chamber or two built of clay-brick, without the oasis, where
dwelt a poor family of their acquaintance. We were in the
end of November (the 21st by my reckoning); the nights
were now cold at this altitude of 4000 feet. The poor people
set dates before us and made coffee; they were neither settlers
upon the soil nor nomads, but Beduw. Weak and broken in
the nomad life, and forsaking the calamities of the desert, they
had become 'dwellers in clay' at one of the Jebel villages, and
Seyadîn or traffickers to the Aarab. They buy dates and corn
in harvest time, to sell later to the hubts or passing market
parties of nomad tribesmen. When spring is come they forsake
the clay-walls and, loading their merchandise upon asses, go forth
to trade among the Aarab. Thus they wander months long,
till their lading is sold; and when the hot summer is in, they

will return with their humble gains of samn and silver to the oasis. From them my companions took up part of their winter provision of dates, for somewhat less than the market price in Hâyil. These poor folk, disherited of the world, spoke to me with human kindness; there was not a word in their talk of the Mohammedan fanaticism. The women, of their own thought, took from my shoulders and mended my mantle which had been rent yesterday at Hâyil; and the house-father put in my hand his own driving-stick made of an almond rod. Whilst I sat with them, my companions went about their other business. Bye and bye there came in a butcher from Hâyil, (I had bought of him three pounds of mutton one morning, for four-pence), and with a loud good humour he praised the Nasrâny in that simple company.

The men were not ready till an hour past midday; then they loaded their dates and we departed. Beyond Gofar we journeyed upon a plain of granite grit; the long Ajja mountain trended with our course upon the right hand. At five we alighted and I boiled them some temmn which I carried, but the sun suddenly setting upon us, they skipt up laughing to patter their prayers, and began to pray as they could, with quaking ribs; and they panted yet with their elvish mirth.—Some wood-gatherers of Hâyil went by us. The double head of the Sumrâ Hâyil was still in sight at a distance of twenty-five miles. Remounting we passed in the darkness the walls and palms of el-Kasr, thirteen miles from Gofar, under the cliffs of Ajja; an hour further we alighted in the desert to sleep.

I saw in the morning the granite flanks of Ajja strangely blotted, as it were with the shadows of clouds, by the running down of erupted basalts; and there are certain black domes upon the crest in the likeness of volcanoes. Two hours later we were in a granitic mountain ground *el-Mukhtelif* Ajja upon the right hand now stands far off and extends not much further. We met here with a young man of el-Kasr riding upon his thelûl in quest of a strayed well-camel. Rock-partridges were everywhere calling and flying in this high granite country, smelling in the sun of the (resinous) sweetness of southern-wood.

About four in the afternoon we went by an outlying hamlet *Biddía*, in the midst of the plain, but encompassed by lesser mountains of granite and basalt. This small settlement, which lies thirty-five miles W. of S. from el-Kasr, was begun not many years ago by projectors from Môgug; there are only two wells and four households. When I asked my companions of the place, they fell a coughing and laughing, and made me signs

that only coughs and rheums there abounded.—A party of
Shammar riding on dromedaries overtook us. They had heard
of Khalîl and spoke friendly, saying that there lay a menzil of
their Aarab not far before us, (where we might sup and sleep).
And we heard from them these happy tidings of the wilderness in
front, "The small cattle have yeaned, and the Aarab have plenty
of léban; they pour out (to drink) till the noon day!" One of
them cried to me: "But why goest thou in the company of
these dogs?"—he would say 'Heteymies'.

A great white snake, *hánash*, lay sleeping in the path: and
the peevish owner put it to the malice of the Nasrâny that I
had not sooner seen the worm, and struck away his camel, which
was nearly treading upon it; and with his lance he beat in
pieces the poisonous vermin. When the daylight was almost
spent my companions climbed upon every height to look for the
black booths of the Aarab. The sun set and we journeyed on
in the night, hoping to espy the Beduin tent-fires. Three hours
later we halted and lay down, weary and supperless, to sleep in
the khála. The night was chill and we could not slumber; the
land-height was here 4000 feet.

We loaded and departed before dawn. Soon after the day
broke we met with Shammar Aarab removing. Great are their
flocks in this dîra, all of sheep, and their camels were a multitude trooping over the plain. Two herdsmen crossed to us
to hear tidings: "What news, they shouted, from the villages?
how many sahs to the real?"—Then, perceiving what I was,
one of them who had a lance lifted it and said to the other,
'Stand back, and he would slay me.' "Nay do not so! wellah!
(exclaimed my rafîks), for this (man) is in the safeguard of Ibn
Rashîd, and we must billah convey him, upon our necks, to
Ch(K)âsim Ibn Barák." Heteymies in presence of high-handed
Shammar, they would have made no manly resistance; and my
going with these rafîks was nearly the same as to wander alone,
save that they were eyes to me in the desert.

In the slow march of the over-loaded camels I went much on
foot; the fanatic who cried Nasrâwy, Nasrâwy! complained
that he could not walk, he must ride himself upon my hired
camel. Though weary, I would not contradict them, lest in
remembering Hâyil they should become my adversaries. I saw
the blown sand of the desert lie in high drifts upon the
mountain sides which encompassed us; they are granite with
some basalt bergs.—We were come at unawares to a menzil of
Shammar. Their sheykh hastened from his booth to meet us,
a wild looking carl, and he had not a kerchief, but only the
woollen cord maasub wound about his tufted locks. He required

of me dokhân; but I told them I had none, the tobacco-bag with
flint and steel had fallen from my camel a little before.—" Give
us tobacco (cried he), and come down and drink kahwa with us,
and if no we will *nô'kh* thy camel, and take it perforce."—
"How (I said), ye believe not in God! I tell you I have none
by God, it is *aŷib* (a shame) man to molest a stranger, and that
only for a pipe of tobacco." Then he let me pass, but they
made me swear solemnly again, that I had none indeed.

As we journeyed in the afternoon and were come into
Heteym country we met with a sheykhly man riding upon his
thelûl: he would see what pasture was sprung hereabout in the
wilderness. The rafîks knew him, and the man said he would
carry me to Kheybar himself, for tômâ. This was one whom I
should see soon again, *Eyâda ibn Ajîuèyn*, an Heteymy sheykh.
My rafîks counselled me to go with him: ' He is a worthy
man, they said, and one with whom I might safely adventure.'
—The first movements of the Arabs from their heart, are the
best, and the least interested, and could the event be foreseen
it were often great prudence to accept them; but I considered
the Emir's words,—that I should go to Kâsim ibn Barák
sheykh of the Beny Rashîd ' who would send me to Kheybar ',
and his menzil was not now far off This Kâsim or Châsim,
or *Jâsim*, they pronounce the name diversely, according to
their tribes' loghrat, my companions said was a great sheykh,
" and one like to Ibn Rashîd " in his country

The sun set as we came to the first Heteym booths, and
there the rafîks unloaded. Kâsim's beyt we heard was " built "
under a brow yonder, and I mounted again with my rafîk
Sâlih, upon his empty camel, to ride thither And in the way
said Sâlih, " When we arrive see that thou get down lightly;
so the Aarab will hold of thee the more, as one inured to the
desert life." Kâsim's tent was but an hejra, small and rent;
I saw his mare tied there, and within were only the hareem.
One of them went to call the sheykh, and Sâlih hastily put
down my bags : he remounted, and without leave-taking would
have ridden away; but seizing his camel by the beard I made
the beast kneel again. " My rafîk, why abandon me thus ?
but Sâlih thou shalt deliver all the Emir's message to Kâsim ; "
—we saw him coming to us from a neighbour beyt.

Kâsim was a slender young man, almost at the middle age.
At first he said that he could not receive me. ' How ! (he
asked), had the Emir sent this stranger to him, to send him on
to Kheybar, when he was at feud with those of Kheybar ! '
Then he reproached Sâlih, who would have ' forsaken me at

strange tents.'—I considered how desperate a thing it were, to be abandoned in the midst of the wilderness of Arabia; where we dread to meet with unknown mankind more than with wild beasts! " You, Kâsim, have heard the word of Ibn Rashîd, and if it cannot be fulfilled at least I have alighted at thy beyt and am weary; here, I said, let me rest this night, *wa ana dakhîlak*, and I enter under thy roof."

He now led me into his booth and bade me repose: then turning all his vehement displeasure against Salih, he laid hands on him and flung him forth—these are violences of the Heteym —and snatched his mantle from him. " Away with thee! he cried, but thy camel shall remain with me, whereupon I may send this stranger to Kheybar; Ullah curse thy father, O thou that forsakedst thy rafîk to cast him upon Aarab." Sâlih took all in patience, for the nomads when they are overborne make no resistance. Kâsim set his sword to Sâlih's throat, that he should avow to him all things without any falsity, and first what tribesman he was. Sâlih now acknowledged himself to be of *Bejaida*, that is a sub-tribe of Bishr; he was therefore of Annezy, but leading his life with Noâmsy Heteymies he passed for an Heteymy. Many poor families both of Annezy and Harb join themselves to that humbler but more thriving nomad lot, which is better assured from enemies; only they mingle not in wedlock with the Heteym. So Kâsim let Sâlih go, and called to kindle the fire, and took up himself a lapful of his mare's provender and littered it down to Sâlih's camel; so he came again and seated himself in the tent with the hypochondriacal humour of a sickly person. "Who is there, said he, will go now and seek us kahwa that we may make a cup for this stranger?—thy name?"—" Khalîl "—" Well, say Khalîl, what shall I do in this case, for wellah, I cannot tell; betwixt us and those of Kheybar and the Dowla there is only debate and cutting of throats: how then says the Emir, that I must send thee to Kheybar?"
—Neighbours came in to drink coffee, and one answered, " If Khalîl give four reals I will set him down, billah, at the edge of the palms of Kheybar and be gone." *Kâsim:* " But Khalîl says rightly he were then as much without Kheybar as before."

The coffee-drinkers showed me a good countenance; " Eigh! Khalîl (said Kâsim), hadst thou complained to me that the man forsook thee, he who came with thee, wellah I would have cut off his head and cast it on this fire: accursed be all the *Anûz* [nation of Annezy]."—" Well, if Kheybar be too difficult, you may send me to Hannas sheykh of the Noâmsy; I heard he is encamped not far off, and he will receive me friendly."—" We shall see in the morning." A scarce dish of

boiled temmn without samn, and a little old rotten léban was
set before me,—the smallest cheer I had seen under worsted
booths; they had no fresh milk because their camel troops
were âzab, or separated from the menzil, and pasturing towards
Baitha Nethîl, westward.

The night closed in darkly over us, with thick clouds and
falling weather, it lightened at once upon three sides without
thunder.   The nomad people said, *"It is the Angels!"*—their
word made me muse of the nomads' vision in the field of
Bethlehem.   " The storm, they murmured, is over the Wady
er-Rummah,"—which they told me lay but half a thelûl journey
from hence.   They marvelled that I should know the name of
this great Wady of middle Nejd: the head, they said, is near
el-Hâyat, in their dîra, one thelûl day distant,—that may be
over plain ground forty-five to seventy miles.   The cold rain fell
by drops upon us through the worn tent-cloth: and when it was
late said Kâsim, " Sleep thou, but I must wake with my eyes
upon his camel there, all night, lest that Annezy (man) come to
steal it away."

When I rose with the dawn Kâsim was making up the fire;
" Good morrow ! he said : well, I will send thee to Hannas ; and
the man shall convey thee that came with thee."—" He betrayed me yesterday, will he not betray me to-day ? he might
even forsake me in the khála."—" But I will make him swear
so that he shall be afraid."   Women came to me hearing I was
a mudowwy, with baggl or dry milk shards, to buy medicines ;
and they said it was a provision for my journey.   Kâsim's
sister came among the rest and sat down beside me.   Kâsim,
she said, was vexed with the rîhh or ague-cake, and what medicine had I ?   These women's veil is a blue calico clout suspended
over the lower face ; her eyes were wonderfully great, and
though lean and pale, I judged that she was very beautiful and
gracious : she leaned delicately to examine my drugs with the
practised hands of a wise woman in simples.   When she could
find no medicine that she knew, she said, with a gentle sweet
voice, " Give then what thou wilt, Khalîl, only that which may
be effectual."   Although so fair, and the great sheykh's sister,
yet no man of the Beduins would have wedded with her ; because the Heteym " are not of the stock " of the Aarab.

Now came Sâlih, and when he saw his camel restored to
him, he was full of joy, and promised all that Kâsim would ; and
he swore mighty oaths to convey me straightway to Hannas.
We mounted and rode forth ; but as we were going I drew
bridle and bound Sâlih by that solemn oath of the desert, aly
el-aûd wa Rubb el-mabûd, that he would perform all these

things: if he would not swear, I would ride no further with him. But Sâlih looking back and trembling cried, "I do swear it, billah, I swear it, only let us hasten and come to our rafîks, who have awaited us at the next tents."

We set out anew with them, and quoth Sâlih, "I was never in such fear of my life as when Châsim set his sword to my neck!" We marched an hour and a half and approached another Heteym menzil of many beyts: as we passed by Sâlih went aside to them to enquire the tidings. Not far beyond we came upon a brow, where two lone booths stood. My companions said the (overloaded) camels were broken, they would discharge them there to pasture an hour. When we were come to the place they halted.

In the first tent was an old wife: she bye and bye brought out to us, where we sat a little aloof, a bowl of milk shards and samn, and then, that which is of most comfort in the droughty heat, a great bowl of her butter-milk. "Canst thou eat this fare? said Sâlih,—the Heteym have much of it, they are good and hospitable." The men rose after their breakfast and loaded upon the camels,—but not my bags!—and drove forth. I spoke to the elder Heteymy, who was a worthy man, but knitting the shoulders and turning up his palms he answered gravely, "What can I do? it is Sâlih's matter, wellah, I may not meddle in it; but thou have no fear, for these are good people, and amongst them there will no evil befall thee." "Also Eyâda ibn Ajjuèyn, said Sâlih, is at little distance."—"But where is thy oath, man?" The third fanatic fellow answered for him, "His oath is not binding, which was made to a Nasrâwy!"—"But what of the Emir? and Kâsim is not yet far off." *Sâlih:* "As for Kâsim we curse both his father and his mother; but thou be not troubled, the Heteym are good folk and this will end well." —To contend with them were little worth; they might then have published it that I was a Nasrâny, I was as good quit of such rafîks,—here were but two women—and they departed.

— "It is true, quoth the old wife, that Eyâda is near, yesterday I heard their dogs bark." In the second tent was but her sick daughter-in-law; their men were out herding. The old wife looked somewhat grim when the hubt had forsaken me; afterwards she came where I sat alone, and said, "Be not sorrowful! *ana khâlatak,* for I am thy mother's sister." Soon after that she went out to bear word to the men in the wilderness of this chance. Near by that place I found the border of a brown vulcanic flood, a kind of trachytic basalt: when the sun was setting I walked out of sight,—lest seeing the stranger not praying at the hour I had been too soon known to them.

Not much after the husband came home, a deaf man with the name of happy augury *Thaifullah* : kindly he welcomed me, and behind him came three grown sons driving-in their camels ; and a great flock of sheep and goats followed them with many lambs and kids. I saw that (notwithstanding their Heteym appearance of poverty) they must be welfaring persons. Thaifullah, as we sat about the evening fire, brought me in a bowl of their evening milk, made hot ;—" We have nothing, he said, here to eat, no dates, no rice, no bread, but drink this which the Lord provideth, though it be a poor supper." I blessed him and said it was the best of all nourishment. " Ay, thus boiled, he answered, it enters into the bones." When he heard how my rafîks forsook me to-day he exclaimed, ' Billah if he had been there, he had cut off their heads.' That poor man was very honourable ; he would hardly fill his galliûn once with a little tittun that I had found in the depth of my bags, although it be so great a solace to them ; neither suffered he his young men to receive any from the (forlorn) guest whom the Lord had committed to them, to-day. These were simple, pious, and not (formal) praying Arabs, having in their mouths no cavilling questions of religion, but they were full of the godly humanity of the wilderness. ' He would carry me in the morning (said my kind host) to Eyâda ibn Ajjuèyn, who would send me to Kheybar.'

It was dim night, and the drooping clouds broke over us with lightning and rain. I said to Thaifullah, " God sends his blessing again upon the earth."—" Ay verily;" he answered devoutly, and kissed his pious hand towards the flashing tempest, and murmured the praises of Ullah.—How good ! seemed to me, how peaceable ! this little plot of the nomad earth under the dripping curtains of a worsted booth, in comparison with Hâyil town !

When the morning rose the women milked their small cattle ; and we sat on whilst the old housewife rocked her blown-up milk-skin upon her knees till the butter came ; they find it in a clot at the mouth of the semîly. I saw soon that little butter seething on the fire, to be turned into samn, and they called me to sup the pleasant milk-skim with my fingers. They throw in now a little meal, which brings down the milkiness ; and the samn or clarified butter may be poured off. The sediment of the meal thus drenched with milky butter is served to the guest ; and it is the most pleasant sweat-meat of the poor nomad life. Afterward the good old woman brought me the

samn (all that her flocks had yielded this morning), in a little
skin (it might be less than a small pint): this was her gift, she
said; and would I leave with them some fever medicine? I
gave her doses of quinine. She brought forth a large bowl of
butter-milk; and when we had drunk a good draught Thaifullah
laid my bags upon a camel of his. We mounted, and rode
southward over the khála.

We journeyed an hour and approached Eyâda's menzil, the
worsted booths were pitched in a shelving hollow overlooking
a wide waste landscape to the south: I saw a vast blackness
beyond,—that was another Harra (the *Harrat Kheybar*)—and
rosy mountains of granite. Sandstones, lying as a tongue
between the crystalline mountains and overlaid by lavas, reach
southward to Kheybar.—" When we come to the tents thus and
thus shalt thou speak to them, said Thaifullah: say thou art a
mudowwy arrived from Hâyil, and that thou wouldst go over to
Kheybar; and for two reals thou shalt find some man who will
convey thee thither."

We alighted and Thaifullah commended me to Eyâda; I was
(he said) a skilful mudowwy,—so he took his camel again and
departed. This was that Heteymy sheykh, whom I had seen
two days before chevying in the wilderness:—he might have
understood then (from some saying of the fanatic) that I was
not a right Moslem, for now when I saluted him and said I
would go to Kheybar with him, he received me roughly. He
was a sturdy carl, and with such ill-blooded looks as I have
remarked in the Fehját, which are also of Heteym. *Eyâda:*
" Well, I said it yesterday, but I cannot send thee to Kheybar."
—Some men were sitting before his tent—" Ho! which of you,
he said, will convey the man to Kheybar, and receive from him
what—? three reals." One answered, " I will carry him, if he
give me this money." I promised, and he went to make ready;
but returning he said, " Give me four reals,—I have a debt,
and this would help me in it." *Eyâda:* " Give him four, and
go with him." I consented, so the sheykh warranted me that
the man would not forsake his rafîk, as did those of the other
day. " Nay, trust me, this is *Ghroceyb*, a sheykh, and a valorous
man."—" Swear, O Ghroceyb, by the life of this stem of grass,
that thou wilt not forsake me, thy rafîk, until thou hast
brought me to Kheybar!"—" I swear to bring thee thither,
but I be dead." *Eyâda:* " He has a thelûl too, that can flee
like a bird." *Ghroceyb:* " See how the sun is already mounted!
let us pass the day here, and to-morrow we will set forward."—
" Nay, but to-day," answered the sheykh, shortly, so that I

wondered at his inhospitable humour, and Ghroceyb at this strangeness. The sheykh did not bid me into his tent, but he brought out to us a great bowl of butter-milk. The hareem now came about me, bringing their little bowls of dry milk shards, and they clamoured for medicines. I have found no Beduins so willing as the Heteym to buy of the mudowwy. After my departure, when they have proved my medicines, they said that Khalîl was a faithful man ; and their good report helped me months later, at my coming by this country again.

Ghroceyb told me that from hence to Baitha Nethîl was half a (thelûl) journey, to Hâyil three, to Teyma four, to el-Ally four and a half ; and we should have three nights out to Kheybar. When we had trotted a mile, a yearling calf of the thelûl, that was grazing in the desert before us, ran with their sidelong slinging gait (the two legs upon a side leaping together) to meet the dam, and followed us lowing,—the mother answered with sobs in her vast throat ; but Ghroceyb dismounted and chased the weanling away. We rode upon a plain of sand. Nigh before us appeared that great craggy blackness—the Harra, and thereupon certain swarty hills and crests, *el-Hélly* : I perceived them to be crater-hills of volcanoes ! A long-ranging inconsiderable mountain, *Bothra*, trended with our course upon the left hand, which I could not doubt to be granitic. Ghroceyb encouraged his thelûl with a pleasant *gluck !* with the tongue under the palate,—I had not heard it before ; and there is a diversity of cattle-calls in the several tribes of the Arabian khála.

We entered upon that black Harra. The lava field is now cast into great waves and troughs, and now it is a labyrinth of lava crags and short lava sand-plains.—This is another member of the vulcanic country of West Arabia, which with few considerable breaches, extends from Tebûk through seven degrees of latitude to the borders of Mecca.

We found clayey water, in a cavern (after the late showers), and Ghroceyb alighted to fill our girby. At half-afternoon we saw a goatherd loitering among the wild lavas. The lad was an Heteymy, he knew Ghroceyb, and showed us where the beyts were pitched, in a deep place not far off. Here Ghroceyb came to his own kindred ; and we alighted at the tent of his brother. The cragged Harra face is there 4300 feet above the sea-level. Their hareem were veiled like those of Kâsim's encampment, and they wore a braided forelock hanging upon their foreheads. In the evening we were regaled with a caldron of temmn, and the host poured us out a whole skinful of thick butter-milk.

One of those men was a hunter; the Heteym and the Sherarát surpass the Beduw in the skill, and are next to the Solubba. In the last season he had killed two ostriches, and sold the skins (to that Damascus feather merchant who comes down yearly with the Haj) for 80 reals : 40 reals for an ostrich skin ! (the worth of a good camel)—a wonderful price it seems to be paid in this country. Of the lineage of the Heteym I could never learn anything in Arabia. They are not of so cheerful temper, and they lack the frank alacrity of mind and the magnanimous dignity of Beduins. Ghroceyb spoke of his people thus, "Jid el-Heteym is *Rashíd* and we—the midland Heteym—are the *Beny Rashíd*. Those Heteymies at the Red Sea bord, under el-Wejh, are the *Gerabís*, our kindred indeed but not friendly with us. The B. Rashîd are as many as the B. Wáhab" (nearly 600 beyts, not much above 2000 souls). Of the Sherarát akin to the Heteym he said, "We may wed with them and they with us,—but there is cattle stealing between us; they are 800 beyt." He told me that in former days, some camels having been reaved by a Noâmsy ghrazzu from the Gerabís, the sheykh Ibn Nômus (father of Hannas), ordained their restitution, saying, "Wellah they be our kindred."

In the early morning Ghroceyb milked our thelûl and brought me this warm bever ; and after that, in the fatigue of the long way to be passed almost without her tasting herbage, her udder would be dried up and the Beduwy fetched in a hurr to cover her; [at such times doubtless in the hope that she may bear a female]. We were called away to breakfast in another booth where they set before us dates fried in samn, and bowls of butter-milk. All was horrid lava-field far before us, and we should be "two nights out without Aarab", and the third at Kheybar.

Gloomy were these days of drooping grey clouds in the golden aired Arabia. We journeyed quickly by the camel paths (*jiddar* pl. *jiddrân*) worn, since ages, in the rolling cinders and wilderness of horrid lavas. Hither come Bishr and Heteym nomads in the early year with their cattle, to seek that rabîa which may be sprung among the lava clefts and pits and little bottoms of vulcanic sand. Before noon we were among the black hills (*hilliân*) which I had viewed before us since yesterday ; they are cones and craters of spent volcanoes. Our path lay under the highest *hilly*, which might be of four hundred or five hundred feet. Some are two-headed,—it is where a side of the crater is broken down. Others are seen ribbed, that is they are guttered down from the head. *All is here as we have seen in the Harrat el-Aueyrid.* We passed over a smooth plain of cinders; and, at the roots of another *hilly,* I saw yellowish soft tufa lying under the scaly crags of lavas. From hence we had sight of the Kharram, a day distant to the westward; lying beyond the Harra in a yellow border of Nefûd; the white sand lay in long drifts upon the high flanks of the mountain.

There was now much ponded rain upon these vulcanic highlands; and in a place I heard the heavy din of falling water! We came to a cold new tarn, and it seemed a fenny mountain lake under the setting sun! from this strange desert water issued a wild brook with the rushing noise of a mill-race. Having gone all the daylight, we drew bridle in a covert place, where we might adventure to kindle our fire. My rafîk was never come so far in this sea of lava, but he knew the great landmarks. He went about to pull an armful of the scanty herbage in the crevices, for his fasting thelûl; I gathered dry stems to set under our pot, poured in water and began our boiling, which was but of temmn. When Ghroceyb came again I bid him mind the cooking; but said he, " What can I do? I, billah, understand it not."—" Yet I never saw the nomad who could not shift for himself upon a journey."—" I eat that which the hareem prepare, and have never put my hand to it."—He had brought for himself only two or three handfuls of dry milk shards! in Ghroceyb was the ague-cake of old fever, and he could eat little or nothing. In this place I found the greatest height which I had passed hitherto in Arabia, nearly 6000 feet. And here I have since understood to be the division of waters between the great wady bottoms of northern Arabia; namely the W. er-Rummah descending from the Harra to the north-eastward, and the W. el-Humth. This night was mild, and sheltered in the wild lavas, as between walls, we were warm till the morning.

We mounted in the morrow twilight; but long after daybreak the heavens seemed shut over us, as a tomb, with gloomy clouds. We were engaged in the horrid lava beds; and were very oftentimes at fault among sharp shelves, or finding before us precipitous places. The vulcanic field is a stony flood which has stiffened; long rolling heads, like horse-manes, of those slaggy waves ride and over-ride the rest: and as they are risen they stand petrified, many being sharply split lengthwise, and the hollow laps are partly fallen down in vast shells and in ruinous heaps as of massy masonry. The lava is not seldom wreathed as it were bunches of cords; the crests are seen also

of sharp glassy lavas, *lába* (in the plural *lúb*) ; lâba is all that
which has a likeness to molten metal.—That this soil was ever
drowned with burning mineral, or of burning mountains, the
Aarab have no tradition. As we rode further I saw certain
golden-red crags standing above the black horror of lavas ; they
were sandstone spires touched by the scattered beams of the
morning sun. In the sheltered lava bottoms, where grow gum-
acacias, we often startled *gatta* fowl (" sand-grouse ") ; they are
dry-fleshed birds and not very good to eat, say the nomads.
There is many times seen upon the lava fields a glistering
under the sun as of distant water; it is but dry clay glazed over
with salt.

Ghroceyb spread forth his hands devoutly ; he knew not the
formal prayers, but wearied the irrational element, with the low-
ings of his human spirit, in this perilous passage. " Give, Lord,
that we see not the evil ! and oh that this be not the day of our
deaths and the loss of the thelûl ! " My rafîk knew not that I
was armed. Ghroceyb, bearing his long matchlock, led on afoot
betwixt running and walking, ever watching for a way before
the thelûl, and gazing wide for dread of any traversing enemies.
Upon a time turning suddenly he surprised me, as I wrote with
a pencil [a reading of the aneroid]. " Is it well, O Khalîl ?
quoth my rafîk, how seest thou (in your magical art of letters),
is there good or else evil toward ? canst thou not write something (a strong spell), for this need ? " Then seeing me ride
on careless and slumbering for weariness he took comfort. My
pistol of six chambers gave me this confidence in Arabia, for
must we contend for our lives I thought it might suffice to
defend me and my company, and Ghroceyb was a brave companion. Ghroceyb's long piece must weigh heavily upon the
strenuous man's sick shoulders, and I spoke to him to hang it
at the saddle-bow of me his rafîk ; to this he consented, ' so I
did not loop the shoulder-cord about the peak ; it must hang
simply, he said, that in any appearance of danger he might take
it again at the instant.'

Two hours after the sunrise we passed the Harra borders, and
came without this lava field upon soil of sandstone. The vulcanic country which we had crossed in seventeen hours is named
Harrat *el-Ethnán*, of the great crater-hill of that name *J. Eth-
nán ;* the dîra is of the Noâmsa Heteym. We came in an hour
by a descending plain of red sand-rock, to a deep cleft, *es-Shotb*,
where we drove down the dromedary at short steps, upon the
shelves and ledges. In the bottom were gum-acacias, and a tree
which I knew not, it has leaves somewhat like the mountain ash.
" The name of it is *thirru*, it has not any use that we know,"

L

said Ghroceyb. Beyond the grove, were some thin effluxions of lava, run down upon the sandstone soil, from the vulcanic field above. By noon we had passed the sand-rock and came again upon the main Harra beyond, which is all one eastward with the former Harra ; and there we went by a few low craters. The whole—which is the *Harrat Kheybar*—lies between north-west and south-east, four days in length ; and that may be, since it reaches to within a thelûl journey of Medina, an hundred great miles. The width is little in comparison, and at the midst it may be passed in a day.

Ghroceyb now said : " But wouldst thou needs go to Kheybar ? —*tûahi*, hearest thou ? shall I not rather carry thee to el-Hâyat ? "—My rafîk was in dread of going to Kheybar, the Dowla being there : those criminals-in-office (I understood it later), might have named him an enemy and seized the poor nomad's thelûl, and cast him into prison ; but el-Hâyat was yet a free village in the jurisdiction of Ibn Rashîd. Ghroceyb I knew afterward to be an homicide, and there lay upon him a grievous debt for blood ; it was therefore he had ridden for four reals with me in this painful voyage. From Eyâda's menzil we might have put the Harra upon our left hand, and passed by easy sand-plains [where I journeyed in the spring] under the granite mountains ; but Ghroceyb would not, for in the open there had been more peril than in this cragged way of the Harra.

An hour from the Shotb, I found the altitude to be 5000 feet. Before mid-afternoon upon our right hand, beyond the flanks of the Harra and the low underlying sand-plain, appeared a world of wild ranging mountains *Jebâl Hejjûr*, twenty-five miles distant, in dîrat of the Wélad Aly. We went all day as fugitives, in this vulcanic country. Sunset comes soon in winter, and then we halted, in a low clay bottom with tall acacias and yellow ponds of rain water. Ghroceyb hopshackled her with a cord ; and loosed out the two days' fasting thelûl, to browse the green branches. There we cooked a little temmn ; and then laid ourselves down upon the fenny soil and stones in a mizzling night-rain to slumber.

When the day began to spring we set forward, and passed over a brook running out from ponded water in the lava-field. The weather was clearer, the melting skies lifted about us. The vulcanic country is from henceforward plain, and always descending and full of jiddrân. Before and below our path, we had now in sight the sharp three-headed mountain, *Atwa ;* that stands beside Kheybar : Ghroceyb greeted the landmark with joy. 'Beyond Atwa was but a night out, he said, for thelûl riders to Medina. Upon our left hand a distant part of the Harra, *Harrat el-Abyad*, showed white under the sun and full of hilliân. Ghroceyb said, "The hills are whitish, the lava-field lies about them; the white stone is burned-like, and heavy as metal." Others say "The heads only of the hilliân are white stone, the rest is black lava."—Those white hills might be lime-stone, which, we know, lies next above the Hisma sand-rock.

Already we saw the flies of the oasis : Kheybar was yet covered from sight by the great descending limb of the Harra ; we felt the air every moment warmer and, for us, faint and breathless. All this country side to Jebâl Hejjûr seyls down by the wady grounds *el-Khâfutha* and *Gumm'ra* to the Wady el-Humth. Ghroceyb showed me a wolf's footprints in the vul-canic sand. At the half-afternoon we were near Kheybar, which lay in the deep yonder, and was yet hidden from us. Then we came upon the fresh traces of a ghrazzu : they had passed down towards Kheybar. We rode in the same jiddar behind them !—the footprints were of two mares and two camels. Ghroceyb made me presently a sign to halt ; he came and took his gun in silence, struck fire to the match and ran out to reconnoitre. He stayed behind a covert of lavas, from whence he returned to tell me he saw two horsemen and two *ráduffa* (radîfs), upon thelûls, riding at a long gunshot before us : they had not seen us. And now, blowing his match, he required very earnestly, 'Were I able with him to resist them ?' —Contrary to the will of Ghroceyb I had stayed this day, at noon, ten minutes, to take some refreshment : but for this we had met with them, as they came crossing from the west-ward, and it is too likely that blood had been shed between us. We stood awhile to give them ground, and when they were hidden by the unequal lava-field, we passed slowly forward. The sun was now going low in the west,—and we would be at Kheybar this night ere the village gate should be shut.

Locusts alighted by our path, and I saw aloft an infinite flight of them drifted over in the evening wind. Ghroceyb asked again, 'If I were afraid of the Dowla.'—"Am I not a Dowlany? they are my friends."—"Wellah *yâ sámy*, my namesake, couldst thou deliver me and quit the thelûl, if they should take me ?"—"Doubt not ; they of the Dowla are of my part."

Now we descended into a large bottom ground in the lava-field, *el-Húrda*, full of green young corn :—that corn I saw ripen before my departure from Kheybar ! Here Ghroceyb dreaded to meet with the ghrazzu,—the robbers might be grazing their mares in the green corn of the settlement. Where we came by suânies, wild doves flew up with great rattling of wings, from the wells of water. I thought these should be the fields of Kheybar, and spoke to Ghroceyb to carry me to the *Jériat Wélad Aly.* There are three villages, named after the land-inheriting Annezy tribes, *Jériat Bishr* (that is Kheybar proper), *Jériat W. Aly,* at the distance of half a mile, and at two miles the hamlet *Jériat el-Fejîr.*—Jériat is said for kériat in the loghrat of these nomads.

Ghroceyb saw only my untimely delay, whilst he dreaded for his thelûl, and was looking at every new turn that we should encounter the enemies who had ridden down before us. I drew bridle, and bade my rafîk—he stepped always a little before me on foot—promise to bring me to none other than the Wélad Aly village. My visiting Kheybar, which they reckon in ' *The Apostle's Country,*' was likely to be a perilous adventure ; and I might be murdered to-night in the tumult, if it went ill with me : but at the W. Aly hamlet, I should have become the guest of the clients of Motlog and Méhsan, great sheykhs of that tribe. Ghroceyb saw me halt, as a man beside himself! and he came hastily, to snatch the thelûl's halter ; then he desperately turned his matchlock against me, and cried, "Akhs! why would I compel him to do me a mischief ? "—" Thou canst not kill thy rafîk ! now promise me and go forward." He promised, but falsely.—Months after, I heard, he had told his friends, when he was at home again ; that ' he had found the stranger a good rafîk, only in the journey's end, as we were about entering Kheybar, I would have taken his thelûl ' !

We passed the corn-fields of the Húrda without new alarms, and came upon the basalt neck of the Harra about the oasis' valleys, which is called *el-figgera* (in the pl. *el-fuggar*) Kheybar. Ghroceyb mounted with me, and he made the thelûl run swiftly, for the light was now failing. I saw ruins upon the figgera of old dry building and ring-walls : some are little yards of the loose basalt blocks, which the Beduw use, to dry their dates in the sun, before stiving the fruit in their sacks. After a mile, we came to a brow, and I saw a palm forest in a green valley of Kheybar below us, but the village not yet. The sun set as we went down by a steep path. At the left hand was an empty watch-tower, one of seven lately built by the now occupying Medina government, upon this side, to check the hostile Annezy [Bishr and Fejîr]. This human landmark seemed to me more inhuman than all the Harra behind us ; for now I remembered Medáin Sâlih and the danger of the long unpaid and some-times beastly Turkish soldiery. How pleasant then seemed to me the sunny drought of the wilderness, how blessed the security of the worsted booths in the wandering villages! These forts are garrisoned in the summer and autumn season.

We came through palm-groves in a valley bottom, *W. Jellás*, named after that old division of Annezy, which having long since forsaken Kheybar, are at this day—we have seen—with the Ruwàlla in the north. The deep ground is mire and rushes and stagnant water ; and there sunk upon our spirits a sickly fenny vapour. In the midst we passed a brook running in a bed of green cresses. Foul was the abandoned soil upon either hand, with only few awry and undergrown stems of palms. The squalid ground is whitish with crusts of bitter salt-warp, *summakha* [written *subbakha*], and stained with filthy rust : whence their fable, that 'this earth purges herself of the much blood of the Yahûd, that was spilt in the conquest of Kheybar.' The thelûl which found no foot-hold under her sliding soles, often halted for fear. We came up between rough walling, built of basalt stones, and rotten palm-stocks, and clots of black clay.—How strange are these dank Kheybar valleys in the waterless Arabia! A heavy presentiment of evil lay upon my heart, as we rode in this deadly drowned atmosphere.

We ascended on firm ground to the entering of Kheybar, that is Jériat Bishr, under the long basalt crag of the ancient citadel *el-Húsn*. In the falling ground upon the left hand stands an antique four-square building of stone, which is the old mesjid from the time of Mohammed ; and in the precinct lie buried the *Ashab en-Neby*,—those few primitive Moslemîn, partisans and acquaintance of the living "apostle", that fell in the (poor) winning of Kheybar.

At the village gate a negro woman met us in the twilight, of whom I enquired, whether *Bou* (*Abu*) *Ras* were in the town ? —I had heard of him from the Moghrebies in Hâyil, as a safe man : he was a Moghreby negro trader settled in those parts ; also I hoped to become his guest. But he was gone from the place, since the entrance of the (tyrannical) Dowla—being, as they say, *shebbaan*, or having gotten now his fill of their poor riches,—to live yet under the free Nejd government at el-Hâyat.—She answered timidly, bidding the strangers a good evening, " She could not tell, and that she knew nothing."

END OF PART ONE

PART TWO

CHAPTER I

WE passed the gates made of rude palm boarding into the street of the Hejâz negro village, and alighted in the dusk before the house of an acquaintance of Ghroceyb. The host, hearing us busy at the door of his lower house, looked down from the casement and asked in the rasping negro voice what men we were? Ghroceyb called to him, and then he came down with his brother to receive the guests. They took my bags upon their shoulders, and led us up by some clay stairs to their dwelling-house, which is, as at el-Ally, an upper chamber, here called *suffa*. The lower floor, in these damp oases, is a place where they leave the orchard tools, and a stable for their few goats which are driven in for the night. This householder was named *Abd el-Hâdy*, 'Servitor of Him who leadeth in the way of Truth,' a young man under the middle age, of fine negro lineaments —These negro-like Arabians are not seldom comely.

Our host's upper room was open at the street side with long casements, *tága*, to the floor ; his roof was but a loose strawing of palm stalks, and above is the house terrace of beaten clay, to which you ascend [they say *erkâ !*] by a ladder of two or three palm beams, laid side by side, with steps hacked in them Abd el-Hâdy's was one of the better cottages, for he was a substantial man. Kheybar is as it were an African village in the Hejâz. Adb el-Hâdy spread his carpet and bade us welcome, and set before us Kheybar dates which are yellow, small and stived together , they are gathered ere fully ripe [their Beduin partner's impatience, and distrust of each other !] and have a drug-like or fenny savour, but are "cooler " than the most dates of the country and not unwholesome. After these days' efforts in the Harra we could not eat; we asked for water to quench our burning thirst. They hang their sweating girbies at the stairhead, and under them is made a hole in the flooring, that the drip may fall through. The water, drawn, they said, from the

spring head under the basalt, tasted of the ditch; it might be
sulphurous. We had left our thelûl kneebound in the street.

Many persons, when they heard say that strangers had
arrived, came up all this evening to visit us;—the villagers
were black men. Ghroceyb told them his tale of the ghrazzu
and the negroes answered " Wellah ! except we sally in the
morning to look for them—! " They feared for the outlying
corn lands, and lest any beast of theirs should be taken.
There came with the rest a tall and swarthy white man, of
a soldierly countenance, bearing a lantern and his yard-long
tobacco-pipe : I saw he was of the mixed inhabitants of the
cities. He sat silent with hollow eyes and smoked tobacco,
often glancing at us; then he passed the *chibûk* to me and
enquired the news. He was not friendly with Abd el-Hâdy,
and waived our host's second cup. The white man sat on
smoking mildly, with his lantern burning; after an hour he
went forth [and this was to denounce us, to the ruffian lieutenant at Kheybar]. My rafîk told me in a whisper, " That was
Ahmed; he has been a soldier and is now a tradesman at
Kheybar."—His brother was *Mohammed en-Nejûmy,* he who
from the morrow became the generous defender of my adversity
at Kheybar : they were citizens of Medina. It was near midnight when the last coffee-drinkers departed ; then I whispered
to Ghroceyb: " Will they serve supper, or is it not time to
sleep ? " " My namesake, I think they have killed for thee;
I saw them bring up a sheep, to the terrace, long ago."—
" Who is the sheykh of the village ? "—"This Abd el-Hâdy is
their sheykh, and thou wilt find him a good man." My rafîk
lied like a (guileful) nomad, to excuse his not carrying me to
the W. Aly village.

Our host and his brother now at length descended from the
house-top, bearing a vast metal tray of the seethed flesh upon
a mess of thùra (it may be a sort of millet) : since the locusts
had destroyed their spring corn, this was the only bread-stuff
left to them at Kheybar.

The new day's light beginning to rise, Ghroceyb went down
to the street in haste ; " Farewell, he said, and was there any
difference between us, forgive it Khalîl ; " and taking my right
hand (and afraid perchance of the stranger's malediction), he
stooped and kissed it. Hâdy, our host's brother, mounted also
upon the croup of his thelûl ; this strong-bodied young negro,
with a long matchlock upon his shoulder, rode forth in his bare
tunic, girded only with the *házam* or gunner's belt. Upon the
baldric are little metal pipes, with their powder charges, and

upon the girdle leather pouches for shot, flint and steel, and a hook whereupon a man—they go commonly barefoot—will hang his sandals. The házams are adorned with copper studs and beset with little rattling chains; there are some young men who may be seen continually *muházamín*, girded and vain-glorious with these tinkling ornaments of war. It is commonly said of tribes well provided with fire-arms "They have many muházamín."—Hâdy rode to find the traces of the ghrazzu of yesterday.

Some of the villagers came up to me immediately to enquire for medicines : they were full of tedious words ; and all was to beg of me and buy none. I left them sitting and went out to see the place, for this was Kheybar.

Our host sent his son to guide me ; the boy led down by a lane and called me to enter a doorway and see a spring. I went in :—it was a mesjid ! and I withdrew hastily. The father (who had instructed the child beforehand), hearing from him when we came again that I had left the place without praying, went down and shut his street door. He returned and took his pistol from the wall, saying, ' Let us go out together and he would show me round the town.' When we were in the street, he led me by an orchard path, out of the place.

We came by a walled path through the palms into an open space of rush-grass and black vulcanic sand, *es-Sefsáfa :* there he showed me the head of a stream which welled strongly from under the figgera. The water is tepid and sulphurous as at el-Ally, and I saw in it little green-back and silver-bellied fishes :—all fish are named *hût* by the Arabians. " Here, he said, is the (summer) menzil of the Dowla, in this ground stand the askars' tents." We sat down, and gazing into my face he asked me, ' Were I afraid of the Dowla ? ' " Is the Dowla better or Ibn Rashîd's government ? "—" The Dowla delivered us from the Beduw,—but is more burdensome."

We passed through a burial ground of black vulcanic mould and salt-warp : the squalid grave-heaps are marked with head-stones of wild basalt. That funeral earth is chapped and ghastly, bulging over her enwombed corses, like a garden soil, in spring-time, which is pushed by the new-spiring plants. All is horror at Kheybar !—nothing there which does not fill a stranger's eye with discomfort.

—" Look, he said, this is the spring of our Lord Aly !—I saw a lukewarm pool and running head of water.—Here our Lord Aly [Fatima's husband] killed *Márhab*, smiting off his head ; and his blade cleft that rock, which thou seest there divided to the earth : "—so we came beyond.—" And here, he

L*

said, is Aly's mesjid " [already mentioned]. The building is
homely, laid in courses of the wild basalt blocks : it is certainly
ancient. Here also the village children are daily taught their
letters, by the sheykh of the religion.

When we had made the circuit, " Let us go, he said, to the
Emir." So the villager named the aga or lieutenant of a score
of Ageyl from Medina. Those thelûl riders were formerly Nejd
Arabians ; but now, because the Dowla's wages are so long in
coming, the quick-spirited Nejders have forsaken that sorry
service. The Ageyl are a mixed crew of a few Nejders
(villagers, mostly of el-Kasîm, and poor Nomads), and of Gallas,
Turks, Albanians, Egyptians, Kurdies and Negroes. The Ageyl
at Kheybar now rode upon their feet : some of their thelûls
were dead, those that remained were at pasture (far off) with
the nomads. They all drew daily rations of corn for their
thelûls alive and dead ; and how else might the poor wretches
live ? who had not touched a cross of their pay (save of a
month or twain) these two years. A few of the government
armed men at Kheybar were zabtîyah, men of the police
service.—" The Aga is a Kurdy," quoth Abd el-Hâdy.

We ascended, in a side street, to a suffa, which was the
soldiers' coffee-room : swords and muskets were hanging upon
the clay walls. Soon after some of them entered ; they were
all dark-coloured Gallas, girded (as townsmen) in their white
tunics. They came in with guns from some trial of their skill,
and welcomed us in their (Medina) manner, and sat down to
make coffee. I wondered whilst we drank together that they
asked me no questions ! We rose soon and departed. As we
stepped down the clay stair, I heard a hoarse voice saying
among them, " I see well, he is *adu* (an enemy) ; "—and I
heard answered, " But let him alone awhile."

It was time I thought to make myself known. When I asked
where was the Kurdy Aga ? my host exclaimed, " You did not
see him ! he sat at the midst of the hearth." That was
Abdullah es-Siruân, chief of the Medina crew of soldiery : his
father was " a Kurdy," but he was a black man with Galla
looks, of the younger middle age,—the son of a (Galla) bond-
woman. I was new to discern this Hejâz world, and the town
manner of the Harameyn. In the street I saw two white faces
coming out of a doorway ; they were infirm soldiery, and the
men, who walked leaning upon long staves of palm-stalks,
seemed of a ghastly pallor in the dreadful blackness of all
things at Kheybar : they came to join hands with me, a white
man, and passed on without speaking. One of them with a
hoary beard was an Albanian, *Muharram ;* the other was an

Egyptian. When we were again at home Abd el-Hâdy locked
his street door; and coming above stairs, "Tell me, said he
art thou a Moslem? and if no I will lay thy things upon a cow
and send thee to a place of safety."—"Host, I am of the
Engleys; my nation, thou mayest have heard say, is friendly
with the Dowla, and I am of them whom ye name the Nasâra."

Abd el-Hâdy went out in the afternoon and left his street-
door open! There came up presently *Sâlem* a Beduin Ageyly,
to enquire for medicines, and a Galla with his arms, *Sirûr;*—
he it was who had named me adu.—"Half a real for the fever
doses!" (salts and quinine), quoth Sâlem. The Galla murmured, 'But soon it would be seen that I should give them for
nothing'; and he added, "This man has little understanding of
the world, for he discerns not persons: ho! what countryman
art thou?"—"I dwell at Damascus."—"Ha! and that is my
country, but thou dost not speak perfectly Áraby; I am thinking
we shall have here a Nasrâny: oho! What brings thee hither?"
—"I would see the old Jews' country."—"The Jews' country!
but this is *dîrat er-Rasûl,* the apostle's country:" so they forsook
me. And Abd el-Hâdy returning, "What, said he, shall we
do? for wellah all the people is persuaded that thou art no
Moslem."—"Do they take me for an enemy! and the aga...?"
—"Ah! he is a *jabbàr,* a hateful tyrant." My host went forth,
and Sirûr came up anew;—he was sent by the aga. 'What was
I?' he demanded.—"An Engleysy, of those that favour the
Dowla."—"Then a Nasrâny; sully aly en-Néby,—come on!"
and with another of the Ageyl the brutal black Galla began to
thrust me to the stairs. Some villagers who arrived saying that
this was the police, I consented to go with them. "Well, bring
him (said the bystanders), but not with violence."—"Tell me,
before we go further, will ye kill me without the house?" I
had secretly taken my pistol under my tunic, at the first alarm.

At the end of the next street one was sitting on a clay
bench to judge me,—that dark-coloured Abyssinian 'Kurdy',
whom I heard to be the soldiers' aga. A rout of villagers came on
behind us, but without cries.—In what land, I thought, am I now
arrived! and who are these that take me (because of Christ's
sweet name!) for an enemy of mankind?—Sirûr cried, in his
bellowing voice, to him on the clay bench, "I have detected
him,—a Nasrâny!" I said, "What is this! I am an Engleysy,
and being of a friendly nation, why am I dealt with thus?"
"By Ullah, he answered, I was afraid to-day, art thou indeed an
Engleysy, art thou not a Muskôvy?"—"I have said it already!"
—"But I believe it not, and how may I trust thee?"—"When I
have answered, here at Kheybar, *I am a Nasrâny,* should I not

be true in the rest? "—" He says well; go back, Abd el-Hâdy, and fetch his baggage, and see that there be nothing left behind" The street was full of mire after the late rain; so I spoke to Abdullah, and he rising led to an open place in the clay village which is called *es-Saheyn*, 'the little pan.'—"By God (added Abdullah es-Siruân,—the man was illiterate), if any books should be found with thee, or the what-they-call-them,—charts of countries, thou shalt never see them more: they must all be sent to the Pasha at Medina. But hast thou not an instrument,—ah! and I might now think of the name,—I have it! the air-measure?—And from whence comest thou?"—"From Hâyil; I have here also a passport from Ibn Rashîd." Abdullah gave it to a boy who learned in the day school,—for few of the grown villagers, and none of those who stood by, knew their letters. *Abdullah:* "Call me here the sheykh *Sâlih*, to read and write for us." A palm-leaf mat was brought out from one of the houses and cast before us upon a clay bench; I sat down upon it with Abdullah.—A throng of the black villagers stood gazing before us.

So Sâlih arrived, the sheykh of this negro village—an elder man, who walked lame—with a long brass inkstand, and a great leaf of paper in his hand. *Siruân:* "Sâlih, thou art to write all these things in order. [My great camel-bags were brought and set down before him.] Now have out the things one by one; and as I call them over, write, sheykh Sâlih Begin: a camel-bridle, a girby, bags of dates, hard milk and temmn;—what is this?"—"A medicine box."—"Open it!" As I lifted the lid all the black people shrunk back and stopped their nostrils. Sirûr took in his hands that which came uppermost, a square compass,—it had been bound in a cloth. "Let it be untied!" quoth Abdullah. The fellow turning it in his hand, said, "Auh! this is *subûny*" (a square of Syrian soap), so Abdullah, to my great comfort, let it pass. But Abd el-Hâdy espying somewhat, stretched forth his hand suddenly, and took up a comb; "Ha! ha!" cries my host (who till now had kindly harboured me; but his lately good mind was turned already to fanatical rancour—the village named him *Abu Summakh*, 'Father Jangles') what is this perilous instrument,—ha! Nasrâny? Abdullah, let him give account of it; and judge thou if it be not some jin devised by them against the Moslemîn!"

Next came up a great tin, which I opened before them: it was full of tea, my only refreshment. "Well, this you may shut again," said Abdullah. Next was a bundle of books. "Aha! exclaimed the great man, the former things—hast thou written them, sheykh Sâlih?—were of no account, but the books!—

thou shalt never have them again " Then they lighted upon
the brass reel of a tape measure. " Ha! he cries, tell me,
and see thou speak the truth (*alemny b'es sahîhh*), is not this
the sky-measure?" " Here, I said to him, I have a paper, which
is a circular passport from the Wàly of Syria."—" Then read
it, sheykh Sâlih." Sâlih pored over the written document
awhile ;—" I have perused it, he answered, but may perceive
only the names, because it is written in *Turki*, [the tongue was
Arabic, but engrossed in the florid Persian manner!], and here
at the foot is the seal of the Pasha,"—and he read his name.
" Ho! ho! (cries Sirûr) that Pasha was long ago ; and he is dead,
I know it well."—A sigh of bodily weariness that would have rest
broke from me. " Wherefore thus ? exclaimed the pious scelerat
Abdullah, only stay thee upon *el-Mowla* (the Lord thy God)."
— To my final confusion, they fetched up from the sack's
bottom the empty pistol case !—in that weapon was all my hope.
" Aha, a pistol case ! cried many voices, and, casting their
bitter eyes upon me, oh thou ! where is the pistol ? " I answered
nothing ;—in this moment of suspense, one exclaimed, " It is
plain that Ibn Rashîd has taken it from him."—" Ay, answered
the black villagers about me, he has given it to Ibn Rashîd ;
Ibn Rashîd has taken it from him, trust us, Abdullah."—A
pistol among them is always preciously preserved in a gay
bolster ; and they could not imagine that I should wear a naked
pistol under my bare shirt. After this I thought ' Will they
search my person ? '—but that is regarded amongst them as
an extreme outrage; and there were here too many witnesses.
He seemed to assent to their words, but I saw he rolled it in
his turbid mind, ' what was become of the Nasrâny's pistol?'
The heavy weapon, worn continually suspended from the neck,
not a little molested me ; and I could not put off my Arab
cloak (which covered it) in the sultry days.—So he said,
" Hast thou money with thee ?—and we may be sure thou hast
some. Tell us plainly, where is it, and do not hide it; this will
be better for thee,—and, that I may be friends with thee ! also it
must be written in the paper ; and tell us hast thou anything
else ?—mark ye O people, I would not that a needle of this
man's be lost ! "—" Reach me that tin where you saw the tea :
in the midst is my purse,—and in it, you see, are six liras ! " The
thief counted them, with much liking, in his black palm ; then
shutting up the purse he put it in his own bosom, saying,
" Sâlih, write down these six liras Fransâwy. I have taken
them for their better keeping ; and his bags will be under key
in my own house."

There came over to me Ahmed, whom I had seen last evening ;

he had been sitting with the old tranquillity amongst the lookers-on, and in the time of this inquisition he nodded many times to me friendly. "*Mâ aleyk, mâ aleyk*, take comfort, he said, there shall no evil happen to thee."—*Abdullah:* "Abd el-Hâdy, let him return to lodge with thee; also he can cure the sick." The negro answered, "I receive again the kafir!—Only let him say the testimony and I will receive him willingly."— "Then he must lodge with the soldiery; thou *Amân*—a Galla Ageyly—take him to your chamber: Khalîl may have his provisions with him and his box of medicines."

I saw the large manly presence standing erect in the backward of the throng—for he had lately arrived—of a very swarthy Arabian; he was sheykhly clad, and carried the sword, and I guessed he might be some chief man of the irregular soldiery. Now he came to me, and dropping (in their sudden manner) upon the hams of the legs, he sat before me with the confident smiling humour of a strong man; and spoke to me pleasantly. I wondered to see his swarthiness,—yet such are commonly the Arabians in the Hejâz—and he not less to see a man so 'white and red'. This was Mohammed en-Nejûmy, Ahmed's brother, who from the morrow became to me as a father at Kheybar. "Go now, said Abdullah, with the soldier."—"Mâ aleyk, mâ aleyk," added some of the better-disposed bystanders. *Abdullah:* "You will remain here a few days, whilst I send a post to the Pasha (of Medina) with the books and papers."—'Ho! ye people, bellows Sirûr, we will send to the Pasha; and if the Pasha's word be to cut his head off, we will chop off thy head Nasrâny." "Trouble not thyself, said some yet standing by, for this fellow's talk,—he is a brute." Hated was the Galla bully in the town, who was valiant only with their hareem, and had been found *khòaf*, a skulking coward, in the late warfare.

So I came with Amân to the small suffa which he inhabited with a comrade, in the next house. They were both *Habûsh*, further-Abyssinians, that is of the land of the Gallas. Lithe figures they are commonly, with a feminine grace and fine lineaments; their hue is a yellow-brown, ruddy brown, deep brown or blackish, and that according to their native districts,— so wide is the country. They have sweet voices and speak not one Galla tongue alike, so that the speech of distant tribes is hardly understood between them. Amân could not well understand his comrade's talk (therefore they spoke together in Arabic), but he spoke nearly one language with Sirûr. Amân taught me many of his Galla words; but to-day I remember no more than *bîsân*, water. Though brought slaves to the Hejâz in

their childhood they forgot not there their country language:
so many are now the Gallas in Mecca and Medina, that
Hábashy is currently spoken from house to house. Some of
the beautiful Galla bondwomen become wives in the citizen
families, even of the great, others are nurses and house
servants; and the Arab town children are bred up amongst
them.—The poor fellows bade me be of good comfort, and all
would now end well, after a little patience: one set bread
before me, and went out to borrow dates for their guest. They
said, " As for this negro people, they are not men but oxen, apes,
sick of the devil and niggards."—These Semite-like Africans
vehemently disdain the Sudân, or negro slave-race. " Great
God!" I have heard them say at Kheybar, " can these woolly
polls be of the children of Adam?"

We heard Mohammed en-Nejûmy upon the clay stairs. He
said, " It is the first time I ever came hither, but for thy sake I
come." At night-fall we went forth together, lighting our way
with flaming palm-branches, to the soldiers' kahwa. Abdullah,
whom my purse had enriched to-day, beckoned me to sit beside
him. Their talk took a good turn, and Mohammed en-Nejûmy
pronounced the famous formula: *kull wáhed aly dînu*, 'every
man in his own religion!'—and he made his gloss, " this is to
say the Yahûdy in his law, the Nasrâny in his law and the
Moslem in his law; aye, and the kafir may be a good faithful
man in his belief." The Nejûmy was an heroic figure, he sat
with his sword upon his knees, bowing and assenting, at every
word to the black villain Abdullah : this is their Turkish
town courtesy. Sometimes (having heard from me that I
understood no Turkish) they spoke together in that language.
Mohammed answered, after every clement saw of the black
lieutenant, the pious praise [though it sounded like an irony],
Ullah yubèyith wejhak, 'the Lord whiten thy visage (in the day
of doom)!' There was some feminine fall in the strong man's
voice,—and where is any little savour of the mother's blood in
right manly worth, it is a pleasant grace. He was not altogether like the Arabs, for he loved to speak in jesting-wise, with
a kindly mirth : though they be full of knavish humour, I never
saw among the Arabians a merry man!

Mohammed and Ahmed were sons of a Kurdy sutler at
Medina; and their mother was an Harb woman of the Ferrâ, a
palm settlement of that Beduin nation in the Hejâz, betwixt
the Harameyn. We drunk round the soldiers' coffee ; yet here
was not the cheerful security of the booths of hair, but town
constraint and Turkish tyranny, and the Egyptian plague of
vermin. They bye and bye were accorded in their sober cups

that the Nasâra might pass everywhere freely, only they may
not visit the Harameyn : and some said, "Be there not many
of Khalîl's religion at Jidda ? the way is passed by riders in
one night-time from Mecca" [many in the Hejâz pronounce
Mekky]. Abdullah said at last, "Wellah, Khalîl is an honest
man, he speaks frankly, and I love him." I was soon weary,
and he sent his bondman to light me back to my lodging. Hearing some rumour, I looked back, and saw that the barefoot negro
came dancing behind me in the street with his drawn sword.

Abdullah said to me at the morning coffee, that I might walk
freely in the village ; and the black hypocrite enquired 'had I
rested well ?' When it was evening, he said, "Rise, we will go
and drink coffee at the house of a good man." We went out,
and some of his soldiers lighted us with flaming palm leaves to
the cottage of one *Ibrahîm el-kâdy*. Whilst we sat in his suffa,
there came up many of the principal villagers. Ibrahîm set his
best dates before us, made up the fire, and began to prepare
kahwa, and he brought the village governor his kerchief full of
their green tobacco.

Then Abdullah opened his black lips—to speak to them of
my being found at Kheybar, a stranger, and one such as they
had not seen in their lives. "What, he said, are these Nasâra ?
— listen all of you ! It is a strong nation : were not two or
three Nasrânies murdered some years ago at Jidda ?—well,
what followed ? There came great war-ships of their nation and
bombarded the place : but you the Kheyâbara know not what
is a ship !—a ship is great, well nigh as the Húsn (the old
acropolis). They began to shoot at us with their artillery, and
we that were in the fortress shot again ; but oh ! where was the
fortress ? or was there, think ye, any man that remained in the
town ? no, they all fled ; and if the Lord had not turned away
that danger, we could not have resisted them. And who were
those that fought against Jidda ? I tell you the Engleys, the
people of this Khalîl : the Engleys are high-handed, ay wellah,
jabâbara ! * * *

* * * Abdullah, though ignorant in school-lore, spoke with
that popular persuasion of the Turkish magistrates, behind
whose fair words lies the crude handling of the sword. The
Arabs and Turks whose books are men's faces, their lively experience of mankind, and whose glosses are the common saws and
thousand old sapient proverbs of their oriental world, touch near
the truth of human things. They are old men in policy in their
youth, and have little later to unlearn ; but especially they have

learned to speak well. Abdullah, and the Medina soldiery, and
the black Kheyâbara spoke Medina Arabic. Their illiberal town
speech resembles the Syrian, but is more full and round, with
some sound of ingenuous Arabian words : the tanwîn is not heard
at Kheybar. I thought the Nejûmy spoke worst among them
all ; it might be he had learned of his father, a stranger, or that
such was the (Hejâz) speech of his Harb village : his brother
spoke better. Medina, besides her motley (now half Indian)
population, is in some quarters a truly Arabian town ; there is
much in her of the Arabian spirit : every year some Arabians
settle there, and I have met with Medina citizens who spoke
nearly as the upland Arabians.

I was his captive, and mornings and evenings must present
myself before Abdullah. The village governor oppressed me
with cups of coffee, and his official chibûk, offered with comely
smiles of his black visage ; until the skeleton three days' hospitality was ended. The soldiery were lodged in free quarters
at Kheybar, where are many empty houses which the owners let
out in the summer months to the salesmen who arrive then
from Medina. Abdullah was lodged in one of the better houses,
the house of a black widow woman, whose prudent and beneficent
humour was very honourably spoken of in the country If any
marketing nomads dismounted at her door, she received them
bountifully ; if any in the village were in want, and she heard
of it, she would send somewhat. Freely she lent her large
dwelling, for she was a loyal woman who thought it reason to
give place to the officer of the Dowla. Although a comely
person in her early middle age, yet she constantly refused to
take another mate, saying, ' She was but the guardian of the
inheritance for her two sons.' She already provided to give
them wives in the next years. The Kheybar custom is to
mortgage certain palm-yards for the bride-money ; but thus the
soil (which cannot bring forth an excessive usury) not seldom
slips, in the end, quite out of the owner's hands. Therefore this
honest negro wife imagined new and better ways : she frankly
sold two béleds, and rode down with the price to Medina ; and
bought a young Galla maiden, well disposed and gracious, for her
elder son's wife : and she would nourish the girl as a daughter
until they should both be of the age of marriage. The Kheyâbara are wont to match with the (black) daughters of their village ;
but the Galla women might be beloved even by white men.
Abdullah once called me to supper : he had a good Medina
mess of goat's flesh and french-beans. When we rose he smiled
to those about him and boasted " *Hâg Ullah!* ' it is God's truth,'

seeing Khalîl has eaten this morsel with me, I could not devise any evil against him!" Another time I came up weary in the afternoon, when the soldiery had already drunk their coffee and departed; yet finding a little in the pot I set it on the coals, and poured out and sipped it.—Abdullah, who sat there with one or two more, exclaimed, "When I see Khalîl drink only that cup, wellah I cannot find it in my heart to wish him evil:"—this was the half-humane black hypocrite!

The Nejûmy, who—since a white man is the black people's "uncle"—was called in the town *Amm Mohammed*, did not forget me; one forenoon I heard his pleasant voice at the stair head: "*Sheykh Khalîl, sheykh Khalîl, hŷ!* come, I want thee." He led me to his house, which was in the next street, at the end of a dark passage, from whence we mounted to his suffa. The light, *eth-thów*, entered the dwelling room at two small casements made high upon the clay wall, and by the open ladder-trap to the roof: it was bare and rude.—" Sit down, sheykh Khalîl, this is my poor place, said he; we live here like the Beduw, but the Lord be praised, very much at our ease, and with plenty of all things:" Amm Mohammed was dwelling here as a trader. A Bishr woman was his housewife; and she made us an excellent dish of moist girdle-cakes, *gors*, sopped in butter and wild honey. "This honey comes to me, said he, from the Beduw, in my buying and selling, and I have friends among them who bring it me from the mountains." The fat and the sweet [in the Hebrew Scriptures—where the fat of beasts is forbidden to be eaten—Fat things, milk and honey, or butter and honey, oil olive and honey] are, they think, all-cure; they comfort the health of the weak-dieted. There is a tribe of savage men upon the wide *Jebel Rodwa* (before Yanba), who "are very long lived and of marvellous vigour in their extreme age; and that is (say the Arabs) because they are nourished of venison (el-bedûn) and wild honey." When we had eaten, "I and thou are now brethren, said the good man; and, sheykh Khalîl, what time thou art hungry come hither to eat, and this house is now as thine own: undo the door and come upstairs, and if I am not within say to this woman, thou wouldst eat dates or a cake of bread, and she will make ready for thee." He told me that at first the negro villagers had looked upon me as a soldier of the Dowla; but he said to them, 'Nay, for were the stranger a soldier he had gone to alight at the Siruân's or else at my beyt.' When, the day after, they began to know me, there had been a sort of panic terror among the black people. 'I was *sáhar*, they said, a warlock, come to bewitch their village': and the hareem said "Oh! look! how red he is!"

Amm Mohammed: "This is a feast day (*Aŷd eth-thahía*), shall we now go and visit the acquaintance ? "—We went from house to house of his village friends : but none of them, in their high and holy day, had slain any head of cattle,—they are reputed niggards ; yet in every household where we came a mess was set before us of girdle-bread sopped in samn. " I warn thee, sheykh Khalîl, said my friend, we must eat thus twenty times before it is evening."

" In these days, whilst we are sending to Medina, said Abdullah the Siruân, thou canst cure the sick soldiery ; we have two at *Umm Kída,* another is here. Sirûr, and you, Sâlem, go with him, take your arms, and let Khalîl see Muharram."—"I cannot walk far."—" It is but the distance of a gunshot from the *Sefsáfa.*"

—We came thither and descended behind the figgera, into another valley *W. es-Sillima,* named thus because in the upper parts there is much wild growth of *slîm* acacia trees. The eyes of the Aarab distinguish four kinds of the desert thorns : *tólh* (the gum-acacia), *sámmara, sillima* and *siđla ;* the leaves of them all are like, but the growth is diverse. The desert smiths cut tólh timber for their wood work, it is heavy and tough ; the other kinds are too brittle to serve them. The sámmara is good for firewood ; it is sweet-smelling, and burns with a clear heat leaving little ash, and the last night's embers are found alive in the morning. They have boasted to me of this good fuel,—" We believe that the Lord has given you many things in your plentiful countries, but surely ye have not there the sámmara ! " W. Sillima descends from the Harra beyond the trachytic mount Atwa, and gives below the basalt headland *Khusshm es-Sefsáfa* into *W. Zeydîeh,* the valley of the greater Kheybar village and the antique citadel. W. Sillima is here a rusty fen, white with the salt-warp, summakha, exhaling a sickly odour and partly overgrown with sharp rushes, *el-gîrt,* which stab the shanks of unwary passengers.—Such is, to the white man, the deadly aspect of all the valley-grounds of Kheybar!

If you question with the villagers, seeing so much waste bottom and barrenness about them, they answer, " There is more already upon our hands than we may labour." The summakha soil, which is not the worst, can be cured, if for two or three seasons the infected salt-crusts be pared with the spade : then the brackish land may be sowed, and every year it will become sweeter. A glaze of salt is seen upon the small clay bottoms in the Harra ; yet of the many springs of Kheybar,

which are warm and with some smack of sulphur, there is not
one brackish: they rise between certain underlying clays and
the basalt, which is fifty feet thick, at the edge of the figgera.
The large Kheybar valleys lie together, like a palm leaf, in the
Harra border: they are gashes in the lava-field—in what
manner formed it were not easy to conjecture—to the shallow
clays beneath. Where an underlying (sandstone) rock comes
to light it is seen scaly (burned) and discoloured.

—We came up by walled ways through palm grounds and
over their brook, to the village Umm Kîda: this is Jériat
W. Aly. The site, upon the high wady-bank of basalt, is
ancient, and more open and cheerful, and in a better air than
the home village. We ascended near the gateway to a suffa,
which was the soldiers' quarters; the men's arms hanged at the
walls, and upon the floor I saw three pallets.—The Turkish
comrades bade us welcome in the hard manner of strangers
serving abroad at wages, and tendered their chibûks. Two of
them were those pale faces, which I had first seen in Kheybar;
the third was *Mohammed*, a Kurdy, from some town near *Tiflis*
(in Russian Armenia). Muharram was a tall extenuated man,
and plainly European. He had worn out forty years in military
service in the Hejâz, about Medina and Mecca, and never the
better: I asked him where was his *fustân?* He answered
smiling, with half a sigh, "There was a time when we wore
the petticoat, and many of the Arnaût were prosperous men at
Medina; but now they are dispersed and dead." He wore yet
his large tasseled red bonnet, which seemed some glorious
thing in the rusty misery of Kheybar! His strength failed
him here, the fever returned upon him: I gave him rhubarb in
minute doses, and quinine. * * *

* * * The guest in the Arabic countries sees the good
disposition of his host, after three days, turned as the backside
of a garment.—Each morning, after I had presented myself to
the village tyrant at the kahwa, I went to breathe the air upon
the figgera above the Sefsáfa. I might sit there in the winter
sun, without the deadly damps of the valley, to meditate my
time away; and read the barometer unespied, and survey the
site of Kheybar, and the brick-red and purple-hued distance of
mountains in the immense Arabian landscape beyond. One
day having transcribed my late readings of the aneroid, I cast
down the old papers, and, lest the wind should betray me, laid
stones on them: but my vision never was good, and there were
eyes that watched me, though I saw no man. As I walked

there another day a man upon a house-top, at Umm Kîda, fired his gun at me. The morning after, seeing two men approach with their matchlocks, I returned to the village: and found Abdullah sitting with malevolent looks. " What is this, he said, that I hear of thee ?—children of Umm Kîda saw you bury papers, I know not what ! They have taken them up, and carried them to the hamlet, where all the people were troubled; and a sheykh, a trusty man, has been over here to complain to me. What were the papers? [in their belief written full of enchantments :]—and now the sheykhs have solemnly burned them." Besides a Beduwy had been to Abdullah accusing the Nasrâny ' that he saw me sitting upon the Harra with a paper in my hand '.

Abdullah told me, that as I returned yesterday, by the path, through the plantations, two young men of Umm Kîda sat behind the clay walling with their matchlocks ready, and disputed whether they should take my life ; and said one to the other, " Let me alone, and I will shoot at him : " but his fellow answered, " Not now, until we see further; for if his blood were shed we know not whom it might hurt." *Abdullah :* " What hast thou done, Khalîl? what is this that I hear of thee ? The chief persons come to me accusing thee ! and I do tell thee the truth, this people is no more well-minded towards thee. Observe that which I say to thee, and go no more beyond the gates of the village ;—I say go not ! I may protect thee in the village, in the daytime : by night go not out of thy chamber, lest some evil befall thee ; and the blame be laid upon me. For Ullah knoweth—and here the malevolent fanaticism kindled in his eyes—who is there might come upon thee with his knife !—a stroke, Khalîl, and thou art dead ! But the slayer was not seen, and the truth of it might never be known. Only in the day visit thine acquaintance, and sit in friendly houses. I have said go not beyond the gates ; but if thou pass them, and thou art one day slain, then am I clean of it ! Canst thou look through walling? a shot from behind some of their (clay) walls may take thy life ; there are some here who would do it, and that as lightly as they shoot at crows, because thou art an alien, and now they have taken thee for an enemy ; and that they have not done it hitherto, wellah it was for my sake." * * *

* * * At first he [Amm Mohammed] called me often to eat with him ; then seeing me bare of necessary things (Abdullah had now my purse) he took me altogether to his house to live with him, in the daytime. Some evenings we went abroad,—

'*nedowwer* (said he,) *el-haky wa el-káhwa*,—seeking pleasant
chat and coffee', to friendly houses. At night, since his home
was but an upper chamber, I withdrew to sleep in Amân's
suffa. At each new sunrising I returned to him: after his
prayers we breakfasted, and when the winter sun began to cast
a little golden heat, taking up our tools, a crowbar, a spade
and a basket, we went forth to an orchard of his; and all this
was devised by Mohammed, that I might not be divided from
him. He carried also (for my sake) his trusty sword, and
issuing from the sordid village I breathed a free air, and found
some respite in his happy company, in the midst of many
apprehensions.

Amm Mohammed set himself to open a water-pit in a palm
ground of his next the troops' summer quarters; the ground-
water lies about a spade deep in the valley bottom of Kheybar,
but the soil rising there and shallowing out under the figgera,
he must break down an arm's length through massy basalt. We
passed the days in this idle business: because he saw his guest
full of weariness he was uneasy when in my turn I took up
the bar. "Sit we down, sheykh Khalîl, a breathing while!
nésma: nay, why make earnest matter of that which is but our
pastime, or what haste is there so all be ended before the
summer?"

A good crowbar is worth at Kheybar five reals; their
(Medina) *husbandmen's-tools are fetched from the coast.* The
upper shells of basalt were easy to be broken through: but next
lies the massy (crystalline) rock, which must be riven and rent
up by force of arms; and doubtless all the old spring-heads of
Kheybar have been opened thus!—Seldom at this season there
arrived a hubt, or company of marketing nomads: then his
wife or son called home Amm Mohammed, and the good man
returned to the village to traffic with them.

Amm Mohammed—endowed with an extraordinary eyesight
—was more than any in this country, a hunter. Sometimes,
when he felt himself enfeebled by this winter's (famine) diet
of bare millet, he would sally, soon after the cold midnight,
in his bare shirt, carrying but his matchlock and his sandals
with him: and he was far off, upon some high place in the
Harra, by the day dawning, from whence he might see over the
wide vulcanic country. When on the morrow I missed the good
man, I sat still in his suffa, full of misgiving till his coming
home again; and that was near mid-day. Only two or three
days of autumn rain had fallen hereabout, and the new blade
was hardly seen to spring; the gazelles and the wild goats
had forsaken this side of the Harra: Amm Mohammed there-

fore found nothing.—At Kheybar they name the stalker of great ground game *gennàs: seyàd* is the light hunter with hawk and hound, to take the desert hare.

He led me with him sometime upon the Harra, to see certain ancient inscriptions;—they were in Kufic, scored upon the basalt rock, and full of *Ullah* and *Mohammed*. Many old Arabic inscriptions may be seen upon the scaly (sandstone) rocks, which rise in the valley, half an hour below the place. I found no more of heathen Arabic than two or three inscriptions, each of a few letters. They are scored upon a terrace of basalt, under the Khusshm es-Sefsáfa, with images of animals: I found the wild ox, but not the elephant, the giraffe, and other great beasts of the African continent, which Amân told me he had seen there. * * *

(*Doughty describes the ruined village el-Gereyeh, and the Húsn, or citadel rock. The villagers, and their ancient partnership in the soil with the Beduins. The Medina soldiery.*)

* * * In the third week of my being in this captivity at Kheybar, the slave-spirited Abdullah wrote to the Pasha of Medina. Since the village governor knew no letters, the black sheykh Sâlih was his scrivener, and wrote after him: " Upon such a day of the last month, when the gates of Kheybar were opened in the morning, we found a stranger without, waiting to enter. He told us that a Beduwy, with whom he arrived in the night, had left him there and departed. When we asked him what man he was? he answered ' an Engleysy '; and he acknowledged himself to be a Nasrâny. And I, not knowing what there might be in this matter have put the stranger in ward, and have seized his baggage, in which we have found some books and a paper from Ibn Rashîd. So we remain in your Lordship's obedience, humbly awaiting the commandments of your good Lordship."—" Now well, said Abdullah; and seal it, Sâlih. Hast thou heard this that I have written, Khalîl ? "—" Write only the truth. When was I found at your gates? I rode openly into Kheybar."—" Nay, but I must write thus, or the

Pasha might lay a blame upon me and say, 'Why didst thou suffer him to enter?'—That Heteymy lodged in the place all night, and he was a gomâny! also his thelûl lay in the street, and I did not apprehend him :—Oh God! where was then my wit? I might [the thief murmured] have taken his drome-dary! Listen, everyone of you here present! for the time to come, ye are to warn me when any strangers arrive; that if there be anything against them, they may be arrested immediately."

Abdullah had in these days seized the cow of an orphan,—for which all the people abhorred him—a poor minor without de-fence, that he might drink her milk himself : so he wrote another letter to the Pasha, " I have sequestered a cow for arrears of taxes, and will send her unto your lordship; the beast is worth fifteen reals at Kheybar, and might be sold for fifty at el-Medina." In a third paper he gave up his account of the village tithing to the Dowla : all the government exactions at Kheybar were together 3600 reals. [For this a regiment of soldiers must march every year to (their deaths at) Kheybar!] Abdullah's men being not fully a score were reckoned in his paysheet at forty. If any man died, he drew the deceased's salary himself, to the end of his term of service. Once every year he will be called to muster his asâkar; but then with some easy deceit, as by hiring or compelling certain of the village, and clothing them for a day or two, he may satisfy the easy passing over of his higher officers ; who full of guilty bribes themselves, look lightly upon other men's criminal cases. Abdullah added a postscript. " It may please your honour to have in remembrance the poor askars that are hungry and naked, and they are looking humbly unto your good Lordship for some relief." In thirty and two months they had not been paid!—what wonder though such wretches, defrauded by the Ottoman government, become robbers! Now they lifted up their weary hearts to God and the Pasha, that a new khúsna, or 'paymaster's chest of treasure ', from Stambûl might be speedily heard of at el-Medina. These were years of wasting warfare in Europe ; of which the rumour was heard confusedly at this unprofitable distance. So Abdullah sealed his letters, which had cost him and his empressed clerk three days' labour, until their black temples ached again.

These were days for me sooner of dying than of life ; and the felonous Abdullah made no speed to deliver me. The govern-ment affairs of the village were treated-of over cups of coffee ; and had Sâlih not arrived betimes, Abdullah sent for him, with authority. The unhappy sheykh with a leg short came then in haste ; and the knocking of his staff might be heard through the length of the street, whilst the audience sat in silence, and the angry blood seemed to boil in the black visage of Abdullah. When he came up, ' Why wast thou not here ere this, sheykh Sâlih ? ' he would say, in a voice which made the old man tremble ; Sâlih answered nothing, only rattling his inkstand he began to pluck out his reed pens. The village sheykh had no leisure now to look to his own affairs ; and for all this pain he received yearly from the government of Medina the solemn mockery of a scarlet mantle : but his lot was now cast in with the Dowla, which he had welcomed ; and he might lose all, and were even in danger of his head, if Ibn Rashîd entered again.

It is the custom of these Orientals, to sit all day in their coffee halls, with only a resting-while at noon. To pass the daylight hours withdrawn from the common converse of men were in their eyes unmanly ; and they look for no reasonable fellowship with the hareem. Women are for the house-service ; and only when his long day is past, will the householder think it time to re-enter to them. Abdullah drank coffee and tobacco in his soldiers' kahwa ; where it often pleased him to entertain his company with tales of his old prowess and prosperity at Medina : and in his mouth was that round kind of utterance of the Arabic coffee-drinkers, with election of words, and dropping with the sap of human life. Their understanding is like the moon, full upon this side of shining shallow light; but all is dimness and deadness upon the side of science. He told us what a gallant horseman he had been,—he was wont to toss a javelin to the height, wellah, of the minarets in Medina ; and how he went like a gentleman in the city, and made his daily devout prayers in the *háram;* nor might he ever be used to the rudeness of thelûl riding, because nature had shaped him a gentle cavalier. He had ridden once in an expedition almost to el-Héjr ; and as they returned he found an hamlet upon a mountain, whose inhabitants till that day, wellah, had not seen strangers. He had met with wild men, when he rode to Yanba,—that was upon the mountain Rodwa ; those hill-folk [Jeheyna] besides a cotton loin-cloth, go naked. One of them an ancient, nearly ninety years of age, ran on before his horse, leaping like a wild goat among the rocks ; and that only of his good will, to be the stranger's guide. He boasted he had bought broken horses for little silver, and sold them soon for much ; so fortunate were his stars at Medina. In the city he had a chest four cubits long ; a cubit deep and wide ; and in his best time it was full of reals, and lightly as they came to his hand, he spent them again. He had a Galla slave-lad at Medina who went gaily clad, and had sweetmeats and money, so that he wondered; but upon a day, his infamy being known, Abdullah drew a sword and pursued his bondsman in the street and wounded him, and sold him the day after to one of his lovers, for five reals —It seems that amongst them a householder may maim or even slay his bond-servant in his anger and go unpunished, and the law is silent; for as Moses said, HE IS HIS CHATTEL. * * *

* * * The Kheyâbara inured to the short tyranny of the Beduins were not broken to this daily yoke of the Dowla. They had no longer sanctuary in their own houses, for Abdullah summoned them from their hearths at his list; their hareem were beaten before their faces ;—and now his imposition of firewood! Abdullah sent for the chief murmurers of the village; and looking gallantly, he sought with the unctuous words of Turkish governors to persuade them. " Are not the soldiers quartered, by order of the Dowla, upon you in this village ? and I say, sirs, they look unto you for their fuel,—what else should maintain this kahwa fire? which is for the honour of Kheybar, and where ye be all welcome. Listen !—under his smiles he looked dangerous, and spoke this proverb which startled me :—the military authority is what ? *It is like a stone, whereupon if anyone fall he will be broken, but upon whom the Dowla shall fall he will be broken in pieces.* I speak to you as a friend, *the Dowla has a mouth gaping wide* [it is a criminal government which devours the subject people], and that cries evermore *hât-hât-hât,* give ! give !—And what is this ? O ye the Kheyâbara, I am mild heretofore ; I have well deserved of you : but if ye provoke me to lay upon you other burdens, ye shall see, and I will show it you ! It had been better for you that you had not complained for the wood ; for now I think to tax your growing tobacco.—I have reckoned that taking one field in eight, I shall raise from Kheybar a thousand reals, and this I have left to you free hitherto. And whatsoever more I may lay upon you, trust me Sirs it will be right well received ; and for such I shall be highly commended at Medina."

Kheybar is three sheykh's sûks.—*Atewy,* a sturdy carl, chief of the upper sûk under the Hûsn, answered for himself and his, that they would no longer give the wood.' Abdullah sent for him ; but Atewy would not come. Abdullah imprisoned two of Atewy's men: Atewy said it should not be so ; and the men of his sûk caught up bucklers and cutlasses, and swore to break up the door and release them. Half of the Ageyl askars at Kheybar could not, for sickness, bear the weight of their

weapons; and the strong negroes, when their blood was moved,
contemned the Sirûân's pitiful band of feeble wretches.
Abdullah sent out his bully Sirûr, with the big brazen voice, to
threaten the rioters: but the Galla coward was amazed at their
settled countenance, and I saw him sneak home to Abdullah;
who hearing that the town was rising, said to the father of his
village housewife, " And wilt thou also forsake me?" The
man answered him, " My head is with thy head!"

Abdullah who had often vaunted his forwardness to the
death, in any quarrel of the Dowla, now called his men to arm;
he took down his pair of horseman's pistols from the wall, with
the ferocity of the Turkish service, and descended to the street;
determined 'to persuade the rioters, and if no wellah he would
shed blood.'—He found the negroes' servile heat somewhat
abated: and since they could not contend with 'the Dowla',
they behaved themselves peaceably· Abdullah also promised
them to release the captives.

Abdullah re-entered the kahwa,—and again he summoned
Atewy; who came now,—and beginning some homely excuses,
" Well, they cared not, he said, though they gave a little wood,
for Abdullah's sake, only they would not be compelled."
Abdullah, turning to me, said "*Wheu!* now hast thou seen,
Khalîl, what sheytâns are the Kheyâbara! and wast thou not
afraid in this hurly-burly? I am at Kheybar for the Dowlat
and these soldiers are under me; but where wert thou to-day,
if I had not been here?"—" My host's roof had sheltered me,
and after that the good will of the people."—'Now let the
Kheyâbara, he cried, see to it, and make him no more turmoils;
or by Ullah he would draw on his boots and ride to Medina!
and the Pasha may send you another governor, not easy as I
am, but one that will break your backs and devour you: and
as for me, wellah, I shall go home with joy to mine own house
and children.' * * *

* * * Abdullah, who knew the simple properties of numbers,
told them upon his fingers in tens; but could not easily keep
the count, through his broken reckoning, rising to thousands.—
And devising to deliver a Turkish bill of his stewardship, he
said, with a fraudulent smile; ' We may be silent upon such
and such little matters, that if the Pasha should find a fault in
our numbers, we may still have somewhat in hand wherewith to
amend it. The unlettered governor made up these dispatches
in the public ear, and turning often to his audience he enquired,
' Did they approve him, Sirs?' and only in some very privy
matter he went up with sheykh Sâlih to indite upon his house-

terrace. Abdullah hired Dakhîl (not the Menhel), one of the best of the black villagers, to carry his government budget, for four reals, to Medina. Dakhîl, who only at Kheybar, besides the Nejûmy, was a hunter, fared on foot : and because of the danger of the way he went clad (though it was mid-winter) in an old (calico) tunic ; he left his upper garment behind him.

Many heavy days must pass over my life at Kheybar, until Dakhîl's coming again; the black people meanwhile looked with doubt and evil meaning upon the Nasrâny,—because the Pasha might send word to put me to death. Felonous were the Turkish looks of the sot Abdullah, whose robber's mind seemed to be suspended betwixt his sanguinary fanaticism and the dread remembrance of Jidda and Damascus : the brutal Sirûr was his privy counsellor.—Gallas have often an extreme hatred of this name, Nasrâny : it may be because their border tribes are in perpetual warfare with the Abyssinian Christians.

Abdullah had another counsellor, whom he called his ' uncle ', —Aly, the religious sheykh, crier to prayers, and the village schoolmaster. Looking upon Aly's mannikin visage, full of strange variance, I thought he might be a little lunatic :—of this deformed rankling complexion, and miserable and curious humour, are all their worst fanatics I enquired of Amm Mohammed ; and he remembered that Aly's mother had died out of her mind. Aly was continually breathing in the ass's ears of Abdullah that the Nasrâny was adu ed-dîn, ' enemy of the faith;' and ' it was due to the Lord (said he) that I should perish by the sword of the Moslemîn. Let Abdullah kill me ! cries the ape-face ; and if it were he durst not himself, he might suffer the thing to be done. And if there came any hurt of it, yet faithful men before all things must observe their duty to Ullah.'—The worst was that the village sheykh Sâlih, other- wise an elder of prudent counsel, put-to his word that Aly had reason !

The Nejûmy hearing of the counsels of Abdullah cared not to dissemble his disdain. He said of Aly, "The hound, the slave ! and all the value of him [accounting him in his contempt à bondman] is ten reals : and as for the covetous fool and very ass Abdullah, the father of him bought the dam of him for fifty reals ! "—But their example heartened the baser spirits of the village, and I heard again they had threatened to shoot at the kafir, as I walked in the (walled) paths of their plantations. Amm Mohammed therefore went no more abroad, when we were together, without his good sword. And despising the black villagers he said, " They are apes, and not children of Adam ; Oh ! which of them durst meddle in my matter ? were it only of a dog or a chicken in my house! But sheykh Khalîl eats with me every day in one dish." The strong man added, ' He would cut him in twain who laid an hand on Khalîl; and if any of them durst sprinkle Khalîl with water, he would sprinkle him with his blood!'

Abdullâh, when we sat with him, smiled with all his Turkish smiles upon the Nejûmy; and Amm Mohammed smiled as good to his black face again. "But (quoth he) let no man think that I am afraid of the Dowla, nor of sixty Dowlas; for I may say, Abdullah, as once said the ostrich to the Beduwy, ' If thou come to take camels, am I not a bird? but comest thou hither a-fowling, behold, Sir! I am a camel.' So if the Aarab trouble me I am a Dowlâny, a citizen of the illustrious Medina, —where I may bear my sword in the streets [which may only officers and any visiting Beduw], because I have served the Dowla. And, if it go hard with me upon the side of the Dowla, I am *Harby*, and may betake me to the *Ferrâ* (of the Beny Amr); that is my mother's village, in the mountains [upon the middle *derb*] between the Harameyn: there I have a patrimony and a house. The people of the Ferrâ are my cousins, and there is no Dowla can fetch me from thence, neither do we know the Dowla; for the entry is strait as a gateway in the jebel, so that three men might keep it against a multitude."— And thus the Nejûmy defended my solitary part, these days and weeks and months at Kheybar;—one man against a thousand! Yet dwelling in the midst of barking tongues, with whom he must continue to live, his honest heart must sometimes quail, (which was of supple temper, as in all the nomad blood). And so far he gave in to the popular humour that certain times, in the eyes of the people, he affected to shun me: for they cried out daily upon him, that he harboured the Nasrâny!—"Ah! Khalîl, he said to me, thou canst not imagine all their malice!"

Neither was this the first time that Mohammed en-Nejûmy had favoured strangers in their trouble.—A Medina tradesman was stripped and wounded in the wilderness as he journeyed to Kheybar; and he arrived naked. The black villagers are inhospitable; and the Medina citizen, sitting on the public benches, waited in vain that some householder would call him. At last Ahmed went by; and the stranger, seeing a white man,—one that (in this country) must needs be a fellow citizen of Medina, said to him, "What shall I do, my townsman? of whom might I borrow a few reals in this place, and buy myself clothing?" *Ahmed:* "At the street's end yonder is sitting a tall white man! ask him:"—that was Mohammed.—"Ah! Sir, said the poor

tradesman, finding him; thou art so swarthy, that I had well
nigh mistaken thee for a Beduwy!" Amm Mohammed led
him kindly to his house and clothed him : and the wounded
man sojourned with his benefactor and Ahmed two or three
months, until they could send him to Medina. "And now
when I come there, and he hears that I am in the city, said
Amm Mohammed, he brings me home, and makes feast and
rejoicing."—This human piety of the man was his thankoffering to the good and merciful Providence, that had prospered him and forgiven him the ignorances of his youth !

Another year,—it was in the time of Ibn Rashîd's government—when the Nejûmy was buying and selling dates and
cotton clothing in the harvest-market at Kheybar, some Annezy
men came one day haling a naked wretch, with a cord about
his neck, through the village street : it was an Heteymy ; and
the Beduins cried furiously against him, that he had withheld the khûwa, ten reals ! and they brought him to see if
any man in Kheybar, as he professed to them, would pay for
him ; and if no, they would draw him out of the town and
kill him. The poor soul pleaded for himself, " The Nejûmy
will redeem me : " so they came on to the Rahabba, where
was at that time Mohammed's lodging, and the Heteymy
called loudly upon him. Mohammed saw him to be some
man whom he knew not : yet he said to the Annezy, "Loose
him."—"We will not let him go, unless we have ten reals
for him."—"But I say, loose him, for my sake."—"We will
not loose him."—"Then go up Ahmed, and bring me ten reals
from the box." " I gave them the money, said Mohammed,
and they released the Heteymy. I clothed him, and gave him
a waterskin, and dates and flour for the journey, and let him
go. A week later the poor man returned with ten reals, and
driving a fat sheep for me."

Mohammed had learned (of a neighbour) at Medina to be a
gunsmith, and in his hands was more than the Arabian ingenuity ; his humanity was ever ready. A Bedûwy in the fruit
harvest was bearing a sack of dates upon Mohammed's stairs;
his foot slipped, and the man had a leg broken. Mohammed,
with no more than his natural wit, which they call *háwas*, set
the bone, and took care of him until he recovered ; and now the
nomad every year brings him a thankoffering of his samn and
dried milk. Mohammed, another time, found one wounded and
bleeding to death : he sewed together the lips of his wound with
silken threads, and gave him a hot infusion of *saffron* to drink,
the quantity of a fenjeyn, two or three ounces, which he tells me
will stay all hæmorrhages. The bleeding ceased, and the man
recovered.

CHAPTER II

AMM MOHAMMED's father was a Kurdy of Upper Syria, from the village Beylàn, near Antioch (where their family yet remain); their name is in that language *Yelduz*, in Arabic Nejûmy, [of *nejm*, star]. The old Nejûmy was purveyor in Medina to the Bashy Bazûk. He brought up his provision convoys himself. by the dangerous passage from Yanbâ : the good man had wedded an Harb woman, and this delivered him from their nation ; moreover he was known upon the road, for his manly hospitable humour, to all the Beduw. He received, for his goods, the soldier's bills on their pay (ever in arrear), with some abatement ; which paper he paid to his merchants at the current rate. And he became a substantial trader in the Holy City.

He was a stern soldier and severe father ; and dying he left to his three sons, who were Bashy Bazûk troopers, no more than the weapons in their right hands and the horses ;—he had six or eight Syrian hackneys in his stable. He left them in the service of the Dowla, and bade them be valiant : he said that this might well suffice them in the world. All his goods and the house he gave to their mother, besides a maintenance to the other women ; and he appointed a near kinsman. to defend her from any recourse against her of his sons.—The horses they sold, and the price was soon wasted in riot by Mohammed, the elder of the young brethren : and then, to replenish his purse, he fell to the last unthrift of gaming. And having thus in a short novelty misspent himself, his time and his substance, he found himself bare : and he had made his brethren poor.

When the Bashy Bazûk were disbanded, Mohammed and Ahmed took up a humble service ; they became dustmen of the temple, and carried out the daily sweeping upon asses, for which they had eightpence daily wages. Besides they hired themselves as journeymen, at sixpence, to trim the palms, to water the soil, to dig, to build walls in the orchards. Weary at length of his illiberal tasks, Mohammed turned to his father's old friends, and borrowed of them an hundred reals. He became now a salesman of cotton wares in the sûk; but the daily gain was too little to maintain him; and in the end he was behind the hand more than four hundred reals.

With the few crowns which remained in his bag he bought a broken mill-horse, and went with her to Kheybar; where the beast browsing (without cost to him) in the wet valleys, was bye and bye healed; and he sold her for the double in Medina. Then he bought a cow at Kheybar, and he sold his cow in the city for double the money. And so going and coming, and beginning to prosper at Kheybar, he was not long after master of a cow, a horse, and a slave; which he sold in like manner, and more after them:—and he became a dealer in clothing and dates in the summer market at Kheybar. When in time he saw himself increased, he paid off two hundred reals of his old indebtedness. Twelve years he had been in this prosperity, and was now chief of the autumn salesmen (from Medina), and settled at Kheybar: for he had dwelt before partly at el-Hâyat and in Medina.

The year after the entering of the Dowla, Ahmed came to live with him. He could not thrive in the Holy City; where passing his time in the coffee houses, and making smoke of his little silver, he was fallen so low that Mohammed sent the real which paid for his brother's riding, in a returning hubt, to Kheybar; —where arriving in great languor he could but say, ' His consolation was, that his good brother should bury him!'—Mohammed, with the advantage of his summer trading, purchased every year (the villagers' right in) a béled for forty or fifty reals. He had besides three houses, bought with his money, and a mare worth sixty reals. His kine were seven, and when they had calved, he would sell some, and restore one hundred reals more to his old creditors. A few goats taken up years ago in his traffic with the nomads, were become a troop; an Heteymy client kept them with his own in the khála. Also his brother had prospered: "See, said Mohammed, he lives in his own house! Ahmed is now a welfaring trader, and has bought himself a béled or two." * * *

* * * Mohammed, though so worthy a man and amiable, was a soldier in his own household. When I blamed him he said, "I snib my wife because a woman must be kept in subjection, for else they will begin to despise their husbands." He chided

every hour his patient and diligent Beduwîa as *melaunat ej-jins*, ' of cursed kind.' He had a mind to take another wife more than this to his liking; for, he said, she was not fair; and in hope of more offspring, though she had thrice borne him children in four or five years,—but two were dead in the sickly air of Kheybar : "a wife, quoth he, should be come of good kin, and be liberal." Son and housewife, he chid them continually ; only to his guest, Amm Mohammed was a mild Arabian. Once I saw him—these are the uncivil manners of the town—rise to strike his son ! The Beduwîa ran between them to shelter her step-son, though to her the lad was not kind. I caught the Nejûmy's arm, yet his force bruised the poor woman ;—and " wellah, she said, smiling in her tears to see the tempest abated, thy hand Mohammed is heavy, and I think has broken some of my bones." Haseyn bore at all times his father's hard usage with an honest submission.

We passed-by one day where Haseyn ploughed a field, and, when I praised the son's diligence, Mohammed smiled ; but in that remembering his hard custom he said, " Nay, he is idle, he will play with the lads of the village and go a gunning "— Each morning when Haseyn returned to his father's suffa, his father began his chiding : " What ! thou good-for-nothing one, should a young man lie and daze till the sun rise over him ? " Hardly then his father suffered him to sit down a moment, to swallow the few dates in his hand ; but he rated him forth to his labour, to keep cows in the *Hálhal*, to dig, to plough, to bring in the ass, to seek his father's strayed mare, to go about the irrigation. Week, month and year, there was no day when Haseyn might sit at home for an hour ; but he must ever avoid out of his father's sight. Sometimes Mohammed sent him out, before the light, fasting, far over the Harra, with some of the village, for wood ; and the lad returned to break his fast at mid-afternoon. If any day his father found his son in the village before the sun was set, he pursued him with outrageous words, in the public hearing; " Graceless ! why come home so soon ? (or, why camest thou not sooner ?) Ha ! stand not, *thôr !* steer, ox, to gape upon me,—*enhaj !* remove out of my sight—thou canst run fast to play; now, *irkud ! ijrî !* run about thy business. Is it to such as thee I should give a wife to-year ? " *Haseyn :* " What wouldst thou have me to do, father ? " —" Out of my sight, *kòr !* Ullah punish that face ! " and he would vomit after him such ordures of the lips (from the sink of the soldiers' quarters at Medina), *akerût, kharra, térras,* or he dismissed his son with *laanat Ullah aleyk,* ' God's curse be with thee.' Haseyn returned to the house, to sup,

M

little before nightfall. Then his father would cry: "Ha!
unthrift, thou hast done nothing to-day but play in the Hálhal!
—he stares upon me like an ox, *bákr!*"—"Nay but father I
have done as thou badest me."—"Durst thou answer me,
chicken! now make haste to eat thy supper, sirra, and begone." Haseyn, a lad under age, ate not with his father and
the guest; but after them of that which remained, with his
father's jâra, whom he called, in their manner, his mother's
sister, *khâlaty*.

Doubtless Mohammed had loved Haseyn, whilst he was still
a child, with the feminine affection of the Arabs; and now he
thought by hardness, to make his son better. But his harsh
dealing and cries in the street made the good man to be
spoken against in the negro village; and for this there was
some little coldness betwixt him and his brother Ahmed.
But the citizen Ahmed was likewise a chider and striker,
and for such his Kheybar wife, Mohammed's housewife's sister,
had forsaken him: he had a town wife at Medina. Why, I
asked, was she not here to keep his house? *Ahmed:* "I bring
my wife to inhabit here! only these blacks can live at Kheybar,
or else, we had taken it from them long ago!" Ahmed's children
died in their youth, and he was unmindful of them · "Ahmed
has no feeling heart," said his brother Mohammed. I counselled
Amm Mohammed to have a better care for his son's health,
and let him be taught letters. "Ay, said his father, I would
that he may be able to read in the koran, against the time
of his marriage, for *then he ought to begin to say his prayers*
(like a man)."

'Ahmed he would say is half-witted, for he spends all that
ever he may get in his buying and selling, for kahwa and
dokhân. Mohammed [in such he resembled the smiths' caste]
used neither. "Is that a wise man, he jested, who will drink
coffee and tan his own bowels?" Yet Ahmed must remember,
amongst his brother's kindness, that the same was he who had
made him bare in the beginning: even now the blameworthy
brother's guilts were visited upon his head, and the generous
sinner went scatheless!—Mohammed, wallowing in the riot of
his ignorant youth at Medina, was requited with the evil which
was sown by the enemy of mankind. Years after he cured
himself with a violent specific, he called it in Arabic "rats'
bane", which had loosened his teeth; a piece of it that
Mohammed showed me was red lead. Though his strong nature
resisted so many evils and the malignity of the Kheybar fevers,
the cruel malady (only made inert) remained in him with
blackness of the great joints. And Ahmed living with him

at Kheybar and extending the indigent hand to his brother's
mess, received from Mohammed's beneficent hand the contagion
which had wasted him from the state of an hale man to his
present infirmity of body.

The rude negro villagers resorted to Ahmed, to drink coffee
and hear his city wisdom; and he bore it very impatiently that
his brother named him mejnûn in the town. " Sheykh Khalîl,
he said to me, how lookest thou upon sheykh Mohammed ? "
" I have not found a better man in all."—" But he is fond and
childish." When Ahmed sickened to death in the last pestilence Mohammed brought a bull to the door, and vowed a vow
to slaughter him, if the Lord would restore his brother. Ahmed
recovered: and then Mohammed killed the bull, his thankoffering, and divided the flesh to their friends;—and it was much
for a poor man! In these days Mohammed killed his yearly
sacrifice of a goat, which he vowed once when Haseyn was sick.
He brought up his goat when the beasts came home in the
evening; and first taking coals in an earthen censer he put on a
crumb of incense, and censed about the victim. I asked wherefore he did this? he answered: " That the sacrifice might be well
pleasing to Ullah; and do ye not so ?" He murmured prayers
turning the goat's head towards Mecca; and with his sword he
cut her throat. When he heard from me that this was not our
custom,—every man to kill his own sacrifice, he seemed to
muse in himself, that we must be but a faint-hearted people.

One early morning, his son going about the irrigation had
found a fox drowned in our well.—Haseyn flung it out upon the
land; and when we came thither, and could not at first sight
find this beast, " No marvel, quoth Mohammed, for what is
more sleighty than a fox? It may be he stiffened himself,
and Haseyn threw him out for dead:"—but we found the
hosenny cast under some nettles, dead indeed. From the snout
to the brush his fur was of such a swart slate colour as the
basalt figgera! only his belly was whitish. Amm Mohammed
drew the unclean carcase out of his ground, holding a foot in a
handful of palm lace.

I told the good man how, for a fox-brush sheykhs in my béled
use to ride furiously, in red mantles, upon horses—the best of
them worth the rent of some village—with an hundred yelling
curs scouring before them; and leaping over walls and dykes
they put their necks and all in adventure: and who is in at the
hosenny's death he is the gallant man. For a moment the
subtil Arabian regarded me with his piercing eyes as if he
would say, " Makest thou mirth of me ! " but soon again relenting

to his frolic humour, "Is this, he laughed, the chevying of
the fox?"—in which he saw no grace. And the good Medina
Moslem seemed to muse in spirit, 'Wherefore had the Lord
endowed the Yahûd and Nasâra with a superfluity of riches,
to so idle uses?' The wolf no less, he said, is a sly beast: upon
a time, he told me, as he kept his mother's goats at the Ferrâ
in his youth, and a (Harb) maiden was herding upon the hill-
side with him, he saw two wolves approach in the plain; then
he hid himself, to watch what they would do. At the foot of
the rocks the old wolf left his fellow; and the other lay down to
await him: that wolf ascended like an expert hunter, pausing,
and casting his eyes to all sides. The trooping goats went feeding at unawares among the higher crags; and Mohammed saw
the wolf take his advantage of ground and the wind, in such
wise that a man might not do better. 'Greylegs' chose out
one of the fattest bucks in the maiden's herd, and winding
about a rock he sprang and bit the innocent by the throat:—
Mohammed's shot thrilled the wolf's heart at the instant; and
then he ran in to cut the bleeding goat's throat (that the flesh
might be lawful meat). * * *

    * * * Mohammed was a perfect marksman. When we came
one morning to our well-ground, and he had his long matchlock
in his hand, there sat three crows upon a *sîdr* (apple-thorn)
tree, that cumbered our ears with their unlucky *krâ-krâ*. "The
cursed ones!" quoth Amm Mohammed, and making ready his
gun, he said he would try if his eyesight were failing: as he
levelled the crows flew up, but one sat on,—through which he
shot his bullet from a wonderful distance. Then he set up a
white bone on the clay wall, it was large as the palm of my
hand, and he shot his ball through the midst from an hundred
paces. He shot again, and his lead pierced the border of the
former hole! Mohammed gave the crow to some Kheyâbara,
who came to look on; and the negro villagers, kindling a fire of
palm sticks, roasted their bird whole, and parted it among them.
—"Like will to like! quoth the Nejûmy, and for them it is good
enough."

    He had this good shooting of an uncommon eyesight, which
was such, that very often he could see the stars at noonday:
his brother, he said, could see them, and so could many more.
He told me he had seen, by moments, three or four little stars
about one of the wandering stars, [Jupiter's moons!] I asked
then, "Sawest thou never a wandering star horned like the
moon?"—"Well, I have seen a star not always round, but like
a blade hanging in the heaven."—Had this vision been in

European star-gazers, the Christian generations had not so long waited for the tube of Galileo! [to lay the first stone—hewn without hands—of the indestructible building of our sciences]. Mohammed saw the moon always very large, and the whole body at once: he was become in his elder years long-sighted. * * *

* * * The remembrance of their younger brother, who had been slain by robbers as he came in a company from Medina to visit his brethren at Kheybar, was yet a burning anguish in Mohammed's breast;—until, with his own robust hands, he might be avenged for the blood! A ghrazzu of *Móngora*, Bíllî Aarab, and five times their number, had set upon them in the way: the younger Nejûmy, who was in the force of his years, played the lion amongst them, until he fell by a pistol shot. Móngora men come not to Kheybar; therefore Mohammed devised in his heart that in what place he might first meet with any tribesman of theirs, he would slay him. A year after, he finding one of them, the Nejûmy led him out, with some pretence, to a desert place; and said shortly to him there, "O thou cursed one! now will I slay thee with this sword."— "Akhs! said the Beduwy, let me speak, Sir, why wilt thou kill me? did I ever injure thee?"—"But thou diest to-day, for the blood of my brother, whom some of you in a ghrazzu have slain, in the way to Kheybar."—"The Lord is my witness! that I had no hand in it, for I was not among them."—"Yet shall thy blood be for his blood, since thou art one of them."— "Nay, hear me, Mohammed en-Nejûmy! and I will tell thee the man's name,—yea by Him which created us! for the man is known to me who did it; and he is one under my hand. Spare now my life, and as the Lord liveth I will make satisfaction, in constraining him that is guilty, and in putting-to of mine own, to the estimation of the midda, 800 reals." Mohammed, whose effort is short, could no more find in his cooling mood to slaughter a man that had never displeased him. He said then, that he forgave him his life, upon this promise to send him the blood-money. So they made the covenant, and Mohammed let him go.

—"That cursed Bellûwy! I never saw him more (quoth he), but now,—ha! wheresoever I may meet with any of them, I will kill him." I dissuaded him—"But there is a wild-fire in my heart, which cannot be appeased till I be avenged for the death of my brother."—"Were it not better if you take any of their tribesmen, to bind him until the blood be redeemed?" But Amm Mohammed could not hear this; the (South) Arabian custom is not to hold men over to ransom : but either they kill their prisoner outright, or, giving him a girby with water and God's curse, they let him go from them. "*Ruhh*, they will say, depart thou enemy! and perish, may it please God, in the khála." They think that a freeman is no chattel and cannot be made a booty. Women are not taken captive in the Arabian warfare, though many times a poor valiant man might come by a fair wife thus, without his spending for bride money.

Mohammed answered, "But now I am rich—the Lord be praised therefore, what need have I of money? might I but quench this heart-burning!"—"Why not forgive it freely, that the God of Mercies may forgive thee thy offences."—"Sayest thou this!—and sheykh Khalîl I did a thing in my youth, for which my heart reproaches me ; but thou who seemest to be a man of (religious) learning declare unto me, whether I be guilty of that blood.—The Bashy Bazûk rode [from Medina] against the Ateyba, and I was in the expedition. We took at first much booty : then the Beduw, gathering from all sides [they have many horsemen], began to press upon us, and our troop [the soldiers ride but slowly upon Syrian hackneys] abandoned the cattle. The Aarab coming on and shooting in our backs, there fell always some among us ; but especially there was a marksman who infested us. He rode upon a mare, radîf, and his fellow carried him out galloping on our flank and in advance : then that marksman alighted, behind some bush, and awaited the time to fire his shot. When he fired, the horseman, who had halted a little aloof, galloped to take him up : they galloped further, and the marksman loaded again. At every shot of his there went down horse or rider, and he killed my mare : then the aga bade his own slave take me up on his horse's croup. 'Thou O young man, said he, canst shoot, gallop forth with my lad and hide thee ; and when thou seest thy time, shoot that Ateyby, who will else be the death of us all.'—'Wellah Captain, I would not be left on my feet, the troop might pass from me.'—'That shall not be, only do this which I bid thee.'

"We hastened forward, said Mohammed, when those Beduins came by on the horse : we rode to some bushes, and there I dismounted and loaded carefully. The marksman rode beyond and went to shroud himself as before ; he alighted, and I was ready and shot at the instant. His companion who saw him wounded, galloped to take him up, and held him in his arms on the saddle, a little while ; and then cast him down,—he was dead! and the Arabs left pursuing us." I asked, ' Wherefore, if he doubted to kill an enemy in the field, had he taken service with the soldiery ? '—" Ah ! it was for tóma : I was yet young and ignorant."

Amm Mohammed had the blood of another such man-slaughter on his mind ; but he spoke of it without discomfort. In a new raid he pursued a Beduwy lad who was flying on foot, to take his matchlock from him,—which might be worth twelve reals ; the weled, seeing himself overtaken by a horseman of the Dowla, fired back his gun from the hip, and the ball passed through the calf of Mohammed's leg, who ' answered the melaun, as he said, *trang*' !—with a pistol shot : the young tribesman fell grovelling, beating his feet, and wallowed snatching the sand in dying throes. Mohammed's leg grew cold, and only then he felt himself to be wounded : he could not dismount, but called a friend to take up the Beduwy's gun for him. Mohammed's father (who was in the expedition) cut off his horseman's boot, which was full of blood, and bound up the hurt : and set him upon a provision camel and brought him home to Medina ; and his wound was whole in forty days.

He showed me also that a bone had been shot away of his left wrist ; that was in after years.—Amm Mohammed was coming up in a convoy of tradesmen from Medina, with ten camel-loads of clothing for Kheybar. As they journeyed, a strong ghrazzu of Harb met with them : then the passengers drove their beasts at a trot, and they themselves hasting as they could on foot, with their guns, fired back against the enemies They ran thus many miles in the burning sun, till their strength began to give out and their powder was almost spent. The Beduw had by this taken the most of the trades-men's loaded camels. Mohammed had quitted his own and the camel of a companion, when a ball shattered the bone of his left forearm. " I saw him, he said, who shot it ! I fired at the melaun again, and my bullet broke all his hand."—The Aarab called now to the Nejûmy (knowing him to be of their kindred), " What hò ! Mohammed son of our sister ! return without fear, and take that which is thine of these camels." He answered them, " I have delivered mine already," and they, " Go in peace."—I asked " How, being a perfect marksman, he had not, in an hour, killed all the pursuers."—' But know, Khalîl, that in this running and fighting we fire almost without taking sight." * * *

* * * The delay of Abdullah's messenger to Medina, was a cloud big with discomfort to me in this darkness of Kheybar. One morning I said to Amm Mohammed at our well-labour,

" What shall I do if ill news arrive to-day ?　Though you put
this sword in my hands, I could not fight against three
hundred."—" Sit we down, said the good man, let us consider,
Khalîl: and now thou hast said a word, so truly, it has made
my heart ache, and I cannot labour more ; *hŷak*, let us home
to the house,"—though half an hour was not yet spent.—He
was very silent, when we sat again in his suffa : and " Look, he
said, Khalîl, if there come an evil tiding from the Pasha, I will
redeem thee from Abdullah—at a price, wellah as a man buys
a slave ; it shall be with my mare, she is worth sixty reals, and
Abdullah covets her.　He is a melaun, a very cursed one,
Khalîl ;—and then I will mount thee with some Beduins, men
of my trust, and let thee go."—" I like not the felon looks of
Abdullah."—" I will go and sound him to-day ; I shall know
his mind, for he will not hide anything from me.　And Khalîl,
if I see the danger instant I will steal thee away, and put thee
in a covert place of the Harra, where none may find thee ; and
leave with thee a girby and dates, that thou mayest be there
some days in security, till news be come from Medina, and I
can send for thee, or else I may come to thee myself."

　　The day passed heavily : after supper the good man rose,
and taking his sword and his mantle, and leaving me in the
upper chamber, he said he would go and ' feel the pulse of the
melaun': he was abroad an hour.　The strong man entered
again with the resolute looks of his friendly worth : and sitting
down, as after a battle, he said, " Khalîl, there is no present
danger ; and Abdullah has spoken a good word for thee to-day,
—' Khalîl, it seems, does not fear Ullah ; he misdoubts me,
and yet I have said it already,—if the Pasha write to me to cut
off Khalîl's head, that I will mount him upon a thelûl and let
him go ; and we will set our seals to paper, and I will take
witness of all the people of Kheybar,—to what ? that Khalîl
broke out of the prison and escaped.—Tell Khalîl, I have not
forgotten es-Sham and Jidda ; and that I am not afraid of a
Pasha, who as he came in yesterday may be recalled to-morrow,
but of Stambûl, and wellah for my own life.' "

　　The post arrived in the night.　Mohammed heard of it,
and went over privily to Dakhîl's house, to enquire the news.
" There is only this, said the messenger, that the Pasha sends
now for his books."

　　On the morrow I was summoned to Abdullah, who bade
sheykh Sâlih read me the Medina governor's letter, where
only was written shortly, " Send all the stranger's books, and
the paper which he brought with him from Ibn Rashîd ; you
are to send the cow also."　The Siruân bade me go with his

hostess to a closet where my bags lay, and bring out the books and papers, and leave not one remaining. This I did, only asking him to spare my loose papers, since the Pasha had not expressly demanded them,—but he would not. I said, " I will also write to the Pasha ; and here is my English passport which I will send with the rest." "No!" he cried, to my astonishment, with a voice of savage rage ; and ' for another word he would break his chibûk over my head ', he cursed me, and cursed "the Engleys, and the father of the Engleys."—The villain would have struck me, but he feared the Nejûmy and Dakhîl, who were present. "Ha, it is thus, I exclaimed, that thou playest with my life ! " Then an hideous tempest burst from the slave's black mouth ; "This Nasrâny ! he yelled, who lives to-day only by my benefit, will chop words with me ; Oh wherefore with my pistol, wherefore, I say, did I not blow out his brains at the first?—wellah as ever I saw thee ! "

Amm Mohammed as we came home said, " Abdullah is a melaun indeed ; and, but we had been there, thou hadst not escaped him to-day."—How much more brutish I thought in my heart had been the abandonment of the Levantine consulate ! that, with a light heart, had betrayed my life to so many cruel deaths !

Even Amm Mohammed heard me with impatience, when I said to him that we were not subject to the Sultan.—The Sultan, who is *Khàlif* (calif), successor to the apostle of Ullah, is the only lawful lord, they think, of the whole world ; and all who yield him no obedience are *âsyîn*, revolted peoples and rebels. The good man was sorry to hear words savouring, it seemed to him, of sedition, in the mouth of Khalîl. He enquired, had we learned yet in our (outlying) countries to maintain bands of trained soldiery, such as are the askars of the Sooltàn ? I answered, that our arts had armed and instructed the Ottoman service, and that without us they would be naked. " It is very well, he responded, that the Engleys, since they be not âsyîn, should labour for the Sooltàn."

When I named the countries of the West, he enquired if there were not Moslemîn living in some of them. I told him, that long ago a rabble of Moghrebies had invaded and possessed themselves of the florid country of *Andalûs.*—Andalusîa was a glorious province of Islam : the Arabian plant grew in the Titanic soil of Europe to more excellent temper and stature ; and there were many *bulbul* voices among them, in that land of the setting sun, gladdened with the genial wine. Yet the Arabs decayed in the fruition of that golden soil, and the robust nephews of them whom their forefathers had dispos-

M*

sessed, descending from the mountains, reconquered their own country. As I said this, "Wellah guwiyîn! then they must be a strong people, answered Amm Mohammed. Thou, Khalîl, hast visited many lands; and wander where thou wilt, since it is thy list, only no more in the Peninsula of the Arabs (*Jezîrat el-Arab*). Thou hast seen already that which may suffice thee; and what a lawless waste land it is! and perilous even for us who were born there; and what is this people's ignorance and their intolerance of every other religion. Where wilt thou be when God have delivered thee out of these troubles? that if ever I come into those parts I might seek thee. Tell me where to send my letter, if ever I would write to thee; and if I inscribe it *Sheykh Khalîl, Béled el-Engleys*, will that find thee?"

"Here is paper, a reed, and ink: Abdullah would not have thee write to the Pasha, but write thou, and I will send the letter by Dakhîl who will not deny me, and he returns to-morrow. See, in writing to the Pasha, that thou lift him up with many high-sounding praises."—"I shall write but plainly, after my conscience."—"Then thou art mejnûn, and that conscience is not good, which makes thee afraid to help thyself in a danger."—"Tell me, is the Pasha a young man of sudden counsels, or a spent old magistrate of Stambûl?"—"He is a grey-beard of equitable mind, a reformer of the official service, and for such he is unwelcome to the ill-deserving. Yet I would have thee praise him, for thus must we do to obtain anything; the more is the pity." I wrote with my pencil in English,—for Mohammed told me there are interpreters at Medina. I related my coming down with the Haj, from Syria, to visit Medáin Sâlih; and, that I had since lived with the Beduw, till I went, after a year, to Hâyil; from whence Ibn Rashîd, at my request, had sent me hither. I complained to the Pasha-governor of this wrongful detention at Kheybar, in spite of my passport from a Wâly of Syria; also certain Beduins of the Dowla coming in, who knew me, had witnessed to the truth of all that I said. I demanded therefore that I might proceed upon my journey and be sent forward with sure persons.

I was sitting in the soldiers' kahwa, when Abdullah wrote his new letter to the Pasha, "My humble duty to your lordship: I send now the stranger's books and papers. I did send the cow to your lordship by some Aarab going down to Medina; but the cow broke from them, and ran back to Kheybar: she is now sick, and therefore I may not yet send her."—"Hast thou written all this, sheykh Sâlih?—he will not be much longer, please Ullah, Bashat el-Medina; for they say another is coming." No man hearing his fable could forbear laughing; only the Siruân looked sadly upon it, for the cow yielded him every day a bowlful of milk, in this low time at Kheybar. Abdullah set his seal to the letters, and delivered them to Dakhîl, who departed before noon. Amm Mohammed, as he was going, put a piece of silver (from me) in Dakhîl's hand, and cast my letter, with my British passport, into the worthy man's budget, upon his back, who feigned thus that he did not see it: the manly villager was not loath to aid a stranger (and a public guest,) whom he saw oppressed in his village by the criminal tyranny of Abdullah.

His inditing the letter to Medina had unsettled Abdullah's brains, so that he fell again into his fever: " Help me quickly! he cries, where is thy book, sheykh Sâlih; and you Beduins sitting here, have ye not some good remedies in the desert?" Sâlih pored over his wise book, till he found him a new caudle and enchantment.—Another time I saw Sâlih busy to cure a mangy thelûl; he sat with a bowl of water before him, and mumbling thereover he spat in it, and mumbled solemnly and spat many times; and after a half hour of this work the water was taken to the sick beast to drink.—Spitting (a despiteful civil defilement) we have seen to be some great matter in their medicine.—Is it, that they spit thus against the malicious jân? Parents bid their young children spit upon them: an Arabian father will often softly say to the infant son in his arms, " Spit upon bâbu! spit thou, my darling."

CHAPTER III

MANY night hours when we could not sleep, I spent in discoursing with my sick Galla comrade, the poor friendly-minded
Amân.   When I enquired of the great land of the Gallas,
" *El-Hábash*," quoth he, is the greatest empire of the werld ;
for who is there a Sooltàn to be compared with the Sooltàn
of el-Hábash ! "—" Well, we found but a little king, on this
side, when the Engleys took his beggarly town, *Mágdala.*"
—Amân bethought him, that in his childhood when he was
brought down with the slave drove they had gone by this
Mágdala.   ' That king, he said, could be no more than a governor
or pasha ; for the great Sooltàn, whose capital is at the distance
of a year's journey, where he inhabits a palace of ivory.   The
governors and lieutenants of his many provinces gather an
imperial tribute,—that is at no certain time ; but as it were
once in three or four years.'

This fable is as much an article of faith with all the Gallas,
as the legend which underlies our most beliefs ; and may rise
in their half-rational conscience of a sort of inarticulate argument :—' Every soil is subject to rulers, there is therefore a
Ruler of Galla-land,—Galla-land the greatest country in all
the world ; but the Sultan of the greatest land is the greatest
Sultan : also a Sultan inhabits richly, therefore that greatest
Sultan inhabits the riches of the (African) world, and his palace
is all of ivory !'   Amân said, ' The country is not settled in villages ; but every man's house is a round dwelling of sticks and
stubble, large and well framed, in the midst of his ground,
which he has taken up of the hill-lands about him.   Such faggot-
work may stand many years [; but is continually in danger to
be consumed by fire, in a moment].   They break and sow as
much soil as they please ; and their grain is not measured for
the abundance.   They have great wealth of kine, so that he is
called a poor man whose stock is only two or three hundred.

Their oxen are big-bodied, and have great horns : the Gallas milk only so many of their cattle as may suffice them for drinking and for butter; they drink beer also, which they make of their plenty of corn. Though it be a high and hilly land, a loin-cloth [as anciently in the Egyptian and Ethiopian countries] is their only garment; but such is the equal temper of the air that they need no more. The hot summer never grieves them; in the winter they feel none other than a wholesome freshness. In their country are lions, but Ullah's mercy has slaked the raging of those terrible wild beasts ; for *the lions sicken every other day with fever, and else they would destroy the world !* The lions slaughter many of their cattle ; but to mankind they do no hurt or rarely. A man seeing a lion in the path should hold his way evenly without faintness of heart, and so pass by him ; not turning his eyes to watch the lion, for that would waken his anger. There are elephants and giraffes ; their horses are of great stature.'—I have heard from the slave drivers that a horse may be purchased in the Galla country for (the value of) a real !

'In Galla-land there is no use of money; the people, he said, have no need to buy anything : they receive foreign trifles from the slave dealers, as beads and the little round in-folding tin mirrors. Such are chiefly the wares which the drivers bring with them,—besides salt, which only fails them in that largess of heaven which is in their country A brick of salt, the load of a light porter, is the price of a slave among them. That salt is dug at Suâkim (by the Red Sea, nearly in face of Jidda), six months distant. The Gallas are hospitable to strangers, who may pass, where they will, through their country. When there is warfare between neighbour tribes, the stranger is safe in what district he is; but if he would pass beyond, he must cross the infested border, at his peril, to another tribe ; and he will again be in surety among them. The Galla country is very open and peaceable; and at what cottage the stranger may alight, he is received to their plenteous hospitality. They ask him whether he would drink of their ale or of their milk ? Some beast is slaughtered, and they will give him the flesh, which he can cook for himself, [since the Gallas are raw-flesh eaters].

' They have wild coffee trees in their country, great as oaks ; and that coffee is the best: the bean is very large. They take up the fallen berries from the ground, and roast them, with samn. Coffee is but for the elders' drinking, and that seldom : they think it becomes not their young men to use the pithless caudle drink. The women make butter, rocking the milk in the

shells of great gourds : they store all their drink in such vessels.
Grain-gold may be seen in the sand of the torrents ; but there
are none who gather it. Among them [as in Arabia] is a smiths'
caste ; the Galla people mingle not with them in wedlock.
The smiths receive payment for their labour, in cattle.' I did
not ascertain from Amân what is their religion : ' he could not
tell ; they pray, he said, and he thought that they turn themselves toward Mecca.' He could not remember that they had
any books among them.

Amân had been stolen, one afternoon as he kept his father's
neat, by men from a neighbour tribe. The raiders went the
same night to lodge in a cottage, where lived a widow woman.
When the good woman had asked the captive boy of his parentage, she said to the guests, that the child's kindred were her
acquaintance, and she would redeem him with an hundred oxen ;
but they would not. A few days later he was sold to the slave
dealer : and began to journey in the drove of boys and girls, to
be sold far off in a strange land. These children with the captive young men and maidens march six months, barefoot, to the
Red Sea : the distance may be 1200 miles. Every night they
come to a station of the slave-drivers, where they sup of flesh
meat and the country beer. Besides the aching weariness of
that immense foot-journey, they had not been mishandled.

' Of what nation were the slave drivers ? '—this he could not
answer : they were white men, and in his opinion Moslemîn ;
but not Arabians, since they were not at home at *Jidda*, which
was then, *and is now, the staple town of African slavery, for the
Turkish Empire :—Jidda where are Frankish consuls !* But you
shall find these worthies, in the pallid solitude of their palaces,
affecting (great Heaven !) the simplicity of new-born babes,—
they will tell you, they are not aware of it ! But I say again,
in your ingenuous ears, *Jidda is the staple town of the Turkish
slavery,* OR ALL THE MOSLEMÎN ARE LIARS.

— At length they came down to the flood of the Nile, which
lay in a great deep of the mountains, and were ferried over upon
a float of reeds and blown goat-skins. Their journey, he said,
is so long because of the hollowness of the country. For they
often pass valley-deeps, where, from one brow, the other seems
not very far off ; yet in descending and ascending they march
a day or two to come thither. Their aged men in Galla-land
use to say, that ' the Nile comes streaming to them in deep
crooked valleys, from bare and unknown country many months
distant.'

"Amân, when I am free, go we to Galla-land ! it will not be
there as here, where for one cow we would give our left hands ! "

The poor Galla had raised himself upon his elbow, with a melancholy distraction, and smiling he seemed to see his country again : he told me his own name in the Galla tongue, when he was a child, in his Galla home. I asked if no anger was left in his heart, against those who had stolen and sold his life to servitude, in the ends of the earth. " Yet one thing, sheykh Khalîl, has recompensed me,—that I remained not in ignorance with the heathen !—Oh the wonderful providence of Ullah ! whereby I am come to this country of the Apostle, and to the knowledge of the religion ! Ah, mightest thou be partaker of the same ! —yet I know that is all of the Lord's will, and this also shall be, in God's good time ! " He told me that few Gallas ever return to their land, when they have recovered their freedom.— " And wilt thou return, Amân ? " " Ah ! he said, my body is grown now to another temper of the air, and to another manner of living."

There is continual warfare on the Galla border with the (hither) Abyssinians ; and therefore *the Abyssinians suffer none to go over with their fire-arms to the Gallas*. The Gallas are warlike, and armed with spear and shield they run furiously upon their enemies in battle.—In the Gallas is a certain haughty gentleness of bearing, even in land of their bondage.

Amân told me the tale of his life, which slave and freed-man he had passed in the Hejâz. He was sometime at Jidda, a custom-house watchman on board ships lying in the road ; the most are great barques carrying Bengal rice, with crews of that country under English captains. Amân spoke with good remembrance of the hearty hospitality of the " Nasâra " seamen. One day, he watched upon a steamship newly arrived from India, and among her passengers was a " Nasrâny ", who " sat weeping—weeping, and his friends could not appease him ". Amân, when he saw his time, enquired the cause ; and the stranger answered him afflictedly, " Eigh me ! I have asked of the Lord, that I might visit the City of His Holy House, and become a Moslem : is not Mecca yonder ? Help me, thou good Moslem, that I may repair thither, and pray in the sacred places !—but ah ! these detain me." When it was dark Amân hailed a wherry ; and privily he sent this stranger to land, and charged the boatman for him.

The Jidda waterman set his fare on shore ; and saw him mounted upon an ass, for Mecca,—one of those which are driven at a run, in a night-time, the forty and five miles or more betwixt the port town and the Holy City.—When the new day was dawning, the " Frenjy " entered Mecca ! Some citizens, the first he met, looking earnestly upon the stranger stayed to

ask him, " Sir, what brings thee hither ?—being it seems a
Nasrâny !" He answered them, " I was a Christian, and I have
required it of the Lord,—that I might enter this Holy City and
become a Moslem !" Then they led him, with joy, to their
houses, and circumcised the man : and that renegade or traveller
was years after dwelling in Mecca, and in Medina.—Amân
thought his godfathers had made a collection for him ; and that
he was become a tradesman in the sûk.—Who may interpret
this and the like strange tales ? which we may often hear related
among them !

Amân drank the strong drink which was served out with his
rations on shipboard; and in his soldiering life he made (secretly)
with his comrade, a spirituous water, letting boiled rice fer-
ment : the name of it is *subia*, and in the Hejâz heat they think
it very refreshing. But the unhappy man thus continually
wounding his conscience, in the end had corroded his infirm
health also, past remedy.—When first he received the long
arrears of his pay, he went to the slave dealers in Jidda, and
bought himself a maiden, of his own people, to wife, for fifty
dollars.—They had but a daughter between them : and another
time, when he removed from Mecca to Jidda, the child fell
from the camel's back ; and of that hurt she died. Amân
seemed not, in the remembrance, to feel a father's pity ! His
wife wasted all that ever he brought home, and after that he put
her away : then she gained her living as a seamstress, but died
within a while ;—" the Lord, he said, have mercy upon her !"
—When next he received his arrears, he remained one year idle
at Mecca, drinking and smoking away his slender thrift in the
coffee houses, until nothing was left ; and then he entered this
Ageyl service.

The best moments of his life, up and down in the Hejâz, he
had passed at Tâyif. " Eigh ! how beautiful (he said) is et-
Tâyif !" He spoke with reverent affection of the Great-sherîf
[he died about this time], a prince of a nature which called forth
the perfect good will of all who served him. Amân told with
wonder of the sherîf's garden [the only garden in Desert
Arabia !] at Tâyif, and of a lion there in a cage, that was meek
only to the sherîf. All the Great-sherîf's wives, he said, were
Galla women ! He spoke also of a certain beneficent widow at
Tâyif, whose bountiful house stands by the wayside ; where she
receives all passengers to the Arabian hospitality.

Since his old " uncle " was dead, Amân had few more hopes
for this life,—he was now a broken man at the middle age ;
and yet he hoped in his " brother ". This was no brother by

nature, but a negro once his fellow servant : and such are by
the benign custom of the Arabian household accounted brethren.
He heard that his negro brother, now a freed-man, was living at
Jerusalem ; and he had a mind to go up to Syria and seek him,
if the Lord would enable him. Amân was dying of a slow con-
sumption and a vesical malady, of the great African continent,
little known in our European art of medicine :—and who is
infirm at Kheybar, he is likely to die. This year there remained
only millet for sick persons' diet : " The [foster] God forgive
me, said poor Amân, that I said it is as wood to eat." With the
pensive looks of them who see the pit before their feet, in the
midst of their days, he sat silent, wrapt in his mantle, all day in
the sun, and drank tobacco.—One's life is full of harms, who is
a sickly man, and his fainting heart of impotent ire, which
alienates, alas ! even the short human kindness of the few
friends about him. At night the poor Galla had no covering
from the cold ; then he rose every hour and blew the fire and
drank tobacco.

The wives of the Kheyâbara were very charitable to the poor
soldiery : it is a hospitable duty of the Arabian hareem towards
all lone strangers among them. For who else should fill a man's
girby at the spring, or grind his corn for him, and bring in firewood ? None offer them silver for this service, because it is
of their hospitality. Only a good wife serving some welfaring
stranger, as Ahmed, is requited once or twice in the year with
a new gown-cloth and a real or two, which he may be willing to
give her. Our neighbour's wife, a goodly young negress, served
the sick Amân, only of her womanly pity, and she sat ofttimes
to watch by him in our suffa. Then *Jummàr* (this was her
name) gazed upon me with great startling eyes ; such a strangeness and terror seemed to her to be in this name 'Nasrâny'!
One day she said, at length, *Andakom hareem, fî?* ' be there
women in your land ? '—" Ullah ! (yes forsooth), mothers,
daughters and wives ;—am I not the son of a woman : or dost
thou take me, silly woman, for *weled eth-thîb,* a son of the wolf ?"
—" Yes, yes, I thought so : but wellah, Khalîl, be the Nasâra
born as we ? ye rise not then—*out of the sea !* "—When I told
this tale to Amm Mohammed he laughed at their fondness.
" So they would make thee, Khalîl, another kind of God's
creature, the sea's offspring ! this foolish people babble without
understanding themselves when they say SEA : their ' sea ' is
they could not tell what kind of monster ! " And Jummàr
meeting us soon after in the street, must hang her bonny floc
head to the loud mirth of Amm Mohammed : for whom I was
hereafter *weled eth-thîb ;* and if I were any time unready at his

dish, he would say pleasantly, "Khalîl, thou art not then *weled eth-thîb !*" A bystander said one day, as I was rolling up a flag of rock from our mine, *Ma fi hail,* 'there is no strength.' Mohammed answered, "Nevertheless we have done somewhat, for there helped me the son of the wolf." "I am no wolfling, I exclaimed, but *weyladak,* a son of thine." "Wellah! answered the good man, surprised and smiling, thou art my son indeed."

Kurds, Albanians, Gallas, Arabs, Negroes, Nasrâny, we were many nations at Kheybar. One day a Beduwy oaf said at Abdullah's hearth, "It is wonderful to see so many diversities of mankind! but what be the Nasâra?—for since they are not of Islam, they cannot be of the children of Adam." I answered, "There was a prophet named Noah, in whose time God drowned the world; but Noah with his sons Sem, Ham, Yâfet, and their wives, floated in a vessel: they are the fathers of mankind. The Kurdies, the Turks, the Engleys, are of Yâfet; you Arabs are children of Sem; and you the Kheyâbara, are of Ham, and this Bîshy."—"Akhs! (exclaimed the fellow) and thou speak such a word again— !" *Abdullah:* "Be not sorry, for I also (thy captain) am of Ham." The Bîshy, a negro Ageyly, was called by the name of his country (in el-Yémen) the *W. Bîshy* [in the opinion of some Oriental scholars "the river Pison" of the Hebrew scriptures, *v. Die alte Geographie Arabiens*]. It is from thence that the sherîf of Mecca draws the most of his (negro) band of soldiery,—called therefore *el-Bîshy,* and they are such as the Ageyl. This Yémany spoke nearly the Hejâz vulgar, in which is not a little base metal; so that it sounds churlish-like in the dainty ears of the inhabitants of Nejd.

We heard again that Muharram lay sick; and said Abdullah, "Go to him, Khalîl; he was much helped by your former medicines."—I found Muharram bedrid, with a small quick pulse: it was the second day he had eaten nothing; he had fever and visceral pains, and would not spend for necessary things. I persuaded him to boil a chicken, and drink the broth with rice, if he could not eat; and gave him six grains of rhubarb with one of laudanum powder, and a little quinine, to be taken in the morning.

The day after I was not called. I had been upon the Harra with Amm Mohammed, and was sitting at night in our chamber with Amân: we talked late, for, the winter chillness entering at our open casement, we could not soon sleep. About midnight we were startled by an untimely voice; one called loudly in the corner of our place, to other askars who lodged there,

'Abdullah bade them come to him.' All was horror at Kheybar,
and I thought the post might be arrived from Medina, with an
order for my execution. I spoke to Amân, who sat up blowing
the embers, to lean out of the casement and enquire of them
what it was. Amân looking out said, *Ey khábar, yâ,* 'Ho,
there, what tidings?' They answered him somewhat, and
said Amân, withdrawing his head, " *Ullah, yurhamhu,* 'May
the Lord have mercy upon him,'—they say Muharram is dead,
and they are sent to provide for his burial, and for the custody
of his goods.' —" I have lately given him medicines! and what
if this graceless people now say, ' Khalîl killed him '; if any of
them come now, we will make fast the door, and do thou lend
me thy musket."—" Khalîl, said the infirm man sitting at the
fire, trust in the Lord, and if thou have done no evil, fear not:
what hast thou to do with this people? they are hounds, apes,
oxen, and their hareem are witches: but lie down again and
sleep."

I went in the morning to the soldiers' kahwa and found
only the Siruân, who then arrived from Muharram's funeral.
"What is this? Khalîl, cries he, Muharram is dead, and they
say it was thy medicines: now, if thou know not the medicines,
give no more to any man.—They say that you have killed him,
and they tell me Muharram said this before he died. [I afterwards ascertained from his comrades that the unhappy man
had not spoken at all of my medicines.] Mohammed el-Kurdy
says that after you had given him the medicine you rinsed
your hands in warm water." I exclaimed in my haste,
"*Mohammed lies!* "—a perilous word. In the time of my being
in Syria, a substantial Christian was violently drawn by the
Mohammed people of Tripoli, where he lived, before the kâdy,
only for this word, uttered in the common hearing; and he had
but spoken it of his false Moslem servant, whose name was
Mohammed. The magistrate sent him, in the packet boat, to
be judged at Beyrût; but we heard that in his night passage,
of a few hours, the Christian had been secretly thrust over-
board!—Abdullah looked at me with eyes which said 'It is
death to blaspheme the Néby!'—"Mohammed, I answered,
the Kurdy, lies, for he was not present."—"I cannot tell,
Khalîl, Abdullah said at last with gloomy looks, the man is
dead; then give no more medicines to any creature;" and the
askars now entering, he said to them, "Khalîl is an angry man,
for this cause of Muharram;—speak we of other matter."

There came up Mohammed the Kurdy and the Egyptian:
they had brought over the dead and buried man's goods, who
yesterday at this time was living amongst them!—his pallet,

his clothes, his red cap, his water-skin. Abdullah sat down to the sale of them; also, 2½ reals were said to be owing for the corpse-washing and burying. Abdullah enquired, 'What of Muharram's money? for all that he had must be sent to his heirs; and has he not a son in Albania?' The dead man's comrades swore stoutly, that they found not above ten reals in his girdle. *Sirûr:* "He had more than fifty! Muharram was rich." The like said others of them (Amân knew that he had as much as seventy reals). *Abdullah:* "Well, I will not enter into nice reckonings;—enough, if we cannot tell what has become of his money.—Who will buy this broidered coat, that is worth ten reals at Medina?" One cried "Half a real." *Sirûr:* "Three quarters!" *A villager:* "I will give two krûsh more." *Abdullah:* "Then none of you shall have this; I reserve it for his heirs. What comes next? a pack of cards:— (and he said with his Turkish smiles) Muharram whilst he lived won the most of his money thus, mesquin!—who will give anything?—I think these were made in Khalîl's country. The picture upon them [a river, a wood, and a German church] is what, Khalîl? Will none buy?—then Khalîl shall have them." —"I would not touch them." They were bidding for the sorry old gamester's wretched blanket and pallet, and contending for his stained linen when I left them.

If a deceased person be named in the presence of pious Mohammedans they will respond, 'May the Lord have mercy upon him!' but meeting with Ahmed in the path by the burial ground, he said, "Muharram is gone, and he owed me two reals, may Ullah confound him!"—I was worn to an extremity; and now the malevolent barked against my life for the charity which I had shown to Muharram! Every day Aly the ass brayed in the ass's ears of Abdullah, 'It was high time to put to death the adversary of the religion, also his delaying [to kill me] was sinful:' and he alleged against me the death of Muharram. I saw the Siruân's irresolute black looks grow daily more dangerous: "Ullah knows, I said to the Nejûmy, what may be brooding in his black heart: a time may come when, the slave's head turning, he will fire his pistols on me." —"Thou camest here as a friend of the Dowla, and what cause had this ass-in-office to meddle at all in thy matter, and to make thee this torment? Wellah if he did me such wrong, since there is none other remedy in our country, I would kill him and escape to the Ferrâ." Amm Mohammed declared publicly 'His own trust in sheykh Khalîl to be such that if I bade him drink even a thing venomous, he would drink it;' and the like said Amân, who did not cease to use my remedies. The better

sort of Kheyâbara now said, that 'Muharram was not dead of
my medicines, but come to the end of his days, he departed by
the decree of Ullah.' * * *

* * * Mohammed had ridden westward, in the Bashy Bazûk
expeditions as far as Yanba; he had ridden in Nejd with
Turkish troops to the Waháby capital, er-Riâth. That was for
some quarrel of the sherîf of Mecca : they lay encamped before
the Nejd city fifteen days, and if Ibn Saûd had not yielded their
demands, they would have besieged him. The army marched
over the khála, with cannon, and provision camels ; and he said
they found water in the Beduin wells for all the cattle, and to
fill their girbies. The Arabian deserts may be passed by armies
strong enough to disperse the resistance of the frenetic but
unwarlike inhabitants; but they should not be soldiers who
cannot endure much and live of a little. The rulers of Egypt
made war twenty years in Arabia ; and they failed finally because they came with great cost to possess so poor a country.
The Roman army sent by Augustus under Aelius Gallus to
make a prey of the chimerical riches of Arabia Felix was
11,000 men, Italians and allies. They marched painfully over
the waterless wastes six months ! wilfully misled, as they supposed, by the Nabateans of Petra, their allies. In the end of
their long marches they took Nejrân by assault : six camps
further southward they met with a great multitude of the
barbarous people assembled against them, at a brookside. In
the battle there fell *many thousands* of the Arabs ! and of the
Romans and allies two soldiers. The Arabians fought, as men
unwont to handle weapons, with slings, swords and lances and
two-edged hatchets. The Romans, at their furthest, were only
two marches from the frankincense country. In returning
upwards the general led the feeble remnant of his soldiery,
in no more than sixty matches, to the port of el-Héjr. The
rest perished of misery in the long and terrible way of the
wilderness : only seven Romans had fallen in battle !—Surely
the knightly Roman deserved better than to be afterward dis-
graced, because he had not fulfilled the dreams of Cæsar's avarice !
Europeans, deceived by the Arabs' loquacity, have in every age a
fantastic opinion of this unknown calamitous country.

Those Italians looking upon that dire waste of Nature in
Arabia, and grudging because they must carry water upon
camels, laid all to the perfidy of their guides. The Roman
general found the inhabitants of the land ' A people unwarlike,
half of them helping their living by merchandise, and half of
them by robbing ' [such they are now]. Those ancient Arabs

wore a cap, and let their locks grow to the full length: the most of them cut the beard, leaving the upper lip, others went unshaven.—"The nomads living in tents of hair-cloth are troublesome borderers," says Pliny, [as they are to-day!] Strabo writing from the mouth of Gallus himself, who was his friend and Prefect of Egypt, describes so well the Arabian desert, that it cannot be bettered. "It is a sandy waste, with only few palms and pits of water: the thorn [acacia] and the tamarisk grow there; the wandering Arabs lodge in tents, and are camel graziers." * * *

* * * The Siruân had bound Amm Mohammed for me, since there was grown this fast friendship between us, saying, "I leave him in thy hands, and of thee I shall require him again;" —and whenever the Nejûmy went abroad I was with him. The villagers have many small kine, which are driven every morning three miles over the figgera, to be herded in a large bottom of wet pasture, the *Hálhal*, a part of W. Jellâs. I went one day thither with Amm Mohammed, to dig up off-sets in the thickets of unhusbanded young palms. The midst of the valley is a quagmire and springs grown up with canes. The sward is not grass, though it seem such, but a minute herb of rushes. This is the pasture of their beasts; though the brackish rush grass, swelling in the cud, is unwholesome for any but the home-born cattle. The small Yémen kine, which may be had at Medina for the price of a good sheep, will die here: even the cattle of el-Hâyat, bred in a drier upland and valued at twelve to fifteen reals, may not thrive at Kheybar; and therefore a good Kheybar cow is worth thirty reals. In the season of their passage plenty of water-fowl are seen in the Hálbal, and in summertime partridges. In these thickets of dry canes the village herd-boys cut their double pipes, *mizamîr*. Almost daily some head of their stock is lost in the thicket, and must be abandoned when they drive the beasts home at evening; yet they doubt not to find it on the morrow. The village housewives come barefoot hither in the hot sun to gather palm sticks (for firing). Mohammed cut down some young palm stems, and we dined of the heart or pith-wood, *jummâr*, which is very wholesome; the rude villagers bring it home for a sweetmeat, and call it, in their negro gibes, 'Kheybar cheese.' Warm was the winter sun in this place, and in the thirsty heat Amm Mohammed shewed me a pit of water;—but it was full of swimming vermin and I would not drink. "Khalîl, said he, we are not

so nice," and with *bismillah!* he laid himself down upon his manly breast and drank a hearty draught. In the beginning of the Hálhal we found scored upon a rock in ancient Arabic letters the words *Mahál el-Wái,* which was interpreted by our (unlettered) coffee-hearth scholars 'the cattle marches'. A little apart from the way, is a site upon the figgera yet named *Súk er-Ruwálla.* There is a spring of their name in Medina; Henakíeh pertained of old to that Annezy tribe, (now far in the north): and 'there be even now some households of their lineage'. Besides kine, there are no great cattle at Kheybar; the few goats were herded under the palms by children or geyatîn.

Another day we went upon the Harra for wood. Amm Mohammed, in his hunting, had seen some sere sammara trees; they were five miles distant. We passed the figgera in the chill of the winter morning and descended to the W Jellás; and Haseyn came driving the pack-ass. In the bottom were wide plashes of ice-cold water. "It will cut your limbs, said Mohammed, you cannot cross the water." I found it so indeed; but they were hardened to these extremities, and the lad helped me over upon his half-drowned beast. Mohammed rode forward upon his mare, and Haseyn drove on under me with mighty strokes, for his father beckoned impatiently. To linger in such places they think perilous, and at every blow the poor lad shrieked to his *jáhash* some of the infamous injuries which his father commonly bestowed upon himself; until we came to the acacia trees. We hurled heavy Harra stones against those dry trunks, and the tree-skeletons fell before us in ruins:—then dashing stones upon them, we beat the timber bones into lengths; and charged our ass and departed.

We held another way homeward, by a dry upland bottom, where I saw ancient walling of field enclosures, under red trachyte bergs, *Umm Rúkaba,* to the Húrda. The Húrda is good corn land, the many ancient wells are sunk ten feet to the basalt rock; the water comes up sweet and light to drink, but is lukewarm. Here Mohammed had bought a well and corn plot of late, and yesterday he sent hither two lads from the town, to drive his two oxen, saying to them, "Go and help Haseyn in the Húrda." They labour with diligence, and eat no more than the dates of him who bids them; at night they lie down wrapped in their cloaks upon the damp earth, by a great fire of sammara in a booth of boughs, with the cattle. They remain thus three days out, and the lads drive day and night, by turns. The land-holders send their yokes of oxen to this three-days' labour every fifteen days. * * *

* * * My Galla comrade had been put by Abdullah in the
room of the deceased Muharram at Umm Kîda;—for Amân, the
freedman of an Albanian petty officer, was accounted of among
them as an Albanian deputy petty officer. I returned now at
night to an empty house. Abdullah was a cursed man, I might
be murdered whilst I slept; and he would write to the Pasha,
'The Nasrâny, it may please your lordship, was found slain
such a morning in his lodging, and by persons unknown.' In
all the Kheybar cottages is a ladder and open trap to the house-
top; and you may walk from end to end of all the house rows
by their terrace roofs, and descend by day or by night at the
trap, into what house-chamber you please : thus neighbours
visit neighbours. I could not pass the night at the Nejûmy's;
for they had but their suffa, so that his son Haseyn went to
sleep abroad in a hired chamber, with other young men in the
like case. Some householders spread matting over their trap,
in the winter night; but this may be lifted without rumour,
and they go always barefoot. There were evil doers not far off,
for one night a neighbour's chickens which roosted upon our
house terrace had been stolen ; the thief, Amân thought, must
be our former Galla comrade : it was a stranger, doubtless,
for these black villagers eat no more of their poultry than the
eggs !—This is a superstition of the Kheyâbara, for which they
themselves cannot render a reason; and besides they will not
eat leeks !

Another day whilst I sat in Ahmed's house there came up
Mohammed the Kurdy to coffee. The Kurdy spoke to us with
a mocking scorn of Muharram's death :—in his fatal afternoon,
"the sick man said, 'Go Mohammed to Abdullah, for I feel
that I am dying and I have somewhat to say to him.'—' Ana
nejjâb, am I thy post-runner? if it please thee to die, what is
that to us?'—the Egyptian lay sick. In the beginning of the
night Muharram was sitting up; we heard a guggle in his
throat,—he sank backward and was dead! We sent word to
Abdullah : who sent over two of the askars, and we made them
a supper of the niggard's goods. All Muharram's stores of
rice and samn went to the pot; and we sat feasting in presence
of our lord [saint] Muharram, who could not forbid this honest
wasting of his substance."—" The niggard's goods are for the
fire " (shall be burned in hell), responded those present. I questioned the Kurdy Mohammed, and he denied before them ; and
the Egyptian denied it, that my medicines had been so much as
mentioned, or cause at all in Muharram's death.—The Kurdy
said of the jebâl in the horizon of Kheybar, that they were but

as cottages, in comparison with the mighty mountains of his own country.

The sick Ageyly of Boreyda died soon after; but I had ceased from the first to give him medicines. 'He found the Nasrâuy's remedies (minute doses of rhubarb) so horrible, he said, that he would no more of them.' In one day he died and was buried. But when the morrow dawned we heard in the village, that the soldier's grave had been violated in the night! —Certain who went by very early had seen the print of women's feet round about the new-made grave. 'And who had done this thing?' asked all the people. "Who, they answered themselves, but the cursed witches! They have taken up the body, to pluck out the heart of him for their hellish orgies." I passed by later with Amm Mohammed, to our garden labour, and as they had said, so it seemed indeed! if the prints which we saw were not the footsteps of elvish children.—Amân carried a good fat cat to a neighbour woman of ours, and he told me with loathing, that she had eaten it greedily, though she was well-faring, and had store of all things in her beyt; she was said to be one of the witches! * * *

CHAPTER IV

DELIVERANCE FROM KHEYBAR

WE looked again for Dakhîl, returning from Medina. I spoke to Mohammed to send one to meet him in the way : that were there tidings out against my life (which Dakhîl would not hide from us), the messenger might bring us word with speed, and I would take to the Harra. " The Siruân shall be disappointed, answered my fatherly friend, if they would attempt anything against thy life ! Wellah if Dakhîl bring an evil word, I have one here ready, who is bound to me, a Beduwy ; and by him I will send thee away in safety."—This was his housewife's brother, a wild grinning wretch, without natural conscience, a notorious camel robber and an homicide. Their father had been a considerable Bishr sheykh ; but in the end they had lost their cattle. This wretch's was the Beduin right of the Hálhal, but that yielded him no advantage, and he was become a gatûny at Kheybar ; where his hope was to help himself by cattle-lifting, in the next hostile marches.—Last year seeing some poor stranger in the summer market, with a few ells of new-bought calico, (for a shirt-cloth,) in his hand, he vehemently coveted it for himself. Then he followed that strange tribesman upon the Harra, and came upon him in the path and murdered him ; and took his cotton, and returned to the village laughing :—he was not afraid of the blood of a stranger ! The wild wretch sat by grinning, when Amm Mohammed told me the tale ; but the housewife said, sighing, "Alas ! my brother is a kafir, so light-headed is he, that he dreads not Ullah." The Nejûmy answered, " Yet the melaun helped our low plight last year, (when there was a dearth at Kheybar) ; he stole sheep and camels, and we feasted many times :—should we leave all the fat to our enemies, and we ourselves perish with hunger ? Sheykh Khalîl, say was this lawful for us or harâm ? "

I thought if, in the next days, I should be a fugitive upon

the vast lava-field, without shelter from the sun, without known landmarks, with water for less than three days, and infirm in body, what hope had I to live?—A day later Dakhîl arrived from Medina, and then, (that which I dreaded,) Amm Mohammed was abroad, to hunt gazelles, upon the Harra; nor had he given me warning overnight,—thus leaving his guest (the Arabs' remiss understanding), in the moment of danger, without defence. The Nejûmy absent, I could not in a great peril have escaped their barbarous wild hands; but after some sharp reckoning with the most forward of them I must have fallen in this subbakha soil, without remedy. Ahmed was too 'religious' to maintain the part of a misbeliever against any mandate from Medina : even though I should sit in his chamber, I thought he would not refuse to undo to the messengers from Abdullah. I sat therefore in Mohammed's suffa, where at the worst I might keep the door until heaven should bring the good man home.—But in this there arrived an hubt of Heteym, clients of his, from the Harra; and they brought their cheeses and samn to the Nejûmy's house, that he might sell the wares for them. Buyers of the black village neighbours came up with them, and Mohammed's door was set open. I looked each moment for the last summons to Abdullah, until nigh mid-day; when Amm Mohammed returned from the Harra, whence he had seen the nomads, far off, descending to Kheybar.—Then the Nejûmy sat down among us, and receiving a driving-stick from one of the nomads, he struck their goods and cried, "Who buys this for so much ?" and he set a just price between them : and taking his reed-pen and paper he recorded their bargains, which were for measures of dates to be delivered (six months later), in the harvest. After an hour, Amm Mohammed was again at leisure; then having shut his door, he said he would go to Abdullah and learn the news.

He returned to tell me that the Pasha wrote thus, " We have now much business with the Haj ; at their departure we will examine and send again the books: in the meanwhile you are to treat the Engleysy honourably and with hospitality." I was summoned to Abdullah in the afternoon : Amm Mohammed went with me, and he carried his sword, which is a strong argument in a valiant hand to persuade men to moderation in these lawless countries. Abdullah repeated that part of the governor's order concerning the books ; of the rest he said nothing.—I afterwards found Dakhîl in the street ; he told me he had been privately called to the (Turkish) Pasha, who enquired of him, ' What did I wandering in this country, and whether the Nasrâny spoke Arabic ? ' (he spoke it very well himself). Dakhîi found him well disposed towards me : he heard also in Medina that at the coming of the Haj, Mohammed Said Pasha, being asked by the Pasha-governor, if he knew me, responded, 'He had seen me at Damascus, and that I came down among the Haj to Medáin Sâlih ; and he wondered to hear that I was in captivity at Kheybar, a man known to be an Engleysy and who had no guilt towards the Dowla, other than to have been always too adventurous to wander in the (dangerous) nomadic countries.'

The few weeks of winter had passed by, and the teeming spring heat was come, in which all things renew themselves : the hamîm month would soon be upon us, when my languishing life, which the Nejûmy compared to a flickering lamp-wick, was likely (he said) to fail at Kheybar. Two months already I had endured this black captivity of Abdullah ; the third moon was now rising in her horns, which I hoped in Heaven would see me finally delivered. The autumn green corn was grown to the yellowing ear ; another score of days—so the Lord delivered them from the locust—and they would gather in their wheat-harvest.

I desired to leave them richer in water at Kheybar. Twenty paces wide of the strong Sefsáfa spring was a knot of tall rushes ; there I hoped to find a new fountain of water. The next land-holders hearkened gladly to my saw, for water is mother of corn and dates, in the oases ; and the sheykh's brother responded that to-morrow he would bring eyyâl, to open the ground.—Under the first spade-stroke we found wet earth, and oozing joints of the basalt rock : then they left their labour, saying we should not speed, because it was begun on a Sunday. They remembered also my words that, in case we found a spring of water, they should give me a milch cow. On the morrow a greater working party assembled. It might be they were in doubt of the cow, and would let the work lie until the Nasrány's departure, for they struck but a stroke or two in my broken ground ; and then went, with crowbars, to try their strength about the old well head, and see if they might not enlarge it. The iron bit in the flaws of the rock ; and stiffly straining and leaning, many together, upon their crowbars, they sprung and rent up the intractable basalt. Others who looked on, whilst the labourers took breath, would bear a hand in it : among them the Nejûmy showed his manly pith and stirred a mighty quarter of basalt. When it came to mid-day they forsook their day's labour. Three forenoons they wrought thus with the zeal of novices : in the second they sacrificed a goat, and sprinkled her blood upon the rock. I had not seen Arabs labour thus in fellowship. In the Arabs are indigent corroded minds full of speech-wisdom; in the negroes' more prosperous bodies are hearts more robust. They also fired the rock, and by the third day the labourers had drawn out many huge stones: now the old well-head was become like a great bath of tepid water, and they began to call it el-hammâm. We had struck a side vein, which increased the old current of water by half as much again,—a benefit for ever to the husbandmen of the valley.

The tepid springs of Kheybar savour upon the tongue of sulphur, with a milky smoothness, save the *Ayn er-Reyih*, which is tasteless. Yellow frogs inhabit these springs, besides the little silver-green fishes. Green filmy webs of water-weed are wrapped about the channels of the lukewarm brooks, in which lie little black turreted snails, like those of W. Thirba and el-Ally [and Palmyra]. I took up the straws of caddis-worms and showed them to Amm Mohammed: he considered the building of those shell-pipes made without hands, and said; " Oh the marvellous works of God ; they are perfect without end ! and well thou sayest, ' that the Kheyâbara are not housed as these little vermin ! ' "

I had nearly outworn the spite of fortune at Kheybar ; and might now spend the sunny hours, without fear, sitting by the spring Ayn er-Reyih, a pleasant place, little without the palms ; and where only the eye has any comfort in all the blackness of Kheybar. Oh, what bliss to the thirsty soul is in that sweet light water, welling soft and warm as milk, [86° F.] from the rock ! And I heard the subtle harmony of Nature, which the profane cannot hear, in that happy stillness and solitude. Small bright dragon-flies, azure, dun and ver-milion, sported over the cistern water ruffled by a morning breath from the figgera, and hemmed in the solemn lava rock. The silver fishes glance beneath, and white shells lie at the bottom of this water world. I have watched there the young of the thób, shining like scaly glass and speckled : this fairest of saurians lay sunning, at the brink, upon a stone ; and oft-times moving upon them and shooting out the tongue he snatched his prey of flies without ever missing.—Glad were we when Jummàr had filled our girby of this sweet water.

The irrigation rights of every plot of land are inscribed in the sheykhs' register of the village ;—the week-day and the hours when the owner with foot and spade may dam off and draw to himself the public water. Amongst these rude Arabian villagers are no clocks nor watches,—nor anything almost of

civil artifice in their houses. They take their wit in the daytime, by the shadowing-round of a little wand set upon the
channel brink.—This is that dial of which we read in Job:
'a servant earnestly desireth the shadow . . . our days on the
earth are a shadow.' In the night they make account of time
more loosely. The village gates are then shut; but the waterers
may pass out to their orchards from some of the next-lying
houses. Amm Mohammed tells me that the husbandmen at
Medina use a metal cup, pierced with a very fine eye,—so
that the cup set floating in a basin may sink justly at the
hour's end. * * *

* * * One afternoon when I went to present myself to the
village tyrant, I saw six carrion beasts, that had been thelûls,
couched before Abdullah's door! the brutes stretched their long
necks faintly upon the ground, and their mangy chines were
humpless. Such could be none other than some unpaid soldiers'
jades from Medina; and I withdrew hastily to the Nejûmy.—
Certain Ageylies had been sent by the Pasha; and the men had
ridden the seventy miles hither in five days!—Such being the
Ageyl, whose forays formerly—some of them have boasted to
me—" made the world cold!" they are now not seldom worsted
by the tribesmen of the desert. In a late expedition of theirs
from Medina, we heard that 'forty were fallen, their baggage
had been taken, and the rest hardly saved themselves.'—I went
back to learn their tidings, and meeting with Abdullah in the
street, he said, " Good news, Khalîl! thy books are come again,
and the Pasha writes, ' send him to Ibn Rashîd '."

On the morrow, Abdullah summoned me; he sat at coffee
in our neighbour Hamdàn's house.—' This letter is for thee,
said he, (giving me a paper) from the Pasha's own hand ' And
opening the sheet, which was folded in our manner, I found
a letter from the Pasha of Medina! written [imperfectly], as
follows, in the French language; with the date of the Christian
year, and signed in the end with his name,—*Sábry*.

[*Ad literam*]   Le 11 janvier 1878
                                  [Medine]

D'aprés l'avertissement de l'autorité local, nous sommes saché
votre arrivée à Khaiber, à cette occasion je suis obligé de faire venir
les lettres de recommendation et les autres papiers à votre charge.
En étudiant à peine possible les livres de compte, les papiers
volants et les cartes, enfin parmi ceux qui sont arrivaient-ici, jai
disserné que votre idée de voyage, corriger la carte, de savoir les

conditions d'état, et de trouver les monuments antiques de l'Arabie
centrale dans le but de publier au monde

je suis bien satisfaisant à votre etude utile pour l'univers dans
ce point, et c'est un bon parti pour vous aussi ; mais vous avez
connu certainement jusqu' aujourd'hui parmi aux alantours des
populations que vous trouvé, il y a tant des Bedouins témeraire, tant
que vous avez le recommendion de quelque personnages, je ne regarde
que ce votre voyage est dangereux parmi les Bédouins sus-indiqué ;
c'est pour cela je m'oblige de vous informé à votre retour à un
moment plutôt possible auprès de Cheïh d'Ibni-Réchite à l'abri de
toute danger, et vous trouvrez ci-join tous vos les lettres qu'il était
chez-nous, et la recommendation au dite Cheïh de ma part, et de là
prenez le chemin dans ces jours à votre destination.

SABRI

" And now, I said to Abdullah, where is that money which
pertains to me,—six lira ! "   The black village governor startled,
changed his Turkish countenance, and looking felly, he said
" We will see to it."   The six Ageylies had ridden from Medina,
by the Pasha's order, only to bring up my books, and they
treated me with regard.   They brought word, that the Pasha
would send other twenty-five Ageylies to Hâyil for this cause.
The chief of the six, a Waháby of East Nejd, was a travelled
man, without fanaticism ; he offered himself to accompany me
whithersoever I would, and he knew, he said, all the ways, in
those parts and far southward in Arabia.

The day after when nothing had been restored to me, I found
Abdullah drinking coffee in sheykh Sâlih's house.   " Why, I
said, hast thou not restored my things ? "—" I will restore them
at thy departure."—" Have you any right to detain them ? "
" Say no more (exclaimed the villain, who had spent my money)
—a Nasrâny to speak to me thus!—or I will give thee a buffet."
—" If thou strike me, it will be at thy peril.   My hosts, how
may this lieutenant of a dozen soldiery rule a village, who cannot
rule himself ? one who neither regards the word of the Pasha of
Medina, nor fears the Sûltàn, nor dreads Ullah himself.   Sâlih,
sheykh of Kheybar, hear how this coward threatens to strike
a guest in thy house ; and will ye suffer it my hosts ? "—
Abdullah rose and struck me brutally in the face.—" Sâlih, I
said to them, and you that sit here, are you free men ?   I am
one man, infirm and a stranger, who have suffered so long, and
unjustly,—you all have seen it ! at this slave's hands, that it
might have whitened my beard : if I should hereafter remember
to complain of him, it is likely he will lose his office."   Auwad,
the kâdy who was a friend, and sat by me, began some conciliating

speech. 'Abdullah, he said, was to blame : Khalîl was also to
blame. There is danger in such differences; let there be no more
said betwixt you both.' *Abdullah :* "Now, shall I send thee to
prison ? "—" I tell thee, that I am not under thy jurisdiction ; "
and I rose to leave them. "Sit down, he cries, and brutally
snatched my cloak, and this askar—he looked through the casement and called up one of his men that passed by—shall lead
thee to prison." I went down with him, and, passing Amm
Mohammed's entry, I went in there, and the fellow left me.

The door was locked, but the Beduin housewife, hearing my
voice, ran down to open : when I had spoken of the matter, she
left me sitting in the house, and, taking the key with her, the
good woman ran to call her husband who was in the palms.
Mohammed returned presently, and we went out to the plantations
together : but finding the chief of the riders from Medina, in the
street, I told him, ' since I could not be safe here that I would
ride with them to the gate of the city. It were no new thing
that an Englishman should come thither ; was there not a cistern,
without the northern gate, named *Birket el-Engleysy ?* '

Mohammed asked ' What had the Pasha written ? he would
hear me read his letter in the Nasrâny language ' : and he stood
to listen with great admiration. ' *Pitta-pitta-pitta !* is such their
speech ? ' laughed he ; and this was his new mirth in the next
coffee meetings. But I found the good man weak as water in
the end of these evils : he had I know not what secret understanding now with the enemy Abdullah ; and, contrary to his
former words, he was unwilling that I should receive my things
until my departure ! The Ageylies stayed other days, and
Abdullah was weary of entertaining them. I gave the Waháby
a letter to the Pasha ; which, as soon as they came again to
town, he delivered.

Kheybar, in the gibing humour of these black villagers, is
jezîrat, ' an island ' : it is hard to come hither, it is not easy to
depart. Until the spring season there are no Aarab upon the
vast enclosing Harra : Kheybar lies upon no common way, and
only in the date-harvest is there any resort of Beduins to their
wadiân and villages. In all the vulcanic country about, there
were now no more than a few booths of Heteym, and the
nearest were a journey distant.—But none of those timid and
oppressed nomads durst for any silver convey the Nasrâny again
to Hâyil ; so aghast are they all of the displeasure of Ibn Rashîd.
I thought now to go to the (Harra) village el-Hâyat, which lies
in the way of them that pass between Ibn Rashîd's country and
Medina : and I might there find carriage to the Jebel.

The Nejûmy blamed my plain speaking : I had no wit, he said, to be a traveller ! " If thou say among the Moslen în, that thou art a Moslem, will your people kill thee, when you return home ? —art thou afraid of this, Khalîl ? " So at the next coffee meetings he said, " I have found a man that will not befriend himself ! I can in no wise persuade sheykh Khalîl : but if all the Moslemîn were like faithful in the religion, I say, the world would not be able to resist us." * * *

* * * The Nejûmy family regarded me with affection : my medicines helped (and they believed had saved) their infant daughter ; I was now like a son in the house, *wullah in-ak mithil weledna yâ Khalîl*, said they both. Mohammed exhorted me, to dwell with him at Kheybar, ' where first after long travels, I had found good friends. I should be no more molested among them for my religion ; in the summer market I might be his salesman, to sit at a stall of mantles and kerchiefs and measure out cubits of calico, for the silver of the poor Beduw. He would buy me then a great-eyed Galla maiden to wife.'— There are none more comely women in the Arabs' peninsula ; they are gracious in the simplest garments, and commonly of a well tempered nature ; and, notwithstanding that which is told of the hither Hábash countries, there is a becoming modesty in their heathen blood.—This was the good Nejûmy, a man most worthy to have been born in a happier country ! * * *

* * * Mohammed asked, " What were the Engleys good for ? " I answered, " They are good rulers."—" Ha ! and what rule they ? since they be not rebels (but friends) to the Sooltàn ? "—" In these parts of the world they rule India ; an empire greater than all the Sultan's Dowlat, and the principal béled of the Moslemîn."—" Eigh ! I remember I once heard an Hindy say, in the Haj, ' God continue the *hakûmat* (government of) el-Engleys ; for a man may walk in what part he will of *el-Hind*, with a bundle of silver ; but here in these holy countries even the pilgrims are in danger of robbers ! ' "—Amm Mohammed contemned the Hindies, " They have no heart, he said, and I make no account of the Engleys, for ruling over never so many of them : I myself have put to flight a score of *Hinûd*,"—and he told me the tale. " It was in my ignorant youth : one morning in the Haj season, going out under the walls (of Medina), to my father's orchard, I saw a company of Hinûd sitting before me upon a hillock,—sixteen persons : there sat a young maiden in the midst of them—very richly attired ! for

N

they were some principal persons. Then I shouted, and lifting
my lance, began to leap and run, against them; the Hindies
cried out, and all rising together they fled to save their lives!—
leaving the maiden alone; and the last to forsake her was a
young man—he perchance that was betrothed to be her
husband."—The gentle damsel held forth her delicate hands,
beseeching him by signs to take only her ornaments: she drew
off her rings, and gave them to the (Beduin-like) robber;—
Mohammed had already plucked off her rich bracelets! But
the young prodigal, looking upon her girlish beauty and her
distress, felt a gentleness rising in his heart and he left her
[unstained].—For such godless work the Arabs have little or no
contrition; this worthy man, whom God had established, even
now in his religious years, felt none.—It may seem to them
that all world's good is *kheyr Ullah* howbeit diversely holden,
in several men's hands; and that the same (whether by sub-
tilty, or warlike endeavour) might well enough be assumed
by another. * * *

* * * Twelve days after I had written to the Pasha, came his
rescript to Abdullah, with a returning hubt; bidding him 'beware
how he behaved himself towards the Engleysy, and to send me
without delay to Ibn Rashîd; and if no Beduins could be
found to accompany me, to send with me some of the Ageyl:
he was to restore my property immediately, and if anything
were missing he must write word again.' The black village
governor was now in dread for himself; he went about the
village to raise that which he had spent of my robbed liras:
and I heard with pain, that (for this) he had sold the orphan's
cow.

He summoned me at night to deliver me mine own. The
packet of books and papers, received a fortnight before from
Medina, was sealed with the Pasha's signet: when opened a koran
was missing and an Arabic psalter! I had promised them to
Amm Mohammed; and where was the camel bag? Abdullah
murmured in his black throat 'Whose could be this infamous
theft?' and sent one for Dakhîl the post.—Dakhîl told us that
'Come to Medina he went, with the things on his back, to the
government palace; but meeting with a principal officer—one
whom they all knew—that personage led him away to drink
coffee in his house. "Now let me see, quoth the officer, what
hast thou brought? and, if that Nasrâny's head should be cut
off, some thing may as well remain with me, before all goes up
to the Pasha."—The great man compelled me, said Dakhîl, so I
let him have the books; and when he saw the Persian camel

bag, "This too, he said, may remain with me." '—" Ullah curse
the father of him!" exclaimed Abdullah: and, many of the
askars' voices answered about him, "Ullah curse him!" I asked,
"Is it a poor man, who has done this?" *Abdullah:* "Poor!
he is rich, the Lord curse him! It is our colonel, Khalîl, at
Medina; where he lives in a great house, and receives a great
government salary, besides all the [dishonest] private gains of
his office."—"The Lord curse him!" exclaimed the Nejûmy.
"The Lord curse him! answered Amân (the most gentle minded
of them all), he has broken the *namûs* of the Dowla!"
Abdullah: "Ah! Khalîl, he is one of the great ones at Medina,
and *gomâny!* (a very adversary). Now what can we do, shall we
send again to Medina?" A villager lately arrived from thence
said, "The colonel is not now in Medina, we heard a little
before our coming away, that he had set out for Mecca."—So
must other days be consumed at Kheybar for this Turkish
villain's wrong! in the meanwhile Sâbry Pasha might be recalled
from Medina!

I sat by the Nejûmy's evening fire, and boiled tea, which he
and his nomad jâra had learned to drink with me, when we
heard one call below stairs; the joyous housewife ran down in
haste, and brought up her brother, who had been long out
cattle lifting, with another gatûny. The wretch came in
jaded, and grinning the teeth: and when he had eaten a morsel,
he began to tell us his adventure;—'That come in the Jeheyna
dîra, they found a troop of camels, and only a child to keep them.
They drove off the cattle; and drove them forth, all that day,
at a run, and the night after; until a little before dawn, when,
having yet a day and a half to Kheybar, they fell at unawares
among tents!—it was a menzil of Harb. The hounds barked
furiously, at the rushing by of camels, the Aarab ran from their
beyts, with their arms. He and his rafîk alighting hastily,
forsook the robbed cattle, and saving no more than their
matchlocks, they betook themselves to the side of a mountain.
From thence they shot down against their pursuers, and those
shot up at them. The Harb bye and bye went home to kahwa;
and the geyatîn escaped to Kheybar on foot with their weary
lives!'

The next day Amm Mohammed called his robber brother-
in-law to supper. The jaded wretch soon rose from the dish
to kindle his pipe, and immediately went home to sleep.—
Mohammed's wife returned later from milking their few goats;
and as she came lighting herself upon the stairs, with a flaming
palm-branch, his keen eye discerned a trouble in her looks.—

"Eigh! woman, he asked, what tidings?" She answered with a sorrowful alacrity, in the Semitic wise, "Well! [a first word of good augury], it may please Ullah: my brother is very sick, and has a flux of the bowels, and is lying in great pain, as if he were to die, and we cannot tell what to do for him:—it is [the poor woman cast down her eyes] as if my brother had been poisoned; when he rose from eating he left us, and before he was come home the pains took him!"—Mohammed responded with good humour, "This is a folly, woman, who has poisoned the melauu? I am well, and sheykh Khalîl is well; and Haseyn and thou have eaten after us of the same mess,—but thy brother is sick of his cattle stealing! Light us forth, and if he be ailing we will bring him hither, and sheykh Khalîl shall cure him with some medicine."

We found him easier; and led him back with us. I gave him grains of laudanum powder, which he swallowed without any mistrusting.—I saw then a remedy of theirs, for the colic pain, which might sometime save life after drugs have failed. The patient lay groaning on his back, and his sister kneaded the belly smoothly with her housemother's hands [they may be as well anointed with warm oil]; she gave him also a broth to drink, of sour milk with a head of (thûm) garlic beaten in it. At midnight we sent him away well again: then I said to Amm Mohammed, "It were easier to die once, than to suffer heart-ache continually."—" The melaun has been twinged thus often-times; and who is there afraid of sheykh Khalîl; if thou bid me, little father Khalîl, I would drink poison."—The restless Beduwy was gone, the third morrow, on foot over the Harra, to seek hospitality (and eat flesh-meat) at el-Hâyat,—forty miles distant.

The Siruân asked a medicine for a chill; and I brought him camphor. "Eigh! said Abdullah, is not this *kafûr* of the dead, wherewith they sprinkle the shrouds as they are borne to the burial?—five drops of this tincture will cut off a man's off-spring. What hast thou done to drink of it, Amm Moham-med!" The good man answered, "Have I not Haseyn, and the little bint? Wellah if sheykh Khalîl have made me from this time childless, I am content, because Khalîl has done it." The black audience were aghast; "Reach me, I said to them, that bottle and I will drink twice five drops." But they murmured, "Akhs! and was this one of the medicines of Khalîl?" * * *

* * * The day was at hand, which should deliver me from

Kheybar. Dâkhil the post was willing to convey me to Hâyil, for two of my gold pieces : but that would leave me with less than eighty shillings—too little to bring me to some friendly soil, out of the midst of Arabia. Eyâd, a Bishr Ageyly, proffered to carry me on his sick thelûl for five reals to Hâyil. I thought to go first (from this famine at Kheybar) to buy victual at el-Hâyat; their oasis had not been wasted by locusts. Those negro Nejd villagers are hospitable, and that which the Arabians think is more than all to the welfare of their tribes and towns, the sheykh was a just and honourable person.—The Nejûmy's wife's brother had returned from thence after the three days' hospitality : and being there, with two or three more loitering Beduwies like himself, he told us that each day a householder had called them ; and " every host killed a bull to their supper ! " " It is true, said the Nejûmy ; a bull there is not worth many reals."—" The villagers of Hâyat are become a whiter people of late years ! quoth the Beduwy ; this is through their often marriages with poor women of Heteym and Jeheyna."

— Eyâd, a Beduwy, and by military adoption a townsman of Medina, was one who had drunk very nigh the dregs, of the mischiefs and vility of one and the other life. A Beduwy (mild by nature to the guest), he had not given his voice for my captivity ; but in the rest he was a lukewarm adulator of Abdullah. —All my papers were come again, *save only the safe-conduct of Ibn Rashíd*, which they had detained ! The slave-hearted Abdullah began now to call me ' Uncle Khalîl ' ; for he thought, ' What, if the Nasrâny afterward remembered his wrongs, and he had this power with the Dowla—' ? How pitiful a behaviour might I have seen from him if our lots had been reversed at Kheybar ! He promised me provision for the way, and half the Ageyly's wages to Hâyil ; but I rejected them both.

Amm Mohammed was displeased because I would not receive from him more than two handfuls of dates :—he was low himself till the harvest, and there remained not a strike of corn in the village. I divided my medicines with the good man, and bought him a tunic and a new gun-stock : these with other reals of mine (which, since they were loose in my pockets, Abdullah had not taken from me), already spent for corn and samn in his house, might suffice that Amm Mohammed should not be barer at my departure, for all the great-hearted goodness which he had shown me in my long tribulation at Kheybar. He said, " Nay, Khalîl, but leave me happy with the remembrance, and take it not away from me by requiting me ! only this

I desire of thee that thou sometimes say, ' *The Lord remember him for good*.' Am I not thy abu, art not thou my son, be we not brethren ? and thou art poor in the midst of a land which thou hast seen to be all hostile to thee. Also Ahmed would not suffer it; what will my brother say ? and there would be talk amongst the Kheyâbara." I answered, "I shall say nothing : " then he consented. So I ever used the Arabian hospitality to my possibility : yet now I sinned in so doing, against that charitable integrity, the human affection, which was in Amm Mohammed; and which, like the waxen powder upon summer fruits, is deflowered under any rude handling. When he received my gift, it seemed to him that I had taken away his good works ! * * *

* * * Abdullah had purchased other camel-bags for me, from a salesman who arrived from Medina. I agreed with Eyâd; and on the morrow we should depart from Kheybar.— When that blissful day dawned, my rafîk found it was the 21st of the moon *Sáfr*, and not lucky to begin our journey; we might set out, he said, the next morning.

I saw then two men brought before Abdullah from Umm Kîda, for resisting the forced cleansing and sweeping in their sûk. Abdullah made them lie upon their breasts, in a public alley, and then, before weeping women, and the village neighbours,—and though the sheykhs entreated for them, he beat them, with green palm rods; and they cried out mainly, till their negro blood was sprinkled on the ground. Amm Mohammed went by driving his kine to the common gathering-place of their cattle without the gates · his half-Beduin (gentle) heart swelled to see this bestial (and in his eyes inhuman) spectacle ! And with loud seditious voice as he returned, he named Abu Aly "very ass, and Yahûdy "! to all whom he found in the village street.

The new sun rising, this was the hour of my deliverance from the long *deyik es-sudr*, the straitness of the breast in affliction, at Kheybar. Eyâd said that all his hire must be paid him, ere the setting out; because he would leave it with his wife. In a menzil of the Aarab, I had not doubted, a Beduwy is commonly a trusty rafîk ; but Eyâd was a rotten one, and therefore I had covenanted to pay him a third in departing, a third at el-Hâyat, and a third at our arriving in Hâyil. Abdullah sought to persuade me with deceitful reasons ; but now I refused Eyâd, who I foresaw from this beginning would be a dangerous companion. *Abdullah :* " Let us not strive, we may find some other, and in all things, I would fain content

Khalîl." Afterwards he said, " I vouch for Eyâd, and if he fail
in anything, the fault be upon my head! Eyâd is an askar of
mine, *the Dowla has a long arm* and for any misdeed I might
cut off his head. Eyâd's arrears of pay are now five or six
hundred reals, and he durst not disobey the Dowla. Say which
way you would take to Hâyil, and to that I will bind him.
You may rest here a day and there a day, at your own liking,
and drink whey, where you find Beduins; and to this Eyâd is
willing because his thelûl is feeble. Wouldst thou as much
as fifteen days for the journey ?—I will give him twenty-six to
go and come."

The Nejûmy, who stood as a looker-on to-day among us, was
loud and raw in his words; and gave his counsel so fondly
before them all, and manifestly to my hurt! that I turned from
him with a heartache. The traveller should sail with every fair
wind in these fanatical countries, and pass forth before good-
will grow cold : I made Eyâd swear before them all to be
faithful to me, and counted the five reals in his hand.

Abdullah had now a request, that an Ageyly Bishr lad,
Merjàn, should go in our company. I knew him to be of a
shallow humour, a sower of trouble, and likely by recounting
my vicissitudes at Kheybar to the Aarab in the way, to hinder
my passage. *Abdullah :* ' He asks it of your kindness, that he
might visit an only sister and his little brother at Hâyil ; whom
he has not seen these many years.' I granted, and had ever
afterward to repent :—there is an impolitic humanity, which is
visited upon us.

The Jew-like Southern Annezy are the worst natured (saving
only the Kahtân) of all the tribes. I marked with discomfort of
heart the craven adulation of Eyâd, in his leavetaking of these
wretches. Although I had suffered wrongs, I said to them (to
the manifest joy of the guilty Abdullah,) the last word of Peace.
—My comrade Amân came along with me. The Nejûmy was
gone before to find his mare ; he would meet us by the way and
ride on a mile with me. We went by a great stone and there
I mounted : Amân took my hand feebly in his dying hand, and
prayed aloud that the Lord would bring me safely to my
journey's end. The poor Galla earnestly charged Eyâd, to have
a care of me, and we set forward. * * *

* * * At little distance the Nejûmy met us,—he was on foot.
He said, his mare had strayed in the palms ; and if he might find
her, he would ride down to the Tubj, to cut male palm blossoms
of the half-wild stems there, to marry them with his female

trees at home. One husband stem (to be known by the doubly robust growth) may suffice among ten female palms.—" Now God be with thee, my father Mohammed, and requite thee."—" God speed thee Khalîl," and he took my hand. Amm Mohammed went back to his own, we passed further; and the world, and death, and the inhumanity of religions parted us for ever!

We beat the pad-footed thelûl over the fenny ground, and the last brooks and plashes. And then I came up from the pestilent Kheybar wadiàn, and the intolerable captivity of the Dowla, to a blissful free air on the brow of the Harra! In the next hour we went by many of the vaults, of wild basalt stones, which I have supposed to be barrows. After ten miles' march we saw a nomad woman standing far off upon a lava rock, and two booths of Heteym. My Beduin rafîks showed me the heads of a mountain southward, el-Baítha, that they said stands a little short of Medina. It was afternoon, we halted and loosed out the thelûl to pasture, and sat down till it should be evening. When the sun was setting we walked towards the tents: but the broken-headed Eyâd left me with Hamed and his loaded thelûl, and went with Merjàn to guest it at the other beyt. The householder of the booth where I was, came home with the flocks and camels; he was a beardless young man. They brought us buttermilk, and we heard the voice of a negress calling in the woman's apartment, *Hamed! yà Hamô!* She was from the village, and was staying with these nomad friends in the desert, to refresh herself with léban. It was presently dark, but the young man went abroad again with the ass to bring in water. He returned after two hours and, without my knowledge, they sacrificed a goat: it was for this he had fetched water. The young Heteymy called me—the adulation of an abject race—*Towîl el-amr*.

After the hospitality Eyâd entered, " Khalîl, he said, hast thou reserved no morsels for me, that am thy rafîk ?"—" Would a rafîk have forsaken me ? " He now counselled to hold a more westerly course, according to the tidings they had heard in the other tent, 'that we might come every day to menzils of the Aarab, and find milk and refreshment; whereas, if I visited el-Hâyat, all the way northward to Hâyil from thence was now bare of Beduins.'—I should thus miss el-Hâyat, and had no provisions: also I assented to them in evil hour! it had been better to have yielded nothing to such treacherous rafîks.

We departed at sunrise, having upon our right hand, in the 'White Harra' (el-Abiath) a distant mountain, which they likewise named *el-Baithá* [other than that in the Hejâz, nigh Medina]. In that jebel, quoth my rafîks, are the highest *sháebán* (seyl-strands) of W. er-Rummah ; but all on this side seyls down to the (great Hejâz) Wady el-Humth. We passed by sharp glassy lavas ; '—*loub*," said my companions. A pair of great lapwing-like fowl, *habâra*, fluttered before us ; I have seldom seen them in the deserts [and only at this season] : they have whitish and dun-speckled feathers. Their eggs (brown and rose, black speckled) I have found in May, laid two together upon the bare wilderness gravel [near Maan] ; they were great as turkey-eggs, and well tasting : the birds might be a kind of bustards. " Their flesh is nesh as cotton between the teeth," quoth the Bishr Sybarite Eyâd. Merjàn and Eyâd lured to them, whistling ; they drew off their long gun-leathers, and stole under the habâras ; but as Beduins will not cast away lead in the air, they returned bye and bye as they went. I never saw the Arabs' gunning help them to any game : only the Nejûmy used to shoot at, (and he could strike down) flying partridges.

From hence the vulcanic field about us was a wilderness of sharp lava stones, where few or no cattle paths [Bishr, *jadda*] appeared ; and nomads go on foot among the rocking blocks un-willingly. A heavy toppling stone split the horny thickness of Hamed's great toe. I alighted that he might ride ; but the negro borrowed a knife and, with a savage resolution, shred away his flesh, and went on walking. In the evening halt, he seared the bloody wound, and said, it would be well enough, for the next marches. As we journeyed the March wind blustered up against us from the north ; and the dry herbage and scudding stems of sere desert bushes, were driven before the blast. Our way was uncertain, and without shelter or water ; the height of this lava-plain is 3400 feet. Merjàn—the lad was tormented with a throbbing ague-cake (*táhal*), after the Kheybar fever, shouted in the afternoon that he saw a flock ; and then all beside his patience he shrieked back curses, because we did not follow him : the flock was but a troop of gazelles. " *Fen el-Aarab*, they said at last, the nomads where ?—*neffera !* deceitful words ; but this is the manner of the Heyteymàn ! they misled us last night, Ullah send them confusion." The negro had drunk out nearly all in my small waterskin : towards evening he untied the neck and would have made a full end of it himself at a draught ; but I said to him, " Nay, for we have gone and thirsted all the day, and no man shall have more than other." The Beduins cried out upon him, " And thinkest thou that we be yet in the Saheyn ? this is the khála and no swaggering-place of the Kheyâbara." Finally, when the sun set, we found a hollow ground and sídr trees to bear off the night wind, which blew so fast and pierced our slender clothing : they rent down the sere white arms of a dead acacia, for our evening fire. Then kneading flour of the little water which remained to us, we made hasty bread under the embers. The March night was cold.

We departed when the day dawned, and held under the sandstone mountain *Gurs:* and oh, joy! this sun being fairly risen, the abhorred land-marks of Kheybar appeared no more. We passed other vaulted cells and old dry walling upon the waste Harra, and an ancient burying-place. "See, said Eyâd, these graves of the auellîn, how they lie heaped over with stones!" We marched in the vulcanic field—' a land whose stones are iron ', and always fasting, till the mid-afternoon, when we found in some black sand-beds footprints of camels. At first my rafîks said the traces were of a râhla five to ten days old; but taking up the jella they thought it might be of five days ago. The droppings led us over the Harra north-westward, towards the outlying plutonic coasts of J Hejjûr.—Footprints in the desert are slowly blotted by insensible wind causing the sand corns to slide; they might otherwise remain perfectly until the next rain.—In a monument lately opened in Egypt, fresh prints of the workmen's soles were found in the fine powder of the floor; and they were of an hundred men's ages past! The Beduins went to an hollow ground, to seek a little ponded rain, and there they filled the girby. That water was full of wiggling white vermin; and we drank—giving God thanks—through a lap of our kerchiefs. [We may see the flaggy hare-lips of the camel fenced with a border of bristles, bent inwardly; and through this brush the brute strains all that he drinks of the foul desert waters!] The Beduin rafîks climbed upon every high rock to look for the nomads: we went on till the sun set, and then alighted in a low ground with acacia trees and bushes; there we found a dàr of the nomads lately forsaken. We were here nigh the borders of the Harra.

As the morrow's sun rose we set forward, and the camel droppings led us toward the Thullân Hejjûr. We came bye and bye to the Harra side, and the lava-border is here like the ice-brink of a glacier; where we descended it was twenty feet in height, and a little beside us eight or ten fathoms. Beyond the Harra we passed forth upon barren steeps of plutonic gravel, furrowed by the secular rains and ascending toward the horrid wilderness of mountains, Jebâl Hejjûr. A napping gazelle-buck, started from a bush before us; and standing an instant at gaze, he had fallen then to the shot of an European,—but the Beduins are always unready. As we journeyed I saw an hole, a yard deep,

digged in the desert earth; the rafîks answered me, 'It was
for a *mejdûr* (*one sick of the small-pox*).'—They kindle a fire in
it, and after raking out the embers the sick is seated in the
hot sand: such may be a salutary sweating-bath. The Arabians dread extremely the homicide disease; and the calamity
of a great sheykh of the Annezy in Kasîm was yet fresh in
men's memories.—His tribesfolk removed from him in haste;
and his own kindred and even his household forsook him!

Leaving the sandstone platform mountain *el-Kh'tâm* upon the
right hand, we came to the desolate mountains, whose knees
and lower crags about us were traps, brown, yellow, grey, slate-
colour, red and purple. Small black eagles, el-agâb, lay upon
the wing above us, gliding like the shadows, which their outstretched wings cast upon the rocky coasts Crows and rákhams
hovered in the lower air, over a forsaken dàr of the nomads:
their embers were yet warm, they had removed this morning.
The Beduin companions crept out with their long matchlocks,
hoping to shoot a crow, and have a pair of shank-bones for pipe-
stems. I asked them if there had fallen a hair or feather to their
shot in the time of their lives? They protested, "Ay wellah,
Khalîl; and the gatta many times." Not long after we espied
the Aarab and the camels. We came up with them a little
after noon, when they first halted to encamp. The sheykh, seeing strangers approach, had remained a little in the hindward;
and he was known to my companions. These nomads were *Ferâ-
dessa, Ibn Simry*, Heteym. We sat down together, and a weled
milked two of the sheykh's nâgas, for us strangers.

This sheykh, when he knew me to be the Nasrâny, began to
bluster, although I was a guest at his milk-bowl. "What!
heathen man, he cries; what! Nasrâny, wherefore comest thou
hither? Dost thou not fear the Aarab's knife? Or thinkest
thou, O Jew-man, that it cannot carve thy throat?—which will
be seen one day. O ye his rafîks, will they not cut the wezand
of him? Where go ye now—to Hâyil? but Ibn Rashîd will kill
him if this (man) come thither again."—The Heteym are not
so civil-minded as the right Beduw; they are often rough
towards their guests, where the Beduw are gentle-natured.
When I saw the man was a good blunt spirit, I derided his
ignorance till he was ashamed; and in this sort you may easily
defeat the malicious simplicity of the Arabs.

We drove on our beast to their camp, and sat down before a
beyt. The householder bye and bye brought us forth a bowl of
léban and another of mereesy; we loosed out the thelûl to pasture, and sat by our baggage in the wind and beating sun till
evening; when the host bade us enter, and we found a supper

set ready for us, of boiled rice. He had been one in the Heteymy hubt which was lately taken by a foray of Jeheyna near the walls of Medina. Upon the morrow this host removed with his kindred, and we became guests of another beyt ; for we would repose this day over in their menzil, where I counted thirty tents. When I gave a sick person rhubarb, his friends were much pleased for " by the smack, said they, it should be a good medicine indeed." A few persons came to us to enquire the news : but not many men were at home by day in the Heteymy menzil : for these nomads are diligent cattle-keepers, more than the Beduw. * * *

    * * * They questioned roughly in the booth, " What are the Nasâra, what is their religion ? " One among them said : " I will tell you the sooth in this as I heard it [in Medina, or in the civil north countries] : The Nasâra inhabit a city closed with iron and encompassed by the sea ! " *Eyâd :* " Talk not so bois- terously, lest ye offend Khalîl ; and he is one that with a word might make this tent to fall about our ears." " Eigh ! they an- swered, could he so indeed ? " I found in their menzil two lives blighted by the morbus gallicus. I enquired from whence had they that malady ? They answered, " From el-Medina."

    At daybreak the nomad people removed. We followed with them westward, in these mountains ; and ascended through a cragged passage, where there seemed to be no footing for camels. Hamed, who had left us, came limping by with one whom he had found to guide him : " Farewell, I said, *akhu Hamda.*" The Kheybar villain looked up pleased and confused, because I had named him (as one of the valiant) by his sister, and he wished me God speed. We were stayed in the midst by some friends, that would milk for us ere we departed from among them. Infinite seemed to me the horrid maze of these desolate and thirsty mountains ! Their name Jebâl Hejjûr may be interpreted the stony mountains :—they are of the Wélad Aly and Bishr,—and by their allowance of these Heteym. In the valley deeps they find, most years, the rabîa and good pasture bushes. These coasts seyl by W. Hejjûr to the W. el-Humth. We were now much westward of our way. The nomads removed southward ; and leaving them we descended, in an hour, to a wady bottom of sand, where we found another Heteym menzil, thirty booths, of *Sueyder,* Ibn Simry. The district (of a kind of middle traps), they name *Yeterôha :* Eyâd's Aarab seldom visited this part of their dîra ; and he had been here but once before. These mountains seyl, they say, by W. Khâfutha, one of the Kheybar valleys.

Merjàn found here some of his own kindred, a household or two of his Bishr clan *Bejaija* or *Bejaida.*—There are many poor families of Beduin tribesmen living (for their more welfare) in the peaceable society of the Heteym. A man, that was his cousin, laid hands on the thelûl, and drew her towards his hospitable beyt.—Our hosts of yesterday sent word of my being in the dîra to a sick sheykh of theirs, *Ibn Heyzán,* who had been hurt by a spear-thrust in a ghrazzu. Amm Mohammed lately sold some ointment of mine to the sick man's friends in Kheybar, which had been found excellent; and his acquaintance desired that I should ride to see him. I consented to wait here one day, until the return of their messenger.

When I took out my medicine book and long brass Arabic inkhorn, men and women gathered about me; it was marvels to them to see me write and read. They whispered, "He sees the invisible ;—at least thou seest more than we poor folk!—it is written there!" The host had two comely daughters; they wondered to look upon the stranger's white skin. The young women's demeanour was easy, with a maidenly modesty; but their eye-glances melted the heart of the beardless lad Merjàn, their cousin, who had already a girl-wife at Kheybar. These nomad-hareem in Nejd were veiled with the face-clout, but only from the mouth downward ; they wore a silver ring in the right nostril, and a braided forelock hanging upon the temples. The goodman went abroad with his hatchet, and we saw them no more till sunset, when he and his wife came dragging-in great lopped boughs of tolh trees :—where we see the trail of boughs in the khála, it is a sign of the nomad menzils. Of these they made a sheep-pen before the beyt; and the small cattle were driven in and folded for the night. They call it *hathîra;* "Shammar, they said, have another name," [*serifat*]. The host now set before us a great dish of rice.

Eyâd was treacherous, and always imagining, since he had his wages, how he might forsake me : the fellow would not willingly go to Hâyil. "Khalîl, shall I leave thee here? wellah the thelûl is not in plight for a long journey."—"Restore then three reals and I will let thee go."—"Ah! how may I, Khalîl? you saw that I left the money at home."—"Then borrow it here."—"Bless me! which of these Aarab has any money, or would lend me one real?"—"All this I said at Kheybar, that thou wouldst betray me; Eyâd, thou shalt carry me to Hâyil, as thou art bounden."—"But here lies no way to Hâyil, we are come out of the path; these Aarab have their faces towards the Auájy, let us go on with them, it is but two marches, and I will leave thee there."—The ill-faith of the Arabs is a gulf,

in the path of the unwary! there is nothing to hope for
in man, amongst them; and their heaven is too far off, or
without sense of human miseries. Now I heard from this
wretch's mouth my own arguments, which he had bravely con-
tradicted at Kheybar! On the morrow Eyâd would set out
with the rising sun : I said, we will remain here to-day, as thou
didst desire yesternight and obtain of me. But he loaded! and
then the villanous rafîk came with his stick, and—it was that
he had learned in the Turkish service—threatened to beat me,
if I did not remove : but he yielded immediately.

In this menzil I found a Solubby household from *W. es-
Suffera*, which is spoken of for its excessive heat, in the Hejâz,
not much north of Mecca. They were here above three
hundred miles from home; but that seems no great distance
to the land-wandering Solubba. The man told me that when
summer was in, they would go to pitch, alone, at some water in
the wilderness : and (having no cattle) they must live then
partly of venison. "You have now asked me for an eye-
medicine, can you go hunting with blear eyes?"—"It is the
young men (*el-eyyâl*) that hunt; and I remain at home."—I
went further by a tent where the Heteymy housewife was
boiling down her léban, in a great cauldron, to mereesy. I sat
down to see it : her pot sputtered, and she asked me, could I
follow the spats with my eyes upward? "For I have heard
say, that the Nasâra cannot look up to heaven." Harshly she
chid 'my unbelief and my enmity to Ullah'; and I answered
her nothing. Then she took up a ladleful of her mereesy
paste, poured samn on it, in a bowl, and bade the stranger
eat, saying cheerfully, "Ah! why dost thou continue without
the religion? and have the Lord against thee and the people
also; only pray as we, and all the people will be thy kindred."
—Such were the nomads' daily words to me in these deserts.

The morning after, when the messenger had not returned,
we loaded betimes. The sun was rising as we rode forth; and
at the camp's end another Bishr householder bade us alight,
for he had made ready for us—no common morrow's hospitality;
but his dish of rice should have been our supper last evening.
Whilst we were eating, a poor woman came crying to me, 'to
cure her daughter and stay here,—we should be her guests; and
she pretended she would give the hakîm a camel when her child
was well.' Eyâd was now as iniquitously bent that I should
remain, as yesterday that I should remove; but I mounted and
rode forth : we began our journey without water. The guest
must not stretch the nomad hospitality, we could not ask them
to fill our small girby with the common juice of the earth; yet

when hosts send to a weyrid they will send also the guest's
water-skin to be filled with their own girbies.

We journeyed an hour or two, over the pathless mountains, to
a brow from whence we overlooked an empty plain, lying before
us to the north.   Only Merjàn had been here once in his childhood ; he knew there were waterpits yonder,—and we must
find them, since we had nothing to drink.   We descended, and
saw old footprints of small cattle ; and hoped they might lead
to the watering.   In that soil of plutonic grit were many
glittering morsels of clear crystal.   Merjàn, looking upon the
landmarks, thought bye and bye that we had passed the water ;
and my rafîks said they would return upon the thelûl to seek
it.   They bade me sit down here and await them : but I thought
the evil in their hearts might persuade them, ere they had
ridden a mile, to leave me to perish wretchedly.—Now couching
the thelûl, they unloaded my bags.   "The way is weary, they
said, to go back upon our feet, it may be long to find the
themeyil ; and a man might see further from the back of the
thelûl."—"I will look for the water with you."—"Nay, but
we will return to thee soon."—"Well go, but leave with me
thy matchlock, Eyâd ; and else we shall not part so."   He laid
down his gun unwillingly, and they mounted and rode from me.

They were out an hour and a half : then, to my comfort,
I saw them returning, and they brought water.—Eyâd now
complained that I had mistrusted him !   'And wellah no man
before had taken his gun from him ; but this is Khalîl !'—
"Being honest rafîks, you shall find me courteous ;—but tell
me, you fired upon your own tribesmen ?"—"Ay, billah ! I an
Auájy shot against the Auájy, and if I dealt so with mine own
kinsmen, what would I not do unto thee ?"—"How then might
I trust thee?"   *Merjàn:* "Thou sayest well, Khalîl, and this
Eyâd is a light-headed coxcomb."   Among the Aarab, friends
will bite at friends thus, betwixt their earnest and game, and it
is well taken.   *Eyâd:* "Come, let us sit down now and drink
tobacco ; for we will not journey all by day, but partly, where
more danger is, in the night-time.   Go Merjàn, gather stalks,
and let us bake our bread here against the evening, when it
were not well to kindle a fire."   The lad rose and went cheerfully ; for such is the duty of the younger among wayfaring
companions in the khála. * * *

* * * An idle hour passed, and we again set forward ; the
land was a sandy plain, bordered north-eastward by distant
mountains.   In the midst, between hills, is a summer watering
place of the Auájy, *Yemmen.*   There are ancient ten-fathom

wells, and well steyned, the work, they say, of the jân.—We have passed again from the plutonic rocks to the (here dark-coloured) red sandstones. A black crater hill appeared now, far in front upon the Harra, J. Ethnàn. This sandy wilderness is of the Auájy; 'white' soil, in which springs the best pasture, and I saw about us almost a thicket of green bushes!—yet the two-third parts of kinds which are not to the sustenance of any creature : we found there fresh foot-prints of ostriches. "Let us hasten, they said, [over this open country]," and Eyâd be-sought me to look in my books, and forecast the peril of our adventure ; ' for *wellah yudayyik súdry*, his breast was straitened, since I had made him lay down his matchlock by me.'

We halted an hour after the stars were shining, in a low place, under a solitary great bush ; and couched the thelûl before us, to shelter our bodies from the chill night wind, now rising to a hurricane, which pierced through their light Hejâz clothing. The Beduin rafîks, to comfort themselves with fire, forgot their daylight fears : they felt round in the darkness for a few sticks. And digging there with my hands, I found jella in the sand,—it was the old mûbrak, or night lair, of a camel ; and doubtless some former passenger had alighted to sleep at our inn of this great desert bush : the beast's dung had been buried by the wind, two or three years. Merjàn gathered his mantle full : the precious fuel soon glowed with a red heat in our sandy hearth, and I boiled tea, which they had not tasted till now.

The windy cold lasted all night, the blast was outrageous. Hardly at dawn could they, with stiffened fingers, kindle a new fire : the rafîks sat on,—there was not warmth in their half naked bodies to march against this wild wind.—A puff whirling about our bush scattered the dying embers, "Akhs ! cries Eyâd, the sot, *Ullah yulâan abu ha'l hubûb*, condemn the father of this blustering blast ; and he added, *Ullah yusullat aly ha'l hattab*, God punish this firewood." We rose at last ; and the Beduin rafîks bathed their bodies yet a moment in the heat, spreading their loose tunics over the dying embers. The baffling March blast raged in our teeth, carrying the sandy grit into our eyes. The companions staggered forward on foot,—we marched north-eastward : after two hours, they halted to kindle another fire. I saw the sky always overcast with thin clouds. Before noon the storm abated ; and the wind chopping round blew mildly in the afternoon, from the contrary part! We approached then the black border of the Harra, under the high crater-hill Ethnàn. Ethnàn stands solitary, in a field of sharp cinder-like and rifted lavas ; the nomads say that this great *hilla* is inaccessible.

Sometimes, after winter rain, they see a light reeking vapour
about the volcano head : and the like is seen in winter mornings
over certain deep rifts in the Harra,—'the smell of it is like
the breath of warm water.' This was confirmed to me by
Amm Mohammed.

In that part there is a (land-mark) valley-ground which lies
through the Harra towards el-Hâyat, *W. Mukheyat.* My small
waterskin might hardly satisfy the thirst of three men in one
summer's march, and this was the second journey; we drank
therefore only a little towards the afternoon, and had nothing
to eat. But my mind was full to see so many seamed, guttered
and naked cinder-hills of craters in the horrid black lavas
before us. The sense of this word hilla, hillaya, is according
to Amm Mohammed, 'that which appears evidently,'—and he
told me, there is a kind of dates of that name at Medina. Eyâd
said thus, "*Halla* is the Harra-hill of black powder and slaggy
matter; *hellayey* is a little Harra-hill; *hillî* or *hellowat* (others
say *hilliân*) are the Harra-hills together."—We marched towards
the same hillies which I had passed with Ghroceyb. When the
sun was near setting the rafîks descried, and greeted (devoutly)
the new moon.

The stars were shining when we halted amidst the hilliân
the eighth evening of our march from Kheybar. They thought
it perilous to kindle a fire here, and we had nothing to eat;—
there should be water, they said, not far off. Eyâd rose to
seek it, but in the night-time he could not find it again.—"I
have been absent, he murmured, twelve years!" He knew his
landmarks in the morning; then he went out, and brought
again our girby full of puddle water. The eye of the sun was
risen (as they said) 'a spear's length,' on height, when feeling
ourselves refreshed with the muddy bever, we set forward in
haste.

They held a course eastward over the lava country, to
Thúrghrud: that is a hamlet of one household upon the wells
of an antique settlement at the further border of the Harra.
Eyâd: "It was found in the last generation by one who
went up and down, like thyself, *yujassas,* spying out the
country:" and he said I should see Thúrghrud in exchange
for el-Hâyat. We went on by a long seyl and black sand-
bed in the lavas, where was sprung a little rabîa : and driving
the wretched thelûl to these green borders we let her graze
forward, or gathering the herbs in our hands as we marched,
we thrust them into her jaws. Where there grew an acacia
I commonly found a little herbage, springing under the north
side of the tree; that is where the lattice of minute leaves

casts a thin shadowing over the sun-stricken land, and the
little autumn moisture is last dried up. I was in advance
and saw camels' footprints! Calling the rafîks I inquired if
these were not of yesterday :—they said they were three days
old. They could not tell me if the traces were of a ghrazzu,—
that is, these Beduin Ageylies did not distinguish whether they
were the smaller footprints of thelûls, passing lightly with
riders, or of grazing camels! But seeing the footing of camel-
calves I could imagine that this was a drove moving between
the pastures. It happened as in the former case when we
found the traces of Ibn Simry's cattle, that a stranger judged
nigher the truth than his Beduin company. The footprints
lay always before us, and near mid-day, when they were in
some doubt whether we should not turn and avoid them, we
saw a camel troop pasturing in a green place, far in front.

The herders lay slumbering upon their faces in the green
grass, and they were not aware of us, till our voice startled
them with the fear of the desert. They rose hastily and with
dread, seeing our shining arms; but hearing the words of peace
(salaam aleyk) they took heart. When Eyâd afterward related
this adventure, "Had they been gôm, he said, we should have
taken wellah all that sight of cattle ! and left not one of them."
So sitting down with them we asked the elder herdsman, ' How
he durst lead his camels hither?' He answered, " *Ullah yetowil
ûmr ha'l weled!* God give that young man [the Emir Ibn
Rashîd] long life, under whose rule we may herd the cattle
without fear. It is not nowadays as it was ten years yore,
but I and my little brother may drive the 'bil to pasture all
this land over." He sent the child to milk for us; and way-
worn, hungry and thirsting, we swallowed every man three or
four pints at a draught : only Merjàn, because of his ague cake,
could not drink much milk. The lads, that were Heteymies,
had been some days out from the menzil, and their camels
were jezzîn. They carried but their sticks and cloaks, and a
bowl between them, and none other provision or arms. When
hungry or thirsting they draw a nâga's udder, and drink their
fill. They showed us where we might seek the nomads in
front, and we left them.

CHAPTER V

DESERT JOURNEY TO HÂYIL. THE NASRÂNY IS DRIVEN
FROM THENCE

WE came in the afternoon to a sandstone platform standing
like an island with cliffs in the basaltic Harra; the rafîks
thought we were at fault, as they looked far over the vulcanic
land and could not see the Aarab. From another high ground
they thought they saw a camel-herd upon a mountain far off :
yet looking with my glass I could not perceive them! We
marched thither, and saw a nomad sitting upon a lava brow,
keeping his camels. The man rose and came to meet us ; and
" What ho! he cries, Khalîl, comest thou hither again?" The
voice I knew, and now I saw it was Eyâda ibn Ajjuèyn, the
Heteymy sheykh, from whose menzil I had departed with
Ghroceyb to cross the Harra, to Kheybar !

Eyâda saluted me, but looked askance upon my rafîks, and
they were strange with him and silent. This is the custom
of the desert, when nomads meeting with nomads are in doubt
of each other whether friends or foemen. We all sat down ;
and said the robust Heteymy, "Khalîl what are these with
thee?"—" Ask them thyself."—" Well lads, what tribesmen be
ye,—that come I suppose from Kheybar?" They answered,
" We are Ageyl and the Bashat el-Medina has sent us to convey
Khalîl to Ibn Rashîd."—" But I see well that ye are Beduw,
and I say what Beduw?"—Eyâd answered, " Yâ Fulàn, O
Someone—for yet I heard not thy name, we said it not hitherto,
because there might be some debate betwixt our tribes."—
" Oho! is that your dread? but fear nothing [at a need he
had made light of them both], eigh, Khalîl! what are they?
—Well then, said he, I suppose ye be all thirsty ; I shall milk
for thee, Khalîl, and then for these, if they would drink!"
When my rafîks had drunk, Eyâd answered, " Now I may tell
thee we are of Bishr."—" It is well enough, we are friends ;
and Khalîl thou art I hear a Nasrâny, but how didst thou

see Kheybar?"—"A cursed place."—"Why wouldst thou go
thither, did I not warn thee?"—"Where is Ghroceyb?"—
"He is not far off, he is well; and Ghroceyb said thou wast
a good rafîk, save that thou and he fell out nigh Kheybar, I
wot never how, and thou wouldst have taken his thelûl."—"This
is his wild talk."—"It is likely, for Khalîl (he spoke to my rafîks)
is an honest man; the medicines our hareem bought of him,
and those of Kâsim's Aarab, they say, have been effectual.
How found ye him? is he a good rafîk?"—"Ay, this ought
we to say, though the man be a Nasrâny! but billah it is the
Moslems many times that should be named Nasâra."—"And
where will ye lodge to-night?"—"We were looking for the
Aarab, but tell us where should we seek their beyts."—"Yonder
(he said, rising up and showing us with his finger), take the low
way, on this hand; and so ye linger not you may be at their
menzil about the sunsetting. I may perhaps go thither myself in the evening, and to-morrow ride with you to Hâyil."—
We wondered to find this welfaring sheykh keeping his own
camels!

We journeyed on by cragged places, near the east border
of the Harra; and the sun was going down when we found
the nomads' booths pitched in a hollow ground. These also
were a *ferîj* (dim. *feraij*, and pl. *ferjàn*), or partition, of
Heteym. A ferîj is thus a nomad hamlet; and commonly the
households in a ferîj are nigh kindred. The most nomad
tribes in Nejd are dispersed thus three parts of the year, till
the lowest summer season; then they come together and pitch
a great standing menzil about some principal watering of their
dîra.

We dismounted before the sheykh's tent; and found a gay
Turkey carpet within, the uncomely behaviour of Heteym, and
a miserable hospitality. They set before us a bowl of milk-
shards, that can only be well broken between mill-stones. Yet
later, these uncivil hosts, who were fanatical young men, brought
us in from the camel-milking nearly two pailfuls of that perfect
refreshment in the desert:—Eyâda came not.

These hosts had heard of the Nasrâny, and of my journey
with Ghroceyb, and knew their kinsman's tale, 'that (though
a good rafîk) Khalîl would have taken the thelûl, when they
were nigh Kheybar.' Another said, 'It was a dangerous passage, and Ghroceyb returning had been in peril of his life; for
as he rode again over the Harra there fell a heavy rain. Then
he held westward to go about the worst of the lava country;
and as he was passing by a sandy seyl, a head of water came

down upon him : his thelûl foundered, and his matchlock fell
from him : Ghroceyb hardly saved himself to land, and drew
out the thelûl, and found his gun again.'

On the morrow we rode two hours, and came to another
hamlet of Heteym.—This day we would give to repose, and
went to alight at a beyt ; and by singular adventure that was
Sâlih's ! he who had forsaken me in these parts when I came
down (now three months ago) from Hâyil. As the man stepped
out to meet us, I called him by his name, and he wondered
to see me. He was girded in his gunner's belt, to go on foot
with a companion to el-Hâyat, two marches distant, to have new
stocks put, by a good sâny (who they heard was come thither),
to their long guns. Sâlih and Eyâd were tribesmen, of one
fendy, and of old acquaintance. The booth beside him was
of that elder Heteymy, the third companion in our autumn
journey. The man coming in soon after saluted me with a
hearty countenance ; and Sâlih forewent his day's journey to
the village for his guests' sake. This part of the vulcanic
country is named *Hebrân*, of a red sandstone berg standing in
the midst of the lavas : northward I saw again the mountains
Bushra or Buthra. Having drunk of their lében, we gave the
hours to repose. The elder Heteymy's wife asked me for a
little meal, and I gave her an handful, which was all I had ;
she sprinkled it in her cauldron of boiling samn and invited me
to the skimming. The housewife poured off the now clarified
samn into her butter-skin ; the sweet lees of flour and butter
she served before us.

I had returned safe, therefore I said nothing ; I could not
have greeted Sâlih with the Scandinavian urbanity, " Thanks
for the last time : " but his wife asked me, " Is Sâlih good,
Khalîl ? " They had a child of six years old ; the little boy,
naked as a worm, lay cowering from the cold in his mother's
arms ;—and he had been thus naked all the winter, at an
altitude (here) of four thousand feet ! It is a wonder they
may outlive such evil days. A man came in who was clothed
as I never saw another nomad, for he had upon him a home-
spun mantle of tent-cloth ; but the wind blew through his
heavy carpet garment. I found a piece of calico for the poor
mother, to make her child a little coat.

When the evening was come Sâlih set before us a boiled kid,
and we fared well. After supper he asked me were I now
appeased ?—*mesquin !* he might be afraid of my evil remembrance and of my magical books. He agreed with Eyâd and
Merjàn that they, in coming-by again from Hâyil, should return
to him, and then all go down together to Kheybar ; where he

would sell his samn for dates, to be received at the harvest. Though one of the hostile Bishr, he was by adoption an Heteymy, and with Eyâd would be safe at Kheybar.—But how might they find these three booths in the wilderness after many days ? Sâlih gave them the *shór* thus ; " The fourth day we remove (when I come again from el-Hâyat), to such a ground : when the cattle have eaten the herb thereabout, we shall remove to such other; after ten or twelve days seek for us between such and such landmarks, and drinking of such waters."—He spoke to ears which knew the names of all bergs and rocks and seyls and hollow grounds in that vast wilderness : Eyâd had wandered there in his youth. * * *

* * * When the morning's light wakened us we arose and departed. We passed by the berg Hebrân, and came to a vast *niggera*, or sunken bay in the lavas : Eyâd brought me to see the place, which they name *Baedi*, as a natural wonder. This is the summer water station of those Sbáa households which wander in the south with Misshel ; when the Auájy pitch at Baitha Nethîl. In the basalt floor, littered with the old jella of the nomads' camels, are two ancient well-pits. Wild doves flew up from them, as we came and looked in ; they are the birds of the desert waters, even of such as be bitter and baneful to the Arabs. We sat to rest out a pleasant hour in the cliff's shadow (for we thought the Aarab beyond could not be far off) : and there a plot of nettles seemed to my eyes a garden in the desert !— those green neighbours and homely inheritors, in every land, of human nature.

We rested our fill ; then I remounted, and they walked forward. Merjàn was weary and angry in the midst of our long journey. I said to him, as we went out, " Step on, lad, or let me pass, you linger under the feet of the thelûl." He murmured, and turning, with a malignant look, levelled his matchlock at my breast. So I said, " Reach me that gun, and I will hang it at the saddle-bow, this will be better for thee : " I spoke to Eyâd to take his matchlock from him and hang it at the peak. Eyâd promised for the lad, " He should never offend me again : forgive him now, Khalîl—because I already alighted—I also must bear with him, and this is ever his nature, full of teen." " Enough and pass over now ;—but if I see the like again, weled, I shall teach thee thy error. Eyâd, was there ever Beduwy who threatened death to his rafîk ? "—" No, by Ullah." " But this (man), cries the splenetic lad, is a Nasrâny,—*with a Nasrâny who need keep any law ? is not this an enemy of Ullah ?* " At that word I wrested his gun from him, and gave it to Eyâd ;

and laying my driving-stick upon the lad (since this is the only
discipline they know at Medina), I swinged him soundly, in
a moment, and made all his back smart. Eyâd from behind
caught my arms; and the lad, set free, came and kicked me in
villanous manner, and making a weapon of his heavy head-cord,
he struck at me in the face: then he caught up a huge stone
and was coming on to break my head, but in this I loosed myself
from Eyâd. "We have all done foolishly (exclaimed Eyâd), eigh!
what will be said when this is told another day?—here! take thy
gun, Merjàn, but go out of Khalîl's sight; and Khalîl be friends
with us, and mount again. Ullah! we were almost at mischief;
and Merjàn is the most narrow-souled of all that ever I saw, and
he was always thus."

We moved on in silence; I said only that at the next menzil
we would leave Merjàn. He was cause, also, that we suffered
thirst in the way; since we must divide with him a third of my
small herdsman's girby. Worse than all was that the peevish
lad continually corrupted the little good nature in Eyâd, with
fanatical whisperings, and drew him from me. I repented of
my misplaced humanity towards him, and of my yielding to such
rafîks to take another way. Yet it had been as good to wink at
the lad's offence, if in so doing I should not have seemed to be
afraid of them. The Turkish argument of the rod might bring
such spirits to better knowledge; but it is well to be at peace
with the Arabs upon any reasonable conditions, that being of a
feminine humour, they are kind friends and implacable enemies.

The Harra is here like a rolling tide of basalt: the long bilges
often rise about pit-like lava bottoms, or *niggeras*, which lie full
of blown sand. Soon after this we came to the edge of the lava-
field; where upon our right hand, a path descended to Thúrghrud, half a journey distant. "Come, I said, we are to go thither."
But Eyâd answered, "The way lies now over difficult lavas! and,
Khalîl, we ought to have held eastward from the morning: yet
I will go thither for thy sake, although we cannot arrive this
night, and we have nothing to eat." Merjàn cried to Eyâd not
to yield, that he himself would not go out of the way to Thúrghrud. *Eyâd:* "If we go forward, we may be with Aarab to-
night: so Sâlih said truly, they are encamped under yonder
mountain." This seemed the best rede for weary men: I gave
Eyâd the word to lead forward. We descended then from the
Harra side into a plain country of granite grit, without blade or
bush. 'Yet here in good years, said Eyâd, they find pasture;
but now the land is máhal, because no autumn rain had fallen
in these parts.'—So we marched some miles, and passed by the
(granitic) Thullân Buthra.

" —But where are we come! exclaimed the rafîks, gazing about them : there can be no Aarab in this khála ; could Sâlih have a mind to deceive us ? " The sun set over our forlorn march ; and we halted in the sandy bed of a seyl to sleep. They hobbled the thelûl's forelegs, and loosed her out in the moonlight ; but there was no pasture. We were fasting since yesterday, and had nothing to eat, and no water. They found a great waif root, and therewith we made a good fire ; the deep ground covered us, under mountains which are named *Ethmâd* (pl. of *Thammad*).

The silent night in the dark khála knit again our human imbecility and misery, at the evening fire, and accorded the day's broken fellowship. Merjàn forgot his spite ; but showing me some swelling wheals, " Dealest thou thus, he said, with thy friend, Khalîl? the chill is come, and with it the smart."— " The fault was thine ; and I bid you remember that on the road there is neither Moslem nor Nasrâny, but we are *rufaká, akhuán*, fellows and brethren."—" Well, Khalîl, let us speak no more of it." Merjàn went out—our last care in the night— to bring in the weary and empty thelûl ; he couched her to bear off the night wind, and we closed our eyes.

The new day rising, we stood up in our sandy beds and were ready to depart. We marched some hours through that dead plain country ; and came among pale granite hills, where only the silver-voiced siskin, *Umm Sâlema*, flitted in the rocky solitude before us. We had no water, and Eyâd went on climbing amongst the bergs at our right hand. Towards noon he made a sign and shouted, 'that Merjàn come to him with our girby'.—They brought down the skin full of water, which Eyâd had found in the hollow of a rock, overlaid with a flat stone ; the work, they supposed, of some Solubby (hunter).— Rubbing milk-shards in the water, we drank mereesy and refreshed ourselves. The height of the country is 4600 feet. We journeyed all day in this poor plight ; the same gritty barrenness of plain-land encumbered with granitic and basalt bergs lay always before us. Once only we found some last year's footprints of a *ráhla*.

They watched the horizon, and went on looking earnestly for the Aarab : at half-afternoon Merjàn. who was very clear sighted, cried out " I see *zól !* "—zôl (pl. *azzuál*), is the looming in the eye of aught which may not be plainly distinguished ; so a blind patient has said to me, "I see the zôl of the sun." Eyâd gazed earnestly and answered, ' He thought billah he did see somewhat.'—Azzuâl in the desert are discerned moving in the farthest offing, but whether wild creatures or cattle, or

Aarab, it cannot be told. When Eyâd and Merjàn had watched awhile, they said, "We see two men riding on one thelûl!" Then they pulled off hastily their gun-leathers, struck fire, and blew the matches and put powder to the touch-holes of their long pieces I saw in Eyâd a sort of haste and trouble! "Why thus?" I asked.—"But they have seen us, and now they come hither!"—My two rafîks went out, singing and leaping to the encounter, and left me with the thelûl; my secret arms put me out of all doubt. Bye and bye they returned saying, that when those riders saw the glance of their guns they held off.—"But let us not linger (they cried) in this neighbourhood:" they mounted the thelûl together and rode from me. I followed weakly on foot, and it came into my mind, that they would forsake me.

The day's light faded, the sun at length kissed the horizon, and our hope went down with the sun: we must lodge again without food or human comfort in the khâla. The Beduin rafîks climbed upon all rocks to look far out over the desert, and I rode in the plain between them. The thelûl went fasting in the mahâl this second day; but now the wilderness began to amend. The sun was sinking when Merjàn shouted, 'He had seen a flock'. Then Eyâd mounted with me, and urging his thelûl we made haste to arrive in the short twilight ere it should be dark night: we trotted a mile, and Merjàn ran beside us. We soon saw a great flock trooping down in a rocky bay of the mountain in front. A maiden and a lad were herding them; and unlike all that I had seen till now, there were no goats in that nomad flock. The brethren may have heard the clatter of our riding in the loose stones, or caught a sight of three men coming, for they had turned their backs! Such meetings are never without dread in the khâla: if we had been land-lopers they were taken tardy; we had bound them, and driven off the slow-footed flock all that night. Perchance such thoughts were in Eyâd, for he had not yet saluted them; and I first hailed the lad,—'Salaam aleyk!' He hearing it was peace, turned friendly; and Eyâd asked him "Fen el-maâziba, where is the place of entertainment?"—we had not seen the booths The young Beduwy answered us, with a cheerful alacrity, "It is not far off."

We knew not what tribesmen they were. The young man left his sister with the flock, and led on before us. It was past prayer time, and none had said his devotion:—they kneeled down now on the sand in the glooming, but (as strangers) not together, and I rode by them;—a neglect of religion which is not marked in the weary wayfarer, for one must dismount to say his formal prayers. It was dusk when we came to their menzil ; and there were but three booths. It had been agreed amongst us that my rafîks should not name me Nasrâny. Gently the host received us into his tent and spread down a gay Turkey carpet in the men's sitting place,—it was doubtless his own and his housewife's only bedding. Then he brought a vast bowl, full of lében, and bade us slack our thirst : so he left us awhile (to prepare the guest-meal). When I asked my rafîks, what Aarab were these, Eyâd whispered, "By their speech they should be Harb."—"And what Harb?"—"We cannot tell yet." Merjàn said in my ear, "Repentest thou now to have brought me with thee, Khalîl? did not my eyes lead thee to this night's entertainment? and thou hadst else lodged again in the khála."

The host came again, and insisted gently, asking, might he take our water, for they had none. My rafîks forbade him with their desert courtesy, knowing it was therewith that he would boil the guest-meal, for us ; but the goodman prevailed : his sacrifice of hospitality, a yearling lamb, had been slain already. Now upon both parts the Beduins told their tribes : these were Beny Sâlem, of Harb in Nejd ; but their native dîra is upon the *sultâny* or highway betwixt the Harameyn. It was my first coming to tents of that Beduin nation; and I had not seen nomad hosts of this noble behaviour. The smiling householder filled again and again his great milk-bowl before us, as he saw it drawn low :—we drank for the thirst of two days, which could not soon be allayed. Seeing me drink deepest of three, the kind host, *maazîb*, exhorted me with *ighrtebig!* 'take thy evening drink,' and he piously lifted the bowl to my lips. "Drink! said he, for here is the good of Ullah, the Lord be praised, and no lack! and coming from the southward, ye have passed much weary country." *Eyâd:* "Wellah it is all máhal, and last night we were khlûa (lone men without human shelter in the khála); this is the second day, till this evening we found you."—"El-hamd illah! the Lord be praised therefore," answered the good householder. Eyâd told them of the ghrazzu. "And Khalîl, said our host, what is he?—a *Méshedy?* (citizen of the town of Aly's violent death or "martyrdom", *Méshed Aly*, before mentioned); methinks his speech, *rótn,* and his hue be like theirs."—"Ay, ay. (answered my rafîks), a Méshedy, an hakîm, he is now returning to Hâyil."—"An uncle's son of his was here very lately, a worthy man ; he came from Hâyil, to sell clothing among the Aarab,—and, Khalîl, dost thou not know him? he was as like to thee, billah, as if ye were brethren."

We lay down to rest ourselves. An hour or two later this generous maazîb and the shepherd, his brother, bore in a mighty charger of rice, and the steaming mutton heaped upon it; their hospitality of the desert was more than one man might carry.— The nomad dish is set upon the carpet, or else on a piece of tent-cloth, that no fallen morsels might be trodden down in the earth: —and if they see but a little milk spilled (in this everlasting dearth and indigence of all things), any born Arabians will be out of countenance. I have heard some sentence of their Néby blaming spilt milk.—The kind maazîb called upon us, saying, *Gûm! hŷakom Ullah wa en-Néby. eflah!* 'rise, take your meat, and the Lord give you life, and His Prophet.' We answered, kneeling about the dish, *Ullah hŷ-îk*, 'May the Lord give thee life':—the host left us to eat. But first Eyâd laid aside three of the best pieces, "for the maazîb, and his wives; they have kept back nothing, he said, for themselves." The nomad house-mothers do always withhold somewhat for themselves and their children, but Eyâd, the fine Beduin gentleman, savoured of the town, rather than of the honest simplicity of the desert. "Ah! nay, what is this ye do? it needeth not, quoth the return-ing host, wellah we have enough; *eflah!* only eat! put your hands to it." "Prithee sit down with us," says Eyâd. "Sit down with us, O maazîb, said we all; without thee we cannot eat." "*Ebbeden*, nay I pray you, never."—Who among Beduins is first satisfied he holds his hand still at the dish; whereas the oasis dweller and the townling, rises and going aside by himself to wash his hands, puts the hungry and slow eaters out of countenance. A Beduwy at the dish, if he have seen the town, will rend off some of the best morsels, and lay them ready to a friend's hand:—Eyâd showed me now this token of a friendly mind.

The Beduw are nimble eaters; their fingers are expert to rend the meat, and they swallow their few handfuls of boiled rice or corn with that bird-like celerity which is in all their deeds. In supping with them, being a weak and slow eater, when I had asked their indulgence, I made no case of this usage; since to enable nature in the worship of the Creator is more than every apefaced devising of human hypocrisy. If any man called me I held that he did it in sincerity; and the Arabs commended that honest plainness in a stranger among them. There is no second giving of thanks to the heavenly Providence; but rising after meat we bless the man, saying (in this dîra) *Unaam Ullah aleyk*, 'the lord be gracious unto thee,' *yâ maazîb*. The dish is borne out, the underset cloth is drawn, and the bowl is fetched to us: we drink and return

to our sitting place at the hearth. Although welfaring and
bountiful the goodman had no coffee ;—coffee Arabs are seldom
of this hospitality.

The guest (we have seen) should depart when the morrow
breaks; and the host sends him away fasting, to journey all
that day in the khála. But if they be his friends, and it is the
season of milk, a good householder will detain the last night's
guests, till his jâra have poured them out a draught. Our Beny
Sâlem maazîb was of no half-hearted hospitality, and when
we rose to depart he gently delayed us. " My wife, he said, is
rocking the semîla, have patience till the butter come, that she
may pour you out a little léban; you twain are Beduw, but
this Méshedy is not, as we, one wont to walk all day in the
wilderness and taste nothing."—The second spring-time was
come about of my sojourning in Arabia; the desert land flowed
again with milk, and I saw with bowings down of the soul to
the divine Nature, this new sweet *rabîa.* " *Ustibbah !* (cries the
good man, with the hollow-voiced franchise of the dry desert),
take thy morning drink."

— I speak many times of the Arabian hospitality, since of
this I have been often questioned in Europe ; and for a memorial
of worthy persons. The hospitality of the worsted booths,—
the gentle entertainment of passengers and strangers in a land
full of misery and fear, we have seen to be religious. I have
heard also this saying in the mouths of town Arabians,—" It
is for the report which passing strangers may sow of them in
the country : for the hosts beyond will be sure to ask of their
guests, ' Where lodged ye the last night; and were ye well
entertained ? ' "

We journeyed now in a plain desert of gritty sand, which is
called *Shaaba ;* beset with a world of trappy and smooth basalt
bergs, so that we could not see far to any part: all this soil
seyls down to the W. er-Rummah. We journeyed an hour and
came by a wide *rautha.* Rautha is any bottom, in the desert,
which is a sinking place of ponded winter rain : the streaming
showers carry down fine sediment from the upper ground, and
the soil is a crusted clay and loam. Rautha may signify garden,
—and such is their cheerful aspect of green shrubs in the
khála: the plural is *riâth,* [which is also the name of the
Waháby metropolis in East Nejd]. I asked Eyâd, " Is not this
soil as good and large as the Teyma oasis? wherefore then has
it not been settled ? "—" I suppose, he answered, that there is
no water, or some wells had been found in it, of the auelîn."
Gá likewise or *khôb'ra* is a naked clay bottom in the desert,

where shallow water is ponded after heavy rain. *Khôbra* (or Khûbbera) is the ancient name of a principal oasis in the Nefûd of Kasîm :—I came there later.

Eyâd with a stone-cast killed a hare; and none can better handle a stone than the Aarab: we halted and they made a fire of sticks. The southern Aarab have seldom a knife, Eyâd borrowed my penknife to cut the throat of his venison; and then he cast in the hare as it was. When their stubble fire was burned out, Eyâd took up his hare, roasted whole in the skin, and broke and divided it; and we found it tender and savoury meat. This is the hunter's kitchen : they stay not to pluck, to flay, to bowel, nor for any tools or vessel; but that is well dressed which comes forth, for hungry men. In the hollow of the carcase the Beduwy found a little blood; this he licked up greedily, with some of the *ferth* or cud, and murmured the mocking desert proverb 'I am *Shurma* (Cleft-lips) quoth the hare.' They do thus in ignorance; Amm Mohammed had done the like in his youth, and had not considered that the blood is forbidden. I said to him, "When a beast is killed, although ye let some blood at the throat, does not nearly all the gore remain in the body ?—and this you eat!" He answered in a frank wonder, "Yes, thou sayest sooth! the gore is left in the body,—and we eat it in the flesh! well then I can see no difference." The desert hare is small, and the delicate body parted among three made us but a slender breakfast. Eyâd in the same place found the gallery (with two holes) of a jerboa; it is the edible spring rat of the droughty wilderness, a little underground creature, not weighing two ounces, with very long hinder legs and a very long tufted tail, silken pelt, and white belly; in form she resembles the pouched rats of Australia. Eyâd digged up the mine with his camel stick and, snatching the feeble prey, he slit her throat with a twig, and threw it on the embers; a moment after he offered us morsels, but we would not taste. The jerboa and the wábar ruminate, say the hunters; Amm Mohammed told me, that they are often shot with the cud in the mouth.

We loosed out the thelûl, and sat on in this pleasant place of pasture. Merjàn lifted the shidád to relieve her, and "Look! laughed he, if her hump be not risen ?"—The constraint of the saddle, and our diligence in feeding her in the slow marches, made the sick beast to seem rather the better. Seeing her old brandmark was the *dubbús*, I enquired 'Have you robbed her then from the Heteym ?' Eyâd was amazed that I should know a wasm! and he boasted that she was of the best blood of the *Benát* (daughters of) *et-Tî* (or *Tîh*); he had bought her from Heteym, a foal, for forty reals: she could then outstrip the most thelûls. Now she was a carrion riding beast of the Ageyl; and such was Eyâd's avarice that he had sent her down twice, freighted like a pack camel, with the Kheybar women's palm-plait to Medina; for which the Beduins there laughed him to scorn.—The Tî or Tîh is a fabulous wild hurr, or dromedary male, in the Sherarát wilderness. 'He has only three ribs, they say, and runs with prodigious swiftness; he may outstrip any horse.' The Sherarát are said to let their dromedaries stray in the desert, that haply they may be covered by the Tîh; and they pretend to discern his offspring by the token of the three ribs. The thelûls of the Sherarát [an 'alien' Arabian kindred] are praised above other in Western Arabia: Ibn Rashîd's armed band are mounted upon the light and fleet *Sheráries.*—Very excellent also, though of little stature, are the (Howeytát) dromedaries in the Nefûd of el-Arîsh.

Eyâd seemed to be a man of very honourable presence, with his comely Jew-like visage, and well-set full black beard; he went well clad, and with the gallant carriage of the sheykhs of the desert. Busy-eyed he was, and a distracted gazer: his speech was less honest than smooth and well sounding. I enquired 'Wherefore he wore not the horns?—the Beduin lovelocks should well become his manly [Annezy] beauty.' *Eyâd:* "I have done with such young men's vanities, since my horn upon this side was shot away, and a second ball cropt the horn on my other;—but that warning was not lost to me! Ay billah! I am out of taste of the Beduin life: one day we abound with the good of Ullah, but on the morrow our halàl may be taken by an enemies' ghrazzu! And if a man have not then good friends, to bring together somewhat for him again, wellah he must go a-begging."

Eyâd had been bred out of his own tribe, among Shammar, and in this dîra where we now came. His father was a substantial sheykh, one who rode upon his own mare; and young Eyâd rode upon a stallion. One day a strong foray of Heteym robbed the camels of his menzil, and Eyâd among the rest galloped to meet them. The Heteymàn (nomads well nourished with milk) are strong-bodied and manly fighters; they are besides well armed, more than the Beduw, and many are marksmen. Eyâd bore before his lance two thelûl riders; and whilst he tilted in among the foemen, who were all thelûl riders, a bullet and a second ball cropt his braided locks; he lost also his horse, and not his young life. "Eyâd, thou playedest the lion!"—"Aha! and canst thou think what said the Heteym?—'By Ullah let that young rider of the horse come over to us when he will, and lie

with our hareem, that they may bring forth valiant sons.' "—
He thought, since we saw him, that Eyâda ibn Ajjuèyn had
been in that raid with them.

"And when thou hast thy arrears, those hundreds of reals,
wilt thou buy thee other halàl? we shall see thee prosperous
and a sheykh again?"—"Prosperous, and a sheykh, it might
well be, were I another; but my head is broken, and I do this
or that many times of a wrong judgment and fondly :—but
become a Beduwy again, nay! I love no more such hazards :
I will buy and sell at Hâyil. If I sell shirt-cloth and cloaks
and *mandîls* (kerchiefs) in the sûk, all the Beduw will come to
me; moreover, being a Beduwy, I shall know how to trade with
them for camels and small cattle. Besides I will be Ibn Rashîd's
man (one of his rajajîl) and receive a salary from him every
month, always sure, and ride in the ghrazzus, and in every one
take something!"—"We shall see thee then a shopkeeper!—
but the best life, man, is to be a Beduwy." *Merjàn:* "Well
said Khalîl, the best life is with the Beduw." *Eyâd:* "But I
will none of it, and 'all is not *Khúthera* and *Tunis*';"—he
could not expound to me his town-learned proverb. * * *

* * * We set forward; and after mid-day we came to six
Shammar booths. The sheykh, a young man, *Braitshàn,* was
known to Eyâd. My rafîks rejoiced to see his coffee-pots in
the ashpit; for they had not tasted kahwa (this fortnight) since
we set out from Kheybar The beyt was large and lofty; which
is the Shammar and Annezy building wise. A mare grazed in
sight; a sign that this was not a poor sheykh's household. The
men who came in from the neighbour tents were also known to
Eyâd; and I was not unknown, for one said presently, "Is not
this Khalîl, the Nasrâny?"—he had seen me at Hâyil. We
should pass this day among them, and my rafîks loosed out the
thelûl to pasture. In the afternoon an old man led us to his
booth to drink more coffee; he had a son an Ageyly at Medina.
"I was lately there, said he, and I found my lad and his comrade
eating their victuals *hâf*, without samn!—it is an ill service that
cannot pay a man his bread."

They mused seeing the Nasrâny amongst them :—'Khalîl, an
adversary of Ullah, and yet like another man!' Eyâd answered
them in mirth, "So it seems that one might live well enough
although he were a kafir!" * * *

* * * We heard that Ibn Rashîd was not at Hâyil. "The
Emir, they said, is *ghrazzai* (upon an expedition) in the north

with the rajajîl; the princes [as Hamûd, Sleymàn] are with
him, and they lie encamped at *Heyennîeh*",—that is a place of
wells in the Nefûd, towards Jauf. The Shammar princes have
fortified it with a block-house; and a man or two are left in
garrison, who are to shoot out at hostile ghrazzus: so that none
shall draw water there, to pass over, contrary to the will of Ibn
Rashîd. We heard that Anèybar was left deputy at Hâyil.—
The sky was overcast whilst we sat, and a heavy shower fell
suddenly. The sun soon shone forth again, and the hareem ran
joyfully from the tents to fill their girbies, under the streaming
granite rocks. The sheykh bade replenish the coffee pots, and
give us a bowl of that sweet water to drink —Braitshàn's mother
boiled us a supper-dish of temmn: the nomad hospitality of
milk was here scant,—but this is commonly seen in a coffee
sheykh's beyt.

Departing betimes on the morrow we journeyed in a country
now perfectly known to Eyâd. The next hollow ground was
like a bed of colocynth gourds, they are in colour and bigness
as oranges. We marched two hours and came to a troop of
camels: the herds were two young men of Shammar. They
asked of the land backward, by which we had passed, 'Was
the rabîa sprung, and which and which plants for pasture had
we seen there?' Then one of them went to a milch nâga to
milk for us; but the other, looking upon me, said, "Is not this
Khalîl, the Nasrâny?" [he too had seen me in Hâyil]! We
were here abreast of the first outlying settlements of the Jebel;
and now looking on our left hand, we had a pleasant sight,
between two rising grounds, of green corn plots. My rafîks
said, "It is *Gussa*, a corn hamlet, and you may see some of
their women yonder; they come abroad to gather green fodder
for the well camels." A young man turned from beside them,
with a grass-hook in his hand; and ran hither to enquire
tidings of us passengers.—Nor he nor might those women be
easily discerned from Beduw! After the first word he asked
us for a galliûn of tobacco;—"But come, he said, with me to
our kasûr; ye shall find dates and coffee, and there rest yourselves." He trussed on his neck what gathered herbs he had
in his cloak, and ran before us to the settlement. We found
their kasûr to be poor low cottages of a single chamber.—Gussa
is a [new] desert grange of the Emir, inhabited only three
months in the year, for the watering of the corn fields (here
from six-fathom square well-pits sunk in the hard earth), till
the harvest; then the husbandmen will go home to their villages:
the site is in a small wady.

Here were but six households of fifteen or twenty persons,

seldom visited by tarkîes (*terágy*). *Aly* our host set before us
dates with some of his spring butter and léban : I wondered at
his alacrity to welcome us,—as if we had been of old acquaintance ! Then he told them, that ' Last night he dreamed of a
tarkîy, which should bring them tobacco ! '—Even here one knew
me ! and said, "Is not this Khalîl, the Nasrâny ? and he has a
paper from Ibn Rashîd, that none may molest him ; I myself saw
it sealed by the Emir." "How sweet, they exclaimed, is dokhàn
when we taste it again !—wellah we are *sherarîb* (tobacco tip-
plers)." I said, "Ye have land, why then do ye not sow it ? "—
"Well, we bib it ; but to sow tobacco, and see the plant growing
in our fields, that were an unseemly thing, *makrúha* !" When we
left them near midday, they counselled us to pass by *Agella*,
another like ' dîra,' or outlying corn settlement ; we might
arrive there ere nightfall.—Beyond their cornfields, I saw young
palms set in the seyl-strand : but wanting water, many were
already sere. Commonly the sappy herb is seen to spring in
any hole (that was perhaps the burrow of some wild creature)
in the hard khála, though the waste soil be all bare : and the
Gussa husbandmen had planted in like wise their palms that
could not be watered ; the ownership was betwixt them and the
Beduw.

As they had shown us we held our way, through a grey
and russet granite country, with more often basalt than the
former trap rocks. Eyâd showed me landmarks, eastward, of
the wells *es-Sákf*, a summer water-station of Shammar. Under
a granite hill I saw lower courses of two cell-heaps, like those
in the Harras ; and in another place eight or more breast-high
wild flagstones of granite, set up in a row.—There was in heathen
times an idol's house in these forlorn mountains.

Seeing the discoloured head of a granite berg above us, the
rafîks climbed there to look for water ; and finding some they
filled our girby. When the sun was setting we came to a
hollow path, which was likely to lead to Agella. The wilderness was again máhal, a rising wind ruffled about us, and clouds
covered the stars with darkness which seemed to bereave the
earth from under our footsteps. My companions would seek
now some sheltered place, and slumber till morning ; but I
encouraged them to go forward, to find the settlement to-
night. We journeyed yet two hours, and I saw some house-
building, though my companions answered me, it was a white
rock : we heard voices and barking dogs soon after, and passed
before a solitary nomad booth. We were come to the " dîrat "
el-Agella. Here were but two cabins of single ground-cham-
bers and wells, and cornplots. The wind was high, we shouted

o

under the first of the house-walls ; and a man came forth who bade us good evening. He fetched us fuel, and we kindled a fire in the lee of his house, and warmed ourselves : then our host brought us dates and butter and léban, and said, ' He was sorry he could not lodge us within doors, and the hour was late to cook anything.' Afterward, taking up his empty vessels, he left us to sleep.

We had gone, they said, by a small settlement, *Háfirat Zeylúl ;* my companions had not been here before Hâyil was now not far off, Eyâd said ; "To-morrow, we will set forward in the *jéhemma,* that is *betwixt the dog and the wolf,*—which is so soon, Khalîl, as thou mayest distinguish between a hound and the wolf, (in the dawning)."—The northern blast (of this last night in March) was keen and rude, and when the day broke, we rose shivering ; they would not remove now till the warm sun was somewhat risen. Yet we had rested through this night better than our hosts ; for as we lay awake in the cold, we heard the shrieking of their well-wheels till the morning light. *Merjàn :* "Have the husbandmen or the Beduw the better life? speak, Khalîl, for we know that thou wast brought up among the Beduw."—"I would sell my palms, if I had any, to buy camels, and dwell with the nomads."—"And I," said he.

As we set forward the *ajjàj* or sand-bearing wind encumbered our eyes. A boy came along with us returning to el-Kasr, which we should pass to-day :—so may any person join himself to what travelling company he will in the open Arabic countries. The wilderness eastward is a plain full of granite bergs, whose heads are often trappy basalt ; more seldom they are crumbling needles of slaty trap rock. Before noon, we were in sight of el-Kasr, under Ajja, which Merjàn in his loghra pronounced *Ejja :* we had passed from the máhal, and a spring greenness was here upon the face of the desert. There are circuits of the common soil about the desert villages where no nomads may drive their cattle upon pain of being accused to the Emir : such township rights are called *h'má* [*confer* Numb. xxxv 2–5]. We saw here a young man of el-Kasr, riding round upon an ass to gather fuel, and to cut fodder for his well camels. Now he crossed to us and cried welcome, and alighted ; that was to pull out a sour milkskin from his wallet—of which he poured us out to drink, saying, "You passengers may be thirsty ?" Then taking forth dates, he spread them on the ground before us, and bade us break our fasts : so remounting cheerfully, he said, "We shall meet again this evening in the village."

The rafîks loosed out the thelûl, and we lay down in the sand of a seyl without shadow from the sun, to repose awhile. The

Ageylies chatted ; and when the village boy heard say between their talk, that there was a Dowlat at Medina,—" El-Medina! cries he, *kus umm-ha !*"—Eyâd and Merjàn looked up like saints, with beatific visages! and told him, with a religious awe, ' He had made himself a kafir! for knew he not that el-Medina is one of the two sanctuaries?' They added that word of the sighing Mohammedan piety, " Ullah, *ammr-ha*, the Lord build up Medina "—I have heard some Beduwy put thereto ' *mûbrak thelûl en-Néby*, the couching place of the prophet's dromedary,' [Christians in the Arabic border-lands will say in their sleeve, *Ullah yuharrak-ha*, ' The Lord consume her with fire!'] It was new lore to the poor lad, who answered half aghast, that 'he meant not to speak anything amiss, and he took refuge in Ullah.' He drew out parched locusts from his scrip, and fell to eat again : locust clouds had passed over the Jebel, he said, two months before, but the damage had been light.

The tôlâ, or new fruit-stalks of their palms, were not yet put forth ; we saw also their corn standing green : so that the harvest in Jebel Shammar may be nearly three weeks later than at Kheybar and Medina.

At half-afternoon we made forward towards the (orchard) walls of el-Kasr, fortified with the lighthouse-like towers of a former age. Eyâd said, 'And if we set out betimes on the morrow, we might arrive in Hâyil, *hâ'l hazza*, about this time.' The villagers were now at rest in their houses, in the hottest of the day, and no man stirring. We went astray in the outer blind lanes of the clay village, with broken walls and cavernous ground of filthy sunny dust. Europeans look upon the Arabic squalor with loathing : to our senses it is heathenish. Some children brought us into the town. At the midst is a small open place with a well-conduit, where we watered the thelûl : that water is sweet, but lukewarm, as all ground-water in Arabia. Then we went to sit down, where the high western wall cast already a little shadow, in the public view ; looking that some householder would call us.

Men stood in their cottage thresholds to look at us Beduins : then one approached,—it seems these villagers take the charge in turn, and we stood up to meet him. He enquired, "What be ye, and whence come ye, and whither will ye ? " we sat down after our answer, and he left us. He came again and said ' *sum !*' and we rose and followed him. The villager led us into his cottage yard ; here we sat on the earth, and he brought us dates, with a little butter and thin whey : when we had eaten he returned, and we were called to the village Kahwa. Here also they knew me, for some had seen me in Hâyil. These morose peasants cumbered me with religious questions; till I was most weary of their insane fanaticism.

El-Kasr, that is *Kasr el-Asheruwát*, is a village of two hundred and fifty to three hundred souls; the large graveyard, without the place, is a wilderness of wild headstones of many generations. Their wells are sunk to a depth (the Beduins say) of thirty fathoms!

We now heard sure tidings of the Emir; his camp had been removed to *Hazzel*, that is an *aed* or jau (watering place made in hollow ground) not distant, eastwards, from Shekàky in the Ruwàlla country (where was this year a plentiful rabîa), 'and all Shammar was with him and the Emir's cattle.' They were not many days out from Hâyil, and the coming again of the Prince and his people would not be for some other weeks. These are the pastoral, and warlike spring excursions of the Shammar Princes. A month or two they lie thus in tents like the Beduw; but the end of their loitering idleness is a vehement activity: for as ever their cattle are murubba, they will mount upon some great ghrazzu, with the rajajîl and a cloud of Beduw, and ride swiftly to surprise their enemies; and after that they come again (commonly with a booty) to Hâyil.—All the desert above Kasr was, they told us, máhal. The rabîa was this year upon the western side of Ajja; and the Emir's troops of mares and horses had been sent to graze about Môgug. Eyâd enquired, 'If anything had been heard of the twenty Ageyl riders from Medina!'

The villagers of Kasr are Beny Temîm: theirs is a very ancient name in Arabia. They were of old time Beduins and villagers, and their settled tribesmen were partly of the nomad life; now they are only villagers. They are more robust than the Beduin neighbours, but churlish, and of little hospitality. In the evening these villagers talked tediously with us strangers, and made no kahwa. Upon a side of their public coffee hall was a raised bank of clay gravel, the *manèm* or travellers' bedstead, a very harsh and stony lodging to those who come in from the austere delicacy of the desert; where in nearly every place is some softness of the pure sand. The nights, which we had found cold in the open wilderness, were here warm in the shelter of walls.—When we departed ere day, I saw many of these Arabian peasants sleeping abroad in their mantles; they lay stretched like hounds in the dust of the village street.

At sunrise we saw the twin heads of the Sumrâ Hâyil, Eyâd responded to all men's questions; "We go with this Khalîl to Hâyil, at the commandment of the Bashat el-Medina;

and are bearers of his sealed letter to Ibn Rashîd; but we know not what is in the writing,—which may be to cut off all our heads!'—also I said in my heart, 'The Turks are treacherous!'—But should I break the Pasha's seal? No! I would sooner hope for a fair event of that hazard. This sealed letter of the governor of Medina, was opened after my returning from Arabia, at a British Consulate; and it contained no more than his commending me to '*The Sheykh*' Ibn Rashîd, and the request that he would send me forward on my journey.

I walked in the mornings two hours, and as much at afternoon, that my companions might ride; and to spare their sickly thelûl I climbed to the saddle, as she stood, like a Beduwy: but the humanity which I showed them, to my possibility, hardened their ungenerous hearts. Seeing them weary, and Eyâd complaining that his soles were worn to the quick, I went on walking barefoot to Gofar, and bade them ride still.—There I beheld once more (oh! blissful sight,) the plum trees and almond trees blossoming in an Arabian oasis. We met with no one in the long main street; the men were now in the fields, or sleeping out the heat of the day in their houses. We went by the *Manôkh*, and I knew it well; but my companions, who had not been this way of late years, were gone on, and so we lost our breakfast. When I called they would not hear; they went to knock at a door far beyond. They sat down at last in the street's end, but we saw no man. "Let us to Hâyil, and mount thou, Khalîl!" said the rafîks. We went on through the ruins of the northern quarter, where I showed them the road; and come near the desert side, I took the next way, but they trod in another. I called them, they called to me, and I went on riding. Upon this Eyâd's light head turning, whether it were he had not tasted tobacco this day, or because he was weary and fasting, he began to curse me; and came running like a madman, 'to take the thelûl.' When I told him I would not suffer it, he stood aloof and cursed on, and seemed to have lost his understanding. A mile beyond he returned to a better mind, and acknowledged to me, that 'until he had drunk tobacco of a morning his heart burned within him, the brain rose in his pan, and he felt like a fiend.'—It were as easy to contain such a spirit as to bind water!

I rode not a little pensively, this third time, in the beaten way to Hâyil; and noted again (with abhorrence, of race) at every few hours' end their "kneeling places";—those little bays of stones set out in the desert soil, where wayfarers overtaken by the canonical hours may patter the formal prayer of their religion.—About midway we met the morning passengers from Hâyil ; and looking upon me with the implacable eyes of their fanaticism, every one who went by uttered the same hard words to my companions, ' Why bring ye him again ? ' Ambar, Aneybar's brother, came next, riding upon an ass in a company ; he went to Gofar, where he had land and palms. But the worthy Galla libertine greeted us with a pleasant good humour,—I was less it might be in disgrace of the princely household than of the fanatical populace. We saw soon above the brow of the desert the white tower-head of the great donjon of the castle, and said Merjàn, " Some think that the younger children of Telâl be yet alive therein. They see the world from their tower, and they are unseen." Upon our right hand lay the palms in the desert, es-Sherafa, founded by Metaab :—so we rode on into the town.

We entered Hâyil near the time of the afternoon prayers. Because the Emir was absent, there was no business ! the most shops were shut. The long market street was silent ; and their town seemed a dead and empty place. I saw the renegade Abdullah sitting at a shop door ; then Ibrahîm and a few more of my acquaintance, and lastly the schoolmaster. The unsavoury pedant stood and cried with many deceitful gestures, " Now, welcome ! and blessed be the Lord !—Khalîl is a Moslem ! " (for else he guessed I had not been so foolhardy as to re-enter Ibn Rashîd's town.) At the street's end I met with Aneybar, lieutenant now in (empty) Hâyil for the Emir ; he came from the Kasr carrying in his hand a gold-hilted back-sword : the great man saluted me cheerfully and passed by. I went to alight before the castle, in the empty Méshab, which was wont to be full of the couching thelûls of visiting Beduins : but in these days since Ibn Rashîd was *ghrazzai*, there came no more Beduins to the town. About half the men of Hâyil were now in the field with Ibn Rashîd ; for, besides his salaried rajajîl, even the salesmen of the sûk are the Prince's servants, to ride with him. This custom of military service has discouraged many traders of the East Nejd provinces, who had otherwise been willing to try their fortunes in Hâyil.

Some malignants of the castle ran together at the news, that the Nasrâny was come again. I saw them stand in the tower gate, with the old coffee-server ; " Heigh ! (they cried) it is he indeed ! now it may please Ullah he will be put to death."— Whilst I was in this astonishment, Aneybar returned ; he had but walked some steps to find his wit. " *Salaam aleyk !* " " *Aleykôm es-salaam,*" he answered me again, betwixt good will and wondering, and cast back the head ; for they have all learned to strut like the Emirs. Aneybar gave me his right hand with a lordly grace: there was the old peace of bread and salt betwixt us.—" From whence, Khalîl? and ye twain with him what be ye?—well go to the coffee hall! and there we will hear more." Aly el-Aŷid went by us, coming from his house, and saluted me heartily.

When we were seated with Aneybar in the great kahwa, he asked again, "And you Beduw with him, what be ye?" Eyâd responded with a craven humility: "We are Heteym."—" Nay ye are not Heteym."—"Tell them, I said, both what ye be, and who sent you hither." *Eyâd:* "We are Ageyl from Medina, and the Pasha sent us to Kheybar to convey this Khalîl, with a letter to Ibn Rashîd."—" Well, Ageyl, and what tribesmen?" —"We must acknowledge we are Beduins, we are Auájy." *Aneybar:* "And, Khalîl, where are your letters?"—I gave him a letter from Abdullah es-Siruàn, and the Pasha's sealed letter. Aneybar, who had not learned to read, gave them to a secretary, a sober and friendly man, who perusing the unflattering titles " *To the sheykh Ibn Rashîd,*" returned them to me unopened.—Mufarrij, the steward, now came in; he took me friendly by the hand, and cried, " Sum!" and led us to the mothîf. There a dish was set before us of Ibn Rashîd's rusty tribute dates, and—their spring hospitality—a bowl of small camel léban. One of the kitchen servers showed me a piece of ancient copper money, which bore the image of an eagle; it had been found at Hâyil, and was Roman.

The makhzan was assigned us in which I had formerly lodged; and my rafîks left me to visit their friends in the town. Children soon gathered to the threshold and took courage to revile me. Also there came to me the princely child Abd el-Azîz, the orphan of Metaab: I saw him fairly grown in these three months; he swaggered now like his uncle with a lofty but not disdainful look, and he resembles the Emir Mohammed. The princely child stood and silently regarded me, he clapt a hand to his little sword, but would not insult the stranger; so he said: " Why returned, Khalîl Nasrâny?"—" Because I hoped it would be pleasant to thine uncle, my darling."—" Nay, Khalîl! nay, Khalîl! the Emir says thou art not to remain here." I saw Zeyd the gate-keeper leading Merjàn by the hand; and he enquired of the lad, who was of a vindictive nature, of all that had happened to me since the day I arrived at Kheybar. Such questions and answers could only be to my hurt: it was a danger I had foreseen, amongst ungenerous Arabs.

We found Aneybar in the coffee-hall at evening : " Khalîl, he said, we cannot send thee forward, and thou must depart to-morrow."—" Well, send me to the Emir in the North with the Medina letter, if I may not abide his coming in Hâyil."— " Here rest to-night, and in the morning (he shot his one palm from the other) depart !—Thou stay here, Khalîl ! the people threatened thee to-day, thou sawest how they pressed on thee at your entering."—" None pressed upon me, many saluted me."— " Life of Ullah ! but I durst not suffer thee to remain in Hâyil, where so many are ready to kill thee, and I must answer to the Emir : sleep here this night, and please Ullah without mishap, and mount when we see the morning light."—Whilst we were speaking there came in a messenger, who arrived from the Emir in the northern wilderness : " And how does the Emir, exclaimed Aneybar, with an affected heartiness of voice ; and where left you him encamped ? " The messenger, a worthy man of the middle age, saluted me, without any religious mis-liking, he was of the strangers at Hâyil from the East provinces. *Aneybar :* " Thou hast heard, Khalîl ? and he showed me these three pauses of his malicious wit, on his fingers, *To-morrow ! —The light !—Depart !* "—" Whither ? "—" From whence thou camest ;—to Kheybar : art thou of the *dîn* (their religion) ? " —" No, I am not."—" And therefore the Arabs are impatient of thy life : wouldst thou be of the dîn, thou mightest live always amongst them."—" Then send me to-morrow, at my proper charge, towards el-Kasîm."

They were displeased when I mentioned the *Dowla :* Aneybar answered hardly, " What Dowla ! here is the land of the Aarab, and the dominion of Ibn Rashîd.—He says Kasîm : but there are no Beduw in the town (to convey him). Khalîl ! we durst not ourselves be seen in Kasîm," and he made me a shrewd sign, sawing with the forefinger upon his black throat.— " Think not to deceive me, Aneybar ; is not a sister of the Emir of Boreyda, a wife of Mohammed ibn Rashîd ? and are not they your allies ? "—" Ullah ! (exclaimed some of them), he knows everything."—*Aneybar :* " Well ! well ! but it cannot be, Khalîl : how sayest thou, sherîf ? "

— This was an old gentleman-beggar, with grey eyes, some fortieth in descent from the Néby, clad like a Turkish citizen, and who had arrived to-day from Medina, where he dwelt. His was an adventurous and gainful trade of hypocrisy : three months or four in a year he dwelt at home ; in the rest he rode, or passed the seas into every far land of the Mohammedan world. In each country he took up a new concubine ; and whereso he passed he glosed so fructuously, and showed them

his large letters patent from kings and princes, and was of that
honourable presence, that he was bidden to the best houses, as
becometh a religious sheykh of the Holy City, and a nephew
of the apostle of Ullah : so he received their pious alms and
returned to the illuminated Medina. Bokhâra was a *villegia-*
tura for this holy man in his circuit, and so were all the cities
beyond as far as Càbul. In Mohammedan India, he went a
begging long enough to learn the vulgar language. Last year
he visited Stambûl, and followed the [not] glorious Mohammedan
arms in Europe ; and the Sultan of Islam had bestowed upon
him his imperial firmàn.—He showed me the *dedale* engrossed
document, with the sign manual of the Calif upon a half
fathom of court paper. And with this broad charter he was
soon to go again upon an Indian voyage.

— When Aneybar had asked his counsel, " *Wellah yà el-*
Mohafûth (answered this hollow spirit), and I say the same,
it cannot be ; for what has this man to do in el-Kasîm ? and
what does he wandering up and down in all the land ; (he
added under his breath), *wa yiktub el-bilâd,* and he writes up
the country." *Aneybar :* " Well, to-morrow, Khalîl, depart ;
and thou Eyâd carry him back to Kheybar."—*Eyâd :* " But it
would be said there, ' Why hast thou brought him again ? '
wellah I durst not do it, Aneybar." Aneybar mused a little.
I answered them, " You hear his words ; and if this rafîk were
willing, yet so feeble is their thelûl, you have seen it yourselves, that she could not carry me."—*Eyâd :* " Wellah ! she
is not able."—" Besides, I said, if you cast me back into
hazards, the Dowla may require my blood, and you must every
year enter some of their towns as Bagdad and Medina : and
when you send to India with your horses, will you not be in the
power of my fellow citizens ? "—*The Sherîf :* " He says truth,
I have been there, and I know the Engleys and their Dowla :
now let me speak to this man in a tongue which he will understand,—he spoke somewhat in Hindostani—what ! an Engleysy
understand not the language of el-Hind ? "—*Aneybar :* " Thou
Eyâd (one of our subject Beduins) ! it is not permitted thee to
say nay ; I command you upon your heads to convey Khalîl to
Kheybar ; and you are to depart to-morrow.—Heigh-ho ! it
should be the hour of prayer ! " Some said, They had heard
the *ithin* already : Aneybar rose, the Sherîf rose solemnly and
all the rest ; and they went out to say their last prayers in the
great mesjid. * * *

* * * When the morning sun rose I had as lief that my night
o*

had continued for ever. There was no going forward for me, nor going backward, and I was spent with fatigues.—We went over to the great coffee-hall. Aneybar sat there, and beside him was the old dry-hearted sherîf, who drank his morrow's cup with an holy serenity. "Eyâd affirms, 1 said, that he cannot, he dare not, and that he will not convey me again to Kheybar."—"To Kheybar thou goest, and that presently."

Eyâd was leading away his sick thelûl to pasture under Ajja, but the Moghréby gatekeeper withheld him by force That Moor's heart, as at my former departure from Hâyil, was full of brutality. "Come, Zeyd, I said to him, be we not both Western men and like countrymen among these Beduw?"— "Only become a Moslem, and we would all love thee; but we know thee to be a most hardened Nasrâny.—Khalîl comes (he said to the bystanders) to dare us! a Nasrâny, here in the land of the Moslemîn! Was it not enough that we once sent thee away in safety, and comest thou hither again!" Round was this burly man's head, with a brutish visage; he had a thick neck, unlike the shot-up growth of the slender Neja Arabians: the rest of him an unwieldy carcase, and half a cart-load of tripes.

In the absence of the princely family, my soul was in the hand of this cyclops of the Méshab. I sat to talk peaceably with him, and the brute-man many times lifted his stick to smite the kafir; but it was hard for Zeyd, to whom I had sometime shown a good turn, to chafe himself against me. The opinions of the Arabs are ever divided, and among three is commonly one mediator:—it were blameworthy to defend the cause of an adversary of Ullah, and yet some of the people of Hâyil that now gathered about us with mild words were a mean for me. The one-eyed stranger stood by, he durst not affront the storm; but when Zeyd left me for a moment, he whispered in my ear, that I should put them off, whom he called in contempt beasts without understanding, Beduw!'—"Only seem thou to consent with them, lest they kill thee; say 'Mohammed is the apostle of Ullah,' and afterward, when thou art come into sure countries, hold it or leave it at thine own liking. This is not to sin before God, when force oppresses us, and there is no deliverance!"

Loitering persons and knavish boys pressed upon me with insolent tongues: but Ibrahîm of Hâyil, he who before so friendly accompanied me out of the town, was ready again to befriend me, and cried to them, "Back with you! for shame, so to thrust upon the man! O fools, have ye not seen him before?"

Amongst them came that Abdullah of the broken arm, the boy-brother of Hamûd. I saw him grow taller, and now he wore a little back-sword; which he pulled out against me, and cried, "O thou cursed Nasrâny, that wilt not leave thy miscreance!" —The one-eyed stranger whispered, "Content them! it is but waste of breath to reason with them. Do ye—he said to the people—stand back! I would speak with this man; and we may yet see some happy event, it may please Ullah." He whispered in my ear, "Eigh! there will be some mischief; only say thou wilt be a Moslem, and quit thyself of them. Show thyself now a prudent man, and let me not see thee die for a word; afterward, when thou hast escaped their hands, *settín séna*, sixty years to them, and *yulaan Ullah abu-hum*, the Lord confound the father of them all! Now, hast thou consented? —ho! ye people, to the mesjid! go and prepare the *muzayyin*: Khalîl is a Moslem!"—The lookers-on turned and were going, then stood still; they believed not his smooth words of that obstinate misbeliever. But when I said to them, "No need to go!"—"Aha! they cried, the accursed Nasrâny, Ullah curse his parentage!"—*Zeyd* (the porter): "But I am thinking we shall make this (man) a Moslem and circumcise him; go in one of you and fetch me a knife from the Kasr:" but none moved, for the people dreaded the Emir and Hamûd (reputed my friend). "Come, Khalîl, for one thing, said Zeyd, we will be friends with thee; say, there is none God but the Lord and His apostle is Mohammed: and art thou poor we will also enrich thee."—"I count your silver as the dust of this méshab:—but which of you miserable Arabs would give a man anything? Though ye gave me this castle, and the *beyt el-mâl*, the pits and the sacks of hoarded silver which ye say to be therein, I could not change my faith."—"*Akhs—akhs—akhs—akhs!*" was uttered from a multitude of throats: I had contemned, in one breath, the right way in religion and the heaped riches of this world! and with horrid outcries they detested the antichrist.

—"Eigh, Nasrâny! said a voice, and what found you at Kheybar, ha?"—"Plenty of dates O man, and fever."—"The more is the pity, cried they all, that he died not there; but akhs! these cursed Nasrânies, they never die, nor sicken as other men: and surely if this (man) were not a Nasrâny, he had been dead long ago."—"Ullah curse the father of him!" murmured many a ferocious voice. Zeyd the porter lifted his huge fist; but Aneybar appeared coming from the sûk, and Ibrahîm cries, "Hold there! and strike not Khalîl."—*Aneybar*: "What ado is here, and (to Zeyd) why is not the Nasrâny mounted?—did I not tell thee?"—"His Beduw were not ready; one of them is gone to bid his kinsfolk farewell, and I gave the other leave to

go and buy somewhat in the sûk."—*Aneybar:* "And you people
will ye not go your ways?—*Sheytàn!* what has any of you to do
with the Nasrâny; Ullah send a punishment upon you all, and
upon him also."

I said to Aneybar, "Let Eyâd take new wages of me and
threaten him, lest he forsake me."—"And what received he
before?"—"Five reals."—"Then give him other five reals.
[Two or three had sufficed for the return journey; but this was
his malice, to make me bare in a hostile land.] When the
thelûl is come, mount,—and Zeyd see thou that the payment is
made;" and loftily the Galla strode from me.—Cruel was the
slave's levity; and when I had nothing left for their cupidity
how might I save myself out of this dreadful country?—*Zeyd:*
"Give those five reals, ha! make haste, or by God—!"—and
with an ugh! of his bestial anger he thrust anew his huge fist
upon my breast. I left all to the counsel of the moment, for a
last need I was well armed; but with a blow, putting to his
great strength, he might have slain me.—Ibrahîm drew me from
them. "Hold! he said, I have the five reals, where is that
Eyâd, and I will count them in his hand. Khalîl, rid thyself
with this and come away, and I am with you.' I gave him the
silver. Ibrahîm led on, with the bridle of the thelûl in his
hand, through the market street, and left me at a shop door
whilst he went to seek Aneybar. Loitering persons gathered at
the threshold where I sat; the worst was that wretched young
Abdullah el-Abeyd; when he had lost his breath with cursing,
he drew his little sword again: but the bystanders blamed him,
and I entered the makhzan.

The tradesman, who was a Meshedy, asked for my galliûn and
bade me be seated; he filled it with hameydy, that honey-like
tobacco and peaceable remedy of human life. "What tidings,
quoth he, in the world?—We have news that the Queen of the
Engleys is deceased; and now her son is king in her room."
Whilst I sat pensive, to hear his words! a strong young swordsman, who remained in Hâyil, came suddenly in and sat down.
I remembered his comely wooden face, the fellow was called a
Moghréby, and was not very happy in his wits. He drew and
felt down the edge of his blade: so said Hands-without-head—
as are so many among them, and sware by Ullah: "Yesterday,
when Khalîl entered, I was running with this sword to kill him,
but some withheld me!" The tradesman responded, "What
has he done to be slain by thee?" *Swordsman:* "And I am
glad that I did it not:"—he seemed now little less rash to
favour me, than before to have murdered me.

Aneybar, who this while strode unquietly up and down, in

the side streets, (he would not be seen to attend upon the Nasrâny), appeared now with Ibrahîm at the door. The Galla deputy of Ibn Rashîd entered and sat down, with a mighty rattling of his sword of office in the scabbard, and laid the blade over his knees. Ibrahîm requested him to insist no more upon the uniquitous payment out of Khalîl's empty purse, or at least to make it less. "No, five reals!" (exclaimed the slave in authority,) he looked very fiercely upon it, and clattered the sword. "God will require it of thee; and give me a schedule of safe conduct, Aneybar." He granted, the trades-man reached him an hand-breadth of paper, and Ibrahîm wrote, 'No man to molest this Nasrâny.' Aneybar inked his signet of brass, and sealed it solemnly, ANEYBAR IBN RASHID.

"The sherîf (I said) is going to Bagdad, he will pass by the camp of the Emir: and there are some Beduw at the gate—I have now heard it, that are willing to convey me to the North, for three reals. If thou compel me to go with Eyâd, thou knowest that I cannot but be cast away: treachery O Aneybar is punished even in this world! May not a stranger pass by your Prince's country? be reasonable, that I may depart from you to-day peaceably, and say, the Lord remember thee for good." The Galla sat arrogantly rattling the gay back-sword in his lap, with a countenance composed to the princely awe; and at every word of mine he clapped his black hand to the hilt. When I ceased he found no answer, but to cry with tyranny, "Have done, or else by God—"! and he showed me a hand-breadth or two of his steel out of the scabbard. "What! he exclaimed, wilt thou not yet be afraid?" Now Eyâd entered, and Ibrahîm counted the money in his hand: Aneybar delivered the paper to Eyâd.—"The Emir gave his passport to me."—"But I will not let thee have it, mount! and Ibrahîm thou canst see him out of the town."

At the end of the sûk the old parasite seyyid or sherîf was sitting square-legged before a threshold, in the dust of the street. "Out, I said in passing, with thy reeds and paper; and I will give thee a writing?" The old fox in a turban winced, and he murmured some koran wisdom between his broken teeth.—There trotted by us a Beduwy upon a robust thelûl. "I was then coming to you, cried the man; and I will convey the Nasrâny to el-Irâk for five reals." *Eyâd:* "Well, and if it be with Aneybar's allowance, I will give up the five reals, which I have; and so shall we all have done well, and Khalîl may depart in peace. Khalîl sit here by the thelûl, whilst I and this Beduwy go back to Aneybar, and make the accord, if it be possible ; wellah ! I am sorry for thy sake."—A former acquaintance, a foreigner from el-Hása, came by and stayed to speak with me ; the man was one of the many industrious strangers in Hâyil, where he sewed cotton quilts for the richer households. "This people, quoth he, are untaught! all things are in the power of Ullah : and now farewell, Khalîl, and God give thee a good ending of this adventure."

Eyâd returned saying, Aneybar would not be entreated, and that he had reviled the poor Beduwy. " Up, let us hasten from them ; and as for Merjàn, I know not what is become of him. I will carry thee to Gofar, and leave thee there.—No, wellah Khalîl, I am not treacherous, but I durst not, I cannot, return with thee to Kheybar : at Gofar I will leave thee, or else with the Aarab."—" If thou betray me, betray me at the houses of hair, and not in the settlements ; but you shall render the silver."—"Nay, I have eaten it ; yet I will do the best that I may for thee."

We journeyed in the beaten path towards Gofar; and after going a mile, " Let us wait, quoth Eyâd, and see if this Merjàn be not coming." At length we saw it was he who approached us with a bundle on his head,—he brought temmn and dates, which his sister (wedded in the town) had given him. Eyâd drew out a leathern budget, in which was some victual for the way that he had received from the Mothîf, (without my knowledge) : it was but a little barley meal and dates of ill kind, in all to the value of about one shilling. We sat down, Merjàn spread his good dates, and we breakfasted ; thus eating together I hoped they might yet be friendly, though only misfortunes could be before me with such unlucky rafîks. I might have journeyed with either of them but not with both together. Eyâd had caught some fanatical suspicion in Hâyil, from the mouth of the old Medina sherîf!—that the Nasâra encroached continually upon the dominion of the Sultàn, and that Khalîl's nation, although not enemies, were not well-wishers, in their hearts, to the religion of Islam. When I would mount ; "Nay, said Eyâd, beginning to swagger, the returning shall not be as our coming; I will ride myself." I said no more ; and cast thus again into the wilderness I must give them line.— My companions boasted, as we went, of promises made to them both in Hâyil.—Aneybar had said, that would they return hither sometime, from serving the Dowla, they might be of Ibn Rashîd's (armed) service ;—Eyâd an horseman of the Emir's riders, and Merjàn one of the rajajîl.

Two women coming out from Hâyil overtook us, as they

went to Gofar. "The Lord be praised (said the poor creatures, with a womanly kindness) that it was not worse. Ah! thou,—is not thy name Khalîl?—they in yonder town are *jabâbara*, men of tyrannous violence, that will cut off a man's head for a light displeasure. Eigh me! did not he so that is now Emir, unto all his brother's children? Thou art well come from them, they are hard and cruel, *kasyín*. And what is this that the people cry, ' *Out upon the Nasrâny!* ' The Nasâra be better than the Moslemîn." *Eyâd* : " It is they themselves that are the Nasâra, wellah, *khubithín*, full of malignity." " It is the Meshâhada that I hate, said Merjàn, may Ullah confound them." It happened that a serving boy in the public kitchen, one of the patients whom I treated (freely) at my former sojourning in Hâyil, was Merjàn's brother. The Meshâhadies he said had been of Aneybar's counsel against me.—Who has travelled in Phœnician and Samaritan Syria may call to mind the inhumanity [the last wretchedness and worldly wickedness of irrational religions,— that man should not eat and drink with his brother!] of those Persian or Assyrian colonists, the *Metówali*.

Forsaking the road we went now towards the east-building of Gofar:—the east and west settlements lie upon two veins of ground-water, a mile or more asunder. The western oasis, where passes the common way, is the greater; but Eyâd went to find some former acquaintance in the other with whom we might lodge. Here also we passed by forsaken palm-grounds and ruinous orchard houses, till we came to the inhabited; and they halted before the friend's dàr. Eyâd and Merjàn sat down to see if the good man (of an inhospitable race, the B. Temîm), would come forth to welcome us. Children gathered to look on, and when some of them knew me, they began to fleer at the Nasrâny. Merjàn cursed them, as only Semites can find it in their hearts, and ran upon the little mouthing knaves with his camel-stick; but now our host coming down his alley saluted Eyâd, and called us to the house. His son bore in my bags to the kahwa : and they strewed down green garden stalks before the thelûl and wild herbage.

A bare dish of dates was set before us; and the good-man made us thin coffee : bye and bye his neighbours entered. All these were B. Temîm, peasant-like bodies in whom is no natural urbanity; but they are lumpish drudgers, living honestly of their own—and that is with a sparing hand. When I said to one of them, " I see you all big of bone and stature, unlike the (slender) inhabitants of Hâyil!"—He answered, dispraising them, "The Shammar are *Beduw!*" Whilst we sat, there came in three swarthy strangers, who riding by to Hâyil alighted here also to drink coffee.—They carried up their zíka to the Prince's treasury; for being few and distant Aarab, his exactors were not come to them these two years: they were of Harb, and their wandering ground was nigh Medina. They mounted again immediately; and from Hâyil they would ride continually to Ibn Rashîd in the northern wilderness.

My rafîks left me alone without a word! I brought in therefore the thelûl furnitures, lest they should lead away their beast and forsake me. Eyâd and Merjàn feared no more that they must give account for me; and their wildness rising at every word, I foresaw how next to desperate, must be my further passage with them: happily for my weary life the milk-season was now in the land. * * *

CHAPTER VI

THE SHAMMAR AND HARB DESERTS IN NEJD

AT daybreak we departed from Gofar: this by my reckoning was the first week in April. Eyâd loosed out our sick thelûl to pasture; and they drove her slowly forward in the desert plain till the sun went down behind Ajja, when we halted under bergs of grey granite. These rocks are fretted into bosses and caves more than the granite of Sinai: the heads of the granite crags are commonly trap rock. Eyâd, kindling a fire, heated his iron ramrod, and branded their mangy thelûl.—I had gone all day on foot; and the Ageylies threatened every hour to cast down my bags, though now light as Merjàn's temmn, which she also carried. We marched four miles further, and espied a camp fire; and coming to the place we found a ruckling troop of camels couched for the night, in the open khála. The herd-lad and his brother sat sheltering in the hollow bank of a seyl, and a watch-fire of sticks was burning before them. The hounds of the Aarab follow not with the herds, the lads could not see beyond their fire-light, and our *salaam* startled them : then falling on our knees we sat down by them,—and with that word we were acquainted. The lads made some of their nâgas stand up, and they milked full bowls and frothing over for us. We heard a night-fowl shriek, where we had left our bags with the thelûl : my rafîks rose and ran back with their sticks, for the bird (which they called *sirrûk*, a thief) might, they said, steal something. When we had thus supped, we lay down upon the pleasant seyl sand to sleep.

As the new day lightened we set forward. A little further we saw a flock of some great sea-fowl grazing before us, upon their tall shanks in the wilderness.—I mused that (here in Nejd) they were but a long flight, on their great waggle wings, from the far seabord ; a morrow's sun might see them beyond this burning dust of Arabia ! At first my light-headed rafîks mistook them for sheep-flocks, although only black fleeces be seen in these parts of Nejd : then having kindled their gun-matches, they went creeping out to approach them ; but bye and bye I saw the great fowl flag their wings over the wide desert, and the gunners returning.—I asked " from whence are these birds ? "—" Wellah from Mecca," [that is from the middle Red Sea bord.]

This soil was waste gravel, baked hard in the everlasting drought, and glowing under the soles of our bare feet ; the air was like a flame, in the sun. An infirm traveller were best to ride always in the climate of Arabia : now by the cruelty of my companions, I went always on foot ; and they themselves would ride. And marching in haste, I must keep them in view, or else they had forsaken the Nasrâny : my plight was such that I thought, after a few days of such efforts, I should rest for ever. So it drew to the burning midst of the afternoon, when, what for the throes in my chest, I thought that the heart would burst. The hot blood at length spouted from my nostrils : I called to the rafîks who went riding together before me to halt, that I might lie down awhile, but they would not hear. Then I took up stones, to receive the dropping gore, lest I should come with a bloody shirt to the next Aarab : besides it might work some alteration in my rafîks' envenomed spirits !—in this haste there fell blood on my hands. When I overtook them, they seeing my bloody hands drew bridle in astonishment ! *Merjàn :* " Now is not this a kafir ! "—" Are ye not more than kafirs, that abandon the rafîk in the way ? " They passed on now more slowly, and I went by the side of the thelûl.—"If, I added, ye abandon the rafîk, what honourable man will hereafter receive you into their tents ? " Merjàn answered, " There is keeping of faith betwixt the Moslemîn, but not with an enemy of Ullah ! "

They halted bye and bye and Eyâd dismounted : Merjàn who was still sitting upon the thelûl's back struck fire with a flint : I thought it might be for their galliûns, since they had bought a little sweet hameydy, with my money, at Hâyil : but Eyâd kindled the cord of his matchlock. I said, " This is what ? " They answered, " A hare ! "—" Where is your hare ? I say, show me this hare ! " Eyâd had yet to put priming to the eye of his piece ; they stumbled in their words, and remained confused. I said to them, " Did I seem to you like this hare ? by the life of Him who created us, in what instant you show me a gun's mouth, I will lay dead your hare's carcases upon this earth : put out the match ! " he did so. The cool of the evening approached ; we marched on slowly in silence, and doubtless they rolled it in their hollow hearts what might signify that vehement word of

the Nasrâny. " Look, I said to them, *rizelleyn !* you two vile
dastards, I tell you plainly, that in what moment you drive me
to an extremity ye are but dead dogs ; and I will take this
carrion thelûl ! "

My adventure in such too unhappy case had been nearly
desperate ; nigher than the Syrian borders I saw no certain
relief. Syria were a great mark to shoot at, and terribly far off ;
and yet upon a good thelûl, fresh watered—for extremities make
men bold, and the often escaping from dangers—I had not
despaired to come forth ; and one watering in the midway,—if
I might once find water, had saved both thelûl and rider.—Or
should I ride towards Teyma ; two hundred miles from hence ?—
But seeing the great landmarks from this side, how might I know
them again !—and if I found any Aarab westward, yet these
would be Bishr, the men's tribesmen. Should I ride eastward in
unknown dîras ? or hold over the fearful Nefûd sand billows to
seek the Sherarát ? Whithersoever I rode I was likely to faint
before I came to any human relief ; and might not strange
Aarab sooner kill the stranger, seeing one arrive thus, than
receive me ? My eyes were dim with the suffered ophthalmia,
and not knowing where to look for them, how in the vastness of
the desert landscape should I descry any Aarab ? If I came by
the mercy of God to any wells, I might drink drop by drop, by
some artifice, but not water the thelûl.

Taking up stones I chafed my blood-stained hands, hoping to
wash them when we should come to the Aarab ; but this was the
time of the spring pasture, when the great cattle are jezzîn, and
oft-times the nomads have no water by them, because there is
léban to drink. Eyâd thought the game turned against him !
when we came to a menzil, I might complain of them and he
would have a scorn.—" Watch, said he, and when any camel
stales, run thou and rinse the hands ; for wellah seeing blood on
thy hands, there will none of the Aarab eat with thee."—The
urine of camels has been sometimes even drunk by town caravaners in their impatience of thirst. I knew certain of the
Medânite tradesmen to the Sherarát, who coming up at midsummer from the W. Sirhàn, and finding the pool dry (above
Maan) where they looked to have watered, filled their bowl thus,
and let in a little blood from the camel's ear. I have told the
tale to some Beduins ; who answered me, " But to drink this
could not help a man, wellah he would die the sooner, it must
so wring his bowels."

It was evening, and now we went again by el-Agella. When
the sun was setting, we saw another camel troop not far off.

The herdsmen trotting round upon some of their lighter beasts were driving-in the great cattle to a sheltered place between two hills; for this night closed starless over our heads with falling weather. When we came to them the young men had halted their camels and were hissing to them to kneel,—*ikh-kh-kh !* The great brutes fall stiffly, with a sob, upon one or both their knees, and underdoubling the crooked hind legs, they sit ponderously down upon their haunches. Then shuffling forward one and the other fore-knee, with a grating of the harsh gravel under their vast carcase-weight, they settle themselves. and with these pains are at rest: the fore bulk-weight is sustained upon the *zôra ;* so they lie still and chaw their cud, till the morning sun. The camel leaves a strange (reptile-like) print (of his knees, of the zôra and of the sharp hind quarters), which may be seen in the hard wilderness soil after even a year or two. The smell of the camel is muskish and a little dog-like, the hinder parts being crusted with urine ; yet is the camel more beautiful in our eyes than the gazelles, because man sees in this creature his whole welfare, in the khála.

The good herding lads milked for us largely: we drunk deep and far into the night ; and of every sup is made ere morning sweet blood, light flesh and stiff sinews. The rain beat on our backs as we sat about their watch-fire of sticks on the pure sand of the desert ; it lightened and thundered. When we were weary we went apart, where we had left our bags, and lay down in our cloaks, in the night wind and the rain. I lay so long musing of the morrow, that my companions might think me sleeping. They rested in the shelter of the next crag, where I heard them say—my quick hearing helping me in these dangers like the keen eyesight of the nomads—that later in the night they would lift their things on the thelûl and be gone. I let them turn over to sleep: then I rose and went to the place where the fire had been.

The herdsmen lay sleeping in the rain; and I thought I would tell the good lads my trouble. Their sister was herding with them, but in presence of strange menfolk she had sat all this evening obscurely in the rain, and far from the cheerful fire Now she was warming herself at the dying embers, and cast a little cry as she saw me coming, for all is fear in the desert. 'Peace ! I said to her, and I would speak with her brethren.' She took the elder by the shoulder, and rolling him, he wakened immediately, for in this weather he was not well asleep. They all sat up, and the young men, rubbing their faces asked, "Oh, what— ? and wherefore would not the stranger let them rest, and why was I not gone to sleep with my rafîks ? " These were manly lads but rude; they had not discerned that I was so much a stranger. I told them, that those with me were Annezy, Ageylies, who had money to carry me to Kheybar; but their purpose was to forsake me, and perhaps they would abandon me this night."—" Look you (said they, holding their mouths for yawning), we are poor young serving men, and have not much understanding in such things; but if we see them do thee a wrong, we will be for thee. Go now and lie down again, lest they miss thee; and fear nothing, for we are nigh thee."

About two hours before the day Eyâd and Merjàn rose, whispering, and they loaded the things on the couching thelûl; then with a little spurn they raised her silently. " Lead out (I heard Eyâd whisper), and we will come again for the guns." I lay still, and when they were passed forth a few steps I rose to disappoint them : I went with their two matchlocks in my hands to the herdsmen's place, and awaked the lads. The treacherous rafîks returning in the dark could not find their arms : then they came over where I sat now with the herdsmen. —" Ah! said they, Khalîl had of them an unjust suspicion; they did but remove a little to find shelter, for where they lay the wind and rain annoyed them." Their filed tongues prevailed with the poor herding lads, whose careless stars were unused to these nice cases; and heartless in the rain, they consented with the stronger part,—that Khalîl had misconstrued the others' simple meaning. " Well, take, they said, your matchlocks, and go sleep again, all of you; and be content Khalîl. And do ye give him no more occasion, said these upland judges :—and wellah we have not napped all this long night ! "

I went forward with the Ageylies, when we saw the morning light; Eyâd rode. We had not gone a mile when he threatened to abandon me there in the khála ; he now threatened openly to shoot me, and raised his camel-stick to strike me; but I laid hand on the thelûl's bridle, and for such another word, I said, I would give him a fall. Merjàn had no part in this violence; he walked wide of us, for being of various humour, in the last hour he had fallen out with Eyâd. [In their friendly discoursing, the asseverations of these Bishr clansmen (in every clause) were in such sort ;—*Merjàn: Wellah, yâ ibn ammy*, of a truth, my cousin ! *Eyâd : Ullah hadîk*, the Lord direct thee !—*Wa hyât rukbátak*, by the life of thy neck !—*Weysh aleyk*, do as thou wilt, what hinders.]—" Well, Khalîl, let be now, said Eyâd, and I swear to thee a menzil of the Aarab is not far off, if the herding lads told us truly."

We marched an hour and found a troop of camels. Whilst their herdsmen milked for us, we met that Aly, who had entertained us before at Gussa! he was here again abroad to gather forage. He told us a wife of his lay sick with fever: "and have you not a remedy, Khalîl, for the entha" (female)? *Eyâd*: "Khalîl has kanakîna, the best of medicines for the fever, I have seen it at Medina, and if a man but drink a little he is well anon: what is the cost, Khalîl?"—"A real." *Aly*: "I thought you would give it me, what is a little medicine, it costs thee nothing, and I will give thee fourpence; did I not that day regale you with dates?" Yet because the young wife was dear to him, Aly said he would go on to the Beduins' menzil, and take up a grown lamb for the payment. We came to a *ferîj* of Shammar about nine in the morning. Eyâd remembered some of those Aarab, and he was remembered by them: we heard also that Braitshàn's booths were now at half an hour's distance from hence upon our right hand. This Shammar host brought us to breakfast the best dates of the Jebel villages, clear as cornelians, with a bowl of his spring léban. Leaving there our baggage, without any mistrust (as amongst Aarab), we went over to Braitshàn's ferîj,—my rafîks hoping there to drink kahwa. A few locusts were flying and alighting in this herbage.

Sitting with Braitshàn in the afternoon, when Eyâd had walked to another booth, and Merjàn was with the thelûl, I spoke to him of my treacherous companions, and to *Ferrah*, an honest old man whom we had found here before. "What is, I asked, your counsel? and I have entered to-day under your roof." They answered each other gravely, "Seeing that Khalîl has required of us the protection, we ought to maintain his right." But within a while they repented of their good disposition, lest it should be said, that they had taken part with the Nasrâny against a 'Míslim'; and they ended with these words, 'They could not go betwixt *khuiàn* (companions in the journey).' They said to Eyâd, when he arrived, 'That since he had carried only my light bags, and I was come down from Hâyil upon my feet, and he had received five reals to convey me to Kheybar, and that in every place he threatened to abandon me; let him render three reals, and leave me with the Aarab, and take the other two for his hire, and go his way.' Eyâd answered, "If I am to blame, it is because of the feebleness of my thelûl."—"Then, why, I exclaimed, didst thou take five reals to carry a passenger upon the mangy carrion?" The Beduins laughed; yet some said, I should not use so sharp

words with my wayfellow,—"Khalîl, the Aarab love the fair
speaking." I knew this was true, and that my plain right
would seem less in their shallow eyes than the rafîks' smooth
words.—*Eyâd :* "Well, be it thus." "Thou hast heard his
promise, said they, return with *khûak,* thy way-brother, and all
shall be well."—Empty words of Arabs ! the sun set ; my rafîks
departed, and I soon followed them.

Our Shammar host had killed the sacrifice of hospitality : his
mutton was served in a great trencher, upon temmn boiled in
the broth. But the man sat aloof, and took no part in our
evening talk ; whether displeased to see a kafir under his tent-
cloth, or because he misliked my Annezy rafîks. I told Aly he
might have the kanakîna, a gift, so he helped me to my right
with Eyâd ; ' He would,' he answered.—I wondered to see him
so much at his ease in the booths of the Aarab ! but his parents
were Beduw, and Aly left an orphan at Gussa, had been bred up
there. He bought of them on credit a good yearling ram to
give me : they call it here *tully,* and the ewe lamb *rôkhal.*

Aly brought me his tully on the morrow, when we were ready
to depart ; and said, " See, O Khalîl, my present ! "—" I looked
for the fulfilment of your last night's words ; and, since you
make them void, I ought not to help him in a little thing, who
recks not though I perish !" The fellow, who weighed not my
grief, held himself scorned by the Nasrâny : my bags were laid
upon the thelûl, and he gazed after us and murmured. The
dewless aurora was rising from those waste hills, without the
voice of any living creature in a weary wilderness ; and I followed forth the riders, Eyâd and Merjàn.

The gravel stones were sharp ; the soil in the sun soon glowed
as an hearth under my bare feet ; the naked pistol (hidden
under my tunic) hanged heavily upon my panting chest ; the
air was breathless, and we had nothing to drink. It was hard
for me to follow on foot, notwithstanding the weak pace of
their thelûl : a little spurn of a rider's heel and she had trotted
out of my seeing ! Hard is this human patience ! showing
myself armed, I might compel them to deliver the dromedary ;
but who would not afterward be afraid to become my rafîk ?
If I provoked them, they (supposing me unarmed), might come
upon me with their weapons ; and must I then take their poor
lives ?—but were that just ?—in this faintness of body and
spirit I could not tell ; I thought that a man should forsake
life rather than justice, and pollute his soul with outrage. I
went training and bearing on my camel-stick,—a new fatigue
—to leave a furrow in the hard gravel soil ; lest if those vile

spirited rafîks rode finally out of my sight, I should be lost in
the khála. I thought that I might come again, upon this trace,
to Braitshàn's booths, and the Aarab. I saw the sun mount to
high noon; and hoped from every new brow to descry pasturing
camels, or some menzil of the Nomads.

An hour further I saw camels that went up slowly through a
hollow ground to the watering. There I came up to my rafîks:
they had stayed to speak with the herdsmen, who asked of the
desert behind us. The Nomads living in the open wilderness
are greedy of tidings; and if herdsmen see passengers go by
peaceably in the desert they will run and cry after them, ' What
news, ho!—Tell us of the soil, that ye have passed through ?—
Which Aarab be there ?—Where lodge they now ?—Of which
waters drink they ?—And, the face of them is whitherward ?—
Which herbs have ye seen ? and what is the soil betwixt them
and us? found ye any bald places (máhal)?—With whom
lodged ye last night ?—heard ye there any new thing, or as ye
came by the way ? " Commonly the desert man delivers himself after this sort with a loud suddenness of tongue, as he is
heated with running; and then only (when he is nigher hand)
will he say more softly, 'Peace be with thee.'—The passengers
are sure to receive him mildly ; and they condescend to all his
asking, with *Wellah Fulàn !* 'Indeed thou Such-an-one.' And
at every meeting with herdmen, they say over, with a set face,
the same things, in the same words, ending with the formal *wa
ent sélim*, 'and thou being in peace.'—The tribesman hardly
bids the strangers farewell, when he has turned the back ; or he
stands off, erect and indifferent, and lets pass the tarkîeh.

I stayed now my hand upon the thelûl; and from the next
high grounds we saw a green plain before us. Our thirst was
great, and Eyâd showed with his finger certain crags which
lay beyond; ' We should find pools in them, he said (after the
late showers): but I marked in the ground [better than the
inept Beduin rafîks] that no rain had fallen here in these days.
We found only red pond-water,—so foul that the thirsting thelûl
refused to drink. I saw there the forsaken site of a winter
encampment : the signs are shallow trenching, and great stones
laid about the old steads of their beyts. Now we espied camels,
which had been hidden by the hollow soil, and then a worsted
village ! My rafîks considered the low building of those tents,
and said, " They must be of Harb ! " As we approached they
exclaimed, " But see how their beyts be stretched nigh together !
they are certainly Heteym."

We met with an herdsman of theirs driving his camels to
water, and hailed him—" Peace ! and ho ! what Aarab be those

yonder ?"—The man answered with an unwonted frankness, "I (am an) Harby dwelling with this ferîj, and they are Heteym." —Eyâd began to doubt! for were they of Kâsim's Heteym (enemies of the Dowla at Kheybar), he thought he were in danger Yet now they could not go back; if he turned from them, his mangy thelûl might be quickly overtaken. The Ageylies rode on therefore, with the formal countenance of guests that arrive at a nomad menzil. The loud dogs of the encampment leapt out against us with hideous affray ; and as we came marching by the beyts, the men and the hareem who sat within, only moving their eyes, silently regarded us passing strangers. We halted before the greater booth in the row, which was of ten or twelve tents.

Eyâd and Merjàn alighted, set down the packs and tied up the knee of the thelûl. Then we walked together, with the solemnity of guests, to the open half of the tent, which is the men's apartment; here at the right hand looking forth : it is not always on the same side among the people of the desert. We entered, and this was the sheykh's beyt. Five or six men were sitting within on the sand, with an earnest demeanour (and that was because some of them knew me) ! They rose to receive us, looking silently upon me, as if they would say, "Art not thou that Nasrâny ? "

The nomad guest—far from his own—enters the strange beyt of hospitality, with demure looks ; in which should appear some gentle token of his own manly worth. We sat down in the booth, but these uncivil hosts—Heteymies—kept their uneasy silence. They made it strange with us ; and my rafîks beat their camel-sticks upon the sand and looked down : the Heteymies gazed side-long and lowering upon us. At length, despising their mumming, and inwardly burning with thirst, I said to the sly fellow who sat beside me, a comely ill-blooded Heteymy and the host's brother, " *Eskîny má*, give me a little water to drink." He rose unwillingly ; and fetched a bowl of foul clay-water When I only sipped this unwholesome bever : " *Rueyht* (he said maliciously), hast allayed thy thirst ? " My companions asked for the water, and the bowl was sent round. " Drink ! said the Heteymies, for there is water enough." At length there was set before us a bowl of mereesy shards and a little léban : then first they broke their unlucky silence. " I think we should know thee (quoth he of the puddle water); art not thou the Nasrâny that came to Kâsim's from Ibn Rashîd ? "

They had alighted yesterday : they call the ground *Âul*, of those crags with water. The (granitic) landscape is named *Ghrólfa ;* and *Sfá*, of a plutonic mountain, which appeared eastward over the plain seven miles distant; and they must send thither to fetch their water. The altitude was here 4600 feet. The flocks were driven in at the going down of the sun; and bye and bye we saw *Maatuk*—that was our host's name—struggling to master a young ram. Eyâd sent Merjàn with the words of course, "Go and withhold him." Merjàn made as though he would help the ram, saying, with the Arabs' smooth (effeminate) dissimulation, 'It should not be, nay by Ullah, we would never suffer it.' "Oho! young man, let me alone, answered the Heteymy, may I not do as I please with mine own?" and he drew his slaughter-sheep to the woman's side.—Two hours later Maatuk bore in the boiled ram brittled, upon a vast trencher of temmn. He staggered under the load and caught his breath, for the hospitable man was asthmatic.

Eyâd said when we were sitting alone, " Khalîl we leave thee here, and *el-Kasîm* lies behind yonder mountains; these are good folk, and they will send thee thither."—" But how may ye, having no water-skin, pass over to the Auájy?"— " Well, we will put in to Thúrghrud for a girby."—" Ullah remember your treachery, the Aarab will blame you who abandon your rafîk, also the Pasha will punish you; and as you have robbed me of those few reals he may confiscate some of your arrears."—" Oh say not so, Khalîl! in this do not afflict me; and at our departure complain not: let not the hosts hear your words, or they will not bring you forward upon your journey."

When the rest were sleeping I saw Maatuk go forth;—I thought this host must be good, although an Heteymy. I went to him and said I would speak with him.—" Shall we sit down here then, and say on,"—for the Arabs think they may the better take counsel in their weak heads when sitting easily upon the béled. I told him how the rafîks had made me journey hitherto on my feet (an hundred miles) from Hâyil; how often they had threatened in the midst of the khála to forsake me, and even to kill me : should I march any longer with them?—no! I was to-day a guest in his tent; I asked him to judge between us, and after that to send me safely to el-Kasîm.—" All this will I do; though I cannot myself send thee to el-Kasîm, but to some Harb whose tents are not far from us, eastward ; and we may find there someone to carry thee thither. Now, when the morning is light and you see these fellows ready to set forward, then say to me, *dakhîlak*, and we shall be for thee, and if they resist we will detain their thelûl."—" Give thy hand, and swear to me."—" Ay, I swear, said he, wullah, wullah!" but he drew back his hand; for how should they keep touch with a Nasrâny!—But in the

night time, whilst I slept, my companions also held their council
with Maatuk: and that was as between men of the same religion,
and Maatuk betrayed me for his pipeful of sweet hameydy tobacco.
When it was day those rafîks laid my bags upon the thelûl,
and I saw Eyâd give to Maatuk a little golden hameydy, for
which the Heteymy thanked him benignly. Then, taking up
their mantles and matchlocks, they raised the thelûl with a
spurn: Merjàn having the bridle in his hand led forth, with
nesellim âleyk. As they made the first steps, I said to Maatuk,
" My host detain them, and *ana dakhîl-ak !*—do justly."—" Ugh !
go with them, answered Maatuk (making it strange), what
justice wouldst thou have, Nasrâny ? "—" Where be thy last
night's promises ? Is there no keeping faith, Heteymy ? listen !
I will not go with them." But I saw that my contention would
be vain ; for there was some intelligence between them.

When Eyâd and Merjàn were almost out of sight, the men
in the tent cried to me, " Hasten after them and your bags, or
they will be quite gone."—" I am your dakhîl, and you are forsworn ; but I will remain here."—" No ! "—and now they began
to thrust me (they were Heteym). Maatuk caught up a tent-
stake, and came on against me ; his brother, the sly villain, ran
upon me from the backward with a cutlass. " Ha ! exclaimed
Maatuk, I shall beat out his brains."—" Kill him—kill him ! "
cried other frenetic voices (they were young men of Harb and
Annezy dwelling in this ferîj). " Let me alone, cries his
brother, and I will chop off the head of a cursed Nasrâny."
" I cannot, I said to them, contend with so many, though ye
be but dastards ; put down your weapons. And pray good
woman ! [to Maatuk's wife who looked to me womanly over her
curtain, and upbraided their violence] pour me out a little léban ;
and let me go from this cursed place."—" Ah ! what wrong, she
said to them, ye do to chase away the stranger ! it is harrâm,
and, Maatuk, he is thy dakhîl : " she hastened to pour me out
to drink. " Drink ! said she, and handed over the bowl, drink !
and may it do thee good ; " and in this she murmured a sweet
proverb of their dîra, *widd el-yhrarîb ahlhu,* " the desire of the
stranger is to his own people ; speed the stranger home."

" Up, I said, Maatuk, and come with me to call the Ageylies back, my strength is lost, and alone I cannot overtake them."
—" I come, and wellah will do thee right with them."—When
we had gone hastily a mile, I said : " I can follow no further,
and must sit down here ; go and call them if you will." Great
is their natural humanity : this Heteymy, who was himself
infirm, bade me rest ; and he limped as fast as he might go and
shouted after them,—he beckoned to my late rafîks ! and they

tardily returned to us. " Maatuk, I said, this is the end of my
journey to-day: Eyâd shall give me here Aneybar's schedule
of safe conduct, and he shall restore me three reals; also,
none of you chop words with me, for I am a weary man, whom
ye have driven to extremities."—*Maatuk* (to Eyâd): "What
say you to this? it seems your rafîk is too weary to go any
more, will ye carry him then on the thelûl?"—"We will not
carry him; we can only sometimes ride upon her ourselves;
yet I will carry him—it is but half a day—to Thúrghrud, and
leave him there!" This I rejected. *Maatuk:* "Well, he shall
stay with us; and I will send Khalîl forward to the Harb with
Ibn Náhal, for his money. Now then I say restore his money,
let it be two reals, and the paper from Ibn Rashîd,—what, man!
it is his own."—*Eyâd:* " I am willing to give up the paper to
Khalîl, so he write me a discharge, which may acquit me before
the Pasha; but I will not restore a real of the silver, I have
spent it,—what, man! wouldst thou have my clothes?"—
Maatuk: " We shall not let thee depart so! give Khalîl one
real, and lay down the schedule."—*Eyâd:* " Well, I accept":
he took out a crown, and "This is all I have left, said he; let
Khalîl give me fourpence, for this is fourpence more than
the mejîdie."—"You may think yourselves well escaped for
fourpence, which is mine own: take that silver, Maatuk, *arrabún*
(earnest-money) of the three reals for conveying me as thou
said'st to the Harb." He received it, but the distrustful wretch
made me give him immediately the other two. I recovered
thus Aneybar's safe-conduct, and that was much for my safety
in the wild country. Eyâd insisted for his written discharge,
and I wrote, "Eyâd, the Ageyly, of Bejaida, Bishr, bound for
five reals by Abdullah Siruân, lieutenant at Kheybar, to convey me to Hâyil, and engaged there by Aneybar, Ibn Rashîd's
deputy, for which he received other five, to carry me again to
Kheybar, here treacherously abandons me at Aul, under Sfá, in
the Shammar dîra." The Ageylies took the seal from my hand,
and set it to themselves twenty times, to make this instrument more sure: then Maatuk made them turn back to the
menzil with my baggage. So Eyâd and Merjàn departed;
yet not without some men's crying out upon them from the
tents, for their untruth to the rafîk.

These Heteymies were heavy-hearted fanatics, without the
urbanity of Beduins: and Maatuk had sold me for a little tobacco. For an hour or two he embalmed his brain with the
reeking drug; after that he said, "Khalîl, *dakhîl-ak*, hast thou
not, I beseech thee, a little dokhân? ah! say not that thou hast

none; give me but a little, and I will restore to thee those three reals, and carry thee on my thelûl to Ibn Náhal."—"I have no dokhân, though you cut off my head."—"Khalîl, yet fill my galliûn once, and I will forgive thee all!"—Had I bought a little tobacco at Hâyil, I had sped well.

One Annezy and three Harb beyts were in this Heteymy ferîj. Some of those strangers asked me in the afternoon, what tribesmen were the rafîks that had forsaken me. I answered, "Auájy and Bejaijy of Bishr."—"Hadst thou said this before to us, they had not parted so! we had seized their thelûl, for they are *gôm*, and we have not eaten with them." Said one: "Whilst they talked I thought the speech of the younger sounded thus, ay billah it was Bejaijy."—"You might overtake them."—"Which way went they?"—"To Baitha Nethîl, and from thence they will cross to the Auájy." Eyâd had this charge, from Kheybar to fetch the Siruân's and the Bîshy's thelûls. [Although those Beduw were enemies of the Dowla, the Ageyl dromedaries had been privately put out to pasture among them.] In that quarter of the wilderness was sprung (this year) a plentiful *rabîa*, after the autumnal rains, "so that the camels might lie down with their fills at noonday."—"How now? (said one to another) wilt thou be my rafîk if the 'bil come home this evening? shall we take our thelûls and ride after them: they will journey slowly with their mangy beast; if the Lord will we may overtake them, and cut their throats."—"Look (I said) I have told you their path, go and take the thelûl if you be able, but you shall not do them any hurt." I was in thought of their riding till the nightfall: but the camels came not.

Of Ibn Náhal's Aarab they had no late tidings. They spoke much in my hearing of Ibn Náhal; and said the hareem—that were the best hearted in this encampment, "His tent is large, so large! and he is rich, so rich,—ouf! all there is liberality: and when thou comest to his tent say, 'Send me, O Ibn Náhal, to el-Kasîm', and he will send thee."

Maatuk and his evil-eyed brother were comely; and their sister—she dwelt in Maatuk's beyt—was one of the goodliest works of nature; only (such are commonly the Heteymàn) not well coloured. She went freshly clad; and her beauty could not be hid by the lurid face-clout: yet in these her flowering years of womanhood she remained unwedded! The thin-witted young Annezy man of the North, who sat all day in the sheykh's beyt, fetched a long breath as oft as she appeared—as it were a dream of their religion—in our sight; and plucking my mantle he would say, "Sawest thou the like ere now!" This sheykhess, when she heard their wonted *ohs!* and *ahs!* cast upon them her flagrant great eyes, and smiled, without any disdain.—She, being in stature as a goddess, yet would there no Beduwy match with her (an Heteymîa) in the way of honourable marriage! But dissolute Beduins will mingle their blood out of wedlock with the beautiful Heteymîas; and I have heard the comely ribald Eyâd mock on thus, making his voice small like a woman's,—" Then will she come and say humbly to the man, 'Marry me, for I am with child, and shield me from the blame.'"

There was an Heteymy in this menzil who returned after an absence : I enquired, ' Where had he been in the meanwhile ? ' —" Wellah, at el-Hâyat : it is but one long day upon the thelûl, and I have wedded there a (black) wife."—" Wherefore thus ? " —" Wellâh I wished for her."—" And what was the bride money ? "— " I have spent nothing."—" Or gave she thee anything ? "—" Ay billah! some palms."—" She has paid for thee ! " " Well, why not ? "—" Will not thy children be black like slaves, *abîd* ? "—" She is blackish-red, her children will be reddish."—" And what hast thou to do with village wives ? "— " Eigh! I shall visit her now and then ; and when I come there go home to mine own house : "—and cries the half-witted nomad, " Read, Khalîl, if this thing which I have done be lawful or unlawful ? " [The negro village el-Hâyat is in the S.-E. borders of the (Kheybar) Harra ; and a journey from thence toward Medina is the palm hamlet Howeyat. The (Annezy) Beduin landlords in both settlements were finally expulsed by Abeyd Ibn Rashîd; because not conforming themselves to the will of the Emir, they had received their Ateyba neighbours—who were his enemies—as their *dakhîls*, and would have protected them against him.]

The camels were azab, Maatuk's thelûl was with them ; and till their coming home we could not set out for Ibn Nâhal. Some Solubba rode-in one morrow on their asses; and our people gave them pots and kettles (which are always of brass), to carry away, for tinning. I found two young Solubbies gelding an ass behind the tents !—(the Aarab have only entire horses). The gipsies said laughing, ' This beast was an ass overmuch, and they had made him chaste ! ' I found an old Solubby sitting in Maatuk's tent, a sturdy greybeard ; his grim little eyes were fastened upon me. I said to him, " What wouldst thou ? "—" I was thinking, that if I met with thee alone in the khâla, I would kill thee."—" Wherefore, old tinker ? "— " For thy clothing and for any small things that might be with thee, Nasrâny ;—if the wolf found thee in the wilderness, wert

thou not afraid?"—The Solubba offend no man, and none do
them hurt. I enquired of these: "Is it true, that ye eat the
sheep or camel which is dead of itself?"—"We eat it, and how
else might we that have no cattle eat meat in the menzils of the
Aarab! Wellah, Khalîl, is this halàl or harrâm?"

A day or two after Maatuk was for no more going to Ibn
Náhal; he said, "Shall I carry thee to el-Hâyat? or else I might
leave thee at Semîra or at Seleyma." But I answered, "To
Ibn Náhal;" and his good wife Noweyr, poor woman, looking
over her tent cloth, spoke for me every day; "Oh! said she, ye
are not good, and Maatuk, Maatuk! why hinder Khalîl? perform thy promise, and *wild el-ghrarîb beledhu aan el-ájnaby:*
(it is a refrain of the Nomad maidens 'speed the stranger on
his way to his own people'; or be it, 'the heart of the stranger
is in his own country, and not in a strange land'.") The good
hareem her neighbours answered with that pious word of fanatical Arabia, 'We have a religion, and they have a religion;
every man is justified in his own religion.' Noweyr was one
of those good women that bring the blessing to an household.
Sometimes I saw her clay-pale face in their tent, without the
veil: though not in prosperous health, she was daily absent in
the khála, from the forenoon till the mid-afternoon; and when
I asked her wherefore she wearied herself thus? she said, and
sighed, "I must fetch water from the Sfá to-day, and to-morrow
visit the camels; and else Maatuk beats me." Maatuk's hospitality was more than any Beduwy had showed me: Noweyr gave
me to drink of her léban; and he bade me reach up my hand
when I was hungry to take of her new mereesy shards, which
were spread to dry in the sun upon their worsted roof. If the
camels came home he milked a great bowlful for the stranger,
saying, it was his sádaka, or meritorious human kindness, for
God's sake In these evenings, I have seen the sporting goats
skip and stand, often two and three together, upon the camels'
steep chines: and the great beasts, that lay chawing the cud in
the open moonlight, took no more heed of them than cattle in
our fields, when crows or starlings light upon them.

Maatuk was afraid to further me, because of Ibn Rashîd: and
they told me a strange tale. A year or two ago, these Heteym
carried on their camels some strangers, whom they called
"Nasâra"!—I know not whither. The Emir hearing of it,
could hardly be entreated not to punish them cruelly, and take
their cattle.—"Ay, this is true, O Khalîl!" added Noweyr.—
"But what Nasrânies! and from whence?"—"Wellah, they
could not tell, the strangers were Nasâra, as they heard." The
Arabs are barren-minded in the emptiness of the desert life, and

retchless of all that pertains not to their living. " Nasâra,"
might signify in their mouths no more than "aliens not of the
orthodox belief." *Maatuk:* " Ibn Rashîd is not thy friend, and
the country is dangerous; abide with me, Khalîl, till the Haj
come and return again, next spring."—" How might I live those
many months? is there food in the khála ? "—" You may keep
my camels."—" But how under the flaming sun, in the long
summer season ? "—" When it is hot thou canst sit in my booth,
and drink léban; and I will give thee a wife "—Hearing his
words, I rejoiced, that the Aarab no longer looked upon me as
some rich stranger amongst them ! When he pronounced ' wife,'
the worthy man caught his breath !—could he offer a bint of
Heteym to so white a man? so he said further, " I will give
thee an *Harbía.*"

" Years ago, quoth Maatuk, there came into our parts a
Moghreby [like Khalîl],—wellah we told little by him ; but the
man bought and sold, and within a while we saw him thriving.
He lived with Harb, and took a wife of their daughters ; and the
Moor had flocks and camels, all gotten at the first and increased
of his traffic in samn and clothing. Now he is dead, his sons
dwell with Harb, and they are well-faring." We sat in the
tent, and they questioned me, ' Where is thy nation ? ' I shewed
them the setting sun, and said we might sail thither in our
shipping, *sefn.*—" Shipping (they said one to another) is *zymát;*
but O Khalîl, it is there, in the West, we have heard to be the
Kafir Nation! and that from thence the great danger shall come
upon el-Islam: beyond how many floods dwell ye, we heard seven;
and how many thelûl journeys be ye behind the Sooltàn ? "—
Coffee-drinking, though the Heteymàn be welfaring more than
the neighbour Beduins, is hardly seen, even in sheykhs' tents,
amongst them : there was none in Maatuk's ferîj Aarab of
Ibn Rashîd, their only enemies are the Ateyba ; and pointing
to the eastward, " All the peril, said Maatuk, is from thence ! "
—These Heteym (unlike their kindred inhabiting nearer Medina)
are never cheesemakers.

He is a free man that may carry all his worldly possession
upon one of his shoulders : now I secretly cast away the superfluous weight of my books, ere a final effort to pass out of Arabia,
and (saving *Die alte Geographie Arabiens,* and Zehme's *Arabien
seit hundert Jahren*) gave them honourable burial in a thób's
hole ; heaped in sand, and laid thereon a great stone.—In this
or another generation, some wallowing camel or the streaming
winter rain may discover to them that dark work of the Nasrány.
Six days the Nomad tents were standing at Âul, to-morrow they

would dislodge ; and Maatuk now consented to carry the stranger to Ibn Náhal: for Noweyr, lifting her pale face above the woman's curtain, many times daily exhorted him, saying, " Eigh, Maatuk ! detain not Khalîl against his liking ; speed the stranger home."

Their camels were come ; and when the morning broke, ' Art thou ready, quoth Maatuk, and I will bring the thelûl : but in faith I know not where Ibn Náhal may be found." Noweyr put a small skin of samn in her husband's wallet ; to be, she said, for the stranger. We mounted, Maatuk's sly brother brought us on our journey ; and hissed his last counsels in my rafîk's ear, which were not certainly to the advantage of the Nasrâny :—" Aye ! aye ! " quoth Maatuk. We rode on a hurr, or dromedary male (little used in these countries), and which is somewhat rougher riding. By this the sun was an hour high ; and we held over the desert toward the Sfá mountain. After two hours we saw another menzil of Heteym, sheykh *Ibn Dammûk*, and their camels pasturing in the plain. Maatuk called the herdsman to us to tell and take the news ; but they had heard nothing lately of Ibn Náhal.

The waste beyond was nearly máhal : we rode by some granite blocks, disposed baywise, and the head laid south-east-ward, as it were towards Mecca : it might be taken in these days for a praying place. But Maatuk answered, " Such works are of the ancients in these dîras,—the B. Taâmir." We saw a very great thób's burrow, and my rafîk alighted to know if the edible monster were ' at home : ' and in that, singing cheerfully, he startled a troop of gazelles. Maatuk shrilled through his teeth, and the beautiful deer bounded easily before us ; then he yelled like a wild man, and they bent themselves to their utmost flight. The scudding gazelles stood still anon, in the hard desert plain of gravel, and gazed back like timid damsels, to know what had made them afraid.—In Syria, I have seen mares, " that had out-stripped gazelles"; but whether this were spoken in the ordinary figure of their Oriental speech, which we call a falsehood, I have not ascertained. The nomads take the fawns with their grey-hounds, which are so swift, that I have seen them overrun the small desert hare almost in a moment. I asked Maatuk, Where was his matchlock ?—He lost it, he answered, to a ghrazzu of Ateyba—that was a year ago ; and now he rode but with that short cutlass, wherewith his brother had once threatened the Nasrâny. He sang in their braying-wise [which one of their ancient poets, Antara, compared to the hum of flies !] as we passed over the desert at a trot, and quavering his voice (*î-î-î-î*) to the wooden jolting of the thelûl saddle. Maatuk told me, (with a sheykh's pride), that those Beduin households in his ferîj had been with him several years. In the midsummer time all the ferjân of the Ibn Barrák Heteym (under the sheykh Kâsim,) assemble and pitch together, near the Wady er-Rummah, " where, said he, one may find water, under the sand, at the depth of this camel stick."—Wide we have seen to be the dispersion of the Heteym : there are some of the B. Rashîd far in the North, near Kuweyt !

Now before us appeared a steep granite mountain, *Genna ;* and far upon our left hand lay the watering *Benâna*, between mountains. We came after mid-day to a great troop of Heteym camels : but here was the worst grazing ground (saving the Sinai country) that I ever beheld in the wilderness ; for there was nothing sprung besides a little wormwood. The herd boys milked their nâgas for us ; but that milk with the froth was like wormwood for bitterness [and such is the goats' milk in this pasture]. The weleds enquired in their headlong manner, " *El-khábar ? weysh el-ellûm ?* What tidings from your parts, what news is there ? "—" Well, it may please Ullah."—" And such and such Aarab, beyond and beside you, where be they now ? where is such a sheykh encamped, and of what waters drink they ? is there word of any ghrazzus ? And the country which you have passed through ?—say is it bare and empty, or such that it may satisfy the cattle ? Which herbs saw ye in it, O Maatuk ? What is heard of the Emir ? and where left ye your households ?—auh ! and the ferjân and Aarab thou hast mentioned, what is reported of their pasture ? "—*Maatuk :* " And what tidings have ye for us, which Aarab are behind you ? what is heard of any ghrazzus ? Where is Ibn Náhal ? where be your booths ? "

An hour or two later we found another herd of Heteym camels : and only two children kept them ! Maatuk made a gesture, stroking down his beard, when we rode from them ; and said, " Thus we might have taken wellah every head of them, had they been our enemies' cattle ! " Yet all this country lies very open to the inroads of Ateyba, who are beyond the W. er-Rummah. Not much later we came to a menzil of Heteym, and alighted for that day.—These tent-dwellers knew me, and said to Maatuk, ' I had journeyed with a tribesman of theirs, Ghroceyb, my name was Khalîl ; and Kâsim's Aarab purchased medicines of me, which they found to be such as I had foretold them ; I was one that deceived not the Aarab.' As for Ibn Náhal, they heard he was gone over " The Wady," into the Ateyba border, (forsaken by them of late years for dread of Ibn Rashîd). The land-height was here 4200 feet, shelving to the W. er-Rummah.

At daybreak we mounted, and came after an hour's riding to other Heteym tents. All the wilderness was barren, almost máhal, and yet, full of the nomads' worsted hamlets at this season. Maatuk found a half-brother in this menzil, with their old mother; and we alighted to sit awhile with them. The man brought fresh goat milk and bade me drink,—making much of it, because his hospitality was *whole milk;* 'The samn, he said, had not been taken.' Butter is the poor nomads' money, wherewith they may buy themselves clothing and town wares; therefore they use to pour out only buttermilk to the guest.—We rode further; the (granite) desert was now sand soil, in which after winter rain there springs the best wild pasture, and we began to find good herbage. We espied a camel troop feeding under the mountain Genna, and crossed to them to enquire the herdsmen's tidings; but Maatuk, who was timid, presently drew bridle, not certainly knowing what they were. "Yonder, I said, be only black camels, they are Harb;" [the great cattle of the south and middle tribes, Harb, Meteyr, Ateybân, are commonly swarthy or black, and none of them dun-coloured]. Maatuk answered, it was God's truth, and wondered from whence had I this lore of the desert. We rode thither and found them to be Harb indeed. The young men told us that Ibn Náhal had alighted by Seleymy to-day; and they milked for us. We rode from them, and saw the heads of the palms of the desert village, and passed by a trap mountain, *Chebád.*

Before us, over a sandy descending plain, appeared a flat mountain *Debby;* and far off behind Debby I saw the blue coast of some wide mountain, *el-Álem.* "Thereby, said Maatuk, lies the way to Medina,—four days' thelûl riding." We went on in the hot noon; and saw another camel troop go feeding under the jebel; we rode to them and alighted to drink more milk and enquire the herdsmen's tidings. They were Harb also, and shewed us a rocky passage in the mountain to go over to Ibn Náhal. But I heard of them an adverse tiding: 'The B. Aly (that is all the Harb N. and E. from hence) were drawing southwards, and the country was left empty, before a ghrazzu of Ibn Saûd and the Ateyba!'—How now might I pass forward to el-Kasîm? We saw a multitude of black booths pitched under Debby; 'They were *Aûf*', answered the herdsmen,—come up hither from the perpetual desolation of their Hejâz marches, between the Harameyn; for they heard that the rabîa was in these parts.—*El-Aûf!* that is, we have seen, a name abhorred even among their brethren; for of Auf are the purse-cutters and pillers of the poor pilgrims. And here, then, according to a distich of the western tribes, I was come to the ends of the (known) world! for says one of their thousand rhymed saws, '*El-Aûf warrahum ma fi shûf,* nothing is seen beyond Auf.' I beheld indeed a desert world of new and dreadful aspect! black camels, and uncouth hostile mountains; and a vast sand wilderness shelving towards the dire imposter's city!

Genna is a landmark of the Beduin herdsmen; in the head are pools of rain-water. Descending in the steep passage, we encountered a gaunt desert man riding upward on a tall thelûl and leading a mare : he bore upon his shoulder the wavering horseman's shelfa. Maatuk shrank timidly in the saddle ; that witch-like armed man was a startling figure, and might be an Aûfy. Roughly he challenged us, and the rocks resounded the magnanimous utterance of his leathern gullet: he seemed a manly soul who had fasted out his life in that place of torment which is the Hejâz between the Harameyn, so that nothing remained of him but the terrific voice!—wonderfully stern and beetle-browed was his dark visage. He espied a booty in my bags ; and he beheld a stranger. "Tell me, he cries, what men be ye ? "—Maatuk made answer meekly, "Heteymy I, and thou ? "—" I Harby, and ugh ! cries the perilous anatomy, who he with thee ? "—" A Shâmy trading among the Aarab."—"Aye well, and I see him to be a Shâmy, by the guise of his clothing." He drew his mare to him, and in that I laid hand to the pistol in my bosom, lest this Death-on-a-horse should have lifted his long spear against us. Maatuk reined aside; but the Harby struck his dromedary, and passed forth.

We looked down from the mountain over a valley-like plain, and saw booths of the Aarab. "Khalîl, quoth Maatuk, the people is ignorant, I shall not say to any of them, 'He is a Nasrâny' ; and say it not thyself. Wellah I may not go with thee to Ibn Náhal's beyt, but will bring thee to Aarab that are pitched by him."—"You shall carry me to Ibn Náhal himself. Are not these tribesmen very strait in religion ? I would not light at another tent; and thou wilt not abandon thy rafîk." —"But Khalîl there is an old controversy betwixt us for camels ; and if I went thither he might seize this thelûl."—" I know well thou speakest falsely."—" Nay, by Him who created this camel-stick ! "—But the nomad was forsworn ! The Nejûmies had said to me at Kheybar, "It is well that Khalîl never met with Harb ; they would certainly have cut his throat : " —they spoke of Harb tribesmen between the sacred cities, wretches black as slaves, that have no better trade than to run behind the caravans clamouring, *bakshish !*

Here I came to upland Harb, and they are tributaries of Ibn Rashîd ; but such distinctions cannot be enquired out in a day from the ignorant. In the Nejd Harb I have found the ancient Arabian mind, more than in Annezy tribesmen. The best of the Ageyl at Kheybar was a young Harby, gentle and magnanimous, of an ascetical humour; he was seldom seen at Abdullah's coffee drinkings, and yet he came in sometimes to Amm Mohammed, who was his half-tribesmen, though in another kindred. One day he said boasting, "We the B. Sâlem are better than ye; for we have nothing Frenjy [of outlandish usage, or wares fetched in by Turks and foreign pilgrims to the Holy Places], saving this tobacco."—Now Maatuk held over to three or four booths, which stood apart in the valley-plain; he alighted before them, and said he would leave me there. An elder woman came out to us, where we sat on the sand beside the yet unloaded thelûl; and then a young wife from the beyt next us. Very cleanly-gay she seemed, amongst Aarab, in her new calico kirtle of blue broidered with red worsted.—Was not this the bride, in her marriage garment, of some Beduin's fortunate youth? She approached with the grace of the desert, and, which is seldom seen, with some dewy freshness in her cheeks,—it might be of an amiable modesty; and she was a lovely human flower in that inhuman desolation. She asked, with a young woman's diffidence, 'What would we?' Maatuk responded to the daughter of Harb, "Salaam, and if ye have here any sick persons, this is an hakîm from es-Sham; one who travels about with his medicines among the Aarab, and is very well skilled, now he seeks who will convey him to el-Kasîm. I leave this Shâmy at your beyt, for I cannot myself carry him further; and ye will send him forward." She called the elder woman to counsel; and they answered, 'Look you! the men are in the khála, and we are women alone. It were better that ye went over to Ibn Náhal!—and see, that is his great booth standing yonder!'— *Maatuk:* "I will leave him here; and when they come home (at evening) your men can see to it." But I made him mount with me to ride to Ibn Náhal.

We alighted at Ibn Náhal's great beyt: and entered with the solemnity and greeting of strangers. Ibn Náhal's son and a few young men were sitting on the sand, in this wide hanging-room of worsted. We sat down and they whispered among them, that 'I was some runaway soldier, of the Dowla' [from the Holy Cities or el-Yémen]: then I heard them whisper, 'Nay, I was that Nasrâny!'—They would not question with us till we had drunk kahwa.

A nomad woman of a grim stature stood upbraiding without Ibn Náhal's great booth! she prophesied bitter words in the air, and no man regarded. Her burden was of the decay of hospitality now-a-days! and Ibn Náhal [a lean soul, under a sleek skin], was gone over to another tent to be out of earshot of the wife-man's brawling. The Beduw commonly bear patiently the human anger, *zaal*, as it were trouble sent by the will of God upon them: the Aarab are light even in their ire, and there is little weight in their vehement words If any Nomad tribesman revile his sheykh, he as a nobleman, will but shrink the shoulders and go further off, or abide till others cry down the injurious mouth. But evil tongues, where the Arabs dwell in towns, cannot so walk at their large: the common railer against the sheukh in Hâyil, or in Boreyda, would be beaten by the sergeants of the Emir.

The coffee mortar rang out merrily for the guests in Ibn Náhal's booth: and now I saw the great man and his coffee companions approaching, with that (half feminine) wavering gait which is of their long clothing and unmuscular bodies. They were coffee lords, men of an elegant leisure in the desert life; also the Harb go gallantly clad amongst Beduins. Khálaf ibn Náhal greeted us strangers with his easy smile, and the wary franchise of these mejlis politicians, and that ringing hollow throat of the dry desert; he proffered a distant hand: we all sat down to drink his kahwa,—and that was not very good. Khálaf whispered to his son, "What is he, a soldier?" The young man smiling awaited that some other should speak: so one of the young companions said, "We think we should know thee." *The son :* "Art not thou the Nasrâny that came last year to Hâyil?" —"I am he."—"I was at Hâyil shortly after, and heard of thee there; and when you entered, by the tokens, I knew thee." Khálaf answered among them, unmoved, "He had visited the Nasâra, that time he traded with camels to Egypt; and they were men of a singular probity. Wellah, in his reckoning with one of them, the Christian having received too much by five-pence, rode half a day after him to make restitution!" He added, "Khalîl travels among the Aarab!—well, I say, why not? he carries about these medicines, and they (the Nasâra) have good remedies. Abu Fâris before him, visited the Aarab; and wellah the princes at Hâyil favoured this Khalîl? Only a thing mislikes me, which I saw in the manners of the Nasâra,—Khalîl, it is not honest! Why do the men and hareem sit so nigh, as it were in the knees of each other?"

Now there came in two young spokesmen of the Seleymy villagers,—although they seemed Beduw. They complained of the injury which Khálaf had done them to-day, sending his camels to graze in their reserve of pasture; and threatened 'that they would mount and ride to Hâyil, to accuse him before the Emir!' Khálaf's son called them out presently to eat in the inner apartment, made (such I had not seen before) in the midst of this very long and great Beduin tent:—that hidden dish is not rightly of the Nejd Aarab, but savours of the town life and Medina. The young men answered in their displeasure, they were not hungry, they came not hither to eat, and that they were here at home. *Khálaf:* " But go in and eat, and afterward we will speak together?" They went unwillingly, and returned anon: and when he saw them again, Khálaf, because he did them wrong, began to scold:—" Do not they of Seleymy receive many benefits from us? buy we not dates of you and corn also? why are ye then ungrateful?—Ullah, curse the fathers of them, fathers of *settatásher kelb* (sixteen dogs)." Another said: " Ullah, curse them, fathers of *ethnasher kelb* (twelve dogs);" forms more liberal perhaps than the " sixty dogs " of the vulgar malice. These were gallants of Harb, bearing about, in their Beduin garments, the savour of Medina. Khálaf said, with only a little remaining bitterness, that to satisfy them, he would remove on the morrow. Seleymy (So-leyma) is a small Shammar settlement of twelve households, their wells are very deep.

When the young men were gone, Khálaf, taking again his elated countenance gave an ear to our business. He led out Maatuk and, threatening the timid Heteymy with the dis-pleasure of Ibn Rashîd, enquired of him of my passing in the country, and of my coming to his menzil. I went to Khálaf, and said to them, " Thou canst send me, as all the people say, to el-Kasîm : I alighted at your beyt, and have tasted of your hospitality, and would repose this day and to-morrow ; and then let some man of your trust accompany me, for his wages, to el-Kasîm." His voice was smooth, but Khálaf's dry heart was full of a politic dissimulation : " *Má úkdar,* I am not able ; and how, he answered, might we send thee to el-Kasîm ?—who would adventure thither ; the people of Aneyza are our enemies."— " Khálaf, no put-offs, you can help me if you will."—" Well, hearken ! become a Moslem, and I will send thee whithersoever thou would'st ; say, ' There is no God, beside Ullah,' and I will send thee to el-Kasîm freely."—" You promise this, before witnesses ?"—" Am I a man to belie my words."—" Hear then all of you ; There is none God but Ullah !—let the thelûl be brought round."—-" Ay ! say also Mohammed is the messenger of Ullah ! "—" That was not in our covenant ; the thelûl Khálaf ! and let me be going."—" I knew not that the Nasrânies could say so ; all my meaning was that you should become a Moslem. Khalîl, you may find some of the *jemmamîl* (camaleers, sing. *jemmál*) of el-Kasîm, that come about, at this season, to sell clothing among the Aarab. Yesterday I heard of one of them in these parts [it was false]; a jemmâl would carry thee back with him for two reals. When you have supped and drunk the evening camel milk, mount again with this Heteymy! and he will convey thee to him ";—but I read in his looks, that it was a fable. He went aside with Maatuk again,—was long talking with him ; and required him, with words like threatenings, to carry me from him. When we had supped, Maatuk called me to mount. I said to Ibn Náhal, "If I am forsaken in this wilderness, or there should no man receive me, and I return to thee, wilt thou then receive me ? "—Khálaf answered, 'he would receive me.'

In the first darkness of the night we rode from him ; seeking a ferîj which Maatuk had espied as we came down from Genna. After an hour, Maatuk said, "Here is sand, shall we alight and sleep ? "—for yet we saw not their watchfires—" Let us ride on : and if all fail tell me what shall become of me, my rafîk ? "—" Khalîl, I have said it already, that I will carry thee again to live with me in my ferîj." Then a hound barked from the dark valley side : we turned up thither, and came before three tents ; where a camel troop lay chawing the cud in the night's peace : their fires were out, and the Aarab were already sleeping. We alighted and set down our bags, and kneebound the thelûl. I would now have advanced to the booths, but Maatuk withheld me,—"It were not well, he whispered ; but abide we here, and give them time, and see if there come not some to call us."

Bye and bye a man approached, and " Ugh ! said he, as he heard our salaam, why come ye not into the beyt ? " This worthy bore in his hand a spear, and a huge scimitar in the other. We found the host within, who sat up blowing the embers in the hearth ; and laid on fuel to give us light. He roused the housewife ; and she reached us over the curtain a bowl of old rotten léban, of which they make sour mereesy. We sipped their sorry night bever, and all should now be peace and confidence ; yet he of the spear and scimitar sat on, holding his weapons in his two hands, and lowered upon us. " How now, friend ! I said at last, is this that thou takest us for robbers, I and my rafîk ? "—" Ugh ! a man cannot stand too much upon his guard, there is ever peril." Maatuk said merrily, " He has a sword and we have another ! " The host answered smiling, " He never quits that huge sword of his and the spear, waking or sleeping ! " So we perceived that the poor fellow was a knight of the moonshine. I said to our host, " I am a hakîm from Damascus, and I go to el-Kasîm : my rafîk leaves me

here, and will you send me thither for my money, four reals ? "
He answered gently, " We will see to-morrow, and I think we
may agree together, whether I myself shall convey thee, or I
find another ; in the meantime, stay with us a day or two."
When we would rest, the housemother, she of the rotten léban,
said a thing to one of us, which made me think we were not
well arrived : she was a forsaken wife of our host's brother. I
asked Maatuk, " If such were the Harb manners ! "—He whispered again, " As thou seest ; and say, Khalîl, shall I leave thee
here, or wilt thou return with me ? "—When the day broke,
Maatuk said to them, "I leave him with you, take care of him :"
so he mounted and rode from us.

Motlog (that was our host's name): " Let us walk down to
Ibn Náhal, and take counsel how we may send thee to el-Kasîm,
but I have a chapped heel and may hardly go." I dressed the
wound with ointment and gave him a sock ; and the Beduwy
drew on a pair of old boots that he had bought in Medina. We
had gone half a mile, when I saw a horseman, with his long
lance, riding against us : a fierce-looking fanatical fellow.—It
was he who alone, of all who sat at Khálaf's, had contraried me
yesterday. This horseman was *Tollog*, my host's elder brother !
and it was his booth wherein we had passed the night ! his was
also that honest forsaken housewife ! It were a jest worthy of
the Arabs and their religion, to tell why the new wedded man
chose to lie abroad at Ibn Náhal's.

" How now ! " cries our horseman staring upon me like a man
aghast. His brother responded simply of the Shâmy hakîm and
the Heteymy.—" Akhs ! which way went that Heteymy ? " (and
balancing his long lance, he sat up) I will gallop after him and
bring him again,—Ullah curse his father ! and knowest thou
that this is a Nasrâny ? " Motlog stood a moment astonished !
then the poor man said nobly, " *Wa low*, and though it be
so . . . ? he is our guest and a stranger ; and that Heteymy is
now too far gone to be overtaken."—Tollog rode further ; he
was a shrew at home and ungracious, but Motlog was a mild
man. We passed by some spring pasture, and Motlog cried to
a child, who was keeping their sheep not far off, to run home
and tell them to remove hither. When the boy was gone a
furlong he waved him back and shouted ' No !' for he had
changed his mind : he was a little broken headed,—and so is
every third man in the desert life. I saw, where we passed
under a granite headland, some ground courses of a dry-built
round chamber such as those which, in the western dîras, I have
supposed to be sepulchres.

P*

Khálaf had removed since yesterday : we found him in his tent stretched upon the sand to slumber—it was noon. The rest made it strange to see me again, but Motlog my host worthily defended me in all. Khálaf turning himself after a while and rising, for the fox was awake, said with easy looks, "Aha ! this is Khalîl back again ; and how Khalîl, that cursed Heteymy forsook thee ? " When he heard that Maatuk had taken wages of me he added : " Had I known this, I would have cut off his head, and seized his thelûl ;—ho ! there, prepare the midday kahwa." His son answered, " We have made it already and drunk round."—"Then make it again, and spare not for kahwa." Khálaf twenty days before had espoused a daughter of the village, and paid the bride money ; and the Beduins whispered in mirth, that she was yet a maid. For this his heart was in bale : and the son, taking occasion to mock the Heteymy, sought in covert words his father's relief, from one called an hakîm. Ibn Náhal said at last kindly, " Since Khalîl has been left at your beyt, send him Motlog whither he desires of thee." * * *

* * * There was here but the deadly semblance of hospitality ; naught but buttermilk, and not so much as the quantity of a cup was set before me in the long day. Happy was I when each other evening their camels came home, and a short draught was brought me of the warm léban. Tollog, the gay horseman, was a glozing fanatical fellow ; in Motlog was some drivelling nobility of mind : the guest's mortal torment was here the miserable hand of Tollog's cast wife. Little of God's peace or blessing was in this wandering hamlet of three brethren ; the jarring contention of their voices lasted from the day rising, till the stars shone above us. Though now their milk-skins overflowed with the spring milk, they were in the hands of the hareem, who boiled all to mereesy, to sell it later at Medina. The Beduw of high Nejd would contemn this ignoble traffic, and the decay of hospitality.

Being without nourishment I fell into a day-long languishing trance. One morrow I saw a ferîj newly pitched upon the valley side, in face of us : when none observed me, I went thither under colour of selling medicines. Few men sat at home, and they questioned with me for my name of Nasrâny ; the women clamoured to know the kinds of my simples, but none poured me out a little léban. I left them and thought I saw other tents pitched beyond : when I had gone a mile, they were but a row of bushes. Though out of sight of friends and

unarmed, I went on, hoping to espy some booths of the Aarab.
I descried a black spot moving far off on the rising plain, and
thought it might be an herd of goats. I would go to them and
drink milk. I crossed to the thin shadow of an acacia tree;
for the sunbeaten soil burned my bare soles; and turning I
saw a tall Beduwy issue from a broken ground and go by, upon
his stalking dromedary; he had not perceived the stranger:
then I made forward a mile or two, to come to the goats. I
found but a young woman with a child herding them.—
'*Salaam!* and could she tell me where certain of the people
were pitched, of such a name?' She answered a little
affrighted, 'She knew them not, they were not of her Aarab.'
—"O maiden milk for me!"—"*Min fen halib*, milk from
whence? we milked them early at the booths; there is naught
now in these goats' udders, and we have no vessel to draw in:"
she said her tents stood yet far beyond. "And is there not
hereby a ferîj, for which I go seeking all this morrow?"—
"Come a little upon the hill side, and I will shew it thee: lo
there! thou mayest see their beyts." My eyes were not so
good; but I marked where she shewed with her finger and
went forward. Having marched half an hour, over wild and
broken ground, I first saw the menzil, when I was nigh upon
them; and turned to go to a greater booth in the circuit, wherein
I espied men sitting.

Their hounds leapt out against me with open throat; the
householder ran with an hatchet, to chase them away from
the stranger (a guest) arriving.—As I sat amongst them, I
perceived that these were not the Beduins I sought. I asked
bye and bye, "Have ye any támr?"—also to eat with them
would be for my security. The good man answered cheerfully, "We have nothing but cheese; and that shall be fetched
immediately." The host was a stranger, a fugitive of Meteyr,
living with these Harb, for an homicide. He sat bruising green
bark of the boughs of certain desert trees; and of the bast he
would twist well-ropes: "There are, said he, some very (*ghra-
mîk*, for '*amîk*) deep *golbán* (sing. *jellîb*, a well) in these dîras."
The poor people treated me honourably, asking mildly and
answering questions. I said, "I came to seek who would carry
me to el-Kasîm for his wages." The man answered, "He had
a good thelûl; and could I pay five reals, he would carry me,
and set me down wellah in the market-place of Aneyza!"

When I came again to my hosts—"Whither wentest thou?
exclaimed Motlog; to go so far from our tents is a great danger
for thee: there are many who finding thee alone would kill

thee, the Beduw are kafirs, Khalîl." When I told him the
man's name, who would carry me to Aneyza, he added, "Have
nothing to do with him! he is a Meteyry If he rode with
thee (radîf), beware of his knife—a Meteyry cannot keep himself
from treachery; or else he might kill thee sleeping: now canst
thou ride four days to el-Kasîm without sleeping!" Such evil-
speaking is common between neighbour tribes; but I think the
Meteyry would have honestly conveyed me to Aneyza. Motlog
had in certain things the gentlest mind of any Arab of my
acquaintance hitherto. When he saw that by moments, I fell
asleep, as I sat, even in the flaming sun, and that I wandered
from the (inhospitable) booths—it was but to seek some rock's
shelter where, in this lethal somnolence and slowness of spirit,
I might close the eyes—he said, ' He perceived that my breast
was straitened (with grief) here among them:' and since I had
taken this journey to heart, and he could not carry me himself
so far as Boreyda, he would seek for someone to-day to convey
me thither;—howbeit that for my sake, he had let pass the
ghrazzu of Ibn Náhal,—for which he had obtained the loan of
another horse.

Besides him a grim councillor for my health was Aly, he of
the spear and scimitar: that untempered iron blade had been
perchance the pompous side arm of some javelin man of the great
officers of Medina,—a personage in the city bestowed the warlike
toy upon the poor soul "Ana sahíbak, I am thy very friend,"
quoth Aly, in the husk voice of long-suffering misery. He was
of the Harb el-Aly: they are next from hence in the N.-E and
not of these Aarab. I asked him: " Where leftest thou thy
wife and thy children and thy camels? " He answered, " I
have naught besides this mantle and my tunic and my weapons:
ana yatîm! I am an orphan!" This fifty years' old poor
Beduin soul was yet in his nonage;—what an hell were it of
hunger and misery, to live over his age again! He had inherited
a possession of palms, with his brother, at Medina; but the
stronger father's son put out his weak-headed brother: and, said
Motlog, "The poor man (reckoned a fool) could have there no
redress."—" And why are these weapons always in his hands? "
—" He is afraid for a thing that happened years ago: Aly and
a friend of his, rising from supper, said they would try a fall.
They wrestled: Aly cast the other, and fell on him;—and it may
be there had somewhat burst in him, for the fallen man lay
dead! None accused Aly; nevertheless the mesquin fled for his
life, and he has gone ever since thus armed, lest the kindred of
the deceased finding him should kill him."

At evening there sat with us a young kinsman of Tollog's new wife. He was from another ferîj; and having spoken many injuries of the Nasâra, he said further, "Thou Tollog, and Motlog! wellah, ye do not well to receive a kafir in your beyts;" and taking for himself all the inner place at the fire,—unlike the gentle customs of the Beduins, he had quite thrust out the guest and the stranger into the evening wind; for here was but a niche made with a lap of the tent cloth, to serve, like the rest of their inhospitality, for the men's sitting-place. I exclaimed, "This must be an Ageyly!"—They answered, "Ay, he is an Ageyly! a proud fellow, Khalîl."—"I have found them hounds, Turks and traitors; by my faith, I have seen of them the vilest of mankind."—"Wellah, Khalîl, it is true."—"What Harby is he?" —"He is *Hâzimy*."—"An *Hâzimy*! then good friends, this ignoble proud fellow is a Solubby!"—"It is sooth, Khalîl, aha-ha-ha!" and they laughed apace. The discomfited young man, when he found his tongue, could but answer, *subbak*, "The Lord rebuke thee." It seemed to them a marvellous thing that I should know this homely matter.—Hâzim, an ancient fendy of Harb, are snibbed as Heteym; and Beduins in their anger will cast against any Heteymy, Sherâry or sâny the reproach of Solubby. Room was now made, and this laughter had reconciled the rest to the Nasrâny.—I had wondered to see great part of Tollog's tent shut close: but on the morrow, when the old ribald housewife and mother of his children sat without boiling samn, there issued from the close booth a new face,—a fair young woman, clean and comely clad! She was Tollog's (new) bright bird in bridal bower; and these were her love-days, without household charge. She came forth with dazing eyes in the burning sunlight.

When the next sun rose, I saw that our three tents were become four. These new comers were Seyadîn, not Solubbies, not sânies but (as we have seen) packmen of poor Beduin kin, carrying wares upon asses among the Aarab. I went to visit the strangers;—"*Salaam!*"—"*Aleykom es-salaam*; and come in Khalîl! art thou here?"—"And who be ye!"—"Rememberest thou not when thou camest with the Heteymies and drank coffee in our kasr, at Gofar?" The poor woman added, "And I mended thy rent mantle." "Khalîl, said the man, where is thy galliûn? I will fill it with hameydy." Beduin-born, all the paths of the desert were known to him; he had peddled as far as Kasîm and he answered me truly in all that I enquired of him:—they are not unkind to whom the world is unkind! there was no spice in them of fanaticism.

CHAPTER VII

THE same morning came two Beduins with camel-loads of temmn; which the men had brought down for Tollog and Motlog, from el-Irâk! They were of Shammar and carriers in Ibn Rashîd's Haj caravan. I wondered how after long journeying they had found our booths: they told me, that since passing Hâyil they had enquired us out, in this sort,—'Where is Ibn Náhal?'—*Answer:* 'We heard of him in the S.-E. country.— Some say he is gone over to the Ateyba marches.—When last we had word of him, he was in such part.—He went lately towards Seleyma.—You shall find his Aarab between such and such landmarks.—He is grazing about Genna.' Whilst they were unloading, a Beduin stranger, but known in this ferîj, arrived upon his camel after an absence: he had lately ridden westward 130 miles, to visit Bishr, amongst whom he had been bred up; but now he dwelt with Harb. The man was of Shammar, and had a forsaken wife living as a widow in our menzil: he came to visit their little son. Motlog counselled me to engage this honest man for the journey to Kasîm. We called him: —He answered, 'Wellah, he feared to pass so open a country, where he might lose his camel to some foraying Ateybân;' but Motlog persuaded him, saying he could buy with his wages a load of dates (so cheap in el-Kasîm) to bring home to his household. He proffered to carry me to *el-Bukkerîeh:* but we agreed for five reals that he should carry me to Boreyda. " Mount, *érkub!* " quoth the man, whose name was *Hàmed;* he loaded my things, and climbed behind me,—and we rode forth. " Ullah bring thee to thy journey's end! said Tollog; Ullah, give that you see not the evil! "

The sun was three hours high: we passed over a basalt coast, and descended to another ferîj; in which was Hàmed's beyt. There he took his water-skin, and a few handfuls of mereesy— all his provision for riding other 450 miles—and to his house-

wife he said no more than this : " Woman, I go with the stranger
to Boreyda." She obeyed silently ; and commonly a Beduwy in
departing bids not his wife farewell :—" Hearest thou ? (said
Hàmed again) follow with these Aarab until my coming home ! "
Then he took their little son in his arms and kissed him.—We
rode at first northward for dread of Ateybân : this wilderness
is granite grit with many black basalt bergs. The marches beyond were now full of dispersed Aarab, B. Sâlem ; we saw their
black booths upon every side. All these Harb were gathering
towards *Semîra*, in the Shammar dîra, to be taxed there, upon a
day appointed, by the collectors of Ibn Rashîd ; because there is
much water for their multitude of cattle. We left the mountain
landmark of Benàny at half a day's distance, west ; and held
forward evenly with the course of W. er-Rummah,—the great
valley now lying at a few miles' distance upon the right hand.
Some black basaltic mountains, not very far off, Hàmed told me,
were beyond the Wady : that great dry waterway bounds the
dîrat of Harb in Nejd ; all beyond is Ateyba country. Twice as
we rode we met with camel herds ; the men milked for us, and
we enquired and told tidings At sun-setting we were journeying under a steep basalt jebel ; and saw a black spot, upon a
mountain sand-drift, far before us, which was a booth of the
nomads : then we saw their camels, and the thought of evening
milk was pleasant to our hearts. " But seest thou ? said Hàmed,
they are all males ! for they are gaunt and have low humps ;—
that is because they serve for carriage : the Aarab let the cows
fatten, and load not upon them." * * *

*(Doughty passes with Hàmed through the desert to Semîra,
meeting with Beny Aly and Harb Aarab.)*

* * * Now before us lay the Nefûd sand of Kasîm, which
begins to be driven-up in long swelling waves, that trend somewhat N. and S. Four miles further we went by the oasis
Ayûn ; embayed in the same sandstone train, which is before
called Sâra. Upon a cliff by the Nefûd side is a clay-built
lighthouse-like watch-tower [the watch-tower is found in all the

villages of Kasîm]. The watchman (who must be clear sighted)
is paid by a common contribution : his duty is to look forth, in
the spring months, from the day rising till the going down of
the sun ; for this is the season, when the villagers who have
called in their few milch goats from the Aarab, send them
forth to pasture without the oasis. We saw the man standing unquietly in his gallery, at the tower head, in the flame of
the sun ; and turning himself to every part, he watched, under
the shadow of his hand, all the fiery waste of sand before
him. Hàmed said, the palms at Ayûn are about half the
palms of Teyma; and here might be 400 or 500 inhabitants.
Ayûn stands at the crossing of the Kasîm cameleers' paths,
to J. Shammar, to the land of the north, and to the Holy Cities.
My rafîk had been well content to leave me here ; where, he
promised, I should meet with carriers to all parts, even to
Kuweyt and Bosra, " wellah, more than in Boreyda."

Some great cattle were feeding before us in the Nefûd—they
were not camels ; but, oh ! happy homely sight, the villagers kine
at pasture in that uncheerful sand wilderness ! I said, " I
would ride to them and seek a draught of cow-milk." Hàmed
answered, " Thou wilt ask it in vain, go not Khalîl ! for these
are not like the Beduw, but people of the *géria*, not knowing
hospitality : before us lies a good village, we shall soon see the
watch-tower, and we will alight there to breakfast." I saw a
distant clay steeple, over the Nefûd southward. Hàmed could
not tell the name of that oasis : he said, " Wellah the *geraïeh*
(towns and villages) be so many in el-Kasîm ! " We came in
two hours to *Gassa*, a palm village, with walls, and the greatest
grown palms that I had seen since Teyma,—and this said Hàmed,
who knew Teyma. When I asked, what were the name Gassa,
he answered, " There is a pumpkin so called : " but the Beduw
are rude etymologers. Their watch-tower—*mergáb* or *garra*—
is founded upon a rock above the village. The base is of rude
stones laid in clay, the upper work is well built of clay bricks.
We were now in Kasîm, the populous (and religious) nefûd
country of the caravaners. We did not enter the place, but
halted at a solitary orchard house under the garra. It was the
time of their barley harvest : this day was near the last in April.
The land-height I found to be now only 2800 feet.

We dismounted ; the householder came out of his yard, to lead
us to the kahwa, and a child bore in my bags : Hàmed brought
away the head-stall and halter of our camel, for here, he said,
was little assurance. The coffee-hall floor was deep Nefûd sand !
When we had drunk two cups, the host called us into his store
room ; where he set before us a platter of dates—none of the

best, and a bowl of water. The people of Kasîm are not lovers of hospitality : the poor Aarab (that are passengers without purses) say despitefully, ' There is nothing there but for thy penny !'—this is true. Kasîm resembles the border lands, ard the inhabitants are become as townsmen: their deep sand country, in the midst of high Arabia, is hardly less settled than Syria. The Kusmân are prudent and adventurous : there is in them much of the thick B. Temîm blood. Almost a third of the people are caravaners, to foreign provinces, to Medina and Mecca, to Kuweyt, Bosra, Bagdad, to the Waháby country, to J. Shammar. And many of them leave home in their youth to seek fortune abroad ; where some (we have seen) serve the Ottoman government in arms: they were till lately the Ageyl at Bagdad, Damascus, and Medina.—All Nejd Arabia, east of Teyma, appertains to the Persian Gulf traffic, and not to Syria: and therefore the (foreign) colour of Nejd is Mesopotamian ! In those borderlands are most of the emigrated from el-Kasîm,—husband-men and small salesmen ; and a few of them are become wealthy merchants.

Arabians of other provinces viewing the many green villages of this country in their winding-sheet of sand, are wont to say half scornfully, ' Kasîm is all Nefûd.' The Nefûd of Kasîm is a sand country through whose midst passes the great Wady [er-Rummah], and everywhere the ground water is nigh at hand. Wells have been digged and palms planted in low grounds [gá, or khóbra], with a loam soil not too brackish or bitter : and such is every oasis-village of el-Kasîm. The chief towns are of the later middle age. The old Kasîm settlements, of which the early Mohammedan geographers make mention, are now, so far as I have enquired, ruined sites and names out of mind. The poor of Kasîm and *el-Wéshm* wander even in their own country ; young field labourers seek service from town to town, where they hear that *el-urruk*, the sweat of their brow, is likely to be well paid. Were el-Kasîm laid waste, this sand country would be, like the lands beyond Jordan, a wilderness full of poor village ruins.

Our host sat with a friend, and had sparred his yard door against any intrusion of loitering persons. These substantial men of Kasîm, wore the large silken Bagdad kerchief, cast negligently over the head and shoulders ; and under this head-gear the red Turkey cap, *tarbúsh.* Our host asked me what countryman I was   "I am a traveller, from Damascus."—" No, thou art not a Shâmy, thy speech is better than so ; for I have been in Syria: tell me, art thou not from some of those vil-lages in the Haurân ? I was there with the Ageyl. What art

thou? thou art not of the Moslemîn; art thou then Yahûdy,
or of the Nasâra?"—"Yes, host, a Mesîhy; will ye therefore
drive me away, and kill me?"—"No! and fear nothing; is not
this el-Kasîm? where the most part have travelled in foreign
lands: they who have seen the world are not like the ignorant,
they will treat thee civilly"—We heard from him that Ibn
Saûd was come as far as *Mejmaâ:* but those rumours had been
false of his riding in Kasîm, and in the Harb country! Our
host desired to buy quinine of the hakîm; I asked half a real;
he would pay but fourpence, and put me in mind of his inhospitable hospitality.—"Wilt thou then accompany me to
Boreyda? and I will give it thee."—"Wherefore should I pay
for kanakîna? in Kasîm thou wilt see it given away (by some
charitable merchants)."

—We rode over a salt-crusted bottom beyond the village:
the well-water at Gassa has a taste of this mineral. In the
oasis, which is greater than er-Rauth, may be three hundred
souls. The dark weather was past, the sun shone out in the
afternoon; and I felt as we journeyed here in the desert of
el-Kasîm, such a stagnant sultry air, as we may commonly find
in the deep Jordan plain below Jericho. At our left hand is
still the low sandstone coast; whereunder I could see palms
and watch-towers of distant hamlets and villages. The soil
is grit-sand with reefs of sand-rock; beside our path are
dunes of deep Nefûd sand. After five miles, we came before
Shuklûk, which is not far from Boreyda; it stands (as I
have not seen another Arabian settlement) without walls! in
the desert side. Here we drew bridle to enquire tidings, and
drink of their sweet water. We heard that *Hásan,* Emir of
Boreyda, whom they commonly call *Weled* (child of) *Mahanna,*
was with his armed band in the wilderness, *ghrazzai.*—
Mahanna, a rich *jemmâl* or camel master at Boreyda, lent money
at usury, till half the town were his debtors; and finally
with the support of the Waháby, he usurped the Emir's
dignity!—Hâmed told me yet more strangely, that the sheykh
of a géria, *Káfer,* near *Kuseyby,* in these parts, is a sâny!
he said the man's wealth had procured him the village
sheykhship. [It is perhaps no free oasis, but under Boreyda or
Hâyil.]

Now I saw the greater dunes of the Nefûd; such are called
tâus and *nef'd* (pl. *anfâd*) by Beduins: and *adanát* and *kethîb*
(pl. *kethbàn*) are words heard in Kasîm. "Not far beyond
the dunes on our right hand (towards Aneyza) lies the W.
er-Rummah," said Hâmed. We journeyed an hour and a
half, and came upon a brow of the Nefûd, as the sun was

going down. And from hence appeared a dream-like spectacle !
—a great clay town built in this waste sand with enclosing
walls and towers and streets and houses! and there beside
a bluish dark wood of ethel trees, upon high dunes! This is
Boreyda! and that square minaret, in the town, is of their
great mesjid. I saw, as it were, Jerusalem in the desert!
[as we look down from the Mount of Olives]. The last upshot
sun-beams enlightened the dim clay city in glorious manner,
and pierced into that dull pageant of tamarisk trees. I asked
my rafîk, " Where are their palms ? " He answered, " Not in
this part, they lie behind yonder great dune towards the Wady
(er-Rummah)."

Hàmed : " And whilst we were in the way, if at any time
I have displeased thee, forgive it me ; and say hast thou
found me a good rafîk? Khalîl, thou seest Boreyda! and
to-day I am to leave thee in this place. And when thou art in
any of their villages, say not, 'I (am) a Nasrâny,' for then they
will utterly hate thee ; but pray as they, so long as thou shalt
sojourn in the country, and in nothing let it be seen that
thou art not of the Moslemîn : do thus, that they may bear thee
also goodwill, and further thee. Look not to find these townlings mild-hearted like the Beduw! but conform thyself to
them ; or they will not suffer thee to abide long time among
them. I do counsel thee for the best—I may not compel thee!
say thou art a *mudowwy,* and tell them what remedies thou
hast, and for which diseases : this also must be thine art to
live by. Thou hast suffered for this name of Nasrâny, and
what has that profited thee? only say now, if thou canst, ' I
(am a) Musslim.' "

We met with some persons of the town, without their walls,
taking the evening air; and as we went by they questioned my
Beduwy rafîk : among them I noted a sinister Galla swordsman
of the Emir. Hàmed answered, ' We were going to the Emir's
hostel.' They said, " It is far, and the sun is now set; were
it not better for you to alight at such an house ? that stands a
little within the gate, and lodge there this night; and you may
go to the Emir in the morning." We rode from them and
passed the town gate : their clay wall [vulg. *ajjidát*] is new, and
not two feet thick. We found no man in the glooming streets ;
the people were gone home to sup, and the shops in the sûk
were shut for the night : their town houses of (sandy) clay are
low-built and crumbling. The camel paced under us with
shuffling steps in the silent and forsaken ways : we went by
the unpaved public place, *mejlis ;* which I saw worn hollow by

the townspeople's feet! and there is the great clay mesjid and
high-built minaret.   Hàmed drew bridle at the yard of the
Emir's hostel, *Munôkh es-Sheukh.*

The porter bore back the rude gates; and we rode in and
dismounted.   The journey from er-Rauth had been nearly
twenty-five miles.   It was not long, before a kitchen lad bade
us, " rise and say God's name ".   He led through dim cloistered
courts; from whence we mounted by great clay stairs, to supper.
The degrees were worn down in the midst, to a gutter, and we
stumbled dangerously in the gloom.   We passed by a gallery
and terraces above, which put me in mind of our convent
buildings : the boy brought us on without light to the end of a
colonnade, where we felt a ruinous floor under us.   And there
he fetched our supper, a churlish wheaten mess, boiled in water
(a sort of Arabian *búrghrol*), without samn : we were guests of
the peasant Emir of Boreyda.   It is the evening meal in Kasîm,
but should be prepared with a little milk and butter; in good
houses this burghrol, cooked in the broth and commonly mixed
with temmn, is served with boiled mutton.—When we had eaten
and washed, we must feel the way back in the dark, in danger
of breaking our necks, which were more than the supper's
worth.—And now Hàmed bade me his short Beduin *adieux :* he
mounted his camel; and I was easy to see my rafîk safely past
the (tyrant's) gates.   The moon was rising; he would ride out
of the town, and lodge in one of the villages.

I asked now to visit " the Emir ",—Hásan's brother, whom
he had left deputy in Boreyda; it was answered, " The hour is
late, and the Emir is in another part of the town ;—*el-bákir !*
in the morning."   The porter, the coffee server, a swordsman,
and other servitors of the guest-house gathered about me : the
yard gates were shut, and they would not suffer me to go forth.
Whilst I sat upon a clay bench, in the little moonlight, I was
startled from my weariness by the abhorred voice of their
barbaric religion! the muéthin crying from the minaret to the
latter prayer.—' Ah ! I mused, my little provident memory! what
a mischance! why had I sat on thus late, and no Emir, and none
here to deliver me, till the morning ? ' I asked quickly, ' Where
was the sleeping place ? ' Those hyenas responded, with a sort
of smothered derision, ' Would I not pray along with them, ere
I went to rest ? '—They shoved me to a room in the dark hostel
building, which had been used for a small kahwa

All was silent within and sounding as a chapel   I groped,
and felt clay pillars, and trod on ashes of a hearth : and lay
down there upon the hard earthen floor.   My pistol was in the

bottom of my bags, which the porter had locked up in another
place: I found my pen-knife, and thought in my heart, they
should not go away with whole skins, if any would do me a
mischief; yet I hoped the night might pass quietly I had
not slumbered an hour when I heard footsteps, of some one
feeling through the floor; "Up, said a voice, and follow me,
thou art called before the sheykhs to the coffee hall: "—he went
before, and I followed by the sound; and found persons sitting
at coffee, who seemed to be of the Emir's guard. They bade
me be seated, and one reached me a cup: then they questioned
me, "Art not thou the Nasrâny that was lately at Hâyil? thou
wast there with some of Annezy; and Aneybar sent thee away
upon their *jurraba* (mangy thelûl): they were to convey thee
to Kheybar?"—"I am he."—"Why then didst thou not go
to Kheybar?"—"You have said it,—because the thelûl was
jurraba; those Beduins could not carry me thither, which
Aneybar well knew, but the slave would not hear:—tell me,
how knowest thou this?"—"I was in Hâyil, and I saw thee
there. Did not Aneybar forbid thy going to Kasîm?"—"I
heard his false words, that ye were enemies, his forbidding I
did not hear; how could the slave forbid me to travel beyond the
borders of Ibn Rashîd?"—At this they laughed and tossed their
shallow heads, and I saw some of their teeth,—a good sign!
The inquisitors added, with their impatient tyranny, "What are
the papers with thee, ha! go and fetch them; for those will we
have instantly, and carry them to the Emir,—and (to a lad) go
thou with the Nasrâny."

The porter unlocked a store-closet where my bags lay. I
drew out the box of medicines; but my weary hands seemed
slow to the bird-witted wretches that had followed me. The
worst of them, a Kahtâny, struck me with his fist, and reviled
and threatened the Nasrâny. "Out, they cried, with all thy
papers!" and snatched them from my hands: "We go with
these, they said now, to the Emir." They passed out; the gates
were shut after them: and I was left alone in the court. The
scelerat remained who had struck me: he came to me presently
with his hand on his sword, and murmured, "Thou kafîr! say
La ilah ill' Ullah; " and there came another and another. I sat
upon the clay bench in the moonlight, and answered them, "To-
morrow I will hear you; and not now, for I am most weary."
Then they plucked at my breast (for money)! I rose, and
they all swarmed about me.—The porter had said a word in
my ear, "If thou hast any silver commit it to me, for these will
rob thee:" but now I saw he was one of them himself! All

the miscreants being upon me, I thought I might exclaim, *Haramíeh*, thieves! ho! honest neighbours!" and see what came of it; but the hour was late, and this part of the town solitary.—None answered to my voice, and if any heard me, doubtless their hearts would shrink within them; for the Arabs [inhabiting a country weakly governed and full of alarms] are commonly dastards. When I cried *thieves!* I saw my tormentors stand a little aghast: "Shout not (they said hoarsely) or by Ullah—!" So I understood that this assailing me was of their own ribald malice, and shouted on; and when I began to move my arms, they were such cowards that, though I was infirm, I might, I perceived, with a short effort have delivered myself from them: yet this had been worse—for then they would return with weapons; and I was enclosed by walls, and could not escape out of the town. Six were the vile crew struggling with me: I thought it best to shout on *haramíeh!* and make ever some little resistance, to delay the time. I hoped every moment that the officer would return from the Emir. Now my light purse was in their brutish hands; and that which most troubled me, the aneroid barometer,—it seemed to them a watch in the starlight! The Kahtâny snatched and burst the cord by which the delicate instrument was suspended from my neck; and ran away with it like a hound with a good bone in his mouth. They had plucked off my mantle and kerchief; and finally the villains left me standing alone in a pair of slops: then they hied all together to the door where my bags lay. But I thought they would not immediately find my pistol in the dark; and so it was.

— Now the Emir's man stood again at the gate, beating and calling loudly to be admitted: and the porter went like a truant to open. "What has happened?" quoth the officer who entered. "They have stripped the Nasrâny."—"Who has done this?" "It was the Kahtâny, in the beginning." "And this fellow, I answered, was one of the nimblest of them!" The rest had fled into the hostel building, when the Emir's man came in. "Oh, the shame! (quoth the officer) that one is robbed in the Kasr of the Emir; and he a man who bears letters from the Sooltân, what have you done? the Lord curse you all together." "Let them, I said, bring my clothes, although they have rent them."—"Others shall be given thee by the Emir." The lurkers came forth at his call from their dark corners; and he bade them, "Bring the stranger his clothes:—and all, he said to me, that they have robbed shall be restored, upon pain of cutting off the hand; wellah the hand of anyone with whom is found aught shall be laid in thy bags for the thing that was stolen I came to lead thee to a lodging prepared for thee; but I must now return to the Emir:—and (naming them) thou, and thou, and thou, do no more thus, to bring on you the displeasure of the Emir." They answered, "We had not done it, but he refused to say, *La ilah ill' Ullah*."— "This is their falsehood!—for to please them I said it four or five times; and hearken! I will say it again, La îlah, ill' Ullah." —*Officer:* " I go, and shall be back anon."—" Leave me no more among robbers."—" Fear not, none of them will do anything further against you"; and he bade the porter close the gates behind him.

He returned soon: and commanded those wretches, from the Emir, "upon pain of the hand," to restore all that they had robbed from the Nasrâny; he bade also the porter, make a fire in the porch, to give us light. The Kahtâny swordsman, who had been the ringleader of them—he was one of the Emir's band—adjured me to give a true account of the money which was in my purse: ' for my words might endanger his hand; and if I said but the sooth, the Lord would show me mercy.'— " Dost thou think, Miserable, that a Christian man should be such as thyself!"—" Here is the purse, quoth the officer; how much money should be therein? take it, and count thy *derâhim* [δραχμ-]." I found their barbarous hands had been in it; for there remained only a few pence! " Such and such lacks."— *Officer:* " Oh! ye who have taken the man's money, go and fetch it, and the Lord curse you." The swordsman went; and came back with the money,—two French gold pieces of 20 francs: all that remained to me in this bitter world. *Officer:* " Say now, is this all thy *fulûs?*"—" That is all."—" Is there any more?" " No!"—The Kahtâny showed me his thanks with a wondering brutish visage. *Officer:* " And what more?"—" Such and such." The wretches went, and came again with the small things and what else they had time, after stripping me (it was by good fortune but a moment), to steal from my bags. *Officer:* " Look now, hast thou all, is there anything missing?"—" Yes, my watch" (the aneroid, which after the pistol was my most care in Arabia); but they exclaimed, " What watch! no, we have restored all to him already." *Officer:* " Oh, you liars, you cursed ones, you thieves, bring this man his watch! or the (guilty) hand is forfeited to the Emir." It was fetched with delays; and of this they made restitution with the most unwillingness: the metal gilt might seem to them fine gold.— To my comfort, I found on the morrow that the instrument was uninjured: I might yet mark in it the height of a fathom.

He said now, 'It was late, and I should pass the night here.'—
"Lend me a sword, if I must sleep in this cursed place ; and if
any set upon me again, should I spare him ? "—" There is no
more danger, and as for these they shall be locked in the coffee-
hall till the morning : " and he led away the offenders.—The
officer had brought my papers : only the safe-conduct of Aneybar
was not among them !

When the day broke the Emir's officer—whose name was
Jeyber—returned to me : I asked anew to visit the Emir.
Jeyber answered, he must first go and speak with him. When
he came again, he laid my bags on his infirm shoulders saying,
he would bring me to my lodging. He led me through an outlying street ; and turned into a vast ruinous yard, before a great
building—now old and crumbling, that had been the Emir's
palace in former days : [the house walls here of loam may hardly
stand above one hundred years]. We ascended by hollow clay
stairs to a great hall above ; where two women, his housewives,
were sitting. Jeyber, tenant of all the rotten palace, was a
tribesman of Khatân. In the end was a further room, which
he gave me for my lodging. "I am weary, and thou more,
said he ; a cup of kahwa will do us both good : " Jeyber sat
down at his hearth, to prepare the morrow's coffee.

In that there came up some principal persons of the town ;
clad in the (heavy) Mesopotamian wise. A great number of the
well-faring sort in Boreyda are *jemmamíl*, camel masters trading in the caravans. They are wheat carriers in Mesopotamia ;
they bring down clothing and temmn to Nejd ; they load dates
and corn of Kasîm (when the prices serve,) for el-Medina. In
autumn they carry samn, which they have taken up from the
country Nomads, to Mecca ; and from thence they draw coffee.
These burly Arabian citizens resemble peasants ! they were
travelled men ; but I found in them an implacable fanaticism.

Jeyber said when they were gone, "Now shall we visit the
Emir ? " We went forth ; and he brought me through a street
to a place, before the Prince's house. A sordid fellow was
sitting there, like Job, in the dust of their street : two or
three more sate with him,—he might be thirty-five years of
age. I enquired, 'Where was Abdullah the Emir ?' They
said "He is the Emir ! "—" Jeyber (I whispered), is this the
Emir ? "—" It is he." I asked the man, "Art thou Weled
Mahanna ? " He answered, "Ay." "Is it (I said) a custom
here, that strangers are robbed in the midst of your town ? I
had eaten of your bread and salt ; and your servants set upon
me in your yard."—"They were Beduw that robbed you."—

"But I lived with the Beduw; and was never robbed in a menzil: I never lost anything in a host's tent. Thou sayest they were Beduins; but they were the Emir's men!"—*Abdullah:* "I say they were Kahtân all of them." He asked to see my 'watch'. "That I have not with me; but here is a telescope!" He put this to his eyes and returned it. I said, "I give it thee; but thou wilt give me other clothing, for my clothing which the Emir's servants have rent."—He would not receive my gift, the peasant would not make the Nasrâny amends; and I had not money to buy more. "To-day, said he, you depart."— "Whither?"—"To Aneyza; and there are certain cameleers— they left us yesterday, that are going to *Siddûs:* they will convey thee thither."—At Siddûs (which they suppose to have been a place of pilgrimage of the idolatrous people of the country, or "Christians", before Mohammed), is an antique "needle" or column, with some scoring or epigraph. But this was Abdullah's guile, he fabled with me of cameleers to Siddûs: and then he cries, "*Min yeshíl*, who will convey the Nasrâny on his camel to *el-Wady?*"—which I afterwards knew to signify the palms at the *Wady er-Rummah:* I said to him, 'I would rest this day, I was too weary for riding.' Abdullah granted (albeit unwillingly); for all the Arabians [inhabitants of a weary land] tender human infirmities.—"Well, as thou wilt; and that may suffice thee."

—There came a young man to bid me to coffee. "They call you, said Abdullah, and go with him." I followed the messenger and Jeyber: we came to some principal house in the town; and there we entered a pleasant coffee-hall. I saw the walls pargetted with fret-work in gypsum; and about the hearth were spread Persian carpets. The sweet *ghrottha* firewood (a tamarisk kind of the Nefûd) glowed in the hearth, and more was laid up in a niche, ready to the coffee maker's hand: and such is the cleanly civil order of all the better citizen households in Kasîm. Here sat a cold fanatical conventicle of well-clad persons; and a young man was writing a letter, after an elder's words. But that did not hinder his casting some reproach, at every pause, upon the Christian stranger, blaspheming that which he called my impure religion.—How crabbed seemed to me his young looks, moved by the bestial spirit within! I took it to be of evil augury, that none blamed him. And contemptible to an European was the solemn silence of these infantile greybeards, in whom was nothing more respectable than their apparel! I heard no comfortable word among them; and wondered why they had called me! After the second cup, I left them sitting; and returned to Jeyber's place, which is called the palace Hajellân: there a boy met me with two dry girdle-breads, from the guest-house. Such sour town bread is crude and tough; and I could not swallow it, even in the days of famine.

The *Kasr Hajellân* was built by Abdullah, son of *Abd-el-Azîz*, princes of Boreyda. Abdullah was murdered by Mahanna, when he usurped the government with the countenance of the Waháby. Mahanna was sheykh over the town for many years, and his children are Hásan (now emir) and Abdullah.

The young sons of the Prince that was slain fled to the neighbour town of Aneyza —And after certain years, in a spring season, when the armed band was encamped with Hásan in the Nefûd, they stole over by night to Boreyda; and lay hid in some of their friends' houses. And on the morrow, when the tyrant passed by, going to his mid-day prayers in the great mesjid, Abdullah's sons ran suddenly upon him with the knife! and they slew him there, in the midst of the street. A horseman, one of the band that remained in the town, mounted and passed the gates, and rode headlong over the Nefûd; till he found the ghrazzu and Hásan.—Hásan hearing this heavy tiding gave the word to mount; and the band rode hastily homeward, to be in Boreyda that night.

Abdullah in the meanwhile who, though he have a leg short, is nimble of his butcherly wit, held fast in the town. In all this fear and trouble, his was yet the stronger part; and the townspeople, long daunted by the tyranny of Mahanna, were unready to favour the young homicides. And so well Abdullah wrought, that ere there was any sedition, he had enclosed the princelings in an house.

It was nightfall when Abdullah, with his armed men, came before their door; and to give light (to the horrid business), a bon-fire was kindled in the street. Abdullah's sons and a few who were their companions within, desperately defended their lives with matchlocks, upon the house head.—Some bolder spirits that came with Abdullah advanced to the gate, under a shield they had made them of a door (of rude palm boarding), with a thick layer of dates crammed upon it. And sheltered thus from weak musketry, they quickly opened a hole, poured-in powder and laid the train. A brand was fetched!—and in the hideous blast every life within the walls perished,—besides one young man, miserably wounded; who (with a sword in his hand) would have leapt down, as they entered, and escaped; and he could not: but still flying hither and thither he cursed-on and detested them, till he fell by a shot.—Hásan arriving in the night, found the slayers of his father already slain, and the town in quiet: and he was Emir of Boreyda.—Others of the princely family of this town I saw afterward dwelling in exile at Aneyza; and one of two old brethren, my patients, now poor and blind, was he who should have been by inheritance Emir of Boreyda!

I wandered in this waste Kasr, which, as a princely residence, might be compared with the Kasr at Hâyil; although less, as the principality of Boreyda is less. But if we compare the towns, Hâyil is a half Beduin town-village, with a foreign sûk; Boreyda is a great civil township of the midland Nejd life. The palace court, large as a market place, is returned to the Nefûd sand! Within the ruinous Kasr I found a coffee-hall having all the height of the one-storied building, with galleries above—in such resembling the halls of ancient England, and of goodly proportion: the walls of sandy clay were adorned with pargetting of jis. This silent and now (it seems) time-worn Kasr, here in the midst of Desert Arabia, had been built in our fathers' days! I admired the gypsum fretwork of their clay walls: such dedale work springs as a plant under the hands of the Semitic artificers, and is an imagery of their minds' vision of Nature!—which they behold not as the Pythagoreans contained in few pure lines, but all-adorned and unenclosed. And is their crust-work from India? We find a skill in raw clay-work in Syria; clay storing-jars, pans, hearths and corn-hutches are seen in all their cottages. In Lebanon the earthen walls and pillars, in some rich peasants' houses, are curiously crusted with clay fretwork, and stained in barbaric wise.

— Admirable seemed the architecture of that clay palace! [the sufficiency of the poorest means, in the Arabs' hands, to a perfect end]. The cornice ornament of these builders is that we call the shark's-tooth, as in the Mothîf at Hâyil. A rank of round-headed blind arches is turned for an appearance of lightness in the outer walling, and painted in green and red ochre. Perchance the builder of Kasr Hajellân was some Bagdad master, *muállem*—that which we may understand of some considerable buildings, standing far from any civil soil in certain desert borders. Years before I had seen a kella among the ruins of 'Utherah in mount Seir, where is a great welling pool, a watering of the Howeytát: it was a rusty building but not ruinous; and Mahmûd from Maan told me, 'The kella had been built in his time, *by the Beduw!*' I asked in great astonishment, "If Beduw had skill in masonry?"— *Mahmûd:* "Nay, but they fetched a muállem from Damascus; who set them to draw the best stones from the ruins, and as he showed them so the Beduins wrought and laid the courses." In that Beduin kella were not a few loopholes and arches, and the

whole frame had been built by his rude prentices without mortar!
In Beduins is an easy wit in any matter not too remote from
their minds; and there are tribes that in a summer's day have
become ploughmen.—Jeyber inhabited the crumbling walls of
the old Mothîf. The new peasant lords of Boreyda keep no public
hospitality; for which they are lightly esteemed by the dwellers
in the desert.

I went out with Jeyber to buy somewhat in the sûk, and see
the town. We passed through a market for cattle forage, mostly
vetches: and beyond were victuallers' shops,—in some of them
I saw hanging huge (mutton—perhaps Mesopotamian) sausages!
and in many were baskets of parched locusts. Here are even
cookshops—yet unknown in the Beduin-like Hâyıl—where one
may have a warm mess of rice and boiled mutton, or else camel
flesh for his penny. A stranger might live at Boreyda, in the
midst of Nomad Arabia, nearly as in Mesopotamia; saving that
here are no coffee taverns. Some of those who sat selling
green stuff in the stalls, were women!—Damascus is not so
civil! and there are only a few poor saleswomen at Aneyza Boreyda, a metropolis of Oasis Arabia, is joined to the northern
settled countries by the trading caravans; and the B. Temîm
townsmen are not unlike the half-blooded Arabs of those border
provinces.

Elvish boys and loiterers in the street gaped upon the Nasrâny stranger; and they gathered as we went. Near the mejlis
or market square there was sitting, on a clay bench, that Galla
swordsman of the Emir, whose visage I had noted yester-
evening, without the gate. The swarthy swordsman reproved
Jeyber, for bringing me out thus before the people; then rising,
with a stick, he laid load upon the dusty mantles of some of
them, in the name of the Emir. Jeyber, liberal minded as a
Beduwy but timid more than townsfolk, hearing this talk, led
me back hastily by bye-streets: I would have gone about to
visit another part of the town, but he brought me again by
solitary ways to his place. He promised, that he would ride with
me on the morrow to Aneyza; " Aneyza, he said, is not far off."
These towns were set down on maps with as much as a journey
between them : but what was there heretofore to trust in maps
of Arabia! Jeyber, whose stature and manners showed the
Beduin blood, was of those Kahtân Beduin strangers, who
were now wandering in el-Kasîm. Poor, among his tribesmen, but of a sheykhly house, he had left the desert life, to
be of the Emir's armed service in Boreyda. The old con-
trariety of fortune was written in his meagre visage; he was
little past the middle age, and his spirits half spent. The mild

Beduin nature sweetened in him his Kahtâny fanaticism; and
I was to-day a thaif-ullah in his household: he maintained
therefore my cause in the town, and was my advocate with the
swine Abdullah. But the fanatical humour was not quenched
in him; for some one saying, "This (man) could not go to
er-Riâth; for they would kill him!" Jeyber responded, half-
smiling, "Ay, they are very austere there; they might not suffer
him amongst them." He spoke also with rancour of the heterodox Mohammedanism of Nejrân [whose inhabitants are in religion *Bayâdiyyeh*, 'like the people of Mascat']. Jeybar had
passed his former life in those southern countries: Wady
Dauâsir, and Wady Bîsha, he said, are full of good villages.

The mid-day heat was come; and he went to slumber in
a further part of the waste building. I had reposed somewhile,
in my chamber, when a creaking of the old door, painted in
vermilion, startled me!—and a sluttish young woman entered.
I asked, wherefore had she broken my rest? Her answer was
like some old biblical talk; *Tekhálliny aném fî hothnak?*
'Suffer me to sleep in thy bosom.'—Who could have sent this
lurid quean? the Arabs are the basest of enemies,—hoped they
to find an occasion to accuse the Nasrâny? But the kind
damsel was not daunted; for when I chided she stood to rate
the stranger; saying, with the loathly voice of misery, 'Aha!
the cursed Nasrâny! and I was about to be slain, by faithful
men; that were in the way, sent from the Emir, to do it! and
I might not now escape them.'—I rose and put this baggage
forth, and fastened the door.—But I wondered at her words,
and mused that only for the name of a Religion, (O Chimæra
of human self-love, malice and fear!) I was fallen daily into
such mischiefs, in Arabia.—Now Jeyber came again from napping; and his hareem related to him the adventure: Jeyber left
us saying, he must go to the Emir.

Soon after this we heard people of the town flocking about
our house, and clamouring under the casements, which opened
backward upon a street, and throwing up stones! and some
noisy persons had broken into the great front yard!—The stair
was immediately full of them: and they bounced at our door
which the women had barred.—"Alas, said the hareem, wring-
ing their hands, what can we do now? for the riotous people
will kill thee; and Jeyber is away." One of them was a townswoman, the other was a Beduwîa: both were good towards the
guest. I sat down saying to them, "My sisters, you must
defend the house with your tongues."—They were ready; and
the townswoman looking out backward chided them that made

this hubbub in the street. "Ha! uncivil people; who be they that throw up stones into the apartment of the hareem? akhs! what would ye?—ye seek what? God send a sorrow upon you! —Oh! ye seek Khalîl the Nasrâny? but here is not Khalîl; ye fools, he is not here: away with you. Go! I say, for shame, and Ullah curse you."—And she that kept the door cried to them that were without, "Aha! what is your will?—akhs! who are these that beat like to break our door? O ye devil-sick and shameless young men! Khalîl is not here; he went forth, go and seek the Nasrâny, go! We have told you Khalîl went forth, we know not whither,—akhs! [they knocked now on the door with stones.] Oh you shameless fellows! would ye break through folks' doors, to the hareem? Ullah send a very pestilence upon you all; and for this the Emir will punish you." Whilst she was speaking there was a confused thrusting and shuffling of feet without our door, the strokes of their sticks and stones sounded hideously upon the wood.—The faithful women's tongues yet delayed them! and I put my hope in the stars, that Jeyber would return with speed But if the besiegers burst in to rend me in pieces, should I spare the foremost of them? The hareem cried on, "Why beat thus, ye cursed people?—akhs! will ye beat down our door indeed?"

At length came Jeyber again; and in the name of the Emir he drove them all forth, and locked them out of his yard.— When he entered, he shrunk up his shoulders and said to me, "They are clamouring to the Emir for thy death! 'No Nasrâny, they say, ever entered Boreyda': there is this outcry in the town, and Abdullah is for favouring the people!—I have now pleaded with him. If, please Ullah, we may pass this night in safety, to-morrow when my thelûl shall be come—and I have sent for her—I will convey thee by solitary lanes out of the place; and bring thee to Aneyza."—As we were speaking, we heard those townspeople swarming anew in his court! the foremost mounted again upon our stairs,—and the door was open. But Jeyber, threatening grievous punishments of the Emir, drove them down once more; and out of his yard. When he returned, he asked his house-wives, with looks of mistrust, who it was had undone the gate (from within)? which he had left barred! He said, he must go out again, to speak with Abdullah; but should not be long absent. I would not let him pass, till he had promised me to lock his gates, and carry the (wooden) key with him. There remained only this poor soul, and the timber of an old door, betwixt me, a lonely alien, and the fanatical wildness of this townspeople. When he came again he said the town was quiet: Abdullah, at his intercession, had forbidden to make more ado, the riotous were gone home; and he had left the gate open.

After this there came up some other of the principal citizens, to visit me: they sat about the hearth in Bagdad gowns and loose kerchiefs and red caps; whilst Jeyber made coffee. Amongst them appeared the great white (Medina) turban—yet spotless, though he slept in it—of that old vagabund issue of the néby! who a month before had been a consenting witness to my mischiefs at Hâyil! "Who art thou?" I asked.—"Oh! dost thou not remember the time, when we were together in Hâyil?"—"And returnest thou so soon from India?"—"I saw the Emir, and ended my business; also I go not to el-Hind, until after the Haj." There came in, on the heels of them, a young sheykh, who arrived then from Hásan's camp; which was at half a journey, in the Nefûd. He sat down among them, and began to question with me in lordly sort; and I enquired of the absent Emir. I found in him a natural malice; and an improbity of face which became the young man's injurious insolence. After these heavy words, he said further, "Art thou Nasrâny or Musslim?"—"Nasrâny, which all this town knows; now leave questioning me."—"Then the Moslemîn will kill thee, please Ullah! Hearest thou? the Moslemîn will kill thee!" and the squalid young man opened a leathern mouth, that grinning on me to his misplaced lap ears, discovered vast red circles of mule's teeth.—Surely the fanatical condition in religion [though logical!] is never far from a radically ill nature; and doubtless the javel was an offspring of generations of depraved Arab wretches. Jeyber, though I was to-day under his roof, smiled a withered half-smile of Kahtâny fanaticism, hearing words which are honey to their ears,—'a kafir to be slain by the Moslemîn!' Because the young man was a sheykh and Hásan's messenger, I sat in some thought of his venomous speaking. When they departed, I said to Jeyber my conceit of that base young fanatic; who answered, shrinking the shoulders, that I had guessed well, for he was a bad one!

— My hap was to travel in Arabia in time of a great strife of the religion [as they understood], with (God and His Apostle's enemies) the Nasâra. And now the idle fanatical people clamoured to the Emir, 'Since Ullah had delivered a Nasrâny into their hands, wherefore might they not put him to death?' At length the sun of this troubled day was at her going down. Then I went out to breathe the cooling air upon the terrace: and finding a broken ladder climbed to a higher part of our roof, to survey this great Arabian town.—But some townspeople in the street immediately, espying me, cried out, "Come down!

Come down! a kafir should not overlook a beled of the Moslemîn." Jeyber brought me a ration of boiled mutton and rice
(which he had purchased in the sûk): when I had eaten he said
we were brethren. He went out again to the Emir.

Jeyber returned all doubtful and pensive! 'The people, he
said, were clamouring again to Abdullah; who answered them,
that they might deal with me as they would: he had told them
already, that they might have slain the Nasrâny in the desert;
but it could not be done in the town.' Jeyber asked me now,
' Would I forsake my bags, and flee secretly from Boreyda on
foot?' I answered "No!—and tell me sooth, Jeyber! hast
thou no mind to betray me?" He promised as he was a faithful man that he would not. "Well, what is the present
danger?"—"I hope no more, for this night, at least in my
house."—"How may I pass the streets in the morning?"—
"We will pass them; the peril is not so much in the town as
of their pursuing."—"How many horsemen be there in Boreyda,
a score?"—"Ay, and more."—"Go quickly and tell Abdullah,
Khalîl says I am *rájol Dowla,* one who is safeguarded (my
papers declare it) by the government of the Sooltàn: if an evil
betide me (a guest) among you, it might draw some trouble
upon yourselves. For were it to be suffered that a traveller,
under the imperial protection, and only passing by your town,
should be done to death, for the name of a religion, which is
tolerated by the Sooltàn? Neither let them think themselves
secure here, in the midst of deserts, for ' *long is the arm of the
Dowla!*' Remember Jidda, and Damascus! and the guilty
punished, by commandment of the Sooltàn!" Jeyber answered,
' He would go and speak these words to Abdullah.'

Jeyber returned with better looks, saying that Abdullah
allowed my words: and had commanded that none should any
more molest the Nasrâny; and promised him, that no evil
should befall me this night. *Jeyber:* "We be now in peace,
blessed be the Lord! go in and rest, Khalîl; to be ready betimes."
I was ready ere the break of day; and thought it an hundred
years till I should be out of Boreyda. At sunrise Jeyber sat
down to prepare coffee; and yet made no haste! the promised
thelûl was not come.—"And when will thy thelûl be here?"—
"At some time before noon."—"How then may we come to
Aneyza to-night?"—"I have told thee, that Aneyza is not far
off." My host also asked for remedies for his old infirmities.
—"At Aneyza!"—"Nay, but now; for I would leave them

here." When he had received his medicines, Jeyber began to make it strange of his thelûl-riding to Aneyza. I thought an host would not forswear himself; but all their life is passed in fraud and deceit.—In this came up the Kahtâny who had been ring-leader in the former night's trouble; and sat down before his tribesman's hearth; where he was wont to drink the morrow's cup. Jeyber would have me believe that the fellow had been swinged yesterday before Abdullah : I saw no such signs in him. The wretch who had lately injured me, would now have maintained my cause! I said to Jeyber's Beduin jâra, who sat with us, " Tell me, is not he possessed by a jin?" The young man answered for himself, "Ay, Khalîl, I am somewhiles a little lunatic." He had come to ask the Nasrâny for medicines,—in which surely he had not trusted one of his own religion.

— A limping footfall sounded on the palace stairs : it was the lame Emir Abdullah who entered! leaning on his staff. Sordid was the (peasant) princeling's tunic and kerchief : he sat down at the hearth, and Jeyber prepared fresh coffee. Abdullah said,—showing me a poor man standing by the door and that came in with him; "This is he that will carry thee on his camel to Aneyza; rise! and bring out thy things."—"Jeyber promises to convey me upon his thelûl." But now my host (who had but fabled) excused himself, saying, ' he would follow us, when his thelûl were come.' Abdullah gave the cameleer his wages, the quarter of a mejîdy, eleven pence.—The man took my bags upon his shoulders, and brought me by a lonely street to a camel couched before his clay cottage. We mounted and rode by lanes out of the town. * * *

CHAPTER VIII

Now we came upon the open Nefûd, where I saw the sand ranging in long banks: *adanat* and *kethîb* is said in this country speech of the light shifting Nefûd sand; *Júrda* is the sand-bank's weather side, the lee side or fold is *lóghraf* [*láhaf*]. *Júrda* or *Jorda* (in the pl. *Jérad* and *Jeràd*) is said of a dune or hillock, in which appear clay-seams, sand and stones, and whereon desert bushes may be growing. The road to Aneyza is a deep-worn drift-way in the uneven Nefûd; but in the sand (lately blotted with wind and rain,) I perceived no footprint of man or cattle!—Bye and bye my cameleer Hásan turned our beast from the path, to go over the dunes: we were the less likely thus to meet with Beduins, not friends of Boreyda. The great tribes of these dîras, Meteyr and Ateyba, are the allies of *Zâmil*, Emir of Aneyza.— Zâmil was already a pleasant name in my ears: I had heard, even amongst his old foes of Harb, that Zâmil was a good gentleman, and that the "Child of Mahanna" (for whom, two years ago, they were in the field with Ibn Rashîd, against Aneyza) was a tyrannical churl: it was because of the Harb enmity that I had not ridden from their menzils, to Aneyza.

The Nefûd sand was here overgrown with a canker-weed which the Aarab reckon unwholesome; and therefore I struck away our camel that put down his long neck to browse; but Hásan said, "Nay; the town camels eat of this herb, for there is little else." We saw a nomad child keeping sheep: and I asked my rafîk, 'When should we come to Aneyza?'— "By the sunsetting." I found the land-height to be not more than 2500 feet. When we had ridden slowly three hours, we fell again into the road, by some great-grown tamarisks. '*Negîl*, quoth Hásan, we will alight here and rest out the hot mid-day hours.' I saw trenches dug under those trees by

466

locust hunters. I asked, " Is it far now ? "—" Aneyza is not far off."—" Tell me truth rafîk, art thou carrying me to Aneyza ? "—" Thou believest not ;—see here ! " (he drew me out a bundle of letters—and yet they seemed worn and old). " All these, he said, are merchants' letters which I am to deliver to-day in Aneyza ; and to fetch the goods from thence."—And had I not seen him accept a letter for Aneyza ! Hásan found somewhat in my words, for he did not halt ; we might be come ten miles from Boreyda. The soil shelved before us ; and under the next tamarisks I saw a little oozing water. We were presently in a wady bottom, not a stone-cast over ; and in crossing we plashed through trickling water ! I asked," What bed is this ? "—*Answer:* " EL-WADY "—that is, we were in (the midst of) the Wady er-Rummah. We came up by oozing (brackish) water to a palm wood unenclosed, where are grave-like pits of a fathom digged beside young palm-sets to the ground water. The plants are watered by hand a year or two, till they have put down roots to the saltish ground moisture.

It is nearly a mile to pass through this palm wood, where only few (older) stems are seen grown aloft above the rest ; because such outlying possessions are first to the destruction, in every warfare. I saw through the trees, an high-built court-wall, wherein the husbandmen may shelter themselves in any alarms ; and Hásan showed me, in an open ground, where Ibn Rashîd's tents stood two years ago, when he came with Weled Mahanna against Aneyza. We met only two negro labourers ; and beyond the palms the road is again in the Nefûd. Little further at our right hand, were some first enclosed properties ; and we drew bridle at a stone trough, a sebîl, set by the landowner in his clay wall, with a channel from his suânies : the trough was dry, for none now passed by that way to or from Boreyda. We heard creaking of well-wheels, and voices of harvesters in a field. " Here, said Hásan, as he put down my bags, is the place of repose : rest in the shadow of this wall, whilst I go to water the camel. And where is the girby ? that I may bring thee to drink ; you might be thirsty before evening, when it will be time to enter the town,— thus says Abdullah ; and now open thy eyes, for fear of the Beduw." I let the man go, but made him leave his spear with me.

When he came again with the waterskin, Hásan said he had loosed out the camel to pasture ; " and wellah Khalîl I must go after her, for see ! the beast has strayed. Reach me my romh, and I will run to turn her, or she will be gone far out in the Nefûd."—" Go, but the spear remains with me." " Ullah !

doubt not thy rafîk, should I go unarmed? give me my lance,
and I will be back to thee in a moment." I thought, that if
the man were faithless and I compelled him to carry me into
Aneyza, he might have cried out to the fanatical townspeople:
'This is the Nasrâny!'—"Our camel will be gone, do not delay
me."—"Wilt thou then forsake me here?"—"No wellah, by
this beard!" I cast his lance upon the sand, which taking up,
he said, "Whilst I am out, if thou have need of anything, go
about the corner of the wall yonder; so thou wilt see a palm
ground, and men working. Rest now in the shadow, and make
thyself a little mereesy, for thou art fasting; and cover these
bags! let no man see them. Aneyza is but a little beyond that
ádan there; thou mayest see the town from thence: I will run
now, and return." I let him pass, and Hásan, hieing after his
camel, was hidden by the sand billows. I thought soon, I would
see what were become of him, and casting away my mantle I
ran barefoot in the Nefûd; and from a sand dune I espied
Hásan riding forth upon his camel—for he had forsaken me!
he fetched a circuit to go about the Wady palms homeward. I
knew then that I was betrayed by the secret commission of
Abdullah, and remembered his word, "Who will carry the
Nasrâny *to the Wady?*"

This was the cruellest fortune which had befallen me in
Arabia! to be abandoned here without a chief town, in the
midst of fanatical Nejd. I had but eight reals left, which
might hardly more than carry me in one course to the nearest
coast. I returned and armed myself; and rent my maps in
small pieces,—lest for such I should be called in question,
amongst lettered citizens.

A negro man and wife came then from the palms, carrying
firewood towards Aneyza: they had seen us pass, and asked me
simply, "Where is thy companion and the camel?"—After this
I went on under the clay walling towards the sound of suânies;
and saw a palm ground and an orchard house. The door was
shut fast: I found another beyond; and through the chinks I
looked in, and espied the owner driving,—a plain-natured face.
I pushed up his gate and entered at a venture with, "Peace be
with thee;" and called for a drink of water. The goodman
stayed a little to see the stranger! then he bade his young
daughter fetch the bowl, and held up his camels to speak with
me. "Drink if thou wilt, said he, but we have no good water."
The taste was bitter and unwholesome; but even this cup of
water would be a bond between us.

I asked him to lend me a camel or an ass, to carry my things
to the town, and I would pay the hire. I told further how I

came hither,—with a cameleer from Boreyda; who whilst I rested in the heat, had forsaken me nigh his gate: that I was an hakîm, and if there were any sick in this place I had medicines to relieve them.—" Well, bide till my lad return with a camel: —I go (he said to his daughter) with this man; here! have my stick and drive, and let not the camels stand.—What be they, O stranger, and where leftest thou thy things? come! thou shouldst not have left them out of sight and unguarded; how, if we should not find them— ? "—They were safe; and taking the great bags on my shoulders, I tottered back over the Nefûd to the good man's gate; rejoicing inwardly, that I might now bear all I possessed in the world. He bade me sit down there (without), whilst he went to fetch an ass.—"Wilt thou pay a piastre and a half (threepence)? " There came now three or four grave elder men from the plantations, and they were going in at the next gate to drink their afternoon kahwa. The goodman stayed them and said, "This is a stranger,—he cannot remain here, and we cannot receive him in our house; he asks for carriage to the town." They answered, he should do well to fetch the ass and send me to Aneyza. "And what art thou? (they said to me)—we go in now to coffee; has anyone heard the íthin? " *Another:* "They have cried to prayers in the town, but we cannot always hear it;—for is not the sun gone down to the âssr? then pray we here together." They took their stand devoutly, and my host joined himself to the row; they called me also, "Come and pray, come! "—"I have prayed already." They marvelled at my words; and so fell to their formal reciting and prostrations. When they rose, my host came to me with troubled looks:—"Thou dost not pray, hmm! " said he: and I saw by those grave men's countenance, they were persuaded that I could be no right Moslem. "Well send him forward," quoth the chief of them, and they entered the gate.

My bags were laid now upon an ass. We departed: and little beyond the first *ádan*, as Hásan had foretold me, was the beginning of cornfields; and palms and fruit trees appeared, and some houses of outlying orchards.—My companion said [he was afraid!] " It is far to the town, and I cannot go there to-night; but I will leave thee with one yonder who is *ibn juâd*, a son of bounty; and in the morning he will send thee to Aneyza."— We came on by a wide road and unwalled, till he drew up his ass at a rude gateway; there was an orchard kouse, and he knocked loud and called, " *Ibrahîm!* " An old father came to the gate, who opened it to the half and stayed—seeing my clothes rent (by the thieves at Boreyda)! and not knowing what strange person I might be :—but he guessed I was some runaway soldier from the Harameyn or el-Yémen, as there had certain passed by Aneyza of late. He of the ass spoke for me; and then that housefather received me. They brought in my bags, to his clay house ; and he locked them in a store closet: so without speaking he beckoned with the hand, and led me out in his orchard, to the "diwân" (their clean sanded sitting-place in the field); and there left me.

Pleasant was the sight of their tilled ground with corn stubbles and green plots of vetches, *jet,* the well-camels' provender ; and borders of a dye-plant, whose yellow blossoms are used by the townswomen to stain the partings of their hair. When this sun was nigh setting, I remembered their unlucky prayer-hour ! and passed hastily to the further side of their palms ; but I was not hidden by the clear-set rows of trees : when I came again in the twilight, they demanded of me, ' Why I prayed not ? and wherefore had I not been with them at the prayers ? ' Then they said over the names of the four orthodox sects of Islam, and questioned with me, " To which of them pertainest thou ; or be'st thou (of some heterodox belief) a *râfuthy ?* "—a word which they pronounced with enmity. I made no answer, and they remained in some astonishment. They brought me, to sup, boiled wheat in a bowl and another of their well water ; there was no greater hospitality in that plain household. I feared the dampish (oasis) air and asked, where was the coffee chamber. *Answer :* " Here is no kahwa, and we drink none." They sat in silence, and looked heavily upon the stranger, who had not prayed.

He who brought me the bowl (not one of them) was a manly young man, of no common behaviour ; and he showed in his words an excellent understanding. I bade him sup with me.— " I have supped."—" Yet eat a morsel, for the bread and salt between us : " he did so. After that, when the rest were away, I told him what I was, and asked him of the town. " Well, he said, thou art here to-night ; and little remains to Aneyza, where they will bring thee in the morning ; I think there is no danger —Zâmil is a good man : besides thou art only passing by them. Say to the Emir to-morrow, in the people's hearing, ' I am a soldier from *Béled el-Asîr* ' (a good province in el-Yémen, which the Turks had lately occupied)."—Whilst we were speaking, the last íthin sounded from the town ! I rose hastily ; but the three or four young men, sons of Ibrahîm, were come again, and began to range themselves to pray ! they called us, and they called to me the stranger with insistence, to take our places with them. I answered : " I am over-weary, I will go and sleep."—*The bread-and-salt Friend:* "Ay-ay, the stranger says well, he is come from a journey ; show him the place without more, where he may lie down."—" I would sleep in the house, and not here abroad."—" But first let him pray ; ho ! thou, come and pray, come ! "—*The Friend:* " Let him alone, and show the weary man to his rest."—" There is but the wood-house."—" Well then to the wood-house, and let him sleep immediately." One of them went with me, and brought me to a threshold : the floor was sunk a foot or two, and I fell in a dark place full of sweet tamarisk boughs. After their praying came all the brethren : they sat before the door in the feeble moonlight, and murmured, ' I had not prayed !—and could this be a Musslim ? ' But I played the sleeper ; and after watching half an hour they left me. How new to us is this religiosity, in rude young men of the people ! but the Semitic religion—so cold, and a strange plant, in the (idolatrous) soil of Europe, is like to a blood passion, in the people of Moses and Mohammed.

An hour before day I heard one of these brethren creeping in —it was to espy if the stranger would say the dawning prayers ! When the morrow was light all the brethren stood before the door ; and they cried to me, *Ma sulleyt,* ' Thou didst not say the prayer ! '—" Friends, I prayed."—" Where washed you then ? " —This I had not considered, for I was not of the dissembler's craft. Another brother came to call me ; and he led me up the house stairs to a small, clean room : where he spread matting on the clay floor, and set before me a dish of very good dates, with a bowl of whey ; and bade me breakfast, with their homely word, *fúk er-ríg* ' Loose the fasting spittle' : (the Bed. say *ríj,* for *rík*). " Drink ! " said he, and lifted to my hands his hospi-table bowl.—After that he brought the ass and loaded my bags. to carry them into the town. We went on in the same walled road, and passed a ruinous open gate of Aneyza. Much of the town wall was there in sight ; which is but a thin shell, with many wide breaches. Such clay walling might be repaired in a few days, and Aneyza can never be taken by famine ; for the wide town walls enclose their palm grounds : the people, at this time, were looking for war with Boreyda.

We went by the first houses, which are of poor folk ; and the young man said he would leave me at one of the next doors, ' where lived a servant of (the Emir) *Zâmil.*' He knocked with the ring, which [as at Damascus] there is set upon all their doors, like a knocker ; and a young negro housewife opened : her goodman (of the butcher's craft,) was at this hour in the sûk. He was bedel or public sergeant, for Zâmil : and to such rude offices, negroes (men of a blunter metal) are commonly chosen.

My baggage was set down in the little camel yard, of their poor but clean clay cottage. *Aly*, the negro householder, came home soon after ; and finding a stranger standing in his court, he approached and kissed the guest, and led me into his small kahwa ; where presently, to the pleasant note of the coffee pestle, a few persons assembled—mostly black men his neighbours. And Aly made coffee, as coffee is made even in poor houses at Aneyza. After the cup, the poor man brought-in on a tray a good breakfast : large was the hospitality of his humble fortune, and he sat down to eat with me.—Homeborn negroes, out of their warmer hearts, do often make good earnest of the shallow Arabian customs ! Before the cottage row I saw a waste place, *el-Gá ;* and some booth or two therein of the miserable Beduins : the plot, left open by the charity of the owner, was provided with a public pool of water running from his suânies. When later I knew them, and his son asked the Nasrâny's counsel, ' What were best to do with the ground ?—because of the draffe cast there, it was noisome to the common health '— I answered, " Make it a public garden : " but that was far from their Arabian understanding.

I went abroad bye and bye with Aly, to seek Zâmil ; though it were *tow,* too early, said my negro host : here is the beginning of the town streets, with a few poor open stalls ; the ways are cleanly. Two furlongs beyond is the sûk, where (at these hours) is a busy concourse of the townspeople : they are all men, since maidens and wives come not openly abroad.—At a cross street, there met us two young gallants. "Ha ! said one of them to Aly, this stranger with thee is a Nasrâny ; "—and turning to me, the coxcombs bid me, " Good morrow, khawâja :" I answered them, " I am no khawâja, but an Engleysy ; and how am I of your acquaintance ? "—" Last night we had word of thy coming from Boreyda : Aly, whither goest thou with him ? " That poor man, who began to be amazed, hearing his guest named Nasrâny, answered, " To Zâmil."—" Zâmil is not yet sitting ; then bring the Nasrâny to drink coffee at my beyt. We are, said they, from Jidda and wont to see (there) all the kinds of Nasâra." They led us upstairs in a great house, by the market-square, which they call in Kasîm *el-Mejlis :* their chamber was spread with Persian carpets.

These young men were of the Aneyza merchants at Jidda. One of them showed me a Winchester (seventeen shooting) rifle ! ' and there were fifty more (they pretended) in Aneyza : with such guns in their hands they were not in dread of warfare [which they thought likely to be renewed,] with Ibn

Rashîd : in the time of the Jehâd they had exercised themselves
as soldiers at Jidda.' They added maliciously, "And if we
have war with Boreyda, wilt thou be our captain ? "

We soon left them. Aly led me over the open market-
square : and by happy adventure the Emir was now sitting in
his place ; that is made under a small porch upon the Mejlis, at
the street corner which leads to his own (clay) house, and in face
of the clothiers' sûk. In the Emir's porch are two clay banks ;
upon one, bespread with a Persian carpet, sat Zâmil, and his
sword lay by him. Zâmil is a small-grown man with a pleasant
weerish visage, and great understanding eyes : as I approached
he looked up mildly. When I stood before him, Zâmil rose a
little in his seat, and took me by the hand, and said kindly,
"Be seated, be seated ! " so he made me sit beside him. I said,
" I come now from Boreyda, and am a hakîm, an Engleysy,
a Nasrâny ; I have these papers with me ; and it may please
thee to send me to the coast." Zâmil perused that which I put
in his hand :—as he read, an uneasy cloud was on his face, for
a moment ! But looking up pleasantly, " It is well, he responded ; in the meantime go not about publishing thyself to
the people, ' I am a Nasrâny ; ' say to them, *ana askary*, I am a
(runaway Ottoman) soldier. Aly, return home with Khalil, and
bring him after midday prayers to kahwa in my house : but
walk not in the public places."

We passed homewards through the clothiers' street, and by
the butchers' market. The busy citizens hardly regarded us ;
yet some man took me by the sleeve ; and turning, I saw one of
those half-feminine slender figures of the Arabians, with painted
eyes, and clad in the Bagdad wise. " O thou, *min eyn*, from
whence ? quoth he, and art thou a Nasrâny ? " I answered,
" Ay : " yet if any asked, " Who is he with thee, Aly ? " the
negro responded stoutly, " A stranger, one that is going to
Kuweyt."—Aneyza seemed a pleasant town, and stored with all
things needful to their civil life : we went on by a well-built
mesjid ; but the great mesjid is upon the public place,—all
building is of clay in the Arabian city.

In these days, the people's talk was of the debate and breach
between the town and Boreyda : although lately Weled Mahanna wrote to Zâmil *ana weled-ak*, ' I am thy child (to serve
and obey thee) ' ; and Zâmil had written, " I am thy friend."
" Wellah, said Aly's gossips at the coffee hearth, there is no
more passage to Boreyda : but in few days the allies of Zâmil
will be come up from the east country, and from the south,
as far as Wady Dauâsir." Then, they told me, I should see the

Q*

passing continually through this street of a multitude of armed men.

After the noon íthin, we went down to Zamil's (homely) house, which is in a blind way out of the mejlis. His coffee room was spread with grass matting (only); and a few persons were sitting with him. Zâmil's elder son, *Abdullah*, sat behind the hearth, to make coffee. Tidings were brought in, that some of the townspeople's asses had been reaved in the Nefûd, by Ateybân (friendly Nomads)!—Zâmil sent for one of his armed riders: and asked him, 'Was his dromedary in the town?'—"All ready."—"Then take some with you, and ride on their traces, that you may overtake them to-day!"—"But if I lose the thelûl—?" (he might fall amongst enemies). Zâmil answered, "The half loss shall be mine;" and the man went out. Zâmil spoke demissly, he seemed not made to command; but this is the mildness of the natural Arab sheykhs.

—*Aly*, uncle of the Emir, entered hastily! Zâmil some years ago appointed him executive Emir in the town; and when Zâmil takes the field, he leaves Aly his lieutenant in Aneyza. Aly is a dealer in camels; he has only few fanatical friends. All made him room, and the great man sat down in the highest place. Zâmil, the Emir and host, sat leaning on a pillow in face of the company; and his son Abdullah sat drinking a pipe of tobacco, by the hearth!—but this would not be tolerated in the street. The coffee was ready, and he who took up the pot and the cups went to pour out first for Zâmil; but the Emir beckoned mildly to serve the Emir Aly. When the coffee had been poured round, Zâmil said to his uncle, "This stranger is an hakîm, a traveller from *es-Sham*: and we will send him, as he desires, to Kuweyt."—Aly full of the Wahâby fanaticism vouchsafed not so much as to cast an eye upon me. "Ugh! quoth he, I heard say the man is a Nasrâny: wouldst thou have a Nasrâny in thy town?" *Zâmil*: "He is a passenger; he may stay a few days, and there can be no hurt!" "Ugh!" answered Aly; and when he had swallowed his two cups he rose up crabbedly, and went forth. Even Zâmil's son was of this Wahâby humour; twenty years might be his age: bold faced was the young man, of little sheykhly promise, and disposed, said the common speech, to be a niggard. Now making his voice big and hostile, he asked me—for his wit stretched no further, "What is thy name?" When all were gone out, Zâmil showed me his fore-arms corroded and inflamed by an itching malady which he had suffered these twenty years!—I have seen the like in a few more persons at Aneyza. He said, like an Arab, "And if thou canst cure this, we will give thee *fulûs!*"

Already some sick persons were come there, to seek the hakîm, when I returned to Aly's ; and one of them offered me an empty *dokân*, or little open shop in a side street by the sûks. —Aly found an ass to carry my bags : and ere the mid-afternoon, I was sitting in my doctor's shop : and mused, should I here find rest in Arabia ? when the muéthin cried to the assr prayers ; there was a trooping of feet, and neighbours went by to a mesjid in the end of the street.—Ay, at this day they go to prayers as hotly, as if they had been companions of the Néby ! I shut my shop with the rest, and sat close ; I thought this shutter would shield me daily from their religious importunity. —" *Ullahu akhbar, Ullahu akhbar !* " chanted the muéthins of the town.

After vespers the town is at leisure ; and principal persons go home to drink the afternoon coffee with their friends. Some of the citizens returning by this street stayed to see the Nasrâny, and enquire what were his medicines ; for nearly all the Arabs are diseased, or imagine themselves to be sick or else bewitched. How quiet was the behaviour of these townsfolk, many of them idle persons and children ! but Zâmil's word was that none should molest Haj Khalîl,—so the good gentleman (who heard I had been many times in the " Holy " City) called me, because it made for my credit and safety among the people. The civil countenance of these midland Arabian citizens is unlike the (Beduish) aspect of the townsmen of Hâyil, that tremble in the sight of Ibn Rashîd : here is a free township under the natural Prince, who converses as a private man, and rules, like a great sheykh of Aarab, amongst his brethren.

Zâmil's descent is from the *Sbeya*, first Beduin colonists of this loam-bottom in the Nefûd. At this day they are not many families in Aneyza ; but theirs is the Emirship, and therefore they say *henna el-úmera*, ' we are the Emirs.' More in number are the families of the *Beny Khâlid*, tribesmen of that ancient Beduin nation, whose name, before the Waháby, was greatest in Nejd ; but above an half of the town are B. Temîm. There are in Aneyza (as in every Arabian place) several wards or parishes under hereditary sheykhs ; but no malcontent factions,—they are all cheerfully subject to Zâmil. The people living in unity, are in no dread of foreign enemies.

Some principal persons went by again, returning from their friends' houses.—One of them approached me, and said, " Hast thou a knowledge of medicine ? " The tremulous figure of the speaker, with some drawing of his face, put me in mind of the Algerine Mohammed Aly, at Medáin Sâlih ! But he that stood here was a gentle son of Temîm, whose good star went before me from this day to the end of my voyage in Arabia! Taking my hand in his hand, which is a kind manner of the Arabs, he said, "Wilt thou visit my sick mother?"

He led me to his house gate not far distant; and entering himself by a side door he came round to open for me: I found within a large coffee-hall, spread with well-wrought grass matting, which is fetched hither from *el-Hása*. The walls were pargetted with fretwork of jis, such as I had seen at Boreyda. A Persian tapet spread before his fire-pit was the guests' sitting place; and he sat down himself behind the hearth to make me coffee. This was *Abdullah el-Kenneyny*, the fortunate son of a good but poor house. He had gone forth a young man from Aneyza; and after the first hazards of fortune, was grown to be one of the most considerable foreign merchants. His traffic was in corn, at Bosra, and he lived willingly abroad; for his heart was not filled in Aneyza, where he despised the Waháby straitness and fanaticism. In these days leaving his merchandise at Bosra to the care of a brother (Sâlih, who they told me little resembles him), Abdullah was come to pass a leisure year at home; where he hoped to refresh his infirm health in the air of the Nefûd.

When I looked in this man's face he smiled kindly.—"And art thou, said he, an Engleysy? but wherefore tell the people so, in this wild fanatical country? I have spent many years in foreign lands, I have dwelt at Bombay, which is under government of the Engleys: thou canst say thus to me, but say it not to the ignorant and foolish people;—what simplicity is this! and incredible to me, in a man of *Europa*. For are we here in a government country? no, but in land of the Aarab, where the name of the Nasâra is an execration. A Nasrâny they think to be a son of the Evil One, and (therefore) deserving of death: an half of this townspeople are Wahábies."—"Should I not speak truth, as well here as in mine own country?"
Abdullah: "We have a tongue to further us and our friends, and to illude our enemies; and indeed the more times the lie is better than the sooth.—Or dreadest thou, that Ullah would visit it upon thee, if thou assentedst to them in appearance? Is there not in everything the good and evil?" [even in lieing and dissembling.]—"I am this second year, in a perilous country, and have no scathe. Thou hast heard the proverb, 'Truth may walk through the world unarmed'."—"But the Engleys are not thus! nay, I have seen them full of policy: in the late warfare between Abdullah and Saûd ibn Saûd, their Resident on the Gulf sent hundreds of sacks of rice,

secretly, to Saûd [the wrongful part; and for such Abdullah
the Waháby abhors the English name].— I see you will not
be persuaded! yet I hope that your life may be preserved:
but they will not suffer you to dwell amongst them! you will
be driven from place to place."—"This seemed to me a good
peaceable town, and are the people so illiberal?"—" As many
among them, as have travelled, are liberal; but the rest no.
Now shall we go to my mother?"

Abdullah led me into an inner room, from whence we ascended to the floor above. He had bought this great new
(clay) house the year before, for a thousand reals, or nearly £200
sterling. The loam brickwork at Aneyza is good, and such
house-walls may stand above one hundred years. His rent, for
the same, had been (before) but fifteen reals; house property
being reckoned in the Arabian countries as money laid up,
and not put out to usury,—a sure and lawful possession.
The yearly fruit of 1000 dollars, lent out at Aneyza, were
120; the loss therefore to the merchant Abdullah, in buying
this house, was each year 100 reals. But dwelling under their
own roof, they think they enjoy some happy security of fortune:
although the walls decay soon, it will not be in their children's
time. In Abdullah's upper storey were many good chambers,
but bare to our eyes, since they have few more moveables than
the Beduw: all the husbandry of his great town-house might
have been carried on the backs of three camels! In the Arabic
countries the use of bed-furniture is unknown; they lie on the
floor, and the wellborn and welfaring have no more than some
thin cotton quilt spread under them, and a coverlet: I saw only
a few chests, in which they bestow their clothing. Their houses,
in this land of sunny warmth, are lighted by open loopholes made
high upon the lofty walls. But Abdullah was not so simply
housed at Bosra; for there—in the great world's side, the Arab
merchants' halls are garnished with chairs: and the Aneyza
tájir sat (like the rest) upon a *takht* or carpeted settle in his
counting-house.

He brought me to a room where I saw his old mother, sitting
on the floor; and clad—so are all the Arabian women, only in
a calico smock dipped in indigo. She covered her old visage,
as we entered, with a veil! Abdullah smiled to me, and looked
to see "a man of Europa" smile. "My mother, said he, I
bring thee el-hakîm; say what aileth thee, and let him see
thine eyes:" and with a gentle hand he folded down her veil.
"Oh! said she, my head; and all this side so aches that I
cannot sleep, my son." Abdullah might be a man of forty; yet
his mother was abashed, that a strange man must look upon her

old blear eyes.—We returned to the coffee room perfect friends. "My mother, said he, is aged and suffering, and I suffer to see her: if thou canst help us, that will be a great comfort to me."

Abdullah added, "I am even now in amazement! that, in such a country, you openly avow yourself to be an Englishman; but how may you pass even one day in safety! You have lived hitherto with the Beduw; ay, but it is otherwise in the townships."—"In such hazards there is nothing, I suppose, more prudent than a wise folly."—"Then, you will not follow better counsel! but here you may trust in me: I will watch for you, and warn you of any alteration in the town." I asked, "And what of the Emir?"—"You may also trust Zâmil; but even Zâmil cannot at all times refrain the unruly multitude."

— In the clay-built chamber of the Arabs, with casements never closed, is a sweet dry air, as of the open field; and the perfume of a serene and hospitable human life, not knowing any churlish superfluity: yet here is not whole human life, for bye and bye we are aware of the absence of women. And their bleak walling is an uncheerfulness in our sight: pictures— those gracious images that adorn our poorest dwellings, were but of the things which are vain in the gross vision of their Mohammedan austerity. The Arabs, who sit on the floor, see the world more indolently than we: they must rise with a double lifting of the body.—In a wall-niche by the fire were Abdullah's books. We were now as brethren, and I took them down one by one: a great tome lay uppermost. I read the Arabic title *Encyclopedia Bustâny, Beyrût,*—Bustâny (born of poor Christian folk in a Lebanon village), a printer, gazetteer, schoolmaster, and man of letters, at Beyrût: every year he sends forth one great volume more, but so long an enterprise may hardly be ended. Abdullah's spectacles fell out at a place which treated of artesian wells: he pored therein daily, and looked to find some mean of raising water upon his thirsty acres, without camel labour.

Abdullah enriched abroad, had lately bought a palm and corn ground at home; and not content with the old he had made in it a new well of eight camels' draught. I turned another leaf and found "Burning Mountain," and a picture of Etna. He was pleased to hear from me of the old Arab usurpers of Sicilian soil, and that this mountain is even now named after their words, *Gibello* (Jebel). I turned to "Telegraph", and Abdullah exclaimed, "Oh! the inventions in Europa! what a marvellous learned subtlety must have been in him who found it!" When he asked further of my profession of medicine; I said, "I am such as your *Solubba* smiths—

better than none, where you may not find a better."—Yet
Abdullah always believed my skill to be greater than so,
because nearly all my reasonable patients were relieved; but
especially his own mother.

Whilst we were discussing, there came in two of the foreign-
living Aneyza townsmen, a substantial citizen and his servant,
clad in the Mesopotamian guise, with head-bands, great as
turbans, of camel wool. The man had been *jemmâl*, a camel
carrier in the Irâk traffic to Syria,—that is in the long trade-
way about by Aleppo; but after the loss of the caravan, before
mentioned, having no more heart for these ventures, he sold his
camels for fields and ploughshares. To-day he was a substantial
farmer in the great new corn settlement, *el-Amâra* (upon the
river a little north of Bosra), and a client of Kenneyny's—one
of the principal grain merchants in the river city. The merchant's dinner tray was presently borne in, and I rose to depart;
but Abdullah made me sit down again to eat with them, though
I had been bidden in another place.—I passed this one good
day in Arabia; and all the rest were evil because of the people's
fanaticism. At night I slept on the cottage terrace of a poor
patient, Aly's neighbour; not liking the unswept dokân for
a lodging, and so far from friends.

At sunrise came Aly, from Zâmil, to bid me to breakfast—
the bread and salt offered to the (Christian and Frankish)
stranger by the gentle philosophic Emir. We drank the morning cup, at the hearth; then his breakfast tray was served, and
we sat down to it in the midst of the floor, the Emir, the
Nasrâny and Aly: for there is no such ignoble observing of
degrees in their homely and religious life.—The breakfast fare
in Aneyza is warm girdle-bread [somewhat bitter to our taste,
yet they do not perceive the bitterness, 'which might be
because a little salt is ground with the corn,' said Abdullah]:
therewith we had dates, and a bowl of sweet (cow) butter. A
bowl of (cow) buttermilk is set by; that the breakfasters may
drink of it after eating, when they rise to rinse the hands; and
for this there is a metal ewer and basin. The water is poured
over the fingers; and without more the breakfasters take leave:
the day begins.

I went to sit in my dokân, where Zâmil sent me bye and
bye, by Aly, a leg of mutton out of the butchers' sûk, "that I
might dine well." Mutton is good at Aneyza: and camel's
flesh is sold to poor folk. A leg of their lean desert mutton,
which might weigh five or six pounds, is sold for sixpence:
this meat, with scotches made in it and hung one day to the
ardent sun, will last good three days. Beduins bring live

gazelle fawns into the town; which are often bought by citizens to be fostered, for their children's pastime : these dearlings of the desert were valued at eightpence.

I had not long been sitting in my dokân before one came to put me out of it! he cried churlishly with averted face—so that I did not know him—to the negro Aly, who stood by, "Out! with these things!" The negro shouted again, "The Nasrâny is here with Zâmil's knowledge : wilt thou strive with Zâmil!" The other (who was Aly the second or executive emir) muttered between his teeth, "Zâmil quoth he, ugh!—the dokân is mine, and I say out! ugh! out of my dokân, out, out!" But the negro cried as loud as he, "Zâmil he is Emir of this town, and what art thou?"—"I am Emir." The emir Aly respected my person—to me he spoke no word, and I was ready to content him; the shop he said was his own. But my friends had not done well to settle me there : the violence of the Waháby Aly, in contempt of the liberal Emir Zâmil, would hearten the town fanatics against the Nasrâny.—This was the comedy of the two Alyes. The white Aly spurned-to the door, and drew the bolt; and the same day he had driven me out of the town, but Zâmil would not hear of it. I remained with my bags in the street, and idle persons came to look on; but the negro Aly vehemently threatened, that 'Zâmil would pluck out the eyes and the tongue of any that molested me!'

The hot morning hours advanced to high noon; and when the muéthins chanted I was still sitting in the street by my things, in the sight of the malevolent people, who again flocked by me to the mesjid.—"Ullah! this is one who prays not," quoth every passing man. After them came a lad of the town, whose looks showed him to be of impure sinister conditions! and bearing a long rod in his hand: therewith of his godly zeal—that is an inhuman envy and cruelty! he had taken upon him to beat in late-lingerers to the prayers. Now he laid hands on the few lads, that loitered to gape upon the Nasrâny, and cried, "Go pray, go pray! may Ullah confound you!" and he drove them before him. Then he threatened Aly, who remained with me; and the poor man, hearing God named, could not choose but obey him. The shallow dastard stood finally grinning upon me,—his rod was lifted! and doubtless he tickled in every vein with the thought of smiting a kafir, for God's sake : but he presently vailed it again,—for are not the Nasâra reputed to be great strikers? In this time of their prayers, some Beduins [they were perhaps Kahtân] issued from a house near by, to load upon their kneeling camels. I went to talk with them and hear their *loghra*: but Beduins in a town are townsmen, and in a journey are hostile; and with maledictions they bade me stand off, saying, " What have we to do with a kafir ? "

Aly would have me speak in the matter of the dokân to Zâmil. I found Zâmil in the afternoon at his house door : and he said, with mild voice, " We will not enter, because the kahwa is full of Beduw " [Meteyr sheykhs, come in to consult with the town, of their riding together against the Kahtân]. We walked in his lane, and sat down under a shadowing wall, in the dust of the street. " Have you lost the dokân ? said Zâmil, well, tell Aly to find you another."

—Yesterday some Aneyza tradesmen to the nomads had been robbed on the Boreyda road, and three camel loads of samn were taken from them—nearly half a ton, worth 200 reals : the thieves were Kahtân. The intruded Kahtân in el-Kasîm were of the Boreyda alliance ; and Zâmil sent a letter thither, complaining of this injury, to Abdullah. Abdullah wrote word again, " It was the wild Beduw : lay not their misdeed to our charge." Zâmil now sent out thirty young men of good houses, possessing thelûls in the town, to scour the Nefûd—[they returned six days later to Aneyza, having seen nothing]. Zâmil spoke not much himself in the town councils : but his mind was full of solicitude ; and it was said of him in these days, that he could not eat.

Aly found me so wretched a tenement, that my friends exclaimed, " It is an house of the rats ! it is not habitable." The negro answered them, He had sought up and down, but that everyone repulsed him saying, " Shall a Nasrâny harbour in my beyt ? " The ruinous house was of a miserable old man, a patient of mine, who demanded an excessive daily hire, although he had received my medicines freely. Aly on the morrow persuaded a young negro neighbour, who had a small upper chamber, empty, to house the hakîm ; promising him that the Nasrâny should cure his purblind father.—I went to lodge there : the old father was a freed-man of *Yahya's* house (afterward my friends). The negro host was a pargetter ; it was his art to adorn the citizens' coffee-halls with chequered daubing and white fretwork, of gypsum. We may see, even in the rudest villages of Arabia, the fantasy they have for whitening ; their clay casements are commonly blanched about with jis : the white is to their sense light and cheerfulness, as black is balefulness. [" A white day to thee ! " is said for " good-morrow " in the border countries : Syrian Moslems use to whiten their clay sepulchres.—Paul cries out, in this sense, " Thou whited walling ! "]

"Now! quoth the young negro, when I entered his dwelling, let them bibble-babble that will, sixty thousand bibble-babblings,"—because for the love of his aged father, he had received the kafir. His narrow kahwa was presently full of town folk : and some of them no inconsiderable persons. It was for the poor man's honour to serve them with coffee, of the best; and that day it cost a shilling, which I was careful to restore to him. All these persons were come in to chat curiously of their maladies with the hakîm, whose counsels should cost them nothing; they hoped to defraud him of the medicines, and had determined in their iniquitous hearts to keep no good will for the Nasrâny again. And I was willing to help them, in aught that I might, without other regard.

At the next sunrise I went to breakfast with Kenneyny: this cheerful hour is not early in that sunny climate, where the light returns with a clear serenity ; and welfaring persons waken to renew the daily pleasures of prayers, coffee, and the friendly discourse of their easy lives. The meal times are commonly at hours when the Arabian people may honestly shun the burden of open hospitality. But the hours of the field labourers are those of the desert : breakfast is brought out to them at high noon, from the master's house, and they sup when the sun is going down. Every principal household possesses a milch cow in this town.

Each morning as I walked in the sûk, some that were sick persons' friends, drew me by the mantle, and led the hakîm to their houses ; where they brought me forth a breakfast-tray of girdle-bread and lében. Thus I breakfasted twice or thrice daily, whilst the wonder lasted, and felt my strength revive. Their most diseases are of the eyes; I saw indeed hundreds of such patients ! in the time of my being at Aneyza. The pupils are commonly clouded by night-chill cataract and small-pox cataract: many lose the sight of one or even both their eyes in childhood by this scourge ; and there is a blindness, which comes upon them, after a cruel aching of years in the side of the forehead.—There is nothing feasible which the wit of some men will not stir them to attempt ; also we hear of eye-prickers in Arabia: but the people have little hope in them. An eye-salver with the needle, from Shuggera, had been the year before at Aneyza. Their other common diseases are rheums and the oasis fever, and the *táhal :* I have seen the tetter among children.

— The small-pox was in the town : the malady, which had not been seen here for seven years, spread lately from some slave children brought up in the returning pilgrim caravan. Some of the town caravaners, with the profit of their sales in Mecca, use

to buy slave children in Jidda, to sell them again in el-Kasîm,
or (with more advantage) in Mesopotamia. They win thus a
few reals: but Aneyza lost thereby, in the time of my being
there—chiefly I think by their inoculation!—"five hundred"
of her free-born children! Nevertheless the infection did not
pass the Wady to Boreyda, nor to any of the Nefûd villages
lying nigh about them. I was called to some of their small-pox
houses, where I found the sick lying in the dark; the custom is
to give them no medicines, "lest they should lose their eyesight."
And thus I entered the dwellings of some of the most fanatical
citizens: my other patients' diseases were commonly old and
radical.—Very cleanly and pleasant are the most homes in this
Arabian town, all of clay building.

The tradesmen's shops are well furnished. The common food
is cheaper at Boreyda; at Aneyza is better cheap of "Mecca
coffee" (from el-Yémen), and of Gulf clothing. Dates, which
in Kasîm are valued by weight, are very good here; and nearly
30 pounds were sold for one real.

There is an appearance of welfare in the seemly clothing of
this townsfolk—men commonly of elated looks and a comely
liberty of carriage. They salute one another in many words,
nearly as the Beduins, with a familiar grace; for not a few of
them, who live in distant orchard houses, come seldom into the
town. But the streets are thronged on Fridays; when all the
townsmen, even the field labourers, come in at mid-day, to pray
in the great mesjid, and hear the koran reading and preaching:
it is as well their market day. The poorer townspeople go clad
like the Aarab; and their kerchiefs are girded with the head-cord.
These sober citizens cut the hair short—none wear the braided
side-locks of the Beduw: the richer sort (as said) have upon
their heads Fez caps, over which they loosely cast a gay kerchief;
that they gird only when they ride abroad. As for the haggu
or waist-band of slender leathern plait [it is called in Kasîm
hágub or brîm] which is worn even by princes in Hâyil, and
by the (Arabian) inhabitants of Medina and Mecca, the only
wearers of it here are the hareem. The substantial townsmen
go training in black mantles of light Irâk worsted: and the
young patricians will spend as much as the cloth is worth, for
a broidered collar in metal thread-work. The embroiderers are
mostly women, in whom is a skill to set forth some careless grace
of running lines, some flowery harmony in needlework—such as
we see woven in the Oriental carpets. Gentle persons in the
streets go balancing in their hands long rods which are brought
from Mecca.

Hareem are unseen, and the men's manners are the more gracious and untroubled : it may be their Asiatic society is manlier, but less virile than the European. They live-on in a pious daily assurance : and little know they of stings which be in our unquiet emulations, and in our foreign religion. Mohammed's sweet-blooded faith has redeemed them from the superfluous study of the world, from the sour-breathing inhospitable wine; and has purified their bodies from nearly every excess of living : only they exceed here, and exceed all in the East, in coffee. Marriage is easy from every man's youth; and there are no such rusty bonds in their wedlock, that any must bear an heavy countenance. The Moslem's breast is enlarged ; he finds few wild branches to prune of his life's vine, —a plant supine and rich in spirit, like the Arabic language. There is a nobility of the religious virtue among them, and nothing stern or rugged, but the hatred of the kafir : few have great hardness in their lives.—But the woman is in bondage, and her heart has little or no refreshment. Women are not seen passing by their streets, in the daytime ; but in the evening twilight (when the men sit at coffee) you shall see many veiled forms flitting to their gossips' houses : and they will hastily return, through an empty sûk, in the time of the last prayers, whilst the men are praying in the mesjids.

A day or two after my being in Aneyza a young man of the patricians came to bid me to dinner, from his father; who was that good man *Abdullah Abd er-Rahmàn, el-Bessàm,* a merchant at Jidda and chief of the house of Bessàm in Aneyza. Abdullah el-Bessàm and Abdullah el-Kenneyny were entire friends, breakfasting and dining together, and going every day to coffee in each other's houses; and they were *filasûfs* with Zâmil. Besides the Kenneyny I found there *Sheykh Nâsir, es-Smíry,* a very swarthy man of elder years, of the Waháby straitness in religion ; and who was of the Aneyza merchants at Jidda. He had lately returned—though not greatly enriched, to live in an hired house at home; and was partner with the Kenneyny in buying every year a few young horses from the Nomads, which they shipped to Bombay for sale. * * *

* * * Sheykh Nâsir was of the B. Khâlid families : there is a Beduishness in them more than in the Temîmies. Though stiff in opinions, he answered me better than any man, and with a natural frankness ; especially when I asked him of the history and topography of these countries : and he first traced for me, with his pen, the situation of the southern *Harras,*—

B. Abdillah, Kesshab, Turr'a, 'Ashîry, 'Ajeyfa, (Rodwa, Jeheyna;) which, with the rest of the vulcanic train described in this work, before my voyage in Arabia, were not heard of in Europe. Not long before he had embarked some of the honest gain of his years of exile under the Red Sea climate, with two more Jidda merchants, in a lading to India. Tidings out of the caravan season may hardly pass the great desert; but he had word in these days, by certain who came up by hap from Mecca, that their vessel had not been heard of since her sailing! and now it was feared that the ship must be lost. These foreign merchants at the ports do never cover their sea and fire risks by an assurance,—such were in their eyes a deed of unbelief! In the meanwhile sheykh Nâsir bore this incertitude of God's hand with the severe serenity of a right Moslem.

— This was the best company in the town: the dinner-tray was set on a stool [the mess is served upon the floor in princes' houses in Hâyil]; and we sat half-kneeling about it. The foreign merchants' meal at Aneyza is more town-like than I had seen in Arabia: besides boiled mutton on temmn, Abdullah had his little dishes of carrots fried in butter, and bowls of custard messes or curded milk.—We sit at leisure at the European board, we chat cheerfully; but such at the Arabs' dish would be a very inept and unreasonable behaviour!—he were not a man but an homicide, who is not speechless in that short battle of the teeth for a day's life of the body. And in what sort (forgive it me, O thrice good friends! in the sacrament of the bread and salt,) a dog or a cat laps up his meat, not taking breath, and is dispatched without any curiosity, and runs after to drink; even so do the Arabs endeavour, that they may come to an end with speed: for in their eyes it were not honest to linger at the dish; whereunto other (humbler) persons look that should eat after them. The good Bessâm, to show the European stranger the more kindness, rent morsels of his mutton and laid them ready to my hand.—*Yerhamak Ullah,* "The Lord be merciful unto thee," say the town guests, every one, in rising from dinner, with a religious mildness and humility. Bessâm himself, and his sons, held the towel to them, without the door, whilst they washed their hands. The company returned to their sitting before the hearth; and his elder son sat there already to make us coffee.

El-Kenneyny bid me come to breakfast with him on the morrow; and we should go out to see his orchard (which they call here *jenèyny* 'pleasure ground'). "Abdullah, quoth sheykh Nâsir, would enquire of thee how water might be raised by some better mean than we now use at Aneyza, where a camel

walking fifteen paces draws but one bucket full! [it may be
nearly three pails, 200 pails in an hour, 1500 to 2000 pails in
the day's labour.] And you, a man of Europa, might be able
to help us! for we suppose you have learned geometry; and
may have read in books which treat of machines, that are so
wonderful in your countries."—Nâsir's Waháby malice would
sow cockle in the clean corn of our friendship, and have made
me see an interested kindness in the Kenneyny! who answered
with an ingenuous asperity, that he desired but to ask Khalíl's
opinion. He had imagined an artesian well flowing with water
enough to irrigate some good part of Aneyza!—I had seen to-
day a hand-cart on wheels, before a smith's forge! a sight not
less strange in an Arabian town, than the camel in Europe;
it was made here for the Kenneyny. The sâny had fastened
the ends of his tires unhandsomely, so that they overlapped:
but his felloes, nave and spokes were very well wrought; and
in all Nejd (for the making of suâny wheels—commonly a large
yard of cross measure), there are perfect wheelwrights. Abdullah's dates had been drawn home on this barrow, in the late
harvest; and the people marvelled to see how two men might
wield the loads of two or three great camels!

The guests rise one after another and depart when the coffee
is drunk, saying, *Yunaam Ullah aleyk*, 'The Lord be gracious
unto thee;' and the host responds gently, *Fî amân illah*, '(go)
in the peace of the Lord.' There are yet two summer hours of
daylight; and the townsmen landowners will walk abroad to
breathe the freshing air, and visit their orchards.

As for the distribution of the day-time in Aneyza: the people
purchase their provision at the market stalls, soon after the
sunrising; the shuttered shops are set open a little later, when
the tradesmen (mostly easy-living persons and landowners)
begin to arrive from breakfast. The running brokers now cry
up and down in the clothiers' street, holding such things in
their hands as are committed to them to sell for ready money, —
long guns, spears, coffee-pots, mantles, fathoms of calico, and
the like. They cry what silver is bidden; and if any person
call them they stay to show their wares. Clothing-pieces
brought down by the caravaners from Bagdad, are often delivered by them to the dellâls, to be sold out of hand. The
tradesmen, in days when no Beduins come in, have little
business: they sit an hour, till the hot forenoon, and then
draw their shop shutters, and go homeward; and bye and bye
all the street will be empty.—At the mid-day íthin the townsmen come flocking forth in all the ways, to enter the mesjids.

Few salesmen return from the mid-day prayers to the sûk ; the most go (like the patricians,) to drink coffee in friends' houses : some, who have jenèynies in the town, withdraw then to sit in the shadows of their palms.

At the half-afternoon íthin, the coffee drinkers rise from the perfumed hearths, and go the third time a-praying to their mesjids. From the public prayers the tradesmen resort to the sûk ; their stalls are set open, the dellâls are again a-foot, and passengers in the bazaar. The patricians go home to dine ; and an hour later all the shops are shut for the day.—Citizens will wander then beyond the town walls, to return at the sun's going down, when the íthin calls men a fourth time to pray in the mesjids !

From these fourth prayers, the people go home : and this is not an hour to visit friends ; for the masters are now sitting to account with the field labourers, in their coffee-halls ; where not seldom there is a warm mess of burghrol set ready for them. But husbandmen, in the far outlying palmsteads, remain there all night ; and needing no roof, they lie down in their mantles under the stars to sleep. Another íthin, after the sun-setting hardly two hours, calls men to the fifth or last public prayers (súlat el-akhír). It is now night ; and many who are weary remain to pray, or not to pray, in their own houses. When they come again from the mesjids, the people have ended the day's religion : there is yet an hour of private friendship (but no more common assemblings) in the coffee-halls of the patricians and foreign merchants.

— El-Kenneyny sent a poor kinsman of his, when we had breakfasted, to accompany me to his jenèyny, half a league distant, within the furthest circuit of town walling : he being an infirm man would follow us upon an ass. [With this kins-man of his, Sleymàn, I have afterward passed the great desert southward to the Mecca country.] We went by long clay lanes with earthen walling, between fields and plantations, in the cool of the morning ; but (in this bitter sun) there springs not a green blade by the (unwatered) way side ! Their cornfields were now stubbles ; and I saw the lately reaped harvest gathered in great heaps, to the stamping places. * * *

* * * Kenneyny's palm and corn-ground might be three and a half acres of sand soil. The farthest bay of the town wall, which fenced him, was there fallen away, in wide breaches : and all without the sûr is sand-sea of the Nefûd. The most had been corn-land, in which he was now setting young palm plants

from the Wady: for every one is paid a real. He had but forty stems of old palms, and they were of slender growth; because of the former " weak " (empoverished) owner's insufficient watering. And such are the most small-landed men in this country; for they and their portions of the dust of this world are devoured (hardly less than in Egypt and Syria,) by rich money-lenders: that is by the long rising over their heads of an insoluble usury. Abdullah's new double well-pit was six fathoms deep, sunk into the underlying crust of sand-rock; and well steyned with dry courses of sandstone, which is hewn near Aneyza. All the cost had been 600 reals, or nearly £120 in silver: the same for four camels' draught would have cost 400 reals. Abdullah valued the ground with his well at about £600, that is above £100 an acre without the water: and this was some of their cheaper land, lying far from the town, They have thick-grown but light-eared harvests of wheat, sown year by year upon the same plots; and corn is always dear in poor Arabia.

Here four nâgas—their camel cattle are black at Aneyza— wrought incessantly: a camel may water one acre nearly from wells of six or eight fathoms. He had opened this great well, hoping in time to purchase some piece more of his neighbour's ground. Abdullah, as all rich landed men, had two courses of well camels; the beasts draw two months till they become lean, and they are two months at pasture in the wilderness. Every morrow Abdullah rode hither to take the air, and oversee his planting: and he had a thought to build himself here an orchard house, that he might breathe the air of the Nefûd,— when he should be come again [but ah! that was not written in the book of life] to Aneyza. Abdullah asked, how could I, "a man of Europa," live in the khála? and in journeying over so great deserts, had I never met with foot robbers, *henshûly!* The summer before this, he and some friends had gone out with tents, to dwell nomadwise in the Nefûd. Welfaring Aneyza citizens have canvas tents, for the yearly pilgrimage and their often caravan passages, made like the booths of the Beduw, that is cottage-wise, and open in front,—the best, I can think, under this climate.

These tilled grounds so far from the town are not fenced; the bounds are marked by mere-stones. Abdullah looked with a provident eye upon this parcel of land, which he planted for his daughters' inheritance: he had purchased palms for his son at Bosra. He would not that the men (which might be) born of him should remain in Arabia! and he said, with a sad presentiment, 'Oh! that he might live over the few years of his children's nonage.'

I found here some of his younger friends. These were *Hàmed es-Sâfy*, of Bagdad, and Abdullah Bessàm, the younger (nephew of the elder Abdullah el-Bessàm) ; and a negro companion of theirs, *Sheykh ibn Ayith*, a lettered sheykh or elder in the religion. After salaams they all held me out their forearms,—that the hakîm might take knowledge of their pulses ! Hàmed and Abdullah, unlike their worthiness of soul, were slender growths : their blood flowed in feeble streams, as their old spent fathers, and the air of great towns, had given them life. Ibn Ayith, of an (ox-like) African complexion, showed a pensive countenance, whilst I held his destiny in my hands !—and required in a small negro voice, ' What did I deem of his remiss health ? ' The poor scholar believed himself to be always ailing ; though his was no lean and discoloured visage ! nor the long neck, narrow breast, and pithless members of those chop-fallen men that live in the twilight of human life, growing only, since their pickerel youth, in their pike's heads, to die later in the world's cold.—The negro litterate was a new man from this day, wherein he heard the hakîm's absolution ; and carried himself upright among his friends (thus they laughed to me), whereas he had drooped formerly. And Ibn Ayith was no pedant fanatic ; but daily conversing with the foreign merchants, he had grown up liberal minded. Poor, he had not travelled, saving that—as all the religious Nejdians, not day-labourers—he had ridden once on pilgrimage (with his bountiful friends, who had entertained him) to Mecca ; " And if I were in thy company, quoth he, I would show thee all the historical places." His toward youth had been fostered in learning, by charitable sheykhs ; and they at this day maintained his scholar's leisure. He was now father of a family ; but besides the house wherein he dwelt, he had no worldly possessions. There was ever room for him at Abdullah el-Bessàm's dish ; and he was ofttimes the good man's scrivener, for Abdullah was less clerk than honourable merchant ; and it is the beginning of their school wisdom to write handsomely. But in Ibn Ayith was no subject behaviour ; I have heard him, with a manly roughness, say the kind Abdullah *nay !* to his beard. There is a pleasant civil liberty in Aneyza, and no lofty looks of their natural rulers in the town ; but many a poor man (in his anger) will contradict, to the face, and rail at the long-suffering prudence of Zâmil !—saying, *Mâ b'ak kheyr*, there is not good in thee.

When I came again, it was noon, the streets were empty, and the shops shut : the íthin sounded, and the people came trooping by to the mesjids. An old Ateyba sheykh passed lateward,

—he was in the town with some of his marketing tribesmen ; and hearing I was the hakîm, he called to me, 'He would have a medicine for the rîh.' One answered, "It might cost thee a real."—"And what though this medicine cost a real, O townling (hâthery), if I have the silver!" There came also some lingering truants, who stayed to smile at the loud and sudden-tongued old Beduwy ; and a merry fellow asked, amidst their laughter, were he well with his wives? "Nay, cries the old heart, and I would, billah, that the hareem had not cause. —Oho! have patience there!" (because some zealots thrust on him).—"Heardest not thou the îthin? go pray!"—"Ay, ay, I heard it, Ullah send you sorrow! am I not talking with this mudowwy?—well, I am coming presently."—A zealot woman went by us : the squalid creature stepped to the Beduin sheykh, and drew him by the mantle. "To the prayer! cries she, old devil-sick Beduwy ; thou to stand here whilst the people pray! —and is it to talk with this misbelieving person?"—"Akhs! do away thy hands! let me go, woman!—I tell thee I have said my prayers." Though he cried akhs-akhs! she held him by the cloth ; and he durst not resist her : yet he said to me, "O thou the mudowwy! where is thy remedy for the rheums?—a wild fire on this woman! that will not let me speak." I bade him return after prayers ; and the sheykh hearing some young children chide with "Warak, warak! why goest thou not in to pray?" he called to me as he was going, "O thou! resist them not, but do as they do; when a man is come to another country, let him observe the usage and not strive—that will be best for thee, and were it only to live in peace with them." Now the stripling with the rod was upon us!—the kestrel would have laid hands on the sheykhly father of the desert. "Oh! hold, and I go," quoth he, and they drove him before them.

My medical practice was in good credit. Each daybreak a flock of miserable persons waited for the hakîm, on the small terrace of my host (before they went to their labour): they importuned me for their sore eyes ; and all might freely use my eye washes. In that there commonly arrived some friendly messenger, to call the stranger to breakfast ; and I left my patients lying on their backs, with smarting eyeballs. The poorer citizens are many, in the general welfare of Aneyza. Such are the field labourers and well drivers, who receive an insufficient monthly wage. The impotent, and the forsaken in age, are destitute indeed ; they must go a-begging through the town. I sometimes met with a tottering and deadly crew in the still streets before midday ; old calamitous widows, childless aged men, indigent divorced wives, and the misshapen and diseased ones of step-dame Nature that had none to relieve them. They creep abroad as a curse in the world, and must knock from door to door, to know if the Lord will send them any good ; and cry lamentably *Yâ ahl el-karîm !* 'O ye of this bountiful household.' But I seldom saw the cheerful hand of bounty which beckoned to them or opened. One morrow when I went to visit the Emir the mesquins were crouching and shuffling at his door ; and Zâmil's son Abdullah came out with somewhat to give them: but I saw his dole was less than his outstretched hand full of dates ! " Go further! and here is for you," quoth the young niggard : he pushed the mesquins and made them turn their backs.

I passed some pleasant evenings in the kahwas of the young friends and neighbours Hàmed and Abdullah ; and they called in Ibn Ayith, who entertained me with discourse of the Arabic letters. Hàmed regaled us with Bagdad nargîlies, and Abdullah made a sugared cooling drink of *támr el-Hind* (tamarind). To Abdullah's kahwa, in the daytime, resorted the best company in the town,—such were the honourable young Bessàm's cheerful popular manners. His mortar rang out like a bell of hospitality, when he prepared coffee. The Aneyza mortar is a little saucer-like hollow in a marble block great as a font-stone : a well-ringing mortar is much esteemed among them. Their great coffee-mortar blocks are hewn not many hours from the town eastward (near el-Mith'nib, toward J. Tueyk). An ell long is every liberal man's pestle of marble in Aneyza : it is smitten in rhythm (and that we hear at all the coffee-hearths of the Arabs). A jealous or miserable householder, who would not have many pressing in to drink with him, must muffle the musical note of his marble or knelling brasswork.

These were the best younger spirits of the (foreign) merchant houses in the town : they were readers in the Encyclopædia, and of the spirituous poets of the Arabian antiquity. Abdullah, when the last of his evening friends had departed, sitting at his petroleum lamp, and forgetting the wife of his youth, would pore on his books and feed his gentle spirit almost till the day appearing. Hàmed, bred at Bagdad, was incredulous of the world old and new ; but he leaned to the new studies. These young merchants sought counsels in medicine, and would learn of me some Frankish words, and our alphabet,—and this because their sea carriage is in the hands of European shippers. A few of these Arabians, dwelling in the trade ports, have learned to endorse their names upon Frankish bills which come to their hands, in Roman letters. Abdullah el-Bessàm's eldest son—he was now in India, and a few more, had learned to read and to speak too in English : yet that was, I can think, but lamely. Others, as the Kenneyny, who have lived in Bombay, can speak the Hindostani. Hàmed wrote from my lips (in his Arabic letters) a long table of English words—such as he thought might serve him in his Gulf passages. His father dwelt, since thirty years, in Bagdad ; and had never revisited Aneyza :— in which time the town is so increased, that one coming again after a long absence might hardly, they say, remember himself there. El-Kenneyny told me that Aneyza was now nearly double of the town fifteen years ago ; and he thought the inhabitants must be to-day 15,000 !

My friends saw me a barefoot hakîm, in rent clothing, as I was come-in from the khála, and had escaped out of Boreyda. The younger Abdullah Bessàm sent me sandals, and they would have put a long wand in my hand ; but I answered them, " He is not poor who hath no need : my poverty is honourable." Kenneyny said to me on a morrow, when we were alone (and for the more kindness finding a Frankish word), " *Mussu* Khalîl, if you lack money—were it an hundred or two hundred reals, you may have this here of me : " but he knew not all my necessity, imagining that I went poorly for a disguise. I gave thanks for his generous words ; but which were thenceforth in my ears as if they had never been uttered. I heard also, that the good Bessàm had taken upon himself to send me forward, to what part I would. I was often bidden to his house, and seldom to Kenneyny's, who (a new man) dreaded over-much the crabbed speech of his Waháby townspeople. The good Bessàm, as oft as he met with me, invited the stranger, benignly, to breakfast on the morrow : and at breakfast he bid me dine the same day with him,—an humanity which was much to thank God for, in these extremities. * * *

CHAPTER IX

LIFE IN ANEYZA

ONE of these mornings word was brought to the town, that Beduins had fallen upon harvesters in the Wady, and carried away their asses : and in the next half hour I saw more than a hundred of the young townsmen hasten-by armed to the Boreyda gate. The poorer sort ran foremost on foot, with long lances; and the well-faring trotted after upon thelûls with their backriders. But an hour had passed; and the light-footed robbers were already two or three leagues distant!

There were yet rumours of warfare with Boreyda and the Kahtân. Were it war between the towns, Hásan and the Boreydians (less in arms and fewer in number) durst not adventure to meet the men of Aneyza in the Nefûd ; but would shelter themselves within their (span-thick) clay wall, leaving their fields and plantations in the power of the enemy,—as it has happened before-time. The adversaries, being neighbours, will no more than devour their fruits, whilst the orchards languish unwatered : they are not foreign enemies likely to lop the heads of the palms, whereby they should be ruined for many years.—This did Ibn Saûd's host in the warfare with Aneyza ; they destroyed the palms in the Wady : so pleasant is the sweet pith-wood to all the Arabians, and they desire to eat of it with a childish greediness.

Kahtân tribesmen were suffered to come marketing to Aneyza ; till a *hubt* of theirs returning one evening with loaded camels, and finding some town children not far from the gate, in the Nefûd, that were driving home their asses, and an *âbd* with them, took the beasts and let the children go : yet they carried away the negro,—and he was a slave of Zâmil's !

A savage tiding was brought in from the north ; and all Aneyza was moved by it, for the persons were well known to them. A great camp of Meteyr Aarab, *sadûk*, or " friends-of-

trust to the town and Zâmil ", (if any of the truthless nomads
can be trusty !) had been set upon at four days' distance from
hence by a strong ghrazzu of Kahtân,—for the pastures of
Kasîm, their capital enemies. Leader of the raid was that
Hayzàn who, not regarding the rites of hospitality, had
threatened me at Hâyil. The nomads (fugitive foemen in every
other cause), will fight to " the dark death " for their pastures
and waters. The Meteyr were surprised in their tents and
outnumbered ; and the Kahtân killed some of them. The rest
saved themselves by flight, and their milch camels ; leaving
the slow-footed flocks, with the booths, and their household
stuff in the power of their enemies; who not regarding the
religion of the desert pierced even women with their lances,
and stripped them, and cut the wezands of three or four young
children ! Among the fallen of Meteyr was a principal sheykh
well known at Aneyza. Hayzàn had borne him through with
his romh !

Those Aarab now withdrew towards Aneyza : where their
sheykhs found the townsmen of a mind to partake with them,
to rid the country of the common pestilence. In their gene-
alogies, el-Meteyr, Ishmaelites, are accounted in the descents
from Keys, and from *Anmâr*, and *Rubîa :* Rubîa, Anmâr,
Múthur, and Eyâd are brethren ; and Rubîa is father of Wâyil,
patriarch of the Annezy. Meteyr are of old Ahl Gibly : and
their home is in the great Harra which lies between the
Harameyn, yet occupied by their tribesmen. Their ancient
villages in that country, upon the *Derb es-Sherky* or east
Haj-road to Mecca, are *El-Feréya, Hâthi, Sfeyna, es-Swergîeh*
in the borders of the *Harrat el-Kisshub ;* and *Hajjir :* but the
most villagers of the Swergîeh valley are at this day *ashrâf,* or
of the " eminent " blood of the Néby. The Meteyr are now in
part Ahl es-Shemâl : for every summer these nomads journey
upward to pasture their cattle in the northern wilderness : their
borders are reckoned nearly to Kuweyt and Bosra; and they
are next in the North to the northern Shammar. Neither are
tributary, but " friendly Aarab," to Ibn Rashîd. The desert
marches of the Meteyr are thus almost 200 leagues over ! [They
are in multitude (among the middle Arabian tribes) next after
the great Beduin nation *'Ateyba,* and may be almost 5000
souls.] Their tents were more than two hundred in el-Kasîm,
at this time. Each year they visit Aneyza ; and Zâmil bestows
a load or two of dates upon their great sheykh, that the town
caravans may pass by them, unhindered.

Other Beduin tribesmen resorting to Aneyza are the *'Ateybân*
(also reckoned to the line of Keys) : neither the Meteyr nor

'Ateyba were friendly with Boreyda. The 'Ateyba marches are all that high wilderness, an hundred leagues over, which lies between el-Kasîm in the north, and the Mecca country : in that vast dîra, of the best desert pastures, there is no settlement ! The 'Ateyba, one of the greatest of Arabian tribes, may be nearly 6000 souls; they are of more stable mind than the most Beduw ; and have been allies (as said), in every fortune, of Abdullah ibn Saûd. There is less fanaticism in their religion than moderation : they dwell between the Waháby and the Háram ; and boast themselves hereditary friends of the Sherîfs of Mecca. Zâmil was all for quietness and peace, in which is the welfare of human life, and God is worshipped; but were it warfare, in his conduct, the people of Aneyza are confident. Now he sent out an hundred thelûl riders of the citizens, in two bands, to scour the Nefûd ; and set over them the son of the Emir Aly, *Yahŷa ;* a manly young man, but like his father of the strait Waháby understanding.

I saw a Kahtâny arrested in the street; the man had come marketing to Aneyza, but being known by his speech, the bystanders laid hands on his thelûl. Some would have drawn him from the saddle; and an Arab overpowered will [his feline and chameleon nature] make no resistance, for that should endanger him. " Come thou with us afore Zâmil," cried they. " Well, he answered, I am with you." They discharged his camel and tied up the beast's knee : the salesmen in the next shops sat on civilly incurious of this adventure.—At Hâyil, in like case, or at Boreyda all had been done by men of the Emir's band, with a tyrannous clamour ; but here is a free township, where the custody of the public peace is left in the hands of all the citizens.—As for the Kahtân Zâmil had not yet proclaimed them enemies of Aneyza ; and nothing was alleged against this Beduwy. They bound him : but the righteous Emir gave judgment to let the man go.

Persons accused of crimes at Aneyza (where is no prison), are bound, until the next sitting of the Emir. Kenneyny told me there had been in his time but one capital punishment,—this was fifteen years ago. The offender was a woman, sister of Mufarrij ! that worthy man whom we have seen steward of the prince's public hall at Hâyil : it was after this misfortune to his house that he left Aneyza to seek some foreign service. —She had enticed to her yard a little maiden, the only daughter of a wealthy family, her neighbours ; and there she smothered the child for the (golden) ornaments of her pretty head, and buried the innocent body. The bereaved father sought to a soothsayer,—in the time of whose "reading" they suppose that the belly of the guilty person should swell. The diviner led on to the woman's house; and showing a place he bade them dig!—There they took up the little corpse! and it was borne to the burial.

— The woman was brought forth to suffer, before the session of the people and elders (musheyikh) assembled with the executive Emir.—In these Arabian towns, the manslayer is bound by the sergeants of the Emir, and delivered to the kindred of the slain, to be dealt with at their list.—Aly bade the father, "Rise up and slay that wicked woman, the murderess of his child." But he who was a religious elder (*muttowwa*), and a mild and godly person, responded, "My little daughter is gone to the mercy of Ullah; although I slay the woman, yet may not this bring again the life of my child!—suffer, Sir, that I spare her: she that is gone, is gone." *Aly :* "But her crime cannot remain unpunished, for that were of too perilous example in the town! Strike thou! I say, and kill her."—Then the muttowwa drew a sword and slew her! Common misdoers and thieves are beaten with palm-leaf rods that are to be green and not in the dry, which (they say) would break fell and bones. There is no cutting off the hand at Aneyza; but any hardened felon is cast out of the township.

After this Zâmil sent his message to the sheykhs of Kahtân in the desert, 'that would they now restore all which had been reaved by their tribesmen, they might return into friendship: and if no, he pronounced them adversaries.' Having thus discharged their consciences, these (civil) townsfolk think they may commit their cause to the arbitrage of Ullah, and their hands shall be clean from blood: and (in general) they take no booty from their enemies! for they say "it were unlawful,"—notwithstanding, I have known to my hurt, that there are many sly thieves in their town! But if a poor man in an expedition bestow some small thing in his saddle-bag, it is indulged, so that it do not appear openly.—And thus, having nothing to gain, the people of Aneyza only take arms to defend their liberties.

One day when I went to visit Zâmil, I found a great silent assembly in his coffee-hall: forty of the townspeople were sitting round by the walls. Then there came in an old man who was sheykh of the religion; and my neighbour told me in my ear, they were here for a Friday afternoon lecture! Coffee was served round; and they all drank out of the same cups.

The Arabs spare not to eat or drink out of the same vessel with any man. And Mohammed could not imagine in his (Arabian) religion, to forbid this earthly communion of the human life; but indeed their incurious custom of all hands dipping in one dish, and all lips kissing in one cup, is laudable rather than very wholesome.

The Imâm's mind was somewhat wasted by the desolate koran reading. I heard in his school discourse no word which sounded to moral edification! He said finally—looking towards me! "And to speak of Aysa bin Miriam,—Jesu was of a truth a Messenger of Ullah : but the Nasâra walk not in the way of Jesu,—they be gone aside, in the perversity of their minds, unto idolatry." And so rising mildly, all the people rose ; and every one went to take his sandals.

The townspeople tolerated me hitherto,—it was Zâmil's will. But the Muttowwa, or public ministers of the religion, from the first, stood contrary ; and this Imâm (a hale and venerable elder of threescore years and ten) had stirred the people, in his Friday noon preaching, in the great mesjid, against the Nasrâny. ' It was, he said, of evil example, that certain principal persons favoured a misbelieving stranger : might they not in so doing provoke the Lord to anger ? and all might see that the seasonable rain was withheld ! '—Cold is the outlaw's life ; and I marked with a natural constraint of heart, an alienation of the street faces, a daily standing off of the faint-hearted, and of certain my seeming friends. I heard it chiefly alleged against me, that I greeted with *Salaam aleyk ;* which they will have to be a salutation of God's people only—the Moslemîn. El-Kenneyny, Bessàm, Zâmil were not spirits to be moved by the words of a dull man in a pulpit ; in whom was but the (implacable) wisdom of the Wahábies of fifty years ago. I noted some alteration in es-Smîry ; and, among my younger friends, in the young Abdullah Bessàm, whose nigh kindred were of the Nejd straitness and intolerance. There was a strife in his single mind, betwixt his hospitable human fellowship, and the duty he owed unto God and the religion : and when he found me alone he asked, "Wellah Khalîl, do the Nasâra hold thus and thus ? contrary to the faith of Islam ! "—Not so Hamed es-Sâfy, the young Bagdady ; who was weary of the tedious Nejd religion : sometimes ere the íthin sounded he shut his outer door ; but if I knocked it was opened (to " *el-docteur* "), when he heard my voice. These Aneyza merchant friends commonly made tea when the Engleysy arrived : they had learned abroad to drink it in the Persian manner. * * *

R

* * * Though there is not a man of medicine in Nejd, yet some modest leech may be found : and I was called to another Bessàm household to meet one who was of this town. That Bessàm, a burly body, was the most travelled of the foreign merchants : by railway he had sped through the breadth of India ; he had dwelt in the land, and in his mouth was the vulgar Hindostany. But no travel in other nations could amend his wooden head ; and like a tub which is shipped round the world he was come home never the better : there is no transmuting such metals ! His wit was thin ; and he had weakly thriven in the world. The salver sat at the Bessàm's coffee hearth ; awaiting me, with the respectable countenance of a village schoolmaster.—His little skill, he said with humility, he had gathered of reading in his few books ; and those were hard to come by. He asked me many simple questions ; and bowed the head to all my answers ; and, glad in his heart to find me friendly, the poor man seemed to wonder that the learning of foreign professors were not more dark, and unattainable !

In these last days the honest soul had inoculated all the children in the town : he acknowledged, ' that there die many thus !—but he had read, that in the cow-pox inoculation [el-'athab] of the Nasâra there die not any ' ! After hearing me he said, he would watch, mornings and evenings, at some of the town gates, when the kine are driven forth or would be returning from pasture ; if haply he might find the pocks on some of their udders. [Already Amm Mohammed had looked for it in vain, at Kheybar.]—I counselled the sheykhs to send this worthy man to the north, to learn the art for the public good ; and so he might vaccinate in these parts of Nejd. Worn as I was, I proffered myself to ride to Bagdad, if they would find me the thelûl, and return with the vaccine matter   But no desire nor hope of common advantage to come can move or unite Arabians : neither love they too well that safeguarding human forethought, which savours to them of untrust in an heavenly Providence. Their religion encourages them to seek medicines,—which God has created in the earth to the service of man ; but they may not flee from the pestilence. Certain of the foreign merchants have sometimes brought home the lymph,—so did Abdullah el-Bessàm, the last year ; yet this hardly passes beyond the walls of their houses.—I heard a new word in that stolid Bessàm's mouth (and perhaps he fetched it from India), " What dost thou, quoth he, in a land where is only diànat el-Mohammedia, Mohammedan religion ? whereas they use to say dîn el-Islam." —India, el-Kenneyny called, " A great spectacle of religions ! "

Amm Mohammed at Kheybar and the Beduw have told me,

there is a disease in camels like that which they understood from me to be the cow-pox.—The small-pox spread fast. One day at noon I found my young negro hostess sorrowing,—she had brought-in her child very sick, from playing in the Gá : and bye and bye their other babe sickened.—I would not remain in that narrow lodging to breathe an infected air : but, leaving there my things, I passed the next days in the streets : and often when the night fell I was yet fasting, and had not where to sleep. But I thought, that to be overtaken here by the disease, would exceed all present evils. None offered to receive me into their houses ; therefore beating in the evening—commonly they knock with an idle rhythm—at the rude door of some poor patient, upon whom I had bestowed medicines, and hearing responded from within, *ugglot*, ' approach ' ! I entered ; and asked leave to lie down on their cottage floor [of deep Nefûd sand] to sleep. The Kenneyny would not be marked to harbour a Nasrâny : to Bessàm I had not revealed my distress. And somewhat I reserved of these Arabian friends' kindness ; that I might take up all, in any extreme need.

The deep sanded (open) terrace roof of the mesjid, by my old dokàn, was a sleeping place for strangers in the town ; but what sanctity of the house of prayer would defend me slumbering ? for with the sword also worship they Ullah.—But now I found some relief, where I looked not for it : there was a man who used my medicines, of few words, sharp-set looks and painted eyes, but the son of a good mother,—a widow woman, who held a small shop of all wares, where I sometimes bought bread. He was a salesman in the clothiers' sûk, and of those few, beside the Emirs and their sons, who carried a sword in Aneyza ; for he was an officer of Zâmil's. He said to me, " I am sorry, Khalîl, to see thee without lodging ; there is an empty house nigh us, and shall we go to see it ? "—Though I found it to be an unswept clay chamber or two ; I went the same day to lodge there : and they were to me good neighbours. Every morrow his mother brought me girdle-bread with a little whey and butter, and filled my water-skin : at the sunsetting (when she knew that commonly—my incurable obliviousness—I had provided nothing; and now the sûk was shut), she had some wheaten mess ready for the stranger in her house, for little money ; and for part she would receive no payment ! it must have been secretly from Zâmil. This aged woman sat before me open-faced, and she treated me as her son : hers was the only town-woman's face that I have seen in middle Nejd,—where only maiden children are not veiled. * * *

* * * My friends, when I enquired of the antiquity of the
country, spoke to me of a ruined site *el-'Eyarîeh,* a little distance
northward upon this side of the W. er-Rummah : and Kenneyny
said "We can take horses and ride thither." I went one
morning afterward with Hâmud Assâfy to borrow horses of a
certain horse-broker *Abdullah,* surnamed [and thus they name
every Abdullah, although he have no child] *Abu Nejm:* Abu
Nejm was a horse-broker for the Indian market. There is no
breeding or sale of horses at Boreyda or Aneyza, nor any town
in Nejd ; but the horse-brokers take up young stallions in the
Aarab tribes, which—unless it be some of not common excellence,
are of no great price among them. Kenneyny would ride out to
meet with us, from another horse-yard, which was nigh his own
plantation.

We found Abu Nejm's few sale horses, with other horses
which he fed on some of his friends' account, in a field among
the last palms north of the town. Two stallions feed head to
head at a square clay bin ; and each horse is tethered by an hind
foot to a peg driven in the ground. Their fodder is green vetches
(*jet*) : and this is their diet since they were brought in lean from
the desert, through the summer weeks ; until the time when the
the Monsoon blows in the Indian seas. Then the broker's horse-
droves pass the long northern wilderness, with camels, bearing
their water, in seventeen marches to Kuweyt; where they are
shipped for Bombay.

An European had smiled to see in this Arab's countenance
the lively impression of his dealing in horses ! Abu Nejm, who
lent me a horse, would ride in our company. Our saddles were
pads without stirrups, for—like the Beduins, they use none
here : yet these townsmen ride with the sharp bit of the border
lands; whereas the nomad horsemen mount without bit or rein,
and sit upon their mares, as they sit on their dromedaries (that
is somewhat rawly), and with a halter only.—I have never heard
a horseman commended among Beduins for his fair riding,
though certain sheykbs are praised as spearsmen. Abu Nejm
went not himself to India ; and it was unknown to him that any
Nasrâny could ride : he called to me therefore, to hold fast to
the pad-brim, and wrap the other hand in the horse's mane.
Bye and bye I made my horse bound under me, and giving rein
let him try his mettle over the sand-billows of the Nefûd,—
"Ullah ! is the hakîm *khayyál,* a horseman ?" exclaimed the
worthy man.

We rode by a threshing-ground; and I saw a team of well-
camels driven in a row with ten kine and an ass inwardly (all
the cattle of that homestead), about a stake, and treading knee-

deep upon the bruised corn-stalks. In that yard-side I saw many
ant-hills; and drew bridle to consider the labour of certain
indigent hareem that were sitting beside them.—I saw the
emmets' last confusion (which they suffered as robbers),—their
hill-colonies subverted, and caught up in the women's meal-
sieves! that (careful only of their desolate living) tossed sky-
high the pismire nation, and mingled people and *musheyikh* in
a homicide ruin of sand and grain.—And each needy wife had
already some handfuls laid up in her spread kerchief, of this
gleaning corn.

We see a long high platform of sand-rock, *Mergab er-Ràfa*,
upon this side of the town. There stone is hewed and squared
for well building, and even for gate-posts, in Aneyza.—Kenneyny
came riding to meet us! and now we fell into an hollow ancient
way through the Nefûd leading to the 'Eyarîeh; and my companions said, there lies such another between el-'Eyarîeh and
el-Owshazîeh ; that is likewise an ancient town site. How may
these impressions abide in unstable sand ?—So far as I have seen
there is little wind in these countries.

Abdullah sat upon a beautiful young stallion of noble blood,
that went sidling proudly under his fair handling : and seeing the
stranger's eyes fixed upon his horse, " Ay, quoth my friend, this
one is good in all." Kenneyny, who with Sheykh Nâsir shipped
three or four young Arabian horses every year to Bombay, told
me that by some they gain ; but another horse may be valued
there so low, that they have less by the sale-money than the first
cost and expenses. Abu Nejm told us his winning or losing was
' as it pleased Ullah : the more whiles he gained, but sometimes
no.' They buy the young desert horses in the winter time,
that ere the next shipping season they may be grown in flesh,
and strong ; and inured by the oasis' diet of sappy vetches, to
the green climate of India.

Between the wealthy ignorance of foreign buyers, and the
Asiatic flattery of the Nejders of the Arab stables in Bombay,
a distinction has been invented of Aneyza and Nejd horses !—
as well might we distinguish between London and Middlesex
pheasants. We have seen that the sale-horses are collected by
town dealers, *min el-Aarab*, from the nomad tribes ; and since
there are few horses in the vast Arabian marches, they are oft-
times fetched from great distances. I have found "Aneyza"
horses in the Bombay stables which were foaled in el-Yémen.—
Perhaps we may understand by *Aneyza horses*, the horses of
Kasîm dealers [of Aneyza and Boreyda] ; and by *Nejd horses*,
the Jebel horses, or those sent to Bombay from Ibn Rashîd's
country. I heard that a Boreyda broker's horse-troop had been

sent out a few days before my coming thither.—Boreyda is a town and small Arabian state ; the Emir governs the neighbour villages, but is not obeyed in the desert. It is likely therefore that the Aneyza horse-coursers' traffic may be the more considerable. [The chief of the best Bombay stable is from Shuggera in el-Wéshm.]

As for the northern or "Gulf" horses, bred in the nomad dîras upon the river countries—although of good stature and swifter, they are not esteemed by the inner Arabians. Their flesh being only "of greenness and water" they could not endure in the sun-stricken languishing country. Their own daughters-of-the-desert, albe they less fairly shaped, are, in the same strains, worth five of the other.—Even the sale-horses are not curried under the pure Arabian climate : they learn first to stand under the strigil in India. Hollow-necked, as the camel, are the Arabian horses : the lofty neck of our thick-blooded horses were a deformity in the eyes of all Arabs. The desert horses, nurtured in a droughty wilderness of hot plain lands beset with small mountains, are not leapers, but very sure of foot to climb in rocky ground. They are good weight carriers : I have heard nomads boast that their mares ' could carry four men '. The Arabians believe faithfully that Ullah created the horse-kind in their soil : el-asl, the root or spring of the horse is, they say, " in the land of the Aarab ". Even Kenneyny was of this superstitious opinion ; although the horse can live only of man's hand in the droughty khála. [Rummaky, a mare, is a word often used in el-Kasîm : Sâlih el-Rasheyd tells me they may say ghrög for a horse ; but that is seldom heard.]

We rode three miles and came upon a hill of hard loam, overlooking the Wady er-Rummah, which might be there two miles over. In the further side appear a few outlying palm plantations and granges : but that air breeds fever and the water is brackish, and they are tilled only by negro husbandmen. All the nigh valley grounds were white with subbakha : in the midst of the Wady is much good loam, grown up with desert bushes and tamarisks ; but it cannot be husbanded because the groundwater—there at the depth of ten feet—is saline and sterile. Below us I saw an enclosure of palms with plots of vetches and stubbles, and a clay cabin or two ; which were sheykh Nâsir's. Here the shallow Rummah bottom reaches north-eastward and almost enfolds Aneyza : at ten hours' distance, or one easy thelûl journey, lies a great rautha, Zighreybîeh, with corn grounds, which are flooded with seyl-water in the winter rains : there is a salt bed, where salt is digged for Aneyza.

The Wady descending through the northern wilderness [which lies waste for hundreds of miles, without settlement] is dammed in a place called *eth-Thueyrát*; that is a thelûl journey or perhaps fifty miles distant from Aneyza, by great dunes of sand which are grown up, they say, in this age.   From thence the hollow Wady ground—wherein is the path of the northern caravans—is named *el-Bátin*; and passengers ride by the ruined sites of two or three villages: there are few wells by the way, and not much water in them.   That vast wilderness was anciently of the B. Taâmir.   The Wady banks are often cliffs of clay and gravel; and from cliff to cliff the valley may be commonly an hour (nearly three miles) over, said Kenneyny.   In the Nefûd plain of Kasîm, the course of the great Wady is sometimes hardly to be discerned by the eyes of strangers.

A few journeying together will not adventure to hold the valley way: they ride then, not far off, in the desert.   All the winding length of the Wady er-Rummah is, according to the vulgar opinion, forty-five days or camel marches (that were almost a thousand miles): it lies through a land-breadth, measured from the heads in the Harrat Kheybar to the outgoing near Bosra, of nearly five hundred miles.—What can we think of this great valley-ground, in a rainless land ?   When the Wady is in flood—that is hardly twice or thrice in a century, the valley flows down as a river.   The streaming tide is large; and where not straitened may be forded, they say, by a dromedary rider.   No man of my time of life had seen the seyl; but the elder generation saw it forty years before, in a season when uncommon rains had fallen in all the high country toward Kheybar.   The flood that passed Aneyza, being locked by the mole of sand at eth-Thueyrát, rose backward and became a wash, which was here at the 'Eyarîeh two miles wide.   And then was seen in Nejd the new spectacle of a lake indeed !—there might be nigh an hundred miles of standing water ; which remained two years and was the repair of all wandering wings of water-fowl not known heretofore, nor had their cries been heard in the air of these desert countries.   After a seyling of the great valley the water rises in the wells at Boreyda and Aneyza ; and this continues for a year or more.

We found upon this higher ground potsherds and broken glass—as in all ruined sites of ancient Arabia, and a few building stones, and bricks: but how far are they now from these arts of old settled countries in Nejd !—This is the site el-'Eyarîeh or *Menzil 'Eyàr*; where they see 'the plots of three or four ancient villages and a space of old inhabited soil greater than Aneyza ': they say, "It is better than the situation of the (new) town." We dismounted, and Abdullah began to say, "Wellah, the Arabs (of our time) are degenerate from the ancients, in all!—we see them live by inheriting their labours" (deep wells in the deserts and other public works)!

— The sword, they say, of *Khâlid bin-Walîd* [that new Joshua of Islam, in the days of Ômar] devoured idolatrous 'Eyarîeh, a town of B. Temîm. The like is reported of Owshazîeh, whose site is three hours eastward: there are now some palm-grounds and orchard houses of Aneyza. *'Eyàr* and *Owshâz*, in the Semitic tradition, are "brethren".—"It is remembered in the old poets of those B. Temîm citizens (quoth my erudite companions) that they had much cattle; and in the spring-time were wont to wander with their flocks and camels in the Nefûd, and dwell in booths like the nomads."—This is that we have seen in Edom and Moab where, from the entering of the spring, the villagers are tent-dwellers in the wilderness about them,—for the summering of their cattle: I have seen poor families in Gilead—which had no tent-cloth—dwelling under great oaks! the leafy pavilions are a covert from the heat by day, and from the nightly dews. Their flocks were driven-in toward the sun-setting, and lay down round about them.

Only the soil remains of the town of 'Eyàr: what were the lives of those old generations more than the flickering leaves! The works of their hands, the thoughts and intents of their hearts,—' their love, their hatred and envy,' are utterly perished! Their religion is forsaken; their place is unvisited as the cemeteries of a former age: only in the autumn landed men of Aneyza, send their servants thither, with asses and panniers, to dig loam for a top-dressing. As we walked we saw white slags lying together; where perhaps had been the workstead of some ancient artificer. When I asked ' had nothing been found here ?' Kenneyny told of some well-sinkers, that were hired to dig a well in a new ground by the 'Eyarîeh [the water is nigh and good]. "They beginning to open their pit, one of them lighted on a great earthen vessel!—it was set in the earth mouth downward [the head of an antique grave]. Then every well-digger cried out that the treasure was his own! none would hear his fellows' reason—and all men have reason! From quick words they fell to hand-strokes; and laid so sharply about them with their mattocks, that in the end but one man was left alive. This workman struck his vessel, with an eager heart!—but in the shattered pot was no more than a clot of the common earth!"—Abdullah said besides, ' that a wedge of fine gold had been taken up here, within their memories. The finder gave it, when he came into the town, for two hundred reals, to one who afterward sold the metal in the North, for better than a thousand.'

We returned : and Kenneyny at the end of a mile or two rode apart to his horse-yard ; where he said he had somewhat to show me another day.—I saw it later, a blackish vein, more than a palm deep and three yards wide, in the yellow sides of a loam pit : plainly the ashes of an antique fire, and in this old hearth they had found potsherds! thereabove lay a fathom of clay ; and upon that a drift of Nefûd sand.—Here had been a seyl-bed before the land was enclosed ; but potsherds so lying under a fathom of silt may be of an high antiquity. What was man then in the midst of Arabia? Some part of the town of Aneyza, as the mejlis and clothiers' street, is built upon an old seyl-ground ; and has been twice wasted by land floods : the last was ninety years before.

I went home with Hàmed and there came-in the younger Abdullah el-Bessàm. They spoke of the ancients, and (as litterates) contemned the vulgar opinion of giants in former ages : nevertheless they thought it appeared by old writings, that men in their grandsires' time had been stronger than now ; for they found that a certain weight was then reckoned a man's load at Aneyza ; which were now above the strength of common labourers : and that not a few of those old folk came to four. score years and ten. There are many long-lived persons at Aneyza, and I saw more grey beards in this one town, than in all parts besides where I passed in Arabia.

But our holiday on horseback to the 'Eyarîeh bred talk. ' We had not ridden there, three or four together, upon a fool's errand ; the Nasrâny in his books of secret science had some old record of this country.' Yet the liberal townsmen bade me daily, Not mind their foolish words ; and they added pro- verbially, *el-Arab, 'akl-hum nâkis*, the Arabs are always short- witted. Yet their crabbed speech vexed the Kenneyny, a spirit so high above theirs, and unwont to suffer injuries.—I found him on the morrow sitting estranged from them and offended : " Ahks, he said, this despiteful people! but my home is in Bosra, and God be thanked! I shall not be much longer with them. Oh! Khalîl, thou canst not think what they call me,—they say, *el-Kenneyny bellowwy!* "—This is some outrageous villany, which is seldom heard amongst nomads ; and is only uttered of anyone when they would speak extremely. The Arabs—the most unclean and devout of lips, of mankind!—curse all under heaven which contradicts their humour ; and the Waháby rancour was stirred against a townsman who was no partizan of their blind faction, but seemed to favour the Nasrâny. I

R*

wondered to see the good man so much moved in his philo-
sophy!—but he quailed before the popular religion; which is
more than law and government, even in a free town. "A pang
is in my heart, says an Oriental poet, because I am disesteemed
by the depraved multitude." Kenneyny was of those that have
lived for the advancement of their people, and are dead before
the time. May his eternal portion be rest and peace!

And seeing the daily darkening and averting of the Waháby
faces, I had a careful outlaw's heart under my bare shirt; though
to none of them had I done anything but good,—and this only
for the name of the young prophet of Galilee and the Christian
tradition! The simpler sort of liberals were bye and bye afraid
to converse with me; and many of my former acquaintance
seemed now to shun, that I should be seen to enter their
friendly houses. And I knew not that this came of the Muttowwa—that (in their Friday sermons) they moved the people
against me! 'It is not reason, said these divines, in a time
when the Sooltàn of Islam is busy in slaughtering the Nasàra,
that any misbelieving Nasràny should be harboured in a faithful town: and they did contrary to their duties who in any
wise favoured him.'—Kenneyny, though timid before the people,
was resolute to save me: he and the good Bessàm were also in
the counsels of Zàmil.—But why, I thought, should I longer
trouble them with my religion? I asked my friends, 'When
would there be any caravan setting forth, that I might depart
with them?' They answered, "Have patience awhile; for
there is none in these days."

A fanatic sometimes threatened me as I returned by the
narrow and lonely ways, near my house: "O kafîr! if it please
the Lord, thou wilt be slain this afternoon or night, or else to-
morrow's day. Ha! son of mischief, how long dost thou refuse
the religion of Islam? We gave thee indeed a time to repent,
with long sufferance and kindness!—now die in thy blind way.
for the Moslemîn are weary of thee. Except thou say the testimony, thou wilt be slain to-day: thou gettest no more grace,
for many have determined to kill thee." Such deadly kind of
arguments were become as they say familiar evils, in this long
tribulation of Arabian travels; yet I came no more home twice
by the same way, in the still (prayer and coffee) hours of the
day or evening; and feeling any presentiment I went secretly
armed: also when I returned (from friends' houses) by night I
folded the Arab cloak about my left arm; and confided, that
as I had lived to the second year a threatened man, I should
yet live and finally escape them. * * *

CHAPTER X

THE CHRISTIAN STRANGER DRIVEN FROM ANEYZA; AND RECALLED

A PLEASANT afternoon resort to me out of the town was Yahŷa's walled homestead. If I knocked there, and any were within, I found a ready welcome; and the sons of the old patriot sat down to make coffee. Sometimes they invited me out to sup; and then, rather than return late in the stagnant heat, I have remained to slumber under a palm-stem, in their orchard; where a carpet was spread for me and I might rest in the peace of God, as in the booths of the Aarab. One evening I walked abroad with them, as they went to say their prayers on the pure Nefûd sand. By their well Hâmed showed me a peppermint plant, and asked if it were not medicine? he brought the (wild) seed from *es-Seyl* [*Kurn el-Menâzil*], an ancient station of the Nejd cara-vans, in the high country before Mecca (whither I came three months later).—I saw one climb over the clay wall from the next plantation! to meet us: it was the young merchant of the rifle! whom I had not since met with, in any good company in the town. The young gallant's tongue was nimble: and he dis-sembled the voice of an enemy. It was dusk when they rose from prayers; then on a sudden we heard shrieks in the Nefûd! The rest ran to the cry: he lingered a moment, and bade me come to coffee on the morrow, in the town; "Thou seest, he said, what are the incessant alarms of our home in the desert!"

— A company of northern (Annezy) Beduins entered the house at that time, with me; the men were his guests. We sat about the hearth and there came-in a child tender and beautiful as a spring blossom! he was slowly recovering from sickness. *Goom hubb amm-ak!* Go, and kiss thine uncle Khalîl, quoth the young man, who was his elder brother; and the sweet boy—that seemed a flower too delicate for the common blasts of the world, kissed me; and afterward he kissed the Beduins, and all the company: this is the Arabs' home tenderness. I wondered to hear that the tribesmen were fifteen years before of this (Kasîm) *dîra!* They had ridden from their menzil in Syria, by the water *el-Házzel* [a far way about, to turn the northern Nefûd], in a fortnight : and left their tents standing, they told me, by *Tódmor* [Palmyra]! Their coming down was about some traffic in camels.

The small camels of Arabia increase in stature in the northern wilderness. Hàmed es-Sàfy sent his thelûl to pasture one year with these Aarab ; and when she was brought in again, he hardly knew her, what for her bulk, and what for the shaggy thickness of her wool. This Annezy tribe, when yet in Kasîm, were very rich in cattle ; for some of the sheykhs had been owners of " a thousand camels " : until there came year after year, upon all the country, many rainless years. Then the desert bushes (patient of the yearly drought) were dried up and blackened, the Nomads' great cattle perished very fast ; and a thelûl of the best blood might be purchased for two reals.—These Aarab forsook the country, and journeying to the north [now full of the tribes and half tribes of Annezy], they occupied a dîrat, among their part friendly and partly hostile kinsmen.

One day when I returned to my lodging, I found that my watch had been stolen ! I left it lying with my medicines. This was a cruel loss, for my fortune was very low ; and by selling the watch I might have had a few reals : suspicion fell upon an infamous neighbour. The town is uncivil in comparison with the desert ! I was but one day in the dokân, and all my vaccination pens were purloined : they were of ivory and had cost ten reals ;—more than I gained (in twice ten months) by the practice of medicine, in Arabia. I thought again upon the Kenneyny's proffer, which I had passed over at that time ; and mused that he had not renewed it ! There are many shrewd haps in Arabia ; and even the daily piastre spent for bread divided me from the coast: and what would become of my life, if by any evil accident I were parted from the worthy persons who were now my friends?

— Handicraftsmen here in a middle Nejd town (of the sanies' caste), are armourers, tinkers, coppersmiths, goldsmiths ; and the workers in wood are turners of bowls, wooden locksmiths, makers of camel saddle-frames, well-wheel-wrights, and (very unhandsome) carpenters [for they are nearly without tools] ; the stone-workers are hewers, well-steyners and sinkers, besides marble-wrights, makers of coffee mortars and the like ; and house-builders and pargeters. We may go on to reckon those that work with the needle, seamsters and seamstresses, embroiderers, sandal makers. The sewimg men and women are, so far as I have known them, of the libertine blood. The gold and silver smiths of Aneyza are excellent artificers in filigrane or thread-work : and certain of them established at Mecca are said to excel all in the sacred town. El-Kenneyny promised that I should see something of this fine Arabian industry; but the waves of their fanatical world soon cast me from him.

The salesmen are clothiers in the sûk, sellers of small wares [in which are raw drugs and camel medicines, sugar-loaves, spices, Syrian soap from Medina, coffee of the Mecca Caravans], and sellers of victual. In the outlying quarters are small general shops—some of them held by women, where are sold onions, eggs, iron nails, salt, (German) matches, girdle-bread [and certain of these poor wives will sell thee a little milk, if they have any]. On Fridays, you shall see veiled women sitting in the mejlis to sell chickens, and milk-skins and girbies that they have tanned and prepared. Ingenuous vocations are husbandry, and camel and horse dealing. All the welfaring families are land owners.—The substantial foreign merchants were fifteen persons.

Hazardry, banquetting, and many running sores and hideous sinks of our great towns are unknown to them. The Arabs, not less frugal than Spartans, are happy in the Epicurean moderation of their religion. Aneyza is a welfaring civil town more than other in Nomadic Arabia : in her B. Temîm citizens, is a spirit of industry, with a good plain understanding—howbeit somewhat soured by the rheum of the Waháby religion.

Seeing that few any more chided the children that cried after me in the street, I thought it an evil sign ; but the Kenneyny had not warned me, and Zâmil was my friend : the days were toward the end of May. One of these forenoons, when I returned to my house, I saw filth cast before the threshold ; and some knavish children had flung stones as I passed by the lonely street. Whilst I sat within, the little knaves came to batter the door; there was a babel of their cries : the boldest climbed by the side walls to the house terrace ; and hurled down stones and clay bricks by the stair head. In this uproar, I heard a skritching of fanatical women, "Yâ Nasrâny ! thou shalt be dead!—they are in the way that will do it!" I sat on an hour whilst the hurly-burly lasted : my door held, and for all their hooting, the knaves had no courage to come down where they must meet with the kafir. At this hour the respectable citizens were reposing at home, or drinking coffee in their friends' houses ; and it was a desolate quarter where I lodged. At length the siege was raised ; for some persons went by who returned from the coffee companies; and finding this ado about Khalîl's door, they drove away the truants,—with those extreme curses which are always ready in the mouths of Arabs.

Later, when I would go again into the town, the lads ran together, with hue and cry : they waylaid the Nasrâny at the corners, and cast stones from the backward; but if the kafir turned, the troop fled back hastily. I saw one coming—a burly man of the people, who was a patient of mine; and called to him, to drive the children away.—" Complain to Zâmil! " muttered the ungracious churl; who to save himself from the stones, shrank through an open door-way and forsook me. We have seen there are none better at stone-casting than the gipsy-like Arabs : their missiles sung about my head, as I walked forward, till I came where the lonely street gave upon the Boreyda road near the Gá : some citizens passed by. The next moment a heavy bat, hurled by some robust arm, flew by my face. Those townsfolk stayed, and cried " ho! "—for the stones fell beyond them; and one, a manly young man, shouted, " What is this, eyyâl ? akhs ! God give you confusion ;—there was a stone, that had Khalîl turned might have slain him, a guest in the town, and under the countenance of the sheykhs and Zâmil."—No one thinks of calling them cowards.

I found the negro Aly, and persuaded him to return with me ; and clear the lonely by-streets about my lodging. And this he did, chasing the eyyâl; and when his blood was warmed, fetching blows with his stick, which in their nimbleness of flies lighted oftener upon the walls. Some neighbours accused the fanatical hareem, and Aly, showing his negro teeth, ran on the hags to have beaten them; but they pitifully entreated, and promised for themselves. Yet holding his stick over one of these, ' Wellah, he cries, the tongue of her, at the word of Zâmil, should be plucked up by the roots!' After this Aly said, " All will now be peace, Khalîl! " And I took the way to the Mejlis ; to drink coffee at Bessàm's house.

Kenneyny was there : they sat at the hearth, though the stagnant air was sultry,—but the Arabians think they taste some refreshment when they rise from the summer fire. Because I found in these friends a cheerfulness of heart, which is the life of man—and that is so short!—I did not reveal to them my trouble, which would have made them look sad. I trusted that these hubbubs would not be renewed in the town : so bye and bye wishing them God's speed, I rose to depart. They have afterward blamed me for sparing to speak, when they might have had recourse immediately to Zâmil.—In returning I found the streets again beset nigh my house ; and that the eyyâl had armed

themselves with brickbats and staves. So I went down to the
sûk, to speak with my neighbour Rasheyd, Zâmil's officer.—
I saw in Rasheyd's shop some old shivers of Ibrahîm Pasha's
bombshells ; which are now used in poor households for mortars,
to bray-in their salt, pepper, and the like. Rasheyd said, 'that
Zâmil had heard of the children's rioting in the town. He had
sent also for the hags, and threatened them ; and Aly had beaten
some of the lads : now there would be quietness, and I might go
home ';—but I thought it was not so. I returned through the
bazaar with the *deyik es-sûdr*—for what heart is not straitened,
being made an outlaw of the humanity about him? were it
even of the lowest savages !—as I marked how many in the
shops and in the way now openly murmured when they saw
me pass. Amongst the hard faces which went by me was Aly,
the executive Emir, bearing his sword ; and Abdullah the
grudging son of Zâmil, who likewise (as a grown child of the
Emir's house) carries a sword in the streets. Then Sheykh
Nâsir came sternly stalking by me, without regard or salutation !—but welcome all the experience of human life. The sun
was set, and the streets were empty, when I came again to
the door of my desolate house ; where weary and fasting, in this
trouble, I lay down and slept immediately.

I thought I had slumbered an hour, when the negro voice
of Aly awakened me ! crying at the gate, " Khalîl !—Khalîl !
the Emir bids thee open." I went to undo for him, and looked
out. It was dark night ; but I perceived, by the shuffling feet
and murmur of voices, that there were many persons. *Aly :*
" The Emir calls thee ; he sits yonder (in the street) ! " I
went, and sat down beside him : could Zâmil, I mused, be
come at these hours ! then hearing his voice, which resembled
Zâmil's, I knew it was another. " Whither, said the voice,
would'st thou go,—to Zílfy ? "—" I am going shortly in the
company of Abdullah el-Bessàm's son to Jidda." " No, no !
and Jidda (he said, brutally laughing) is very far off : but where
wilt thou go this night ? "—" Aly, what sheykh is this ? "—" It
is Aly the Emir." Then a light was brought : I saw his face
which, with a Waháby brutishness, resembled Zâmil's ; and
with him were some of his ruffian ministers.—" Emir Aly, Ullah
lead thy parents into paradise ! Thou knowest that I am sick ;
and I have certain debts for medicines here in the town ; and
to-day I have tasted nothing. If I have deserved well of some
of you, let me rest here until the morning ; and then send
me away in peace."—" Nay, thy camel is ready at the corner
of the street ; and this is thy cameleer : up ! have out thy
things, and that quickly. Ho ! some of you, go in with Khalîl,

to hasten him."—"And whither will ye send me, so suddenly? and I have no money!"—"Ha-ha! what is that to us, I say come off" : as I regarded him fixedly, the villain struck me with his fist in the face.—If the angry instinct betray me, the rest (I thought) would fall with their weapons upon the Nasrâny :— Aly had pulled his sword from the sheath to the half. "This, I said to him, you may put up again ; what need of violence ?"

Rasheyd, Zâmil's officer, whose house joined to mine from the backward—though by the doors it was a street about, had heard a rumour ; and he came round to visit me. Glad I was to see him enter, with the sword, which he wore for Zâmil. I enquired, of him, if Aly's commandment were good ? for I could not think that my friends among the chief citizens were consenting to it ; and that the philosophical Zâmil would send by night to put me out of the town ! When I told Rasheyd that the Wahâby Aly had struck me ; he said to me apart, "Do not provoke him, only make haste, and doubtless this word is from Zâmil : for Aly would not be come of himself to compel thee." Emir Aly called from without, "Tell Khalîl to hasten ! is he not ready ?" Then he came in himself ; and Rasheyd helped me to lift the things into the bags, for I was feeble. "Whither, he said to the Emir Aly, art thou sending Khalîl ?" "To Khubbera."—"El-Helàlîeh were better, or er-Russ ; for these lie in the path of caravans."—"He goes to Khubbera." "Since, I said, you drive me away, you will pay the cameleer ; for I have little money." Emir Aly : "Pay the man his hire and make haste ; give him three reals, Khalîl."—Rasheyd : "Half a real is the hire to Khubbera : make it less, Emir Aly."—"Then be it two reals, I shall pay the other myself."—"But tell me, are there none the better for my medicines in your town ?"—"We wish for no medicines."—"Have I not done well and honestly in Aneyza ? answer me, upon your conscience." Emir Aly : "Well, thou hast."—"Then what dealing is this ?" But he cried, "Art thou ready ? now mount !" In the meanwhile, his ruffian ministers had stolen my sandals (left without the chamber door) ; and the honest negro Aly cried out for me, accusing them of the theft, "O ye, give Khalîl his sandals again !" I spoke to the brutal Emir ; who answered, "There are no sandals : " and over this new mishap of the Nasrâny [it is no small suffering to go barefoot on the desert soil glowing in the sun] he laughed apace. "Now, art thou ready ? he cries, mount then, mount ! but first pay the man his hire."—After this, I had not five reals left ; my watch was stolen : and I was in the midst of Arabia.

Rasheyd departed : the things were brought out and laid upon the couching camel ; and I mounted. The Emir Aly with his crew followed me as far as the Mejlis. "Tell me (I said to him), to whom shall I go at Khubbera?"—"To the Emir, and remember his name is Abdullah el-Aly."—"Well, give me a letter for him."—"I will give thee none." I heard Aly talking in a low voice with the cameleer behind me;—words (of an adversary), which doubtless boded me no good, or he had spoken openly : when I called to him again, he was gone home. The negro Aly, my old host, was yet with me ; he would see me friendly to the town's end.—But where, I mused, were now my friends ? The negro said, that Zâmil gave the word for my departure at these hours, to avoid any further tumult in the town ; also the night passage were safer, in the desert. Perhaps the day's hubbub had been magnified to Zâmil ; they themselves are always ready !

Aly told me, that a letter from the Muttowwa of Boreyda had been lately brought to Zâmil and the sheykhs of Aneyza ; *exhorting them, in the name of the common faith, to send away the Nasrâny !*—"Is this driver to trust ? and are they good people at Khubbera ? " Aly answered with ayes, and added, " Write back to me ; and it is not far : you will be there about dawn, and in all this, believe me Khalîl, I am sorry for thy sake." He promised to go himself early to Kenneyny, with a request from me, to send ' those few reals on account of medicines ' : but he went not (as I afterward learned) ; for the negro had been bred among Arabs, whose promises are but words in the air, and forged to serve themselves at the moment. —" Let this cameleer swear to keep faith with me." *Aly* : Ay, come here thou Hásan ! and swear thus and thus." Hásan swore all that he would ; and at the town walls the negro departed. There we passed forth to the dark Nefûd ; and a cool night air met us breathing from the open sand wilderness, which a little revived me to ride : we were now in the beginning of the stagnant summer heat of the lower Rummah country.

After an hour's riding we went by a forsaken orchard and ruined buildings,—there are many such outlying homesteads. The night was dim and overcast so that we could not see ground under the camel's tread. We rode in a hollow way of the Nefûd ; but lost it after some miles. " It is well, said Hásan ; for so we shall be in less danger of any lurking Beduins." We descended at the right hand, and rode on by a firmer plain-ground—the Wady er-Rummah ; and there I saw plashes of ponded water, which remained from the last days' showers at Aneyza. The early summer in Kasîm enters with sweet April showers : the season was already sultry, with heavy skies, from which some days there fell light rain ; and they looked that this weather should continue till June. Last year, I had seen, in the khála, a hundred leagues to the westward, only barren heat and drought at this season ; and (some afternoons) dust-driving gusts and winds.

We felt our camel tread again upon the deep Nefûd ; and riding on with a little starlight above us, to the middle night we went by a grove of their bushy fuel-tree, *ghrotha*. The excellence of this firewood, which is of tamarisk kind, has been vaunted—my friends told me, by some of their (elder) poets ; " ardent, and enduring fire (they say,) as the burning *ghrotha :* " and, according to sheykh Nâsir, " a covered fire of this timber may last months long, slowly burning : which has been oft proved in their time ; for Aneyza caravans returning over the deserts have found embers of their former fires remaining as much as thirty days afterward." The sere wood glows with a clear red flame ; and a brand will burn as a torch : they prefer it to the sammara fuel,—-that we have seen in so much estimation at Kheybar.

Hásan my back-rider, was of the woodman's trade. He mounted from his cottage in the night time ; at dawn he came to the trees, and broke sere boughs, and loaded ; and could be at home again in Aneyza by the half-afternoon. He was partner in the wooden beast under us—an unbroken dromedary, with Zâmil, who had advanced half the price, fifteen reals. Small were his gains in this painful and perilous industry ; and yet the fellow had been good for nothing else. I asked him wherefore he took of me for this night's journey as much as he gained, doing the like, in eight or nine days ? ' The Nefûd, he answered, was now full of unfriendly Aarab, and he feared to lose the thelûl ; he would not otherwise have adventured, although he had disobeyed Zâmil.—He told me, this sending me away was determined to-night, in a council of the sheykhs ; he said over their names, and among them were none of my acquaintance. Hásan had heard their talk ; for Zâmil sent early to call him, and bade him be ready to carry Haj Khalîl : the Emir said at first, to *el-Búkeríeh*—for the better opportunity of passing caravans ; but the rest were for Khubbera.

— Hásan dismounted about a thing I had not seen hitherto used in the Arab countries, although night passengers and Beduins are not seldom betrayed by the braying of their thelûls : he whipped his halter about the great sheep-like brute's muzzle ! which cut off further complainings. I was never racked by camel riding as in this night's work, seated on a sharp pack-saddle : the snatching gait of the untaught thelûl, wont only to carry firewood, was through the long hours of darkness, an agony. What could I think of Zâmil ?—was I heretofore so much mistaken in the man ?

Hásan at length drew bridle ; I opened my eyes and saw the new sun looking over the shoulder of the Nefûd : the fellow alighted to say his prayer ; also the light revealed to me the squalid ape-like visage of this companion of the way. We were gone somewhat wide in the night time ; and Hásan, who might be thirty years of age, had not passed the Nefûd to Khubbera since his childhood. From the next dune we saw the heads of the palms of el-Helàlîeh. The sand sea lay in great banks and troughs : over these, we were now riding ; and when the sun was risen from the earth, the clay-built town of Khubbera [or Khóbra] appeared before us, without palms or greenness. The tilled lands are not in sight ; they lie, five miles long, in the bottom of the Wady er-Rummah, and thereof is the name of their *géria*. Amidst the low-built Nefûd town, stands a high clay watch-tower. *Hásan :* " Say not when thou comest to the place, 'I am a Nasrâny,' because they might not receive thee."— " Have they not heard of the Nasrâny, from Aneyza ?"—" It may be ; for at this time there is much carriage of grain to the Bessàms, who are lenders there also."

We saw plashes, a little beside our way. " Let us to the water," quoth Hásan.—" There is water in the girby, and we are come to the inhabited."—" But I am to set thee down there ; for thus the Emir Aly bade me."—Again I saw my life betrayed ! and this would be worse than when the Boreyda cameleer (of the same name) forsook me nigh Aneyza ; for in Aneyza was the hope of Zâmil : Khubbera, a poor town of peasant folk, and ancient colony of Kahtân, is under Boreyda ; the place was yet a mile distant.—" Thou shalt set me down in the midst of the town ; for this thou hast received my reals." Hásan notwithstanding made his beast kneel under us ; I alighted, and he came to unload my bags. I put him away, and taking out a bundle in which was my pistol, the wretch saw the naked steel in my hands !—" Rafîk, if thou art afraid to enter, I shall ride alone to the town gate, and unload ; and so come thou and take thy thelûl again : but make me no resistance, lest I shoot her ; because thou betrayest my life." " I carry this romh, answered the javel, to help me against any who would take my thelûl."—I went to unmuzzle the brute ; that with the halter in my hand I might lead her to Khubbera.

A man of the town was at some store-houses not far off ; he had marked our contention, and came running : " Oh ! what is it? (he asked); peace be with you." I told him the matter, and so did Hásan, who said no word of my being a Nasrâny: nor had the other seen me armed. The townsman gave it that the stranger had reason; so we mounted and rode to the walls. But the untrained thelûl refused to pass the gates: alighting therefore we shackled her legs with a cord, and left her; and I compelled Hásan to take my bags upon his shoulders, and carry them in before me.—So we came to the wide public place; and he cast them down there and would have forsaken me; but I would not suffer it. Some townspeople who came to us ruled, That I had right, and Hásan must bear the things to the kahwat of the emir.

I heard said behind me, "It is some stranger;" and as so many of these townspeople are cameleers and almost yearly pilgrims to the holy places, they have seen many strangers.— We entered the coffee hall; where an old blind man was sitting alone—Aly, father of the Emir; who rising as he heard this concourse, and feeling by the walls, went about to prepare coffee. The men that entered after me sat down each one after his age and condition, under the walls, on three sides of their small coffee-chamber. Not much after them there came in the Emir himself, who returned from the fields a well-disposed and manly fellah. They sent out to call my rafîk to coffee; but Hásan having put down my things was stolen out of their gate again. The company sat silent, till the coffee should be ready; and when some of them would have questioned me the rest answered, "But not yet." Certain of the young men already laid their heads together, and looking up between their whispers they gazed upon me. I saw they were bye and bye persuaded, that I could be none other than that stranger who had passed by Boreyda—the wandering Nasrâny.

Driven thus from Aneyza, I was in great weariness; and being here without money in the midst of Arabia, I mused of the Kenneyny, and the Bessàm, so lately my good friends!— Could they have forsaken me? Would Kenneyny not send me money? and how long would this people suffer me to continue amongst them? Which of them would carry me any whither, but for payment? and that I must begin to require for my remedies, from all who were not poor: it might suffice me to purchase bread,—lodging I could obtain freely. I perceived by the grave looking of the better sort, and the side glances of the rest, when I told my name, that they all knew me. One asked already, 'Had I not medicines?' but others responded for me, "To-morrow will be time for these enquiries." I heard the emir himself say under his breath, 'they would send me to the Helâlîeh, or the *Bükerîeh*.'—Their coffee was of the worst: my Khubbera hosts seemed to be poor householders. When the coffee-server had poured out a second time the company rose to depart.

Only old Aly remained. He crept over where I was, and let himself down on his hands beside the hakîm; and gazing with his squalid eyeballs enquired, if with some medicine I could not help his sight? I saw that the eyes were not perished. "Ay, help my father! said the emir, coming in again; and though it were but a little yet that would be dear to me." I asked the emir, "Am I in safety here?"—"I answer for it; stay some days and cure my father, also we shall see how it will be." Old Aly promised that he would send me freely to er-Russ—few miles distant; from whence I might ride in the next (Mecca) samn kâfily, to Jidda. The men of er-Russ [pronounce *ér-Russ*] are nearly all caravaners. I enquired when the caravan would set forth? "It may be some time yet; but we will ascertain for thee."—"I have not fully five reals [20s.] and these bags; may that suffice?"—"Ay, responded the old man, I think we may find some one to mount thee for that money."

Whilst we were speaking, there came in, with bully voices and a clanking of swords and long guns, some strangers; who were thelûl troopers of the Boreyda Prince's band, and such as we have seen the rajajîl at Hâyil. The honest swaggerers had ridden in the night time; the desert being now full of thieves. They leaned up matchlocks to the wall, hanged their swords on the tenters, and sat down before the hearth with ruffling smiles; and they saluted me also: but I saw these rude men with apprehension; lest they should have a commission from Hásan to molest me: after coffee they mounted to an upper room to sleep. And on the morrow I was easy to hear that the riders had departed very early, for er-Russ: these messengers of Weled Mahanna were riding round to the oases in the principality [of Boreyda], to summon the village sheykhs to a common council.

Old Aly gave me an empty house next him, for my lodging, and had my bags carried thither. At noon the blind sire led me himself, upon his clay stairs, to an upper room; where I found a slender repast prepared for me, dates and girdle-bread and water. He had been emir, or we might say mayor of Khubbera under Boreyda, until his blindness; when his son succeeded him, a man now of the middle age; of whom the old man spoke to all as '*the emir*'. The ancient had taken to himself a young wife of late; and when strange man-folk were not there, she sat always beside her old lord; and seemed to love him well. They had between them a little son; but the child was blear-eyed, with a running ophthalmia. The grey-beard bade the young mother sit down with the child, by the hâkim; and cherishing their little son, with his aged hands, he drew him before me.

Old Aly began to discourse with me of religion; enforcing himself to be tolerant the while. He joyed devoutly to hear, there was an holy rule of men's lives also in the Christians' religion.—"Eigh me! ye be good people, but not in the right way, that is pleasing unto Ullah; and therefore it profiteth nothing. The Lord give thee to know the truth and say, There is none God but the Lord, and Mohammed is the apostle of the Lord."—A deaf man entering suddenly, troubled our talk; demanding ere he sat down, would I cure his malady? "And what, I asked, wouldst thou give the hakîm, if he show thee a remedy?" The fellow answered, "Nothing surely! Wouldst thou be paid for only telling a man,—wilt thou not tell me? eigh!" and his wrath began to rise. *Aly* · "Young man, such be not words to speak to the hakîm, who will help thee if he may."—"Well tell him, I said, to make a horn of paper, wide in the mouth, and lay the little end to his ear; and he shall hear the better."—The fellow, who deemed the Nasrâny put a scorn upon him, bore my saying hardly. "Nay, if the thing be rightly considered, quoth the ancient sheykh, it may seem reasonable; only do thou after Khalîl's bidding." But the deaf would sit no longer. 'The cursed Nasrâny, whose life (he murmured) was in their hand, to deride him thus!' and with baleful looks he flung out from us. —A young man, who had come in, lamented to me the natural misery of his country; "where there is nothing, ᵼaid he, besides the incessant hugger-mugger of the suânies. I have a brother settled, and welfaring in the north; and if I knew where I might likewise speed, wellah I would go thither, and return no more."—"And leave thy old father and mother to die! and forget thine acquaintance?"—"But my friends would be of them among whom I sojourned."—Such is the mind of many of the inhabitants of el-Kasîm.

On the morrow there arrived two young men riding upon a thelûl, to seek cures of the mudowwy; the one for his eyes, and his rafîk for an old visceral malady. They were from the farthest palm and corn lands of Khubbera,—loam bottoms or rauthas in the Wady; that last to the midway betwixt this town and er-Russ. When they heard, that they must lay down the price of the medicines, elevenpence—which is a field labourer's wages (besides his rations) for three days—they chose to suffer their diseases for other years, whilst it pleased Ullah, rather than adventure the silver.—"Nay, but cure us, and we will pay at the full : if thy remedies help us, will not the sick come riding to thee from all the villages?" But I would not hear; and, with many reproaches, the sorry young men mounted, to ride home again.

I found my medical credit high at Khubbera : for one of my Aneyza patients was their townswoman : the Nasrány's eye-washes somewhat cleared her sight; and the fame had passed the Nefûd. I was soon called away to visit a sick person. At the kahwa door, the boy who led the hakîm bade me stand— contrary to the custom of Arabian hospitality—whilst he went in to tell them. I heard the child say, "The kafir is come;" and their response in like sort,—I entered then! and sat down among them; and blamed that householder's uncivil usage. Because I had reason, the peasants were speechless and out of countenance; the coffee maker hastened to pour me out a cup : and so rising I left them.—I wondered that all Khubbera should be so silent! I saw none in the streets; I heard no cheerful knelling of coffee-pestles in their clay town. In these days the most were absent, for the treading out and winnowing of their corn : the harvest was light, because their corn had been beaten by hail little before the ear ripened. The house-building of Khubbera is rude; and the place is not unlike certain village-towns of Upland Syria. I passed through long uncheerful streets of half-ruinous clay cottages; but besides some butchers' stalls and a smith's forge, I saw no shop or merchandise in the town. Their mosque stands by the mejlis, and is of low clay building : thereby I saw a brackish well—only a fathom deep, where they wash before prayers. They have no water to drink in the town, for the ground is brackish; but the housewives must go out to fill their girbies from wells at some distance. The watch-tower of Khubbera, built of clay—great beneath as a small chamber, and spiring upward to the height of the gallery, is in the midst of the acre-great Mejlis : and therein [as in all Kasîm towns] is held the Friday's market; when the nomads, coming also to pray at noon in the mesjid, bring camels and small cattle and samn.

— It was near mid-day : and seeing but three persons sitting on a clay bench in the vast forsaken Mejlis, I went to sit down by them. One of these had the aspect of, a man of the stone age; a wild grinning seized by moments upon his half human visage. I questioned the others who sat on yawning and in-different : and they began to ask me of my religion. The elf-

like fellow exclaimed: "Now were a knife brought and put to
the wezand of him!—which billah may be done lawfully, for the
Muttowwa says so; and the Nasrâny not confessing, *la ilah ill'
Ullah!* pronounce, *Bismillah er-rahman, er-rahîm* (in the name
of God the pitiful, the god of the bowels of mercies), and cut
his gullet; and *gug-gug-gug!*—this kafir's blood would gurgle
like the blood of a sheep or camel when we carve her halse.
I will run now and borrow a knife."—"Nay, said they, thou
mayest not do so." I asked them, "Is not he a Beduwy?—
but what think ye, my friends? says the wild wretch well or
no?"—"We cannot tell: THIS IS THE RELIGION! Khalîl; but we
would have no violence,—yes, he is a Beduwy."—"What is thy
tribe, O thou sick of a devil?"—"I Harby."—"Thou liest! the
Harb are honest folk: but I think, my friends, this is an *Aûfy*."
—"Yes, God's life! I am of Aûf; how knowest thou this, Nas-
rây?—does he know everything!"—"Then my friends, this
fellow is a cut-purse, and cut-throat of the pilgrims that go
down to Mecca, and accursed of God and mankind!" The
rest answered, "Wellah they are cursed, and thou sayest well:
we have a religion, Khalîl, and so have ye." But the Aûfy
laughed to the ears, ha-ha-hî-hî-hî! for joy that he and his
people were men to be accounted-of in the world. "Ay billah,
quoth he, we be the Haj-cutters."—They laughed now upon
him; and so I left them.

When I complained of the Aûfy's words to the emir, he
said—wagging the stick in his hand, "Fear nothing! and in
the meanwhile cure the old man my father: wellah, if any
speak a word against thee, I will beat him until there is no
breath left in him!—The people said of the emir, "He is poor
and indebted:" much of their harvest even here is grown for
the Bessàm; who take of them ten or twelve in the hundred:
if paid in kind they are to receive for every real of usury one-
third of a real more. After this I saw not the emir; and his
son told me he was gone to el-Búkerîeh, to ride from thence in
the night-time to Boreyda: they journey in the dark, for fear
of the Beduw. Last year Abdullah the emir and fifteen men of
Khubbera returning from the Haj, and having only few miles
to ride home, after they left the Boreyda caravan, had been
stripped and robbed of their thelûls, by hostile Beduw.

The townspeople that I saw at Khubbera was fellahîn-like
bodies, ungracious, inhospitable. No man called the stranger
to coffee; I had not seen the like in Arabia, even among the
black people at Kheybar: in this place may be nigh 600 houses.
Many of their men were formerly Ageylies at Medina; but the
Turkish military pay being very long withheld of late, they

had forsaken the service. Khubbera is a site without any natural amenity, enclosed by a clay wall: and strange it is, in this desert town, to hear no creaking and shrilling of suânies! —The emir and his old father were the best of all that I met with in this place.

— 'The Kenneyny, I thought, will not forsake me!' but now a second day had passed. I saw the third sun rise to the hot noon; and then, with a weary heart, I went to repose in my lodging. Bye and bye I heard some knocking at the door, and young men's voices without,—" Open, Khalîl! Zâmil has sent for thee." I drew the bolt; and saw the cameleer Hásan standing by the threshold!—" Hast thou brought me a letter?" —'I have brought none." I led him in to Aly, that the fatherly man might hear his tale.—'Zâmil recalled me, to send me by the kâfily which was to set out for Jîdda.'—But we knew that the convoy could not be ready for certain weeks! and I asked Aly, should I mount with no more to assure me than the words of this Hásan?—it had been better for the old man that I continued here awhile, for his eyes' sake. "Well, said he, go Khalîl, and doubt not at all; go in peace!" I asked for vials, and made eye-washes to leave with him: the old sire was pleased with this grateful remembrance.

Some young men took up my bags of good will, and bore them through the streets; and many came along with us to the gates, where Hásan had left his thelûl.—When we were riding forth I saluted the bystanders: but all those Kahtanites were not of like good mind; for some recommended me to *Iblîs*, the most were silent; and mocking children answered my parting word with *maa samawwy!*—instead of the goodly Semitic valediction *maa salaamy*, ' go in peace '.

We came riding four miles over the Nefûd, to the Helâlîeh: the solitary mountain Sàg, which has the shape of a pine-apple, appeared upon our left hand, many miles distant. The rock, say the Arabs, is hard and ruddy-black :—it might be a plutonic outlyer in the border of the sand country. As we approached, I saw other palms, and a high watch-tower, two miles beyond ; of another oasis, el-Búkerîeh : between these settlements is a place where they find " men's bones " mingled with cinders, and the bones of small cattle ; which the people ascribe to the B. Helàl—of whom is the name of the village, where we now arrived. El-Búkerîeh is a station of the cameleers ; and they are traffickers to the Beduw. Some of them are well enriched ; and they traded at first with money borrowed of the Bessàm.

The villagers of Helàlîeh and of Búkerîeh (ancient Sbeya

colonies) would sooner be under Zâmil and Aneyza than subject to Hásan Weled Mahanna—whom they call *jabbár:* they pay tax to Boreyda; five in the hundred. Of these five, one-fourth is for the emir or mayor of the place; an half of the rest was formerly Ibn Saûd's, and the remnant was the revenue of the princes of Boreyda; but now Weled Mahanna detains the former portion of the Wahâby.—Their corn is valued by measure, the dates are sold by weight. At the Helàlîeh are many old wells " of the B. Helàl ". Some miles to the westward is *Tholfa,* an ancient village, and near the midway is an hamlet *Shehîeh:* at half a journey from Bûkerîeh upon that side are certain winter granges and plantations of Boreyda.—One cried to us, as we entered the town, " Who is he with thee, Hásan ? " —" A Nasrâny dog, answered the fellow [the only Nejd Arabian who ever put upon me such an injury], or I cannot tell what; and I am carrying him again to Aneyza as Zâmil bids me."— Such an unlucky malignant wight as my cameleer, whose strange looking discomforts the soul, is called in this country *mìshûr,* bewitched, enchanted. When I complained of the elf here in his native village—though from a child he had dwelt at Aneyza, they answered me, " Ay, he is mîshûr, *mesquin !* "— We rode through the streets and alighted where some friendly villagers showed us the kahwa.

Many persons entered with us ; and they left the highest place for the guest, which is next the coffee maker. A well-clad and smiling host came soon, with the coffee berries in his hand : but bye and bye he said a word to me as bitter as his coffee, " How farest thou ? O *adu* (thou enemy of) Ullah ! " Adu is a book word ; but he was a koran reader.—" I am too simple to be troubled with so wise a man : is every camel too a Moslem ? " " A camel, responded the village pedant, is a creature of Ullah, irrational ; and cannot be of any religion."— " Then account me a camel: also I pray Ullah send thee some of the aches that are in my weary bones ; and now leave finding fault in me, who am here to drink coffee." The rest laughed, and that is peace and assurance with the Arabs: they answered him, " He says reason ; and trouble not Khalîl, who is over weary."—But the koran reader would move some great divinity matter· " Wherefore dost thou not forsake, Nasrâny, your impure religion (*dîn négis*) ; and turn to the right religion of the Moslemîn ? and confess with us, ' There is an only God and Mohammed is his Sent One ' ?—And, with violent looks, he cries, I say to thee abjure ! Khalîl." I thought it time to appease him the beginning of Mawmetry was an Arabian faction, and so they ever think it a sword matter.—" O What-

is-thy-name, have done thou; for I am of too little understanding to attain to your high things." It tickled the village
reader's ears to hear himself extolled by a son of the ingenious
Nasâra. "No more, I added: the Same who cast me upon
these coasts, may esteem an upright life to be a prayer before
Him. As for me, was I not born a Christian, by the providence
of Ullah? and His providence is good; therefore it was good
for me to be born a Christian! and good for me to be born, it is
good for me to live a Christian; and when it shall please God,
to die a Christian: and if I were afraid to die, I were not a
Christian!" Some exclaimed, "He has well spoken, and none
ought to molest him." The pedant murmured, "But if Khalîl
knew letters—so much as to read his own scriptures, he would
have discerned the truth, that Mohammed is Seal of the prophets
and the apostle of Ullah."

Even here my remedies purchased me some relief; for a
patient led me away to breakfast. We returned to the kahwa;
and about mid-afternoon the village company, which sat thick
as flies in that small sultry chamber, went forth to sit in the
street dust, under the shadowing wall of the Mejlis. They bade
me be of good comfort, and no evil should betide me: for here,
said they, the Arabs are *muhâkimîn*, 'under rulers.' [The
Arabs love not to be in all things so straitly governed. I remember a young man of el-Wéshm, of honest parentage, who
complained; that in his Province a man durst not kill one outright, though he found him lying with his sister, nor the adul-
terer in his house: for not only must he make satisfaction, to
the kindred of the slain; but he would be punished by the laws!]
Some led me through the orchards; and I saw that their wells
were deep as those of Aneyza.

In the evening twilight I rode forth with Hásan. The moon
was rising, and he halted at an outlying plantation; where
there waited two Meteyr Beduins, that would go in company
with us,—driving a few sheep to their menzil near Aneyza. The
mother of Hásan and some of her kindred brought him on the
way. They spoke under their breath; and I heard the hag bid
her son 'deal with the Nasrâny as he found good,—so that he
delivered himself!'—Glad I was of the Beduin fellowship; and
to hear the desert men's voices, as they climbed over the wall,
saying they were our rafîks.—We journeyed in the moon-light;
and I sat crosswise, so that I might watch the shadow of Hásan's
lance, whom I made to ride upon his feet. I saw by the stars
that our course lay eastward over the Nefûd billows. After two
hours we descended into the Wady er-Rummah.—The Beduin
companions were of the mixed Aarab, which remain in this dîra

since the departure of Annezy. They dwell here together under the protection of Zâmil; and are called *Aarab Zâmil*. They are poor tribe's-folk of Meteyr and of Ateyba, that wanting camels have become keepers of small cattle in the Nefûd, where are wells everywhere and not deep: they live at the service of the oases, and earn a little money as herdsmen of the suâny and caravan camels. Menzils of these mixed Arabs remove together: they have no enemies; and they bring their causes to Zâmil.

An hour after middle night we halted in a deep place among the dunes; and being now past the danger of the way they would slumber here awhile.—Rising before dawn, we rode on by the Wady er-Rummah; which lay before us like a long plain of firm sand, with much greenness of desert bushes and growth of ghróttha: and now I saw this tree, in the daylight, to be a low weeping kind of tamarisk. The sprays are bitter, rather than—as the common desert tamarisk—saline: the Kasîm camels wreathe to it their long necks to crop mouthfuls in the march.—The fiery sun soon rose on that Nefûd horizon: the Beduins departed from us towards their menzil; and we rode forth in the Wady bottom, which seemed to be nearly an hour over. We could not be many miles from Aneyza:—I heard then a silver descant of some little bird, that flitting over the desert bushes, warbled a musical note which ascended on the gamut! and this so sweetly, that I could not have dreamed the like.

I sought to learn, from my brutish companion, what were Zâmil's will concerning me. I asked, whither he carried me? Hásan answered, ' To the town; ' and I should lodge in that great house upon the Gá,—the house of Rasheyd, a northern merchant, now absent from Aneyza. We were already in sight of an outlying corn ground; and Hásan held over towards a plantation of palms, which appeared beyond. When we came thither, he dismounted to speak with some whose voices we heard in the coffee-bower,—a shed of sticks and palm branches, which is also the husbandmen's shelter.—Hásan told them, that Zâmil's word had been to set me down here! Those of the garden had not heard of it: after some talk, one Ibrahîm, the chief of them, invited me to dismount and come in; and he would ride himself with Hásan to the town, to speak with Zâmil. They told me that Aneyza might be seen from the next dunes. This outlying property of palms lies in a bay of the Wady, at little distance (southward) from el-'Eyarîeh.

They were busy here to tread out the grain: the threshing-floor was but a plot of the common ground; and I saw a row of twelve oxen driven round about a stake, whereto the inmost beast is bound.· The ears of corn can be little better than bruised from the stalks thus, and the grain is afterward beaten out by women of the household with wooden mallets. Their winnowing is but the casting up this bruised straw to the air by handfuls. A great sack of the ears and grain was loaded upon a thelûl, and sent home many times in the day, to Rasheyd's town house.

The high-walled court or kasr of this ground was a four-square building in clay, sixty paces upon a side, with low corner towers. In the midst is the well of seven fathoms to the rock, steyned with dry masonry, a double camel-yard, and stalling for kine and asses; chambers of a slave woman caretaker and her son, rude store-houses in the towers, and the well-driver's beyt. The cost of this castle-like clay yard had been a hundred reals, for labour; and of the well five hundred. An only gateway into this close was barred at nightfall. Such redoubts—impregnable in the weak Arabian warfare, are made in all outlying properties. The farm beasts were driven in at the going down of the sun.

At mid-afternoon I espied two horsemen descending from the Nefûd. It was Kenneyny with es-Sâfy, who came to visit me. —Abdullah told me that neither he nor Bessâm, nor any of the friends, had notice that night of my forced departure from Aneyza. They first heard it in the morning; when Hâmed, who had bidden the hakîm to breakfast, awaited me an hour, and wondered why I did not arrive. As it became known that the Nasrâny had been driven away in the night, the towns-people talked of it in the sûk: many of them blamed the sheykhs. Kenneyny and Bessâm did not learn all the truth till evening; when they went to Zâmil, and enquired, ' Wherefore had he sent me away thus, and without their knowledge ? ' Zâmil answered, 'That such had been the will of the mejlis,' and he could not contradict them. My friends said, ' But if Khalîl should die, would not blame be laid to Aneyza ?—since the Nasrâny had been received into the town. Khalîl was ibn juâd, and it became them to provide for his safe departure.' Bessâm, to whom nothing could be refused, asked Zâmil to recall Khalîl;—' who might, added el-Kenneyny, remain in one of the outlying jeneynies if he could not be received again into the town [because of the Waháby malice], until some kâfily were setting forth.' Zâmil consented, and sent for Hásan ; and bade him ride back to Khubbera, to fetch again Haj Khalîl. My friends made the man mount immediately; and they named to Zâmil these palms of Rasheyd.

Abdullah said that none would molest me here; I might take rest, until he found means for my safe departure: and whither, he asked, would I go?—"To Jidda." He said, 'he should labour to obtain this also for me, from Zâmil; and of what had I present need?'—I enquired should I see him again?— "Perhaps no; thou knowest what is this people's tongue!" Then I requested the good man to advance money upon my bill; a draft-book was in my bags, against the time of my arriving at the coast; and I wrote a cheque for the sum of a few reals. Silver for the Kenneyny in his philosophical hours was *néjis ed-dínya* " world's dross"; nevertheless the merchant now desired Hâmed (my disciple in English) to peruse the ciphers! But that was surely of friendly purpose to instruct me; for with an austere countenance he said further, " Trust not, Khalîl, to any man! not even to me." In his remembrance might be my imprudent custom, to speak always plainly; even in matter of religion. Here, he said, I was in no danger of the crabbed Emir Aly: when I told my friend that the Wahâby mule had struck me, " God, he exclaimed, so smite Aly! "—The bill, for which he sent me on the morrow the just exchange in silver, came to my hands after a year in Europe: it had been paid at Beyrût.—Spanish crowns are the currency of Kasîm: I have asked, how could the foreign merchants carry their fortunes (in silver) over the wilderness? it was answered, " in the strong pilgrimage caravans." * * *

CHAPTER XI

THE KAHTÂN EXPELLED FROM EL-KASÎM

* * * THESE were sultry days ; and in the hours of most heat I commonly found (in our arbour) 97° F., with heavy skies. The wells are of five, four and three fathoms, as they lie lower towards the Wady ; and a furlong beyond, the water is so nigh that young palm-sets in pits should need no watering, after a year or two. The thermometer in the well-water—which in this air seemed cool, showed 87° F. A well sunk at the brim of the Nefûd yields fresh ground-water ; but wells made (lower) in the gá are somewhat brackish. Corn, they say, comes up better in brackish ground ; and green corn yellowing in sweet land may be restored by a timely sprinkling of salt. All the wells reek in the night air : the thermometer and the tongue may discern between well-waters that lie only a few rods asunder : the water is cooler which rises from the sandstone, and that is warmer which is yielded from crevices of the rock.

Of all wells in Aneyza, there is but one of purely sweet water !—the sheykhs send thither to fill their girbies in the low summer season. It is in the possession of a family whose head, Abu Daûd, one of the emigrated Kusmân, lived at Damascus ; where he was now sheykh of the Ageyl, and leader of the rear guard in the Haj caravan. [Abu Daûd told me, he had returned but once, in twenty-five years, for a month, to visit his native place !]—Water from Rasheyd's two wells was raised incessantly by the labour of five nâgas ; and ran down in sandy channels (whereby they sowed water-melons, in little pits, with camel jella) to a small pool, likewise bedded in the loamy sand. These civil Arabians have not learned to burn lime, and build themselves conduits and cisterns. The irrigation pond in Kasîm lies commonly under the dim shadow of an undressed vine ; which planted in the sand by water will shoot upon a trellis to a green wood. We have seen vines a covert for well-walks at Teyma. The camels labour here under an awning of palm branches.

The driving at the wells, which began in the early hours after midnight, lasts till near nine, when the day's heat is already great.—At the sun-rising you may see women (of the well-driver's family) sit with their baskets in the end of the shelving well walk, to feed the toiling camels : they wrap a handful of vetches in as much dry forage cut in the desert ; and at every turn the nâga receives from her feeder's hands the bundle thrust into her mouth. The well-cattle wrought anew from two in the afternoon, till near seven at evening, when they were fed again. The well-driver, who must break every night his natural rest, and his wife to cut trefoil and feed the camels, received three reals and a piastre—say thirteen shillings, by the month ; and they must buy their own victual. A son drove the by-well, and the boy's sisters fed his pair of camels. They lived leanly with drawn brows and tasting little rest, in a land of idle rest. [Whenever I asked any of these poor souls, How might he endure perpetually ? he has answered the stranger (with a sigh), That he was inured thereto from a child, and—*min Ullah !* the Lord enabled him.]—But the labouring lads in the jeneyny fared not amiss ; they received 4*d.* a day besides their rations : they have less when hired by the month. I saw the young Shuggery, a good and diligent workman, agree to serve Rasheyd six months for nine reals and his rations ; and he asked for a tunic (two-thirds of a real more), which was not denied him. There is no mention in these covenants of harbour ; but where one will lie down on the sand, under the stars of God, there is good night-lodging (the most months of the twelve), in this summer country.

The lads went out to labour from the sunrise . and when later the well-pool is let out, *yurussún el-má*, they distributed the water running down in the channels ; and thus all the pans of the field, and the furrows of the palms are flushed, twice in the day.—Of this word *russ* is the name of the Kasîm oasis er-Russ. The *jet* was flooded twice a week ; and this trefoil, grown to a foot high, may be cut every fifteen days [as at Damascus], —the soil was sand. The eyyâl wrought sheltered in the bower, as we have seen, in the sultry afternoons and heard tales, till vespers. Then one of them cried to prayers ; the rest ran to wash, and commonly they bathed themselves in the well. It was a wonder then to see them not doubt to leap down, one upon the neck of another, from an height of thirty feet ! to the water ; and they plashed and swam sometime in that narrow room : they clambered up again, like lizards, holding by their fingers and toes in the joints of the stone-work. After they had prayed together, the young men laboured abroad again till the sun was setting; when they prayed, and their supper was brought to them, from the town. Supper is the chief meal in Arabia; and here it was a plentiful warm mess of sod wheaten stuff, good for hungry men.

The work-day ended with the sun, the rest is *keyif*: only after a long hour must they say the last prayers. The lads of the garden (without coffee or tobacco) sing the evening time away; or run chasing each other like colts, through the dim desert. On moonlight nights they played to the next palm-yards; and ofttimes all the eyyâl came again with loud singing, and beating the tambûr. The ruder merrymake of the young Arab servants and husbandmen was without villany; and they kept this round for two or three hours: or else all sitting down in a ring together at the kasr gate, the Shuggery entertained his fellows with some new tales of marvellous adventures.

In every oasis, are many date-kinds. The most at Aneyza are the *rótb* or ' moist' (good for plain diet), of the palm which is called the *es-Shúkra*, or Shuggera, of that Wéshm oasis. They have besides a dry kind, both cool and sweet, which is carried as sweetmeat in their caravan journeys. Only the date-palm is planted in Arabia: the *dôm*, or branched nut-palm, is a wilding [in the Hejâz and Tehâma],—in sites of old settlements, where the ground-water is near; and in some low desert valleys. The nut's woody rind (thrice the bigness of a goose's egg) is eaten; and dry it has the taste of ginger-bread.—When later in the year I was in Bombay, I found a young man of Shuggera at the Arab stables: we walked through the suburbs together, and I showed him some cocoa-nut palms,—" Ye have none such, I said, in Nejd ! " " Nay, he responded austerely, not these: there is no *báraka* with them ! "—a word spoken in the (eternal) Semitic meaning, " All is vanity which is not bread."

The fruit-stalks hanged already—with full clusters of green berries—in the crowns of the female palms: the promise was of an abundant harvest, which is mostly seen after the scarcity and destruction of a locust-year. Every cluster, which had in-closed in it a spray of the male blossom, was lapped about with a wisp of dry forage; and this defended the sets from early flights of locusts. The Nejd husbandman is every year a loser by the former and latter locusts, which are bred in the land; besides what clouds of them are drifted over him by the winds from he knows not whither. This year there were few hitherto and weak flights; but sometimes with the smooth wind that follows the sun-rising the flickering *jarâd* drove in upon us: and then the lads, with palm branches of a spear's length, ran hooting in the orchard and brushed them out of the trees and clover. The

s

fluttering insects rising before them with a *whir-r-r!* were borne forth to the Nefûd. The good lads took up the bodies of the slain crying, "They are good and fat;" and ran to the arbour to toast them. If I were there, they invited me to the feast: one morrow, because the hakîm said nay, none any more desired to eat; but they cast out their scorched locusts on the sand, in the sun, where the flies devoured them.—"The jarâd, I said, devour the Beduw, and the Beduw devour the jarâd!"—words which seemed oracles to that simple audience; and Sâlih repeated Khalîl's proverb in the town.

The poor field labourers of Rasheyd's garden were my friends: ere the third day, they had forgiven me my alien religion, saying they thought it might be as good as their own; and they would I might live always with them. Ay, quoth the honest well-driver, "The Nasâra are of a godly religion, only they acknowledge not the Rasûl; for they say, *Mohammed is a Beduwy* [I thought the poor soul shot not wide from the mark,—Mohammedism is Arabism in religion]: there is no other fault in them; and I heard the sheykhs saying this, in the town."— Some days a dull 'bewitched' lad laboured here, whom the rest mocked as *Kahtâny*—another word of reproach among them [as much as *man-eater*], because he was from Khubbera. Other two were not honest, for they rifled my bags in the night time in Rasheyd's kasr: they stole sugar—the good Kenneyny's gift; and so outrageously! that they had made an end of the loaf in few days. A younger son of Rasheyd had a hand in their villany. The lads were soon after dismissed; and we heard they had been beaten by the Emir Aly.

— It was past ten o'clock one of these nights, and dim moonlight, when Ibrahîm and Fáhd were ready with the last load of corn:—then came Ibrahîm and said to me, "We are now going home to stay in the town; and the jeneyny will be forsaken." This was a weary tiding of ungenerous Arabs two hours before midnight when I was about to sleep!—"What shall I do?"— "Go with us; and we will set thee down at the Kenneyny's palm-ground, or at his house."—"His jeneyny is open and not inhabited; and you know that I may not return to the town: Zâmil sent me here."—"Ullah curse both thee and Zâmil! thou goest with us: come! or I will shoot thee with a pistol! [They now laid my things upon an ass.]—Drive on Fáhd!—Come! Khalîl, here are thieves; and we durst not leave thee in the jeneyny alone."—"Why then in Kenneyny's outlying ground?" —"By Ullah! we will forsake thee in the midst of the Nefûd!" —"If you had warned me to-day, I had sent word to Zâmil, and to Kenneyny: now I must remain here—at least till the morning." Then the slave snatched my mantle ; and in that he struck me on the face : he caught up a heavy stone, and drew back to hurl this against my head. I knew the dastardly heart of these wretches,—the most kinds of savage men are not so ignoble !—that his wilful stone-cast might cost me one of my eyes ; and it might cost my life, if I the Nasrâny lifted a hand upon one of the Moslemîn ! Here were no witnesses of age ; and doubtless they had concerted their villany beforehand. Whilst I felt secretly in the bags for my pistol, lest I should see anything worse, I spoke to the lubber Fáhd, ' that he should remember his father's honour.' A younger son of Rasheyd—the sugar-thief, braved about the Nasrâny with injuries ; and, ere I was aware in the dark, Ibrahîm struck me from behind a second time with his fist, upon the face and neck. In this by chance there came to us a young man, from the next plantation. He was a patient of mine ; and hearing how the matter stood, he said to them, " Will ye carry him away by night ? and we know not whither ! Let Khalîl remain here at least till the morning." Ibrahîm, seeing I should now be even with him, sought words to excuse his violence : the slave pretended, that the Nasrâny had snibbed him (a Moslem) saying *Laanat Ullah aleyk*, ' The curse of God be upon thee ! '—And he cried, " Were we here in Egypt, I had slain thee ! "—Haply he would visit upon the Nasrâny the outrages of the Suez Canal !

An Aneyza caravan was now journeying from Bosra ; and in it rode the sire Rasheyd. Sâlih was called away the next forenoon by a Meteyry ; a man wont to ride post for the foreign merchants to the north. But in his last coming down he lost their budget and his own thelûl ; for he was resting a day in the Meteyr menzil, when they were surprised by the murderous ghrazzu of Kahtân. He told us, that the foreriders of the kâfily were come in ; and the caravan—which had lodged last night at *Zilfy*, would arrive at midday. This messenger of good tidings, who had sped from the town, hied by us like a roebuck : I sat breathless under the sultry clouded heaven, and wondered at his light running. Ibrahîm said, " This Beduwy is nimble, because of the camel milk which is yet in his bones ! "—The caravan [of more than 200 camels] was fifteen days out from Bosra ; they had rested every noon-day under awnings.

— The day of the coming again of a great caravan is a day of feasting in the town. The returned-home are visited by friends and acquaintance in their houses ; where an afternoon guest-meal is served. Rasheyd now sat solemnly in that great clay beyt, which he had built for himself and the heirs of his body; where he received also the friendly visitation of Zâmil. He had brought down seventeen loads (three tons nearly) of clothing, from his son at Kuweyt, to sell in Aneyza, for a debt of his— 3000 reals—which he must pay to the heirs of a friend deceased, *el-Káthy*. His old servants in this plantation went hastily to Aneyza to kiss the master's hand: and ere evening portions were sent out to them from his family supper.

I heard the story of Rasheyd from our well-driver. The Arabs covet to have many children; and when his merchandise prospered, this new man bought him wives; and 'had the most years his four women in child at once: and soon after they were delivered he put out the babes to suck, so that his hareem might conceive again: since forty years he wrought thus'.—"Rasheyd's children should be an hundred then, or more! but how many has he?" The poor well driver was somewhat amazed at my putting him to the count; and he answered simply, "But many of the babes die." The sire, by this butcherly husbandry in his good days, was now father of a flock; and, beside his sons, there were numbered to him fifteen daughters.—In his great Aneyza household were more than thirty persons.

The third morrow came Rasheyd himself, riding upon a (Mesopotamian) white ass, from the town, to view his date trees in Nejd. The old multiplier alighted solemnly and ruffling in his holiday attire, a gay yellow gown, and silken kerchief of Bagdad lapped about his pilled skull. He bore in his belt—as a wayfarer come from his long journey—a kiddamîyyah and a horse-pistol; or it might be (since none go armed at home) the old Tom-fool had armed himself because of the Nasrâny! He was a comely person of good stature, and very swarthy: his old eyes were painted. He roamed on his toes in the garden walks, like the hoopoes, to see his palms and his vetches. Rasheyd came after an hour to the arbour, where I sat—he had not yet saluted the kafir; and sitting down, ' Was I (he asked) that Nasrâny?— he had heard of me.' I made the old tradesman some tea; and it did his sorry heart good to heap in the fenjeyn my egg-great morsels of sugar.—I regaled him thus as oft as he came hither; and I heard the old worldling said at home, 'That Khalîl is an honest person; and wellah had made him tea with much sugar.'

He said, to soothe my weariness, 'It would not be long, please Ullah, till I might depart with a kâfily.' Then he put off his gay garments, and went abroad again in his shirt and cotton cap.—He returned to the arbour in the hot noon; and sitting down the old man stripped himself; and having only the tunic upon his knee, he began to purge his butcher's skin from the plague of Egypt accrued in the caravan voyage. Before the half afternoon he wandered again in the garden, and communed with the workmen like a poor man of their sort. Rasheyd looked upon every one of their tools, and he wrought somewhat himself; and began to cleanse the stinking bed of the pool. Coming again thirsty, he went to drink of my girby, which was hanging to the air upon a palm branch; and untying the neck he drank his draught from the mouth, like any poor camel-driver or Beduwy.—The maintenance of this outlying possession cost him yearly 200 reals; the greater part was for camel labour. The fruits were not yet fully so much worth.

No worldly prosperity, nor his much converse abroad, could gentilize Rasheyd's ignoble understanding; he was a Waháby after the straitest Nejd fanaticism. A son of this Come-up-from-the-shambles was, we saw, the Occidental traveller! Another son, he who had been the merchant in Aden, came down with him in the caravan: he opened a shop in the sûk, and began selling those camel-loads of clothing stuffs. The most buyers in the town were now Meteyr tribesmen; and one of those "locusts" was so light-handed, that he filched a mantle of Rasheyd's goods, worth 10s., for which the old man made fare and chided with his sons. That son arrived one day from the town, to ask the hakîm's counsel; he was a vile and deceit-ful person, full of Asiatic fawning promises. 'He would visit Aden again (for my sake); and sail in the same ship with me. He left a wife there, and a little son; he had obtained that his boy was registered a British subject: if I would, he would accompany me to India.'—I sojourned in his father's plantation; and they had not made me coffee.

— 'What, said some one sitting in Rasheyd's hall (in the town), could bring a Nasrâny from the magnific cities of Europa into this poor and barren soil of Nejd?' The old merchant responded, "I know the manners of them! this is a Frenjy, and very likely a poor man who has hired out his wife, to win money against his coming home; for, trust me, they do so all of them."—The tale was whispered by his young sons in the jeneyny: and one afternoon the Shuggery asked me of it before them all, and added, "But I could not believe it." "Such imaginations, I exclaimed, could only harbour in the dunghill heart of a churl; and be uttered by a slave!" He whispered, "Khalîl speak not so openly, for here sits his son (the sugar-thief)! and the boy is a tale-bearer."—When the Shuggery had excused himself, I asked, "Are ye guiltless of such disorders?" He answered, "There are adulteries and fornication among them, secretly."

We should think their hareem less modest than precious. The Arabs are jealous and dissolute; and every Moslem woman, since she may be divorced with a word, fears to raise even a wondering cogitation in such matter. Many poor hareem could not be persuaded by their nearest friends, who had called the hakîm, to fold down so much of the face-cloth from their temples as to show me their blear eyes. A poor young creature of the people was disobedient to her mother, sooner than discover a painful swelling below the knee. Even aged negro women [here they go veiled], that were wall-eyed with ophthalmia, would not discover their black foreheads in hope of some relief. And they have pitifully answered for themselves, ' If it be not the Lord's will here, yet should they receive their sight—where miserable mankind hope to inherit that good which they have lacked in this world!—f' il-jínna in the paradise.' Yehŷa's wife was prudent therein also: for when she had asked her old lord, she with a modest conveyance through the side-long large sleeves of the woman's garment, showed her painful swollen knees to the hakîm. This is their strange fashion of clothing: the woman's sleeves in Kasîm are so wonderfully wide, that if an arm be raised the gown hangs open to the knee. One must go therefore with heedfulness of her poor garment, holding the sleeves gathered under her arms; but poor townswomen that labour abroad and Beduin housewives are often surprised by unseemly accidents. Hareem alone will sit thus in the sultry heat; and cover themselves at the approach of strangers.

The days were long till the setting out of the samn caravan: Zâmil had delayed the town expedition, with Meteyr, against the intruded Kahtân, until the coming home of the great northern kâfily. The caravan for Mecca would not set out till that contention were determined. To this palm ground, two and a half miles from Aneyza, there came none of my acquaintance to visit the Nasrâny. Their friendship is like the voice of a bird upon the spray: if a rumour frighten her she will return no more. I had no tidings of Bessâm or of Kenneyny! Only from time to time some sick persons resorted hither, to seek counsel of the hakîm; who told me the Kenneyny sent them or Zâmil, saying, "In Khalîl's hand is a báraka; and it may be that the Lord will relieve thee."

The small-pox was nearly at an end in the town. Sâlih had lost a fair boy, a grief which he bore with the manly short sorrow of the Moslemîn. A daughter of Kenneyny died; and it was unknown to him, three days!—till he enquired for her: then they of his household and his friends said to him, "The Lord has taken the child; and yesterday we laid her in the

grave."—But Abdullah blamed them with a sorrowful severity;
"Oh! wherefore, he said, did ye not tell me?"—at least he
would have seen her dead face. It pained me also that I was
not called,—I might have been a mean to save her. * * *

* * * When I had been more than three weeks in this
desolation, I wrote on a leaf of paper, *katálny et-taab wa ej-jú'a*,
' I am slain with weariness and hunger '; and sent these words
to Kenneyny.—I hoped ere long to remove, with Zâmil's allowance, to some of the friends' grounds; were it Bessâm's
jeneyny, on the north-east part of the town [there is the *black
stone*, mentioned by some of their ancient poets, and ' whereof,
they say, Aneyza itself is named ']; or the palms of the good
father Yahỹa, so kind to my guiltless cause. My message was
delivered: and at sunrise on the morrow came Abdullah's
serving lad, who brought girdle-bread and butter, with a skin
of butter-milk; and his master's word bidding me be of good
comfort; and they (the friends) would ere long be able to
provide for my departure.—I could not obtain a little butter
milk (the wine of this languishing country) from the town.
Sâlih answered, 'That though some hareem might be secretly
milk-sellers in Aneyza, yet could not he, nor any of his household, have an hand in procuring it for me.' Some poor families
of Meteyr came to pitch by the water-pits of abandoned stubbles
nigh us; and I went out to seek a little milk of them for dates
or medicines. Their women wondered to see the (English)
colour of the stranger's hair; and said one to another, "Is this
a grey-haired man, that has tinged his beard with saffron?"—
"Nay, thou mayest see it is his nature; this is certainly a red-
man, *min ha'l shottût*, from those rivers (of Mesopotamia); and
have we not seen folk there of this hue?—but where, O man, is
thy béled?"

The sheukh of Meteyr were now in Aneyza, to consult finally
with Zâmil and the sheykhs for the common warfare. The
Kahtân thought themselves secure, in the khála, that no townsfolk would ride against them in this burning season; and as for
el-Meteyr, they set little by them as adversaries.—Zâmil sent
word to those who had thelûls in the town, to be ready to
mount with him on the morrow. He had " written " for this
expedition " six hundred " thelûls. The ghrazzu of the confederate Beduw was " three hundred thelûls, and two hundred
(led) horses ".

The day after el-Meteyr set forward at mid-afternoon. But
Zâmil did not ride in one company with his nomad friends:
the Beduins, say the townspeople, are altogether deceitful—as

we have seen in the defeat of Saûd the Waháby. And I heard that some felony of the Aarab had been suffered two years before by Aneyza! It is only Ibn Rashîd, riding among the rajajîl and villagers, who may foray in assurance with his subject Beduw.

Zâmil rode out the next day, with " more than a thousand " of the town: and they say, " When Zâmil ·mounts, Aneyza is confident." He left Aly to govern at home: and the shops in the sûk were shut ; there would be no more buying or selling, till the expedition came home again. The morning market is not held, nor is any butcher's meat killed in these days. Although so many were in the field with Zâmil, yet ' the streets, said Sâlih, seemed full of people, so that you should not miss them ' ! I enquired, " And what if anyone open his dokan— ? " *Answer :* " The emir Aly would send to shut it : but if he persisted such an one would be called before the emir, and beaten : " only small general shops need not be closed, which are held by any old broken men or widows.

The Emir writes the names of those who are to ride in a ghrazzu ; they are mostly the younger men of households able to maintain a thelûl. Military service falls upon the substantial citizens—since there can be no warfaring a-foot in the khála : we hear not that the Waháby, poor in all military discipline, had ever foot soldiers. The popular sort that remain at home, mind their daily labour ; and they are a guard for the town. The Emir's sergeant summons all whose names have been enrolled to mount with Zâmil (on the morrow). Two men ride upon a warfaring thelûl ; the radîf is commonly a brother, a cousin, or client [often a Beduwy] or servant of the owner.— If one who was called be hindered, he may send another upon his dromedary with a backrider. If he be not found in the muster with the Emir, and have sent none in his room, it may be overlooked in a principal person ; but, in such case, any of the lesser citizens might be compelled. Zâmil was an easy man to excuse them who excused themselves ; for if one said, " Wellah, Sir, for such and such causes, I cannot ride," the Emir commonly answered him, " Stay then."

It was falsely reported that the Kenneyny was in the expedition. The infirm man sent his two thelûls with riders (which may be found among the poor townsmen and Beduins). None of Rasheyd's sons were in the field : Sâlih said, " We have two cousins that have ridden for us all."—A kinsman of Zâmil, who was with him, afterward told me their strength was 800 men, and the Meteyr were 300. Some said, that Aneyza sent 200 thelûls, that is 400 riders ; others said 500 men.—We may conjecture that Zâmil called for 300 thelûls of the town ; and there went forth 200, with 400 men, which were about a third of all the grown male citizens; and of Meteyr rode nearly 150 tribesmen. With the town were not above 20 led mares, of sheykhly persons. Kahtân were reckoned (in their double-seeing wise) 800 men ; perhaps they were as many as 400, but (as southern Aarab) possessing few firearms. They had many horses, and were rich in great cattle : it was reported, ' Their mares were 150 '; but say they had 70 horses.

The townsmen rode in three troops, with the ensigns of the three great wards of Aneyza ; but the town banners are five or six, when there is warfare at home.

Early in the afternoon I heard this parley in the garden, between Fáhd and a poor Meteyry,—who having no thelûl could not follow with his tribesmen. *Fáhd :* " By this they are well in the way ! and please Ullah they will bring back the heads of them."—" Please Ullah ! the Lord is bountiful ! and kill the children from two years old and upward ; and the hareem shall lament ! " I said to them, " Hold your mouths, kafirs ! and worse than kafirs." *The Beduwy :* " But the Kahtân killed our children—they killed even women ! " The Meteyr were come in to encamp nigh the town walls ; and two small menzils of theirs were now our neighbours. These southern Aarab were such as other Beduw. I heard in their mouths the same nomad Arabic ; yet I could discern that they were of foreign dîras. I saw their girbies suspended in cane-stick trivets. Some of them came to me for medicines : they seemed not to be hospitable ; they saw me tolerated by Zâmil, and were not fanatical.

In these parts the town-dwellers name themselves to the Aarab, and are named of them again, *el-Moslemîn,*—a word used like *Cristiani* in the priests'-countries of Europe ; first to distinguish the human generation, and then in an illiberal straitness of the religious sense. One day I saw camels feeding towards the Wady ; and in the hope of drinking milk I adventured barefoot to them, over Rasheyd's stubbles and the glowing sand : and hailed the herdsmen ! The weleds stood still; and when I came to them they said, after a little astonishment, " The nagas, O man, are not in milk nor, billah, our own : these be the town camels ; and we are herding them for the *Moslemîn.*" One said, " Auh ! be'st thou the hakîm ? wilt thou give me a medicine ?—And if thou come to our booths when the cattle are watered, I will milk for thee mine own nâga ; and I have but her : were our cattle here, the Beduins would milk for thee daily."—The long day passed ; then another, which seemed

s*

without end ; and a third was to me as three days : it had been told me, 'that my friends were all in the ghrazzu ',—and now Aly reigned in the town! Sâlih bade me be easy; but fair words in the Arabs are not to trust : they think it pious to persuade a man to his rest.

Tidings of this foray came to Boreyda, and messengers rode out to warn the Kahtân. Zâmil made no secret of the town warfare, which was not slackness in such a politic man, but his long-suffering prudence. ' He would give the enemies time, said Sâlih, to sue for peace ' :—how unlike the hawks of er-Riâth and Jebel Shammar!

— The Kahtân were lately at *el-'Ayûn ;* and the ghrazzu held thither. But in the way Zâmil heard that their menzils were upon *ed-Dellamîeh,* a water between the mountain Sàk and er-Russ. The town rode all that day and much of the night also. By the next afternoon they were nigh er-Russ ; and alighted to rest, and pitched their (canvas) tents and (carpet) awnings. Now they heard that the enemy was upon the wells *Dókhany,* a march to the southward. As they rode on the morrow they met bye and bye with the Meteyr; and they all alighted together at noon.—The scouts of Meteyr brought them word, that they had seen the booths of the Aarab, upon *Dókhany !* and so many they could be none other than the Kahtân ; who might be taken at unawares!—The young litterates of Aneyza boasted one to another at the coffee fires, " We shall fight then to-morrow upon the old field of *Jebel Kezâz,* by *Dókhany ;* where the Tubb'a (lord the king, signeur) of el-Yémen fought against the *Wáilyîn* (sons of Wâil, that is the Annezy),—*Koleyb, sheykh Rabî'a ;* and with them B. Temîm and Keys " [Kahtân against Ishmael :—that was little before the héjra]. The berg Kezâz is ' an hour ' from the bed of the Wady er-Rummah.

Zâmil and the town set forward on the morrow, when the stars were yet shining : the Meteyr had mounted a while before them, and Dókhany was at little distance. In this quarrel it was the Beduins which should fall upon their capital foemen ; and Zâmil would be at hand to support them. The town fetched a compass to envelope Kahtân from the southward.

Meteyr came upon their enemies as the day lightened : the Kahtân ran from the beyts, with their arms, sheykhs leapt upon their mares ; and the people encouraged themselves with shout-ing. Then seeing they were beset by Meteyr they contemned them, and cried, *jàb-hum Ullah,* " A godsend ! "—but this was a day of reckoning upon both parts to the dreary death. The

Meteyr had "two hundred" mares under them; but they were of the less esteemed northern brood. The *Kahatîn* in the beginning were sixty horse-riders. Then thirty more horsemen joined them from another great menzil of theirs pitched at little distance. The Kahtân were now more than the ghrazzu of Meteyr, who finally gave ground.

— Then first the Kahtân looked about them; and were ware of the town bands coming on! The Kahatîn, of whom not many were fallen, shouted one to another, in suspense of heart, "Eigh! is it Ibn Rashîd?—but no! for Ibn Rashîd rides with one bàrak: but these ride like townsfolk.—Ullah! they are *hâthr!*"—Now as the town approached some knew them, and cried, "These be the Kusmân!—they are the *Zuâmil* (Zâmils, or the people of Zâmil)." When they saw it was so, they hasted to save their milch-camels.

— Zâmil, yet distant, seeing Beduin horsemen driving off the camels, exclaimed, "Are not these the *Moslemîn* [those of our part]?" "Nay! answered him a sheykh of Meteyr (who came riding with the town to be a shower of the way in the khála), they are billah el-Kahtân"! The town cavaliers were too few to gallop out against them. And now the Kahtân giving themselves to save the great cattle forsook their menzil: where they left booths, household stuff, and wives and children in the power of their foemen.

The horsemen of Meteyr pursued the flying Kahtân; who turned once more and repulsed them: then the Aneyza cavaliers sallied to sustain their friends. The rest of the Meteyr, who alighted, ran in to spoil the enemies' tents.—And he and he, whose house-wives were lately pierced with the spears of Kahtân, or whose babes those fiend-like men slew, did now the like by their foemen; they thrust through as many hareem, and slit the throats of their little ones before the mothers' faces, crying to them, "Oh, wherefore did your men so with our little ones the other day!" Some frantic women ran on the spoilers with tent-staves; and the Meteyries, with weapons in their hands, and in the tempest of their blood, spared them not at all.—Thus there perished five or six wives, and as many children of Kahtân.

In their most tribulation a woman hid her husband's silver, 600 reals [that was very much for any Beduwy]! in a girby; and stript off her blue smock—all they wear besides the haggu on their hunger-starved bodies: and hanging the watₑr-skin on her shoulder, she set her little son to ride upon the other. Then she ran from her tent with a lamentable cry, *weyléy*, *weyléy!* woe is me! and fled naked through the tumult of the enemies. The Meteyr, who saw it, supposed that one of the people had spoiled the woman, and thought shame to follow her; yet some called to her, to fling down that she bore on her shoulder: but she, playing the mad woman, cried out, 'She was undone!—was it not enough to strip a sheykh's daughter? and would they have even this water, which she carried for the life of her child!' Others shouted, to let the woman pass: and she fled fast, and went by them all;—and saved her goodman's fortune, with this cost of his wife's modesty.

There fell thirty men of Kahtân,—the most were slain in the flight; and of Meteyr ten.—These returned to bury their dead: but the human charity is here unknown to heap a little earth over the dead foemen!

A woman messenger came in from the flying Kahtân, to Zâmil. The town now alighted at the wells (where they would rear up the awnings and drink coffee): she sought safe conduct for some of their sheykhs, to come and speak with him; which Zâmil granted.—Then the men returned and kissing him as suppliants, they entreated him, 'since their flocks, and the tents and stuff, were now (as he might see) in the hands of Meteyr, to suffer them to come to the water, that they might drink and not perish.' They had sweated for their lives, and that summer's day was one of greatest heat; and having no girbies, they must suffer, in flying through the desert, an extremity of thirst. But who might trust to words of Beduin enemies! and therefore they bound themselves with a solemn oath,—*Aleyk âhad Ullah wa amân Ullah, in mâ akhûnak! elkhàyin yakhûnhu Ullah*—"The covenant of the Lord be with thee, and His peace! I will not surely betray thee! who betrayeth, the Lord shall him betray."

Such was the defeat of the intruded Kahtân, lately formidable even to Ibn Rashîd. Ibn Saûd had set upon them last summer here at Dókhany! but the Kahtân repulsed the decayed Waháby!—This good success was ascribed to the fortune of Zâmil: the townsmen had made no use of their weapons. The Meteyr sent messengers from the field to Ibn Rashîd, with a gift of two mares out of the booty of Kahtân.—Even Boreyda would be glad, that the malignant strange tribesmen were cast out of the country.—Many Kahtân perished in their flight through the khála: even lighter wounds, in that extremity of weariness and thirst, became mortal. They fled southward three days, lest their old foes, hearing of their calamity, should fall upon them: we heard, that some Ateyba had met with them, and taken "two hundred" of the saved milch camels. Certain of them who came in to el-Ethellah said, that they were destroyed and had lost 'an hundred men':—so dearly they bought the time past [now two full years] of their playing the wolf in Nejd !

When I asked what would become of the Kahtân? the Shuggery answered, "The Beduw are hounds,—that die not; and these are sheyatîn. They will find twenty shifts ; and after a year or two be in good plight again."—" What can they do now ? "—" They will milk the nâgas for food, and sell some camels in the villages, to buy themselves dates and cooking vessels. And they will not be long-time lodged on the ground, without shelter from the sun : for the hareem will shear the cattle that remain to them, and spin day and night; and in few weeks set up their new woven booths! besides the other Kahtân in the south will help them."—We heard after this, that the defeated Kahtân had made peace with the Ateybân ; and reconciled themselves with Ibn Saûd! But how might they thus assure themselves ? had the Kahtân promised to be confederate with them against Ibn Rashîd?

— Hayzàn was fallen! their young Absalom ; 'a young man of a thievish false nature,' said his Beduin foes : it was he who threatened me, last year, in a guest-chamber at Hâyil: Hayzàn was slain for that Meteyry sheykh, who lately fell by his hand in the north. A sheykhly kinsman of the dead sought him in the battle : they ran together; and Hayzàn was borne through the body with a deadly wide wound. The young man was very robust for a Beduwy, and his strong hand had not swerved ; but his lance-thrust was fended by a shirt of mail which his foemen wore privily under his cotton tunic. That Meteyry was a manly rider upon a good horse, and after Hayzàn, he bore down other five sheykhs.—When the fortune of the day was determined by the coming of "the Zuâmil," he with his brother and his son, yet a stripling [principal sheykhs' sons soon become horsemen, and ride with their elders to the field], and a few of his Aarab, made prize of eighty milch camels ! In that day he had been struck by lances and shot in the breast, eleven times ; but the dints pierced not his " Davidian " shirt of antique chain work. They say, that the stroke of a gun-shot leaves upon the body fenced by such harness, only a grievous bruise.

A brother of Hayzàn, Terkey, was fallen ; and their sheykhly sister. She was stripped, and thrust through with a spear!— because Kahtân had stripped and slain a Meteyry sheykh's daughter. The old Kahtân sheykh—father of these evil-starred

brethren, hardly escaped upon a thelûl. Hayzàn, mortally
wounded, was stayed up in the saddle, in the flight, till evening ; and when they came to the next *golbân* (south of Dókhany,)
the young sheykh gave up the ghost: and his companions cast
his warm body into one of those well-pits.

In the Kahtân camp was found a poor foreigner,—a young
Móghreby derwish ! who committed himself to the charity of
the townspeople. In the last pilgrimage he came to Mecca ;
and had afterward joined himself to a returning kâfily of
Kusmân, hoping to go up from their country to el-Irâk. But
as they marched he was lost in that immense wilderness : and
some wandering Kahtân found him,—what sweetness to be
found, in such extreme case, by the hand of God's providence !
Yet the Kahtân, who saved him, not regarding the religious
bounty of the desert, made the young Moor their thrall ; and
constrained him to keep sheep : and as often as they approached
any village they bound him, that he should not escape them.—
They had so dealt with me, and worse, if (which I once purposed)
I had journeyed with some of them.—The returning " Moslemîn "
brought the young Moghreby with them to Aneyza, where he
remained a guest in the town, until they might send him forward. He had been with Kahtân since the winter, and said
with simplicity, " I knew not that life, but they made me a
Beduwy, and wellah I am become a Beduwy "—And in truth if
one live any time with the Aarab, he will have all his life after
a feeling of the desert.

— The fifth evening we saw a nomad horseman on the brow
of the Nefûd, who descended to the booths : that was the first
of them who returned from the warfare. Zâmil and the town
came again on the morrow ; and we heard them, riding home
under our horizon, more than two hours, with a warlike beating
of tambûrs ; they arrived, in three troops, under their banners.
All the Beduins came not yet : there was a wrangling among
them—it is ever so, in the division of the booty. A Beduwy
will challenge his own wheresoever he find it ; and as Meteyr
had been lately " taken " in the north by Kahtân, many a man
lighted on his own cattle again, in the hand of a tribesman. The
same afternoon we saw sheep driven in : they were few, and the
most of them had been their own. Those who now returned
from the battle brought heavy tidings,—six men were fallen of
the menzils nigh us ! that were thirty households. As they
heard it, the house-wives of the dead ran forth wailing, and
overthrew their widowed booths. The Beduins removed when
the morrow lightened, and returned to the khála.—This was

the calamity of Kahtân! and there was peace between Boreyda and Aneyza.

Now in Aneyza the jemamîl made ready their gear; for the samn kâfily was soon to set out for Mecca. The *zemmel*, bearing camels, were fetched in from the nomads; and we saw them daily roaming at pasture in the Nefûd about us. A caravan departed in these days with dates and corn for Medina.

Zâmil and Kenneyny rode out one day to the Wady together, where Zâmil has a possession; and they proposed to return by Rasheyd's plantation, to visit Khalîl. But in the hot noon they napped under the palms: Abdullah woke quaking with ague! and they rode the next way home.

One evening there came a company of young patricians from Aneyza; to see some sheep of theirs, which the Beduin herds had brought in, with a disease in the fleece. The gallants stripped off gay kerchiefs and mantles; and standing in the well-troughs, they themselves washed their beasts. When it was night, they lay down on the Nefûd sand to sleep, before the shepherds' tents. Some of them were of the fanatical Bessâms; and with these came a younger son of the good Abdullah. The lad saluted me affectuously from his father; who sent me word, 'that the kâfily would set out for Mecca shortly; and I should ride with Abd-er-Rahmàn (his elder son)'; I had languished now six weeks in Rasheyd's plantation.

Ere they departed on the morrow, one of the young fanatical Bessâms said to me.—" Oh that thou wouldst believe in Mohammed! Khalîl, is it true, that ye are daily looking for the coming again of the Messîh, from heaven? and if Aysa bid thee then believe on Mohammed, wilt thou obey him, and be a Moslem? But I am sure that the Lord Aysa will so command thee! I would that he may come quickly; and we shall see it!"—The same day there visited us the two young men of Rasheyd's kindred that had ridden in the ghrazzu: they were very swarty, and plainly of the servile blood. One of them, who had been an Ageyly in Damascus, told me that he lately bought a horse of perfect form and strength in el-Yémen, for five hundred reals; and he hoped to sell him in es-Sham for as much again. Coffee was prepared for any who visited the jeneyny, by the young sons of Rasheyd; and in these days—the last in June—they brought cool clusters of white grapes, which were ripening in the vine.

The great sheykh of Meteyr also visited me: he was sent by Zâmil. Though under the middle age, he began to have the dropsy, and could not suffer a little fatigue: the infirm man came riding softly upon a carpet, which was bound in his thelûl-saddle. The *istiska* is better known as a horse sickness among them : he knew not what ailed him,—have not all men a good understanding of the diseases and nurture of their cattle rather than of themselves and their children ! he received my word with a heavy-heart. The horse sweats much, and is not less than man impatient of thirst : and the beginning of this evil may be, in both, a surfeit of cold water in a chilled skin. When he heard his malady would be long he said, " Yâ Khalîl ! wilt thou not go with us ? *henna rahîl,* the Aarab journey to-morrow (to their summer dîra, in the north): thou shalt lodge in my booth ; and they will serve thee well. We will milk for thee : and when thou hast cured me I will also reward thee."— "Have patience in God ! "—" I know that the blessing is from Ullah ; but come Khalîl: thou wilt be in surety with us ; and I will send thee again to Aneyza, or if it like thee better to Kuweyt or to Bosra."—" I am shortly to set out with the samn caravan." —" Well, that will be—we heard it now in the town—the ninth day from to-day ; come with us, and I will send thee ere that day : thereto I plight my faith."—It had been pleasant, in this stagnant heat, to breathe the air of the khála and be free again, among the Aarab; and regaled with léban I might recover strength. I sent therefore to ask counsel of the Kenneyny: and my friend wrote again that I could adventure with them. But the time was short, and I durst not trust in the Beduin faith.

I had passed many days of those few years whose sum is our human life, in Arabia ; and was now at the midst of the Penin-sula. A month !—and I might be come again to European shipping. From hence to the coast may be counted 450 desert miles, a voyage of at least twenty great marches in the uneasy camel-saddle, in the midsummer flame of the sun ; which is a suffering even to the homeborn Arabs. Also my bodily languor was such now, that I might not long sit upright ; besides I fore-saw a final danger, since I must needs leave the Mecca kâfily at a last station before the (forbidden) city. There was come upon me besides a great disquietude : for one day twelve months before, as I entered a booth (in Wady Thirba), in the noon heat, when the Nomads slumber, I had been bitten by their grey-hound, in the knee. I washed the wound ; which in a few days was healed, but a red button remained ; which now (justly at the year's end) broke, and became an ulcer ; then many like ulcers rose upon the lower limbs (and one on the wrist of the left hand).—Ah ! what horror, to die like a rabid hound in a hostile land.

The friends Kenneyny and Bessàm purchased a thelûl, in the
Friday market, for my riding down to Jidda, where the beast,
they thought, might fetch as much as they gave ; and if no,
one of their kinsmen, who was to come up from Jidda in the
returning kâfily would ride home upon her.—I received then a
letter from the good Bessàm : 'All (he wrote) is ready ; but
because of the uncivil mind [Waháby malice] of the people he
would not now be able to send me in his son's company ! I must
excuse it. But they had provided that I should ride in the
company of Sleymàn el-Kenneyny, to whom I might look for
that which was needful [water, cooking, and the noon shelter]
by the way.'—He ended in requesting me to send back a little
quinine : and above his seal was written—" God's blessing be
with all the faithful Moslemîn."

I sent to Zâmil asking that it might be permitted me to come
one day to town, to purchase somewhat for the journey, and
bid my friends farewell : but my small request could not be
vouchsafed,—so much of the Waháby misery is in the good
people of Aneyza.

The husbandmen of the garden—kind as the poor are kind,
when they went into Aneyza on Fridays, purchased necessary
things for me : the butcher's family showed me no hospitable
service.—Hàmed el-Yehŷa came one of these last evenings, to
visit me, riding upon his mare. This first of my returning
friends—a little glozing in his words, excused himself, that he
had not come sooner to see me. The hakîm being now about
to depart, he would have medicines for his mother, who sent me
his saddlebag-ful of a sort of ginger cakes (which they prepare
for the caravan journeys), and scorched gobbets of fresh meat,
that will last good a month. Hàmed was a manly young
franklin with fresh looks, the son of his mother—but also the
son of his father, of great strength, of an easy affectuous nature,
inclined to be gentle and liberal : his beard was not yet begun
to spring. The old mare was his own : to be a horseman also
belongeth to nobility. He came well clad, as when these townsmen ride abroad ; his brave silken kerchief was girded with the
head-band and perfumed with attar of rose, from Mecca. The
young cavalier led a foal with him, which he told me he found
tied in a Kahtân booth : Hàmed brought the colt home ; and
said, excusing himself, ' that it had otherwise perished !' The
colt now ran playing after the dry mare, as if she were his
kindly dam. The mare had adopted the strange foal ! and
wreathing back her neck she gazed for him, and snorted softly
with affection.

We supped together ; and Hàmed told of their meeting with

the Kahtân. He rode upon his mare, armed with a (Frankish) double gun ; but complained to me that one on horseback could not re-load. This was, I answered, their loose riding upon a pad (*maârakka*) ; I bade him use stirrups, and he held it a good counsel.—Such was the dust of the battle, that Hâmed could not number the Kahtân tents, which he supposed might be 300. The Mecca caravans pass by Dókhany ; but this year he said we should shun it, because of the fetor of the unburied carcases (of Kahtân). I enquired, if the kâfily marched through all the day's heat !—" Nay, for then the (molten) samn might leak through the butter-skins." He thought we should journey by night, for fear of Kahtân ; and that our kâfily would be joined at er-Russ with the butter convoy descending from Boreyda. He sat on another hour with me, in the moonlight : Hâmed would not, he protested, that our friendship were so soon divided,—after my departure we might yet write one to the other. So mounting again, he said, ' he would ride out to the gathering place of the kâfily to bid me God-speed, on the day of our departure ' :—but I met with him no more.

It is the custom in these countries, that all who are to journey in a kâfily should assemble at a certain place, without the town : where being mustered by the vigil of the day of their departure ; when the sun is risen they will set forth.

CHAPTER XII

SET OUT FROM EL-KASÎM, WITH THE BUTTER CARAVAN
FOR MECCA

ON the morrow, when the sun was setting, there came a messenger for me, from Abdullah el-Kenneyny; with the thelûl upon which I should ride to Jidda. We mounted; and Rasheyd's labourers who had left their day's toil, and the poor slave woman, approached to take my hand; and they blessed me as we rode forth. We held over to the Kenneyny's plantation: where I heard I should pass the morrow. The way was not two miles; but we arrived, after the short twilight, in the dark: there my rafîk forsook me; and I lay down in that lonely palm ground to sleep, by the well side.

At the sun-rising I saw Abdullah el-Kenneyny! who arrived riding upon an ass, before the great heat. A moment later came Abdullah el-Bessâm, on foot: " Ah! Khalîl, said he, taking my hand, we are abashed, for the things thou hast suffered, and that it should have been here! but thou knowest we were overborne by this foolish people." Kenneyny asked for more of that remedy which was good for his mother's eyes; and I distributed to them my medicines. Now came Hâmed es-Sâfy; and these friends sat on with me till the sun was half an hour high, when they rose to return to breakfast, saying they would see me later. In the afternoon came es-Sâfy again; who would perfect his writing of English words.—None of my other friends and acquaintance came to visit the excommunicated Nasrâny.

The good Kenneyny arrived again riding upon the ass, in the cooling of the afternoon, with his son Mohammed. He was feeble to-day, as one who is spent in body and spirit; and I saw him almost trembling, whilst he sat to talk with me: and the child playing and babbling about us, Abdullah bade him be still, for he could not bear it. I entreated him to forget whatsoever inquietude my coming to Aneyza had caused him: he made no answer.

547

It was now evening; and Sleymàn arrived, upon a thelûl, with his little son. He was riding-by to the caravan menzil, and would speak the last words with his kinsman, who lent him money for this traffic. Abdullah called to him, to set down the child; and take up Khalîl and his bags.—I mounted with Sleymàn; and we rode through a breach of the town wall, which bounded Kenneyny's tillage. Abdullah walked thus far with us: and here we drew bridle to take leave of him: I gave hearty thanks, with the Semitic blessings; and bade this gentle and beneficent son of Temîm a long farewell. He stood sad and silent: the infirm man's mortal spirit was cut off (Cruel stars!) from that Future, wherefore he had travailed—and which we should see! [Three months later Abdullah el-Kenneyny went down in the pilgrimage to Mecca: and returned, by sea, to Bosra. But his strength failed him; and he sought in vain a better air at *Abu Shahr*, on the Persian Coast.—In the summer of the third year after, Sleymàn, a younger son of Abdullah el-Bessàm, wrote to me, from Jidda; " Poor el-Kenneyny died some months ago, to our grief, at Bosra: he was a good man and very popular."]

We went on riding an hour or two in that hollow roadway worn in the Nefûd, by which I had once journeyed in the night-time in the way to Khubbera. It was dark when we came to the caravan menzil; where Sleymàn hailed his drivers, that had arrived before us, with the loads. They brought us to our place in the camp; which, for every fellowship, is where they have alighted and couched their camels. Here was a coffee fire, and I saw Sleymàn's goat-skins of samn (which were twenty-four or one ton nearly) laid by in order: four of them, each of fifteen sah (of el-Kasîm), are a camel's burden, worth thirty reals, for which they looked to receive sixty in Mecca.—Many persons from Aneyza were passing this last night in the camp with their outfaring friends and brethren. This assembling place of the Mecca kâfily is by the outlying palms *'Auhellàn;* where are said to be certain *ancient caves hewn in the sand-rock!* I only then heard of it, and time was not left me to search out the truth in the matter.

— But now I learned, that no one in the caravan was going to Jidda! they were all for Mecca. Abdullah el-Kenneyny had charged Sleymàn; and the good Bessàm had charged his son (*Abd-er-Rahmàn*) for me, that at the station next before Mecca [whether in Wady Laymûn, or the Seyl] they should seek an *'adamy,* to convey me (without entering the *hadûd* or sacred limit) to Jidda.—The good Kenneyny, who had never ridden on pilgrimage, could not know the way ; and his per-spicuous mind did not foresee my final peril, in that passage.

In our butter kâfily were 170 camels,—bearing nearly 30 tons of samn—and seventy men, of whom forty rode on thelûls, —the rest were drivers. We were sorted in small companies ; every master with his friends and hired servants. In each fellowship is carried a tent or awning, for a shelter over their head at the noon stations, and to shadow the samn,—that is molten in the goat-skins (*jerm*, pl. *jerûm*) in the hot hours : the *jerûm* must be thickly smeared within with date syrup. Each skinful, the best part of an hundredweight, is suspended by a loop (made fast at the two ends) from the saddle-tree. Some-times a jerm bursts in the caravan journeys, and the precious humour is poured out like water upon the dust of the khála : somewhiles the bearing-camels thrust by acacia trees, and jerms are pricked and ripped by the thorny boughs. It was well that there rode a botcher in the kâfily ; who in the evening station amended the daily accidents to butter-skins and girbies.—All this samn, worth more than £2000 in Mecca, had been taken up, since the spring, in their traffic with the Beduw : the Aneyza merchants store it for the time in marble troughs.

There is an emir, named by Zâmil, over such a great town caravan : he is one of the princely kin ; and receives for every camel a real.—El-Kenneyny had obtained a letter from Zâmil, commending me to the emir ; and charging him to provide for my safety, when I should leave the kâfily " at the Aŷn ".—We sat on chatting about the coffee fire, till we were weary ; and then lay down to sleep there, on the Nefûd sand.

Rising with the dawn, there was yet time to drink coffee. The emir and some young Aneyza tradesmen in Mecca, that would return with the kâfily, had remained all night in the town : they would overtake us riding upon their fleet *'omanías*. [The thelûls of the Gulf province 'Omân or ' Amân ' are of great force and stature ; but less patient of famine and thirst than some lesser kinds. A good 'omanîa, worth 50 to 70 reals at Aneyza, may hardly be bought in the pilgrim season at Mecca— where they are much esteemed—for 150 reals.] When the sun was up the caravaners loaded, and set forward. Wé soon after fell into the Wady er-Rummah ; in which we journeyed till two hours before noon : and alighted on a shaeb, *es-Shibbebieh*, to rest out the midday heat (*yugyilûn*). In that place are some winter granges of Aneyza, of ruinous clay building, with high-walled yards. They are inhabited by well-drivers' families, from the autumn seed time till the early harvest. Here we drew brackish water, and filled our girbies. The day's sultry heat was great; and I found under the awnings 105° F. Principal persons have canvas tents made Beduin-wise, others have awnings of Bagdad carpets. I saw but one or two round tents— bargains from the coast, and a few ragged tilts of hair-cloth [that I heard were of the Kahtân booty!] in poorer fellowships.—Sleymàn el-Kenneyny's six loads of samn were partly Abdullah's: he was a jemmâl, and the beasts were his own.

It might be three o'clock ere they removed,—and the hot sun was going down from the meridian: the signal is made with a great shout of the Emir's servant, ES-SHÎ-ÎL! In the next instant all awnings are struck, the camels are led-in and couched, the caravaners carry out the heavy butter-skins; and it is a running labour, with heaving above their strength, to load on their beasts, before the kâfily is moving: for the thelûl riders are presently setting forth; and who is unready will be left in the hindward. The emir's servant stands like a shepherd before the kâfily—spreading his arms to withhold the foremost! till the rest shall be come up: or, running round, he cries out on the disobedient. Now they march; and—for the fear of the desert—the companies journey nigh together. Our path southward was in the Wady Rummah, which is a wide plain of firmer sand in the Nefûd. The Abàn mountains are in sight to the westward, covered with haze. [The Abànát may be seen, lifted up in the morning twilight, from the dunes about Aneyza.] At sun-setting we alighted by other outlying granges—that are of er-Russ, el-Hajnowwy, without the Wady: we were there nearly abreast of Khubbera.

Their tents are not pitched at night; but in each company the awning is now a sitting carpet under the stars; and it will be later for the master to lie on. One in every fellowship who is cook goes out to gather sticks for fuel; another leads away the beasts to browse, for the short half-hour which rests till it is dark night. With Sleymàn went three drivers: the first of them, a poor townsman of Aneyza, played the cook in our company; another was a Beduwy.—After an hour, the supper dish (of seethed wheaten stuff) is set before us. Having eaten, we sip coffee: they sit somewhile to chat and drink tobacco; and then wrapt in our cloaks we lie down on the sand, to sleep out the short hours which remain till toward sunrising.

An hour before the dawn we heard shouted, 'THE REMOVE!' The people rise in haste; the smouldering watch-fires are blown to a flame, and more sticks are cast on to give us light: there is a harsh hubbub of men labouring; and the ruckling and braying of a multitude of camels. Yet a minute or two, and all is up: riders are mounted; and they which remain afoot look busily about them on the dim earth, that nothing be left.—They drive forth; and a new day's march begins; to last through the long heat till evening. After three hours journeying, in the desert plain, we passed before er-Russ;—whose villagers, two generations ago, spared not to fell their palm stems for a bulwark, and manfully resisted all the assaults of Ibrahîm Pasha's army. The Emir sent a thelûl rider to the place for tidings: who returned with word, that the samn caravaners of er-Russ were gone down with the Boreyda kâfily, which had passed-by them two days ago. Er-Russ (which they say is greater than Khubbera) appears as three oases lying north and south, not far asunder. In the first, er-Rueytha, is the town; in the second, er-Rafya, a village and high watch-tower showing above the palms; the third and least is called Shinàny. Er-Russ is the last settlement southward and gate of el-Kasîm proper.—We are here at the border of the Nefûd; and bye and bye the plain is harsh gravel under our feet: we re-enter that granitic and basaltic middle region of Arabia, *which lasts from the mountains of Shammar to Mecca.* The corn grounds of er-Russ are in the Wâdy er-Rummah; their palms are above.

I saw the Abànát—now half a day distant westward, to be a low jebel coast, such as Ajja, trending south. There are two mountains one behind other; and the bed of the Wâdy (there of no great width) lies betwixt them. The northern is named *el-Eswad,* and oftener *el-Esmar,* the brown and swart coloured; and the southerly, which is higher, *el-Ahmar,* the red mountain: this is perhaps granite; and that basaltic.

We came at noon to *Umm T'yeh,* other outlying granges of er-Russ, and inhabited; where some of us, riding-in to water, found a plot of growing tobacco! The men of Aneyza returned laughing, to tell of this adventure in the caravan menzil: for it was high noon, and the kâfily halted yonder.—From this *mogyil* we rose early; and journeyed forth through a plain wilderness full of basaltic and grey-red granite bergs [such as we have seen in the Harb and Shammar dîras westward]. Finally when the sun was descending, with ruddy yellow light behind the Abàn mountains, we halted to encamp.

Zâmil's letter, commending me to *Ibrahîm,* the young caravan emir, was brought to me by a client of the Bessam to-day. Ibrahîm—he succeeded his father, who till lately had been emir of the town caravans—a sister's son of Zâmil, was a manly young sheykh of twenty years, of a gallant countenance; and like Zâmil in his youth, though not of like parts : a smiling dissembler, confident and self-minded; and the Wahâby rust was in his soul. Such are the most young franklins in the free oases, always masking as it were in holiday apparel : but upon any turn of fortune, you find them haply to be sordid and iniquitous Arabs. Ibrahîm receiving Zâmil's letter from my hand, put it hastily into his bosom unopened ; for he would read what his uncle wrote to him concerning the Nasrâny, bye and bye in a corner ! He showed me daily pleasant looks : and sometimes as we journeyed, seeing me drooping in the saddle, he would ride to me, and put his new-kindled galliûn in my hand : and some days, he bade me come to sup with him, in the evening menzil. The young tradesmen that returned to Mecca, where they had shops, and a few of the master-caravaners mounted on thelûls, rode with Ibrahîm, in advance of the marching kâfily : now and then they alighted to kindle a fire of sticks, and make coffee. I rode, with less fatigue, among our burden camels —Ibrahîm told me, laughing, that he first heard of me in Kuweyt (where he then arrived with a caravan): —' That there was come a Nasrâny to Hâyil, *túlahu theláthy armâh*, three spears' length (they said) of stature ! for certain days the stranger had not spoken ! after that he found a mine for Ibn Rashîd, and then another !'—We lodged this night under the berg *el-Kîr*, little short of the peak *Jebel Kezâz*,— Dókhany being an hour distant, at our right hand ; where are shallow water pits, and some ground-work of old building.

We journeyed on the morrow with the same high country about us, beset with bergs of basaltic traps and granite. [The steppe rises continually from el-Kasîm to et-Tâyif.] We came early to the brackish pits *er-Rukka ;* and drew and replenished our girbies: this thick well-water was full of old wafted droppings of the nomads' cattle; but who will not drink in the desert, the water of the desert, must perish. Here is a four-square clay kella, with high walls and corner towers, built by those of er-Russ, for shelter when they come hither to dig gun-salt,—wherewith the soil is always infected about old water stations. We drank and rested out an hour, but with little refreshment: for the simûm—the hot land wind—was blowing, as the breath of an oven ; which is so light and emptied of oxygen that it cannot fill the chest or freshen the blood ; and there comes upon man and cattle a faintness of heart.—I felt some relief in breathing through a wetted sponge.

Remounting we left *Jebel Ummry* at the right hand, a mountain landmark of basalt which is long in sight.—I wondered seeing before us three men in the khàla ! they were wood-cutters from *Therrîeh*, a desert village few hours distant to the westward; and thereby the Aneyza caravans pass some years. Not many miles north of Therrîeh is another village, Miskeh : these are poor corn settlements, without palms,—Miskeh is the greater, where are hardly fifty houses. West of Therrîeh is a hamlet, *Thorèyih*, in the mountain, *Shâba*. The people of these villages are of mixed kindred from el-Kasîm, and of the nomads, and of negro blood : others say they are old colonies of Heteym. An 'Ateyby sheykh, *Múthkir*, who rode rafîk in our caravan [his tribesmen are the Aarab of this vast wilderness], said, "those villagers are descended from Múthur." The nomads about them are sometimes Meteyr, sometimes Harb (intruded from the westward), sometimes 'Ateybân; but formerly those migrated Annezy were their neighbours that are now in the Syrian desert. —Far to the eastward are other three desert villages, *es-Shaara*, *Doàdamy* and *Goayîeh*, which lie in the Haj way from Shuggera : the inhabitants are *Beny Zeyd ;* and, it is said, 'their jid was a Solubby !'—Passing always through the same plain wilderness encumbered with plutonic bergs and mountains, we alighted at evening under the peak *Ferjeyn ;* where also I saw some old ground-courses, of great stones.

On the morrow we journeyed through the same high steppe, full of sharp rocks, bergs and jebâl, of trap and granite. At noon we felt no more the fiery heat of yesterday ; and I read in the aneroid that we were come to an altitude of nearly five thousand feet ! where the bright summer air was light and refreshing. Now on our left hand are the mountains *Minnîeh*, at our right a considerable mountain of granite, *Tokhfa*. Our *mogŷil* was by the watering *el-Ghrôl*, in an hollow ground amidst trap mountains: that soil is green with growth of harsh desert bushes; and here are two-fathom *golbân* of the ancients, well steyned. The water, which is sweet and light, is the only good and wholesome to drink in all this way, of fifteen journeys, between el-Kasîm and the Mecca country.—A day eastward from hence is a mountain, *Gabbily ;* whose rocks are said to be hewn in strange manner.

This high wilderness is the best wild pasture land that I have seen in Arabia : the bushes are few, but it is a 'white country' overgrown with the desert grass, *nussy*.—What may be the cause that this Arabian desolation should smile more than other desolations of like soil, not far off ? I enquired of the Ateyba men who rode in the kâfily with Múthkir ; and they answered, *that this wilderness is sprinkled in the season by yearly showers.*— Is it not therefore because the land lies in the border of the monsoon or tropical rains? which fall heavily in the early autumn, and commonly last five or six weeks at et-Tâyif. Everywhere we see some growth of acacias, signs doubtless of ground-water not far under: and yet in so vast a land-breadth (of three hundred miles) there is no settlement! [This may be because the water is seldom or never sweet.] Of late years the land, lying so open to the inroads of Ibn Rashîd, has been partly abandoned by the Aarab; and the forsaken water-pits are choked, for lack of cleansing.—After the watering, we journeyed till evening: and alighted in a place called *es-She'ab*, near the basalt mountain and water *Kabshàn*. The land-height is all one since yesterday.

The fifth morning we journeyed in the same high country, full of bergs, mostly granitic; and often of strange forms, as the granite rock is spread sheet-wise and even dome-wise and scale-wise: a basalt berg with a strange vein in it called ' the wolf's path ' is a landmark by the way. Ere noon we crossed traces of a great ghrazzu; which was that late foray, they said, of Ibn Rashîd against 'Ateyba.—Ere noon there was an alarm! and the kâfily halted: some thought they had seen Aarab. All looked to their arms; many fired-off their long guns to load afresh; the weary drivers on foot, braving with their spears, began to leap and dance: the companies drew together; and the caravan advanced in better order. Sleymàn, who among the first had plucked off his gun-case, rode now with lighted matchlock in his lap, cursing and grinding the teeth with malevolence. The like did the most of them; for this is the caravan fanaticism, to cry to heaven for the perdition of their natural enemies!—the human wolves of the desert. Ibrahîm sent out scouts to descry the hovering foes: who bye and bye returned with word that they found them to be but desert trees! Then we heard it shouted, by the Emir's servant, ' To advance freely! ' At our noon menzil we were still at the height of 4550 feet.—We rode in the afternoon through the like plain desert, full of standing hay, but most desolate: the basalt rocks now exceed the granites. And already two or three desert plants appeared, which were new to my eyes,—the modest blossoms of another climate: we saw no signs of human occupation. When the sun was setting they alighted in a place called *Umm Meshe'aib;* the altitude is 4500 feet. We passed to-day the highest ground of the great middle desert.—In the beginning of the twilight a meteor shone brightly about us for a moment, with a beautiful blue light; and then drooping in the sky broke into many lesser stars.

I found Múthkir. in all the menzils under Ibrahîm's awning:

for he alighted with the emir.   The Beduin sheykh rode with
us to safe-guard the caravan in all encounters with his ('Ateyba)
tribesmen : and he and his two or three followers were as eyes
to us in the khála.—Nevertheless the Kasîm caravaners, continually passing the main deserts from their youth, are themselves expert in land-craft.   There was one among us, Sâlih
(the only Arabian that I have seen cumbered with a wen in the
throat), who had passed this way to and from Mecca, he thought,
almost an hundred times,—that were more than four years,
or fifty thousand miles of desert journeys : and he had ridden
and gone not less in the north between his Kasîm town and
the Gulf and river provinces.   Sâlih could tell the name of
every considerable rock which is seen by the long wayside.
They know their paths, but not the vast wilderness beyond the
landmarks.

How pleasant is the easy humour of all Beduins! in comparison with the harsher temper of townsfolk : I was bye and
bye friends with Múthkir.   When we spoke of the traces of Ibn
Rashîd's foray, he said, " Thou hast been at Hâyil, and art a
mudowwy : eigh !   Khalîl, could'st thou not in some wise quit us
from Ibn Rashîd—*el-Hâchim!* and we would billah reward thee :
it is he who afflicts 'Ateyba.''   He said further, " In the [north]
parts from whence we be come there are none our friends, but
only Aneyza": and when I enquired, Were his Aarab good folk?
he answered " Eigh !—such are they, as the people of Aneyza.''
Then he asked, ' If he visited me in my béled, what things
would I give him ?—a mare and a maiden to wife ?'—"And what
wilt thou give me, Múthkir, when I alight at thy beyt ? "   At
this word the Beduin was troubled, because his black booth of
ragged hair-cloth was not very far off; so he answered, he
would give me a bint, and she should be a fair one, to wife.—
" But I have given thee a mare, Múthkir."—" Well, Khalîl, I
will give thee a camel.   We go to Mekky, and thou to Jidda ;
and then whither wilt thou go ? "—"To India, it may please
Ullah."—Ibrahîm said, ' He had a mind to visit India with me ;
would I wait for him at Jidda ? till his coming down again in
the Haj—after four months ! '

We removed an hour before dawn ; and the light showed a
landscape more open before us, with many acacia trees.   Of all
the wells hitherto there are none so deep as four fathoms : this
land, said Múthkir, is full of *golbán* and waterpits of the Aarab.
When it rains, he told me, the seyls die shortly in the soil ; but
if in any year it rain a flood, the whole steppe seyls down (westward) to the Wady er-Rummah.   The country is full of cattle-

paths,—it may be partly made by the wild goats and gazelles. Leaving on our right hand the cragged *J. She'aba,* wherein "are many bedûn," we passed by a tent-like granite landmark, *Wareysieh ;* and came to lodge at noon between black basaltic mountains, full of peaks and of seyl strands ;—on this side was *Thul'aan en-Nîr,* and on that *She'ar.*

At each midday halt, the town camels are loosed out to pasture. The weary brutes roam in the desert, but hardly take anything into their parched mouths : they crop only a few mouthfuls by the way in the early morning, whilst the night coolness is yet upon the ground. The great brutes, that go fainting under their loads, sweat greatly, and for thirst continue nearly without eating till seventeen days be ended ; when they are discharged at Mecca. But these beasts from Nejd suffer anew in the stagnant air of the Tehâma ; where they have but few days to rest : so they endure, almost without refreshment ; till they arrive again very feeble at Aneyza. Our hardened drivers [all Arabs will—somewhat faint-heartedly—bemoan the aching life of this world !] told me with groans, that their travail in the journey was very sore; one of them rode in the morning and two walked ; in the afternoon one walked and two rode. The march of the Kasîm caravaners is not like the slowpaced procession of the Syrian Haj ; for they drive strenuously in the summer heat, from water to water. The great desert waterings are far asunder ; and they must arrive ere the fourth day, or the beasts would faint.

The caravaners, after three days, were all beside their short Semitic patience ; they cry out upon their beasts with the passionate voices of men in despair. The drivers beat forward the lingering cattle, and go on goading them with the heel of their spears, execrating, lamenting and yelling with words of evil augury, *Yâ mâl et-teyr—hut !* eigh ! thou carrion for crows, *Yâ mâl eth-thubbah,* eigh ! butcher's meat : if any stay an instant, to crop a stalk, they cry, *Yâ mâl ej-jû'a,* O thou hunger's own ! *Yelaan Ullah abu hâ 'l ras,* or *hâ 'l kalb* or *hâ 'l hulk,* May the Lord confound the father of thy head, of thy heart, of thy long halse.—Drivers of camels must have their eyes continually upon the loaded beasts : for a camel coming to any sandy place is likely to fall on his knees to wallow there, and ease his itching skin ;—and then all must go to wreck ! They discern not their food by sight alone, but in smelling ; and a camel will halt at any white stone or bleached *jella,* as if it were some blanched bone,—which if they may find at anytime they take it up in their mouth, and champ somewhile with a melancholy air ; and that is "for the saltiness ", say the Arabs. The caravaners in the march are each day of more waspish humour and fewer words; there is naught said now but with great *by-gods:* and the drivers, whose mouths are bitter with thirst, will hardly answer each other with other than crabbed and vaunting speech; as 'I am the son of my father! I the brother of my little sister!' 'Am I the slave of thy father (that I should serve or obey thee)?' And an angry soul will cry out on his neighbour, *Ullah la yubárak fík, la yujíb 'lak el-kheyr,* 'The Lord bless thee not, and send thee no good.'

The heat in our mid-day halt was 102° F. under the awnings, and rising early we made haste to come to the watering; where we arrived two hours before the sunsetting. This is *'Afíf,* an ancient well of ten fathoms to the water, and steyned with dry building of the wild basalt blocks.—Sleymàn, and the other master caravaners, had ridden out before the approaching kâfily, with their tackle; each one contending to arrive before other at the well's mouth, and occupy places for the watering. When we rode-in they stood there already by their gear; which is a thick stake pight in the ground, and made fast with stones : the head is a fork, and in that they mount their draw-reel, *maḥal,* —as the nomads use at any deep golbân, where they could not else draw water. The cord is drawn by two men running out backward; a third standing at the well-brink receives the full bucket, as it comes up; and runs to empty it into the camel trough,—a leather or carpet-piece spread upon a hollow, which they have scraped with stick or stone and their hands in the hard gravel soil. When so many camels must be watered at a single *jelíb,* there is a great ado of men drawing with all their might and chanting in cadence, like the Beduw. I went to drink at the camel troughs, but they bade me beware; 'I might chance to slip in the mire, and fall over the well brink,' which [as in all desert golbân] is even with the soil. The well-drawers' task is not without peril; and they are weary. At their last coming down, an unhappy man missed his footing,—and fell in ! He was hastily taken up—for Arabs in the sight of such mischiefs are of a sudden and generous humanity ! and many are wont from their youth to go down in all manner of wells :—His back was broken : and when the caravan departed, the sick man's friends laid him upon a camel; but he died in the march. —To the first at the well succeeded other drawers; and they were not all sped in three hours. This ancient well-mouth is mounded round with earth once cast up in the digging : thus the waterers, who run backward, draw easily; and the stinking sludge returns not to infect the well.

By that well side, I saw the first token of human life in this vast wilderness,—the fresh ashes of a hunter's fire ! whereby lay the greatest pair of gazelle horns that I have seen at any time. The men were Solubba ; and some in the kâfily had seen their asses' footprints to-day. It is a marvel even to the Arabs, how these human solitaries can live by their shooting, in the khála. The Solubby may bear besides his long matchlock only a little water ; but their custom is to drink a fill of water, or mereesy two hours before dawn : and then setting out, they are not athirst till noon. I now learned to do the like ; and that early draught sustained me until we halted at midday, though in the meanwhile my companions had drunk thrice.—They would hardly reach me the bowl, when they poured out for themselves to drink ; and then it was with grudges and cursing : if Sley-màn were out of hearing, they would even deny the Nasrâny altogether. Sleymàn, who was not good, said, " We all suffer by the way, I cannot amend it, and these are Arabs : Abdullah would find no better, were he here with his beard (himself). See you this boy, Khalîl ? he is one from the streets of Aneyza : that other (a Beduwy lad, of Annezy in the North) has slain, they say, his own father ; and he (the cook) yonder ! is a poor fol-lower from the town : wellah, if I chided them, they would for-sake me at the next halt ! "—It were breath lost to seek to drink water in another fellowship : one day I rode by a townsman who alighted to drink ; and ere he put up the bowl I asked him to pour out a little for me also. His wife had been a patient of mine, and haply he thought I might remember his debt for medi-cines ; for hastily tying again the neck of his girby, he affected not to know me. When I called him by name !—he could no longer refuse ; but undoing the mouth of the skin, he poured me out a little of the desert water, saying, " Such is the road and the toil, that no man remembers other ; but the word is *imshy hâl-ak !* help thyself forward."— A niggard of his girby is called *Bîa'a el-má*, Water-seller, by his angry neighbours. My thelûl was of little stature, wooden and weak : in walking she could not keep pace with the rest ; and I had much ado to drive her. The beast, said Sleymàn, was hide-bound ; he would make scotches in her sides, when they were come down to Mecca.

I found here the night air, at the coolest, 72° F. ; the deep well-water being then 79° F. The land-height is 4600 feet : there were flies and gnats about the water.—The cattle were drenched again towards morning : then we were ready to set forward, but no signal was given. The sun rose ; and a little after we heard a welcôme shout of the emir's servant, *El-yôm nej-î-î-îm !* We shall abide here to-day.

— There are two paths for the kâfilies going down from el-Kasîm to Mecca; the west derb with more and better waterings, —in which the butter caravan of Boreyda and er-Russ were journeying before us—is called *es-Sultâny*, the 'highway'. The middle derb, wherein we marched, is held by convoys that would pass expeditely : it is far between waterings, and there is the less likelihood of strife with Aarab summering upon any of them.—The caravaners durst not adventure to water their camels, in presence of the (fickle) Beduw : in such hap they may require the nomads to remove, who on their part will listen to the bidding of townsfolk with very evil mind. But if the Beduw be strong in number, the townspeople must make a shift to draw in haste with arms in their hands : and drive-on their half-refreshed beasts to the next cattle-pits, which in this wilderness are mostly bitter.—There is a third path, east of us, *derb Wady Sbeya*, with few and small *maweyrids ;* which is trodden by flying companies of thelûl riders. Last year the good Abdullah el-Bessâm, returning home by that way from Jidda, found the well-pit choked, when he came to one of those disused waterings, *Jelib ibn Haddîf ;* and he with his fellowship laboured a day to clear it. The several derbs lie mostwhat so nigh together, that we might view their landmarks upon both sides.

'Afîf, where we rested, is an hollow ground like el-Ghrôl, encompassed by low basaltic mountains. I saw the rude basalt stones of this well's mouth in the desert encrusted white, and deeply scored by the nomads' soft ropes! Hereabout grows great plenty of that tall joint-grass (*thurrm*), which we have seen upon the Syrian Haj road. The fasting camels were driven out to pasture ; and the 'Ateyba Beduins, companions of Múthkir, went up into the *mergab*—which was the next height of basalt—to keep watch. Great was the day's heat upon the kerchiefed heads of them who herded the camels ; for the sun which may be borne in journeying, that is whilst we are passing through the air, is intolerable even to Nomads who stand still : our Beduin hind sighed to me, "Oh! this sun!" which boiled his shallow brains. Towards evening a sign being made from the mergab! the caravan camels were hastily driven in. The scouts had descried *zôl*, as they supposed, of some Aarab : but not long after they could distinguish them to be four Solubbies, riding on asses.

We set forward from 'Afîf before the new day. When the sun came up we had left the low mountain train of *Átula* on our left hand ; and the wilderness in advance appeared more open : it is overgrown with hay ; and yet, Múthkir tells me, they

have better pastures! The mountains are now few: instead of
bergs and peaks, we see but rocks.—I was riding in the van;
and a great white gazelle-buck stood up in his lair before us:
The *thobby*, which was thick grown as a great he-goat, after a
few steps stood still, to gaze on this unwonted procession of
men and camels; then he ran slowly from us. The well-mounted
young gallants did off their gun-leathers; and pricked after the
quarry on their crop-eared thelûls, which run jetting the long
necks like birds:—to return when they were weary, from a
vain pursuit! Desert hares started everywhere as we passed,
and ran to cover under the next bushes,—the pretty tips yet
betraying them of their most long ears.

For two days southward the desert land is called *es-Shiffa*,
which is counted three days wide; others say 'Es-Shiffa lies
between er-Russ and 'Afîf; and all beyond is *el-Házzam*, for
two and a half journeys:' Múthkir holds that the Házzam
and the Shiffa are one. In all this vast land-breadth I had not
seen the furrow of a seyl!—Our mountain marks are now *Mér-
dumma*, on the left; and at our right hand three conical bergs
together, *Methàlitha*. *Jebel es-Sh'eyb*, which appears beyond,
lies upon the *derb es-Sultàny*: there is good water [this is
Gadyta of the old itineraries,—*v. Die alte Geogr. Arabiens;*
wherein we find mentioned also *Dathyna*, that is the water-pits
Dafîna; and *Ḳoba*, which is *Goba*, a good watering]: *J. Meshaf*
stands before us. Our *mogŷil* was between the mountains
'*Ajjilla* and *eth-Th'al;* the site is called *Shebrûm*, a bottom
ground with acacia trees, and where grows great plenty of a
low prickly herb, with purple blossoms, of the same name. In
this neighbourhood are cattle-pits of the Aarab, *Sh'brámy*.

Here at the midst of the Sheffa is an head, says Múthkir
(though it be little apparent), of *Wady Jerrîr*. This is the
main affluent from the east country of the Wady er-Rummah;
that in some of their ancient poems is feigned to say; 'My
side valleys give me to sip; there is but Wady Jerrîr which
allays my thirst',—words that seem to witness of the (here)
tropical rains! In the course of this valley, which is north-
westward, are many water-holes of the Beduw. Some interpret
Rummah 'old fretted rope' [which might be said of its much
winding].—We journeyed again towards evening: the landscape
is become an open plain about us; and the last mountain northward is vanished from our horizon.—Where we lodged at the
sunset I found the land height to be 4100 feet.

We removed not before dawn: at sunrise I observed the
same altitude, and again at mid-day; when the air under the
awnings was 107° F. This open district is called *ed-D'aika*,

which they interpret 'plain without bergs of mixed earth and good pasture.' Eastward we saw a far-off jebel; and the head of a solitary mountain, *Khâl*, before us. Later we passed between the *Seffua* and *'Aridàn* mountains and *Thennŷib*, which is a landmark and watering-place upon the derb es-Sultâny.— Near the sunsetting we rode over a wide ground crusted with salt; and the caravan alighted beyond.

Arriving where he would encamp, the emir draws bridle and, smiting her neck, hisses to his dromedary to kneel; and the great infirm creature, with groans and bowing the knees, will make some turns like a hound ere her couching down.—Strange is the centaur-like gaunt figure of the Arab dromedary rider regarded from the backward; for under the mantled man appears—as they were his demesurate pair of straddling (camel) legs. The master caravaners ride-in after the emir to take their menzils,—having a care that the lodgings shall be disposed in circuit: then the burden camels are driven up to their places and unloaded. The unruly camel yields to kneel, being caught by the beard: if a couched camel resist, rolling and braying, lay hold on the cartilage of his nose, and he will be all tame. We may think there is peril of his teeth, Arabs know there is none; for the great brute is of mild nature, though he show no affection to mankind. Beduins gather sappy plants and thrust them into their camels' jaws,—which I have done also a thousand times; and never heard that anyone was bitten. [I have once—in Sinai—seen a muzzled camel.] Though they snap at each other in the march it is but a feint. a grown camel has not the upper front teeth.

Our morrow's course—the tenth from Aneyza—was toward the flat-topped and black (basaltic) conical Jebel Khâl; and a swelling three-headed (granitic) mountain *Thúlm*.—The Nejd pilgrims cry out joyfully in their journey, when they see these jebâl, 'that, thanks be to God, they are now at the midway!' In the midst is the *maweyrid Shurrma*, where we alighted three hours before mid-day: here are cattle pits, but of so bitter water, that the Kusmàn could not drink. "We shall come, they said, to another watering to-morrow." There was little left in their girbies. I chose to drink here, enforcing myself to swallow the noisome bever, rather than strive with Sleymàn's drivers: the taste was like alum. But the cooks filled up some flagging skins of 'Afîf water; and thus mingled it might serve they thought, to boil the suppers. The three shallow pits [one is choked], with water at a fathom, are dry-steyned. In the midst of our watering, the wells were drawn dry; and the rest of the thirsting camels were driven up an hour later to drink, when the water was risen in them again. The land-height is the same as in our yesterday's march.

Journeying from Shurrma, we began to cross salty bottoms; and were approaching that great vulcanic country, the *Harrat el-Kisshub*. We pass wide-lying miry grounds, encrusted with subbakha; and white as it were with hoarfrost: at other times we rode over black plutonic gravel; and I thought I saw clear pebbles shining amongst the stones. In this desert landscape, of one height and aspect, are many *sammar* (acacia) trees: but the most were sere, and I saw none grown to timber.—A coast loomed behind Khâl: "Look! Khalîl, said my companions, yonder is the Harrat el-Kisshub!" a haze dimmed the Harra mountains, which I soon perceived to be crater-hills, *hillián*. In this march I rode by certain round shallow pits, a foot deep, but wide as the beginning of water-holes; and lying in pairs together. I hailed one of the kâfily as he trotted by; who responded, when I showed him the place, "Here they have taken out gold!" I asked Múthkir of it in the evening: "Ay Khalîl, he answered, we find many *rasûm*, 'traces,' in our dîra, —they are of the *auellín*."

On the morrow we removed very early to come this day to water. When the light began to spring, I saw that our course lay even with the Harra border, some miles distant. The lower parts were shrouded in the morning haze, where above I saw the tops of crater hills. The derb es-Sultâny lies for a day and a half over this lava field. We coast it; which is better for the camels' soles, that are worn to the quick in a long voyage. [Múthkir tells me, the lavas of the *Harrat Terr'a*, which joins to the Kisshub, are so sharp that only asses may pass them: and therein are villages and palms of 'Ateyba Aarab.] A foot-sore beast must be discharged; and his load parted among them will break the backs of the other camels. Some Nejd caravaners are so much in dread of this accident, that in the halts they cure their camels' worn feet with urine.—Might not the camels be shod with leather? there is a stave in the moallakát [LEBEID, 23] which seems to show that such shoes were used by the (more ingenious) ancient Arabians.

Betwixt us and the lava country is the hard blackish crusted mire of yesterday; a flat without herb or stone, without foot-print, and white with *subbakha:* tongues of this salty land stretch back eastward beyond our path. A little before noon we first saw footprints of nomad cattle, from the Harra-ward;—where-under is a good watering, in face of us. In the mid-day halt our thirst was great: the people had nothing to drink, save of that

sour and black water from Shurrma ; and we could not come to
the wells, till nightfall, or early on the morrow. I found the
heat of the air under the awnings 107° F. ; and the simûm was
blowing. In the caravan fellowships they eat dates in the mogŷil, and what little burghrol or temmn may be left over from
their suppers. Masters and drivers sit at meat together ; but to-
day none could eat for thirst. I went to the awnings of Ibrahîm
and Bessâm—each of them carried as many as ten girbies—to
seek a fenjeyn of coffee or of water. The young men granted
these sips of water and no more ; for such are Arabians on the
journey : I saw they had yet many full waterskins !

That nooning was short, because of the people's thirst,—and
the water yet distant. As we rode forth I turned and saw my
companions drinking covertly ! besides they had drunk their fills
in my absence, after protesting to me that there was not any ;
and I had thirsted all day. I thought, might I drink this once,
I could suffer till the morning. I called to the fellows to pour
me out a little ; ' we were rafîks, and this was the will of Abdullah el-Kenneyny ' : but they denied me with horrible cursing ; and Sleymân made merchant's ears. I alighted, for ' need
hath no peer ', and returned to take it whether they would or
no. The Beduwy, wagging his club and beginning to dance,
would maintain their unworthy purpose : but Sleymân (who
feared strife) bade them then pour out for Khalîl.—It was sweet
water from 'Afîf, which they had kept back and hidden this
second day from the Nasrâny : they had yet to drink of it twice
in the afternoon march.—Sleymân was under the middle age, of
little stature, of a sickly nature, with some sparkles of cheerful
malice, and disposed to fanaticism. I had been banished from
Aneyza, and among these townsmen were many of the Wabâby
sort ; but the most saluted me in the long marches with a friendly
word, "How fares Khalîl, art thou over weary ? well ! we shall
be soon at our journey's end." Once only I had heard an injurious word ; that was in the evening rest at 'Afîf, when
crossing in the dark towards Ibrahîm and Mûthkir I lighted on
some strange fellowship, and stumbled at the butter skins.
" Whither O kafir," cried their hostile voices ; but others called
to them ' to hold their mouths !—and pass by, mind them not
Khalîl.'

Sleymân told me he had sometime to do with the English
shippers, on the Gulf : " they were good people, and better than
the Turks. Trust thy goods, quoth he, to the Engleys ; for they
will save thee harmless, if anything should be damaged or lost.
But as for Turkish shipping, you must give to the labourers, and
again ere they will receive your goods aboard ; besides the officer

looks for his fee, and the seamen will embezzle somewhat on the ship's voyage : but with the English you shall find right dealing and good order. And yet by Ullah, if any Engleys take service with the Osmully, they become bribe-catchers, and are worse than the Turks!"—The brazen sun, in the afternoon march, was covered with clouds : and when we had ridden in these heavenly shadows three hours, leaving the mountains *el-Kamîm* and *Hakràn* behind our backs, I saw some stir in the head of our kâfily ; and thelûl-riders parted at a gallop! They hastened forward to seek some cattle-pits, lying not far beside the way. When they came to the place, every man leapt down in a water-hole, to fill his girby ; where they stood up to their middles in the slimy water : each thirsty soul immediately swallowed his bowlful ; and only then they stayed to consider that the water was mawkish!

This is *Hazzeym es-Seyd*, a grove of acacia trees,—very beautiful in the empty khála! and here are many cattle-pits of a fathom and a half, to the water ; which rises of the rain.—Now we looked back, and saw the kâfily heading hither! the thirsty drivers had forsaken their path. Ibrahîm, when the camels were driven in, gave the word to encamp. That water was welcome more than wholesome ;—the most were troubled with diarrhœa in the night. I felt no harm ;—nor yesterday, after drinking the Shurrma water : which made me remember with thankful mind, that in these years spent in countries, where in a manner all suffer, I had never sickened.

In the night-time Ibrahîm sent some thelûl-riders to spy out that water before us, where we had hoped to arrive yesterday ; and bring word if any Aarab were lodged upon it.—The sun rose and we yet rested in this pleasant site. And some went out with their long matchlocks amongst the thorny green trees, to shoot at doves [which haunt the *maweyrids*, but are seldom seen flying in the khála]: but by the counsel of Múthkir, Ibrahîm sent bye and bye to forbid any more firing of guns ; for the sound might draw enemies upon us.—When the sun was half an hour high, we saw our scouts returning ; who rode in with tidings, that they had seen only few Beduw at the water, which were 'Àteybàn ; and had spoken with one they found in the desert, who invited them to come and drink milk. We remained still in our places ; and the awnings were set up.—A nâga fàtir was slaughtered ; and distributed among the fellowships, that had purchased the portions of meat. Three or four such slaughter-beasts were driven down in the kâfily : and in this sort the weary caravaners taste flesh meat, every few days.

The caravan removed at noon : the salt flats reaching back to
the vulcanic coast, lay always before us; and to the left the
desert horizon. We passed on between the low *J. Hakràn* and
the skirts of the Harra. At sunset the caravan entered a
cragged bay in an outflow of the Harra: that lava rock is
heavy and basaltic.   Here is a watering place of many wells,—
el-Moy, or *el-Moy She'ab*, or *Ameah Hakràn*, a principal *maurid*
of the Aarab.

The Beduins were departed : yet we alighted in the twilight
somewhat short of the place ; for 'the country in these months
is full of thieves'.   But every fellowship sent one to the wells
with a girby, to fetch them to drink.   The caravaners now
encamped in a smaller circuit, for the fear of the desert: the
coffee and cooking fires were kindled ; it was presently dark
night, and watches were set.   In each company one wakes for
the rest ; and they make three watches till dawn.   If any pass
by the dim fire-lights, or one is seen approaching, a dozen cruel
throats cry out together, *Min hâtha*, 'Who is there, who ?'
And all the fellowships within hearing shout hideously again,
Ethbah-hu ! kill-kill him! So the beginning of the night is
full of their calling and cursing ; since some will cross hither
and thither, to visit their friends.   When I went through the
camp to seek Ibrahîm and Múthkir, and the son of Bessàm ;
huge were the outcries, *Ethbah-hu !*—*Min hu hâtha ?* the answer
is *Ana sahib*, It is I, a friend ; or *Tâyib, mâ fî shey*, It is well,
there is nothing.—Sleymàn tells me, that in their yearly pilgrimage caravan, in which is carried much merchandise and
silver, they keep these night watches in all the long way of the
desert.

At break of day the Kusmàn, with arms in their hands!
drove the camels to water : and their labour was soon sped, for
the wells were many.   The kâfily departed two hours after the
sunrise, the thirteenth from Aneyza. We had not met with
mankind since el-Kasîm ! but now a few Beduins appeared
driving their cattle to water. The same steppe is about us :
many heads of quartz, like glistering white heaps, are seen in
this soil.   We passed by a *dar*, or old worn camping-ground of
the Aarab ; and cattle-pits of bitter water. The high coast of
the Harrat el-Kisshub trends continually with our march; I
could see in it green acacias, and drift-sand banked up high
from the desert: the crater-hills appeared dimly through the
sunny haze.   [These great lavas have overflowed plutonic rocks :
—those of Kheybar and the 'Aueyrid a soil of sandstones.]
The salt-flats yet lie between our caravan path and the Harra.—
Such is the squalid landscape which we see in going down from

Nejd to Mecca! The height of all this wilderness is 4200 feet nearly. We halted at high noon, sun-beaten and in haste to rear-up the awnings. A Beduwy came riding to us from the wilderness upon his thelûl. The man, who was a friendly 'Ateyby, brought word that the kâfily of Boreyda was at the water *Marràn*, under the Harra yonder.—The simûm rose, in our afternoon march, and blustered from the westward. At the sun's going down we alighted for the night: but some in the caravan, hearing that cattle-pits were not far off, rode out to fill their girbies: they returned empty, for the water was bitter and tasted, they told us, of sulphur.

On the morrow, we saw everywhere traces of the Nomads. The height of the desert soil is that which I have found daily for a hundred miles behind us. Our path lies through a belt of couutry, *er-Rukkaba*, which the Arabs say 'is the highest in all the way, where there always meets them a cold air,'—when they come up from the (tropical) Teháma. Notwithstanding their opinion I found the altitude at noon and before sunset no more than 4300 feet. The heat was lighter, and we look here upon a new and greener aspect of the desert: this high plain reaches south-eastward to et-Tâyif. Each day, when the sun as we journeyed was most hot over our heads, I nodded in the saddle and swooned for an hour or two: but looking up this noonday methought I saw by the sun that we were returning backward! I thought, in those moments, it was a sun-stroke; or that the fatigues of Arabian travel had at length troubled my understanding: bus the bitter sweat on my forehead was presently turned to a dew of comfort, in the cogitation, that we were past the summer tropic; and the northing of the sun must reverse our bearings. I saw in the offing a great mountain bank, eastward, *J. Hatthon*, of the *B'goom* Aarab; and beyond is the village *Túrraba:* under the mountain are, they say, some ancient ruins. West of our path stands the black basaltic jebel, *Néfur et-Tarîk.* The Harra has vanished from our sight: before us lies the water *Mehàditha.*—This night was fresher than other: the altitude being nearly 4600 feet. At dawn I found 73° F. and chill water in the girbies.

The morrow's journey lay yet over the Rukkaba, always an open plain: the height increases iu the next hours to nearly five thousand feet. I saw the acacia bushes cropped close, and trodden round in the sand—by the beautiful feet of gazelles! At our mogýil the heat under the awnings was 102° F.—In the evening march we saw sheep flocks of the Aarab; and naked children keeping them. The little Beduins—nut-brown skinned under the scourge of the southern sun—were of slender growth. We espied their camels before us : the herdsmen approached to enquire tidings; and a horseman, who sat upon his mare's bare chine, thrust boldly in among us. We saw now their black booths : these Aarab were *Sheyabîn*, of 'Ateyba. The sun was low; and turning a little aside from the nomad menzil we alighted to encamp.—And there presently came over to us some of the nomad women, who asked to buy clothing of the caravaners : but the Kusmàn said it was but to spy out our encampment, and where they might pilfer something in the night. Their keen eyes noted my whiter skin ; and they asked quickly " Who he ? —who is that stranger with you ? "

On the morrow we journeyed in the midst of the nomad flocks —here all white fleeces. In this (now tropical) desert, I saw some solitary tall plants of a jointed and ribbed flowering cactus, *el-ghrullathî*, which is a cattle-medicine : the Aarab smear it in the nostrils of their sick camels. The soil is sand and gravel of the crystalline rocks.—Two hours before noon, we rode by the head of another basaltic lava stream ; and met camels of the same Sheyabîn breasting up from the maweyrid *Sh'aara*, lying nigh before us. These 'Ateyba camels are brown coloured, with a few blackish ones among them ; and all of little stature : the herdsmen were free and well-spoken weleds.—Riding by a worsted booth standing alone, I saw only a Beduin wife and her child that sat within, and said *Salaam !* she answered again with a cheerful " Welcome—welcome."—In approaching nomads, our caravaners—ever in distrust of the desert folk—unsling their long guns, draw off the leathers, blow the matches ; and ride with the weapons ready on their knees.

Before us is a solitary black jebel, *Biss*, which is perhaps of basalt.—And now we see again the main Harra ; that we are approaching, to water at Sh'aara. Múthkir tells me, ' the great Harrat el-Kisshub is of a round figure [some say, It is one to two days to go over] ; and that the Kisshub is not solitary, but a member of the train of Harras between Mecca and Medina : the Kisshub and the Ahràr el-Medina are not widely separated.' There met us a slender Beduin lad coming up after the cattle ; and beautiful was the face of that young waterer, in his Mecca tunic of blue !—but to Northern eyes it is the woman's colour : the black locks hanged down dishevelled upon his man-maidenly shoulders. " Hoy, weled ! (cries our rude Annezy driver, who as a Beduwy hated all Beduw not his own tribesfolk).—I say fellows, is this one a male or a female ? " The poor weled's heart swelled with a vehement disdain ; his ingenuous eyes looked fiercely upon us, and he almost burst out to weep.—Sh'aara, where we now arrived, is a bay in the Harra that is here called *A'ashiry.* The end of the lava, thirty feet in height, I found to overlie granite rock,—which is whitish, slacked, and crumbling, with the suffered heat: the head of lava has stayed at the edge of the granite reef. Sh'aara is a sh'aeb or seyl-strand which they reckon to the *Wady 'Adzîz* and *Wady el-'Agîg.* Here are many narrow-mouthed wells of the ancients, and dry-steyned with lava stones; but some are choked. We heard from the Aarab that the Boreyda caravan watered here last noon: since yesterday the desert paths are one. I found the altitude, 4900 feet.

The caravaners passed this night under arms. Our slumbers were full of shouted alarms, and the firing of matchlocks; so that we lay in jeopardy of our own shot, till the morning. If any Beduin thief were taken they would hale him to the Emir's tent; and his punishment, they told me, would be "to beat him to death". Almost daily there is somewhat missed in the kâfily; and very likely when we mounted ere day, it was left behind upon the dim earth.—In the next menzil the owner, standing up in his place, will shout, through his hollow hands, 'that he has lost such a thing; which if anyone have found, let him now restore it, and remember Ullah'.

Some of the Beduins came to us in the morning; who as soon as they eyed me, enquired very earnestly, what man I were. Our caravaners asked them of the price of samn in Mecca. When we removed, after watering again the camels, a Beduin pressed hardily through the kâfily: he was ill clad as the best of them, but of comely carriage beside the harsh conditions of drudging townsfolk. Our bold-tongued Annezy driver cursed the father that begat him, and bade him stand off! but the 'Ateyby drew out his cutlass to the half and, with a smile of the Beduin urbanity, went on among them: he was not afraid of townlings in his own dîra. We journeyed again: and the coast of the Harra appeared riding high upon the plain at our right hand. We found a child herding lambs, who had no clothes, but a girdle of leathern thongs. [Afterward I saw hareem wearing the like over their smocks: it may be a South Arabian guise of the *haggu.*] The child wept, that he and his lambs were overtaken by so great a company of strangers: but stoutly gathering his little flock, he drove aside and turned his blubbered cheeks from us.

Here we passed from the large and pleasant plains of Nejd; and entered a cragged mountain region of traps and basalts, *er-Rî'a,* where the altitude is nearly 5000 feet. [*Rî'a* we have seen to signify a gap and wild passage in the jebel,—I find no like word in our lowland language.] In the Rî'a grow certain gnarled bushes, *nèbba*, which I had seen last in the limestone hills of Syria : and we passed by the blackened sites of (Meccan) charcoal burners. Further in this strait we rode by cairns : some of them, which show a rude building, might be sepulchres of principal persons in old time,—the Rî'a is a passage betwixt great regions. If I asked any in the caravan, What be these heaps ? they answered, " Works of the kafirs, that were in the land before the Moslemîn :—how Khalîl ! were they not of thy people ? " Others said, " They are of the Beny Helál."

From this passage we ascended to the left, by a steep seyl, encumbered with rocks and acacia trees. Not much above, is a narrow brow ; where I saw a cairn, and courses of old dry building ; and read under my cloak the altitude 5500 feet, which is the greatest in all the road. There sat Ibrahîm with his companions ; and the emir's servant stood telling the camels—passing one by one, which he noted in a paper ; for upon every camel (as said) is levied a real. Few steps further the way descended again, by another torrent.—I looked in vain for ancient scored inscriptions : here are but hard traps and grey-red granite, with basalt veins.

The aspect of this country is direful. We were descending to Mecca—now not far off—and I knew not by what adventure I should live or might die on the morrow : there was not anyone of much regard in all the caravan company. Sleymàn's good-will was mostwhat of the thought, that he must answer for the Nasrâny, to his kinsman Abdullah. Abd-er-Rahmàn was my friend in the kâfily,—in that he obeyed his good father : he was amiable in himself ; and his was not a vulgar mind, but *mesquin*. I felt by his answers to-day, that he was full of care in my behalf.

It was noon when we came forth upon a high soil, straitened betwixt mountains, like a broad upland wady. This ground, from which the Nejd caravans go down in a march or two short stages, to Mecca, is called *es-Seyl :* I found the height to be 5060 feet.—The great Wady el-Humth whereunto seyls the Harb country on both sides, and the Harras between Mecca and Tebûk, is said to spring from the Wady Laymûn, which lies a little below, on the right hand : the altitude considered, this is not impossible.

We have passed from Nejd ; and here is another nature of Arabia ! We rode a mile in the narrow *Seyl* plain, by thickets

T*

of rushy grass, of man's height! with much growth of peppermint; and on little leas,—for this herbage is browsed by the
caravan camels which pass-by daily between Mecca and Tâyif.
Now the kâfily halted, and we alighted : digging here with their
hands they find at a span deep the pure rain water. From hence
I heard to be but a march to Tâyif : and some prudent and
honest persons in the kâfily persuaded me to go thither, saying,
'It was likely we should find some Mecca cameleers ascending
to et-Tâyif, and they would commit me to them,—so I might
arrive at et-Tâyif this night; and they heard the Sherîf (of
Mecca) was now at et-Tâyif : and when I should be come thither,
if I asked it of the Sherîf, he would send me down safely to
Jidda.'

— What pleasure to visit Tâyif! the Eden of Mecca, with
sweet and cool air, and running water; where are gardens of
roses, and vineyards and orchards. But these excellencies are
magnified in the common speech, for I heard some of the Kusmàn saying, 'They tell wonders of et-Tâyif!—well, we have
been there; and one will find it to be less than the report.'—
The maladies of Arabia had increased in me by the way; the
lower limbs were already full of the ulcers, that are called ḥub or
bízr or bethra et-támr, 'the date button,' on the Persian Gulf
coast [because they rise commonly near the time of date har-
vest]. The boil, which is like the Aleppo button, is known in
many parts of the Arabic world,—in Barbary, in Egypt ('Nile
sores'): and in India ('Delhi boil'): it is everywhere ascribed
to the drinking of unwholesome water. The flat sores may be
washed with carbolic acid, and anointed with fish oil; but the
evil will run its course, there is no remedy: the time with me
was nearly five months.—Sores springing of themselves are
common among the Beduw. [Comp. also Deut. xxviii. 35.] For
such it seemed better to descend immediately to Jidda; also I
rolled in my heart, that which I had read of (old) Mecca Sherîfs:
besides, were it well for me to go to et-Tâyif, why had not el-
Bessàm—who had praised to me the goodness of the late Sherîf
—given me such counsel at Aneyza? Now there sat a new
Sherîf : he is also Emir of Mecca; and I could not know that
he would be just to a Nasrâny.

The Kusmàn were busy here to bathe themselves, and put off
their secular clothing : and it was time, for the tunics of the
drivers and masters were already of a rusty leaden hue, by their
daily lifting the loads ot butterskins.—Sitting at the water-holes,
each one helped other, pouring full bowls over his neighbour's
head. And then, every man taking from his bundle two or
three yards of new calico or towel stuff, they girded themselves.

This is the *ihrâm,* or pilgrims' loin-cloth, which covers them to
the knee; and a lap may be cast over the shoulder. They are
henceforth bare-headed and half-naked; and in this guise must
every soul enter the sacred precincts: but if one be of the town
or garrison, it is his duty only after a certain absence. In the
men of our Nejd caravan, a company of butter-chandlers, that
descend yearly with this merchandise, could be no fresh trans-
ports of heart. They see but fatigues before them in the Holy
City; and I heard some say, 'that the heat now in Mekky
[with clouded simûm weather] would be intolerable': they
are all day in the sûks, to sell their wares; and in the sultry
nights they taste no refreshing, until they be come again
hither. The fellowships would lodge in hired chambers: those
few persons in the caravan who were tradesmen in the City
would go home; and so would the son of Bessâm: his good
father had a house in town; and an old slave-woman was left
there, to keep it.

This is a worn camping-ground of many generations of pilgrims and caravaners; and in summer the noon station of passengers between the Holy City and et-Tâyif. Foul râkhams
were hawking up and down; and I thought I saw mortar clods
in this desert place, and some old substruction of brick building!
—My Aneyza friends tell me, that this is the old station *Kurn
el-menâzil;* which they interpret of the interlacing stays of the
ancient booths, standing many together in little space. I went
barefoot upon the pleasant sward in the mid-day sun,—which at
this height is temperate; for what sweetness it is, after years
passed in droughty countries, to tread again upon the green sod!
Only the Nasrâny remained clad among them; yet none of the
Kusmân barked upon me: they were themselves about to
arrive at Mecca; and I might seem to them a friend, in comparison with the malignant Beduin people of this country [*el-
Hathèyl*].

I found Bessâm's son, girded only in the ihrâm, sitting under
his awning. "Khalîl, quoth he, yonder—by good fortune! are
some cameleers from et-Tâyif: I have spoken with one of them;
and the man—who is known—is willing to convey thee to
Jidda."—"And who do I see with them?"—"They are *Jáwwa.*
[Java pilgrims so much despised by the Arabians: for the Malay
faces seem to them hardly human! I have heard Amm Mohammed say at Kheybar, 'Though I were to spend my lifetime in
the *Bèled ej-Jáwwa,* I could not—! wellah I could not wive
with any of their hareem.' Those religious strangers had been
at Tâyif, to visit the Sherîf; and the time was at hand of their

going-up, in the 'little pilgrimage', to Medina.] Khalîl, the adventure is from Ullah : wellah I am in doubt if we may find anyone at *el-'Ayn*, to accompany thee to the coast. And I must leave the kâfily ere the next halt; for we (the young companions with Ibrahîm) will ride this night to Mecca; and not to-morrow in the sun, because we are bare-headed. Shall we send for Sleymàn, and call the cameleer?—but, Khalîl, agree with him quickly; for we are about to depart, and will leave thee here."

— That cameleer was a young man of wretched aspect! one of the multitude of pack-beast carriers of the Arabic countries, whose sordid lives are consumed with daily misery of slender fare and broken nights on the road. In his wooden head seemed to harbour no better than the wit of a camel, so barrenly he spoke. *Abd-er-Rahmàn:* " And from the 'Ayn carry this passenger to Jidda, by the Wâdy Fâtima."—" I will carry him by Mecca, it is the nigher way." *Abd-er-Rahmàn, and Sleymàn:* " Nay, nay ! but by the Wâdy,—Abd-er-Rahmàn added ; This one goes not to Mecca,"—words which he spoke with a fanatical strangeness, that betrayed my life; and thereto Sleymàn rolled his head ! So that the dull cameleer began to imagine there must be somewhat amiss !—he gaped on him who should be his charge, and wondered to see me so white a man ! I cut short the words of such tepid friends : I would ride from the 'Ayn in one course to Jidda, whereas the drudge asked many days. The camels of this country are feeble, and of not much greater stature than horses. Such camels move the Nejd men's derision : they say, the Mecca cameleers' march is *mìthil, en-nimml,* ' at the ant's pace '.

That jemmâl departed malcontent, and often regarding me, whom he saw to be unlike any of the kinds of pilgrims. [As he went he asked in our kâfily, what man I were ; and some answered him, of their natural malice and treachery, *A Nas-rány!* When he heard that, the fellow said, ' *Wullah-Bullah,* he would not have conveyed me,— no, not for an hundred reals !] " Khalîl, there was a good occasion, but thou hast let it pass !" quoth Abd-er-Rahmàn.—" And is it to such a pitiful fellow you would commend my life, one that could not shield me from an insult,—is this the man of your confidence? one whom I find to be unknown to all here : I might as well ride alone to Jidda." *Sleymàn:* " Khalîl, wheresoever you ride in these parts, they will know by your saddle-frame that you are come from the east [Middle Nejd]."—And likewise the camel-furnitures of these lowland Mecca caravaners seemed to us to be of a strange ill fashion.

Whilst we were speaking Ibrahîm's servant shouted to re-move! The now half-naked and bare-headed caravaners loaded hastily : riders mounted ; and the Nejd kâfily set forward.—We were descending to Mecca ! and some of the rude drivers *yulubbún* [the devout cry of the pilgrims at Arafát]; that is, looking to heaven they say aloud *Lubbeyk! Lubbeyk!* which might signify, 'to do Thy will, to do Thy will (O Lord) !' This was not a cheerful song in my ears : my life was also in doubt for those worse than unwary words of the son of Bessâm. Such tidings spread apace and kindle the cruel flame of fanaticism ; yet I hoped, as we had set out before them, that we should arrive at the ʿAyn ere that unlucky Mecca jemmâl. I asked our Annezy driver, why he craked so ? And he—"Auh ! how fares Khalîl ? to-morrow we shall be in Mekky ! and thus we cry, because our voyage is almost ended,—Lubbeyk-lubbeyk !"

The ihrâm or pilgrims' loin-cloth remains doubtless from the antique religions of the Kaaba. I have found a tradition among Beduins, that a loin-cloth of stuff which they call *yémeny* was their ancient clothing.—Women entering the sacred borders are likewise to be girded with the ihrâm ; but in the religion of Islam they cover themselves with a sheet-like veil. Even the soldiery riding in the (Syrian or Egyptian) Haj caravans, and the officers and the Pasha himself take the ihrâm : they enter the town like bathing men,—there is none excused. [The pilgrims must remain thus half-naked in Mecca certain days; and may not cover themselves by night ! until their turning again from Arafát.] At Mecca there is, nearly all months, a tropical heat : and perhaps the pilgrims suffer less from chills, even when the pilgrimage is made in winter, than from the sun poring upon their weak pates, wont to be covered with heavy coifs and turbans. But if the health of anyone may not bear it, the Lord is pitiful, it is remitted to him ; and let him sacrifice a sheep at Mecca.

I saw another in our kâfily who had not taken the ihrâm,—a sickly young trader, lately returned from Bosra, to visit his Kasîm home; and now he went down, with a little merchandise, to Mecca. The young man had learned, in fifteen years' sojourn-ing in the north, to despise Nejd, " Are they not (he laughed to me) a fanatic and foolish people ? ha-ha ! they wear no shoes, and are like the Beduins. I am a stranger, Khalîl, as thou art, and have not put on the ihrâm, I might take cold ; and it is but to kill a sheep at Mekky." I perceived in his illiberal nicety and lying, and his clay visage, that he was not of the ingenuous blood. He had brought down a strange piece of merchandise in our kâfily, a white ass of Mesopotamia ; and looked to have a double price for her in Mecca,—where, as in other cities of the Arabic East, the ass is a riding-beast for grave and considerable persons. [*Confer* Judg. v. 10.] I said to Abd-er-Rahmàn, who was weakly, "And why hast thou taken the ihràm?" He answered, 'that if he felt the worse by the way, he would put on his clothing again ; and sacrifice a sheep in Mecca.'—These are not pilgrims who visit the sacred city : they perform only the ordinary devotion at the Kaaba ; and then they will clothe themselves, to go about their affairs.

From the Seyl we descend continually in a stony valley-bed betwixt black plutonic mountains, and half a mile wide : it is a vast seyl-bottom of grit and rolling-stones, with a few acacia trees. This landscape brought the Scandinavian *fjelde* to my remembrance. The carcase of the planet is alike, everywhere : it is but the outward clothing that is diverse,—the gift of the sun and rain. They know none other name for this iron valley than *Wady es-Seyl*. In all yonder horrid mountains are *Aarab Hathèyl* [gentile pl. *el-Hetheylân*],—an ancient name ; and it is said of them in the country, "they are a lineage by themselves, and not of kindred with the neighbour tribes." When Mecca and Tâyif cameleers meet with strangers coming down from Nejd, they will commonly warn them with such passing words, " *Ware the Hathèyl! they are robbers.*" The valley way was trodden down by camels' feet ! The Boreyda caravan had passed before us with two hundred camels,—but here I saw the footprints of a thousand ! I knew not that this is the Mecca highway to Tâyif, where there go-by many trains of camels daily. When the sun was setting we alighted—our last menzil—among the great stones of the torrent-valley. The height was now only 3700 feet.

—It had been provided by the good Bessàm, in case none other could be found at the station before Mecca, that his own man (who served his son Abd-er-Rahmàn by the way) should ride down with me to Jidda. Abd-er-Rahmàn now called this servant ; but the fellow, who had said " Ay-ay " daily in our long voyage, now answered with *lilla*, 'nay-nay—thus the Arabs do commonly fail you at the time !—He would ride, quoth he, with the rest to Mecca.' Abd-er-Rahmàn was much displeased and troubled ; his man's answer confounded us. "Why then didst thou promise to ride with Khalîl? go now, I entreat thee, said he ; and Khalîl's payment is ready : thou canst not say nay." Likewise Ibrahîm the Emir persuaded the man ;—but he had no authority to compel him. The fellow answered shortly, " I am free, and I go not to Jidda ! " and so he left us. Then Ibrahîm sent for another in the kâfily, a poor man of good understanding: and when he came he bade him ride with Khalîl to Jidda; but he beginning to excuse himself, they said, " Nothing hastens thee, for a day or two, to be at Mecca ; only set a price—and no nay ! " He asked five reals ; and with this slender assurance they dismissed him : " Let me, I said, bind the man, by paying him earnest-money." Ibrahîm answered, " There is no need tonight ;—in the morning ! " I knew then in my heart that this was a brittle covenant; and had learned to put no trust in the evening promises of Arabs.—" Yâ Múthkir ! let one of your Beduins ride with me to Jidda."—" Well, Khalîl, if that might help thee ; but they know not the way." Ibrahîm, Abd-er-Rahmàn and the young companions were to mount presently, after supper, and ride to Mecca,—and then they would abandon me in this sinister passage. I understood later, that they had deferred riding till the morning light:—which came all too soon ! And then we set forward.

It needed not that I should await that Promiser of over-night ; who had no thoughts of fulfilling Ibrahîm and Abd-er-Rahmàn's words,—and they knew this. Though to-day was the seventeenth of our long marches from Aneyza ; yet, in the sameness of the landscape, it seemed to me, until yesterday, when we passed es-Sh'aara, as if we had stood still.—The caravan would be at Mecca by mid-day : I must leave them now in an hour, and nothing was provided.

We passed by a few Beduins who were moving upward : light-bodied, black-skinned and hungry-looking wretches: their poor stuff was loaded upon the little camels of this country. I saw the desolate valley-sides hoary with standing hay--these mountains lie under the autumn (monsoon) rains—and among the steep rocks were mountain sheep of the nomads ; all white fleeces, and of other kind than the great sheep in Nejd. Now in the midst of the wady we passed through a grove of a tree-like strange canker-weed (el-'esha), full of green puff-leaves ! the leafy bubbles, big as grape-shot, hang in noisome-looking clusters, and enclose a roll of seed. This herb is of no service, they say, to man or cattle ; but the country people gather the sap, and sell it, for a medicine, to the Persian pilgrims ; and the Beduins make charcoal of the light stems for their gunpowder. There met us a train of passengers, ascending to Tâyif, who had set out this night from Mecca. The hareem were seated in litters, like bedsteads with an awning, charged as a houdah upon camel-back · they seemed much better to ride-in than the side cradles of Syria.

I was now to pass a circuit in whose pretended divine law is no refuge for the alien; whose people shut up the ways of the common earth; and where any felon of theirs in comparison with a Nasrâny is one of the people of Ullah. I had looked to my pistol in the night; and taken store of loose shot about me; since I had no thought of assenting to a fond religion. If my hard adventure were to break through barbarous opposition; there lay thirty leagues before me, to pass upon this wooden thelûl, to the coast; by unknown paths, in valleys inhabited by *ashrâf* [sherîfs], the seed of Mohammed.—I would follow down the seyl-strands, which must needs lead out upon the seabord. But I had no food nor water; and there was no strength left in me.—Ibrahîm who trotted by, gazed wistfully under my kerchief; and wondered (like a heartless Arab) to see me ride with tranquillity. He enquired, "How I did? and quoth he, seest thou yonder bent of the Wâdy? when we arrive there, we shall be in sight of '*Ayn ez-Zeyma*."—"And wilt thou then provide for me, as may befall?"—"Ay, Khalîl;" and he rode further: I saw not Abd-er-Rahmân! he was in the van with the companions.

The thelûl of one who was riding a little before me fell on a stone, and put a limb out of joint,—an accident which is without remedy! Then the next riders made lots hastily for the meat; and dismounting, they ran-in to cut the fallen beast's throat: and began with their knives to hack the not fully dead carcase. In this haste and straitness, they carved the flesh in the skin; and every weary man hied with what gore-dropping gobbet his hand had gotten, to hang it at his saddle bow; and that should be their supper-meat at Mecca! they re-mounted immediately, and hastened forward. Between the fall of the thelûl, and an end of their butchery, the caravan camels had not marched above two hundred paces!—Now I saw the clay banks of 'Ayn ez-Zeyma! green with thúra;—and where, I thought, in few minutes, my body might be likewise made a bloody spectacle. We rode over a banked channel in which a spring is led from one to the other valley-side. Besides the fields of corn, here are but few orchards; and a dozen stems of sickly palms; the rest were dead for fault of watering: the people of the hamlet are Hathèyl. I read the altitude, under my cloak, 2780 feet.

Here is not the Hejâz, but the Tehâma; and according to all Arabians, *Mecca is a city of the Tehâma.* Mecca is closed-in by mountains, which pertain to this which we should call a middle region; nevertheless the heads of those lowland jebâl (whose border may be seen from the sea) reach not to the brow of Nejd.

In the (southern) valley-side stands a great clay kella, now ruinous; which was a fort of the old Wahábies, to keep this gate of Nejd : and here I saw a first coffee-station *Kahwa* (vulg. *Gahwa*) of the Mecca country. This hospice is but a shelter of rude clay walling and posts, with a loose thatch of palm branches cast up.—Therein sat Ibrahîm and the thelûl riders of our káfily ; when I arrived tardily, with the loaded camels. Sleymàn el-Kenneyny coming forth led up my riding-beast by the bridle to this open inn. The Kusmàn called *Khalîl !* and I alighted; but Abd-er-Rahmàn met me with a careful face.— I heard a savage voice within say, "*He shall be a Moslem*" : and saw it was some man of the country,—who drew out his bright *khánjar !* "Nay ! answered the Kusmàn, nay ! not so." I went in, and sat down by Ibrahîm : and Abd-er-Rahmàn whispered to me, "It is a godsend, that we have found one here who is from our house at Jidda ! for this young man, *Abd-el-Azîz*, is a nephew of my father. He was going up, with a load of carpets, to et-Tâyif ; but I have engaged him to return with thee to Jidda : only give him a present,—three reals. Khalîl, it has been difficult !—for some in the Kahwa would make trouble : they heard last night of the coming of a Nasrâny ; but by good adventure a principal slave of the Sherîf is here, who has made all well for you. Come with me and thank him : and we (of the káfily) must depart immediately."—I found a venerable negro sitting on the ground ; who rose to take me by the hand : his name was *Ma'abûb*. Ibrahîm, Sleymàn, and the rest of the Kusmàn now went out to mount their thelûls ; when I looked again they had ridden away. The son of Bessàm remained with me, who cried, "Mount ! and Abd-el-Azîz mount behind Khalîl !"—" Let me first fill the girby." "There is water lower in the valley, only mount." "Mount, man ! " I said ; and as he was up I struck-on the thelûl : but there was no spirit in the jaded beast, when a short trot had saved me.

I heard a voice of ill augury behind us, "Dismount, dismount !—Let me alone I say, and I will kill the kafir." I looked round, and saw him of the knife very nigh upon us ; who with the blade in his hand, now laid hold on the bridle.—" Ho ! Jew, come down ! ho ! Nasrâny (yells this fiend) ; I say down ! " I was for moving on ; and but my dromedary was weak I had then overthrown him, and outgone that danger. Other persons were coming,—" *Nôkh, nôkh !* cries Abd-er-Rahmàn, make her kneel and alight ! Khalîl." This I did without show of reluctance. He of the knife approached me, with teeth set fast, "to slay, he hissed, the Yahûdy-Nasrâny " ; but the servitor of the sherîf, who hastened to us, entreated him to hold his hand.—I whispered then to the son of Bessâm, "Go call back some of the kâfily with their guns; and let see if the guest of Aneyza may not pass. Can these arrest me in a public way, without the *hadûd?*" (borders of the sacred township). But he whispered, "Only say, Khalîl, thou art a Moslem, it is but a word, to appease them; and to-morrow thou wilt be at Jidda: thou thyself seest—! and wellah I am in dread that some of these will kill thee."—"If it please God I will pass, whether they will or no." "Eigh Khalîl! said he in that demiss voice of the Arabs, when the tide is turning against them, what can I do? I must ride after the kâfily; look! I am left behind."—He mounted without more; and forsook his father's friend among murderers.

A throng of loitering Mecca cameleers, that (after their night march) were here resting-out the hot hours, had come from the Kahwa, with some idle persons of the hamlet, to see this novelty. They gathered in a row before me, about thirty together, clad in tunics of blue cotton. I saw the butcherly sword-knife, with metal scabbard, of the country, *jambîeh*, shining in all their greasy leathern girdles. Those Mecca faces were black as the hues of the damned, in the day of doom: the men stood silent, and holding their swarthy hands to their weapons.

The servitor of the Sherîf (who was infirm and old), went back out of the sun, to sit down, And after this short respite the mad wretch came with his knife again and his cry, 'that he would slay the Yahûdy-Nasrâny'; and I remained standing silently. The villain was a sherîf; for thus I had heard Maabûb name him: these persons of the seed of Mohammed 'are not to be spoken against,' and have a privilege, in the public opinion, above the common lot of mankind. The Mecca cameleers seemed not to encourage him; but much less were they on my side. [The sherîf was a nomad: his fellows in this violence were one or two thievish Hathèylies of the hamlet; and a camel driver, his rafîk, who was a Beduwy. His purpose and theirs was, having murdered the kafir—a deed also of "religious" merit! to possess the thelûl, and my things.]

When he came thus with his knife, and saw me stand still, with a hand in my bosom, he stayed with wonder and discouragement. Commonly among three Arabians is one mediator; their spirits are soon spent, and indifferent bystanders incline to lenity and good counsel: I waited therefore that some would open his mouth on my behalf!—but there was no man. I looked in the sclerat's eyes; and totter-headed, as are so many poor nomads, he might not abide it; but, heaving up his khánjar, he fetched a great breath (he was infirm, as are not few in that barren life, at the middle age) and made feints with the weapon at my chest; so with a sigh he brought down his arm and drew it to him again. Then he lifted the knife and measured his stroke : he was an undergrown man ; and watching his eyes I hoped to parry the stab on my left arm,—though I stood but faintly on my feet, I might strike him away with the other hand ; and when wounded justly defend myself with my pistol, and break through them. Maabûb had risen, and came lamely again in haste ; and drew away the robber sherîf : and holding him by the hand, "What is this, he said, sherîf Sâlem ? you promised me to do nothing by violence ! Remember Jidda bombarded !—and that was for the blood of some of this stranger's people ; take heed what thou doest. They are the Engleys, who for one that is slain of them will send great battleships; and beat down a city. And thinkest thou our lord the Sherîf would spare thee, a bringer of these troubles upon him ? —Do thou nothing against the life of this person, who is guilty of no crime, neither was he found within the precincts of Mecca. —No ! sherîf Sâlem, for *Hasseyn* (the Sherîf Emir of Mecca) our master's sake. Is the stranger a Nasrâny ? he never denied it : be there not Nasâra at Jidda ? "

Maabûb made him promise peace. Nevertheless the wolvish nomad sherîf was not so, with a word, to be disappointed of his prey : for when the old negro went back to his shelter, he approached anew with the knife ; and swore by Ullah that now would he murder the Nasrâny. Maabûb seeing that, cried to him, to remember his right mind ! and the bystanders made as though they would hinder him. Sâlem being no longer countenanced by them, and his spirits beginning to faint—so God gives to the shrewd cow a short horn—suffered himself to be persuaded. But leaping to the thelûl, which was all he levelled at, " At least, cries he, this is *náhab*, rapine ! " He flung down my coverlet from the saddle, and began to lift the great bags. Then one of his companions snatched my headband and kerchief ; but others blamed him. A light-footed Hathèyly ran to his house with the coverlet ; others (from the backward) plucked at my mantle: the Mecca cameleers stood still in this hurly-burly. I took all in patience ; and having no more need, here under the tropic, I let go my cloak also. Maabûb came limping again towards us. He took my saddle-bags to himself ; and dragging them apart, made me now sit by him. Sâlem repenting—when he saw the booty gone from him—that he had not killed the stranger, drew his knife anew ; and made toward me, with hard-set (but halting) resolution appearing in his squalid visage and crying out, that he would put to death the Yahûdy-Nasrâny.

but now the bystanders withheld him. *Maabûb*: "I tell thee, Sherîf Sâlem, that if thou have any cause against this stranger, it must be laid before our lord the Sherîf; thou mayst do nothing violently."—"Oh! but this is one who would have stolen through our lord's country."—"Thou canst accuse him; he must in any wise go before our lord Hasseyn. I commit him to thee Sâlem, *teslîm*, in trust: bring him safely to Hasseyn, at et-Tâyif." The rest about us assenting to Maabûb's reasons, Sâlem yielded,—saying, "I hope it may please the Sherîf to hang this Nasrâny, or cut off his head; and that he will bestow upon me the thelûl."—Notwithstanding the fatigue and danger of returning on my steps, it seemed to me some amends that I should visit et-Tâyif.

CHAPTER XIII

TÂYIF. THE SHERÎF, EMIR OF MECCA

THUS, Maabûb who had appeased the storm, committed me to the wolf! He made the thieves bring the things that they had snatched from me; but they were so nimble that all could not be recovered. The great bags were laid again upon the weary thelûl, which was led back with us; and the throng of camel-men dispersed to the Kahwa shadows and their old repose. —Maabûb left me with the mad sherîf! and I knew not whither he went.

Sâlem, rolling his wooden head with the soberness of a robber bound over to keep the peace, said now, ' It were best to lock up my bags.' He found a storehouse, at the Kahwa sheds; and laid them in there, and fastened the door, leaving me to sit on the threshold : the shadow of the lintel was as much as might cover my head from the noonday sun.—He eyed me wistfully. " Well, Sâlem (I said), how now? I hope we may yet be friends." " Wellah, quoth he—after a silence, I thought to have slain thee to-day ! "—The ungracious nomad hated my life, because of the booty; for afterward he showed himself to be little curious of my religion ! Sâlem called me now more friendly, " Khalîl, Khalîl ! " and not Nasrâny.

— He left me awhile ; and there came young men of the place to gaze on the Nasrâny, as if it were some perilous beast that had been taken in the toils. " Akhs !—look at him ! this is he, who had almost slipped through our hands. What think ye ?—he will be hanged ? or will they cut his throat ?—Auh ! come and see ! here he sits, Ullah curse his father !—Thou cursed one ! akhs ! was it thus thou wouldst steal through the béled of the Moslemîn ? " Some asked me, " And if any of us came to the land of the Nasâra, would your people put us to death with torments ? "—Such being their opinion of us, they in comparison showed me a forbearance and humanity ! After them came one saying, he heard I was a hakîm; and could I cure his old wound? I bade him return at evening and I would dress it. "Thou wilt not be here then!" cries the savage wretch,—with what meaning I could not tell. Whatsoever I answered, they said it was not so; "for thou art a kafir, the son of a hound, and dost lie." It did their hearts good to gainsay the Nasrâny; and in so doing it seemed to them they confuted his pestilent religion.

I was a passenger, I told them, with a general passport of the Sultan's government. One who came then from the Kahwa cried out, 'that he would know whether I were verily from the part of the Dowla, or a Muskôvy,—the man was like one who had been a soldier: I let him have my papers; and he went away with them: but soon returning the fellow said, 'I lied like a false Nasrâny, the writings were not such as I affirmed.' Then the ruffian—for this was all his drift—demanded with flagrant eyes, 'Had I money?'—a perilous word! so many of them are made robbers by misery, the Mother of misdeed.— When Sâlem came again they questioned me continually of the thelûl; greedily desiring that this might become their booty. I answered shortly, 'It is the Bessâms'.'—'He says el-Bessâm! are not the Bessâm great merchants? and wellah melûk, like to princes, at Jidda!'

— Sâlem, who was returning from a visit to Mecca, had heard by adventure at the Kahwa station, of the coming down of a Nasrâny: at first I thought he had it from some in the Boreyda caravan. "It was not from them of Boreyda, he answered,— Ullah confound all the Kusmàn! that bring us kafirs: and billah last year we turned back the Boreyda kâfily from this place."—The Kasîm kâfilies sometimes, and commonly the caravans from Ibn Rashîd's country, pass down to Mecca by the Wady Laymûn. I supposed that Sâlem had some charge here; and he pretended, 'that the oversight of the station had been committed to him by the Sherîf'.—Sâlem was a nomad sherîf going home to his menzil: but he would not that I should call him Beduwy. I have since found the nomad sherîfs take it very hardly if any name them Beduw; and much less would the ashràf that are settled in villages be named fellahîn. Such plain speech is too blunt in their noble hearing: a nomad sherîf told me this friendly,—"It is not well, he said, for they are ashràf."

Now Sâlem bade me rise, and led to an arbour of boughs, in whose shadow some of the camel-men were slumbering out the hot mid-day. Still was the air in this Tehâma valley, and I could not put off my cloak, which covered the pistol; yet I felt no extreme heat. When Salem and the rest were sleeping, a poor old woman crept in; who had somewhat to say to me, for she asked aloud, 'Could I speak Hindy?' Perhaps she was a bond-servant going up with a Mecca family to et-Tâyif,—the Hara-meyn are full of Moslems of Hindostany speech: it might be she was of India. [In the Nejd quarter of Jidda is a spital of such poor Indian creatures.] Some negro bondsmen, that returned from their field labour, came about the door to look in upon me: I said to them, 'Who robbed you from your friends, and your own land?—I am an Engleysy, and had we met with them that carried you over the sea, we had set you free, and given you palms in a béled of ours.' The poor black men answered in such Arabic as they could, 'They had heard tell of it'; and they began to chat between them in their African language.—One of the light sleepers startled! and sat up; and rolling his eyes he swore by Ullah, 'He had lost through the Engleys, that took and burned a ship of his partners.' I told them we had a treaty with the Sooltân to suppress slavery. 'I lied, responded more than one ferocious voice; when, Nasrâny, did the Sooltân forbid slavery?' 'Nay, he may speak the truth, said another; for the Nasâra lie not.'— 'But he lies!' exclaimed he of the burned ship.—'By this you may know if I lie;—when I come to Jidda, bring a bondman to my Konsulato: and let thy bondservant say he would be free, and he shall be free indeed!'—'Dog! cries the fellow, thou liar!—*are there not thousands of slaves at Jidda, that every day are bought and sold?* wherefore, thou dog! be they not all made free? if thou sayest sooth:' and he ground the teeth, and shook his villain hands in my face.

Sâlem wakened late, when the most had departed: only a few simple persons loitered before our door; and some made bold to enter. He rose up full of angry words against them. 'Away with you! he cries, Ullah curse you all together; Old woman, long is thy tongue—what! should a concubine make talk:—and up, go forth, thou slave! Ullah curse thy father! shall a bondman come in hither?'—This holy seed of Mohammed had leave to curse the poor lay people. But he showed now a fair-weather countenance to me his prisoner: perhaps the sweet sleep had helped his madman's brains. Sâlem even sent for a little milk for me (which they will sell here, so nigh the city): but he made me pay for it excessively; besides a real for a bottle of hay, not worth sixpence, which they strewed down to my thelûl and their camels. Dry grass from the valley-sides above, twisted rope-wise (as we see it in the Neapolitan country), is sold at this station to the cameleers.

It was now mid-afternoon : an ancient man entered ; and he spoke long and earnestly with Sâlem He allowed it just to take a kafir's life, but perilous : ' the booty also was good he said, but to take it were perilous ; ay, all this, quoth the honest grey-beard, striking my camel-bags with his stick, is *tóm'a.* But thou Sâlem bring him before Hasseyn, and put not thyself in danger.' *Sâlem :* " Ay wellah, it is all tóm'a ; but what is the most tóm'a of all ?—is it not the Nasrâny's face ? look on him ! is not this tóm'a ? " I rallied the old man (who was per-haps an Hathèyly of the hamlet, or a sherîf) for his opinion, ' that the Nasâra are God's adversaries.' His wits were not nimble ; and he listened a moment to my words,—then he answered soberly, " I can have no dealings with a kafir, except thou repent : " so he turned from me, and said to Sâlem, " Eigh ! how plausible be these Nasrânies ! but beware of them, Sâlem ! I will tell thee a thing,—it was in the Egyptian times. There came hither a hakîm with the soldiery : wellah Sâlem, I found him sitting in one of the orchards yonder !—*Salaam aleyk !* quoth he, and I unwittingly answered, *Aleykom es-salaam !*— afterward I heard he was a Nasrâny ! akhs !—but this is certain, that one Moslem may chase ten Nasâra, or a score of them ; which is ofttimes seen, and even an hundred together ; and Sâlem it is *ithin* (by the permission of) *Ullah !* " " Well, I hope Hasseyn will bestow on me the thelûl ! " was Sâlem's nomad-like answer.

— Seeing some loads of India rice, for Tâyif, that were set down before the Kahwa, I found an argument to the capacity of the rude camel-men ; and touching them with my stick en-quired, " What sacks be these ? and the letters on them ? if any of you (ignorant persons) could read letters ? Shall I tell you ?—this is rice of the Engleys, in sacks of the Engleys ; and the marks are words of the Engleys. Ye go well clad !—though hareem wear this blue colour in the north ! but what tunics are these ?—I tell you, the cotton on your backs was spun and wove in mills of the Engleys Ye have not considered that ye are fed in part and clothed by the Engleys ! " Some con-tradicted ; the most found that I said well. Such talk helped to drive the time, disarmed their insolence, and damped the murderous mind in Salem. But what that miscreant rolled in his lunatic spirit concerning me I could not tell : I had caught some suspicion that they would murder me in this place. If I asked of our going to Tâyif, his head might turn, and I should see his knife again ; and I knew not what were become of

Maabûb.—They count thirty hours from hence to et-Tâyif, for
their ant-paced camel trains: it seemed unlikely that such a
hyena could so long abstain from my blood.

Late in the day he came to me with Maabûb and Abd-el-
Azîz; who had rested in another part of the Kahwa!—surely
if there had been right worth in them (there was none in
Abd-el-Azîz), they had not left me alone in this case. Maabûb
told me, I should depart at evening with the caravan men; and
so he left me again. Then Sâlem, with a mock zeal, would
have an inventory taken of my goods—and see the spoil! he
called some of the unlettered cameleers to be witnesses. I
drew out all that was in my bags, and cast it before them : but
" *El-f̓lûs, ·el-f̓lûs!* cries Sâlem with ferocious insistence, thy
money! thy money! that there may be afterward no question,
—show it all to me, Nasrâny!"—"Well, reach me that medicine
box; and here, I said, are my few reals wrapped in a cloth!"

The camel-men gathered sticks; and made watch fires: they
took flour and water, and kneaded dough, and baked *'abûd*
under the ashes; for it was toward evening. At length I saw
this daylight almost spent: then the men rose, and lifted the
loads upon their beasts. These town caravaners' camels march
in a train, all tied, as in Syria.—My bags also were laid upon
the Bessâm's thelûl: and Sâlem bade me mount with his companion, *Fheyd*, the Beduin or half-Beduin master of these
camels.—"Mount in the shidâd! Khalîl Nasrâny." [But thus
the radîf might stab me from the backward, in the night!] I
said, I would sit back-rider; and was too weary to maintain
myself in the saddle. My words prevailed! for all Arabs
tender the infirmity of human life,—even in their enemies.
Yet Sâlem was a perilous coxcomb; for if anyone reviled the
Nasrâny in his hearing, he made me cats' eyes and felt for his
knife again.

In this wise we departed; and the Nasrâny would be hanged,
as they supposed, by just judgment of the Sherîf, at et-Tâyif:
all night we should pace upward to the height of the Seyl.
Fheyd was in the saddle; and the villain, in his superstition,
was adread of the *Nasrâny!* Though malignant, and ye t more
greedy, there remained a human kindness in him; for understanding that I was thirsty he dismounted, and went to his
camels to fetch me water. Though I heard he was of the
Nomads, and his manners were such, yet he spoke nearly that
bastard Arabic of the great government towns, Damascus,
Bagdad, Mecca. But unreasonable was his impatience, because
I a weary man could not strike forward the jaded thelûl to his

liking,—he thought that the Nasrâny lingered to escape from them!

A little before us, marched some Mecca passengers to et-Tâyif, with camel-litters. That convoy was a man's household : the goodman, swarthy as the people of India and under the middle age, was a wealthy merchant in Mecca. He went beside his hareem on foot, in his white tunic only and turban; to stretch his tawny limbs—which were very well made—and breathe himself in the mountain air. [The heat in Mecca was such, that a young Turkish army surgeon, whom I saw at et-Tâyif, told me he had marked there, in these days, 46° C.] Our train of nine camels drew slowly by them : but when the smooth Mecca merchant heard that the stranger riding with the camel-men was a Nasrâny, he cried, " Akhs! a Nasrâny in these parts!" and with the horrid inurbanity of their (jealous) religion, he added, " Ullah curse his father!" and stared on me with a face worthy of the koran!

The caravan men rode on their pack-beasts eating their poor suppers, of the bread they had made. Sâlem, who lay stretched nomad-wise on a camel, reached me a piece, as I went by him; which beginning to eat I bade him remember, "that from henceforth there was bread and salt between us,—and see, I said, that thou art not false, Sâlem."—" Nay, wellah, I am not *khayin*, no Khalîl." The sickly wretch suffered old visceral pains, which may have been a cause of his splenetic humour.— He bye and bye blamed my nodding; and bade me sit fast. " Awake, Khalîl! and look up! Close not thine eyes all this night!—I tell thee thou mayest not slumber a moment; these are perilous passages and full of thieves,—the Hathèyl! that steal on sleepers : awake! thou must not sleep." The camels now marched more slowly; for the drivers lay slumbering upon their loads: thus we passed upward through the weary night. Fheyd left riding with me at midnight, when he went to stretch himself on the back of one of his train of nine camels; and a driver lad succeeded him. Thus these unhappy men slumber two nights in three : and yawn out the daylight hours,—which are too hot for their loaded beasts—at the 'Ayn station or at the Seyl.

The camels march on of themselves, at the ants pace.— " Khalil! quoth the driver lad, who now sat in my saddle, beware of thieves!" Towards morning, we both nodded and slumbered, and the thelûl wandering from the path carried us under an acacia :—happy I was, in these often adventures of night-travelling in Arabia, never to have hurt an eye! My tunic was rent!—I waked; and looking round saw one on foot

come nigh behind us.—"What is that?" quoth the strange
man, and leaping up he snatched at the worsted girdle which
I wore in riding! I shook my fellow-rider awake, and struck
on the thelûl; and asked the raw lad, 'If that man were one
of the cameleers?'—"Didst thou not see him among them?
but this is a thief and would have thy money." The jaded
thelûl trotted a few paces and stayed. The man was presently
nigh behind me again: his purpose might be to pull me down;
but were he an Hathèyly or what else, I could not tell. If I
struck him, and the fellow were a cameleer, would they not
say, 'that the Nasrâny had beaten a Moslem'? He would not
go back; and the lad in the saddle was heavy with sleep. I
found no better rede than to show him my pistol—but I took
this for an extreme ill fortune: so he went his way.—I heard
we should rest at the rising of the morning star: the planet
was an hour high, and the day dawning when we reached the
Seyl ground: where I alighted with Sâlem, under the spreading
boughs of a great old acacia tree.

There are many such menzil trees and shadows of rocks,
in that open station, where is no Kahwa: we lay down to
slumber, and bye and bye the sun rose. The sun comes up
with heat in this latitude; and the sleeper must shift his
place, as the shadows wear round. "Khalîl (quoth the tor-
mentor) what is this much slumbering?—but the thing that
thou hast at thy breast, what is it? show it all to me."—"I
have showed you all in my saddle-bags; it is infamous to search
a man's person."—"Aha! said a hoarse voice behind me, he
has a pistol; and he would have shot at me last night."—It was
a great mishap, that this wretch should be one of the cameleers;
and the persons about me were of such hardened malice in their
wayworn lives, that I could not waken in them any honourable
human sense. *Sâlem:* "Show me, without more, all that thou
hast with thee there (in thy bosom)!"—There came about us
more than a dozen cameleers.

The mad sherîf had the knife again in his hand! and his old
gall rising, "Show me all that thou hast, cries he, and leave
nothing; or now will I kill thee."—Where was Maabûb? whom
I had not seen since yester-evening: in him was the faintness
and ineptitude of Arab friends.—"Remember the bread and
salt which we have eaten together, Sâlem!"—"Show it all to
me, or now by Ullah I will slay thee with this knife." More
bystanders gathered from the shadowing places: some of them
cried out, "Let us hack him in morsels, the cursed one! what
hinders?—fellows, let us hack him in morsels!"—"Have
patience a moment, and send these away." Sâlem, lifting his

knife, cried, "Except thou show me all at the instant, I will slay thee!" But rising and a little retiring from them I said "Let none think to take away my pistol!"—which I drew from my bosom.

What should I do now? the world was before me; I thought, Shall I fire, if the miscreants come upon me; and no shot amiss? I might in the first horror reload,—my thelûl was at hand: and if I could break away from more than a score of persons, what then?—repass the Rî'a, and seek Sh'aara again? where 'Ateybân often come-in to water; which failing I might ride at adventure: and though I met with no man in the wilderness, in two or three days, it were easier to end thus than to be presently rent in pieces. I stood between my jaded thelûl, that could not have saved her rider, and the sordid crew of camel-men advancing, to close me in: they had no fire-arms.—Fheyd approached, and I gave back pace for pace: he opened his arms to embrace me!—there was but a moment, I must slay him, or render the weapon, my only defence; and my life would be at the discretion of these wretches.—I bade him come forward boldly. There was not time to shake out the shot, the pistol was yet suspended from my neck, by a strong lace: I offered the butt to his hands.— Fheyd seized the weapon! they were now in assurance of their lives and the booty: he snatched the cord and burst it. Then came his companion Sâlem; and they spoiled me of all that I had; and first my aneroid came into their brutish hands; then my purse, that the black-hearted Siruân had long worn in his Turkish bosom at Kheybar.—Sâlem feeling no reals therein gave it over to his confederate Fheyd; to whom fell also my pocket thermometer: which when they found to be but a toy of wood and glass, he restored it to me again, protesting with nefarious solemnity, that other than this he had nothing of mine! Then these robbers sat down to divide the prey in their hands. The lookers-on showed a cruel countenance still; and reviling and threatening me, seemed to await Sâlem's rising, to begin 'hewing in pieces the Nasrâny'.

Sâlem and his confederate Fheyd were the most dangerous Arabs that I have met with; for the natural humanity of the Arabians was corrupted in them, by the strong contagion of the government towns.—I saw how impudently the robber sherîf attributed all the best of the stealth to himself! Sâlem turned over the pistol-machine in his hand: such Turks' tools he had seen before at Mecca. But as he numbered the ends of the bullets in the chambers, the miscreant was dismayed; and thanked his God, which had delivered him from these six deaths! He considered the perilous instrument, and gazed on me; and seemed to balance in his heart, whether he should not prove its shooting against the Nasrâny. "Akhs—akhs! cried some hard hostile voices, look how he carried this pistol to kill the Moslemîn! Come now and we will hew him piecemeal:— how those accursed Nasrânies are full of wicked wiles!—O thou! how many Moslems hast thou killed with that pistol?" "My friends, I have not fired it in the land of the Arabs.— Sâlem, remember 'Ayn ez-Zeyma! thou camest with a knife to kill me, but did I turn it against thee? Render therefore thanks to Ullah! and remember the bread and the salt, Sâlem."

— He bade his drudge Fheyd, shoot off the pistol; and I dreaded he might make me his mark. Fheyd fired the first shots in the air: the chambers had been loaded nearly two years; but one after another they were shot off,—and that was with a wonderful resonance! in this silent place of rocks. Sâlem said, rising, "Leave one of them!" This last shot he reserved for me; and I felt it miserable to die here by their barbarous hands without defence. "Fheyd, he said again, is all sure?—and one remains?"

Sâlem glared upon me, and perhaps had indignation, that I did not say, *dakhílak:* the tranquillity of the kafir troubled him. When he was weary, he went to sit down and called me, "Sit, quoth he, beside me."—"You hear the savage words of these persons; remember, Sâlem, you must answer for me to the Sherîf."—"The Sherîf will hang thee, Nasrâny! Ullah curse the Yahûd and Nasâra." Some of the camel-men said, "Thou wast safe in thine own country, thou mightest have continued there; but since thou art come into the land of the Moslemîn, God has delivered thee into our hands to die:—so perish all the Nasâra! and be burned in hell with your father, Sheytàn." "Look! I said to them, good fellows—for the most fault is your ignorance, ye think I shall be hanged to-morrow: but what if the Sherîf esteem me more than you all, who revile me to-day! If you deal cruelly with me, you will be called to an account Believe my words! Hasseyn will receive me as one of the ullema; but with you men of the people, his subjects, he will deal without regard." "Thou shalt be hanged, they cried again, O thou cursed one!" and after this they dispersed to their several halting places.

— Soon afterward there came over to us the Mecca burgess; who now had alighted under some trees at little distance. From this smooth personage, a flower of merchants in the holy city —though I appealed to his better mind, that he should speak to Sâlem, I could not draw a human word; and he abstained from evil. He gazed his fill; and forsook me to go again to his hareem. I watched him depart, and the robber sherîf was upbraiding me, that I had "hidden" the things and my pistol! —in this I received a shock! and became numbed to the world : I sat in a swoon and felt that my body rocked and shivered; and thought now, they had mortally wounded me with a knife, or shot! for I could not hear, I saw light thick and confusedly. But coming slowly to myself, so soon as I might see ground I saw there no blood : I felt a numbness and deadness at the nape of the neck. Afterward I knew that Fheyd had inhumanly struck me there with his driving-stick, —and again, with all his force.

I looked up and found them sitting by me. I said faintly, "Why have you done this?" *Fheyd :* "Because thou didst withhold the pistol." "Is the pistol mine or thine? I might have shot thee dead! but I remembered the mercy of Ullah." A caravaner sat by us eating,—one that ceased not to rail against me : he was the man who assailed me in the night, and had brought so much mischief upon me. I suddenly caught his hand with the bread; and putting some in my mouth, I said to him, "Enough, man! there is bread and salt between us." The wretch allowed it, and said not another word. I have never found any but Sâlem a truce-breaker of the bread and salt,—but he was of the spirituality.

— There came one riding to us on an ass! it was Abd-el-Azîz! He and Maabûb had heard the shots, as they sat resting at some distance yonder! For they, who were journeying together to et-Tâyif, had arrived here in the night-time; and I was not aware of it. Maabûb now sent this young man (unworthy of the name of Bessâm) to know what the shots meant, and what were become of the Nasrâny —whether he yet lived? Abd-el-Azîz seeing the pistol in Sâlem's hands and his prisoner alive, asked, 'Wherefore had he taken away the man's pistol?' I said to him, "You see how these ignorant men threaten me : speak some word to them for thine uncle Abdullah's sake." But he, with sour fanatical looks; "Am I a Frenjy?"—and mounting again, he rode out of sight.

After these haps; Sâlem having now the spoil in his hands, and fearing to lose it again at et-Tâyif, had a mind to send me down to Jidda, on the Bessâm's thelûl.—"Ha! Khalîl, we are become brothers; Khalîl, are we not now good friends? there is nothing more betwixt us. What sayest thou? wilt thou then that we send thee to Jidda, and I myself ride with thee on the thelûl?"—But I answered, "I go to visit the Sherîf, at Tâyif; and you to accuse me there, and clear yourselves before him; at

Jidda you would be put in prison." Some bystanders cried, "Let him go to et-Tâyif."

—A messenger returned from Maabûb, bidding Sâlem, Khalîl and Fheyd come to him. As we went I looked back, and saw Fheyd busy to rifle my camel-bags!—after that he followed us. The young Bessàm was sitting under the shadow of some rocks with Maabûb.—" Are you men? quoth Maabûb, are you men? who have so dealt with this stranger!" I told him how they robbed me, and what I had suffered at their hands: I was yet (and long afterward) stunned by the blows on the neck. *Maabûb*: "Sherîf Sâlem, thou art to bring this stranger to our lord Hasseyn at et-Tâyif, and do him no wrong by the way. How canst thou rob and wound one who is committed to thy trust, like the worst Beduin thieves? but I think verily that none of the Beduw would do the like. *Sâlem*: "Is not this a Nasrâny? he might kill us all by the way; we did but take his pistol, because we were afraid." *Maabûb*: "Have you taken his silver from him and his other things, because ye were afraid?—I know thee, Sâlem! but thou wilt have to give account to our lord the Sherîf:"—so he dismissed us; and we returned to our place.

It came into my mind, bye and bye, to go again to Maabûb: the sand was as burning coals under my bare feet, so that after every few steps I must fall on my knees to taste a moment's relief.—Maabûb was Umbrella-bearer of the Sherîf; and an old faithful servitor of his brother, the late Sherîf. "Wherefore, I asked, had he so strangely forsaken me hitherto? Or how could he commit me to that murderous Sâlem! whom he himself called *a mad sherîf;* did he look to see me alive at Tâyif! —I am now without defence, at the next turn he may stab me; do thou therefore ride with me on the thelûl!"—"Khalil, because of an infirmity [sarcocele] I cannot mount in a saddle." When I said, I would requite his pains, the worthy negro answered, "That be far from me! for it is my duty, which I owe to our lord, the Sherîf: but if thou have a remedy for my disease, I pray thee, remember me at et-Tâyif."—The young Bessàm had fever, with a daily crisis. It came on him at noon; and then he who lately would not speak a word to shelter the Frenjy's life, with a puling voice (as they are craven and unmanly), besought me to succour him. I answered, 'At et-Tâyif!' Had he aided me at the first, for his good uncle's sake, I had not now been too faint to seek for remedies. I promised, if he would ride with me to-night, to give him a medicine to cut the fever, to-morrow: but Arabs put no trust in distant promises.

It drew to the mid-afternoon, when I heard we should remove;

and then the foolish young Bessàm bade me rise and help to
load the carpets on his camel. I did not deny him; but had
not much strength; and Maabûb, blaming the rashness of the
young man, would have me sit still in the shadow —Maabûb
rode seated on the load of carpets; and when the camel arose
under him, the heavy old negro was nigh falling Once more
I asked him, not to forsake me; and to remember how many
were the dark hours before us on the road.

I returned hastily to our menzil tree. The caravaners had
departed; and the robber sherîf, who remained with the thelûl,
was chafing at my delay: he mounted in the saddle, and I
mounted again back-rider.—Sâlem had a new companion, who
rode along with us, one Ibrahîm of Medina, lately landed at
Jidda; and who would soon ride homeward in the 'little pilgrimage'. Ibrahîm hearing what countryman I was began to
say, "That an Engleysy came in the vessel with him to Jidda;
—who was wellah a good and perfect Moslem! yesterday he
entered Mecca, and performed his devotion:—and this Engleysy
that I tell you of, sherîf Sâlem, is now sojourning at Mecca,
to visit the holy places."—Ibrahîm was one who lying under
our awning tree, where he had arrived late, had many times
disdained me, crying out despitefully, "Dog! dog! thou dog!"
But as we rode he began to smile upon the Nasrâny betwixt
friendly and fiendly: at last quoth he, "Thou wast at Hâyil;
and dost thou not remember me?—I have spoken with thee
there; and thou art Khalîl."—How strange are these meetings
again in the immensity of empty Arabia! but there is much
resort to Hâyil; and I had passed a long month there. The
light-bodied Arabian will journey, upon his thelûl, at foot-pace,
hundreds of leagues for no great purpose: and little more
troubles him than the remembrance that he is absent from his
household and children. "Thou hast known me then a long
time in these countries; now say on before these strangers, if
thou canst allege aught against me."—"Well none, but thy
misreligion."

Ibrahîm rode upon a dromedary; his back-rider was an
envenomed cameleer; who at every pause of their words shook
his stick at me: and when he walked he would sometimes leap
two paces, as it were to run upon the kafir. There was a danger
iu Sâlem's seeing another do me wrong,—that in such he would
not be out-done, and I might see his knife again: so I said to
Ibrahîm (and stroked my beard), "By thy beard, man! and for
our old acquaintance at Hâyil—!" Ibrahîm acknowledged the
token; and began to show the Nasrâny a more friendly countenance. "Ibrahîm, did you hear that the Engleys are a bad

people? "—" Nay, *kullesh táyib*, good every whit."—" Are they the Sultan's friends, or foes? "—" His friends: the Engleys help him in the wars." *Sálem:* "Well Khalîl, let this pass; but tell me, what is the religion of the Nasâra? I thought surely it was some horrible thing!"—" Fear God and love thy neighbour, this is the Christian religion,—the way of Aysa bin-Miriam, from the spirit of Ullah."—" Who is Aysa?—hast thou heard this name, Ibrahîm? "—" Ullah curse Aysa and the father of Aysa, cries Ibrahîm's radîf. Akhs! what have we to do with thy religion, Nasrâny? " Ibrahîm answered him very soberly, " But thou with this word makest thyself a kafir, blaspheming a prophet of the prophets of Ullah!" The cameleer answered, half-aghast, "The Lord be my refuge!—I knew not that Aysa was a prophet of the Lord!" "What think'st thou, Sâlem? "— " Wellah Khalîl, I cannot tell: but how sayest thou, *Spirit of Ullah!*—is this your kafir talk? "—" You may read it in the koran,—say, Ibrahîm? "—" Ay indeed, Khalîl."

There were many passengers in the way; some of whom bestowed on me an execration as we rode-by them, and Sâlem lent his doting ears to all their idle speech: his mind wavered at every new word.—" Do not listen to them, Sâlem, it is they who are the Nasâra! " He answered, like a Nomad, "Ay billah, they are Beduw and kafirs;—but such is their ignorance in these parts! " Ibrahîm's radîf could not wholly forget his malevolence; and Sâlem's brains were beginning again to unsettle: for when I said, " But of all this ye shall be better instructed to-morrow: " he cried out, "Thou liest like a false Nasrâny, the Sherîf will cut off thy head to-morrow, or hang thee:—and, Ibrahîm, I hope that our lord will recompense me with the thelûl."

We came to a seyl bed, of granite-grit, with some growth of pleasant herbs and peppermints; and where holes may be digged to the sweet water with the hands. Here the afternoon wayfarers to Tâyif alight, to drink and wash themselves to prayerward. [This site is said to be *'Okátz*, the yearly parliament and vaunting place of the tribes of Arabia before Islâm: the altitude is between 5000 and 6000 feet.] As we halted Abd-el-Azîz and Maabûb journeyed by us; and I went to ask the young Bessâm if he would ride with me to-night,—and I would reward him? He excused himself, because of the fever: but that did not hinder his riding upon an ass.—Sâlem was very busy-headed to know what I had spoken with them; and we remounted.

Now we ascended through strait places of rocks; and came upon a paved way, which lasts for some miles, with steps and

u

passages opened by blasting!—this path had been lately made by Turkish engineers at the Government cost. After that we journeyed in a pleasant steppe which continues to et-Tâyif.

We had outmarched the slow caravan, and were now alone in the wilderness: Ibrahîm accompanied us,—I had a doubtful mind of him. They said they would ride forward : my wooden dromedary was cruelly beat and made to run ; and that was to me an anguish.—Sâlem, had responded to some who asked the cause of our haste, as we outwent them on the path, 'that he would be rid of the Nasrâny : ' he murmured savage words ; so that I began to doubt whether these who rode with me were not accorded to murder the Nasrâny, when beyond sight. The spoilers had not left me so much as a penknife : at the Seyl I had secretly bound a stone in my kerchief, for a weapon.

At length the sun set : it is presently twilight ; and Ibrahîm enquired of Sâlem, wherefore he rode thus, without ever slacking. *Sâlem :* "But let us outride them and sleep an hour at the midway, till the camels come by us.—Khalîl, awake thou and sleep not ! (for I nodded on his back ;) Auh ! hold thine eyes open ! this is a perilous way for thee : " but I slumbered on, and was often in danger of falling. Bye and bye looking up, I saw that he gazed back upon me ! So he said more softly, "Sleepest thou, Khalîl Nasrâny ?—what is this ! when I told thee *no ;* thou art not afraid ! "—" Is not Ullah in every place ? "—" Ay, wellah Khalîl." Such pious words are honeycombs to the Arabs, and their rude hearts are surprised with religion.—" Dreadest thou not to die ! "—" I have not so lived, Moslêm, that I must fear to die." The wretch regarded me ! and I beheld again his hardly human visage : the cheeks were scotched with three gashes upon a side ! It is a custom in these parts, as in negro Africa ; where by such marks men's tribes may be distinguished.

Pleasant is the summer evening air of this high wilderness. We passed by a watering-place amongst trees, and would have halted : but Ibrahîm answered not to our call !—he had out-ridden us in the gloom. Sâlem, notwithstanding the fair words which lately passed between them, now named him "impudent fellow " and cursed him. " And who is the man, Sâlem ? I thought surely he had been a friend of thine."—" What makes him my friend ?—Sheytàn ! I know of him only that he is from Medina."—Bye and bye we came up with him in the darkness ; and Ibrahîm said, ' They had but ridden forward to pray. And here, quoth he, is a good place ; let us alight and sup.' They had bread, and I had dates : we sat down to eat

together. Only the radîf held aloof, fearing it might be unlawful to eat with a kafir : but when, at their bidding, he had par-
taken with us, even this man's malice abated.—I asked Ibrahîm,
Did he know the Nejûmy family at Medina ?   " Well, he said,
I know them,—they are but smiths."

We mounted and rode forward, through the open plain ; and
saw many glimpsing camp-fires of nomads. Sâlem was for
turning aside to some of them ; where, said he, we might drink
a little milk. It had been dangerous for the kafir, and I was
glad when we passed them by ; although I desired to see the
country Aarab.—We came at length to the manôkh or midway
halting-place of passengers : in the dim night I could see some
high clay building, and a thicket of trees. Not far off are
other outlying granges and hamlets of et-Tâyif. We heard
asses braying, and hounds barking in nomad menzils about us.
We alighted and lay down here on the sand in our mantles ; and
slumbered two hours : and then the trains of caravan camels,
slowly marching in the path, which is beaten hollow, came by us
again : the cameleers lay asleep upon their loads. We remounted,
and passing before them in the darkness we soon after lost the
road : Ibrahîm said now, they would ride on to et-Tâyif, without
sleeping ; and we saw him no more.

In the grey of the morning I could see that we were come to
orchard walls ; and in the growing light enclosures of vines, and
fig trees ; but only few and unthriving stems of palms [which
will not prosper at Tâyif, where both the soil and the water are
sweet]. And now we fell into a road—a road in Arabia ! I had
not seen a road and green hedges since Damascus. We passed
by a house or two built by the way-side ; and no more such as
the clay beyts of Arabia, but painted and glazed houses of
Turkey. We were nigh et-Tâyif ; and went before the villa of
the late Sherîf, where he had in his life-time a pleasure-ground,
with flowers ! [The Sherîfs are commonly Stambûl bred men.]
—The garden was already gone to decay.

Sâlem turned the thelûl into a field, upon our right hand ; and
we alighted and sat down to await the day. He left me to go
and look about us ; and I heard a bugle-call,—Tâyif is a
garrisoned place. When Sâlem returned he found me slumbering ; and asked, if I were not afraid ? We remounted and
had ado to drive the dromedary over a luke-warm brook, running
strongly. So we came to a hamlet of ashrâf, which stands a
little before et-Tâyif ; and drew bridle a moment ere the
sunrising, at the beyt of a cousin of Sâlem.

He called to them within, by name !—none answered. The

goodman was on a journey; and his wives could not come forth to us. But they, hearing Sâlem's voice, sent a boy, who bore in our things to the house; and we followed him This poor home in the Mecca country was a small court of high clay walling; with a chamber or two, built under the walls There we found two (sherîf) women; and they were workers of such worsted coverlets in yarns and colours as we have seen at Teyma.—And it was a nomad household; for the hareem told me they lived in tents, some months of the year, and drank milk of the small cattle and camels. Nomad-like was also the bareness of the beyt, and their misery: for the goodman had left them naught save a little meal; of which they presently baked a cake of hardly four ounces, for the guests' breakfast. Their voices sounded hollow with hunger, and were broken with sighing; but the poor noble-women spoke to us with a constant womanly mildness: and I wondered at these courtly manners, which I had not seen hitherto in Arabia. They are the poor children of Mohammed. The Sultàn of Islam might reverently kiss the hand of the least sherîf; as his wont is to kiss the hand of the elder of the family of the Sherîfs of Mecca (who are his pensioners—and in a manner his captives), at Stambûl.

It had been agreed between us, that no word should be said of my alien religion. Sâlem spoke of me as a stranger he had met with in the way. It was new to me, in these jealous countries, to be entertained by two lone hareem. This pair of pensive women (an elder and younger) were sister-wives of one, whom we should esteem an indigent person. There was no coffee in that poor place; but at Sâlem's request they sent out to borrow of their neighbours: the boy returned with six or seven beans; and of these they boiled for us, in an earthen vessel (as coffee is made here), a thin mixture,—which we could not drink! When the sun was fairly risen, Sâlem said he would now go to the Sherîf's audience; and he left me. —I asked the elder hostess of the Sherîf. She responded, "Hasseyn is a good man, who has lived at Stambûl from his youth; and the best learned of all the learned men here: yet is he not fully such as Abdullah (his brother), our last Sherîf, who died this year,—the Lord have him in His mercy! And he is not white as Abdullah; for his mother was a (Galla) bondwoman."—It seemed that the colour displeased them, for they repeated, "His mother was a bond-woman!—but Hasseyn is a good man and just; he has a good heart."

Long hours passed in this company of sighing (hunger-stricken) women; who having no household cares were busy, hilst I slumbered, with their worsted work.—It was toward high noon, when Sâlem entered. "Good tidings! 'nuncle Khalîl, quoth he: our lord the Sherîf sends thee to lodge in the house of a Tourk. Up! let us be going; and we have little further to ride" He bore out the bags himself, and laid them on my fainting thelûl, and we departed. From the next rising-ground I saw et-Tâyif! the aspect is gloomy, for all their building is of slate-coloured stone. At the entering of the town stands the white palace of the Sherîf, of two stories; and in face of it a new and loftier building with latticed balconies, and the roof full of chimneys, which is the palace of Abdillah Pasha, Hasseyn's brother. In the midst of the town appears a great and high building, like a prison; that is the soldiers' quarters.

— The town now before my eyes! after nigh two years' wandering in the deserts, was a wonderful vision. Beside our way I saw men blasting the (granite) rock for building-stone.— The site of Tâyif is in the border of the plutonic steppe, over which I had lately journeyed, a hundred leagues from el-Kasîm. I beheld also a black and cragged landscape, with low mountains, beyond the town. We fell again into the road from the Seyl, and passed that lukewarm brook; which flows from yonder monsoon mountains, and is one of the abounding springs which water this ancient oasis. The water-bearers—that wonted sight of Eastern towns! went up staggering from the stream, under their huge burdens of full goat-skins;—there are some of their mighty shoulders that can wield a camel load! Here a Turkish soldier met us, with rude smiles; and said, he came to lead me to the house where I should lodge. The man, a Syrian from the (Turkish) country about Antioch, was the military servant of an officer of the Sherîf: that officer at the Sherîf's bidding would receive me into his house.

The gate, where we entered, is called *Bab es-Seyl;* and within is the open place before the Sherîf's modest palace. The streets are rudely built, the better houses are daubed with plaster: and the aspect of the town, which is fully inhabited only in the summer months, is ruinous. The ways are unpaved: and we see here the street dogs of Turkish countries. A servant from the Sherîf waited for me in the street, and led forward to a wicket gate: he bade me dismount,—and here, heaven be praised! he dismissed Sâlem. "I will bring thee presently, quoth the smiling servitor, a knife and a fork; also the Sherîf bids me ask, wouldst thou drink a little tea and sugar?"— these were gentle thoughts of the homely humanity of the Prince of Mecca!

Then the fainting thelûl, which had carried me more than

four hundred and fifty miles without refreshment, was led away to the Sherîf's stables; and my bags were borne up the house stairs. The host, *Colonel Mohammed*, awaited me on the landing; and brought me into his chamber. The tunic was rent on my back, my mantle was old and torn ; the hair was grown down under my kerchief to the shoulders, and the beard fallen and unkempt ; I had bloodshot eyes, half blinded, and the scorched skin was cracked to the quick upon my face. A barber was sent for, and the bath made ready : and after a cup of tea, it cost the good colonel some pains to reduce me to the likeness of the civil multitude. Whilst the barber was doing, the stalwart Turkish official anointed my face with cooling ointments ; and his hands were gentle as a woman's,—but I saw no breakfast in that hospice ! After this he clad me, my weariness and faintness being such, like a block, in white cotton military attire; and set on my head a fez cap.

This worthy officer, whose name and style was *Mohammed Kheiry, Effendy, yâwer* (aide de camp) *es-Sherîf*, told me the Sherîf's service is better (being duly paid) than to serve the Dowla : he was *Bîm-bashy*, or captain of a thousand, in the imperial army. Colonel Mohammed was of the *Wilayat Konia* in Anatoly. He detested the corrupt officiality of Stambûl, and called them traitors ; because in the late peace-making they had ceded provinces, which were the patrimony of Islam : the great embezzling Pashas, he exclaimed, betrayed the army. With stern military frankness he denounced their Byzantine vices, and the (alleged) drunkenness of the late Sultan !—In Colonel Mohammed's mouth was doubtless the common talk of Turkish officers in Mecca and et-Tâyif. But he spoke, with an honest pride, of the provincial life in his native country; where is maintained the homely simplicity of the old Turkish manners. He told me of his bringing up, and the charge of his good mother, " My son, speak nothing but the truth ! abhor all manner of vicious living." He remembered from his childhood, ' when some had (but) broken into an orchard by night and stolen apples, how much talk was made of it '! Such is said to be the primitive temper of those peoples !— And have here a little tale, told me by a true man,—the thing happened amongst Turkoman and Turkish peasants in his own village, nigh Antioch. " An old husbandman found a purse in his field ; and it was heavy with silver. But he having no malice, hanged it on a pole, and went on crying down the village street, ' Did ye hear, my neighbours who, has lost this purse here ? ' And when none answered, the poor old man delivered the strange purse to the Christian priest; bidding him keep it well, until the owner should call for it."

— Heavy footfalls sounded on the stair; and there entered two Turkish officers. The first, a tall martial figure, the host's namesake, and whom he called his brother, was the Sherîf's second aide de camp; and the friends had been brothers in arms these twenty years. With him came a cavalry aga; an Albanian of a bony and terrible visage, which he used to rule his barbarous soldiery; but the poor man was milder than he seemed, and of very good heart. He boasted himself to be of the stock of Great "Alexander of the horns twain"; but was come in friendly wise to visit me, a neighbour of Europa. He spoke his mind—five or six words coming confusedly to the birth together, in a valiant shout: and when I could not find the sense; for he babbled some few terms that were in his remembrance of Ionian Italian and of the border Hellenes, he framed sounds, and made gestures! and looking stoutly, was pleased to seem to discourse with a stranger in foreign languages. The Captain (who knew not letters) would have me write his name too, *Mahmûd Aga el-Arnaûty, Abu Sammachaery* (of) *Praevaesa, Jûz-bashy.* Seven years he had served in these parts; but he understood not the words of the inglorious Arabs, —he gloried to be of the military service of the Sûltàn! though he seldom-times received his salary. This worthy was years before (he told me) a *kawàs* of the French Consulate in Corfu; where he had seen the English red frieze coats. "*Hî Angli —huh-huh!* the English (be right strong) quoth he. But the Albanians, *huh!*—the Albanians have a great heart!—heart makes the man!—makes him good to fight!—Aha; they have it strong and steadfast here!" and he smote the right hand upon his magnanimous chest. The good fellow looked hollow, and was in affliction: Colonel Mohammed told me his wife died suddenly of late; and that he was left alone with their children. —The other, Mohammed Aga, was a man curious to observe and hard to please, of polite understanding more than my host: he spoke Arabic smoothly and well for a Turk. In the last months they had seen the Dowla almost destroyed in Europe: they told me, 'there was yet but a truce and no sure peace; that England was of their part, and had in these days sent an army by sea from India,—which passed by Jidda—an hundred thousand men!' Besides, the Nemsy (Austria) was for the Sûltàn; and they looked for new warfare.

Toward evening, after a Turkish meal with my host, there

entered a kawâs of the Sherîf; who brought a change of clothing for me.—And when they had clad me as an Arab sheykh; Colonel Mohammed led me through the twilight street, to the Sherîf's audience: the ways were at this hour empty.

Some *Bisha* guards stand on the palace stairs; and they made the reverence as we passed to the Sherîf's officer: other men-at-arms stand at the stair's head. There is a waiting chamber; and my host left me, whilst he went forward to the Sherîf. But soon returning he brought me into the hall of audience; where the Sherîf Emir of Mecca sits daily at certain hours—in the time of his summer residence at et-Tâyif—much like a great Arabian sheykh among the *musheyikh*. Here the elders, and chief citizens, and strangers, and his kinsmen, are daily assembled with the Sherîf: for this is the mejlis, and coffee-parliament of an Arabian Prince; who is easy of access and of popular manners, as was Mohammed himself.

The great chamber was now void of guests: only the Sherîf sat there with his younger brother, Abdillah Pasha, a white man and strongly grown like a Turk, with the gentle Arabian manners. Hasseyn Pasha [the Sherîf bears this Ottoman title!] is a man of a pleasant face, with a sober alacrity of the eyes and humane demeanour; and he speaks with a mild and cheerful voice: his age might be forty-five years. He seemed, as he sat, a manly tall personage of a brown colour; and large of breast and limb. The Sherîf was clad in the citizen-wise of the Ottoman towns, in a long blue *jubba* of pale woollen cloth. He sat upright on his diwan, like an European, with a comely sober countenance; and smoked tobacco in a pipe like the "old Turks". The simple earthen bowl was set in a saucer before him: his white jasmine stem was almost a spear's length. —He looked up pleasantly, and received me with a gracious gravity. A chair was set for me in face of the Sherîf: then Col. Mohammed withdrew, and a servitor brought me a cup of coffee.

The Sherîf enquired with a quiet voice, "Did I drink coffee?" I said, "We deem this which grows in Arabia to be the best of all; and we believe that the coffee plant was brought into Arabia from beyond the (Red) Sea."—"Ay, I think that it was from Abyssinia: are they not very great coffee-drinkers where you have been, in Nejd?" Then the Sherîf asked me of the aggression at 'Ayn ez-Zeyma; and of the new aggression at the Seyl. "It were enough, he said, to make any man afraid. [Alas! Hasseyn himself fell shortly, by the knife of an assassin, —it was the second year after, at Jidda: and with the same affectuous cheerfulness and equanimity with which he had lived,

he breathed forth his innocent spirit ; in the arms of a countryman of ours, Dr. Gregory Wortabet, then resident Ottoman
Officer of Health for the Red Sea.]—But now you have arrived,
he added kindly ; and the jeopardy (of your long voyage) is
past. Take your rest at Tâyif, and when you are refreshed I
will send you down to the English Consul at Jidda." He asked,
' Had I never thought of visiting et-Tâyif ?—it had been better,
he added, if I were come hither at first from the Seyl ; and he
would have sent me to Jidda.' The good Sherîf said further,
"Neither is this the only time that Europeans have been here ;
for—I think it was last year—there came one with the consul
of Hollanda, to visit an inscription near the Seyl ;—I will give
charge that it may be shown to you, as you return." I answered,
' I knew of one (Burckhardt) who came hither in the time of
the Egyptian warfare.'—The Sherîf looked upon me with a
friendly astonishment ! [from whence, he wondered, had I this
knowledge of their home affairs ?]—The subtle Sherîf of Mecca,
who was beguiled and dispatched by the old Albanian fox
Mohammed Aly, might be grand uncle of this worthy Prince.
"And how, he asked, had I been able to live with the
Beduw, and to tolerate their diet ?—And found you the Beduw
to be such as is reported of them [in the town romances], or
fall they short of the popular opinion [of their magnanimity]?
—Did you help at the watering? and draw up the buckets
hand over hand—thus ?" And with the Arabian hilarity the
good Sherîf laid-by his demesurate pipe-stem ; and he made
himself the gestures of the nomad waterers ! (which he had
seen in an expedition). There is not I think a natural Arabian
Prince—but it were some sour Waháby—who might not have
done the like ; they are all pleasant men.—"I had not strength
to lift with them." He responded, with a look of human kindness, " Ay, you have suffered much !"
He enquired then of my journey ; and I answered of Medáin
Sâlih, Teyma, Hâyil : he was much surprised to hear that I had
passed a month—so long had been the tolerance of a tyrant!—
in Ibn Rashîd's town. He asked me of Mohammed ibn Rashîd,
' Did I take him for a good man ?'—plainly the Sherîf, notwithstanding the yearly presents which he receives from thence,
thought not this of him : and when I answered a little beside
his expectation, "He is a worthy man," Hasseyn was not
satisfied. Then we spoke of Aneyza ; and the Sherîf enquired
of Zâmil, " Is he a good man ?" Finally he asked, ' if the
garments [his princely gift] in which I sat clad before him
pleased me ?' and if my host showed me (which he seemed to
distrust) a reasonable hospitality ? Above an hour had passed ;

then Colonel Mohammed, who had been waiting without, came forward; and I rose to take my leave. The Sherîf spoke to my host, for me; and especially that I should walk freely in et-Tâyif, and without the walls; and visit all that I would.—Colonel Mohammed kissed the venerable hand of the Sherîf, and we departed. * * *

* * * On the morrow . . . Col. Mohammed entered,—and then Sâlem: whom the Sherîf had commanded to restore all that he and his confederate robbed from me. The miserable thief brought the pistol (now broken!), the aneroid, and four reals, which he confessed to have stolen himself from my bags. He said now, "Forgive me, Khalîl! and, ah! remember the *zád* (food) and the *melh* (salt) which is between us." "And why didst thou not remember them at the Seyl, when thou tookest the knife, a second time, to kill me?" *Col. Mohammed* "Khalîl says justly; why then didst thou not remember the bread and salt?"—"I am guilty, but I hope the Sherîf may overlook it; and be not thou against me, Khalîl!" I asked for the purse and the other small things. But Sâlem denying that they had anything more! Col. Mohammed drove him out, and bade him fetch them instantly.—"The cursed one! quoth my host, as he went forth: the Sherîf has determined after your departure to put him in irons, as well as the other man who struck you. He will punish them with severity,—but not now, because their kindred might molest you as you go down to Jidda. And the Sherîf has written an injunction, which will be sent round to all the tribes and villages within his dominion, ' *That in future, if there should arrive any stranger among them they are to send him safely to the Sherîf* ' : for who knows if some European may not be found another time passing through the Sherîf's country; and he might be mishandled by the ignorant people. Also the Sherîf would have no after-questions with their governments."

(*After resting for four days at Tâyif Doughty sets forth on the last stage of his journey, with a guard of three men appointed by the Sherîf. He reaches Jidda without mishap, and is there " called to the open hospitality of the British Consulate.*")

THE END.

SHORT GLOSSARY OF ARABIC TERMS

Abd, slave; in Arabia, any one of servile condition, whether bond or free; a black man.

'Abûd, hasty bread baked under the embers.

Adu, enemy.

'Agab, the small brown eagle of the desert.

Agîd, the leader of a foray.

Akhu, brother.

Akkâm, a camel driver in the pilgrimage.

Asîly, one of noble stock.

Askar, soldier.

el-Assr, mid-afternoon.

Ayb, shame.

Ayn, spring; also eye.

Azîz, beloved.

Bab, gate.

Baggl, dry milk shards.

Bakhîl, niggard.

Bakhûr, incense.

Báraka, blessing.

Battál, idle, bad.

Bédan, the ibex.

Bélah, the ripening date berries.

Béled, the country soil, also a settlement, and at Kheybar, a palm-yard.

Benát, pl. of *bint*.

Beny, pl. of *ibn*, son : said of a tribe ; which are accounted as children, of a common ancestor.

Berkôa, woman's face-cloth ; veil.

Bersîm, vetches.

Beyt, abode, booth, house.

el-'Bil, the camels of a nomad tribe.

Billah, by Ullah !

Bint, daughter, maiden.

Bîr, well-pit.

Birket, cistern.

Bismillah, in the name of Ullah.

Boghàz, strait, between cliffs.

Bórghrol, prepared wheat, of which porridge is made, in Syria.

Brîk, metal ewer.

Bunn, coffee-powder.

Bustàn (Persian, heard only in townsmen's speech), an orchard.

Dàb, snake.

Dalîl, a guide, a shower of the way.

Dar, a house, a court, a camping-ground of nomads.

Dawwa, medicine; also condiments.

Dellàl, coffee-pots.

Dellâl, running broker, in the bazar.

Derb, the beaten way, path.

Deyik es-sudr, constraint of heart.

Dibba, pumpkin.

Dîn, religion; also national custom.

Dîra, a nomad tribe's circuit, or oasis settlement.

Dokân, shop.

Dowla, the Ottoman Government.

Dowlàny, a Government man.

Dubbûs, mace.
Dúbbush, small cattle.

Ebbeden, never.
Entha, female.
Ethel, (sing. éthla), tamarisk timber.
Eyyâl, children.

Fáras, mare.
Fàtir, a decrepit camel.
Fendy, a kindred, within a nomad tribe.
Fenjeyn, coffee-cup.
Ferîj, a nomad hamlet.
Ferth, cud.
Futûr, breakfast.

Gaila, time of midday heat.
Galliûn, tobacco pipe.
Gâra, oasis soil.
Géria, village.
Ghrazzai, a-wayfaring, upon a foray.
Ghrazzu, a foray, rode (It. razzia).
Ghrôttha, a tamarisk rind.
Girby, water-skin.
Gôm, enemies (sing. gomâny).

Habâra, a bustard.
l-Hábash, Abyssinia.
Haggu, Nomad girdle or waist-cord, commonly of braided thongs, worn next the body.
Hâil, strength.
Haj, the pilgrimage to Mecca (or other Holy Place).
Haj, or Hajjy, a pilgrim.
Hakîm (wise man), a professor of medicine.
Hâkim, ruler.
Halàl, the lawful.
Halîb, milk.
Hamîm, the first Summer heat, in the Hejâz.
el - Hâram, "the forbidden" (namely, to Unbelievers); the temple courts of Mecca and Medina; which are called,

therefore, in the dual, el-Hára-mèyn, the two Hárams.
Harâm, that which is unlawful, in the Religion.
Harâmy, law-breaker, thief.
Harreem, plur. of horma, a woman.
Harr, hot.
Hátab, firewood.
Hàthr, people of the settlements, not Nomads.
Hawd, camel's watering-trough.
Házam, gunner's belt.
Hejra, small Summer, or flitting tent.
Helw, sweet.
Henshûly, desert,thieves.
Hess, voice.
Hijab, amulet.
Hubt, a company of marketing nomads.
el-Hummu, a dry dead heat.
Hurr; dromedary male.

Ibn, son.
Ihràm, the loin-cloth of pilgrims that enter Mecca.
Istiska, the dropsy.
Ithin, the religious cry to prayer.

Jaddar, cattle path in the Harra.
Jâhil, ignorant.
Jan (pl. of jin), demons.
Jâra, Bed, housewife
Jarâd, locusts.
Jebel, mountain.
Jehâd, war, for the (Moham-medan) religion.
Jella, camel-dung.
Jellîb, a well.
Jémel, camel.
Jemmâl, camel-master.
Jenéyny, pleasure-ground, palm-orchard.
Jerîd, javelin.
Jet, vetch.
Jezzîn (pl. of jazy), said of the great cattle, when, in spring-time, they drink no water.

Jid (gransire), patriarch or high father of a nomad tribe or oasis.

Jídery, small-pox.

Jin, demon (pl. *jan*.).

Jinna, (the Garden of) Paradise.

Júa, hunger.

Jubba, long Turkish coat of cloth, worn in the Ottoman Government towns.

Kàdy, a justice.

Kabâil, tribes, pl. of *kabîla*.

Kabîla, a tribe.

Kâfila, a caravan.

Kàfir, a reprobate, one not of the saving religion.

Karîm, bountiful.

Kassâd, a riming poet in the nomad tribes.

Kassîda, the lay of a *kassâd*.

Kéllâ, redoubt, or stronghold, upon the Haj-way.

Kéyif, pleasance, solace.

Kelb, dog

Khábar, the news.

Khála, the empty desert.

Khánjar, girdle-knife.

Khátm, seal.

Khayin, treacherous.

Kheyr, good.

Khíbel, lunatic.

el-Kibd, the liver.

Kitâb, book.

Kúfl, Bed., convoy.

Maazîb, host.

Maazîba, the place of entertainment.

Máhal, an extreme barrenness of the desert soil.

Mákbara, burying-ground.

Manêm, sleeping-place.

Manôkh, place where their camels kneel; and passengers alighting are received to the public hospitality.

Márhaba, welcome.

Marra, woman.

Matara, leathern bucket-like saddle-bottle for water, carried by riding pilgrims.

Matîn, sound and strong, firm.

Medàin, cities; plur. of *medina*.

Mejdûr, one sick of the small-pox.

Mejîdy, Turkish silver dollar.

Mejlis, the assembly, or council of elders; the open market-place in Kasîm towns.

Mejnûn (one sick, by possession of the jins), a foolish person.

Ménzil, alighting place. camping-ground.

Mereesy, dry milk-shards.

Mérgab, the watch-tower in Kasim villages; also any high look-out rock in the wilderness.

Mésjid, mosque.

Míl, needle, pillar.

Min? Who?

Míry, tribute.

Móghreby, a man of the Móghrib, or Land of the Sunsetting, an Occidental, a Moor.

el-Mowla, the Lord God.

Muállem, teacher.

Muderris, a well-studied man.

Mudówwy, man of medicine.

Muetthin, he who utters the formal cry, (*el-íthin*), to prayers.

Muhâfiz, guardian.

Muhakimîn, the governed.

Muhazimîn, they who go girdled with the gunner's belt.

Mujeddir, vaccinator.

Mukaad, sitting place (of the men), in an Arab house or nomad booth.

Mukàry, a carrier for hire.

Mukkarîn, deceitful persons.

Mukowwem, a camel-master in the Haj.

Múksir, the crated camel-litter of sheykly Beduin women.

Munâkh, v. Manôkh.

Musâfir, a wayfaring man.

Mushrakîn, (they who attribute partners, *skurka*, i.e., fellow-gods, to the Only GOD ;) said of Christians, and idolaters.

Muslemîn, pl. of *Muslim*.

Muslim, lit. one who is submitted (to God).

Muttowwa, religious elder (in Wáhaby Arabia).

Muwelladin, the home-born, of brought-in strange blood ; such are persons of the servile condition amongst them, in the second generation.

Nâga, cow camel.

Náhab, rapine.

Naksh, scored inscriptions.

Nasr, victory.

Néby, prophet.

Nefs, spirit, wind.

Nejis, foul, impious.

Nejm, a star.

Nimmr, leopard.

Nîs, the porcupine.

Rabèyby, one-stringed viol of the Arabians.

Rabía, the tender spring of herbs, in the wilderness.

Radîf, (dromedary) back-rider.

Rafîk, a way-fellow.

Ráhla, a remove, between the camps of nomads.

Ráhma, mercy.

Rajajîl, armed men of the Prince's band at Hayîl.

Rájil, a man.

Rákham, small white carrion eagle.

Ras, head.

Rasûl, messenger, apostle.

Rautha, pl. *riâth* ; a green site of bushes, where winter rain is ponded, in the desert.

er-Rihh, said by the Nomads for all kinds of rheums.

Rommh, horseman's lance.

Rubb, lord.

Rubbâ, a fellowship.

Saat, an hour.

Sáhar, a magician.

Sâiehh, a religious world's wanderer.

Sajjèydy, a kneeling carpet.

Salaam, peace.

Sámn, clarified butter.

Sâny, a smith.

Sebîl, the way, path of the religious life.

Semîly, milk skin.

Seyf, sword.

Seyl, torrent, generally a dry bed, which flows only rarely, after rain : the Arabs use also the word as a verb, and say, the Land *seyls* towards. . . .

Shahûd (witnesses), martyrs.

Shelfa, Beduin horseman's lance.

Sherîf, nobleman of the blood of Mohammed.

Sheykh, an elder, a nobleman, the head of a tribe, a village headman.

Shidâd, camel riding-saddle.

Simûm, the hot land-wind, commonly regarded as poisonous.

Suâny, draw-wheel frames of the irrigation wells, in Nejd oases.

Subbakha, salt-crust upon the desert soil.

Suffa, the upper chamber, at Kheybar, so-called.

Sûk, street or bazaar.

es-Súlat, the prayer.

Sûr, town wall.

Tájir, tradesman.

Támr, dates.

Tarkîy, a small wayfaring company of nomads ; pl. *terâgy*.

Temmn, a kind of rice, from Mesopotamia.

Thaif, a guest.

Thelûl, a dromedary.

Themîla, shallow water-hole of the Beduw ; such as is digged with a stick and their hands.

Thíb, wolf.

Timathíl (images :) inscriptions are sometimes thus called by the Nomads.

Tóma, cupidity, gain.

Ullema, learned men, the religious doctors.

Wády, a low valley-ground.

Waháby, the Wáhabbies, (new Arabian Puritan zealots,) are thus named after their Founder. Mohammed, ibn *'Abd-el-Wáháb*, of East Nejd.

Wasm, cattle-brand ; also the like token of any family, kindred, or tribesfolk.

Wellah, by Ullah !

Weylèy ! woe is me.

Wéyrid, a watering.

Zaal, displeasure, sorrow.

Zàd, food.

Zélamat, a carle, a man of the people.